# BLOOM'S PERIOD STUDIES

BLOOM'S PERIOD STUDIES

# The Eighteenth-Century English Novel

Edited and with an introduction by
## Harold Bloom
Sterling Professor of the Humanities
Yale University

CHELSEA HOUSE
PUBLISHERS
A Haights Cross Communications Company

Philadelphia

A Haights Cross Communications ⌁ Company

Printed and bound in the United States of America.
10  9  8  7  6  5  4  3  2  1

Library of Congress Cataloging-in-Publication Data

The Eighteenth-Century English Novel / edited and with an introduction by Harold Bloom.
        p. cm. — (Bloom's period studies)
    Includes bibliographical references and index.
    ISBN 0-7910-7896-5
  1.  English fiction—18th century—History and criticism.  I. Bloom, Harold. II. Series.
    PR853.E445 2003
    823'.509—dc22

                                    2003028170

Contributing Editor: Janyce Marson

Cover designed by Keith Trego

Layout by EJB Publishing Services

# Contents

# Editor's Note

My Introduction traces the fortunes of the Protestant will in Eighteenth-Century English prose fiction, from Defoe's *Robinson Crusoe* and *Moll Flanders* to Fanny Burney's *Evelina*. Along the way, I offer interpretations of Swift's *A Tale of a Tub* and *Gulliver's Travels*, of Richardson's *Clarissa* and Fielding's *Tom Jones*, and of the very varied triad of Sterne's *Tristam Shandy*, Goldsmith's *The Vicar of Wakefield*, and Smollett's *Humphrey Clinker*.

James R. Foster surveys the pre-Romantic novel of Sentiment from Aphra Behn to Marivaux, while Margaret Anne Doody meditates upon the dream-lives of women in Gothic romances.

Sterne's comic version of the Longinian Sublime is seen as indebted to Cervantes by Jonathan Lamb, after which Sheridan Baker analyzes the triumphant comedy of Fielding, and Paula R. Backscheider contextualizes Defoe's *Moll Flanders* for us.

The architecture of Bath, major social resort, is presented by Simon Varey as an induction to the fictive art of Richardson and Fielding, after which Jonathan Lamb brings together the Book of Job and *Tristam Shandy*, following Sterne's own lead.

Patrick Reilly sees *Tom Jones* as Fielding's grand assault upon hypocrisy and self-deception, while John M. Warner uncovers Smollett as one of James Joyce's precursors.

*Clarissa*, in my judgment the supreme novel in English literature, is expounded by Lois E. Bueler as two plot-lines, Clarissa as "tested woman" and Lovelace as Don Juan after which David E. Hoegberg salutes Aphra Behn's *Oroonoko*, which our current political correctness insists is a canonical work.

Michael Seidel shrewdly explores the ambiguities of truth-telling in *Gulliver's Travels*, after which Thomas Keymer approaches *Tristam Shandy* in the clime of its literary marketplace.

# Introduction

## DANIEL DEFOE

### I

*Of his prayers and the like we take no account, since they are a source of pleasure to him, and he looks upon them as so much recreation.*
—Karl Marx on *Robinson Crusoe*

> *I got so tired of the very colors!*
> *One day I dyed a baby goat bright red*
> *with my red berries, just to see*
> *something a little different.*
> *And then his mother wouldn't recognize him.*
> —Elizabeth Bishop, "Crusoe in England"

Had Karl Marx written *Robinson Crusoe*, it would have had even more moral vigor, but at the expense of the image of freedom it still provides for us. Had Elizabeth Bishop composed it, Defoe's narrative would have been enhanced as image and as impulse, but at the expense of its Puritan plainness, its persuasive search for some evidences of redemption. Certainly one of Defoe's novelistic virtues is precisely what Ian Watt and Martin Price have emphasized it to be: the puzzles of daily moral choice are omnipresent. Robinson Crusoe and Moll Flanders are human—all-too-human—and suffer what Calvin and Freud alike regarded as the economics of the spirit.

Defoe comes so early in the development of the modern novel as a literary form that there is always a temptation to historicize rather than to read him. But historicisms old and new are poor substitutes for reading, and I do not find it useful to place *Robinson Crusoe* and *Moll Flanders* in their

1

contemporary context when I reread them, as I have just done. Ian Watt usefully remarked that "Defoe's heroes ... keep us more fully informed of their present stocks of money and commodities than any other characters in fiction." I suspect that this had more to do with Defoe than with his age, and that Defoe would have been no less obsessed with economic motives if he had written in the era of Queen Victoria. He was a hard man who had led a hard life: raised as a Dissenter in the London of the Great Plague and the Great Fire; enduring Newgate prison and the pillory in bankrupt middle age; working as a secret agent and a scandalous journalist until imprisoned again for debt and treason. Defoe died old and so may be accounted as a survivor, but he had endured a good share of reality, and his novels reflect that endurance.

Dr. Johnson once said that only three books ought to have been still longer than they were: *Don Quixote*, *The Pilgrim's Progress*, and *Robinson Crusoe*. Defoe has authentic affinities with Bunyan, but there is nothing quixotic about Robinson Crusoe or Moll Flanders. All of Defoe's protagonists are pragmatic and prudent, because they have to be; there is no play in the world as they know it.

## II

I did not read *Robinson Crusoe* as a child, and so missed an experience that continues to be all but universal; it remains a book that cannot fail with children. Yet, as Dickens observed, it is also "the only instance of an universally popular book that could make no one laugh and could make no one cry." Crusoe's singular tone, his self-baffled affect, does not bother children, who appear to empathize with a near-perfect solipsist who nevertheless exhibits energy and inventiveness throughout a quarter-century of solitude. Perhaps Crusoe's survival argues implicitly against every child's fear of dependency and prophesies the longed-for individuality that is still to come. Or perhaps every child's loneliness is answered in Crusoe's remarkable strength at sustaining solitude.

Though the identification of Defoe with Crusoe is never wholly overt, the reader senses its prevalence throughout the narrative. Defoe seems to me the least ironic of writers, and yet Crusoe's story is informed by an overwhelming irony. A restless wanderer, driven to travel and adventure by forces that he (and the reader) cannot comprehend, Crusoe is confined to an isolation that ought to madden him by turning him towards an unbearable inwardness. Yet his sanity prevails, despite his apparent imprisonment. Defoe had borne much; Newgate and the pillory were nightmare experiences. Crusoe bears more, yet Defoe will not describe his hero's suffering as being psychic. As Virginia Woolf noted, Defoe "takes the opposite way from the psychologist's—he describes the effect of emotion on the body, not on the mind." Nowhere is this stronger than in Crusoe's agony as he views a shipwreck:

> Such certainly was the Case of these Men, of whom I could not so much as see room to suppose any of them were sav'd; nothing could make it rational, so much as to wish, or expect that they did not all perish there; except the Possibility only of their being taken up by another Ship in Company, and this was but meer Possibility indeed; for I saw not the least Signal or Appearance of any such Thing.
>
> I cannot explain by any possible Energy of Words what a strange longing or hankering of Desires I felt in my Soul upon this Sight; breaking out sometimes thus; O that there had been but one or two; nay, or but one Soul sav'd out of this Ship, to have escap'd to me, that I might but have had one Companion, one Fellow-Creature to have spoken to me, and to have convers'd with! In all the Time of my solitary Life, I never felt so earnest, so strong a Desire after the Society of my Fellow-Creatures, or so deep a Regret at the want of it.
>
> There are some secret moving Springs in the Affections, which when they are set a going by some Object in view; or be it some Object, though not in view, yet rendred present to the Mind by the Power of Imagination, that Motion carries out the Soul by its Impetuosity to such violent eager embracings of the Object, that the Absence of it is insupportable.
>
> Such were these earnest Wishings, That but one Man had been sav'd! *O that it had been but One!* I believe I repeated the Words, *0 that it had been but One!* a thousand Times; and the Desires were so mov'd by it, that when I spoke the Words, my Hands would clinch together, and my Fingers press the Palms of my Hands, that if I had had any soft Thing in my Hand, it wou'd have crusht it involuntarily; and my Teeth in my Head wou'd strike together, and set against one another so strong, that for some time I cou'd not part them again.

These are the reactions of a compulsive craftsman who has found his freedom but cannot bear its full sublimity. Crusoe, himself the least sublime of personages, is embedded throughout in a sublime situation best epitomized by the ghastly cannibal feasts he spies upon and from which he rescues his man Friday. Against his superior technology and Puritan resolve, the cannibals offer almost no resistance, so that the rapid conversion of the cannibal Friday to Protestant theology and diet is not unconvincing. What may baffle the average rereader is Crusoe's comparative dearth of Protestant inwardness. It is not that Marx was accurate and that Crusoe becomes Protestant only upon the Sabbath, but rather that Defoe's God is himself a technocrat and an individualist, not much given to the nicer emotions. Defoe's God can be visualized as a giant tradesman, coping with the universe as Crusoe makes do on his island, but with teeming millions of adoring Fridays where Crusoe enjoys the devotion of just one.

III

With *Robinson Crusoe*, aesthetic judgment seems redundant; the book's status as popular myth is too permanent, and so the critic must ground arms. *Moll Flanders* is another matter and provokes a remarkably wide range of critical response, from the late poet-critic Allen Tate, who once told me it was a great novel of Tolstoyan intensity, to equally qualified readers who deny that it is a novel at all. The overpraisers include James Joyce, who spoke of "the unforgettable harlot Moll Flanders," and William Faulkner, who coupled *Moby-Dick* and *Moll Flanders* as works he would like to have written (together with one of Milne's Pooh books!). Rereading *Moll Flanders* leaves me a touch baffled as I thought it had been better, it being one of those books that are much more vivid in parts than as a unit so that the memory holds on to episodes and to impressions, investing them with an aura that much of the narrative does not possess. The status of the narrative is curiously wavering; one is not always certain one is reading a novel rather than a colorful tract of the Puritan persuasion. Moll is a formidable person who sustains our interest and our good will. But the story she tells seems alternately formed and formless, and frequently confuses the rival authorities of fiction and supposed fact.

Martin Price notes how little thematic unity Defoe imposes upon the stuff of existence that constitutes *Moll Flanders*. As a man who had suffered Newgate, Defoe gives us only one key indication of his novel's vision; Moll was born in Newgate and will do anything to avoid ending there. The quest for cash is simply her equivalent of Crusoe's literal quest to survive physically upon his island, except that Moll is more imaginative than the strangely compulsive Crusoe. He does only what he must, she does more, and we begin to see that her obsession has in it an actual taste for adventures. This taste surprises her, but then, as Price observes, she is always "surprised by herself and with herself." She learns by what she does, and almost everything she does is marked by gusto. Her vehemence is her most winning quality, but most of her qualities are attractive. Male readers are charmed by her, particularly male readers who both exalt and debase women, among whom Joyce and Faulkner remain the most prominent.

Puritan force, the drive for the soul's exuberant self-recognition, is as much exemplified by Moll as by Bunyan's protagonist. I suspect that was why William Hazlitt, the greatest literary critic to emerge from the tradition of

Protestant Dissent, had so violent a negative reaction to *Moll Flanders*, which otherwise I would have expected him to admire. But, on some level, he evidently felt that she was a great discredit to Puritan sensibility. Charles Lamb greatly esteemed her and understood how authentic the Puritan dialectic was in her, pointing to "the intervening flashes of religious visitation upon the rude and uninstructed soul" and judging this to "come near to the tenderness of Bunyan." Infuriated, Hazlitt responded, "Mr. Lamb admires *Moll Flanders*; would he marry Moll Flanders?" to which the only response a loyal Hazlittian could make is, "Would that Hazlitt had married a Moll Flanders, and been happy for once in a relationship with a woman." All proportion abandoned Hazlitt when he wrote about *Moll Flanders*:

> We ... may, nevertheless, add, for the satisfaction of the inquisitive reader, that *Moll Flanders* is utterly vile and detestable: Mrs. Flanders was evidently born in sin. The best parts are the account of her childhood, which is pretty and affecting; the fluctuation of her feelings between remorse and hardened impenitence in Newgate; and the incident of her leading off the horse from the inn-door, though she had no place to put it in after she had stolen it. This was carrying the love of thieving to an *ideal* pitch and making it perfectly disinterested and mechanical.

Hazlitt did not understand Moll because he could not bear to see the Puritan impulse displaced into "carrying the love of thieving to an *ideal* pitch." Brilliant as the horse-stealing is, it is surpassed by Moll's famous second theft, the episode of the child's necklace:

> I went out now by Day-light, and wandred about I knew not whither, and in search of I knew not what, when the Devil put a Snare in my way of a dreadful Nature indeed, and such a one as I have never had before or since; going thro' *Aldersgate-street* there was a pretty little Child had been at a Dancing School, and was going home, all alone, and my Prompter, like a true Devil, set me upon this innocent Creature; I talk'd to it, and it prattl'd to me again, and I took it by the Hand and led it a long till I came to a pav'd Alley that goes into *Bartholomew Close*, and I led it in there; the Child said that was not its way home; I said, yes, my Dear it is, I'll show you the way home; the Child had a little Necklace on of Gold Beads, and I had my Eye upon that, and in the dark of the Alley I stoop'd, pretending to mend the Child's Clog that was loose, and took off her Necklace and the Child never felt it, and so led the Child on again: Here, I say, the Devil put me upon killing the child

in the dark Alley, that it might not Cry; but the very thought frighted me so that I was ready to drop down, but I turn'd the Child about and bade it go back again, for that was not its way home; the Child said so she would, and I went thro' into *Bartholomew Close*, and then turn'd round to another Passage that goes into *Long-lane*, so away into *Charterhouse-Yard and* out into *St. John's-street*, then crossing into *Smithfield*, went down *Chick-lane* and into *Field-lane* to *Holbourn-bridge*, when mixing with the Crowd of People usually passing there, it was not possible to have been found out; and thus I enterpriz'd my second Sally into the World.

The thoughts of this Booty put out all the thoughts of the first, and the Reflections I had made wore quickly off; Poverty, as I have said, harden'd my Heart, and my own Necessities made me regardless of any thing: The last Affair left no great Concern upon me, for as I did the poor Child no harm, I only said to my self, I had given the Parents a just Reproof for their Negligence in leaving the poor little Lamb to come home by it self, and it would teach them to take more Care of it another time.

This String of Beads was worth about Twelve or Fourteen Pounds; I suppose it might have been formerly the Mother's, for it was too big for the Child's wear, but that, perhaps, the Vanity of the Mother to have her Child look Fine at the Dancing School, had made her let the Child wear it; and no doubt the Child had a Maid sent to take care of it, but she, like a careless jade, was taken up perhaps with some Fellow that had met her by the way, and so the poor Baby wandred till it fell into my Hands.

However, I did the Child no harm; I did not so much as fright it, for I had a great many tender Thoughts about me yet, and did nothing but what, as I may say, meer Necessity drove me to.

The remarkable moment, which horrifies us and must have scandalized Hazlitt, is when Moll says, "the Devil put me upon killing the Child in the dark Alley, that it might not Cry; but the very thought frighted me so that I was ready to drop down." We do not believe that Moll will slay the child, but she frightens us because of her capacity for surprising herself. We are reminded that we do not understand Moll, *because Defoe does not understand her*. That is his novel's most peculiar strength and its most peculiar weakness. Gide's Lafcadio, contemplating his own crime, murmurs that it is not about events that he is curious, but only about himself. That is in the spirit of Defoe's Moll. The Protestant sensibility stands back from itself, and watches the spirits of good and of evil contend for it, with the detachment of a certain estrangement, a certain wonder at the immense energies that God has placed in one's soul.

JONATHAN SWIFT

I

Twice a year, for many years now, I reread Swift's *A Tale of a Tub*, not because I judge it to be the most powerful prose work in the language (which it is) but because it is good for me, though I dislike this great book as much as I admire it. A literary critic who is speculative, Gnostic, still imbued with High Romantic enthusiasm even in his later middle age, needs to read *A Tale of a Tub* as often as he can bear to do so. Swift is the most savage and merciless satirist and ironist in the history of Western literature, and one of his particularly favorite victims is the critic given to Gnostic speculations and Romantic enthusiasms.

*A Tale of a Tub* is a queerly shaped work, by design a parody of the seventeenth-century "anatomy," as exemplified by Sir Thomas Browne's *Pseudodoxia Epidemica* or Robert Burton's magnificent *The Anatomy of Melancholy*. The most important section of the *Tale* outrageously is not even part of the book, but is the attached fragment, *A Discourse Concerning the Mechanical Operation of the Spirit*. The philosopher Descartes, one of the leaders of the Bowmen among the Moderns in their confrontation with the Ancients in Swift's *The Battle of the Books*, is the inventor of the dualism that always will haunt the West, a dualism called "the Ghost in the Machine" by the analytical philosopher, Gilbert Ryle, and more grimly named *The Mechanical Operation of the Spirit* by Jonathan Swift. In *The Battle of the Books*, Descartes expiates his radical dualism by dying of an Aristotelian arrow intended for Bacon:

> Then *Aristotle* observing Bacon advance with a furious Mien, drew his Bow to the Head, and let fly his Arrow, which mist the valiant *Modern*, and went hizzing over his Head; but *Des-Cartes* it hit; The Steel Point quickly found a *Defect* in his *Head-piece*; it pierced the Leather and the Past-board, and went in at his Right Eye. The Torture of the Pain, whirled the valiant *Bow-man* round, till Death, like a Star of superior Influence, drew him into his own *Vortex*.

Not even the dignity of an heroic death is granted to poor Descartes, who pays for his cognitive defect and perishes via an anti-Baconian shaft, swallowed up into a vortex that parodies his own account of perception. Yet even this poor fate is better than the extraordinarily ferocious drubbing received by the Cartesian dualism in *The Mechanical Operation of the Spirit*:

> But, if this Plant has found a Root in the Fields of *Empire*, and of *Knowledge*, it has fixt deeper, and spread yet farther upon *Holy*

*Ground*. Wherein, though it hath pass'd under the general Name of *Enthusiasm*, and perhaps arisen from the same Original, yet hath it produced certain Branches of a very different Nature, however often mistaken for each other. The Word in its universal Acceptation, may be defined, *A lifting up of the Soul or its Faculties above Matter*. This Description will hold good in general; but I am only to understand it, as applied to *Religion*; wherein there are three general Ways of ejaculating the Soul, or transporting it beyond the Sphere of Matter. The first, is the immediate Act of God, and is called, *Prophecy* or *Inspiration*. The second, is the immediate Act of the Devil, and is termed *Possession*. The third, is the Product of natural Causes, the effect of strong imagination, Spleen, violent Anger, Fear, Grief, Pain, and the like. These three have been abundantly treated on by Authors, and therefore shall not employ my Enquiry. But, the fourth Method of *Religious Enthusiasm*, or launching out of the Soul, as it is purely an Effect of Artifice and *Mechanick Operation*, has been sparingly handled, or not at all, by any Writer; because tho' it is an Art of great Antiquity, yet having been confined to few Persons, it long wanted those Advancements and Refinements, which it afterwards met with, since it has grown so Epidemick, and fallen into so many cultivating Hands.

All four "methods" reduce the spirit or soul to a gaseous vapor, the only status possible for any transcendental entity in the cosmos of Hobbes and Descartes, where the soul must be ejaculated in sublime transport "beyond the Sphere of Matter." Within *A Tale of a Tub* proper, Swift keeps a very precarious balance indeed as he plays obsessively with the image of the spirit mechanically operated. So operated, the wretched soul is capable of only one mode of movement: digression. What Freud called the drive is to Swift merely digression. Digression is a turning aside, a kind of walking in which you never go straight. Digress enough, in discourse or in living, and you will go mad. *A Tale of a Tub* is nothing but digression, because Swift bitterly believes there is nothing else in a Cartesian universe. Spirit digressing is an oxymoronic operation, and so falls from spirit to gaseous vapor. Vapor properly moves only by turning aside, by digressing.

Swift's principal victims, all high priests of digression, he calls "the Learned *Aeolists*," acolytes of the god of the winds, among whom he counts: "All Pretenders to Inspiration whatsoever." His savage indignation, so constant in him as a writer, maintains a consistent fury whenever the *Aeolists* are his subject. They are introduced as apocalyptics for whom origin and end intermix:

The Learned *Aeolists*, maintain the Original Cause of all Things to be *Wind*, from which Principle this whole Universe was at first produced, and into which it must at last be resolved; that the same Breath which had kindled, and blew up the Flame of Nature, should one Day blow it *out*.

As he is kindled by the Aeolists, Swift's Tale-teller mounts to an intensity worthy of his subject, and attains an irony that is itself a kind of hysteria:

> It is from this Custom of the Priests, that some Authors maintain these *Aeolists*, to have been very antient in the World. Because, the Delivery of their Mysteries, which I have just now mention'd, appears exactly the same with that of other antient Oracles, whose Inspirations were owing to certain subterraneous *Effluviums of Wind*, delivered with the same Pain to the Priest, and much about the *same* Influence on the People. It is true indeed, that these were frequently managed and directed by *Female* Officers, whose Organs were understood to be better disposed for the Admission of those Oracular *Gusts*, as entring and passing up thro' a Receptacle of greater Capacity, and causing also a Pruriency by the Way, such as with due Management; hath been refined from a Carnal, into a Spiritual Extasie. And to strengthen this profound Conjecture, it is farther insisted, that this Custom of *Female* Priests is kept up still in certain refined Colleges of our *Modern Aeolists*, who are agreed to receive their Inspiration, derived thro' the Receptacle aforesaid, like their Ancestors, the Sibyls.

This ends in a passing blow at the Quakers, but its power is dangerously close to its horror of becoming what it is working so hard to reject. Rather like King Lear, the Tale-teller fears the ascent of vapors from abdomen to head, fears that hysteria, the womb or mother, will unman him:

> O how this mother swells up toward my heart!
> *Hysterica passio*, down, thou climbing sorrow,
> Thy element's below.—

Swift cannot be, does not want to be, the Tale-teller, but the Tale-teller may be, in part, Swift's failed defense against the madness of digression, and the digressiveness that is madness. Compulsiveness of and in the Tale-teller becomes a terrifying counter-Sublime of counter-Enthusiasm, a digressiveness turned against digressiveness, a vapor against vapors:

Besides, there is something Individual in human Minds, that
easily kindles at the accidental Approach and Collision of certain
Circumstances, which tho' of paltry and mean Appearance, do
often flame out into the greatest Emergencies of Life. For great
Turns are not always given by strong Hands, but by lucky
Adaption, and at proper Seasons; and it is of no import, where the
Fire was kindled, if the Vapor has once got up into the Brain. For
the *upper Region* of Man, is furnished like the *middle Region* of the
Air; The Materials are formed from Causes of the widest
Difference, yet produce at last the same Substance and Effect.
Mists arise from the Earth, Steams from Dunghils, Exhalations
from the Sea, and Smoak from Fire; yet all Clouds are the same
in Composition, as well as Consequences: and the Fumes issuing
from a Jakes, will furnish as comely and useful a Vapor, as Incense
from an Altar. Thus far, I suppose, will easily be granted me; and
then it will follow, that as the Face of Nature never produces
Rain, but when it is overcast and disturbed, so Human
Understanding, seated in the Brain, must be troubled and
overspread by Vapours, ascending from the lower Faculties, to
water the Invention, and render it fruitful.

Are these the accents of satire? The passage itself is overcast and
disturbed, not so much troubled and overspread by vapors ascending from
below, as it is by the not wholly repressed anxiety that *anyone*, including the
Tale-teller and Swift, is vulnerable to the Mechanical Operation of the Spirit.
King Henry IV of France (Henry of Navarre), rightly called "the Great," is
the subject of the next paragraph, which tells of grand preparations for battle,
perhaps to advance "a Scheme for Universal Monarchy," until the
assassination of Henry IV released the spirit or mighty vapor from the royal
body:

Now, is the Reader exceeding curious to learn, from whence this
*Vapour* took its Rise, which had so long set the Nations at a Gaze?
What secret Wheel, what hidden Spring could put into Motion
so wonderful an Engine? It was afterwards discovered, that the
Movement of this whole Machine had been directed by an absent
*Female*, whose Eyes had raised a Protuberancy, and before
Emission, she was removed into an Enemy's Country. What
should an unhappy Prince do in such ticklish Circumstances as
these?

What indeed? This is genial, and quite relaxed, for Swift, but his
subsequent analysis is darker, rhetorically and in moral substance:

Having to no purpose used all peaceable Endeavours, the collected part of the *Semen*, raised and enflamed, became adust, converted to Choler, turned head upon the spinal Duct, and ascended to the Brain. The very same Principle that influences a *Bully* to break the Windows of a Whore, who has jilted him, naturally stirs up a Great Prince to raise mighty Armies, and dream of nothing but Sieges, Battles, and Victories.

As a reduction, this continues to have its exuberance, but the phrase, "raised and enflamed" is at the center, and is yet another Swiftian assault upon Enthusiasm, another classical irony set against a romantic Sublime. The Author or Tale-teller forsakes digressiveness to become Swift at his calmest and most deadly, a transformation itself digressive. Swift cannot be censured for wanting it every which way, since he is battling not for our right reason, but for our sanity, and ruggedly he fights for us, against us, and for himself, against himself.

## II

The terrible greatness of *A Tale of a Tub* has much to do with our sense of its excess, with its force being so exuberantly beyond its form (or its calculated formlessness). *Gulliver's Travels*, the later and lesser work, has survived for the common reader, whereas Swift's early masterpiece has not. Like its descendant, Carlyle's Sartor Resartus, *A Tale of a Tub* demands too much of the reader, but it more than rewards those demands, and it now seems unclear whether Sartor Resartus does or not. Gulliver's first two voyages are loved by children (of all ages), while the third and fourth voyages, being more clearly by the Swift who wrote *A Tale of a Tub*, now make their appeal only to those who would benefit most from an immersion in the *Tub*.

Gulliver himself is both the strength and the weakness of the book, and his character is particularly ambiguous in the great fourth voyage, to the country of the rational Houyhnhnms and the bestial Yahoos, who are and are not, respectively, horses and humans. The inability to resist a societal perspectivism is at once Gulliver's true weakness, and his curious strength as an observer. Swift's barely concealed apprehension that the self is an abyss, that the ego is a fiction masking our fundamental nothingness, is exemplified by Gulliver, but on a level of commonplaceness far more bathetic than anything reductive in the Tale-teller. Poor Gulliver is a good enough man, but almost devoid of imagination. One way of describing him might be to name him the least Nietzschean character ever to appear in any narrative. Though a ceaseless traveler, Gulliver lacks any desire to be elsewhere, or to be different. His pride is blind, and all too easily magnifies to pomposity, or declines to a self-contempt that is more truly a contempt for all other humans. If the Tale-teller is a Swiftian parody of one side of Swift, the anti-Cartesian, anti-Hobbesian, then Gulliver is a Swiftian parody of the great ironist's own misanthropy.

The reader of "A Voyage to Lilliput" is unlikely to forget the fatuity of Gulliver at the close of chapter 6:

> I am here obliged to vindicate the Reputation of an excellent Lady, who was an innocent Sufferer upon my Account. The Treasurer took a Fancy to be jealous of his Wife, from the Malice of some evil Tongues, who informed him that her Grace had taken a violent Affection for my Person; and the Court-Scandal ran for some Time that she once came privately to my Lodging. This I solemnly declare to be a most infamous Falshood, without any Grounds, farther than that her Grace was pleased to treat me with all innocent Marks of Freedom and Friendship. I own she came often to my House, but always publickly ... I should not have dwelt so long upon this Particular, if it had been a Point wherein the Reputation of a great Lady is so nearly concerned, to say nothing of my own; although I had the Honour to be a *Nardac*, which the Treasurer himself is not; for all the World knows he is only a *Clumglum*, a Title inferior by one Degree, as that of a Marquess is to a Duke in *England*; yet I allow he preceded me in right of his Post.

The great *Nardac* has so fallen into the societal perspective of Lilliput, that he sublimely forgets he is twelve times the size of the *Clumglum*'s virtuous wife, who therefore would have been quite safe with him were they naked and alone. Escaping back to England, Gulliver has learned nothing and sets forth on "A Voyage to Brobdingnag," land of the giants, where he learns less than nothing:

> The Learning of this People is very defective; consisting only in Morality, History, Poetry and Mathematicks; wherein they must be allowed to excel. But, the last of these is wholly applied to what may be useful in Life; to the Improvement of Agriculture and all mechanical Arts; so that among us it would be little esteemed. And as to Ideas, Entities, Abstractions and Transcendentals, I could never drive the least Conception into their Heads.
>
> No Law of that Country must exceed in Words the Number of Letters in their Alphabet; which consists only of two and twenty. But indeed, few of them extend even to that Length. They are expressed in the most plain and simple Terms, wherein

those People are not Mercurial enough to discover above one Interpretation. And, to write a Comment upon any Law, is a capital Crime. As to the Decision of civil Causes, or Proceedings against Criminals, their Precedents are so few, that they have little Reason to boast of any extraordinary Skill in either.

Effective as this is, it seems too weak an irony for Swift, and we are pleased when the dull Gulliver abandons Brobdingnag behind him. The Third Voyage, more properly Swiftian, takes us first to Laputa, the floating island, at once a parody of a Platonic academy yet also a kind of science fiction punishment machine, always ready to crush earthlings who might assert liberty:

> If any Town should engage in Rebellion or Mutiny, fall into violent Factions, or refuse to pay the usual Tribute; the King hath two Methods of reducing them to Obedience. The first and the mildest Course is by keeping the Island hovering over such a Town, and the Lands about it; whereby he can deprive them of the Benefit of the Sun and the Rain, and consequently afflict the Inhabitants with Dearth and Diseases. And if the Crime deserve it, they are at the same time pelted from above with great Stones, against which they have no Defence, but by creeping into Cellars or Caves, while the Roofs of their Houses are beaten to Pieces. But if they still continue obstinate, or offer to raise Insurrections; he proceeds to the last Remedy, by letting the Island drop directly upon their Heads, which makes a universal Destruction both of Houses and Men. However, this is an Extremity to which the Prince is seldom driven, neither indeed is he willing to put it in Execution; nor dare his Ministers advise him to an Action, which as it would render them odious to the People, so it would be a great Damage to their own Estates that lie all below; for the Island is the King's Demesn.

The maddening lack of affect on Gulliver's part begins to tell upon us here; the stolid narrator is absurdly inadequate to the grim force of his own recital, grimmer for us now even than it could have been for the prophetic Swift. Gulliver inexorably and blandly goes on to *Lagado*, where he observes the grand Academy of Projectors, Swift's famous spoof of the British Royal Society, but here the ironies go curiously flat, and I suspect we are left with the irony of irony, which wearies because by repetition it seems to become compulsive. Yet it may be that here, as subsequently with the immortal but senile and noxious *Struldbrugs*, the irony of irony is highly deliberate, in order to prepare Gulliver, and the battered reader, for the great shock of

reversal that lies just ahead in the Country of the Houyhnhnms, which is also
the land of the Yahoos, "a strange Sort of Animal."

Critical reactions to Gulliver's fourth voyage have an astonishing
range, from Thackeray calling its moral "horrible, shameful unmanly,
blasphemous" to T.S. Eliot regarding it as a grand triumph for the human
spirit. Eliot's judgment seems to me as odd as Thackeray's, and presumably
both writers believed that the Yahoos were intended as a just representation
of the natural man, with Thackeray humanistically disagreeing, and the neo-
Christian Eliot all too happy to concur. If that were the proper reading of
Swift, we would have to conclude that the great satirist had drowned in his
own misanthropy, and had suffered the terrible irony, after just evading the
becoming one with his Tale-teller, of joining himself to the uneducable
Gulliver. Fit retribution perhaps, but it is unwise to underestimate the deep
cunning of Swift.

Martin Price accurately reminds us that Swift's attitudes do not depend
solely upon Christian morals, but stem also from a traditional secular
wisdom. Peace and decency are wholly compatible with Christian teaching,
but are secular virtues as well. Whatever the Yahoos represent, they are *not* a
vision of secular humanity devoid of divine grace, since they offend the
classical view of man quite as profoundly as they seem to suit an ascetic
horror of our supposedly natural condition.

Clearly, it is the virtues of the Houyhnhnms, and not the squalors of
the Yahoos, that constitute a burden for critics and for common readers. I
myself agree with Price, when he remarks of the Houyhnhnms: "They are
rational horses, neither ideal men nor a satire upon others' ideals for man."
Certainly they cannot represent a human rational ideal, since none of us
would wish to lack all impulse, or any imagination whatsoever. Nor do they
seem a plausible satire upon the Deistic vision, a satire worthier of Blake than
of Swift, and in any case contradicted by everything that truly is admirable
about these cognitively advanced horses. A rational horse is a kind of
oxymoron, and Swift's irony is therefore more difficult than ever to interpret:

> My Master heard me with great Appearances of Uneasiness in his
> Countenance; because *Doubting* or *not believing*, are so little
> known in this Country, that the Inhabitants cannot tell how to
> behave themselves under such Circumstances. And I remember
> in frequent Discourses with my Master concerning the Nature of
> Manhood, in other Parts of the World; having Occasion to talk
> of *Lying*, and *false Representation*, it was with much Difficulty that
> he comprehended what I meant; although he had otherwise a
> most acute Judgment. For he argued thus; That the Use of
> Speech was to make us understand one another, and to receive
> Information of Facts; now if any one *said the Thing which was not*,

these Ends were defeated; because I cannot properly be said to understand him; and I am so far from receiving information, that he leaves me worse than in Ignorance; for I am led to believe a Thing *Black* when it is *White*, and *Short* when it is *Long*. And these were all the Notions he had concerning the Faculty of *Lying*, so perfectly well understood, and so universally practised among human Creatures.

Are we altogether to admire Gulliver's Master here, when that noble Houyhnhnm not only does not know how to react to the human propensity to say *the thing which was not*, but lacks even the minimal imagination that might allow him to apprehend the human need for fictions, a "sickness not ignoble," as Keats observed in *The Fall of Hyperion*? Since the noble Houyhnhnm finds the notion "that the *Yahoos* were the only governing Animals" in Gulliver's country "altogether past his Conception," are we again to admire him for an inability that would make it impossible for us to read *Gulliver's Travels* (or *King Lear*, for that matter)? The virtues of Swift's rational horses would not take us very far, if we imported them into our condition, but can that really be one of Swift's meanings? And what are we to do with Swiftian ironies that are too overt already, and become aesthetically intolerable if we take up the stance of the sublimely rational Houyhnhnm?

My Master likewise mentioned another Quality, which his Servants had discovered in several *Yahoos*, and to him was wholly unaccountable. He said, a Fancy would sometimes take a *Yahoo*, to retire into a Corner, to lie down and howl, and groan, and spurn away all that came near him, although he were young and fat, and wanted neither Food nor Water; nor did the Servants imagine what could possibly ail him. And the only Remedy they found was to set him to hard Work, after which he would infallibly come to himself. To this I was silent out of Partiality to my own Kind; yet here I could plainly discover the true Seeds of *Spleen*, which only seizeth on the *Lazy*, the *Luxurious*, and the *Rich*; who, if they were forced to undergo the *same Regimen*, I would undertake for the Cure.

His Honour had farther observed, that a Female-*Yahoo* would often stand behind a Bank or a Bush, to gaze on the young Males passing by, and then appear, and hide, using many antick Gestures and Grimaces; at which time it was observed, that she had a most *offensive Smell*; and when any of the Males advanced, would slowly retire, looking often back, and with a counterfeit Shew of Fear, run off into some convenient Place where she knew the Male would follow her.

Swift rather dubiously seems to want it every which way at once, so that the Yahoos both are and are not representations of ourselves, and the Houyhnhnms are and are not wholly admirable or ideal. Or is it the nature of irony itself, which must weary us, or finally make us long for a true sublime, even if it should turn out to be grotesque? Fearfully strong writer that he was, Swift as ironist resembles Kafka far more than say Orwell, among modern authors. We do not know precisely how to read "In the Penal Colony" or *The Trial*, and we certainly do not know exactly how to interpret Gulliver's fourth voyage. What most merits' interpretation in Kafka is the extraordinary perversity of imagination with which he so deliberately makes himself uninterpretable. Is Swift a similar problem for the reader? What is the proper response to the dismaying conclusion of *Gulliver's Travels*?

> Having thus answered the *only* Objection that can be raised against me as a Traveller; I here take a final Leave of my Courteous Readers, and return to enjoy my own Speculations in my little Garden at *Redriff*; to apply those excellent Lessons of Virtue which I learned among the *Houyhnhnms*; to instruct the *Yahoos* of my own Family as far as I shall find them docible Animals; to behold my Figure often in a Glass, and thus if possible habituate my self by Time to tolerate the Sight of a human Creature: To lament the Brutality of *Houyhnhnms* in my own Country, but always treat their Persons with Respect, for the Sake of my noble Master, his Family, his Friends, and the whole *Houyhnhnm* Race, whom these of ours have the Honour to resemble in all their Lineaments, however their Intellectuals came to degenerate.
>
> I began last Week to permit my Wife to sit at Dinner with me, at the Farthest End of a long Table; and to answer (but with the utmost Brevity) the few Questions I ask her. Yet the Smell of a *Yahoo* continuing very offensive, I always keep my Nose well stopt with Rue, Lavender, or Tobacco-Leaves. And although it be hard for a Man late in Life to remove old Habits; I am not altogether out of Hopes in some Time to suffer a Neighbour *Yahoo* in my Company, without the Apprehensions I am yet under of his Teeth or his Claws.

Who are those "Courteous Readers" of whom Gulliver takes his final leave here? We pity the poor fellow, but we do not so much pity Mrs. Gulliver as wonder how she can tolerate the insufferable wretch. Yet the final paragraphs have a continued power that justifies their fame, even as we continue to see Gulliver as deranged:

My Reconcilement to the *Yahoo*-kind in general might not be so difficult, if they would be content with those Vices and Follies only which Nature hath entitled them to. I am not in the least provoked at the Sight of a Lawyer, a Pick-pocket, a Colonel, a Fool, a Lord, a Gamster, a Politician, a Whoremunger, a Physician, an Evidence, a Suborner, an Attorney, a Traytor, or the like: This is all according to the due Course of Things: But, when I behold a Lump of Deformity, and Diseases both in Body and Mind, smitten with *Pride*, it immediately breaks all the Measures of my Patience; neither shall I be ever able to comprehend how such an Animal and such a Vice could tally together. The wise and virtuous *Houyhnhnms*, who abound in all Excellencies that can adorn a rational Creature, have no Name for this Vice in their Language, whereby they describe the detestable Qualities of their *Yahoos*; among which they were not able to distinguish this of Pride, for want of thoroughly understanding Human Nature, as it sheweth it self in other Countries, where that Animal presides. But I, who had more Experience, could plainly observe some Rudiments of it among the wild *Yahoos*.

But the *Houyhnhnms*, who live under the Government of Reason, are no more proud of the good Qualities they possess, than I should be for not wanting a Leg or an Arm, which no Man in his Wits would boast of, although he must be miserable without them. I dwell the longer upon this Subject from the Desire I have to make the Society of an *English Yahoo* by any Means not insupportable; and therefore I here intreat those who have any Tincture of this absurd Vice, that they will not presume to appear in my Sight.

What takes precedence here, the palpable hit at the obscenity of false human pride, or the madness of Gulliver, who thinks he is a Yahoo, longs to be a Houyhnhnm, and could not bear to be convinced that he is neither? As in *A Tale of a Tub*, Swift audaciously plays at the farthest limits of irony, limits that make satire impossible, because no norm exists to which we might hope to return.

SAMUEL RICHARDSON

I

I first read *Clarissa* as a Cornell undergraduate in the late 1940s, under the skilled direction of my teacher, William M. Sale, Jr., a fierce partisan of

Richardson and a remarkable critic of fiction. Since I cannot read a novel other than the way that Sale taught me, it is not surprising that many years later I hold on fast to his canonical judgment that *Clarissa* is the finest novel in the English language. Rereading it through the years, I find it the only novel that can rival even Proust, despite Proust's evident advantages. The long and astonishing sequence that ends the novel, Clarissa's protracted death and its aftermath, is clearly at one of the limits of the novel as an art. I find myself fighting not to weep just before the moment of Clarissa's death, but as a critic I submit that these would be *cognitive* tears, and would say little about me but much about Richardson's extraordinary powers of representation. It remains a mystery that Richardson, with no strong novelistic precursors, should have been able to make Clarissa Harlowe the most persuasive instance of a kind of secular saint, a strong heroine, in the entire subsequent history of the Western novel.

Ian Watt, still our best historian of the rise of the novel, emphasizes that one of Richardson's major advances upon Defoe was in solving the problem of plot by centering it upon a single action: courtship between the sexes. That action necessarily entails Richardson's other grand innovation: the novelistic representation of the protagonists' inwardness, a mode of mimesis in which Richardson had only the one inevitable precursor, Shakespeare. If Jan Hendrik van den Berg is right, then historical psychology is essentially the study of the growing inner self, from Luther's "inner man" (1520) through Shakespeare's almost fully secularized tragic heroes on to Rousseau's and Wordsworth's solitary egos confronting, with ecstasy, the estrangement of things in a "sense of nature." *Clarissa* (1747–48) preceded all of Rousseau's publications, so that while Rousseau could have had something to tell Richardson about the sentiments and sensibility of inwardness, he did not teach the first great English novelist about the fictional representation of the inner life.

Whether anyone since has surpassed Richardson in this mimetic mode seems to me at least doubtful. George Eliot's Dorothea Brooke, Henry James's Isabel Archer, D.H. Lawrence's Ursula Brangwen, and even Virginia Woolf's Clarissa Dalloway, do not take us farther into the portrayal of a single consciousness than the original Clarissa brings us, and perhaps they all of them retreat to some degree from her full inwardness. Price remarks that "Richardson has transformed highly particularized characters so that their dense and familiar social setting fades away in the course of the slow disclosure of consequences." That transformation, in Clarissa and to some extent in Lovelace, replaces the social and historical context with a not less than tragic inwardness. If Clarissa is a saint and a martyr, then what she bears heroic witness to is not so much supernatural faith in Christ as it is natural faith in the heroic integrity of her own perpetually growing inner self.

## II

Richardson's power as a novelist centers in the wildly antithetical and fiercely ambivalent relationship between Clarissa and Lovelace, who destroy both themselves and one another in what may be the most equivocal instance of a mutual passion in all of Western literature. I do not venture that assertion lightly, but no single love affair in Shakespeare, Tolstoy, or Proust seems comparable in its strength and complexity to the terrible agon that consumes Clarissa and Lovelace. We can no more speculate upon what a marriage between Richardson's protagonists might have been than we can visualize a world harmoniously ruled by a perpetually united Antony and Cleopatra. Lovelace and Clarissa are mighty opposites yet uncannily complementary, and it is Richardson's consummate art to have so created them that they must undo one another.

I begin with Lovelace, if only because his power of being, immense as it is, finally is eclipsed by the transcendental transformation of the gorgeously dying Clarissa. But that indeed is a finality; until Clarissa begins to die, the sheer force of her resistance to Lovelace compels him to become even more himself. Conversely, Lovelace's aggression greatly strengthens Clarissa, though the cost of her confirmation is her life. In the novel's most terrible irony, the slow dying of Clarissa directly causes a steady waning in Lovelace, a dwindling down from a heroic Satanist to a self-ruined libertine, drowning in remorse and confusion.

A.D. McKillop usefully traced Lovelace's literary ancestry to the libertine man-of-fashion in Restoration comedy and to the Herculean hero of Dryden's dramas, such as *Aureng-Zebe* and *The Conquest of Granada*. This lineage accounts both for some of Lovelace's obvious faults and for his few but authentic virtues: healthy disdain for societal appearances and for false morality, a curiously wistful longing for true virtue, and a brutal honesty. But a fusion of a Restoration witty rake and Herculean rhetorician is no more a match for Clarissa Harlowe than a Jacobean hero-villain would have been, and part of the novel's fascination is in watching Lovelace slowly realize that Clarissa is necessarily an apocalyptic defeat for him. The turning point is not the rape, but a moment late in Letter 266, when Lovelace suddenly apprehends the dialectical entrapment that he and Clarissa constitute for one another:

> A horrid dear creature!—By my soul, she made me shudder! She had need, indeed, to talk of *her* unhappiness, in falling into the hands of the only *man* in the world who could have used her as I have used her! She is the only *woman* in the world who could have shocked and disturbed me as she has done—So we are upon a foot in that respect. And I think I have the *worst* of it by much.

Since very little has been my joy; very much my trouble: and *her* punishment, as she calls it, is *over*: but when *mine* will, or what it *may be*, who can tell?

Here, only recapitulating (think, then, how I must be affected at the time), I was forced to leave off, and sing a song to myself. I aimed at a lively air; but I croaked rather than sung: and fell into the old dismal thirtieth of January strain. I hemmed up for a sprightlier note; but it would not do: and at last I ended, like a malefactor, in a dead psalm melody.

High-ho!—I gape like an unfledged kite in its nest, wanting to swallow a chicken, bobbed at its mouth by its marauding dam!—

What a devil ails me!—I can neither think nor write!—

Lie down, pen, for a moment!—

The devil that ails him is the beginning of his own end, his falling outwards and downwards from his last shreds of a libertine ideology into the dreadful inner space of his defeat by Clarissa, his enforced realization that self-willing and self-assertion are permanently over for him. Clarissa, a great Puritan withholder of esteem will not accept him at his own evaluation, and he begins to know that pragmatically they have destroyed one another. His actual death is a release from the death-in-life he has suffered since Clarissa's death:

He was delirious, at times, in the two last hours; and then several times cried out, Take her away! Take her away! but named nobody. And sometimes praised some lady (that Clarissa, I suppose, whom he had called upon when he received his death's wound) calling her, Sweet Excellence! Divine Creature! Fair Sufferer!—And once he said, Look down, blessed Spirit, look down!—And there stopped—his lips however moving.

At nine in the morning, he was seized with convulsions, and fainted away; and it was a quarter of an hour before he came out of them.

His few last words I must not omit, as they show an ultimate composure; which may administer some consolation to his honourable friends.

*Blessed*—said he, addressing himself no doubt to Heaven; for his dying eyes were lifted up—a strong convulsion prevented him for a few moments saying more—But recovering, he again with great fervour (lifting up his eyes, and his spread hands) pronounced the word *Blessed*—Then, in a seeming ejaculation, he spoke inwardly so as not to be understood: at last, he distinctly pronounced these three words,

LET THIS EXPIATE!

And then, his head sinking on his pillow, he expired; at about half an hour after ten.

Lovelace dies in his own acquired religion, which is the worship of the blessed Clarissa, whom he personally has converted into something considerably more than a saint or even an angel. Being himself pure will and having been conquered by an even purer one, he worships his conqueror as God. Dying as a Clarissian rather than a Christian, as it were; Lovelace sustains his final pride, a peculiar sense of glory that has gone beyond remorse and has little left in it of mere love. This is hardly expiation in any moral or spiritual sense whatsoever, as Richardson on some level must have known, but is certainly an aesthetic expiation, worthy of Baudelaire or of Proust.

## III

Clarissa, as is radiantly appropriate, ends many trajectories beyond her lover's destination. I dissent from the entire critical tradition, from Watt and Price to my younger contemporaries, that has overemphasized Clarissa's supposed self-deceptions. Dr. Samuel Johnson first noted that Clarissa could not confront the truth of having fallen in love with Lovelace, but that hardly seems to me a duplicity in her, however unknowing. We cannot choose whom we are free to love, but Clarissa wars more strongly against every mode of overdetermination than any comparable character in secular fiction. What matters to her, and this is her greatness, is that her will cannot be violated, even by her own affections. *She refuses to see herself as anyone's victim*—whether Lovelace's, her family's, or her own turning against the self.

Lovelace becomes a wounded narcissist, and so is aggressive down to the end. But Clarissa could honestly say, if she wanted to, that it is not her narcissism but her eros that has been crucified. If Lovelace indeed represented her desire for what she did not have, and was not in herself, then her desire died, not so paradoxically, with the violation of her body. Lovelace becomes still more naturalistic after the rape, but she is transformed into a dualist and begins the process of dying to the body of this life. The issue has nothing to do with society and little to do with conventional reality. It is an aesthetic issue, the ancient agon of the Sublime mode, which always seeks to answer the triple question: more? equal to? less than? She was never less than Lovelace, hoped vainly he could be reformed into her equal, and knows now that she is far more than he is, and more indeed than anyone else in her world. At that height of the Sublime, she can only commence dying.

If her will is to remain inviolate, then its independence and integrity must be manifested by a death that is anything but a revenge, whether it be against Lovelace, her family, herself, or even against time. Rather, *her* death is the true expiation, which can bring forgiveness upon everyone else involved, though I surmise that she is more interested in forgiving herself even as she forgives the bewildered Lovelace. A Puritan saint, as Shaw's St. Joan shows, is rather more interested in her own integrity than in anyone else's suffering. The cost for Clarissa or for Shaw's St. Joan is an absolute, inner isolation, but is that not the essence of Protestantism?

There is nothing like Clarissa's virtually endless death-scene in all of literature, and while no one would wish it longer I do not wish it any shorter. Extraordinary as the actual moment of death is, in Letter 481, the most characteristic revelation of Clarissa's apotheosis is in Letter 475:

> Her breath being very short, she desired another pillow; and having two before, this made her in a manner sit up in her bed; and she spoke then with more distinctness; and seeing us greatly concerned, forgot her own sufferings to comfort us; and a charming lecture she gave us, though a brief one, upon the happiness of a timely preparation and upon the hazards of a late repentance, when the mind, as she observed, was so much weakened, as well as the body, as to render a poor soul unable to contend with its own infirmities.
>
> I beseech ye, my good friends, proceeded she, mourn not for one who mourns not, nor has cause to mourn, for herself. On the contrary, rejoice with me that all my worldly troubles are so near their end. Believe me, sirs, that I would not, if I might, choose to live, although the pleasantest part of my life were to come over again: and yet eighteen years of it, out of nineteen, have been very pleasant. To be so much exposed to temptation, and to be so liable to fail in the trial, who would not rejoice that all her dangers are over!—All I wished was pardon and blessing from my dear parents. Easy as my departure seems to promise to be, it would have been still easier had I had that pleasure. BUT GOD ALMIGHTY WOULD NOT LET ME DEPEND FOR COMFORT UPON ANY BUT HIMSELF.

This is certainly the purest Protestantism, and we might still be tempted to call this pride, particularly since Clarissa reminds us that she is all of nineteen years old. But we do Clarissa violence to name her total knowledge as a form of pride. The Protestant will by now has been blamed for practically everything that has gone wrong in our spiritual, intellectual, economic, and political life, as well as our sexual life, and the United States is the evening land of Protestantism and so the final stage for the travails of its will. Clarissa, as she dies, shows us the other side, the glory of the Protestant will. If God would not let Clarissa depend for comfort upon any but himself, then he gave her the ultimate accolade of the Protestant will: to accept esteem only where it chose to bestow esteem, and only on its own terms.

HENRY FIELDING

I

Martin Price remarks that "Fielding can reward his heroes because they do not seek a reward." As a critical observation, this is in Fielding's own spirit and tells us again what kind of novel Fielding invented, a comic *Odyssey*, ancestor of Smollett and Dickens, and of Joyce's *Ulysses*. My teacher Frederick W. Hilles liked to compare *Tom Jones* to *Ulysses*, while acknowledging that Fielding the narrator was neither invisible nor indifferent. Certainly Fielding was a fabulous artificer, which must be why he provoked so formidable a critical enemy as Dr. Samuel Johnson, who loved Alexander Pope while despising the most Popean of all novelists. Johnson vastly preferred Samuel Richardson to Fielding, a preference I myself share, though without prejudice to Fielding, since Richardson's *Clarissa* seems to me still the strongest novel in the language, surpassing even Austen's *Emma*, Eliot's *Middlemarch*, and James's *Portrait of a Lady*, all of them its descendants. *Tom Jones* founds another line, the rival tradition that includes Dickens and Joyce, novelists as exuberant as Fielding, and metaphysically and psychologically more problematic.

Samuel Johnson evidently resented what he took to be Fielding's simplistic vision, a resentment understandable in a great moralist who believed that human life was everywhere a condition in which much was to be endured, and little to be enjoyed. No one can match Johnson as a compelling moralist, but he necessarily undervalued Fielding's moral shrewdness. The true issue between Richardson and Fielding was in modes of representation, in their different views of mimesis. It is as though Richardson and Fielding split Shakespeare between them, with Richardson absorbing the Shakespearean power to portray inwardness, and Fielding inheriting Shakespeare's uncanny ease in depicting a romance world that becomes more real than reality.

Johnson told the protesting Boswell that "there is more knowledge of the heart in one letter of Richardson's, than in all *Tom Jones*." To Johnson, the personages in Fielding were "characters of manners," but in Richardson they were "characters of nature." This distinction is at least critical; one feels that many modern scholars who prefer Fielding to Richardson do so upon Coleridge's affective premises: "and how charming, how wholesome,

Fielding always is! To take him up after Richardson is like emerging from a sick-room heated by stoves into an open lawn on a breezy day in May." That has the same persuasiveness as Richardson's explanation of why he would not read *Tom Jones*: "I was told, that it was a rambling Collection of Waking Dreams, in which Probability was not observed."

The seven volumes of Clarissa were published throughout the year from December 1747 through December 1748; *Tom Jones* came out in February 1749. Rivalry between the two novels was inevitable, and both seem to have sold very well. Between them, they established the modern novel, still the dominant literary form now, after two and a half centuries. Ian Watt, the definitive chronicler of *The Rise of the Novel* (1957), probably achieved the most balanced judgment on Fielding's crucial strengths and limitations:

> In his effort to infuse the new genre with something of the Shakespearean virtues, Fielding departed too far from formal realism to initiate a viable tradition, but his work serves as a perpetual reminder that if the new genre was to challenge older literary forms it had to find a way of conveying not only a convincing impression but a wise assessment of life, an assessment that could only come from taking a much wider view than Defoe or Richardson or the affairs of mankind.

## II

What is Shakespearean about *Tom Jones*? The violent, daemonic, mindless energy of Squire Western, or the bodily ego rampant, is certainly part of the answer. Martin Price calls Western the finest English comic character after Falstaff, and the judgment seems indisputable. Yet here also a shadow falls. Falstaff, like his precursor, the Wife of Bath, is a heroic vitalist, raising vitalism, as she does, to the sublime of wit. Like Falstaff, the Wife is a great parodist, and a dangerously sophisticated Bible interpreter, as Talbot Donaldson demonstrates. But Western is energy without mind, and so is himself a living parody of vitalism. Fielding's genius nevertheless is so incarnated in Western that he breaks the limits of representation, and leaps out of the novel into that supermimetic domain where Falstaff and the Wife of Bath join Don Quixote and Sancho Panza. Western's simplicity is so exuberant and physical that it achieves a new kind of complexity, as in this astonishing comic reversal:

> *Western* had been long impatient for the Event of this Conference, and was just now arrived at the Door to listen; when having heard the last Sentiments of his Daughter's Heart, he lost

all Temper, and bursting open the Door in a Rage, cried out.—
"It is a Lie. It is a d-n'd Lie. It is all owing to that d-d'd Rascal
*Juones*; and if she could get at un, she'd ha un any Hour of the
Day." Here *Allworthy* interposed, and addressing himself to the
Squire with some Anger in his Look, he said, "Mr. *Western*, you
have not kept your Word with me. You promised to abstain from
all Violence."—"Why so I did," cries *Western*, "as long as it was
possible; but to hear a Wench telling such confounded Lies.—
Zounds! Doth she think if she can make Vools of other Volk, she
can make one of me?—No, no, I know her better than thee dost."
"I am sorry to tell you, Sir," answered *Allworthy*, "it doth not
appear by your Behaviour to this young Lady, that you know her
at all. I ask Pardon for what I say; but I think our Intimacy, your
own Desires, and the Occasion justify me. She is your Daughter,
Mr. *Western*, and I think she doth Honour to your Name. If I was
capable of Envy, I should sooner envy you on this Account, than
any other Man whatever."—"Odrabbit it," cries the Squire, "I
wish she was thine with all my Heart—wouldst soon be glad to be
rid of the Trouble o' her."—"Indeed, my good Friend," answered
*Allworthy*, "you yourself are the Cause of all the Trouble you
complain of. Place that Confidence in the young Lady which she
so well deserves, and I am certain you will be the happiest Father
on Earth."—"I Confidence in her!" cries the Squire.—"'Sblood!
what Confidence can I place in her, when she won't do as I would
ha her? Let her gi but Consent to marry as I would ha her, and
I'll place as much Confidence in her as wouldst ha me."—"You
have no Right, Neighbour," answered *Allworthy*, "to insist on any
such Consent. A negative Voice your Daughter allows you, and
God and Nature have thought proper to allow you no more." "A
negative Voice?" cries the Squire—"Ay! ay! I'll shew you what a
negative Voice I ha. Go along, go into your Chamber, go, you
Stubborn."—"Indeed, Mr. *Western*," said *Allworthy*,—"Indeed,
you use her cruelly—I cannot bear to see this—You shall, you
must behave to her in a kinder Manner. She deserves the best of
Treatment." "Yes, yes," said the Squire, "I know what she
deserves: Now she's gone, I'll shew you what she deserves—See
here, Sir, here is a Letter from my Cousin, my Lady *Bellaston*, in
which she is so kind to gi me to understand, that the Fellow is got
out of Prison again; and here she advises me to take all the Care
I can o' the Wench. Odzookers! Neighbour *Allworthy*, you don't
know what it is to govern a Daughter."

The Squire ended his Speech with some Compliments to his
own Sagacity; and then *Allworthy*, after a formal Preface,

acquainted him with the whole Discovery which he had made concerning *Jones*, with his Anger to *Blifil*, and with every Particular which hath been disclosed to the Reader in the preceding Chapters.

Men over-violent in their Dispositions, are, for the most Part, as changeable in them. No sooner then was *Western* informed of Mr. *Allworthy*'s Intention to make *Jones* his Heir, then he joined heartily with the Uncle in every Commendation of the Nephew, and became as eager for her Marriage with *Jones*, as he had before been to couple her to *Blifil*.

Here Mr. *Allworthy* was again forced to interpose, and to relate what had passed between him and *Sophia*, at which he testified great Surprize.

The Squire was silent a Moment, and looked wild with Astonishment at this Account—At last he cried out, "Why what can be the Meaning of this, Neighbour *Allworthy*? Vond o un she was, that I'll be sworn to.—Odzookers! I have hit o't. As sure as a Gun I have hit o the very right o't. It's all along o Zister. The Girl hath got a Hankering after this son of a Whore of a Lord. I vound'em together at my Cousin, my Lady *Bellaston*'s. He hath turned the Head o' her that's certain—but d-n me if he shall ha her—I'll ha no Lords nor Courtiers in my Vamily."

Western is equally passionate, within moments, in swearing that Sophia shall *not* have Jones, and that she *shall*. We are delighted by his stance, either way, and most delighted at his childish ease in moving from one position to the other without pause, embarrassment, or reflection. A passionate infant, Squire Western is sublime on the page, or on the screen, where as played by Hugh Griffith he ran off with the Osborne-Richardson *Tom Jones*; but in mere reality he would be a monster. As a representation he is triumphant because like the much greater Falstaff he is free of the superego. We rejoice in Western because he is freedom gone wild, including freedom from nasty plotting; yet his mindlessness almost frightens us.

Price is as accurate as ever when he observes that "Fielding controls his characters by limiting them," but Western is the grand exception, being out of control and extravagant, beyond all limits. No other eighteenth-century novel could accommodate Western, which is another indication of the power of *Tom Jones*. Something primeval in the mode of romance survives in Western the wild man, who hardly seems to belong to a post-Swiftian novel that still exalts the Augustan vision. Fielding, like Pope and Swift, joins the Enlightenment consciousness and ideas of order to an ongoing sense of the demands of energy. Johnson, who shared with Fielding the heritage of Pope and Swift, may have felt, obscurely but accurately, that Fielding, like Swift, gave too much away to the daemonic force of vitalism. "This kind of writing may be termed not improperly the Comedy of Romance," Johnson said of Fielding, thus relegating Fielding to the dark and enchanted ground not yet purified by reason. Johnson meant to condemn, perhaps, but guides us instead to Fielding's most surprising strength.

## Laurence Sterne's *Tristram Shandy*

### I

Sterne remarked, in a letter, that *Tristram Shandy* "was made and formed to baffle all criticism," but he probably knew better. Dr. Johnson, greatest of critics, insisted that *Tristram Shandy* would not last, a hopelessly wrong prophecy. Sterne gives the critic and reader everything to do, and can anyone resist, one wonders, a novel in which the hero-narrator declares (volume 1, chapter 14) that "I have been at it these six weeks, making all the speed I possibly could,—and am not yet born"? Published in nine short volumes from 1760 to 1767, *Tristram Shandy* is the masterpiece of what Northrop Frye has taught us to call the Age of Sensibility, the era of Rousseau, and of a secularized, vernacular, "Orientalized" Bible, described by Bishop Lowth (*Lectures on the Sacred Poetry of the Hebrews*, 1753) as the true source of the "language of the passions." It is also the era of John Locke, much as we still live in the Age of Sigmund Freud. Johnson, who also opposed the poetry of Thomas Gray and of his own personal friend, William Collins, was quite consistent in setting himself against *Tristram Shandy*. Henry Fielding may have subverted novelistic forms, but Sterne subverts the entire Augustan mode of representation and truly ends the cultural enterprise in which Pope had triumphed.

It cannot be accidental that so many of the best contemporary Spanish-American novels are Shandean, whether or not the particular writer actually has read Sterne. One such distinguished novelist, when told by me how grand a fantasist he seemed, amiably assured me that his intentions were merely realistic. In the presence of extraordinary actuality, Wallace Stevens observed, consciousness could take the place of imagination. For Sterne, consciousness itself was the extraordinary actuality, so that sensibility became one with imagination. Dualism, Cartesian and Lockean, comes to us now mostly in Freudian guise. "Shandean guise" would do as well, since Sterne is a thoroughgoing Freudian five generations before Freud. The fundamental Freudian frontier concepts—the drive, the bodily ego, the nonrepressive defenses of introjection and projection—are conceptually exemplified in *Tristram Shandy*, as is the central Freudian idea or trope of repression or defense. Most readers of Sterne see this at once, and many of his critics have reflected upon it. A Freudian exegesis of *Tristram Shandy* therefore becomes a redundancy. Far more vital is the question: What is Sterne trying to do for himself, as a novelist, by his dualistic, solipsistic, psychological emphasis?

That there is an aesthetic and moral program in the Shandean philosophy, most critics agree, but phrasing it has led to some unfortunate banalities. You can sum up Pope's or Fielding's designs upon the reader rather more easily than you can express Sterne's. This is not simply a rhetorical dilemma; Sterne is a great ironist and parodist, but so are Pope and Fielding, while Swift excels even Sterne in such modes. But if all three of the great Augustans are cognitively subtle, Sterne is preternaturally subtle, to the point of being daemonic. Swift is ferocious, yet Sterne is uncanny; his artistry is indeed diabolic as Martin Price comments, comparing it to the skill of Ionesco. The spirit of the comparison is right, but Ionesco hardly can work on Sterne's scale, which is both vast and minute. I prefer Richard Lanham's comparison of Sterne to Chaucer, who also is too wise to fall into an Arnoldian high seriousness. Like Chaucer and Cervantes, Sterne is very serious about play, but he is even more playful about form than they are.

## II

What is love, to an almost perfect solipsist? Can it be more than sex? Is sex all, and does every trembling hand make us squeak, like dolls, the wished-for word? Sterne is reductive enough to muse on the question, and to intimate an affirmative answer:

> I had escaped, continued the corporal, all that time from falling in love, and had gone on to the end of the chapter, had it not been predestined otherwise—there is no resisting our fate.
> It was on a *Sunday*, in the afternoon, as I told your honour—
> The old man and his wife had walked out—
> Every thing was still and hush as midnight about the house—
> There was not so much as a duck or a duckling about the yard—
> —When the fair *Beguine* came in to see me.
> My wound was then in a fair way of doing well—the inflammation had been gone off for some time, but it was succeeded with an itching both above and below my knee, so insufferable, that I had not shut my eyes the whole night for it.
> Let me see it, said she, kneeling down upon the ground parallel to my knee, and laying her hand upon the part below it— It only wants rubbing a little, said the *Beguine*; so covering it with the bed cloaths, she began with the fore-finger of her right-hand to rub under my knee, guiding her fore-finger backwards and forwards by the edge of the flannel which kept on the dressing.

In five or six minutes I felt slightly the end of the second finger—and presently it was laid flat with the other, and she continued rubbing in that way round and round for a good while; it then came into my head, that I should fall in love—I blush'd when I saw how white a hand she had—I shall never, an' please your honour, behold another hand so white whilst I live—

—Not in that place: said my uncle *Toby*—

Though it was the most serious despair in nature to the corporal—he could not forbear smiling.

The young *Beguine*, continued the corporal, perceiving it was of great service to me—from rubbing, for some time, with two fingers—proceeded to rub at length, with three—till by little and little she brought down the fourth, and then rubb'd with her whole hand: I will never say another word, an' please your honour, upon hands again—but it was softer than satin—

—Prithee, *Trim*, commend it as much as thou wilt, said my uncle *Toby*, I shall hear thy story with the more delight—The corporal thank'd his master most unfeignedly; but having nothing to say upon the *Beguine*'s hand, but the same over again—he proceeded to the effects of it.

The fair *Beguine*, said the corporal, continued rubbing with her whole hand under my knee—till I fear'd her zeal would weary her—"I would do a thousand times more," said she, "for the love of Christ"—In saying which she pass'd her hand across the flannel, to the part above my knee, which I had equally complained of, and rubb'd it also.

I perceived, then, I was beginning to be in love—

As she continued rub-rub-rubbing—I felt it spread from under her hand, an' please your honour, to every part of my frame—The more she rubb'd, and the longer strokes she took—the more the fire kindled in my veins—till at length, by two or three strokes longer than the rest—my passion rose to the highest pitch—I seiz'd her hand—

—And then, thou clapped'st it to thy lips, *Trim*, said my uncle *Toby*—and madest a speech.

Whether the corporal's amour terminated precisely in the way my uncle Toby described it, is not material; it is enough that it contain'd in it the essence of all the love-romances which ever have been wrote since the beginning of the world. (8, 22)

To be in love is to be aroused; no more, no less. Sterne, something of an invalid, was abnormally sensitive, as W.B.C. Watkins remarked, "—partly because he was inevitably self-conscious physically to an abnormal degree.

He was acutely aware of the very circulation of his blood and the beating of his heart." Much of Sterne's alleged prurience is actually his heightened vulnerability, cognitive and bodily, to sexual stimuli. The sense of "Sensibility" in Sterne is fully sexual, and aids us in seeing the true nature of the cultural term, both morally and aesthetically. A susceptibility to tender feelings, however fine, and whether one's own or those of others, becomes objectified as a quality or stance that turns away from the Stoic and Augustan ideal of reason in affective response. This is Sensibility or "the Sentimental" ideologically free from either right-wing celebration of bourgeois morality or left-wing idealization or proletarian or pastoral natural virtues. Its politics, though Whiggish in origin, diffuse into a universal and histrionic vision of the force and beauty of the habits of the heart. Martin Price terms it "a vehement, often defiant assertion of the value of man's feelings." Overtly self-conscious and dramatic, yet insisting upon its sincerity, the stance of Sensibility is a kind of sexualization of all the other effects, as Sterne most clearly knew, showed, and told. Richard Lanham sums this up when he writes that "For Sterne, we finally become not only insatiable pleasure-seekers but, by our nature, incurable poseurs."

All Shandeans have their favorite episodes, and I am tempted to cite all of volume 7, throughout which Tristram/Sterne flees from Death by taking a Sentimental journey through France. One could vote for the story of Amandus and Amanda, or for the concluding country-dance with Nanette, two superb moments in volume 7. But, if we are pleasure-seeking poseurs, we cannot do better than chapter 15 of volume 8, which precedes the Widow Wadman's direct attempt to light Uncle Toby at both ends at once, in the sentry-box:

> It is a great pity—but 'tis certain from every day's observation of man, that he may be set on fire like a candle, at either end—provided there is a sufficient wick standing out; if there is not—there's an end of the affair; and if there is—by lighting it at the bottom, as the flame in that case has the misfortune generally to put out itself—there's an end of the affair again.
>
> For my part, could I always have the ordering of it which way I would be burnt myself—for I cannot bear the thoughts of being burnt like a beast—I would oblige a housewife constantly to light me at the top; for then I should burn down decently to the socket; that is, from my head to my heart, from my heart to my liver, from my liver to my bowels, and so on by the meseraick veins and arteries, through all the turns and lateral insertions of the intestines and their tunicles to the blind gut—
>
> —I beseech you, doctor *Slop*, quoth my uncle *Toby*, interrupting him as he mentioned the *blind gut*, in a discourse

with my father the night my mother was brought to bed of me—
I beseech you, quoth my uncle *Toby*, to tell me which is the blind
gut; for, old as I am, I vow I do not know to this day where it lies.

The *blind gut*, answered doctor *Slop*, lies betwixt the *Illion* and
*Colon*—

—In a man? said my father.

—'Tis precisely the same, cried doctor *Slop*, in a woman—
That's more than I know; quoth my father. (8, 15)

We confront again Sterne's marvelous sense of the dualistic perplexities
of human existence. Man is not exactly the Puritan candle of the Lord, burning
with a preternatural will-to-holiness, but a sexual candle altogether, burning
with the natural will-to-live. When Tristram/Sterne asks to be lit at the top,
presumably with cognitive fire, then he asks also to "burn down decently to the
socket." Sterne's fierce metaphor rejects the Cartesian ghost-in-the-machine
(Gilbert Ryle's fine formulation) and desires instead a conflagration of the
mind through the senses. Though he is perhaps the most satirical of all
vitalists, Sterne's final affinities seem to be with Rabelais and Blake, visionaries
who sought to redeem us through an improvement in sensual enjoyment.

## Oliver Goldsmith

### I

Oliver Goldsmith, versatile and graceful in every genre, compels a critic to
speculate upon the disproportion between the writer-as-person and the
writer-as-writer. Some (not all) of the most accomplished writers I have
known have been the most colorless of personalities, or if more vivid and
interesting as people, then they have been remarkably unpleasant or foolish
or merely mawkish. Goldsmith appears to have been a luckless individual and
even what Freud called a "moral masochist," a victim of his own death-drive
at the age of forty-four. Indeed, Goldsmith is a fairly classic instance of many
Freudian insights, and both *The Vicar of Wakefield* and *She Stoops to Conquer*
sustain immediate illumination when Freudian categories are applied to
them. What Freud termed "the most prevalent form of degradation in erotic
life" is a clear guide to young Marlow's backwardness with well-born women,
and exuberant aggressivity with inn barmaids, college bedmakers, and others
of whom he remarks: "They are of us you know." And the lumpish Tony
Lumpkin becomes an even more persuasive representation when his descent
into the company of the alehouse is seen, again in Freudian guise, as a
reaction-formation to his dreadful mother, Mrs. Hardcastle.

Goldsmith aped Johnson in most things, even to the copying of the
critic's manner, according to Boswell. Johnson spoke the last word upon his

friend and follower: "If nobody was suffered to abuse poor Goldy but those who could write as well, he would have few censors." Yet it is a curious sadness that the best lines in any poem by Goldsmith, the concluding passage of *The Deserted Village*, were written by Johnson himself:

> That trade's proud empire hastes to swift decay,
> As ocean sweeps the laboured mole away;
> While self-dependent power can time defy,
> As rocks resist the billows and the sky.

An ironical reading might interpret that humanly constructed breakwater, "the laboured mole," as Goldsmith's ego, in contrast to Johnsonian self-dependence, the great critic's rock-like ego. Still, Goldsmith's laboured breakwater has defied time also, though not quite with the massive Johnsonian force. Goldsmith's writing survives on its curious grace, curious both because it resists strict definition and because it extends across the genres: from the Popean verse of *The Traveller*, through the Bunyanesque revision of the Book of Job in the sentimental novel *The Vicar of Wakefield*, on to the elegiac pastoralism of *The Deserted Village*, the permanently successful stage comedy *She Stoops to Conquer*, and the urbane good nature of the posthumously published poem *Retaliation*, a gentle satire upon the members of Dr. Johnson's Club.

The strongest case for Goldsmith was made by William Hazlitt, second only to Johnson in my estimate, among all critics in the language:

> Goldsmith, both in verse and prose, was one of the most delightful writers in the language.... His ease is quite unconscious. Everything in him is spontaneous, unstudied, yet elegant, harmonious, graceful, nearly faultless.

A kind of natural or unconscious artist, Goldsmith prevails by disarming his reader. He seems the least tendentious of all authors, writing as though he had no design upon us. Even now he has not lost his audience, although critics sometimes treat his works as period pieces. He is strangely close to popular literature, though he hardly can sustain comparison with the far more powerful Bunyan. Perhaps he moves us now primarily as an instance of our continuity with a past that we seem otherwise wholly to have abandoned.

## II

The canonical status of *The Vicar of Wakefield* is beyond doubt, though I do not advise rereading it side by side with Bunyan's far stronger *The*

*Pilgrim's Progress* as I have just done. But then, Bunyan is so powerful a visionary as to claim the company of Milton and Blake. Goldsmith gives us a gentle theodicy in the *Vicar*, and theodicy is hardly a gentle mode. Henry James, writing an introduction to the novel in 1900, called it "the spoiled child of our literature," a work so amiable that it seemed to him "happy in the manner in which a happy man is happy—a man, say, who has married an angel or been appointed to a sinecure."

Like the Book of Job, the *Vicar* brings a good man, here Dr. Primrose, into the power of Satan, here Squire Thornhill. Some recent revisionist readings of the *Vicar* have attempted to give us a Dr. Primrose who is more self-righteous than virtuous, more smugly egoistical than innocent. These seem to me weak misreadings because they overlook Goldsmith's most surprising revision of the Book of Job. With singular audacity, Goldsmith makes his Job the narrator. Whatever you have Job do, you ought not to make him the hero of a first-person narrative. Consider the aesthetic and spiritual effect that even the opening would then have upon us:

> I was a man in the land of Uz, and my name was Job; I was perfect
> and upright, and I feared God, and eschewed evil.

No one proclaims his own virtues without alienating us, and no one recites his own sufferings without embarrassing us. The opening of *The Vicar of Wakefield* is not quite like that of a first-person Book of Job, but it is problematic enough:

> I was ever of opinion, that the honest man who married and
> brought up a large family, did more service than he who
> continued single and only talked of population. From this
> motive, I had scarce taken orders a year, before I began to think
> seriously of matrimony, and chose my wife, as she did her
> wedding-gown, not for a fine glossy surface, but such qualities as
> would wear well.

At best, poor Primrose sounds a pompous fool; at worst, a bore rampant. Why did Goldsmith take the risk? Was Primrose intended to be a satiric butt and Burchell a reality instructor? Dickens evidently did not think so, and something of Primrose got into Mr. Pickwick. Unlike Goethe and Dickens, we do not find Primrose to be altogether comically lovable. However, we also ought not to fault him. Perhaps he does represent a secularization of the figure of Job or a Johnsonian allegory of an education in true humility, but I suspect that he is primarily Goldsmith's introjection of Job. This is not to suggest a composite figure, Job/Primrose-Goldsmith as it were, but to intimate that Primrose is a loving self-satire on Goldsmith's part, or an amiable Jobean parody directed against the feckless writer's own penchant for catastrophe.

Goldsmith takes the risk of first-person narration because he knows that the Vicar Primrose is his own somewhat ironic self-portrait and that his personal Jobean tribulations do not exactly achieve sublimity. Yet Goldsmith, in life, and the Vicar, in the novel, cannot refrain from self-praise, from a kind of snobbery of virtue, even as they are altogether the passive victims of fortune. Goldsmith, though an impossible personality, was a literary genius, but Dr. Primrose is simply not very clever. An unintelligent Job startles us, if only by reminding us what a formidable moral psychologist and reasoner the biblical Job was, so much so that he finally infuriated John Calvin, his greatest commentator. Calvin, in his sermons on the Book of Job, is finally provoked to cry out that God would have had to make new worlds to satisfy Job. No one would say that God would have had to make new worlds to satisfy Dr. Primrose. Goldsmith himself, I suspect, was about halfway between Job and the Vicar in this regard.

## III

*The Citizen of the World, The Vicar of Wakefield*, and the three major poems may be the best of Goldsmith, but I myself prefer *She Stoops to Conquer*. It has held the stage for more than two hundred years and may well be the authentic instance of a popular drama in English after Shakespeare. Though it was intended as a parody upon what Goldsmith called Sentimental as opposed to Laughing Comedy, we have lost the satire without losing the value of the work. It remains very funny and evidently always will be funny. Goldsmith did not intend farce, but that is what *She Stoops to Conquer* assuredly is: major farce. There is something Shakespearean about Kate Hardcastle, though to compare her to the Rosalind of *As You Like It* is an offence against literary tact, as is any comparison of Tony Lumpkin to Puck.

Goldsmith had the literary good sense to keep his farce simple, reductive, and almost primitive; the portrait of Mrs. Hardcastle has a kind of unrelenting savagery about it. And Tony Lumpkin's ordeal-by-fright for her is not less than sadistic, with a cruelty in which we are compelled to share:

> TONY. Never fear me. Here she comes. Vanish. She's got from the pond, and draggled up to the waist like a mermaid. *Enter Mrs Hardcastle.*
>
> MRS HARDCASTLE. Oh, Tony, I'm killed. Shook. Battered to death. I shall never survive it. That last jolt that laid us against the quickset hedge has done my business.
>
> TONY. Alack, mama, it was all your own fault. You would be for running away by night, without knowing one inch of the way.

MRS HARDCASTLE. I wish we were at home again. I never met so
many accidents in so short a journey. Drenched in the mud,
overturned in a ditch, stuck fast in a slough, jolted to a jelly,
and at last to lose our way. Whereabouts do you think we
are, Tony?

TONY. By my guess we should be upon Crack-skull Common,
about forty miles from home.

MRS HARDCASTLE. O lud! O lud! the most notorious spot in all the
country. We only want a robbery to make a complete night
on't.

TONY. Don't be afraid, mama, don't be afraid. Two of the five that
kept here are hanged, and the other three may not find us.
Don't be afraid. Is that a man that's galloping behind us?
No; it's only a tree. Don't be afraid.

MRS HARDCASTLE. The fright will certainly kill me.

TONY. Do you see anything like a black hat moving behind the
thicket?

MRS HARDCASTLE. O death!

TONY. No, it's only a cow. Don't be afraid, mama; don't be afraid.

MRS HARDCASTLE. As I'm alive, Tony, I see a man coming towards
us. Ah! I'm sure on't. If he perceives us we are undone.

TONY (*aside*). Father-in-law, by all that's unlucky, come to take
one of his night walks. (*To her*) Ah, it's a highwayman, with
pistols as long as my arm. A damned ill-looking fellow.

MRS HARDCASTLE. Good heaven defend us! He approaches.

TONY. Do you hide yourself in that thicket, and leave me to
manage him. If there be any danger I'll cough and cry,
Hem! When I cough be sure to keep close.
*Mrs Hardcastle hides behind a tree in the Back Scene.*

To find a comparable savagery, one would have to turn to W.S.
Gilbert. There is a touch of Gilbert to *She Stoops to Conquer*, if only because
we are already in that cosmos of nonsense that is shadowed by the Freudian
reality principle. Freud, writing on "Humor" in 1928, heard in it the voice
of the super-ego, speaking "kindly words of comfort to the intimidated
ego." This does not take us far when we consider Shakespearean comedy at
its most complex, *As You Like It* or *All's Well That Ends Well*. But it
beautifully enlightens us as to Goldsmith's holiday from the superego in *She
Stoops to Conquer*. Goldsmith was very uncomfortable as Job, even as that
most amiable and silly of Jobs, Dr. Primrose. But he was supremely
comfortable as Tony Lumpkin, his kindly word of comfort to his own
intimidated ego.

## Tobias Smollett

Despite the vigor and humor of *Humphry Clinker*, Smollett is currently the most neglected of the major eighteenth-century British novelists. Since he is not of the aesthetic eminence of Richardson, Fielding, and Sterne, one would not expect him to provoke the intense critical interest that they perpetually sustain. But *Humphry Clinker*, in my judgment, is a stronger novel than Defoe's *Moll Flanders* or Goldsmith's *The Vicar of Wakefield*, and compares favorably also with Fanny Burney's *Evelina*. Since it is now less read and studied than any of those three, its eclipse perhaps indicates that something in Smollett is not available to what is dominant in our current sensibility. The era of Thomas Pynchon, apocalyptic and beyond the resources of any satiric vision, is not a time for accommodating Smollett's rough tumble of an expedition towards a yearned-for health.

Smollett, a surgeon, probably knew he had not long to live even as he composed *Humphry Clinker*. Resident in Italy from 1768 on, for his health, Smollett died there in 1771, just fifty, some three months after *Humphry Clinker* was published. The expedition that is the novel, winding from Wales up through the length of England well into Smollett's native Scotland, is the author's long farewell to life, rendering Britain with a peculiar vividness as he remembers it from abroad.

Why the novel is named for Humphry Clinker rather than its central figure, Matthew Bramble, who clearly is Smollett's surrogate, never has been clear to me, except that Clinker is a representative of the future and may be Smollett's wistful introjection of a life he would not survive to know. Clinker and Bramble rise together from the water, a natural son and the father he has saved from drowning, and both undergo a change of name into the same name: Matthew Loyd. This curious mutual baptism seems to have been a mythic transference for Smollett, since Matthew Loyd was Bramble's *former* name, and will be his son Humphry Clinker's *future* name. It is as though the slowly dying Smollett required a double vision of survival: as a Matthew Bramble largely purged of an irascibility close to madness, and as Humphry Clinker, a kindly and innocent youth restored to a lost heritage.

I have found that many of my friends and students, generally very good readers, shy away from *Humphry Clinker* and from Smollett in general, because they are repelled by his mode, which at its strongest tends toward grotesque farce. The mode by definition is not pleasant, but, like the much greater Swift, Smollett is a master in this peculiar subgenre. It is hardly accidental that Thomas Rowlandson illustrated Smollett in the early 1790s, because there is a profound affinity between the novelist and the caricaturist. Smollett's reality, at its most intense, is phantasmagoric, and there are moments early on in *Humphry Clinker* when the irritable (and well-named) Bramble seems close to madness. His speculations on the origins of the waters at Bath are not less than disgusting, and he is more than weary of mankind: "My curiosity is quite satisfied: I have done with the science of men, and must now endeavour to amuse myself with the novelty of things." Everywhere he finds only "food for spleen, and subject for ridicule."

Bramble satirizes everything he encounters, and is himself an instance of the mocker mocked or the satirist satirized. One can cultivate an amused affection for him, but he is not Don Quixote, and the vivid but unlikable Lismahago, my favorite character in the book, is no Sancho Panza. Smollett evidently identifies with Bramble, but we cannot do so, and surely Smollett intended it that way. We may enjoy farce, but we do not wish to find ourselves acting in one as we stumble on in our lives. I think of my favorite farce in the language, Marlowe's *The Jew of Malta*. I have acted on stage just once in my life, playing Falstaff in an emergency, an amateur pressed into service, and played the witty knight more or less in the style of the late, great Zero Mostel playing Leopold Bloom in *Ulysses in Nighttown*. The one part I would love to play on stage is Barabas, bloody Jew of Malta, but in life obviously I would prefer being Falstaff to being Barabas.

When a novel conducts itself as realistic farce, which is Smollett's mode, we are denied the pleasures of introjection and identification. But a novel is wiser to forsake realism when it moves into farce. Sometimes I wish, reading Smollett, that he had been able to read the Evelyn Waugh of *Decline and Fall*, *Vile Bodies*, *A Handful of Dust*, because I think that Waugh would have been a good influence upon him. But that is to wish Smollett other than Smollett; one of his strengths is that he drives realistic representation almost beyond its proper limits, in order to extend the empire of farce. Perhaps his own fierce temperament required the extension, for he was more than a little mad, in this resembling certain elements of temperament in Swift, Sterne, and Dr. Samuel Johnson.

Sterne, in *A Sentimental Journey*, robustly satirizes Smollett as "the learned Smelfungus," who "set out with the spleen and jaundice, and every object he passed by was discoloured or distorted." Coming out of the Pantheon, Smelfungus comments, "'Tis nothing but a huge cock pit," and all his travel adventures lead to similar judgments, provoking Sterne to a good retort: "I'll tell it, cried Smelfungus, to the world. You had better tell it, said I, to your physician." All of us would rather travel with Sterne than with Smollett, but reading Smollett remains a uniquely valuable experience. Let us take him at his most ferociously grotesque, in the account of the sufferings of Lismahago and the still more unfortunate Murphy at the horrid hands of the Miami Indians:

> By dint of her interrogations, however, we learned, that he and
> ensign Murphy had made their escape from the French hospital
> at Montreal, and taken to the woods, in hope of reaching some

English settlement; but mistaking their route, they fell in with a party of Miamis, who carried them away in captivity. The intention of these Indians was to give one of them as an adopted son to a venerable sachem, who had lost his own in the course of the war, and to sacrifice the other according to the custom of the country. Murphy, as being the younger and handsomer of the two, was designed to fill the place of the deceased, not only as the son of the sachem, but as the spouse of a beautiful squaw, to whom his predecessor had been betrothed; but in passing through the different whigwhams or villages of the Miamis, poor Murphy was so mangled by the women and children, who have the privilege of torturing all prisoners in their passage, that, by the time they arrived at the place of the sachem's residence, he was rendered altogether unfit for the purposes of marriage: it was determined therefore, in the assembly of the warriors, that ensign Murphy should be brought to the stake, and that the lady should be given to lieutenant Lismahago, who had likewise received his share of torments, though they had not produced emasculation.—A joint of one finger had been cut, or rather sawed off with a rusty knife; one of his great toes was crushed into a mash betwixt two stones; some of his teeth were drawn, or dug out with a crooked nail; splintered reeds had been thrust up his nostrils and other tender parts; and the calves of his legs had been blown up with mines of gunpowder dug in the flesh with the sharp point of the tomahawk.

The Indians themselves allowed that Murphy died with great heroism, singing, as his death song, the *Drimmendoo*, in concert with Mr. Lismahago, who was present at the solemnity. After the warriors and the matrons had made a hearty meal upon the muscular flesh which they pared from the victim, and had applied a great variety of tortures, which he bore without flinching, an old lady, with a sharp knife, scooped out one of his eyes, and put a burning coal in the socket. The pain of this operation was so exquisite that he could not help bellowing, upon which the audience raised a shout of exultation, and one of the warriors stealing behind him, gave him the *coup de grace* with a hatchet.

Lismahago's bride, the squaw Squinkinacoosta, distinguished herself on this occasion.—She shewed a great superiority of genius in the tortures which she contrived and executed with her own hands.—She vied with the stoutest warrior in eating the flesh of the sacrifice; and after all the other females were fuddled with dram-drinking, she was not so intoxicated but that she was able to play the game of the platter with the conjuring sachem, and afterwards go through the ceremony of her own wedding, which was consummated that same evening. The captain had lived very happily with this accomplished squaw for two years, during which she bore him a son, who is now the representative of his mother's tribe; but, at length, to his unspeakable grief, she had died of a fever, occasioned by eating too much raw bear, which they had killed in a hunting excursion.

This is both dreadfully funny and funnily dreadful, and is quite marvelous writing, though evidently not to all tastes. If it were written by Mark Twain, we would know how to take it, but Smollett renders it with a dangerous relish, which makes us a little uncertain, since we do not wish to be quite as rancid as the learned Smelfungus, or even as the dreadful Lismahago for that matter. Reading Smollett is sometimes like eating too much raw bear, but that only acknowledges how authentic and strong his flavor is.

To have inspired Rowlandson and fostered Charles Dickens (who took his origins in a blend of Smollett and Ben Jonson) is enough merit for any one writer. Smollett is to Dickens what Marlowe was to Shakespeare, a forerunner so swallowed up by an enormous inheritor that the precursor sometimes seems a minnow devoured by a whale. But, considered in himself, Smollett has something of Marlowe's eminence. Each carried satirical farce and subversive melodrama to a new limit, and that too is merit enough.

### Fanny Burney's *Evelina*

*Evelina or the History of a Young Lady's Entrance into the World* (1778) earned the approbation of Dr. Samuel Johnson, who remains in my judgment, as in that of many others, the best critic in Western literary history. These days *Evelina* seems to attract mostly feminist critics, though it is hardly a precursor of their ideologies and sensibilities. A reader who knows the novels of Samuel Richardson will recognize immediately how indebted Fanny Burney was to him, and any reader of Jane Austen will be interested in *Evelina* in order to contrast the very different ways in which Richardson influenced the two women novelists. In itself, *Evelina* provides a rather mixed aesthetic experience upon rereading, at least to me. Its largest strength is in its humor and in Fanny Burney's quite extraordinary ear for modes of speech. What is rather disappointing is Evelina herself, who records the wit and spirits of others, while herself manifesting a steady goodness that is not ideally suited for fictional representation.

*Entrance* is indeed the novel's central metaphor, and Evelina enters the social world as a kind of lesser Sir Charles Grandison, rather than as a lesser Clarissa. This is not to say that Evelina's advent in the book does not please us. Fanny Burney shrewdly delays, and we do not have direct acquaintance with Evelina until the lively start of Letter 8:

> This house seems to be the house of joy; every face wears a smile, and a laugh is at every body's service. It is quite amusing to walk about and see the general confusion; a room leading to the garden is fitting up for Captain Mirvan's study. Lady Howard does not sit a moment in a place; Miss Mirvan is making caps; every body so busy!—such flying from room to room!—so many orders given, and retracted, and given again! nothing but hurry and perturbation.

Ronald Paulson praises *Evelina* as a careful balance of the old and the new, of Smollettian satire and a pre-Austenian ironic sensibility. I am surprised always when Smollett's effect upon Fanny Burney is judiciously demonstrated, as it certainly is by Paulson, precisely because Evelina cannot be visualized as journeying in the superbly irascible company of Matthew Bramble, whereas one can imagine her in dignified converse with Sir Charles Grandison. That seems another indication of a trouble in *Evelina* as a novel, the trouble alas being Evelina herself. In a world of roughness and wit, she remains the perpetual anomaly, too good for her context and too undivided to fascinate her reader. One implicit defense of Evelina is the polemic of Susan Staves, who views the heroine's dominant affect as being one of acute anxiety, since she is frequently in danger of sexual (or quasi-sexual) assault. Staves has a telling and lovely sentence: "Evelina's progress through the public places of London is about as tranquil as the progress of a fair-haired girl through modern Naples." Surrounded by Smollettian characters, the non-Smollettian Evelina must struggle incessantly to maintain her delicacy. That is clearly the case, and yet again, this creates a problem for the reader. Delicacy under assault is very difficult to represent except in a comic mode, since more of our imaginative sympathy is given to rambunctiousness than to virtue.

This makes it highly problematic, at least for me, to read *Evelina* either as a study in the dynamics of fear or as a chronicle of assault. If I find Evelina herself a touch too bland in her benignity, nevertheless she seems to me commendably tough, and rather less traumatized than some feminist critics take her to be. Historical changes in psychology are very real, and eighteenth-century men and women (of the same social class) have more in common with one another than say eighteenth-century women intellectuals have in common with our contemporary feminist critics. Evelina (and Fanny Burney) are less obsessed by Electra complexes, and less dismayed by female difficulties, than many among us, and a curious kind of anachronism is too frequently indulged these days.

Like her creator, Fanny Burney, who knew so well how to live in the forceful literary world of her father's companions, Evelina is ultimately stronger and shrewder than any of the men, and nearly all of the women, in her own universe. They may assault her delicacy, but she outwits them, and subtly triumphs over them. Her goodness does not exclude the skills of a grand manipulator. She is an anomaly in her sensibility, but not in her admirably poised social sense, and her manifold virtues coexist with an enigmatic cunning, suitable to the social psychology of her era.

JAMES R. FOSTER

# Sentiment from Afra Behn to Marivaux

J'étais remplie de sentiment: j'avais le cœur plus fin et plus avancé que l'esprit, quoique ce dernier ne le fût déjà pas mal.

—Marianne

1

In England sensibility made its novelistic debut in the love stories that came from the pens of authors who are little known, or known principally for their coarse comedies or scandalous court chronicles. The most important influence upon these writers came from a group of French women who wrote in the last decades of the seventeenth and the first of the eighteenth century, and whose novels, for the most part, were modelled after the *Princess of Cleves*.

Although history was still present in many of these French narratives, it was little more than a frame for a story of love and adventure. The rôle of the heroine was nearly always more important than that of the hero. The authors gave much attention to delineations of the tender passion and accompanying states of mind—tearful moods, anxiety, and melancholy. And they took care to avoid the incredibility and prolixity of the heroic-gallant romance. Usually they showed a partiality for material from private and everyday life, yet they were not above using the old novelistic themes, such as piracy, great storms, false deaths, hidden identities, disguises, and lovers who wander in search of each other. Occasionally a bit of landscape, or a

From *History of the Pre-Romantic Novel in England.* © 1949 by The Modern Language Association of America.

ruined and gloomy chateau, or a ghost got into the story. But their chief theme was love, which passion they were in the habit of presenting as it had been set forth in the *Princess of Cleves*, a novel Clara Reeve cannot approve since "it influences young minds in favour of a certain *fatality* in love matters which encourages them to plead errors of the imagination, for faults of the heart, which if indulged will undermine both their virtue and their peace."[1]

In the Countess Marie-Cathérine d'Aulnoy's *Histoire de Hipolite, Comte de Douglas* (1690),[2] which is quite typical, these old time-honored novelistic themes are interwoven with the newer sentimental situations, moods, and characters. As usual the historical is subordinated to the main attraction, which is the account of the ordeals of a heroine in love and in need of help and sympathy. The world is seen from her point of view, and her emotions are carefully noted.

> Julia's father, the Earl of Warwick, who is an ardent Catholic, is forced to flee from Henry VIII and England. He is captured by a pirate and reported to be dead. News of this kills Julia's mother, who leaves Julia with the Douglases. They rear her as sister to their Lucile and Hypolitus. Julia and Hypolitus fall in love and are unhappy because they think that they are brother and sister. Bedford asks for Julia's hand, but she does not love him and begs to be allowed to go to France and enter a convent.
>
> Now she is told who her parents were and desires to remain near Hypolitus, but the ambitious Douglas, wishing to break up the affair, sends his son to Italy. Hypolitus makes a false departure and at night returns secretly to meet Julia. Bedford, who arrives to abduct Julia, surprises the lovers. Hypolitus must go. At sea he fights the pirates, and one of them turns out to be Julia's long-lost father. False letters accuse Julia of being untrue: she is hurried into marriage with Bedford. Her lover, disguised as a higgler, pays her a visit. The jealous Bedford places her in a convent, but Hypolitus gains entrance as a student. However, he has to return home as his father is reported to be dying.
>
> When Bedford threatens to make her change convents, Julia flees to Florence, where a senator bothers her with his amorous entreaties and an unknown person abducts her. Escaping to a peasant's hut, she disguises herself as a pilgrim and takes the name of Silvio. Her husband, dressed as a woman, poniards her, but she recovers from her wound, and when it is found out that Bedford had married an Italian lady, she is free to wed her Hypolitus.

This was the pattern that pleased the readers of that day, and it was imitated many times by both French and English novelists.

The first long English epistolary novel to deal with domestic life is not so full of adventure as *Hypolitus*, but it reflects the new interest in bourgeois characters and everyday life shown by some of the contemporary French novels, as, for example, *L'Illustre Parisienne* (1679). It is the *Adventures of Lindamira, a Lady of Quality* (1702),[3] and its chief subject is the love of Lindamira and Cleomidon, a barrister of Lincoln's Inn who must wed a rich lady chosen by his uncle or lose a good estate. Lindamira, too magnanimous to stand in her lover's way, deliberately leads him to believe that she is fickle. So he marries his uncle's choice, but of course is very unhappy. After a time his wife's death frees him, and when he finds that Lindamira has loved him all along, he proposes marriage and is accepted. Although the names are still rather old-fashioned, the characters are well drawn. The letters are fairly natural, and the plot is simple and limited to ordinary events, except for the inset story which describes the adventures of Lindamira and her cousin in French court society and feebly echoes the tone of the heroic-gallant novel.[4] Sentiment is rather restrained, and there is an air about the work that would lead one to surmise that a woman wrote it.

Afra Behn (1640–89) must be numbered among the pioneers of sentiment if for no other reason than that she was the first English imitator of the famous *Lettres d'une Religieuse Portugaise*.[5] She was acquainted with the heroic-gallant novel and on occasion could repeat its clichés and love jargon. And she translated, or helped translate, Fontenelle's *Pluralité des Mondes* and *Histoire des Oracles*.[6] Her ebony Apollo in *Oroonoko, or the History of the Royal Slave* (1688) was almost the first noble savage. As he was "in the first stage of innocence," he was instinctively virtuous, and his honesty and magnanimity contrasted sharply with the duplicity and meanness of civilized Europeans he came in contact with. He was educated by an exiled French gentleman of "very little religion but with admirable morals." In Surinam the natives were like deistic primitives—harmless, innocent, and happy children of nature.

If, as is probable, the *Love Letters betwixt a Nobleman and his Sister* (1683) is Afra Behn's,[7] she was the author of two imitations of the *Portuguese Letters*, for the *Love Letters to a Gentleman* (1671) is certainly hers. Whether the "gentleman" who inspired the passion in this book—supposed to be genuine letters of the author—was wholly fictitious, or her atheistic lover, John Hoyle, or William Scot, the radical spy who had gone with her to Surinam, or a composite of both and other unsavory consorts, is not known.[8] One finds something approaching the sentimental story in a few of her tales or novelle of love, such as *The Lucky Mistake*, where there is much swooning. But most of these are after the Spanish novel of intrigue, or, like her plays, picture a dissolute aristocratic society. A French critic of one of these tales which was translated in 1761 wrote: "Ce dernier petit ouvrage dans les mains d'un homme de génie, tel que l'auteur de *Clarisse* ou M. l'Abbé Prevost, eût fait couler bien des larmes."[9] In fact, although there is no denying the sincere ring of the passion in *Love Letters to a Gentleman,* Afra Behn was only a novice at sentiment and lacked the delicacy of taste and awareness of sentimental values which would have made her stories popular in the eighteenth century. They were reprinted a few times but, except for *Oroonoko,* were soon almost forgotten. This novel had many admirers, yet few sentimental readers could have enjoyed the gruesome scene in which the hero is hacked to pieces, or the reference to the stench of Imoinda's corpse.[10]

Mary de la Riviere Manley (1672–1724), the "Sappho" of the *Tatler,* also lacked modesty and delicacy. She did not resemble the Lesbian poetess so much as she did the garrulous midwife in the *New Atalantis* (1709–10) who was on the visiting committee and board of review to cover the political and amorous scandal of Queen Anne's England. Her special talent was for scandal mongering, and she made the most out of her listening post in the house of the notorious Barbara Villiers, Duchess of Cleveland.[11] In the *Adventures of Rivella* (1714) Mrs. Manley claimed that she was a peerless lover and had made some notable discoveries in the tender passion, but the love she described was more often a brazen and lusty wench than a gentle sentimental lady. Yet once she tried to take love seriously. *A Letter from a supposed Nun in Portugal,* her imitation of the *Portuguese Letters,* was the only one of her narratives that gained the complete approval of sentimental readers. However, a more lasting impression was made by her *Letters to a Friend, or a Stage-Coach Journey to Exeter,* and she deserves credit for seeing the narrative possibilities of the travelling stagecoach even though her book was but an imitation of Mme. d'Aulnoy's travelogue, called by the English translators *The Ingenious and Diverting Letters of a Lady: Travels in Spain.*[12]

Sentimentality, particularly as developed in the contemporary French novel, played a far more important rôle in the narratives of Penelope Aubin (fl. 1718–29). In 1729 she translated Marguerite de Lussan's *La Comtesse de Gondez* without naming the author. The novel was a delicate and graceful sentimental account of the struggle between love and duty in a woman's heart. She also translated—very freely—Robert des Challes's collection of sentimental stories, *Les Illustres Françaises* (1712). Although Des Challes followed in the main the lead of the imitators of the *Princess of Cleves,* he discarded the historical frame and presented contemporary figures and scenes. He made notable advances in characterization. Penelope Aubin called her translation *The Illustrious French Lovers* (1727). In one of the stories the hero, Des Prés, marries Marie secretly, but his parents break up the union and take him away by force. Like Prevost's Des Grieux in *Manon Lescaut,* he is imprisoned in St. Lazare. There are other but on the whole rather superficial similarities between the story and Prevost's masterpiece. It is interesting to note that Mrs. Aubin gave the Christian name of Manon to Mlle. du Puits, the heroine of another one of these stories, and changed the original ending by having Manon's lover forgive a brief defection and take her back. A third story, that of M. de Contamini, is something of an anticipation of *Pamela* because it shows that a poor maid if virtuous may get a good husband.

Prevost may have seen Penelope Aubin, for she was alive when he first came to England in 1728.[13] At least he talked to people who had known her, for she moved, or had moved, in the French circles he came in contact with while in London. She must have died before the summer of 1734 because Prevost's biographical sketch of her appeared in one of the last numbers of the *Pour et Contre* he edited from England.[14] According to this sketch, she was born in London, where her father, a French officer (doubtless a refugee), had come to live. But he had not prospered, and Penelope was brought up in poor circumstances. Prevost thought her writings showed that she had a heart capable of feeling the tenderest passions but surmised that poverty and her lack of beauty had robbed her of any chance she might have had of attracting a lover. Her first novel sold well because people wished to see what a woman would write. As the novelty of feminine authorship wore off, the public received her subsequent novels coldly, so coldly that she declared she would never write another. So she turned her attention to converting her fellow man. She wrote sermons, but finding no parson to purchase them, she rented a hall and preached them herself. Again novelty brought success. People filled her conventicle and willingly paid a shilling to hear her. Within a few weeks she had gained a small fortune, but unfortunately she died before she could benefit from it.

This sketch is not without bias and can hardly be considered accurate on all points. For one thing, the ending does not agree with an anecdote told elsewhere by Prevost[15] describing her as dying penniless, or at least with funds in such a condition that her creditors, giving up all hopes of collecting, decided that the only way they could recover part of their losses was to publish a *histoire galante* she had given them in partial payment. For some reason Prevost did not approve of her, but this does not mean that he did not read her novels.[16] He could have obtained the idea of his famous cavern in *Cleveland* from her *Life of Mme. de Beaumont, a French Lady; who Lived in a Cave in Wales above Fourteen Years Undiscovered, being Forced to fly France for her Religion; and of the cruel Usage she had there ...* (1718).[17] The heroine is brought up in the Protestant faith, but when her parents die, her guardians try to force her to become a Catholic and do put her in a convent. A lover helps her escape, but his intolerant family threatens her with imprisonment unless she abjures Protestantism. So she and her lover, now her husband, fly to England. However, they become separated, and she and her daughter live in a cavern in Wales until he, after an adventurous career in Muscovy, finds them. The theme of the French religious refugee was Mrs. Aubin's favorite. *The Life of Charlotta Du Pont, an English Lady, Taken from her own Memoirs* (1739) is about a refugee then living in Bristol.

Some of Mrs. Aubin's novels show the influence of Defoe. She exploited the romantic features of foreign settings—Africa, Turkey, America, Persia—and having shipwrecked her characters in uninhabited parts, tried to make the experience seem credible. For the sake of further variety she threw in romantic love stories, and as she entertained she hoped to point a moral. Her virtuous heroine is sorely tried but always eludes the snares of the seducer, finds a perfect lover and, with him, worldly goods. In *Strange Adventures of the Count de Vinevil and his Family* (1721) it takes a fire and an assassination to save Ardelisa from Osmin, the lustful Turk, but she escapes him and brings away with her a lady who had been an unwilling inmate of his harem. The sensitive Violetta feels deeply the shame of her harem experience and her loss of honor. However, she finds a generous captain who dismisses her past as no obstacle to marriage. Yet her delicacy is such that she will not wed him until Osmin dies, which he does with considerate promptitude.

There is a shipwreck in this novel and another in her most popular work, *The Noble Slaves, or The Lives and Adventures of Two Lords and Two Ladies* (1722),[18] which ran through several editions and appeared in Elizabeth Griffith's *Collection of Novels* in 1777. Its plot and characters have a Spanish cast, and the story moves about over many lands and seas and has minor personages of nearly every race, each relating his experiences. Her best work, *The Life and Adventures of the Lady Lucy* (1726), which has a sequel called *Young Count Albertus* (1728), is a story of the Irish Rebellion. Lady Lucy's father fights on the side of James II and is killed. After the Battle of the Boyne the troops of King William break into her castle, and she and her mother are in great peril. However, one of William's officers, a German prince, rescues them and later marries Lady Lucy. In Flanders he becomes insanely jealous of a kinsman, kills him, wounds his pregnant wife, and leaves her in a forest. After many adventures and a long separation he and Lady Lucy come together again.[19]

There is something like Penelope Aubin's odd blend of sentiment, romantic adventure, and Defoe in William Rufus Chetwood's *Voyages and Adventures of Captain Robert Boyle* (1726).[20] Mrs. Villars, the heroine, is the sport of the wildest caprices of fortune; and her charms are so potent that they fill men's minds with burning desire and dubious schemes.

> Through trickery Captain Bourn, her first would-be ravisher, gets her on his ship and sails off with her. However, her maid and the crew save her. Then she falls into the hands of an Irish renegade, Hamet, but before he can make her a regular member of his harem, Robin Boyle cleverly steals her away and wins her heart. Robin's intentions are honorable, but as she is dressed as a boy, the French captain who picked up the runaway couple, and later the French ambassador in Morocco, insist on putting them

in the same bedroom. Robin's passion gets out of hand and throws him into a raging fever. Considering that the situation demanded extra-ordinary measures, she grants him her favors and so saves his life. Her heart was tender, and as she did not deliberately flout the moral code, her action was perhaps not without some redeemable attributes. Besides, Robin had promised to marry her at the first opportunity. However, before he could make his word good, they were separated and she fell again into the hands of Hamet and other rude men. Yet she always escaped in the nick of time, for as the author writes, "there is a ruling Providence that regulates every action of our lives, when they tend to virtue."

The rôle of lover sits less naturally upon Robin than that of privateer and adventurer, for when his fits of depression and longing for Mrs. Villars come upon him, it seems a little out of character. The chief matter of the book is Defoe-like nautical and exotic adventure. To this the author added stories of Spanish love and intrigue; and it should be noted that his Indians are not noble savages.

2

Eliza Haywood (1693?–1756) wrote many novels and over a long period of time. As in the case of Mary Manley, her scandalous works drew attention away from her other writings. Often both writers were pilloried together. The pious declared that to read the novels of Mrs. Manley and Mrs. Haywood was as iniquitous as secret dram drinking, and even sinners like Letty Pilkington, who tried to blackmail Mary Manley's aging sustainer, Alderman Barber, into subscribing for her poems, put on an air of moral superiority when either novelist was mentioned.[21] Often Mrs. Haywood was singled out, as when the portrait of Henrietta Howard, mistress of the Prince of Wales, in the *Secret History of the Present Intrigues of the Court of Carimania* (1727), offended Swift and precipitated Pope's coarse attack upon her in the *Dunciad.* The notorious Rev. William Dodd in *The Sisters* mentions her novels as exerting a bad influence upon his heroines, Lucy and Caroline. And as late as 1768, when a version of her *The Agreeable Caledonian* appeared under the title of *Clementina, or the History of an Italian Lady who made her Escape from a Monastery for the Love of a Scots Nobleman,* a reviewer hailed it with: "This is the republication of a dull, profligate Haywoodian production in which all the males are rogues, and all the females whores, without a glimpse of plot, fable, or sentiment."[22]

Like Mrs. Manley she imitated or translated several French narratives. Many of her short amatory romances, like *Love in Excess, or, the Fatal Inquiry* and others included in her *Secret Histories, Novels, and Poems* (1725),[23] show plainly that she was well acquainted with contemporary French novels. Her *Fatal Secret; or, Constancy in Distress* (1724) is in the style of Mme. de Gomez.[24] Mrs. Haywood translated this writer's *La Belle Assemblée* and *L'Entretien des Beaux Esprits*. Clara Reeve thought Mrs. Haywood's version of the first, which was entitled *La Belle Assemblée; or, the Adventures of Six Days* (1724–26), "a very unexceptionable and entertaining work" and declared that it was very popular.[25] French influence is conspicuous in *The Mercenary Lovers* (1726), *The Life of Mme. de Villesache* (1727), and *Philidore and Placentia; or, l'amour trop Délicate* (1727), yet in the last story the episode in which the hero and heroine are stranded on a desert island seems to have come from Defoe's *Captain Singleton*. Mrs. Haywood did a version of the *Portuguese Letters* which she called *Letters of a Lady of Quality to a Chevalier* (1721). She based it upon the paraphrase of Edmé Boursault.

After her return from a trip to France she made a translation of De Mouhy's *La Paysanne Parvenue*, an imitation of Marivaux's *Marianne*. She called it *The Virtuous Villager, or the Virgin's Victory; Being Memoirs of a very great Lady at the Court of France, Written by Herself ... translated from the original by the Author of "La Belle Assemblée"* (1742). The fact that she prefers to refer to herself here as the translator of Mme. de Gomez's book might mean that she realized her name as a writer of scandals no longer had its former market value. In fact, she had about decided to give up scandal-mongering and was now turning to a new model, Marivaux—not Richardson, as has been claimed. Yet she used Richardson as a springboard and traded on his fame, either in humble works like *A Present for a Servant-Maid*, which tells how to make an omelet or to preserve one's chastity, or in the naughty *Anti-Pamela, or Feign'd Innocence Detected in a Series of Syrena's Adventures* (1741), which deserves to be placed beside Fielding's *Shamela*. *Anti-Pamela* is a very improper story about the sayings and doings of Syrena, "a predestined prostitute," and her pandering mother. Its cynicism concerning virginity, which doubtless made Richardson wince, reappears in Mrs. Haywood's last novel, *The Invisible Spy* (1755), an imitation of De Mouhy's *La Mouche* and Lesage's *Diable Boiteux*. Curiously enough, the starchy old maid, Clara Reeve, overlooking the bawdry for the sake of the moral, declared this novel its author's best. In fact, she condoned Eliza as a victim of the bad example set by Afra Behn and Mary Manley, and praised her for recovering a lost reputation and devoting "the remainder of her life and labours to the service of virtue."[26]

Indeed, such an about-face seems to be indicated by the absence of coarseness and scandal in *The Fortunate Foundlings* (1744). Mrs. Haywood made her heroine Louisa like Marianne and put her in situations somewhat like those in Marivaux's novel. She is brought up very carefully by a kind gentleman whose benevolence turns to amorous desire, and she is forced to flee to escape his attempts on her virtue. As she has no one to go to, she throws herself upon the mercies of the world. Beginning humbly as a milliner's apprentice, she soon—rather too soon—becomes the mistress of the rules of politeness at the leading courts of Europe. An honorable lover, who saves her from a rake, wins her affections and proposes marriage, but she is too magnanimous to accept, for he is of a higher station, and she can bring him nothing but herself. She takes refuge in a convent. Here she becomes so popular that the abbess lays a plot to induce her to become a nun. But the scheme fails and Louisa goes to Paris where she meets the "kind" gentleman who had caused her so much trouble. He turns out to be her father. Like Cécile in *Cleveland*, she had had her own father for a lover. Now she can marry the good youth who had saved her from the rake.

The less interesting part of the story describes how Louisa's brother, the other foundling, becomes a brave colonel and marries the girl of his choice. There is less overplotting and more unity in this novel than in the usual Haywood narrative, yet there are still some of the old "love-in-excess" inset stories.[27]

In *Life's Progress through the Passions, or, the Adventures of Natura* (1748) the author makes Natura's life almost too varied—and as one might expect, very rich in feminine relationships. A nun, a jailer's wife, a prostitute, a girl in a convent, a spoiled lady, Maria, who prefers a footman to Natura, and finally the good Charlotte stir up all the passions known to Faculty Psychology. Like Prevost's Cleveland and Defoe's Captain Carleton, Natura is pestered by over-zealous priests, and these stir up other passions. But it will not do. The reader simply cannot become interested in Eliza's man of straw. However, the book contains a few landscapes—among the first in the English novel. It is possible that the author admired the landscapes of Mary Collyer's *Letters from Felicia to Charlotte*, published four years before.

The *History of Miss Betsy Thoughtless* (1751) is its author's best work. At times Betsy reminds one of Marivaux's Marianne. Both girls are coquettish, live to please, instinctively keep themselves unsullied, and lack strong passions. And like Marianne, Betsy had inherited the good fortune of fictional orphans. Luck and happy coincidence always preserve the chastity which she often put in peril by her disregard of conventional safeguards and her easygoing, incautious, and indulgent attitude toward friends and companions. Even Betsy's greatest mistake, the marrying of a currish scoundrel to please her brothers, turned out to be a blessing in disguise, for it made her resolve never again to be vain, yielding, free and easy, or to disregard what questionable actions, situations, and companions might make others think. She became a changed woman, but her luck was still with her, for her husband killed himself and Charles Trueworthy's wife died, and she and her lover were free to marry.

Although Betsy occasionally wept out of sympathy and was benevolent enough to adopt a poor waif, she was not quite tender or sensitive enough to be a typical sentimental heroine. Certainly her aversion to living in the country was not sentimental. In her opinion, to live away from London was like being buried alive; and she laughed at her lover when he described country life as ideal. "What!" she cried, "be cooped up like a tame dove, only to coo,—and bill,—and breed?"

The fine characterization of Betsy and the many realistic glimpses of London life make this a remarkable novel. The influence of *Marianne* is quite apparent and certainly of much more importance than the few slight borrowings from Richardson, Fielding, and Prevost.[28] Even if Fanny Burney has nowhere explicitly stated that she had read this novel, she surely had, and the proof of it is in *Evelina* and *Cecilia*.

Celia of the Woods is the chief threat to the happiness of the lovers in *The History of Jemmy and Jenny Jessamy* (1753), and her history is another satire of *Pamela*.

> While a student at Oxford Jemmy had met Celia, who seemed to be an innocent, simple country girl. Yet she was rather extraordinary because her love for him ripened so quickly that at their second meeting she begged him not to ruin her, for "she could not bear the thoughts of being naughty." This was a strange kind of resistance, and it soon collapsed. However Jemmy could not keep the crucial appointment because of his father's death, and he let the affair die. Afterwards, by using Pamela's methods, Celia married her Mr. B. in the form of an old doting baronet. Now when Jemmy sees her at the great Auction House in the Covent Garden Piazza, she is ravishing as Lady Hardy. She still remembers her disappointment at the broken tryst and hastens to make another with Jemmy. He meets her but finds only the ghost of his former passion left. With innocence goes the charm. So the affair languishes and finally expires with some moral advice and a parting letter from Jemmy. He learns that she has other lovers too, and that her doting husband passes over her infidelities without daring to reprimand her.

Eliza Haywood was ingenious and nearly always started off with a good idea, yet she could hardly ever keep from overplotting. The risqué never entirely lost its attraction for her, but she tried to adapt to the taste of the new sentimental reading public when she was convinced that most of it no longer cared for coarseness and the intrigues of jades of quality and ruttish court puppies but wished to read about the loves and adventures of a girl like Pamela or Marianne. And as her mind was more in harmony with Marivaux's than with Richardson's, Mrs. Haywood preferred Marianne to Pamela.[29]

3

The *Vie de Marianne; ou, les Aventures de la Comtesse de ...* (1731–41), which is in the direct line of descent from the *Princess of Cleves*, got a lively and appreciative reception in England, and although the vogue of Marivaux (1688–1763) began to decline in the seventeen fifties, his influence remained a force to reckon with throughout the century and beyond. In 1765 Horace Walpole wrote Gray that neither Crébillon's nor Marivaux's "taste for trifles" pleased him any longer, and he believed that Crébillon was "entirely out of fashion" and Marivaux "a proverb." *"Marivauder"* and *"marivaudage"* had become "established terms for being prolix and tiresome." Yet not everyone was tired of Marivaux's hair-splitting analyses and pirouetting on a sixpence. As late as 1785 Clara Reeve scolded Mary Collyer for leaving some of the *marivaudage* out of one of her versions of the *Vie de Marianne*. "In this piece of patchwork," Miss Reeve wrote, "many of the fine reflections, the most valuable part of the work, are omitted."[30] In Fanny Burney's *Early Diary*, Fanny tells how her friend, Mr. Seaton, discovering a copy of *Marianne* on the Burney table, asked her whether she had read *Le Paysan Parvenu*, and gave it as his opinion that these two novels were the best ever written, "for they are pictures of nature, and therefore excel your Clarissas and Grandisons far away."[31]

Clara Reeve in the passage just cited declared that she liked Marivaux's pictures of real life, his polished language, and his sentiments, but thought the *Paysan Parvenu* "somewhat exceptionable" since "French morality is not suitable to an old English palate." But *Marianne* had "no such abatements; she needs no foil, but shines by her own light." And here Miss Reeve spoke for all her sister novelists.

Marivaux was a close friend of Mme. de Lambert and a habitué of her salon, where he met such men as Fontenelle and Montesquieu, and women like Mme. de Murat and Mlle. de la Force. The ideas aired here kept him abreast of the times. However, he was not much of a philosopher. In *Marianne* he wrote that the intellect was too much of a fanciful dreamer to be depended on in learning about ourselves. The real clue to human nature was sentiment. His point of view was conditioned by deistic ideas, yet in his novels these were pushed into the background by the all-absorbing interest which he took in human conduct. Doubtless his insistent disapproval of authoritarian ethics and religion derived from deistic anticlericalism, as did also the large number of false devotees and selfish and stupid spiritual directors in his novels. But there was no bitter hate: he even censured Montesquieu for his harsh treatment of the church in the *Lettres Persanes*. The nearest Marivaux came to primitivism was in his sympathetic portrayal of good peasants, like the Villots in *Marianne*, and in the philosophical play, *L'Isle des Esclaves* (1725). Here masters and slaves on their desert island rid themselves of the injustices they habitually caused each other to suffer, injustices produced by artificial society. These disappear along with class distinctions when all the persons on the island return to a state of innocence. But one finds no noble savages in Marivaux. Any impulse to embrace the belief in man's essential goodness was checked when he lost all his fortune in the Law crash. Yet he could not believe in the theory of total depravity. Although in his opinion there was more of the rational and less of the instinctive in the conscience than the deists maintained, he was impressed with and influenced by Shaftesbury's concept of moral beauty.

He was interested in the common people; his sympathy for them was genuine. Because all men are interdependent, he thought the rich under a moral obligation to relieve the poor. The rich man or the aristocrat who had nothing to recommend him but power or rank disgusted him. *Marianne* is partly an attack on the privileges of birth. Portions of this novel reveal a surprising interest in domestic life and its problems, yet Marivaux did not, like Richardson, look upon the middle class as possessing nearly all of the virtues. According to the French writer, it was a hybrid, half noble and half plebeian—*"noble par imitation, peuple par caractère."* In *Marianne* he gave realistic pictures of the social conditions of the poor and studies of the mentalities of the common people. The needy and unfortunate aroused his compassion, but he conceived no radical doctrine to better the lot of the poor. Instead he urged individual benevolence.

The delicate persiflage—already slightly old-fashioned—of Mme. de Lambert's salon, the lay morality discussed here and the cult of sensibility practiced here, all were extremely congenial to him. In his writings he reflected the tone and ideas of this circle. It was the source of that theory of sentimental morality he set forth in the *Spectateur Français* (1722–23), *L'Indigent Philosophe* (1728), and the *Cabinet du Philosophe* (1734). He believed that human worth and generosity increased with sensibility, which softens the brutality of the raw instincts and endows sexual desire with the dignity and delicacy that make love the most beautiful of human experiences. Benevolence must be based on sympathy, understanding, and sincere generosity. It must not be cold, calculating, or patronizing, but as delicate and tactful as the aid offered to Marianne by Mme. de Mirvan, thought to be modelled on Mme. de Lambert, and Mme. Dorsin, perhaps meant to be Mme. de Tencin. A morality based on feeling must not be foolishly impetuous or maudlin, but moderated and tempered by reason and common sense. And its soul is the good heart—the index of virtue and the true source of happiness.

Although sentiment and sentimental points of view can be found scattered throughout the works of Marivaux, *Marianne* is the only novel exactly to the taste of the sentimental palate. His first narratives are satirical. Parts of *La Voiture Embourbée* (1714) seem to make fun of the Scudéry romance, and *Pharsamon*, written in 1712 but not published until 1737, when it was called the *Don Quixote Moderne*, does so unquestionably.

A Mr. Lockman Englished this work in 1749 as *Pharsamond, or the Knight Errant*. Expressing the opinion that burlesque was not the author's forte, a reviewer sounded the sour note which always greeted an imitation of Cervantes' masterpiece and chided the translator for giving the characters English names.[32] The novel has its points. It is interesting to note that the hero, Jean Bagnol *alias* Pharsamond, is perfectly content that the military features of the heroic age died with it. His only regret is the passing of the old kind of love-making. He wants a mistress who is imperious and unyielding, and finds one such in Mlle. Babet *alias* Cidalise, whose head had been turned by the same novels that had thrown him off balance. She plays the desired rôle *con amore*. The pair do wild romantic things, spout old-fashioned lovers' talk, strike theatrical poses, and work up many a grand scene. But they are hounded by the anticlimax. Something flat, common-place, and utterly unpoetic always intrudes to spoil the romance. Jean's transports are never completed. He thought that perhaps the eternal comic had also broken in upon the great moments of the great heroes but wondered why the writers of the good books had failed to record any such *contretemps*. A female Quixote was a novelty and Mlle. Babet was excellent. For magnetic charm Mme. Felonde, the coquettish widow who finally captured Jean, was even better. Her rôle is comparable to Colonel Brandon's in *Sense and Sensibility*. The *Quixote Moderne* influenced Smollett's *Launcelot Greaves* and Charlotte Lennox's *Female Quixote*. Clarice in *Les Effets Surprenans de la Sympathie* (1713–14) is still another piquant feminine portrait and about the only redeeming feature of the novel, which is a poor imitation of the very romances Marivaux had been parodying.

Even less than these early novels did the *Paysan Parvenu* (1735–36) conform to the sentimental pattern or please the sentimental reader. To the feminine reader it appeared that the surprising successes of Jacob, the *parvenu*, were meant to lay bare weaknesses which the author seemingly supposed were common to the female sex. Almost any woman would feel the attraction of a handsome well-sexed fellow, but how many women would overlook a valet's poverty, his not-too-delicate sense of honor, his lack of birth and education, and accept him as fit to be a lover and husband? Marivaux made his Jacob irresistible. After Geneviève, the maid, came Mlle. Habert, the false devotee, and then Mme. de Ferval, the gay sensualist, and the wealthy Mme. de Fécour, and finally the *amour tendresse* of Mme. de Vambures. Jacob did not have to scheme or struggle: he did not, like Marianne, have to guard his virtue. Consequently few of the situations in the novel are moving, not even Jacob's little benevolent acts. The reader cannot become really interested in Jacob's becoming more refined as he rose in the world and came in contact with good manners and taste, because one feels that this too is little but veneer and not true culture gained through study and reflection. So he does not win the reader's esteem, and the women at whose expense he has gained his "education" lose prestige. Some of the more delicate readers objected to the suggestiveness of parts of the novel, as for example, Jacob's affair with Mme. de Ferval, which is somewhat in the Crébillon manner, although more discreet.[33] It was not the success of the valet but the good fortune of the orphan that caught the sentimental imagination. *Marianne* is sentimental although not of the tragic-passionate type of sensibility. There is elasticity and restraint so that wit and light irony, and even a touch of libertinage, can appear. The characters nearly always keep control of themselves, and although endowed with tender souls, never raise their voices to outlandish volume in complaint against destiny. Marivaux is writing a comedy despite the fact that the atmosphere in the inset *Nun's Tale* is of unusual gloom and the heroine cries out that she was born to be the most unfortunate person in the world.

Marianne was born with a *sensible* heart and a sound head, with a t aste for the proper, the refined, and the beautiful. She is elegant and fine and shrewd but not passionate or exalted or Quixotic. She never forgets herself or the proprieties when she weeps, which she does occasionally, or when she faints, which is seldom. Her delicacy is instinctive and her coquetry a form of her dominant quality, self-esteem. She wishes to be delectable in her own eyes first and then to inspire in others the desire to love and admire her. She could not be called exactly crafty or designing, yet her virtuous actions somehow always manage to be seen, and by persons able to reward or help. She is too ready-witted to be caught badly off balance. By feigning not to understand what the bad M. de Climal means to convey, she makes him wonder whether she really does. When he kisses her ear in the coach, she prefers to take it as an accidental bump and asks him if she has hurt him. She knows that she is clever and her moral position is strong. But she is not unstudied or naïve enough to be an ingenue: like her contemporaries she did not let a fear of false-modesty deter her from exhibiting her good qualities however intimate or trivial. Her Narcissus-like fondness for contemplating herself and her sentiments is perfectly unashamed and is always a tonic for her.

All this may not be extremely heroic or saintly, but it is very human. Marivaux attempts to explain her *savoir faire* by having her say that women have two kinds of *Esprit*. One is reason, but as Marianne was not yet sixteen, this could not have been of much help. The other is wit. This is found even in the stupidest woman and is born of vanity and the desire to please. It is called coquetry, and Marianne had a goodly supply of it. Perhaps Marivaux meant to suggest that the surprising awareness of masculine intentions is a feminine instinct too. Such an instinct is certainly in nature, but in novels young ladies like Marianne and Pamela must not seem to possess too much of it since it is generally thought to preclude innocence.

The subject of the novel is the ordeal of a virtuous and charming orphan.

Marianne, now a countess well along in years, tells the story of her life. Her parents, killed by robbers near Bordeaux, were of good family, probably noble, and she was brought up carefully by a kind curate and his good sister. The curate dies and so does his sister after taking Marianne to Paris, where a grasping inn-keeper initiates her into the cruel world by stealing half the money left her by her foster-parents. A priest tries to get her a place, and the unctuous M. de Climal does get her one. "Disinterested" sympathy makes him willing to pay part of her expenses if she will help in Mme. Dutour's shop. As there seems to be nothing else to do, Marianne accepts. The brusque merchants wound her "delicatesse" and she is ashamed of being a mere linen maid. Should she take the dresses and finery offered by De Climal, whose motives no longer appear so unselfish to her? Yes, if she does not have to pay with her favors. Does not the fact that his pursuit causes her trouble put him a little in debt to her? She thinks so.

The men in church eye her and she flirts with them. Valville sees her and loves. A sprained ankle got while dodging his coach gives her an opportunity to clinch the affair. Carrying her into his house and calling a surgeon, he has her small hurt attended to and is much pleased with the turn of her ankle. As she is afraid he will find out that she lives with the lowly Dutour and despise her, she insists upon leaving in a hired carriage. Sometime later De Climal is disagreeably surprised to find the lovers together, especially as Valville is his nephew. And later when Valville discovers his uncle in the act of urging Marianne to become his mistress, it is the nephew's turn to be vexed, and he retires with the wrong impression, but of course his uncle's naughty proposal is rejected. Then the benevolence ends; Marianne is turned out into the world. Besides she has to return De Climal's presents, even the nice frocks that fitted her so well. It is not easy.

Mme. de Miran, Valville's mother and De Climal's sister, sees her weeping in a convent chapel and is so touched that she becomes a mother to her. Like a dutiful daughter Marianne confesses her love for Valville to her, gives her his love letters, and to show her disregard for personal advantage agrees to give him up. All of this culminates in a touching scene of tender sentiment and weeping lovers. Soon "mother" comes around to the opinion that a marriage with a girl like Marianne might not be so bad for her son. So she introduces her into society, taking her first to the home of the beautiful and benevolent Mme. Dorsin. It is thought best to pass Marianne off as a relative, but Mme. Dutour recognizes her, and spreading the word around, causes an overproud host to dismiss the poor girl from his house. Now De Climal dies. He was not so bad after all, for before he went he cleared Marianne's reputation, left her a respectable annuity, and obtained her forgiveness.

Next, some of Valville's stiff-necked relatives abduct her from her convent, carry her to a minister of justice they have bribed to tell her that she must either marry his clerk or take the veil, and might have ruined everything had not Mme. de Miran come to the rescue. All present are moved to tears when Marianne expresses her willingness to give up Valville. Indeed, so much virtue inspires the minister to free her from her pledge and return her to Mme. de Miran. When everything points to an early wedding with Valville, he falls in love with Marianne's convent companion, Mlle. Varthon. Although deeply hurt, Marianne has wisdom enough not to show it. In fact, she is very magnanimous to her inconstant lover. She will not encourage another suitor, a military gentleman of fifty who is attracted by her intelligence and virtue, and she even contemplates taking the veil. Her somewhat extravagant love for Mme. de Miran helps her regain her balance, so that when Valville comes to his senses, he is forced to see that Marianne's moral advantage over him is considerable. When he begs for forgiveness, she has another opportunity to demonstrate her nobleness of soul, and under the most flattering of circumstances.

Family relations, especially filial and parental ingratitude and selfishness, are prominent in the inset story, *The Nun's Tale.* Mlle. Tervire's mother, a selfish widow, runs off with a wealthy man and leaves Tervire with a grandmother. When this lady dies, she lives with the good farmer Villot. The bad mother sets on a false devotee to force Tervire to take the veil, but the plot fails because an unhappy nun warns her. Another vicious plan, to marry her to a rich old baron with the asthma, is ruined by the baron's heir who hides in Tervire's bedroom and manages to have himself discovered there. As a reward for kindness, a great aunt makes Tervire her heir, but a love affair with her cousin Dursan is spoiled by his bad mother, who sends her away to Paris. On arriving, she finds that her mother, again a widow, is being mistreated by an ungrateful son and a heartless daughter-in-law and is in dire need of help. Tervire immediately forgives her mother and does all she can to assist her. The mother soon dies and the unfortunate girl's lover proves false. There is nothing to do but take the veil. Yet she hates convent life. She tells Marianne of its seamy side—the enmity, jealousy, cliquishness, anger, slander, cabals—and reveals that she herself was held in solitary confinement for a whole year simply for receiving her lover's letters.

*Marianne* had many imitators but few of them were clever enough to reproduce its author's style. Happily the simple and realistic plot of domestic or everyday life, the characters from the middle class, and the truly novel sketches of bourgeois and popular manners, even the famous quarrel between Mme. Dutour and the coachman, deplored by some, found admirers. But mere copyists could not, of course, hold Marivaux's fine balance or produce characters so ingeniously conceived. Yet they could and did tell sentimental stories of virtue in distress patterned after *Marianne.*

It was very popular in England, where many preferred to read it in French. For those who did not there were English translations. Even before *Pamela* was published, about half of *Marianne* had appeared in a literal translation called *The Life of Marianne; or, the Adventures of the Countess de ...,* which was begun in 1736 and completed in 1742. According to Clara Reeve, this was a poor translation but nevertheless "was read by everybody with avidity."[34] Another version entitled *The Virtuous Orphan; or, the Life of Marianne, Countess of ...* (1742) was reprinted in the *Novelist's Magazine* in 1784 and was undoubtedly the work of Mary Collyer, as was also a slightly different version of this published in 1746 and called *The Life and Adventures of Indiana, the Virtuous Orphan. The Fortunate Orphan; or, Memoirs of the Countess of Marlau,* an English translation of a version by the Chevalier de Mouhy, was printed the same year.

4

Among those who helped to spread the influence of Marivaux were De Mouhy and De La Place. The Chevalier de Mouhy (Charles de Fieux) (1701–84) is one of those mediocre figures whose writings are accurate indicators of the novels most in vogue at a certain time. He was a poor ugly hunchback who came to Paris to live by the pen. He called himself "chevalier" and posed as a cavalry officer. Begging letters made him known to Voltaire, who employed him as courier, secretary, and leader of his claque. But a ridiculous egoism egged him on to write foolish things about his benefactor. De Mouhy wanted money more than anything else in the world and let no nice scruples stand in the way. So he wrote four score novels, hoping to make quantity make up for quality. He visited cafés, drawing rooms, and theatres, and gathered up all that he heard. When he got home he turned it into novels. Always a great plagiarist, he even copied himself, for whenever he scored a success he followed it up with a sequel. His wares were widely advertised: he even hawked them himself, and begged until one bought to be rid of him. The critics despised him and his confreres made fun of him, but nearly everybody read him.

The author of a sketch of De Mouhy which appeared in the *European Magazine* called him a "literary Hercules" who at eighty-one was still turning out novels.[35] After giving rather reluctant praise to some of his work, this writer criticized the style of his usual production as "diffusive, unconnected, and rampant," the action as "improbable and awkwardly contrived," and the whole as "often insipid and boring." Other critics had been more severe than this, but De Mouhy could ignore them because the public always asked for more of his narratives. He had readers in Holland and England as well as in France: indeed, he was one of the first of the circulating-library novelists.

When the vogue of Marivaux and Crébillon *fils* was highest, he copied them. His best work, *La Mouche* (1736), which Eliza Haywood published (and probably translated) as *The Busy Body, a Successful Spy* (1742), is of the licentious Crébillon type. There is license also in the *Mille et une Faveurs*, after Galland, and in the novel Englished as *Female Banishment; or, the Woman Hater* (1759).[36]

Next he paid tribute to the vogue of Abbé Prevost with an imitation of the *Man of Quality* which he called Mémoires et Aventures d'une Dame de Qualité qui s'est retirée du Monde (1747). He also composed something like a parody of Prevost's novel in *Mémoires d'une Fille de Qualité qui s'est pas retirée du Monde* (1748). And there is a great deal of Prevost, along with some of Marivaux, in the popular *Les Délices du Sentiment* (1735), which was praised in the biographical sketch just cited and translated as *Les Délices du Sentiment, or the Passionate Lovers. In a series of Letters which have recently passed between two celebrated characters....* (1782).

His most influential novel was *La Paysanne Parvenue* (1735), an imitation of *Marianne*. In 1742 Eliza Haywood made a version of this entitled *The Virtuous Villager*. A translation which was made in 1740–41 was reprinted in the *Novelist's Magazine* under the title of *The Fortunate Country Maid; or, Memoirs of the Marchioness of L-V-*.[37] Both these versions were reprinted many times, and Clara Reeve mentions them as "well known to the readers of circulating libraries."[38] This novel is not so poor as some of the critics have claimed. At any rate De Mouhy is much franker about his indebtedness than novelists of those days usually were. When one of Jenny's lovers buys books for her, among them *Marianne*, "which instructs and amuses," the author has his heroine remark on the similarity between herself and Marivaux's sentimental orphan. And he has her point out that Mme. de

G** is like Mme. de Miran, M. de G** like De Climal, and her favored lover like Valville. Jenny says that she would like to meet Marivaux because his novel is so charming and so full of wit and delicacy.

As Jenny is the daughter of a lady's maid and a woodcutter, she is lower socially than Marianne.[39] A few traits of the peasant shepherdess of romance still cling to Jenny: she has a lover Colin, calls herself Silviana, falls into a wolf-pit, and climbs a tree to escape a seducer. But she does not romanticize peasant life. Villages always seem to her wretched and mean. She is no fool like her neighbor Charlotte, who becomes the victim of an artful Pandarus and a lustful duke. In one English version this duke indulges in such expletives as "adsniggers" and shouts, "Depend upon it, I'll never follow the example of—; who in order to gratify his passion, was guilty of a thousand follies, and then to crown the work married his own maid. A very virtuous wife, perhaps you'll say; but I don't much admire the artful methods she made use of to gain her ends." Jenny, if not as delicate as Marianne, is more impressionable and emotional. When she flees for refuge to a convent, she shudders at a death's head placed at the foot of a crucifix and weeps at the sad tale of the unwilling nun, Agnes. At the height of her ordeals she becomes subject to fits and vapors. An empiric pronounces her mad, but an emetic restores her. She faints often and complains that she is pursued by a malign destiny.

This attention to intense mental states did not go unnoticed by the novelists. The real villain of the piece is a woman, Jenny's rival, Mlle. d'Elbieux. After this virago ceases persecuting Jenny, she turns her attention to making life unbearable for her husband. When with child she is as full of whimsy as Commodore Trunnion's spouse. One of her whims is to pull the beard of a certain Capuchin friar whose "nose for highness and sharpness might dispute precedency with all the noses in the universe." And what she does to the friar's whiskers puts "all the beards, not even those of the good nuns excepted ... in commotion." De Mouhy liked to garnish his dish with such piquant bits. Another such is the anecdote of the fair penitent who became mysteriously pregnant—a case which would have delighted "Doctor" John Hill, Fielding's enemy and the author of *Lucina sine Concubitu.*

*Marianne* in the form of *L'Orpheline Anglaise, ou Histoire de Charlotte Summers, imitée de l'Anglais de M.N.*** (1751) by Pierre-Antoine de La Place (1707–93) became an eighteenth-century international best seller. De La Place was an indefatigable but undistinguished "translator" of English novels.[40] His style is diffuse and sloppy. Like many another French translator of those days, his knowledge of English was not too good. He is said to have rendered *Love's Last Shift* as *La Derniére Chemise de L'Amour.* He was a great talker and floater of canards. It was he who was responsible for the ghastly story of Prevost's double death. According to him, Prevost, having suffered a stroke, was thought dead but revived for a terrible moment under the scalpel of the surgeon making the autopsy. De La Place sought to supply the French demand for English plays and novels with free translations or imitations accommodated to the French taste.[41] *Laideur Aimable* (1752) seems to be his own although it is commonly attributed to Sarah Scott, who wrote an *Agreeable Ugliness* in 1754.[42]

The original of *L'Orpheline Anglaise* was an anonymous *History of Charlotte Summers, the Fortunate Parish Girl* (1749).[43] The *Monthly Review* did not like this novel: "... all that we can say of this performance, is, that the author has kept his name unknown, which is an instance of his discretion: and that it is sold by Charles Corbet in Fleet-Street."[44] The readers, however, did like it. Lady Mary Wortley Montagu confessed that she could not lay it down, although she was convinced that the author did not know how to draw the virtuous character he intended to.[45] Grimm wrote that the author was Fielding; Richardson must have thought the same.[46] At any rate he pretended to be offended by what the author had said about him in one of the introductory essays, and complained about it in a letter to Lady Bradshaigh.[47] He must have been still more vexed when she replied and, citing the offending passage, declared that she did not find in it anything which resembled what he had told her.[48] The opinion sometimes expressed that Sarah Fielding was the author is based on nothing but conjecture. It is not known who wrote the book.[49]

In his version De La Place kept the introductory essays, which were modelled after those in *Tom Jones,* but cut out realistic bits like the curious description of Charlotte's adolescent diet of lime, wax, tobacco pipes, and coal cinders, and, of course, could not render dialect like that of the Welsh constable with his pronoun "hur" or Hodge's tribute to Charlotte's beauty—"Wauns, mistress, I think no wonder the Rogues quarrelled about that sweet face.... Ods dickens, it is enough to spoil a Parson's Preaching; efackins, I think you are in the Right, not to care to be stared at; if I look much longer, I shall forget my Moll. Ads Niggars!" He does nothing with the bit of Parson Adams that is in Goodheart, Lady Bountiful's chaplain, and throwing out the inset story of Jenny Jenkins, inserts a very sentimental story of his own, the *Histoire de Fanny Arthur.* But he dared not change the main lines of the story, which follow *Marianne.*

The plot of the *History of Charlotte Summers* runs as follows.

> Lady Bountiful on a visit to London sees Charlotte Summers, a poor mistreated parish girl, and is so touched by her pitiful appearance that she takes her home with her to Wales. A bad governess destroys Charlotte's happiness by circulating lies about her origin, but all is righted when her old nurse tells the authentic story of the poor girl's parents. Her mother, a bishop's daughter, had foolishly submitted to a secret marriage with

Captain Summers, who soon became dissolute and so desperate for funds that he even asked his wife to step aside to allow him to make a rich marriage. This she refused to do, yet she supported her delinquent spouse while he was in prison by painting fans. Finally he abandoned her and was reported dead. Her good friend and adviser, Richard Dick, contrived to get her on a ship and off to Maryland, where she became the wife of Governor Morgan. Charlotte had been left behind with Dick, and when he died, was thrown on the parish.

Charlotte, now grown to young womanhood under the care and protection of Lady Bountiful, arouses the passions of the dissolute Croft, who enters her bedroom at night but is discovered in time by Lady Bountiful's valiant son Thomas and pays dearly for his rashness. Thomas loves Charlotte and she returns his love, but the pride of his mother and the determination of his sweetheart to do nothing which her benefactress would not approve of bring the affair to an impasse. Charlotte decides that the best way to repay the generosity of Lady Bountiful and to alleviate the situation is to leave. She slips from the castle on a moonlight night, consciousness of her innocence enabling her to brave the dangers of goblins, ghosts, and the road. But she is not to escape without a scare. Three bandits rob her and would have done worse had not farmer Hodge delivered her.

At Hodge's house her beauty wounds many a rustic heart. Both Dick and George woo her, and this causes a quarrel which ends with her being haled before Judge Worthy. Like Marianne, she always wins friends. The judge's wife takes her part and will find a place for her in London. Thomas, hearing of Charlotte's presence at the Worthy's, flies to her, but she is hidden and a Fanny Arthur passed off as the lady he had heard of. In London Charlotte has many narrow escapes. Her landlady, Mrs. Weller, betrays her to a Captain Price, who would have been her undoing had not the watch chanced to pass by. Another wretched creature tries to deliver her over to a false benefactor, the old Mr. D**, who has her arrested and will not release her until she promises to be his mistress. But a good sergeant protects her, and her mother, recently arrived from America, gets word of her plight through the now repentant Captain Price, and takes her into her home. Lady Morgan, now a widow, recognizes Charlotte as her daughter, and the father soon turns up rich and repentant—and Lady Bountiful no longer will keep Charlotte and Thomas apart.

This novel conforms quite closely to the sentimental pattern. It tells of female tribulations; there are tears and tender tableaux, the most notable being the recognition scene. Charlotte faints when she sees her father—a sign of "sympathy of blood," and she cries out, "My blood confesses its dear Original, and my Heart tells me I behold my Father."

Novels like the *History of Charlotte Summers* and the French version of it broadened Marivaux's influence considerably. It has been said that there is a bit of *Marianne* in nearly every eighteenth-century French and English novel. One has only to try to trace out the numerous lines of influence to be convinced that there is much truth in the statement. Eliza Haywood's imitations, already noted, were only the first of a goodly number. Even though Richardson and Marivaux were different in personality and manner, there are enough similarities between *Pamela* and *Marianne* to encourage the conjecture of a possible borrowing. One striking parallel is the returning of the fine gift clothes when the heroines reach the breaking point with Mr. B. and M. de Climal. It is likely that had it not been for Marivaux, *Pamela* would never have been written.

Many a Marianne, whether coming directly from *Marianne* or copied from the *History of Charlotte Summers* or the *Paysanne Parvenue*, refused the flattering but immoral offers of a man of superior position, fell in love with the son or other near relative of her benefactress, and proved her delicacy and disregard of personal advantage by sacrificing her passion—temporarily—on the altar of gratitude and friendship. Replicas of her are the heroines of *The Female Foundling, translated from the French* (1750) and *La Campagne*, translated into French by M. de Puysieux in 1767. She is a servant girl and a little like Pamela in the *History of Betty Barnes* (1752), the *Life of Patty Saunders* (1752), and the *Life of Lucy Wellers* (1754).[50] Usually she is an orphan, as in *The Supposed Daughter, or Innocent Impostor* (1756), but she is illegitimate in *Emily; or, the History of a Natural Daughter* (1756).[51] The author of the *History of Miss Indiana Danby* (1765), who also wrote novels with Pamela Howard and Eliza Granville as heroines, got the name Indiana and much of her story from Mary Collyer's version of *Marianne*. The situation of Indiana in love with her own brother doubtless is from Prevost, who was also levied upon in a French version of the *History of Charlotte Summers* entitled *Maria, ou les Véritable Mémoires d'une dame illustre par son merite, traduit de l'Anglais* (1765). One will find Marivaux's influence strong in the novels of Mrs. A. Woodfin,[52] a mediocre writer who once kept a school in Bullen Court in the Strand, in the anonymous *History of Miss Lucinda Courtney* (1764) and *History of Miss Charlotte Seymour* (1764), and in Elizabeth Helme's *Louisa, or the Cottage on the Moor* (1787). In the popular novel of the type written by Agnes Maria Bennett, Marianne becomes a Cinderella or a Griselda. This author's *Juvenile Indiscretions* (1786), *Agnes de*

*Courci* (1789), *Ellen, Countess of Castle Howell* (1794), and *The Beggar Girl and her Benefactors* (1797) were very popular. Her most famous novel is *Anna, or Memoirs of a Welsh Heiress* (1785),[53] an imitation of Fanny Burney's *Cecilia* and the *History of Charlotte Summers*.

Many another English novelist was influenced by Marivaux, and not all of them by any means were mere run-of-the-mill scribblers like some of these just mentioned. Sarah Fielding, Charlotte Lennox, Mary Collyer, Frances Brooke, Sophia Lee, Harriet Lee, and Fanny Burney at one time or another paid the highest compliment to *Marianne* and imitated it.

## NOTES

1. *Progress of Romance* (1785), I, 115. The most notable of these French authors are Mmes. de Villedieu, d'Aulnoy, de Murat, du Noyer, Durand, and Mlles. Bernard, L'Heritiere, de la Force, and de La Roche-Guilhem. They were the forerunners of Marivaux, Prevost, Mme. de Tencin, Marguerite de Lussan, Mme. de Gomez, Mme. Riccoboni, and others like them who wrote sentimental novels in the eighteenth century.

2. The title of the English translation is *Hypolitus Earl of Douglas* (1708). In 1773 a critic (*Critical Review*, XXXVI [1773], 112), praised another English version of it just then published. Clara Reeve, *Progress of Romance* (1785), II, 60, thought the novel wild and improbable but admitted that it had many admirers.

3. In the edition of 1715 it was called *The Lover's Secretary, or the Adventures of Lindamira, a Lady of Quality, written by herself to her friend in the country*. The novel was "revised and corrected" by Thomas Brown, and he was perhaps the author. He was familiar with the contemporary French novel and translated Mme. d'Aulnoy's *Mémoires de la Cour d'Espagne* (1690).

4. This part does not square with the preface, which declares the novel an anti-romance dealing with "Domestic Intrigues managed according to the humours" of Londoners and other Englishmen. Aunt Xantippe, who with a tedious pedant named Sir Formal Trifle supplies the comic relief, tries to teach Lindamira Stoical self-discipline and cure her weakness for the romances, "those foolish books."

5. Long recognized as a sentimental masterpiece and an important source of romanticism. See P. and J. Larat, "Les *Lettres d'une religieuse portugaise* et la sensibilité française," *Revue de Littérature comparée*, VIII (1928), 619–639; also Wolfgang von Wurzbach, *Geschichte des Französischen Romans* (Heidelberg, 1912), p. 356ff. Sir Roger L'Estrange's translations, *Five Love-Letters from a Nun to a Cavalier* (1678) and *Seven Portuguese Letters* (1678 81), ran through several editions, usually being printed with a sequel, *Answers of the Chevalier Del.* The *Portuguese Letters* were used in Paul Chamberlen's *Love in its Empire: Illustrated in Seven Novels* (1721) in support of the theme of love versus duty. Jane Barker in *The Lining of the Patchwork Screen* (1726) described further adventures of the Nun and her escape from the convent. The *Love Letters betwixt a Nobleman and his Sister* furnished material for a novel, *The Illegal Lovers: a true Secret History, being an Amour between a Person of Condition and his Sister* (1728). But this was just the beginning. The influence of the *Portuguese Letters* ran right on through the eighteenth century. Their affinity with the sentiment expressed in Pope's "Eloise and Abelard" has been noted. Eloisa's famous lines run:

> Curse on all laws but those which Love has made!
> Love, free as air, at sight of human ties,
> Spreads his light wings, and in a moment flies.
> . . . . . . . . . .
> O happy state! when Souls each other draw,
> When love is liberty, and Nature law.

6. She called the translation of the last *The History of Oracles, and the Cheats of Pagan Priests*. It was published in 1688, the year in which *Oroonoko* appeared. *Oroonoko* was almost the first novel to preach the religion of humanity.

7. The *Monthly Review*, I (1749), 394, in a footnote to a review of a Grubstreet pamphlet describing the lawsuit between Lord Grey, the Philander of the *Letters*, and Lady Harriet Berkeley, the Silvia, asserts that this piece was generally numbered among her works.

8. For these men see H. G. Platt, Jr., "Astrea and Celadon: an Untouched Portrait of Aphra Behn," *PMLA*, XLIX (1934), 544–560.

9. *Année Littéraire* (1761), III, 188.

10. See E. D. Seeber, "*Oroonoko* in France in the Eighteenth Century," *PMLA*, LI (1936), 953–960.

11. In Mrs. Manley's *Lady's Packet Broke Open* one can read of the awful retribution meted out to the aging Barbara Villiers through her marriage with the unspeakable Beau Fielding. When the Duchess visited Mme. de Mazarin's gaming salon, she liked to have Mrs. Manley along, for she was convinced that the writer gave her good luck. Here Mrs. Manley could have heard the *liberlins* discussing radical ideas, but it is doubtful whether she was particularly interested. Yet there are some interesting political discussions in *Vertue Rewarded; or the Irish Princess* (1693), which has been attributed to her. This novel also describes some coarse adventures of military life, and it contains a story somewhat similar to *Pamela*, and another which is a sentimental account of a virtuous savage.

12. This book was also used by Defoe in *Memoirs of Captain Carleton*. Many novelists borrowed the device of the stagecoach from the *Stage-Coach Journey*. It was Mrs. Manley's book, or an imitation or version of it entitled *The Stage-Coach, Containing the Characters of Mr. Manley, and the History of his Fellow Travellers* (1753), that Smollett referred to in Chapter I of *Count Fathom*. John Steinbeck's *The Wayward Bus* (1947) presents a modern version of the stagecoach device.

13. She was a friend of Mrs. Elizabeth Rowe, author of the popular *Friendship in Death* (1728) and *Letters Moral and Entertaining* (1729–33).

14. IV, No. 58.

15. *Œuvres Choisies*, XXXV, 356.

16. Could it have been that Prevost did not approve of her friend Mrs. Rowe or Mrs. Rowe's friend, the deeply religious hymn writer, Dr. Watts, who was detested by the deists?

17. This was reprinted three times, once under the title of *Belinda; or, Happiness the Reward of Constancy*.

18. Sea adventures also figure in her *Life and Amorous Adventures of Lucinda, an English Lady* (1722).

19. Claire-élaine Engel, *Figures et Aventures du XVIII⁶ Siècle: Voyages et Découvertes de l' Abbé Prevost* (Paris, 1939), gives an excellent account of Mrs. Aubin and her novels (pp. 120–122 and 181–188). She suggests that perhaps Prevost got the name for the title hero of the *Doyen de Killerine* from Lord Coleraine, to whom Mrs. Aubin dedicated *Lady Lucy*. Prevost's *Mémoires de M. de Montcal* also is on the subject of the Irish Rebellion.

20. Chetwood (d. 1766) was a bookseller, hack writer, and at one time a prompter at Drury Lane Theater. He disputes with Defoe and Benjamin Victor the authorship of this novel but is certainly the author of the *Voyages, Dangerous Adventures, and Imminent Escapes of Captain R. Falconer* (1720), the *Voyages, Travels, and Adventures of Captain W.O.G. Vaughan* (1736), and some novelas translated or adapted from the Spanish.

21. See the *Memoirs of Mrs. Letitia Pilkington* (1748–54), ed. 1928, pp. 308–309.

22. *Critical Review*, XXV (1768), 59.

23. This collection was reprinted several times.

24. Cooper's *Select Novels* of 1745 contains English versions of some of Mme. de Gomez's novels.

25. *Progress of Romance* (1785), I, 117.

26. *Ibid.*, I, 121.

27. It is said that scandals in the Duke of Rutland's family furnished Mrs. Haywood with some ideas for her plot. Crébillon *fils* made an adaptation of the novel which he called *Les Heureux Orphelins*. This in turn became the base for a version by Edward Kimber, author of the picaresque *Life and Adventures of Joe Thompson*, which he called *The Happy Orphans, or the Authentic History of Persons in High Life* (1759). The reviewer of this in the *Critical Review*, VII (1759), 174–175, had heard that it was a piracy taken almost verbatim from Mrs. Haywood's *Fortunate Foundlings*, "that farrago of adventures," but discovered on examination that about the only similarity was in the plot. He supposed the book was a translation because it was full of gallicisms, a fact he deplored.

28. The investigation of Betsy's reputation by Charles's aunt is like Lady Davers's examination of Pamela. The frail Flora is somewhat like Fielding's Fanny Matthews just as Charles is a little like Booth. And Mrs. Haywood imitates the humorous chapter headings of *Tom Jones*. It is thought that her attack on Fielding here (ed. 1762, I, 76–77) was provoked by a dispute she had with him over her unauthorized reworking of *Tom Thumb*. The situation of the false death-bed marriage could have come from Prevost's *Mémoires d'un Honnête Homme* (1745), which seems also to have provided the model for Mrs. Haywood's false Magdalen, Mlle. de Roquilar.

29. The *Novelist's Magazine* (1780–88) reprinted *Betsy Thoughtless, The Invisible Spy* and *Jemmy and Jenny Jessamy*. Mrs. Haywood's most notable imitator is Mrs. Davys whose *Familiar Letters betwixt a Gentleman and a Lady* is modelled after the *Portuguese Letters*. She also wrote *The Reformed Coquet; or, Memoirs of Amoranda* (1724) and *The Accomplished Rake; or, Modern Fine Gentleman* (1727).

30. *Progress of Romance* (1785), I, 129.

31. Ed. 1907; year 1768, p. 36.

32. *Monthly Review*, II (1749), 91–92.

33. For editions of his novels and an excellent study of the novelist see Ruth Kirby Jamieson, *Marivaux, a Study in Sensibility* (New York, 1941). The first four parts of the *Paysan Parvenu* appeared in English in 1735 as *The Paysan Parvenu, or the Fortunate Peasant*, and there seems to have been but one other translation.

34. *Progress of Romance* (1785), I, 129.

35. I (1782), 99.

36. This relates how a Gaulish king takes to hating women and locks them all up in a walled city until one of them can prove herself truly sincere and chaste. After hearing many confessions—the real purpose of the book—a nonpareil of virtue is found.

37. There was another edition, probably a pirated one, published the same year. Its title runs: *The Fortunate Country Maid; Being the Entertaining Memoirs of the Present Celebrated Marchioness of L-V- who from a Cottage became a Lady of the First Quality in the*

*Court of France; Wherein are display'd the Various and Vile Artifices employ'd by Men of Intrigue for Seducing Young Women, with Suitable Reflections.* One wonders whether De Mouhy, pander to the Maréchal de Belle-Isle, could have been responsible for the moral title, and whether he was perfectly qualified to provide the "suitable reflections."

An imitation of De Mouhy's novel called *Love in a Nunnery; or the Secret History of Miss Charlotte Hamilton (ca.* 1742) was reviewed unfavorably in the *Monthly Review,* XLVI (1772), 78.

A third-rate novelist who called himself, or herself, Adolphus Bannoc wrote a version of *La Paysanne Parvenue* called *The Fortunate Villager, or the Adventures of Sir Andrew Thompson (ca.* 1757). See the disdainful review of this and the same author's *The Apparition, or, the Female Cavalier,* etc., in the *Critical Review,* III (1757), 187.

38. *Progress of Romance* (1785), I, 130.

39. More men succumb to Jenny's charms than to Marianne's. While trying to abduct Jenny, the Chevalier d'Elbieux is driven to violence and is badly wounded. His wounds will not heal until she comes to him. When he realizes that he cannot marry her, he becomes a Capuchin monk and tries to forget. But he cannot and faints dead away when he recognizes her among those listening to one of his sermons. Saint Fal's passion is gentler and finally turns into resignation. As for the rich ogre Gripart, who had Jenny at the altar twice only to have untimely interruptions break up the ceremony—he is soulless.

The hero's most dangerous rival is his own father, the husband of Jenny's benefactress. The moment he sees Jenny, he schemes to take her in keeping. He spirits her off to hired lodgings and has his servants crown her with a "bought head" and apply rouge to cheeks which needed it not. She is able to get a message through to Mme. de G++, who promptly spoils her husband's evil plans. Moreover, by clever maneuvering she finally breaks her husband of his habit of keeping. At the end of the novel she gives her son permission to wed Jenny.

40. See Lillian Cobb, *Pierre-Antoine de La Place: sa vie et son œuvre (1707–1793)* (Paris, 1928).

41. De La Place's *Collection de Romans et Contes, imités de l'Anglais* (1788) contains versions of *Oroonoko, David Simple, The Old English Baron, The Two Mentors,* the *History of Charlotte Summers,* etc.

42. Sarah Robinson Scott was the sister of Lady Elizabeth Montagu and was just as beautiful as she until smallpox marks ruined her complexion. Mrs. Scott helped write *Millenium Hall* (1762), which tells the life histories of some ladies living in a Protestant "convent" like the one envisioned by Sir Charles Grandison. The benevolent Jamaica planter who is the hero of her *Man of Real Sensibility* (1765) finds inspiration and new hope in Millenium Hall after he had suffered from a series of misfortunes. Her *History of Cornelia* (1750) is in part an imitation of *Marianne.* Cornelia, an unprotected orphan, flees from the incestuous passion of her uncle Octavio, who is pander to the King of France. After walking all night she faints from weariness but is resuscitated by the good Bernardo, with whom she falls in love. In Paris she takes lodgings only to find that she is in a bagnio. Her pleadings turn the first man who enters her room into a savior and she escapes. After living for a while with a milliner, she becomes a lady's secretary. Then she is abducted and imprisoned, but again escaping she lives with virtuous cottagers. Finally after adventures in Italy and elsewhere she and Bernardo flee to Spain and marry. Now both inherit wealth and spend it on various benevolent enterprises. Her bad uncle falls from favor, becomes a Capuchin monk, and dies of melancholy.

*Agreeable Ugliness* tells the story of a plain but sensible girl and her pretty hare-brained sister who is spoiled by her mother and makes a failure of life. Obediently the plain sister marries the middle-aged Dorigny although she loves another. She wishes to withdraw from Paris with its carnivals and its corruption and live in the quiet simplicity of the country. When she becomes a widow, she marries her true lover. The situation of the hero's father, on the verge of marrying the heroine and only ceding her to his son when moved by her virtues, comes by way of De Mouhy's *Paysanne Parvenue*.

Mrs. Scott was influenced by Richardson as well as by Marivaux. For her other writings see Walter M. Crittenden, *The Life and Writings of Mrs. Sarah Scott, Novelist (1723–1795)* (Philadelphia, 1932).

43. Corbet put out a corrected edition in 1750. Two editions appeared in 1753, and perhaps it was printed again before the greater popularity of De La Place's version snowed it under. The English title appears in George Colman's list (1760). Surveys of French libraries before 1800 show that *L'Orpheline Anglaise* ranks fifth as regards circulation among all the French and English novels of 1740–60 and fourth among French translations or adaptations of English novels.

44. II (1750), 352.

45. *Letters* (ed. 1892), p. 209.

46. Grimm, *Correspondance Littéraire* (ed. 1829), I, 39.

47. In the essay entitled "A Time to Laugh and a Time to Cry" the author represented a "judicious acquaintance" as having said that Fielding tickled him until he "had like to die of laughing," while Richardson, who had "a peculiar melancholy cast to his temper," moved him so that he "had like to have died crying." After calling Fielding and Richardson "inimitable moderns," the author declared he loved them both.

48. Her letter is dated March 27, 1750.

49. In the introductory chapter the author calls himself a young beginner, "the first begotten of the poetic issue of the Father of *Joseph Andrews* and *Tom Jones* ... or perhaps just a bye-blow."

50. A critic in the *Monthly Review*, x (1754), 75, disdainfully ranks Lucy Wellers as a "formidable rival to those excellent ladies, Charlotte Summers, Patty Saunders, Fanny Seymour, Sophia Shakespeare, etc., etc."

51. This novel is somewhat above the average. It was translated into French in 1756, and an abstract of it appeared in the *Bibliothèque Universelle des Romans* (Jan. 1778), II, 87–140. Instead of marrying her lover, Emily's mother concealed her pregnancy and became the rich Lady Coverly. Emily was brought up carefully by a widow, but when this good woman died, she had to live in the home of a fatuous scribbler and bookseller whose daughters were silly and affected. Later she got a place as companion to a proud but benevolent old lady whose nephew, Sir George Freelove, found Emily charming. She rejected his offer of taking her in keeping and even his proposal of marriage, but as this affair was misrepresented to Emily's mistress, the poor girl had to leave. While in the service of the sickly Mrs. Languish, Emily discovered her mother, who was quite ill. In fact, after a tender recognition scene and a penitential speech, she died. Later Emily found her father, lately arrived from Minorca and very wealthy. And as Sir George's aunt no longer objected, Emily became Lady Freelove.

52. She wrote *Memoirs, or the History of a Scotch Family* (1756), *The History of Sally Sable* (1758), *The Auction* (1759) and *The Discovery, or Memoirs of Miss Marianne Middleton* and *The History of Miss Harriet Watson*, which were published in the sixties.

53. There was a fourth edition of *Anna* in 1788 and others later. The reviewer of the French version of it (*Mercure de France*, Aug. 1788, p. 225) liked the novel but wished that Prevost, whose methods of translating English fiction he considered ideal, had translated it.

MARGARET ANNE DOODY

# Deserts, Ruins and Troubled Waters: Female Dreams in Fiction and the Development of the Gothic Novel

My Harriet has been telling me how much she suffered lately
from a dream, which she permitted to give strength and terror to
her apprehensions from Mr. Greville. Guard, my dear Ladies,
against these imbecillities of tender minds. In these instances, if
no other, will you give a superiority to our Sex....[1]

So says Richardson's Sir Charles Grandison, airily dismissing Harriet's
disturbing sequence of nightmares. Sir Charles voices the accepted rational
and masculine view. In eighteenth-century English fiction, until the
appearance of the Gothic novel, it is women, not men, who have dreams.
Masculine characters rarely dream; those who do are usually simpletons
whose dreams can be jocosely interpreted. Heroes are not dreamers.

This certainly marks a change from earlier literature. In Elizabethan
and Jacobean drama, for instance, men have very vivid dreams. In the
seventeenth century all sorts of men regarded dreams as significant, bearing
a message from God. Men with diverse religious views, such as Laud and
Bunyan, thought their dreams worth recording. The credit given to dreams
became associated with religious wars, fanaticism, and all kinds of irrational
and useless behavior. In the eyes of later generations, reality is the thing.
Defoe alone among the novelists maintains an old tradition, believing in the
spiritual import of dreams and prophetic apparitions. His central characters,
male and female, have revelatory dreams. But Defoe was considered a writer

From *Genre*, vol. X, no. 4 (Winter 1977): 529–72. © 1977 by The University of Oklahoma.

for the low, the unenlightened. In polite eighteenth-century fiction, men—if they are admirable, if they are strong—must be shown to be in touch with reality; they exert rational control without idiosyncratic private assistance from the Voice of God and without any awkward manifestations of the unconscious self. Men belong to the scientific world rather than to that of superstition; hence, they do not have prophetic dreams or premonitions. They exercise masculine authority in a world whose ways, even if sometimes distasteful, are comprehensible. They are either essentially in control, or they are failures, deserving of pity or contempt. The strong man does not have the dreams or nightmares which reveal self-division or perturbation. The only real exception is Lovelace, whose remarkable dream is a sign of (deserved) disintegration and dereliction, and who appears in a novel which has its roots in seventeenth-century comprehension of experience. Even there, the dream is connected with, and serves as a punishment for, Lovelace's moral madness. As Michael DePorte has shown, eighteenth-century psychology saw dreaming and madness as closely connected, and was frightened of both.

> The mystical view of dreams implies a high correlation between subjective and objective: it insists that the universal can be manifested in the most personal experience; it validates idiosyncratic insight. The view of dreams as temporary madness, on the other hand, reflects a profound distrust of subjectivity. Again and again Augustan writers identify the tendency toward insanity with the tendency toward the subjective.... The lunatic is typically represented as ... a person with no sense of limit. In this respect the eighteenth century's attitude toward madness is almost exactly the reverse of that of modern psychiatry, with its growing stress on the connection between insanity and an underdeveloped sense of self.[2]

Masculine novelists must show the world of men as objective, not subjective. The same considerations do not apply, or not quite in the same way, to the presentation of women. Richardson, whose guiding interest was in the subjective, necessarily wrote about women. Clarissa, in her dreams and madness, is not morally reprehensible. *Grandison*, more completely a novel of its time than *Clarissa*, has a hero who is supposed to epitomize all the current conceptions of good masculinity; it is the women around the hero who have weaknesses and perturbation. It is the women who have dreams. Sir Charles teases Harriet about having allowed herself to be affected by "a dream, a resverie," and the embarrassed heroine confesses apologetically, "I own I should have made a very silly, a very pusilanimous [sic] man" (III, 248). Dreaming is feminine; men are not to be subjected to inner terrors.

Women, weaker than men, not in control of their environment, are permitted to have dreams. The censorship of dreaming doesn't quite apply to them. Officially, in the eighteenth century, women are thought of as weak and superstitious; they have something of an archaic consciousness, not enjoying the full benefits of masculine reason and masculine knowledge of reality. Their dreaming is not necessarily insanity, nor is it the sign of an unbecoming and ignoble weakness. A female character can be shown as dreaming—or having nightmares or delusions—without forfeiting the reader's respect. The "imbecillities of tender minds" are not unattractive. A female dreamer does not seem comic, nor need the fact that she dreams be interpreted as a distasteful psychic dereliction. Women are often seen as living an inward life rather different from that of men, whose consciousness is more definitely related to the objective world and to action within it. Women, less able to plan and execute actions, are seen as living a life closer to the dream-like, and closer to the dream-life.

That this is so can be seen in Pope's presentations of both Belinda and Eloisa. The dreams of both are related to their sexual natures, and to disturbances about their sexual nature. It has often been pointed out that the imagery in *Eloisa to Abelard* prefigures the Gothic manner:

> methinks we wandring go
> Thro' dreary wastes, and weep each other's woe;
> Where round some mould'ring tow'r pale ivy creeps,
> And low-brow'd rocks hang nodding o'er the deeps. (ll. 241–44)

This imagery—the imagery of the sublime—is certainly present in the national consciousness, but can be used freely here precisely because the poet is dealing with a woman's experience. When we read *The Dunciad* we may wonder if the sublime and the dreamlike are not both thought of as dangerously associated with the feminine; it is the "mighty Mother" who threatens masculine rational objectivity. In *Eloisa* Pope treats his subject sympathetically. There is no need to ask about meaning or sense aside from the psychological. Eloisa need not be asked to do anything in the objective world because she cannot. There is no event in the poem; the poem is Eloisa, that passive victim and active dreamer whose sexual nature is inseparably associated with pain, dread and guilt. When the feminine is feminine, there is no need for hostility. We do not need to ask, while reading about Eloisa's dream, if the character is evincing the inferiority of her sex and the superiority of the other—ultimately, she is, perhaps, but we need take her only as she is, attending to her experience. The poem was popular with women, especially with the ladies of the town, who must have taken the work as a vindication of feminine passion.

When women writers themselves describe feminine dreams, the effects are both similar to and different from those in Pope's poems. In writing novels the women writers, although dealing with the objective everyday world, felt free to include dream experience as part of the heroine's life. Unlike Defoe, they do not follow the old tradition which relates the dream to the promptings of God or the Devil. Female novelists interest themselves in the psychology of the heroine; her subjective life has meaning, and her dreams cry out for interpretation, but not the old religious meaning or spiritual interpretation. The reader's sympathetic understanding of the dream rises from an understanding of the character in her situation. The dreams delineated by women writers are much lonelier and more complex than those which Pope describes. What gives rise to the dream may not be quite what we expect, and the dreamcontent is powerfully related to the sense of individuality under attack. Women's heroines usually are not as simply hopeful as Belinda or as simply grief-sticken as Eloisa. In an apparently placid situation the heroine's relationship to a lover or to marriage may be fraught with anxiety amounting to dread. The heroine has a strong but divided sense of self, and the self is usually suffering from something more complicated than simple desire or simple grief. Some sort of good self-realization is being thwarted, and tension and terror arise from a sense of incomplete and unsatisfactory alternatives. The pain is related to the woman's sexual nature; the sexual nature and the whole sense of identity do not coincide satisfactorily, and the individual is threatened with severe loss.

One of the most interesting examples of the disturbing feminine dream occurs in Jane Barker's *Love Intrigues: The History of the Amours of Bosvil and Galesta* (1713). The heroine is in a constant state of uneasy suspense about her relationship to Bosvil and his on-again-off-again courtship (if that is what it is). When Bosvil appears to have abandoned her, the heroine goes for solitary rambles and begins to write poetry. Deciding to dedicate herself to her work, she writes verses on an ash tree in a grove:

> *Methinks these Shades, strange Thoughts suggest,*
> *Which heat my Head, and cool my Breast;*
> *And mind me of a Laurel Crest.*

> *Methinks I hear the Muses sing,*
> *And see'em all dance in a Ring;*
> *And call upon me to take wing.*

> *We will (say they) assist thy Flight,*
> *Till thou reach fair ORINDA's Height,*
> *If thou can'st this World's Follies slight.*

> *Then gentle Maid cast off they Chain,*

*Which links thee to thy faithless Swain,*
*And vow a Virgin to remain.*

After this self-dedication, Galesia devotes herself to poetry and study: "Thus I thought to become *Apollo's* Darling Daughter, and Maid of Honour to the Muses."[3] Her activities become important in themselves, but when Bosvil returns and appears to be on the point of a declaration she drops her studies. Things are apparently going prosperously, but she is still in a state of suspense about herself and her future. While in this state of suspense, she has an important dream:

> I thought my self safe landed on Love's Shore, where no cross Wind, unseen Accident, cou'd oppose my Passage to *Hymen's* Palace, or wrack me in this Harbour of true Satisfaction.... Now my Thoughts swam in a Sea of Joy, which meeting with the Torrent of the foresaid Vexations, made a kind of dangerous Rencounter, ready to overset my Reason. I pass'd some Nights without Sleep, and Days without Food, by reason of this secret Satisfaction. At last, being overcome with a little Drowsiness, I fell asleep in a Corner of our Garden, and dream'd, that on a suddain, an angry Power carried me away, and made me climb a high mountain: at last brought me to that Shade where I had heretofore writ those Verses on the Bark of an Ash, as I told you, in which I seem'd to prefer the Muses, and a studious Life, before that of Marriage, and Business. Whereupon,
> —*My uncouth Guardian said,*
> —*Unlucky Maid!*
> *Since, since thou has the Muses chose,*
> Hymen *and Fortune are thy Foes.* (pp. 32–33)

In a later edition of this novel (1719) the dream is more surprisingly revealing:

> ... a mountain where I met *Bosvil*, who endeavour'd to tumble me down, but I thought the aforesaid Power snatch'd me away, and brought me to that Shade....[4]

The dream is not related only to Galesia's lover, or even primarily to her repressed passion for him. The dream is related to her own sense of an enforced choice, and to a decision she must make about her own nature. If she is "Apollo's Daughter," she must give over the desire for marriage, for sexual fulfillment. She recognizes and fears the penalty of sexual frustration even while her own sense of herself makes her unhappily reject the man she loves. Her own will does not govern the nature of the alternatives. In the second (and unexpurgated?) version of the dream, the high mountain represents a freedom from anxiety, a sexual aspiration fulfilled—but it cannot be obtained after all; she is transported back to the "Shade" of her intellect. In some fashion she knows that the affair with Bosvil will never mature (as it does not—the subtitle of the story is ironic). What makes the dream terrifying is the helplessness, the sense of being "snatch'd away" from fulfillment and being compelled to confront the truth about herself. A modern psychological allegorist must inevitably see the "power" as representing not just Fate (though external conditions make this division inevitable), nor the irresistible power of Apollo, but Galesia's inner nature which makes a bitter choice her will does not know how to make. She had made a life for herself without Bosvil, and this has been more than a substitute for him. She had decided on a single life (in which she could use her intellect)—although she didn't expect herself to take her at her word. Her dream-journey travels over the landscape of her divided self—and the dream vision powerfully intimates anxiety and loss.

In the sequel, *A Patch-Work Screen for the Ladies* (1723), loss and perturbation are repeated. Here the heroine is living her single life, in fulfillment of the prophecy. The kind brother with whom she studied medicine, her only intellectual companion, dies. The heroine is disdainful about the superstitions of other girls, which include "Our little Follies of telling our Dreams; laying Things under each other's Heads to dream of our Amours ... drawing Husbands in the Ashes; St. *Agnes's* Fast; and all such childish Auguries,"[5] but she is impressed by her own dreams of the lost brother, remembering "that I even wish'd for that which is *the Horror of Nature*, that I might see his *Ghost*" (p. 13). Telling dreams is a silly feminine pastime, the mature Galesia indicates—but what about the force of experience in some dreams? The life Galesia knew seems lost. She has to go with her widowed mother to London, where she spends most of her time working in the garret, or on the roof of their humble lodging, gazing over the city:

> Out of this Garret, there was a Door went out to the Leads; on which I us'd frequently to walk to take the Air, or rather the Smoke.... Here it was that I wish'd sometimes to be of *Don Quixote's* Sentiments, that I might take the *Tops* of *Chimneys*, for *Bodies* of *Trees*; and the *rising Smoke* for *Branches*; the *Gutters* of *Houses*, for *Tarras-Walks*; and the *Roofs* for stupendous *Rocks* and *Mountains*. However, though I could not beguile my Fancy thus, yet here I was alone, or, as the Philosopher says, never *less alone*. Here I entertain'd my Thoughts, and indulg'd my solitary Fancy. (p. 67)

Such reverie is not like that of Eloisa, simply and strongly connected with erotic passion; rather, it is connected with a sense of solitary identity, both losing and finding itself. Galesia contemplates London rather as Mrs. Radcliffe's Ellena will contemplate the mountains and valleys from her turret in the convent; imprisoned, the self can create meaning from inner impressions. Galesia's mountaintop in her dream has now become the rooftop where she finds herself, and, in looking down from her height, she can transcend reality for a while, although not without a fear of that outer world which would be too powerful for her if she were to descend to it.

There is an eighteenth-century heroine who is very firmly "of *Don Quixote's* Sentiments." Arabella in *The Female Quixote* (1752) determinedly lives her life in a kind of dream reverie. By imagining that the real world is like that of her favorite romances, she interprets everything as she pleases, in the only manner which appears to allow importance to feminine nature. Unlike Don Quixote's illusions the attractive Arabella's much simpler ones are almost entirely related to her sexual nature. Her desire for and fear of men both have real meaning; men rule her world, and pay little attention to the female identity. The dream-life is also well-designed to protect her from her basic anxiety: that she is a woman and thus does not count for much, that all her actions will be controlled and that everything about her is to be made safe and dull.

As the Countess informs the heroine, good respectable women do not have adventures, and they have no histories.[6] That nothing should ever happen to one, that a strong consciousness should never be allowed to emerge—this is the most frightening anxiety of all. It is no wonder that the adolescent girl defers recognition of this for as long as possible, and that she does not care for images of safe plateaux. She makes a history for herself and reconstructs the landscape into the landscape of romance and dream. In the long conversation with the divine who ultimately helps to convert her to right-mindedness, Arabella gives up her imagery only under protest:

> What then should have hinder'd him from placing me in a Chariot? Driving it into the pathless Desart? And immuring me in a Castle, among Woods and Mountains? Or hiding me perhaps in the Caverns of a Rock? Or confining me in some Island of an immense Lake?
>
> From all this, Madam, interrupted the Clergyman, he is hinder'd by Impossibility.
>
> He cannot carry you to any of these dreadful Places, because there is no such Castle, Desart, Cavern, or Lake.
>
> You will pardon me, Sir, said *Arabella*, if I recur to your own Principles:

Universal Negatives are seldom safe, and are least to be allow'd where the Disputes are about Objects of Sense; where one Position cannot be inferr'd from another.

That there is a Castle, any Man who has seen it may safely affirm. But you cannot with equal Reason, maintain that there is no Castle, because you have not seen it.

Castles indeed, are the Works of Art; and are therefore subject to Decay. But Lakes, and Caverns, and Desarts, must always remain.[7]

We rather agree with Arabella, that "Lakes, and Caverns, and Desarts must always remain"—that they certainly remain as part of the landscape of the mind. This is strikingly borne out by a passage in a highly realistic novel which appeared about the same time. The heroine of Eliza Haywood's *The History of Miss Betsy Thoughtless* (1751) portrays an archetypal young coquette, but there is more to her than that; she has a strong personality, and the author represents her sympathetically, making the reader understand the causes of Betsy's "thoughtlessness" and appreciate the mixed and often irrational and unconscious motives for her actions. After several false flirtations, and after losing Trueworth, the man she really loves, Betsy is in an emotional condition to accept the control of her guardians, who wish to settle her in marriage. A marriage is soon arranged between Betsy and the apparently pleasant and wealthy Mr. Munden—whom Betsy does not dislike, but whom she does not really know. The girl suddenly realizes that she is engaged:

Miss Betsy had not as yet had time to meditate on what she had given her promise to perform:—the joy she found her compliance had given all her friends,—the endearing things they said to her upon the occasion, and the transport mr. [*sic*] Munden had expressed, on seeing himself so near the end of all his wishes, had kept up her spirits, and she imagined, while in their presence, that her inclination had dictated the consent her lips had uttered.

But when she was alone,—shut up in her own appartment [*sic*];—when she no longer received the kind caresses of her smiling friends, nor the flattering raptures of her future husband, all the lively ideas, which their conversation and manner of behaviour towards her had inspired, vanished at once, and gave place to fancies, which might justly bear the name of splenatic [*sic*].

"I must now look upon myself," said she, "as already married:—I have promised,—it is too late to think of retracting—

a few days hence, I suppose, will oblige me to the performance of my promise, and I may say with Monimia in the play:

'I have bound up for myself a weight of cares,
And how the burthen will be borne, none knows.'

"I wonder," continued she, "what can make the generality of women so fond of marrying?—It looks to me like an infatuation.—Just as if it were not a greater pleasure to be courted, complimented, admired, and addressed by a number, than be confined to one, who from a slave becomes a master, and perhaps uses his authority in a manner disagreeable enough.

"And yet it is expected from us.—One has no sooner left off one's bib and apron, than people cry,—'Miss will soon be married,'—and this man, and that man, is presently picked out for a husband.—Mighty ridiculous!—they want to deprive us of all the pleasures of life, just when one begins to have a relish for them."

In this humour she went to bed, nor did sleep present her with images more pleasing;—sometimes she imagined herself standing on the brink of muddy, troubled waters;—at others, that she was wandering through desarts, overgrown with thorns and briars, or seeking to find a passage through some ruin'd building, whose tottering roof seemed ready to fall upon her head, and crush her to pieces.

These gloomy representations, amidst her broken slumbers, when vanished, left behind them an uncommon heaviness upon her waking mind:—she rose,—but it was only to throw herself into a chair, where she sat for a considerable time, like one quite stupid and dead to all sensations of every kind.[8]

Like Galesia's, this dream results from an apprehension of the self under attack, and from a sense of severe loss which cannot be exactly defined. The heroine has been disturbed by a sense that there are alternatives which her world does not acknowledge as real. Her questioning is accompanied by sharp resentment: "they want to deprive us of all the pleasures of life, just when one begins to have a relish for them." Her articulate resentment does not make her less helpless; the dream urges upon her the truth about her loneliness and danger, facts which are too large to be contained in (or dismissed by) her unhappy articulate ruminations. In Betsy's dream the images of Arabella's romance are present, but transformed and given new vividness by dread. The dreamer is trying to go somewhere—away from or towards something?—but her passage is slow and fearful. She is threatened by "annihilation"; the world is terribly unsafe. The subjective consciousness tells her truths which her real everyday world will not acknowledge. In this novel the author has identified the heroine's condition and her dream with the difficulties attendant upon woman's role and woman's lot. The author, through her heroine, makes a generalization which the reader is intended to recognize. The dreamer does not merely present an idiosyncratic individual problem. Frightening images, "gloomy representations" are the necessary and appropriate symbols of the consciousness of unhappy women—imprisoned by social conventions, threatened by slavery, and plagued by loneliness. Betsy's world cheerfully bears her off to the marriage with Munden, a union disastrous in all respects. Her intuitions were right, but there seemed to be no way for her to make her intuitions count in the real world.

Betsy's dream embodying her fear of marriage finds an interesting parallel in the experience of another and much more admirable heroine, the creation of a first-rate male novelist. Richardson's Harriet Byron dreams very vividly before her approaching marriage—a marriage not to a man she barely knows, but to the man she most desires. Richardson, never a simple novelist, does not imagine that an apparently idyllic prospect is a simple matter for the woman concerned.[9] Harriet is at the point of her life where she should be most happy; the man whom she feared she had lost to the beautiful Italian, Clementina, has been set free to return to her and express his love. Yet, now that she is faced with a reality instead of the unrequited love she has been nourishing for so long, her unconscious mind reveals that she is far from being totally at one with herself in her response to a new, unexpected and very demanding "happiness." It is she who has insisted on continuing in a state of suspense, telling Sir Charles that she wishes him to hear from Italy before she marries him, thus giving her rival time to change her mind; Sir Charles is sure all is settled.

In her shifting nightmare visions, objective fears (that her rejected suitor may attack Sir Charles) mingle with less exact and less obvious ones. Her resentment of Sir Charles for his love of Clementina, her guilt about taking him from somebody else, and her fear of the man himself, with his total righteousness and domineering masculinity—all these mingle in shifting visions which express a very tense (and intense) life going on beneath the surface of the happily engaged girl. Her earlier anxious puzzling over the case of Clementina (who, she has thought, "deserved" Sir Charles more than she) is not at an end. The land she has never seen asserts itself in her dreams, as Italy and England (that is, Clementina and Harriet) exchange their natures. Everything is shifting, unstable, expressive of different kinds of loss. Harriet's series of dreams arises from a highly charged sexual state, and present a panic about identity and about the future. She later tells Sir Charles about part of it (not the whole), and Grandison can dismiss it as "a dream, a resverie" unworthy the attention of an intelligent being. That is not what Harriet or the reader feels—we, like the heroine are compelled to experience something frightening and significant:

... going immediately from my pen to my rest, I had it broken and disturbed by dreadful, shocking, wandering dreams. The terror they gave me, several times awakened me; but still, as I closed my eyes, I fell into them again. Whence, my dear, proceed these ideal vagaries, which for the time, realize pain or pleasure to us, according to their hue or complexion, or rather according to our own?

But such *contradictory* vagaries never did I know in my slumbers. Incoherencies of incoherence!—For example—I was married to the best of men: I was *not* married: I was rejected with scorn, as a presumptuous creature. I sought to hide myself in holes and corners. I was dragged out of a subterraneous cavern, which the sea had made when it once broke bounds, and seemed the dwelling of howling and conflicting winds; and when I expected to be punished for my audaciousness, and for repining at my lot, I was turned into an Angel of light; stars of diamonds, like a glory, encompassing my head: A dear little baby was put into my arms. Once it was Lucy's; another time it was Emily's; and at another time Lady Clementina's!—I was fond of it, beyond expression.

I again dreamed I was married: Sir Charles again was the man. He did not love me. My grandmamma and aunt, on their knees, and with tears, besought him to love their child; and pleaded to him my Love of him of long standing, begun in gratitude; and that he was the only man I ever loved. O how I wept in my dream! ...

My sobs, and my distress and *theirs*, awakened me; but I dropt asleep, and fell into the very same resverie. He upbraided me with being the cause that he had not Lady Clementina. He said, and *so* sternly! I am sure he cannot look so sternly, that he thought me a much better creature than I proved to be: Yet methought, in my own heart, I was not altered. I fell down at his feet. I called it my misfortune, that he could not love me.... And then I said, Love and Hatred are not always in one's power. If you cannot love the poor creature who kneels before you, *that* shall be a cause sufficient with me for a divorce.... I will bind myself never, never to marry again; but you shall be free—And God bless you, and her you can love better than your poor Harriet. Fool! I weep as I write!...

In another part of my resverie he loved me dearly; but when he nearly approached me, or I him, he always became a ghost, and flitted from me. Scenes once changed from England to Italy, from Italy to England: Italy, I thought, was a dreary wild, covered with snow, and pinched with frost: England, on the contrary, was a country glorious to the eye; gilded with a sun not too fervid; the air perfumed with odours, wafted by the most balmy Zephyrs from orange-trees, citrons, myrtles, and jasmines. In Italy, at one time, Jeronymo's wounds were healed; at another, they were breaking out afresh.... There was a fourth brother, I thought; and he, taking part with the cruel Laurana, was killed by the General....

But still, what was more shocking, and which so terrified me that I awoke in a horror which put an end to all my resveries (for I slept no more that night)—Sir Charles, I thought, was assassinated by Greville. Greville fled his country for it, and became a vagabond, a Cain, the Accursed, I thought, of God and Man—I, your poor Harriet, a widow.... (*Grandison*, III, 148–49)

The reader is invited to unravel the dreams, to answer Harriet's question "whence proceed these ideal vagaries?" They are all related to the heroine's experience, and make a good deal of sense. Harriet has long desired Sir Charles and has feared that he rightly judges her as inferior to her rival. The first part of her dreaming expresses fear of rejection, her sense of guilt and unworthiness. The sequence winds from the image-filled sets of strong sensational impressions (cavern, sea, winds, diamonds, baby) to a rationalized scenario in the terms of social realities (in the social world, the worst final rejection is to be divorced, and this Sir Charles could inflict upon her). That rationalized dream allows an imagined dialogue, but the images insisting on worth have been negated. The reassuring picture of herself crowned like the Virgin Mary, and blessed with a child which belongs to all the rejected women, gives way to a scene of humiliating feminine supplication. Then the dreaming plunges again into disintegrated and wild impressions and images which words cannot reach. Sir Charles is a ghost—or she is—so they cannot approach each other. Scenes change. Italy (which she has feared) is cold; England (herself) becomes warmly Mediterranean; this must be at least in part Harriet's assertion that she has as much warmth and passion as the Italian lady. The dreams become more violent. In real life, Clementina's brother Jeronymo (whom Harriet has never met) has been wounded in a manner that implies he has lost, if not his manhood, any future hope of exercising that manhood. This Italian Fisher-King, who has adopted Sir Charles as his brother, is in the dream evidently another manifestation of the unsatisfactory lover himself. Clementina's "fourth brother" is actually Sir Charles, the adopted brother; here he is imagined as being cruel to Clementina, in company with Clementina's worst persecutor, her cousin Laurana. If the cruel cousin had made Clementina's insanity worse, it was Sir Charles, unsatisfactory suitor of the Italian girl, who caused her madness in the first place. Harriet is at once identifying herself with Clementina, tormented by Sir Charles, and also "killing off" the Sir Charles who was once the lover of Clementina. But in killing the "bad" Sir Charles who did what Harriet did not like, the dreamer is also killing the "good" Sir Charles whom she loves—so there is a real connection between what precedes her last dream of horror and that dream itself. The last dream, which awoke her in "horror," is a more rational one. The anger, frustration, and vengefulness are projected entirely upon Greville—who in real life poses the only threat to Sir Charles's safety. In that last dream Harriet's suitor abandons her unwillingly, but the loss is more final, more certain, than the others.

In her dreaming the English girl who is engaged to the best of men has actually adapted a nightmare of her rival as described in a letter which Harriet has read. Clementina, who has gone mad from love for the man who is not a Catholic and whom her family will not, in effect, permit her to marry, also dreams out of a sense of loss. Her loss, one which is very real, is associated with severe doubt about her own identity, and with an anxious sense of guilt. At one important point, Sir Charles has said a final farewell to the family and left Bologna without Clementina's being allowed to know of his departure. When she does not see him, she imagines that her irascible brother, the General, has murdered their guest:

> She took Camilla under the arm—Don't you know, Camilla, said she, what you heard said of Somebody's threatening Somebody?—Don't let anybody hear us.... I want to take a walk with you into the garden, Camilla.
>
> It is a dark night, madam.... Be pleased to tell me, madam, what we are to walk in the garden for?
>
> Why, Camilla, I had a horrid dream last night; and I cannot be easy till I go into the garden.
>
> What, madam, was your dream?
>
> In the Orange-grove, I thought I stumbled over the body of a dead man!
>
> And who was it, madam?
>
> Don't you know who was threatened? And was not Somebody here tonight? And was not Somebody to sup here? And *is* he here?
>
> The General then went to her. My dearest Clementina; my beloved sister; set your heart at rest. Somebody is safe: Shall be safe.
>
> She took first one of his hands, then the other; and looking in the palms of them, They are not bloody, said she.—What have you done with him, then? Where is he?
>
> Where is who?—

You know whom I ask after; but you want some-thing against me. (II, 241)

Neither Clementina's nor Harriet's dream is prophetic; although each is used to heighten suspense (about possible violence to Sir Charles), that is not the main function. Each of these dreams is most strongly related to the psychological state of the dreamer, accurately depicting the acute fears of her helpless condition. These dreams are true, not as prophecies of the future but as expressions of a subjective reality and of the imperfections in both subjective and objective worlds. We see in them what an outer, uncontrollable world has done to the inner life, and not a mere reprehensible derangement. It is noticeable that Clementina's dream is shorter than Harriet's, less complex, betraying no impulse to rationalize or re-arrange; in her dreams, as in everything else, Clementina tends to accept what is given her. In her dream she expresses her knowledge of the violence of the oppressive family which is trying to "kill" what she desires. Confusing dream with reality, in the liberty of her madness, she can look for tokens of bloodshed on the hands of her family, thus accusing them as her unconscious mind accuses them; she does not feel *safe* with her family. With the foolish but not senseless cunning born of "insane" secret insight, she refuses to utter the name of the man she loves, as her family are punishing her for loving him; she treats the family as a tribunal before which she must not commit herself: "you want something against me." She would prefer to go into the imprisoning and maze-like garden rather than to stay and talk. She would rather find the corpse than talk to the murderers.

Both dreams invite the reader to participate in the dreamer's vision; he must not accept either dream as presenting literal scientific truth of fact, but he must allow images and emotions to play on his sensibility. The combined imagery of "garden," "dark night," "Orange-grove" and "dead man" is powerful: darkness over Eden, life and fruitfulness giving way to death, fear, sexual loss. That potent image-cluster recurs, elaborated, in Harriet's dream with its magnificent sequence of images: "subterraneous cavern," "howling winds," "diamonds," "baby," "tears," "ghost," "dreary wild," "snow," "frost," "sun," "orange trees, citrons, myrtles and jasmines"—all ending again with the corpse of Sir Charles. Clementina mad and miserable, Harriet sane and happily engaged, both inhabit a dream-world of loneliness, helplessness and dread which the reader is invited to share and understand. Dreams assist them in their struggle for self-knowledge, for fuller being. Dreams are not trifling or contemptible—if the dreamer is a woman. Even Richardson, with his strong respect for the value of subjectivity, could not show a good man having dreams or being affected by them. In a man such dreaming would be (as Harriet shamefacedly admits) "pusillanimous." But that is hardly a defect in a woman, and her dreams and fantasies can be fully expressed, because they pose no threat to the public rational order. If Sir Charles were to dream, the ranged arch of empire might fall.

Richardson's enquiring and sympathetic view of feminine dreaming extends to a view of madness—feminine madness—which is curiously out of keeping with the general notions of his time. DePorte quite truly says that the Augustan age distrusted a subjectivity of which madness was the final expression, and identified madness with egotism: "The lunatic is typically represented as a person with no sense of limit." This never quite applied, I think, to women; their breaking down is often seen more tenderly, as in the case of Belvidera in *Venice Preserved*. Fictional women often go mad because more is put upon them than they can bear; they are often fragile, deficient in egotism rather than guilty of an excessive sense of self. This tradition of feminine madness (especially in drama) permitted Richardson to draw the sympathetic and virtuous Clarissa and Clementina. There is an important difference between his presentation of female madness and that of the stage-plays. Richardson's heroines' madness does not mark the end of their lives. Madness is a phase through which the heroine lives and from which she learns; it arises from an insufficient and underdeveloped sense of self, and pushes the woman onward to a stronger and more integrated state of being. Derangement has its creative aspects, as Jung and R.D. Laing were later to point out. The intensity of the heroines' experience supplies something which commonplace life denies, and which social life tends (often wrongly) to deny to women. After Richardson, other eighteenth-century novelists of both sexes could feel safely justified in portraying the good heroine going mad and emerging from this experience with some access of strength.

Masculine madness is a much more tricky subject; indeed, in most eighteenth-century literature it could not be presented at all, save as a sign of consummate folly, or of vice reaping its reward. To say a *man* is mad is the perfect insult (see *The Dunciad*). Smollett met with failure in *Launcelot Greaves* because his hero—a young Quixote—could not be accommodated either by the novel form or by novel readers; the author eventually plays safe by indicating that the hero's derangement is just a game, a sham role he can drop at will. It is the heroine who has the more distressing experience of being shut away in a madhouse, and the hero who gallantly rescues her. Smollett's interests lay beyond, while including, the satiric, but he perpetually has to return to the acceptability of satire. His interest in pathological states is a remarkable feature of his works, although he never quite managed to give full embodiment to his perceptions.

Madness or derangement in a man is associated with the ideas of failure and ridicule; in orthodox eighteenth-century literature its point is satiric and not psychological. Launcelot Greaves moves through an outer world, not, like Arabella Stanley and Female Quixote, through inner regions. Geoffrey Wildgoose, the Spiritual Quixote, has no identity beyond being a satiric caricature of the absurdities of Methodism as his author sees them. It is no wonder that Mackenzie's *The Man of Feeling* (1771) seems such an odd novel, and has puzzled so many readers, some holding that it exalts sensibility while showing the cruelty of a world which denies it, others holding that it ridicules sensibility by showing the absurdity of its excess in relation to the real world. The novel does both, unevenly. Mackenzie, a good but not a great novelist, could not get out of the problem he had set himself, for he was too much a man of his age not to want to laugh at a man who can't manage the real world. There is no possible end except killing the hero off before he does anything of importance, like getting married. A man who is so pusillanimous is too mentally impotent to be fully sexual.[10] *Tristram Shandy* deals with a kind of madness by recreating Renaissance comedy about theories and the workings of the reason. In comically asserting the madness of us all, it gets away from madness as suffering, or madness as threat. The world is irrational (but entertaining) and we are absurd if we take ourselves too seriously. In that kind of festive madness born of science, women have no place. (The dull Mrs. Shandy has no hobby-horse.) The novel talks about suffering, while insulating us from it, just as all good surrealist farce does. We don't worry about the mental states of the Marx brothers in their films, or the Monty Python characters—neither do we feel grief or dread about Walter and Toby. *Tristram Shandy* is a brilliant manifestation of a comic art which makes masculine responsibility tolerable. It essentially affirms what it appears to deny. Sterne's way of dealing with masculine aberration is the only one that can work perfectly in mid-eighteenth-century literature.

The difference between concepts of men and women in the period can be seen in the simple and striking fact that feminine madness is not funny, whereas masculine madness is an almost irresistible source of jest. Female madness is not funny because women never have quite the sort of sanity that is demanded of men. They never have rational control of the world, so when they lose rational control of themselves they are not contradicting their essential nature. A woman may be deranged without losing credibility, sexual attractiveness, or value. The women novelists themselves become fond of presenting female characters who temporarily lose their reason and enter into a heightened state of morbid perceptiveness. In a realistic novel the heroine's venture into an hallucinatory state is perhaps the wildest "adventure" she can be allowed (compare Arabella); the women novelists also found in the presentation of an extraordinarily irrational state a means of expressing the extreme of feminine pain, and of giving that full value as an experience without the encumbrance of sententious precepts about contentment, good conduct, and good sense. As in the cases of the dreaming heroines, we have the pattern of uneasy loss leading to a crisis which precipitates an anguished vision. The bounds of reality dissolve, and the heroine is left alone in delirious terror which is more insistent and prevalent than a dream—the nightmare terror takes control for a while of vision, actions, and speech.

The heroine of Fanny Burney's *Cecilia, or Memoirs of an Heiress* (1782), a woman of pleasant good sense in a society which is neither kind nor sensible, is subjected to increasing presures by people who see her only as "an Heiress." Constantly robbed of value and always threatened by the loss of the man she loves, she undergoes an anxiety which even her secret marriage to her lover, Delvile, does not solve. Already suffering from guilt and from uncertainty about the future, she then hears that Delvile has been injured in a duel. She, like the dreamers but more violently, then loses self-control and acts out her worst fears as she rushes frantically about the London streets in search of her husband, obsessed by the idea that he is both injured and in danger from the law:

> [T]he coachman, too much intoxicated to perceive her rising frenzy, persisted in detaining her.
>
> "I am going to France!" cried she, still more wildly, "why do you stop me? he will die if I do not see him, he will bleed to death!"
>
> The coachman, still unmoved, began to grow very abusive ... and Mr. Simkins, much astonished, entreated her not to be frightened: she was, however, in no condition to listen to him; with a strength hitherto unknown to her, she forcibly disengaged herself from her persecutors; yet her senses were wholly disordered; she forgot her situation, her intention, and herself; the single idea of Delvile's danger took sole possession of her brain....
>
> ... She called aloud upon Delvile as she flew to the end of the street. No Delvile was there !—she turned the corner; yet saw nothing of him; she still went on, though unknowing whither, the distraction of her mind every instant growing greater, from the inflammation of fatigue, heat, and disappointment. She was spoken to repeatedly; she was even caught once or twice by her riding habit; but she forced herself along by her own vehement rapidity, not hearing what was said, not heeding what was thought. Delvile, bleeding by the arm of Belfield, was the image before her eyes, and took such full possession of her senses, that still, as she ran on, she fancied it in view. She scarce touched the ground; she scarce felt her own motion; she seemed as if endued with supernatural speed, gliding from place to place, from street to street; with no consciousness of any plan, and following no other direction than that of darting forward whereever there was most room, and turning back when she met with any obstruction;

till quite spent and exhausted, she abruptly ran into a yet open
shop, where, breathless, and panting, she sunk upon the floor....[11]

In the pawn-broker's shop Cecilia is given refuge, and treated as a
madwoman; the woman of the house, having locked her in a chamber, brings
her a quantity of straw, "having heard that mad people were fond of it."
Cecilia can recognize no one; her maid is astonished and afflicted by what
she finds:

> She wept bitterly while she enquired at the bed-side how her lady
> did, but wept still more, when, without answering, or seeming to
> know her, Cecilia started up, and called out, "I must be removed
> this moment! I must go to St. James's-square,—if I stay an instant
> longer, the passing-bell will toll, and then how shall I be in time
> for the funeral?" (v, 333).

Such scenes do not seem out of place in this comic narrative because the
author's comedy throughout is closely related to frustration, and to irritation
of the nerves. The comic figures are baleful; the suspense in scene after scene
arises from the frustration of the heroine's wishes, or the relentless
application of pressure to the heroine and her weak if well-meaning lover.
Almost always surrounded by crowds, Cecilia has always been alone, and the
scene in which, in her delirium, she rushes through the crowded streets is a
repetition and culmination of many previous scenes involving desire
thwarted, and anxious hurrying forward impeded. Most notably it reflects
the long episode in which Cecilia tried to make her way secretly to London
for a clandestine marriage, only to have her journey obstructed by the
meeting with "friends," the comic figures who dog her steps and obstruct her
purposes. At least in the delirious running she gains a kind of relief—a relief
possible only once she "forgot her situation, her intention, and herself"; she
acquires speed for the first time. She can run with the feeling of supernatural
ease as one does in a nightmare, and goes hurrying towards what she desires
and fears, the image of her husband bleeding and dying. Real London totally
disappears and the nightmare takes over the vision of waking life.

Fanny Burney was evidently impressed and moved by her own scene
here; her next heroine also falls victim to delirium, and the visions of
Camilla's madness are set out at greater length and are much more complex
and forceful, drawing the reader into the experience.

Camilla's dream-visions make sense and have their effect because of
their context; panic and pain are heightened because of the heroine's growing
and intolerable sense of loss, loneliness and guilt. Camilla, believing herself
responsible for her father's having been imprisoned for debt, returns to her
uncle's home, which has always sheltered her, to find it "despoiled and

forsaken"; her uncle has sold everything and moved away in his determination to help the Tyrold family repay their debts. Camilla, frightened to go home and now "all at war with herself," goes to the home of her unhappily married sister Eugenia, but Eugenia's brutal husband Bellamy turns her away. Camilla then reluctantly begins her journey towards her parents, but stops at a small inn, as she wants to write to her mother and be sure she is forgiven before she returns. There is no answer to the letter in which she explains her situation—without a home, without money. She begins to fall ill, and to hope for death. Then a murdered man is brought to the inn. Camilla passes the room in which the corpse lies, goes in and, moved by "enthusiastic selfcompulsion," lifts up the cloth that covers the face, and sees it is Bellamy. She faints, and is taken to a room, there to lie neglected and deathly ill. She no longer desires death, but is profoundly frightened of it—she fears she has added suicide to her previous sins: "self-murdered through wilful self-neglect." After begging for a clergyman to be sent for, she tries in vain to compose herself:

> It was dark, and she was alone; the corpse she had just quitted seemed still bleeding in full view. She closed her eyes, but still saw it; she opened them, but it was always there. She felt nearly stiff with horrour, chilled, frozen, with speechless apprehension.
>
> A slumber, feverish nearly to delirium, at length surprised her harassed faculties; but not to afford them rest. Death, in a visible figure, ghastly, pallid, severe, appeared before her, and with its hand, sharp and forked, struck abruptly upon her breast. She screamed—but it was heavy as cold, and she could not remove it. She trembled; she shrunk from its touch; but it had iced her heart-strings. Every vein was congealed; every stiffened limb stretched to its full length, was hard as marble: and when again she made a feeble effort to rid her oppressed lungs of the dire weight that had fallen upon them, a voice hollow, deep, and distant, dreadfully pierced her ear, calling out: "Thou has but thy own wish! Rejoice, thou murmurer, for thou diest!" Clearer, shriller, another voice quick vibrated in the air: "Whither goest thou," it cried, "and whence comest thou?"
>
> A voice from within, over which she thought she had no controul, though it seemed issuing from her vitals, low, hoarse, and tremulous, answered, "Whither I go, let me rest ! Whence I come from let me not look back! Those who gave me birth, I have deserted; my life, my vital powers I have rejected." Quick then another voice assailed her, so near, so loud, so terrible ... she shrieked at its horrible sound. "Prematurely," it cried, "thou art

come, uncalled, unbidden; thy task unfulfilled, thy peace unearned. Follow, follow me! the Records of Eternity are opened. Come! write with thy own hand they claims, thy merits to mercy!" A repelling self-accusation instantaneously overwhelmed her. "O, no! no! no!" she exclaimed, "let me not sign my own miserable insufficiency !" In vain was her appeal. A force unseen, yet irresistible, impelled her forward. She saw the immense volumes of Eternity, and her own hand involuntarily grasped a pen of iron, and with a velocity uncontroulable wrote these words: "Without resignation, I have prayed for death: from impatience of displeasure, I have desired annihilation[....]" Her head would have sunk upon the guilty characters; but her eyelids refused to close, and kept them glaring before her. They became, then, illuminated with burning sulphur. She looked another way; but they partook of the same motion; she cast her eyes upwards, but she saw the characters still [....] Loud again sounded the same direful voice: "These are thy deserts; write now thy claims:—and next,—and quick,—turn over the immortal leaves, and read thy doom." ... "Oh, no!" she cried, "Oh, no!" ... "O, let me yet return! O, Earth, with all thy sorrows, take, take me once again [....]" In vain again she called;—pleaded, knelt, wept in vain. The time, she found, was past; she had slighted it while in her power; it would return to her no more; and a thousand voices at once, with awful vibration, answered aloud to every prayer, "Death was thy own desire!" Again, unlicensed by her will, her hand seized the iron instrument. The book was open that demanded her claims. She wrote with difficulty ... but saw that her pen made no mark! She looked upon the page, when she thought she had finished, ... but the paper was blank! ... Voices then, by hundreds, by thousands, by millions, from side to side, above, below, around, called out, echoed and re-echoed, "Turn over, turn over ... and read thy eternal doom!" In the same instant, the leaf, untouched, burst open ... and ... she awoke.[12]

Camilla's vision (the chapter is called "A Vision") is, despite some awkward phrasing, probably the most impressively horrifying of all the dreams I have cited. The author seems determined to deal with the very source of Burke's Sublime: the fear of death. The sensations of dying are acutely painful, with no control and no central identity; her consciousness is apparently broken up, scattered over her body and over the universe. Her whole being becomes a tribunal of voices. Camilla is being tried by an invisible Inquisition of her scattered self. The marble immobility is horrifying, but not as horrifying as the judgment which is condemning her, not to Hell but to "annihilation," the absolute loss. She grasps at an identity which will not stay. The image of writing with an iron pen and making no mark is a particularly striking emblem of waste, and of lack of personal significance—she has made no impression on life. The act of writing, itself so much an act of conscious intellect, seems to foreshadow a fate truly worse than death, a future of impotent consciousness which tries to communicate its worth and is condemned ever to fail. (It may be remarked that this seems particularly an author's image of hell.)

The author has drawn upon the older religious tradition of the inspired dream here, yet the whole is intimately related to Camilla's psychology and situation, and what emerges is not simply didactic. Ostensibly, the author is concerned with making the reader vividly aware of the heroine's fault, her sin of egotistical self-destructiveness, like that of the later Marianne Dashwood. Yet this does not explain what the dream-vision feels like in its context in the novel. Camilla's life has been one of perpetual frustration, which the reader has shared. The man whom she loves has fallen victim to his jealous mania and has rejected her. Camilla has made a few trifling errors, for the most part the result of unscrupulous other people misunderstanding or manipulating her. Her family's financial trouble has come largely from her scapegrace brother Lionel who has blackmailed Camilla into lending him money and shielding him. Nothing in her life has gone right, and the novel, while apparently pursuing the educational story of a young lady who, although led into a few indiscretions, was amiable and educable, has actually become a gigantic defence of the tormented Camilla against the rest of the unjust world. The abandonment into which she has been plunged is a form of suffering much worse than she can conceivably be said to merit: Fanny Burney's description of her torments is of a piece with that author's constant intuition (or suspicion) that it is a woman's lot to be thwarted, isolated, and unrecognized. Camilla's delirious dreamvision resembles the dreams of Charlotte Brontë's Lucy Snow when that heroine lies ill with fever in the pensionnat. Both heroines express an unmerited sense of total failure, a haunting sense of being unloved, unlovable, worthless and meaningless. Fanny Burney here differs from the other novelists of her century in not presenting her heroine's tormenting dream as arising from a primarily sexual problem; Camilla's dread is born of a half-acquiescent, half-rebellious judgment that her life has been meaningless. The dream is a frightening account of the greatest imaginable frustration and loss, and an expression of the total guilt which seems the feminine emotion appropriate to eternity.

I have perhaps cheated somewhat in discussing *Camilla* here, before the Gothic novels, for it is certainly true that the Gothic novel was under way before Fanny Burney's third work (1796), and it seems that she had begun to be influenced by Gothic devices here, as she certainly was in her last novel. It also seems evident that the women writers of Gothic novels were strongly affected by *Cecilia* (which contains, among other things, the scene of the secret wedding frighteningly interrupted, so like that in *The Italian*). But certainly *Cecilia* and *Camilla* belong, with *Betsy Thoughtless* and *Grandison*, to the class of comic social novels. The heroine moves in the recognizable world of daily common life, and has to learn to cope with her own feelings and with society. It is true of *Camilla* as of all the other dream-containing novels I have mentioned that the heroine has to wake up (is allowed to wake up) from her dream—or nightmare—or vision. There is a real world to come back to, and the horrid landscapes and frightful, if exciting, images exist only momentarily. The authors who deal with dreams can do so only temporarily; not too much can be made of a heroine's dream, for after all it is only a dream. The passages I have quoted stand out a trifle oddly in the novels in which they occur, for they introduce suggestions which cannot be fully taken up by the author. Certain levels of consciousness don't repay investigation in a certain type of novel. Charlotte Lennox deals with the matter in an original way, and is the most consistent in presenting her heroine's whole career in terms of her wilful waking dream—but in her anti-romance (also a salute to the romance) Charlotte Lennox uses satiric control to keep the wholly disturbing at a distance. Satiric control works well in the novel she created, for she succeeds in making us forget alternatives, but there were other novelists who wanted to say that Arabella's contradictory fears, of being violently ravished or of being left hopelessly repressed and dull, were entirely relevant to what happens in the real world. Richardson certainly believed in the truthful intuitions of both kinds of fear. It was left to later (I certainly do not say superior) novelists to deal extensively with fear, desire and repression in terms of the nightmare images used by earlier novelists only occasionally to provide momentary glimpses into the perturbed depths of the feminine psyche. That is, the occasionally-glimpsed landscape of feminine dream was to become the entire setting in another, non-realistic, type of novel.

That the first writers of the Gothic novel in English were women does not seem a mere coincidence. Clara Reeve, Sophia Lee, Charlotte Smith, Ann Radcliffe—with this last name we come to the point at which the Gothic novel is fully developed, however much later writers may have contributed to embellish and alter it in their own fashions. The only notable exception is of course Horace Walpole whose *Castle of Otranto* (1764) gives us the trappings of the Gothic story without its essence. He who can be stirred to fear by any page of that work must have a constitution more pusillanimous than most. As Clara Reeve noted with some puzzlement, the story is full of silly machinery and ridiculous images which produce a comic effect.[13] Walpole refuses to give way to any belief in the reality, at any level, of what he was writing; Reason was certainly on the throne. It isn't witty, it isn't gentlemanly, to be agitated. The source was a dream, and wit can conquer dreams. Walpole gave some of the old-time trappings a literary respectability which was to become useful later; he could not use them. Clara Reeve, without a quarter of Walpole's talent, and suffering the additional disadvantage of a heavily conscious adherence to propriety, wrote a dull novel which is almost redeemed by some vivid passages in which fear is handled and not fobbed off. Our eyes are not upon a heroine who has to learn, but upon a strange older world not subject to modern rationality.

The writers of the Gothic novel could give their full attention to the world of dream and nightmare—indeed, the "real world" for characters in a Gothic novel is one of nightmare. There is no longer a commonsense order against which the dream briefly flickers; rather, the world of rational order briefly flickers in and out of the dreamlike. There is no ordinary world to wake up in. The extraordinary world of Gothic romances differs markedly from the realms of the old seventeenth-century productions. What strikes the reader who moves from the eighteenth-century Gothic works to the romances of, for instance, Madeleine de Scudéry is the great *calm* of the older works. Everything is spacious, everything is leisurely. The sublime exists to be contemplated, not to horrify. The description of the burning city at the beginning of *Le Grand Cyrus* (1653–55) is an impressive version of an aweful sight, but it is not intended to send a thrill of dread along the nerves. It is not seen as threat, but as stupendous spectacle—which the hero himself has caused. There is in the old romances a great deal of battle and bloodshed, but little sense of violence. Throughout, a beautiful grandeur saves us from a sense of oppression. These works are as much tributes to the beauty of reason as, say, the work of Bernini. One is not helpless because everything is explicable and harmonious. The power of the characters to expound and define (they are among the most articulate characters known to fiction) is just as heroically impressive as the heroines' beauty or the heroes' prowess. Experience is wonderful, not tormenting. We feast on grandeur, and do not shrink before the mysterious. Emotions are intense but not perturbing.

The feelings which the new form, the Gothic romance, deals with constantly—feelings which sharply set it off from the older sort of romance—are inner rage and unspecified (and unspecifiable) guilt. These passions are essentially related to all sorts of other emotions—fear, anxiety, loneliness—which are unstable, powerful, and unpleasantly associated with helplessness and with some kind of sense of inferiority. It will, I think, be acknowledged that all the dreams of heroines to which I have referred bear a weight or inner rage and/or guilt in each case. The one instance that looks like an exception, Arabella's fantasy, is certainly not an exception; the heroine adopts the manners of her favorite heroines in order to justify her expressions of anger and disdain. Her fantasy is a feeble (and unreasonable) rebellion. Inner rage and overwhelming guilt are, in eighteenth-century circumstances, very feminine emotions—women have to suppress rage because they cannot control things; women feel guilty because they continually fail to live up to expectations. If they are to be judged by anybody (Apollo, Mrs. Tyrold, Sir Charles) they will be found wanting. The Gothic romances find an embodiment for these feelings, and work them out using the dream-language to new purposes.

All the imagery we have met in these fictional dreams of women is to be found in the Gothic novel: mountain, forest, ghost, desert, cavern, lake, troubled waters, ruined building with tottering roof, subterraneous cavern, sea, "howling and conflicting winds," snowy wastes, the bleeding lover, orange groves, corpse, iron instruments, invisible voices and dread tribunals—and, with these, sudden changes of place, preternatural speed, irresistible forces. In the Gothic novel these things are not the illusions which result from momentary feminine weakness—they constitute objects and facts in the "real" outer world, whose nature it is to create dread.

The first English novel in which the dream-world expands to take on the contours of the whole world is not the witty *Otranto* nor the cautious *Old English Baron* but that wild tale by Sophia Lee, *The Recess* (1783–85). This work, one of the first English historical novels,[14] tells the story of two women, the legitimate but concealed daughters of Mary Queen of Scots; the historical unreality of these beings, whose lives are not to be found recorded on any page of history, works, oddly, in the novel as a kind of substantiation of these buried lives. Matilda and Ellinor are brought up in a subterraneous cavern, their identity a danger to their mother, to themselves, and to all who come into contact with them. They live secluded in this Recess, a place beautiful but claustrophobic, a combined palace and prison, womb and grave. St. Vincent's Abbey was destroyed in the Reformation; part of the Abbey has been rebuilt as a palatial residence, but the secret refuge is buried under ruins. In their furnished cavern, the children see the very beams of the sun only dimly, as it is filtered through "casements of painted glass" (I, 3). Their adult ventures into the world above their subliminal shelter lead both to release and disaster. Leicester comes upon the girls on one of their rare excursions above ground; he falls in love with Matilda (and she, most ardently, with him). He contrives to marry her secretly, and takes her and her sister about with him in disguise. The unacknowledged wife and her sister even serve in the court of their greatest enemy, Queen Elizabeth, who of course does not know who they are. As Ellinor says later of this life, "we were all an illusion" (II, 165).

Part of the fascination of the novel is that the girls, the story's centers of consciousness, lead in a sense the life of phantoms—they cannot be real, they must not be known. They are the mystery of this Gothic novel; it is the villains who endeavor to discover them. Their lives are a perpetual image of guilt; their existence is not only a threat to themselves and their lovers but a Damocles' sword hanging over the life of their mother, the imprisoned Queen. Mary's daughters see her only once, through a grated window; they thrust their hands through the bars, but cannot touch their mother or talk with her.

Every action is doomed to loss—and dread; every relationship is fated to be fractured by history. When Queen Elizabeth discovers Matilda's identity and her marriage, Leicester flies with her to the Continent—where they are betrayed by Matilda's own relative, who allows the Queen's agents to come upon them at dead of night; Matilda's husband is murdered before her eyes. There is no happy mistake, or restoration, or awakening; Matilda's only consolation is in watching by the coffin of her dead love. Her pretended friend, Mortimer, offers to rescue her; Matilda awaits him in the convent chapel at midnight, listening to the bell strike through the cold air while she rests her head upon Leicester's coffin, from which she refuses to be parted, much to Mortimer's chagrin. As the reader expects, the rescuer has his own designs upon Matilda, and she is a prisoner in the ship which carries her to Jamaica. The novel is full of rapid movement, of dream-like wandering from scene to scene; apparent release from one frightening situation proves only an introduction to another, although the images change with dreamlike completeness which yet is continuity.

Matilda, pregnant with Leicester's child, is comforted by the presence of the faithful Rose Cecil, who has been herself in love with Leicester and has followed him through the world. Like the dreaming Harriet Byron, Matilda is rescued from the fear of sea and wind by being presented with a baby, the child which her rival could not have. After Matilda has given birth, Rose's mind begins to give way to increasing melancholy which leads to an unexpected and rapid climax:

> One evening ... I perceived her more than usually disturbed. Neither my prayers, nor the pouring rain could bring her from the balcony, where for hours she told her weary steps. I started at last from a momentary slumber on her re-entering the cabin. The dim lamp burning in it, shewed her with a slow and tottering pace approaching the last asylum of Lord Leicester; sinking by this repository of her breaking heart, she clasped her hands upon her bosom with a most speaking sense of woe; while over it her fair locks fell wild and dishevelled, heavy with the midnight rain, and shivering to its beatings. The wet drapery of her white garments spread far over the floor, and combined to form so perfect an image of desolation, as froze up all my faculties. I struggled for articulation. A feeble cry alone escaped me. She started at the sound from her icy stupor, and glanced her eyes every where, with that acuteness of perception which marks a disturbed imagination.... Springing up with etherial lightness, even while her feeble frame shivered with agony and affection, she fixed on my convulsed features a long, long look, then waving majestically

a last adieu, rushed again into the balcony. Unable to move a
limb, my harrowed soul seemed, through the jar of the elements,
to distinguish her dreadful plunge into the world of waters. (II,
100–01)

This striking scene is an embodiment of feminine pain. The heroine, like the
female dreamers, is conscious of danger but is unable to move or speak.
Matilda shares the consciousness of her admirable rival, who seems like a
dreamer's other self; Rose seems rather like Harriet in the earlier parts of her
nightmare. At the end of the scene Rose dissolves into the elements; the
plunge into the depths offers the final release from the sense of woe. The
central characters, the two sisters, are perpetually hovering above depths into
which they fear or desire to descend.

Ellinor's account of her life is even more violent than Matilda's, with
more inner loss involved. One of the novel's points is that the two sisters in
their adult life are separate in views and circumstances. When we read
Ellinor's narrative we find with surprise that the sisters have always been
different, and Matilda's views of events can no longer be seen as the only
ones. It is an interesting shock to discover that Ellinor, while always loving
her sister, never trusted Leicester. Ellinor herself is in love with Essex—
another love which is doomed to disaster—and cannot see his faults of
weakness which accompany the charm. Ellinor has more to bear than her
sister. After Matilda's flight, she is left to bear the brunt of the anger of
Elizabeth and Burleigh. Ellinor is imprisoned—in St. Vincent's Abbey:

[H]e ordered his servants to bear me into the grated room at the
end of the eastern cloister. You cannot but remember the dismal
place. Half sunk in ruin, and overhung with ivy, and trees of
growth almost immemorial, it appeared the very cell of
melancholy.... The pale gleams of the moon seemed every
moment to people the dungeon they glanced through—my pulse
beat with redoubled strength and quickness—the whole cloister
resounded the long night with distant feet, but they came not to
me—fearfully I often started when sinking into a lethargy, rather
than slumber, by the echo of some remote voice, which fancy
continually told me I knew, but it died away ere memory could
assign it an owner.... (II, 214–15)

Ellinor's reason slowly starts to give way under this treatment, and her
tortured experience is closely associated with fear of a most undesired
marriage, and with guilty responsibility. Burleigh forces her into marriage
with the unloveable Lord Arlington, after making her sign a dishonest
document swearing that neither she nor Matilda is the child of Queen Mary.

Ellinor signs—with the death warrant for her mother before her eyes; she does not know that "our sainted mother was led to execution, almost at the very moment I was defaming you and myself to save her" (II, 236). Ellinor's fearful midnight marriage increases her despair: "Wedded—lost—annihilated" (II, 235). The news of her mother's execution overthrows a reason which she never quite recovers:

> Severed at once from every tie both of nature and of choice, dead while yet breathing, the deep melancholy which seized upon my brain soon tinctured my whole mass of blood—my intellects strangely blackened and confused, frequently realized scenes and objects that ever existed, annihilating many which daily passed before my eyes.... There were moments when I started as from a deep sleep, (and oh, how deep a sleep is that of the soul!)—turned my dubious eyes around with vague remembrance—touched my own hand, to be convinced I yet existed—trembled at the sound of my own voice, or raising my uncertain eye toward the blue vault of Heaven, found in the all-chearing sun a stranger.—Alas! my sister, look no more in this sad recital for the equal-minded rational Ellinor you once saw me; sensations too acute for either endurance or expression, from this fatal period blotted every noble faculty, often substituting impulse for judgment. Always sensible of my wandering the moment it was past, shame continually succeeded, and united every misery of madness and reason. (II, 237–38)

Ellinor's narrative, which often does break into rambling, provides a contrast to Matilda's more straightforward account. Ellinor's life is a nightmare within the nightmare, and she subsides into dreaming:

> I dreamt of Essex—Ah, what did I say? I dreamt of Essex—Alas, I have dreamt of him my whole life long!—Something strangely intervenes between myself and my meaning. (II, 243)

Life is a painful dream, with fits of hectic joy. Ellinor recovers after Arlington's death, escapes to Ireland and Essex, but these lovers are soon separated again. Essex, who matches Ellinor in "substituting impulse for judgment," is led to his foolish return to the Queen and his mad rush upon London—and to the Tower and the block. Ellinor is brought to see him the night before his execution, but merciful insanity intervenes and she does not know him, or realize what is happening. After his death she is doomed to repeat the experience of his execution over and over again, going through the Tower and even the Queen's palace, looking for her lover:

"Somebody told me, continued the lovely wanderer, that he was in the Tower, but I have looked there for him till I am weary—is there a colder, safer prison, then? But is a prison a place for your *favorite*, and can you condemn him to the grave?—Ah, gracious Heaven, strike off his head—his beauteous head!—Seal up those sparkling eyes forever.—Oh, no, I thought not, said she with an altered voice.—So you hid him *here* after all, only to torment me. But Essex will not see me suffer—will you, my Lord ? So—so—so"—the slow progress of her eyes round the room, shewed, she in imagination followed his steps.—"Yes—yes,—added she, with revived spirits, I thought that voice would prevail, for who could ever resist it?—and only I need die then; well, I do not mind that—I will steal into his prison and suffer in his place, but be sure you don't tell him so, for he loves *me*—ah! dearly does he love me, but I alone need sigh at that, you know.... Oh, now I remember it, resumed she, I do not mind how you have me murdered, but let me be buried in Fotheringay; and be sure I have *women* to attend me; *be sure* of that—you know the reason." (III, 182–83)

The Queen takes Ellinor, in this mad visitation, for a supernatural accuser. But Ellinor herself suffers from guilt, because she feels she has failed in her responsibility to her mother and to Essex. The fulfillment of any desire is colored with guilt:

"Me married to him! resumed our friend, replying to some imaginary speech,—oh, no, I took warning by my sister!—I will have no more bloody marriages: you see I have no ring, wildly displaying her hands, except a black one; a *black* one indeed, if you knew all—but I need not tell *you* that—have I, my Lord?" (III, 184)

Pitiless Fate impels the tale to its inevitable end, the obliteration of Mary's unacknowledged descendants. What is feared is not worse than what happens. The aberrations of Ellinor's mind are merciful in comparison to the reality. Unlike Clementina, or Cecilia, Ellinor cannot be brought back to the comfort of the real world, because there is no comfort in her real world, and her madness is a simple reflection of what exists outside herself. It is true that Ellinor is self-divided; indeed, she keeps slipping into the identities of her mother and her lover: "I fear I begin again to wander, for my hand writing appears to my own eyes that of Essex" (II, 275). But Ellinor's self-division is not the expression of a merely individual psychological difficulty. Her varying identities have a common substance: her mother, her lover, herself,

Matilda, Leicester all suffer under a common tyranny. The only way of escaping this tyranny in the real world is by concealment of oneself (in the subterranean life) or by annihilation in death (courted in different ways by Rose Cecil and Essex). The buried life (as symbolized by the life of the Recess itself) is confining, dim, unsatisfactory: "how deep a sleep is that of the soul!" But life in the world is irrational and brutal; consciousness is punished rather than rewarded. The only choice seems to be between two dreams—lethargic reverie, or nightmare.

This novel, which is, with all its defects, often interesting and even striking, can claim the distinction of being a pioneer work in two literary kinds. It is the first fully developed English Gothic novel, and it is also one of the first recognizable historical novels in English. The two facts seem connected. This Gothic story about sixteenth-century characters is a judgment of the real world; history is a chronicle of pain and sorrow. Institutions, power, political activities are the nightmarish cruel realities from which no one can escape. All the characters are trapped in their own historical situation; what we have here may not be exactly the history of the textbooks, but we are presented with an historical situation. The past affects the present. The past (Henry's dissolution of the monasteries, the suppression of Catholicism, Mary's flight) really has happened. The actions, loyalties, motives of all the characters are affected by what has happened before they come upon the scene, and by contemporary realities over which the individual rarely has control. The world functions on power which is both necessary and deeply destructive. The woman who is powerful (Elizabeth) perverts her nature in exercising power; the men who wish to use power drive themselves on to feverish activity and are ultimately ridden over by history. The women whom the author sees as good (Mary of Scotland, Matilda, Ellinor, Rose, young Mary) are more passive (not entirely passive), but they are inevitably implicated in events which they affect but cannot control. Like the heroines of Jane Barker, Richardson, and Fanny Burney, the heroines are moved by guilt and fear—but in this case guilt and fear are not just the property of dreaming young ladies, although it is the female characters who give expression to these emotions. The men are un-Grandisonian; they rage, and are helpless, and fail in their grand designs. Guilt and fear are diffused throughout the whole historical dream and all of it—ruined monastery, pomp and pageantry at Kenilworth, axe and Tower and palace—is at once both real and nightmarish, both inescapable and absurd. It is in the Gothic novel that women writers could first accuse the "real world" of falsehood and deep disorder. Or perhaps, they rather asked whether masculine control is not just another delusion in the nightmare of absurd historical reality in which we are all involved. The visions of horror are not private—they have become public.

The visions of horror are certainly related to public issues rather than to purely private life in the works of Charlotte Smith. It is evident in her first novel, *Emmeline* (1788) that the writer has recognized in the development of Gothic effects a feminine tradition particularly suited to the discussion of women's difficulties and their social causes. In this she anticipates Mary Wollstonecraft's achievement in *The Wrongs of Woman*. (Mary Wollstonecraft herself, in a less advanced stage of her feminist career, reviewed *Emmeline* rather severely, seeing in it too much sympathy with certain kinds of female dreams and desires. Such reading encourages the search for *"adventures"* at the expense of duty and contentment; one remembers Mrs. Lennox's Arabella.)[15]

The Gothic elements in *Emmeline* appear only sporadically; the author is primarily interested in contemporary social problems, and uses all the elements of fiction which will serve her turn, without fully developing any. As some early readers noticed, she is indebted to Fanny Burney's earlier novels for social comedy and for plot complication. Mrs. Smith in her first work stands uneasily between old and new. Her heroine has nightmares rather than living in nightmare, but at one point the author does make an interesting transition between dream and reality, in which the reality seems a continuation of the dream. This is the scene in which Emmeline, aroused from bad dreams ("horrid visions" rather like Harriet Byron's concerning Greville's attack on Sir Charles), waits by the window for the dawn. The atmosphere, with the starlight, the dimly seen garden and the "low, hollow murmur of the sea" is well created. In the faint and uncertain light the heroine sees the figure of a man who moves like a phantom over the lawn; "on perceiving the first rays of the morning, he 'started like a guilty thing,' and swiftly stepped away to his concealment" (*Emmeline*, pp. 465–66).

There is no prolonged mystery; the mysterious stranger is soon identified as the man with whom Emmeline's friend, the unhappy Adelina, committed adultery; Fitz-Edward has come to watch the house of the woman he loves but dares not approach. His Hamlet's-ghost appearance is an emblem of his forlorn, penitential and helpless condition, for both he and Adelina are in a shadowy social and emotional limbo. Emmeline's own case, the unwilling engagement to a man she does not wish to marry, is thematically related to that of the unhappily married Adelina. The self-division, uncertainty and even horror inspired by the prospect of marriage as seen in the dreams of earlier heroines are, in this novel, projected upon outward circumstances.

The atmosphere surrounding Fitz-Edward's appearance suggests the unhappiness caused by oppressive reality—marriage laws, position of women, bonds of custom. Truth cannot come by daylight; the world pushes some emotional realities into shadows. The novel patently argues about these things; the miseries of bad marriages are forcefully described, and the novelist depicts both the adulteress and her lover with a good deal of sympathy. By the end of the novel the virtuous heroine has broken her engagement, and it is indicated that Adelina, now a widow, will marry her lover with her family's eventual approval. The author certainly tells us what she wants to see changed. She is always interested in the objective world, the political world.

In this novel she is not sure of all her effects; she wants to be both realistic and Gothic, and the Gothic moments tend to be spasmodic and self-contained. It was not until after the advent of Mrs. Radcliffe's works that Charlotte Smith discovered how to make the elements of Gothic romance work in harmony with her radical themes. Mrs. Radcliffe is of course not consciously "a radical" at all, but in her works that which inspires horror is given a pure and consistent objective reality; it is not dropped in for merely perfunctory effect, and it has a significance which is always in some sense a historical significance. Charlotte Smith took, I think, what she needed from Mrs. Radcliffe, which was not what she could take from Sophia Lee's inward-turning passionate wraiths. Charlotte Smith is not extremely interested in the inner life of characters; her interests lie outward, and she wants to change the world, to make it less painful rather than to analyze pain as Sophia Lee does. She needed a more objective means of sanctifying anger and purging guilt in the presentation of her well-intentioned heroes and heroines caught in the turbulence of contemporary history. Her best Gothic effects are to be found in *Desmond* (1792), especially in the sequence in which the hero and heroine plunge about the fortified manor one of the last die-hard aristocrats of revolutionary France. There, historical reality provides appropriate Gothic imagery for all oppression and greed, an objective correlative for what men in power have done to other men and to women in the true nightmare which is history. The intuitions of Mrs. Haywood's splenetic Betsy are vindicated indeed. The private protests of feminine dreams have become public, rational, schematic objections to institutions and traditions clearly seen and defined. It is not surprising that the English Gothic novel, with its roots in the dreams of women, should become, along one line of its evolution, the novel of feminine radical protest.

The achievement of Mrs. Smith in her major works was to be of importance for later writers. In a highly original manner she relates individual difficulties, states of mind, and views to larger cultural conditions. Her insight into the significance of the Gothic is a result of this desire to connect. Scott is indebted to her, and so too, although less directly, is George Eliot. Yet, with all her originality and even brilliance, Mrs. Smith is merely a writer of great talent, not a genius. She possesses the limitations of her qualities which are intellectual rather than powerfully imaginative. The melancholy which Scott noted as one of her most marked characteristics is subtly at odds with her urge to put things right. In defining matters clearly and programatically, she tidies away the nightmare. Once the cause of nightmare is rationally defined as social oppression, then the visions of terror are merely symptoms of a wrong that can be put right. The sublime, the horrifying, lose their mysterious hold on us; the force of imagination, the power of the inner life, are rendered negligible. In the development of the Gothic novel it is Ann Radcliffe who is the major innovator, in subtle ways as well as obvious ones. She has been accused of disappointing readers with too-careful explanations of her mysteries, but of course she never really tidies up the suggestive horror at all, any more than she removes Vesuvius from the landscape of Vivaldi's Naples.

In Mrs. Radcliffe's novels we find the world of nightmare made into an objective art which is neither self-indulgent nor dogmatic. She uses the objective third-person narrator to convey the impression of truth; we are not, as in *The Recess*, locked into the subjectivity of a female victim. The Gothic atmosphere is all-pervasive, not residing in occasional pieces of machinery as in the tricksy *Otranto* or the sedate *Old English Baron*. Her novel represents an expansion and clarification of the motifs of fear and anxiety, and the imagery acquires a new conviction from careful and consistent use. In her first novel, *The Castles of Athlin and Dunbayne* (1789), there is a deliberate economy of effect, as if she were dubious about cheapening her resources. The action is simpler than that in any of her other novels, and the major setting, the castle of Dunbayne, is a stark place in barren surroundings; the author is trying to capture the bare grandeur of her idea of ancient Scotland, with its clan warfare, clan loyalties and primitive way of life.

The hero, Osbert, is at the novel's outset a victim of history; his father, the chief of Athlin has been killed by the haughty Malcolm of Dunbayne, and the clan hopes for revenge when the young Earl is of an age to lead his clan "to conquest and revenge."[16] This rather lonely young man is both martial and imaginative:

> He delighted in the terrible and in the grand, more than in the softer land-scape; and wrapt in the bright visions of fancy, would often lose himself in awful solitudes.
>
> It was in one of these rambles, that having strayed for some miles over hills covered with heath, from whence the eye was presented with only the bold outlines of uncultivated nature, rocks piled on rocks, cataracts and vast moors unmarked by the foot of traveller, he lost the path which he had himself made; he looked in vain for the objects which had directed him; and his heart, for the first time, felt the repulse of fear. No vestige of a human being was to be seen; and the dreadful silence of the place was interrupted only by the roar of distant torrents, and by the screams of the birds which flew over his head. He shouted, and his voice was answered only by deep echoes from the mountains.

He remained for some time in a silent dread not wholly unpleasing, but which was soon heightened to a degree of terror not to be endured; and he turned his steps backward, forlorn, and almost without hope. His memory gave him back no image of the past; and having wandered some time, he came to a narrow past, which he entered, overcome with fatigue and fruitless search.... (pp. 9–10)

We have here the desert, the silent anxiety-filled wilderness which is the landscape of nightmare. The phrase "His memory gave him back no image of the past" is more than an elegant periphrasis for "he could not remember having seen any of this landscape before"; the phrase itself suggests the horrors of a mind without recollection, with no recallable past, finding itself arbitrarily placed in a scene utterly alien—the condition of dream. But the dream is reality, and the figure who stands in the place of the dreamer is masculine. At last an eighteenth-century hero experiences real terror.

When Osbert leads the expected attack on the castle of Dunbayne, himself fired with ardent belief in his cause, his clansmen are surprised by the enemy. The attack is a failure, and Osbert and his friend, the valiant young Alleyn, are imprisoned, separately, in the dungeons of the castle. Here, both young men experience fear—and helplessness:

Reflection, at length, afforded him time to examine his prison: it was a square room, which formed the summit of a tower built on the east side of the castle, round which the bleak winds howled mournfully; the inside of the apartment was old, and falling to decay: a small mattress, which lay in one corner of the room, a broken matted chair, and a tottering table, composed its furniture; two small and strongly grated windows, which admitted a sufficient degree of light and air, afforded him on one side a view into an inner court, and on the other a dreary prospect of the wild and barren Highlands.

Alleyn was conveyed through dark and winding passages to a distant part of the castle, where at length a small door, barred with iron, opened and disclosed to him an abode, whence light and hope were equally excluded. He shuddered as he entered, and the door was closed upon him. (pp. 35–36)

After an interview with the cruelly vengeful Baron, Osbert feels "perfect misery" and even thinks of suicide:

the cool fortitude in which he had so lately gloried, disappeared; and he was on the point of resigning his virtue and his life by means of a short dagger, which he wore concealed under his vest.... (p. 39)

The perturbation of this novel's heroes is in marked contrast to the sedate emotions of Mrs. Reeve's Edmund, who, in the haunted room, is *almost* allowed to feel fear:

> He recollected the other door, and resolved to see where it led to; the key was rusted into the lock, and resisted his attempts; he set the lamp on the ground, and exerting all his strength opened the door, and at the same instant the wind of it blew out the lamp, and left him in utter darkness. At the same moment he heard a hollow rustling noise like that of a person coming through a narrow passage. Till this moment not one idea of fear had approached the mind of Edmund; but just then, all the concurrent circumstances of this situation struck upon his heart, and gave him a new and disagreeable sensation. He paused a while; and, recollecting himself, cried out aloud—What should I fear? I have not wilfully offended God, or man; why, then, should I doubt protection? But I have not yet implored the divine assistance; how then can I expect it! Upon this, he kneeled down and prayed earnestly, resigning himself wholly to the will of Heaven; while he was yet speaking, his courage returned, and he resumed his usual confidence....[17]

It is the *reader's* fear with which the author plays briefly, while not quite allowing her *hero* to be fully afraid. His usual confidence governs Edmund through the rest of the action—even in the long sequence of dreams he is touched not by horror but by blessings: "Every succeeding idea was happiness without allay; and his mind was not idle a moment till the morning sun awakened him." The dream-sequence is not fearful, but assures him of his true identity and inheritance. Edmund has no reason to fear—he is good old English manliness (with suitable if anachronistic Protestant rational piety). He waits for his appropriate reward. But Osbert, although courageous, is really afraid. His cool fortitude can disappear. Here is a man who is subject to failure, distress, captivity—just like the heroine (whom he will eventually meet, a fellow-prisoner in this castle). These moments in which the hero experiences terror seem so natural in Mrs. Radcliffe's novel that no one is likely to remark them as offering anything startlingly new. The author makes no pother about it—she certainly is not making any dogmatic statement, feminist or otherwise. She serenely takes it for granted that terror is so important an experience that all human beings can have it—that the nightmare apprehensions are universally true, and related to real life. Inner rage, guilt, anxiety and dread are not the exclusive property of women. In showing this, in making this truth objective, she brings the Gothic novel to maturity as a genre with something important to say about the unknown darkness which shadows all our lives. Her characterization is simple and conventional (necessarily, for her purpose); her notion of what can be felt by human beings (for which the characters act as signals) is unconventional and profound.

In her next novel, *A Sicilian Romance* (1790), Mrs. Radcliffe is confident enough to attempt more elaborate effects. Lovers are rapt from each other with the speed of nightmare; we move from landscape to landscape, from warm to cold, from height to depth, from brilliant light to eerie dark, whirling about a wild exotic world as Harriet Byron did in her dreams. There is a luxuriance of striking images: the ancient castle of Mazzini; the sea; the "dark rocky coast of Calabria"; "Mount Etna, crowned with eternal snows, and shooting from among the clouds"; the festivity of the ball with the illuminated forest in the background: "long vistas ... terminated by pyramids of lamps that presented to the eye one bright column of flame." We have the wicked marchioness' pavilion by the sea-shore, "hung with white silk ... richly fringed with gold" where "alternate wreaths of lamps and of roses entwined the columns" in contrast to the bleak haunted gallery, the piles of fallen stone and the dark dungeons. We move from the haunted castle to the Abbey of St. Augustine, where to the sound of the organ's "high and solemn peal" the dying nun "covered with a white veil" is borne to the altar by white-robed nuns "each carrying, in her hand a lighted taper." There is the tempest at sea, the shipwreck, the bandits' cavern filled with the bodies of their victims, the living tomb of the real marchioness. And at the end there is the impressive setting where Ferdinand at last finds the members of his real family gathered together, an image which combines flame and darkness, sea and rock, stronghold and tempest:

> At length he discerned, amid the darkness from afar, a red light waving in the wind: it varied with the blast, but never totally disappeared. He pushed his horse into a gallop, and made towards it.
>
> The flame continued to direct his course; and on a nearer approach, he perceived, by the red reflection of its fires, streaming a long radiance upon the waters beneath—a light-house situated upon a point of rock which overhung the sea.[18]

(Virginia Woolf is not the first female novelist to direct us to the Lighthouse.) In *A Sicilian Romance* there is a variety of impressively intense dream-like sensations—dream-like in their intensity, in their unquestionable reality. Guilt and sorrow are the substance of the tale, and the innocent characters, Ferdinand, Julia and Emilia, children of the wicked father and his ill-used first wife, bear the burden of the mystery of ancient unknown evil. Julia and Ferdinand, troubled by the strange lights and sounds which appear to emanate from the disused wing of the castle, determine to discover what lies behind the deserted gallery. Ferdinand breaks the lock and they enter: "The gallery was in many parts falling to decay, the ceiling was broke, and the window-shutters shattered, which, together with the dampness of the walls, gave the place an air of wild desolation" (I, 90). In this novel it is *home*—that home which young ladies are supposed to love and cherish— which is wild and unsafe.

When they see a light passing by a large stair-case at the end of the gallery, Ferdinand determines to follow it; he goes down, and through a passage which grows narrower and less passable: "fragments of loose stone made it now difficult to proceed." He finds a door, and on the other side of it a staircase leading up to the south tower:

> After a momentary hesitation, he determined to ascend the staircase, but its ruinous condition made this an adventure of some difficulty. The steps were decayed and broken, and the looseness of the stones rendered a footing very insecure. Impelled by an irresistible curiosity, he was undismayed, and began the ascent. He had not proceeded very far, when the stones of a step which his foot had just quitted, loosened by his weight, gave way; and dragging with them those adjoining, formed a chasm in the staircase that terrified even Ferdinand, who was left tottering on the suspended half of the steps, in momentary expectation of falling to the bottom with the stone on which he rested. In the terror which this occasioned, he attempted to save himself by catching at a kind of beam which projected over the stars, when the lamp dropped from his hand, and he was left in total darkness. Terror now usurped the place of every other interest.... (I, 92–93).

What was once the dream-experience of a terrified woman like Betsy Thoughtless, "seeking to find a passage through some ruin'd building," is now the experience of a hero, and equally terrifying. The effect is even more remarkable in the context of the whole novel. This dilapidated and threatening region of the castle contains the heart of the mystery, the mother, imprisoned by her cruel husband and condemned to a perpetual living death beneath these ruins. The children circle around and about their mother, like creatures perplexed in a maze, but they do not know what is at the heart of the maze—their ignorance condemns her to continued burial. Later, when Ferdinand is, at his father's command, cast into a dungeon, he hears a sound which frightens him, changing dejection to horror:

It returned at intervals in hollow sighings, and seemed to come from some person in deep distress. So much did fear operate upon his mind, that he was uncertain whether it arose from within or from without. He looked around his dungeon, but could distinguish no object through the impenetrable darkness. As he listened in deep amazement, the sound was repeated in moans more hollow. Terror now occupied his mind, and disturbed his reason; he started from his posture, and, determined to be satisfied whether any person beside himself was in the dungeon, groped, with arms extended, along the walls. The place was empty; but coming to a particular spot, the sound suddenly arose more distinctly to his ear. (I, 223)

Ferdinand comes to believe that his dungeon is haunted by some malign spirit, and thinks it must be the spirit of a man his father had murdered, come for purposes of vengeance upon the whole family: "At this conviction, horror thrilled his nerves" (I, 224). Much later, we find out that the mother had heard someone in a dungeon nearby, and had tried to call out to her fellow-prisoner, not knowing he was her son.

The macabre theme has a psychological resonance as, in different ways at different times, Ferdinand and Julia both pursue and unwittingly reject the buried mother. The theme culminates in the most powerful and surprising scene in the novel, when Julia, after making her way through the robbers' cavern, forces her way along narrow tortuous passages, without an object save escape:

She groped along the winding walls for some time, when she perceived the way was obstructed. She now discovered that another door interrupted her progress, and sought for the bolts which might fasten it. These she found; and strengthened by desperation forced them back. The door opened, and she beheld in a small room, which received its feeble light from a window above, the pale and emaciated figure of a woman, seated, with half-closed eyes, in a kind of elbow-chair. (II, 158)

Themselves prisoners and victims. Ferdinand and Julia are also ignorant accomplices in the crime against their mother, that unsuspected living ghost. They feel guilty. Julia feels that sharing her mother's prison for life would not be too small a compensation, while Ferdinand, mistaking his mother's voice for that of a vengeful spirit threatening father and children, has felt a horror which threatened to overturn his reason. The irony of the tale is that the children are guilty while innocent: they have not rescued their mother; they have feared what they would love. The novel's fable is a large image of guilt—guilt and fear are in the children's case undeserved and inescapable. The whole story makes the nightmare realm of guilt, rage and loss an appropriate environment for both sexes.

Of Mrs. Radcliffe's later novels it is scarcely necessary to treat, for they are better known. In what is probably her best work, *The Italian* (1797) the reader shares the separate experience of both Ellena and Vivaldi, and the hero's experience is even more frightening than the heroine's. Everyone remembers Vivaldi's being brought into the fortress of the Inquisition, and the scenes of his interrogation before mysterious tribunals, in the depths of the labyrinth behind iron doors. These scenes touch on our terror of being tried, of facing accusation without defence, of being tainted with unspecified guilt while innocent of crime. In these scenes before the tribunal, with unseen speakers and strange instruments of torture, the iron implements and accusing voices of Camilla's dream are represented in a new guise; the tribunal is full of father figures, masculine justice is presented as it appears in the historical institution whose nature is to create guilt—and the reader is at full liberty to shout "No!" instead of acquiescing in the judgment. The Inquisition is given the fearful reality of the local habitation and the earthly name. It is capable of shocking the mind with the dread of what is fearfully unreasonable and painful in consciousness, from which one cannot be dismissed by awakening, while at the same time conveying the fact that the public world is inescapably harsh, crushing the individual in the name of order and reason, attempting to make both masculine and feminine sexual identity and inner existence into guilt. The hero is really afraid, and, when he "at length found a respite from thought and from suffering in sleep,"[19] he has a frightening dream in which the unknown monk appears, holding a bloodstained poniard. When he awakens he finds "the same figure standing before him" although in this reality into which the dream has melted, the monk does not at first seem to be holding a dagger. It is only after the strange conversation with Vivaldi that the intruder shows him a poniard and asks him to look at the blood upon it: "Mark those spots ... Here is some print of truth! To-morrow night you will meet me in the chambers of death!" (p. 323). Clementina had looked for marks of blood that were not there: reality and dreaming melancholy were separate. Now within the environment of nightmare man as well as woman is the victim, and dream and reality are indistinguishable.

The Gothic novel as Mrs. Radcliffe developed it takes the images of nightmare and gives them a strong embodiment; they are the framework of life, they are reality. The images and their concomitant emotions are no longer the figments of a particular feminine consciousness within the novel, nor do they, as in *The Recess*, provide an environment for feminine consciousness alone. They cannot be dismissed as symptoms of a peculiar psychological state. This is not to deny the value of the more realistic novel dealing with fully-developed psychological characters in a social world—I certainly do not hold that Mrs. Radcliffe is superior to Richardson. But the eighteenth-century novel could not go beyond a certain point in developing the consciousness of human beings as long as it maintained very rigid notions of the strength of the male sex and subscribed to very limiting beliefs about superior rational consciousness and about the orderliness of the real world—notions and beliefs which inhibited any apprehension of deep disorders and fears. The Gothic novel has a value in this alone in making accessible what was strange and elusive, and so paying full attention to what had been underdeveloped in the work of earlier novelists. The dream scenes I have cited—especially those from *Grandison* and *Camilla*—are unsatisfactory, not because they are bad (on the contrary) but because they are so powerful that they threaten the stability of the world which the novelist would like us to inhabit; we cannot shrug these things off so easily once they have passed.

Mrs. Radcliffe admits that the world of Nature and of Man is dangerous, and that danger is in the nature of things. She admits dread as a natural experience—and the readers themselves take their part in it, for we need, like the boy in the old tale, to learn what fear is, "to shiver and to shake." Adolescent heroines had previously been shown as troubled by dubious fears and mysterious dreads upon their coming to maturity. Mrs. Radcliffe also associates fear with maturing, and assumes, quite calmly, that men can be afraid. A whole tradition of intrepid heroes bites the dust as soon as Osbert (uninteresting in himself, but interesting for his experience) undergoes helplessness and terror, even (at one juncture) to the point of fainting. The late-Renaissance conventions of masculine control in an orderly universe within which men regulate events—these are swept aside. It was good that this should be so, not because previous fictional conventions had produced works untrue or bad in themselves, but because at this point they could yield nothing new. The novel had been too much affected by certain beliefs, hemming itself into a tight corner with too little room for truth. Masculinity was to be found only in virtuous assurance or amiable eccentricity. We could have been stuck with the tiresome procession, emerging from the works of poorer novelists, of good untroubled heroes and virtuous heroines.

In the Gothic novels, heroes and heroines share the nightmare—and the nightmare is real. At least, that is what they can share as soon as Mrs. Radcliffe's first work had appeared in 1789. It has not, I think been sufficiently recognized what a liberating effect this was to have on subsequent novelists and subsequent heroes—whether or not the novels deal in the Gothic. Charlotte Smith in *Desmond* plucked up the courage to present a hero who is anxious and self-divided, impressed by dream, reverie and recollection; at the same time he is a hero confronting the outrageous ghastliness of history, past and present. He, like the later Vivaldi, and so many heroes after them, tries to make sense of a world which is (unlike the worlds of Tom Jones and Grandison) not readily amenable to good sense. After Mrs. Radcliffe, there need be no more condescension about "the imbecillities of tender minds"; it is not stupid or feeble or criminal to recognize that the outer world and the world within are mysterious and perturbing. Without Mrs. Radcliffe's novels, Scott could not have written as he did; his heroes explore the unknown, and experience that fear of present and future which allows the author to give every place and event its full meaning. That some of his heroes are unusually passive the author himself remarked (in his jovial review of his own works); they are thus because thus the author can tell the truth about human life in the onrush of history, which expresses man's needs and desires but over which no man or woman has very much control.

Scott's most exotic hero, Ravenswood in *The Bride of Lammermoor* (1819), is a tormented and divided man, both strong and weak, no mere flaccid victim but ultimately a victim indeed. This good young man, the sexually exciting lover so fascinating and disturbing to Lucy, has his own weaknesses, unfulfilled desires and fear of loss—he is no Lovelace, for not only does he mean well but in himself he has scarcely the illusion of control, still less of the power to manipulate men and women. In his forlorn castle at Wolf's Crag, the remnant of a dead ancestral power, he is one of the victims in the dungeons of history.

The later novelists of the nineteenth century did not need to flinch in presenting their heroes as wanderers through a strange and puzzling world, men who feel guilt without being villainous, men who know weakness, self-division, terror and failure. One could make a long list of names culled from the Victorian novel of heroes who know weakness and fear: Henry Esmond, Author Clennam, Pip, Paul Emanuel, Lydgate, Clym Yeobright. These men are interesting. Men could not be fully present in the novel until they could be shown as self-divided, wary, torn by their own unconscious and divided motives, even weak, erring and guilty—and shown thus without being exhibited as villains or failures. It was the Gothic novel, in all its implication, that saved men from being seen as the sex without a full consciousness. The Gothic novel gave them the freedom to have—and to live in—nightmares.

## Notes

1. Samuel Richardson, *Sir Charles Grandison* (Oxford English Novels Edition, London, 1972), Part III, p. 242.

2. Michael V. DePorte, *Nightmares and Hobbyhorses: Swift, Sterne, and Augustan Ideas of Madness* (San Marino: The Huntington Library, 1974), p. 31.

3. Jane Barker, *Love Intrigues* (New York: Garland Press Reprint, Foundation of the Novel series), pp. 14–15.

4. Barker, *The Entertaining Novels of Mrs. Jane Barker* (2 vols., London: 1719), II, 29.

5. Barker, *A Patch-Work Screen for the Ladies* (New York: Garland Press Reprint, Foundation of the Novel series), pp. 10–11.

6. See ch. vii, Book VIII of *The Female Quixote*.

7. Charlotte Lennox, *The Female Quixote* (Oxford English Novels Edition, London, 1970), pp. 372–73. Some critics have suggested that the chapter from which this passage comes (Book IX, ch. xi) was written wholly or in part by Dr. Johnson; Duncan Isles considers the claim "by no means adequately supported" although admitting the influence of Johnson's "ideas and phraseology" in the chapter. See Isles's Appendix to the above edition, p. 421.

8. Eliza Haywood, *The History of Miss Betsy Thoughtless* (4 vols., London: 3rd edition, 1752) IV, 22–25.

9. Conversations with women of various ages have led me to believe that dreams of fear are extremely common before marriage, and are quite separate from fear (if any) of sex. Young women who have had pre-marital sex, often for some years, with the man they intend to marry, seem to be just as much afflicted with nightmare prior to marriage as were women of a previous generation who went virgin to the bridal, and their fear-dreams embody the same images.

10. I am indebted to George Starr's discussion of *The Man of Feeling*; see above, pp. 512–17.

11. Frances Burney, *Cecilia, or Memoirs of an Heiress* (5 vols., London: 1782), V, 319–22.

12. Frances Burney (D'Arblay), *Camilla, or A Picture of Youth* (Oxford English Novels Edition, London, 1972), pp. 874–76. As the author uses the three dots for special punctuation in this passage, I have put my own marks of ellipsis in brackets.

13. See Clara Reeve's Preface to the Second Edition of her novel, in *The Old English Baron* (Oxford English Novels Edition, London, 1967), pp. 4–5.

14. Sophia Lee was indebted to the Continental novel, especially to Prévost *The Recess* caused some stir; it went through a good number of editions and appeared in several translations. Despite its anachronisms and its juggling of facts, it was hailed by some English reviews for its historicity in introducing credible characterizations of Queen Elizabeth, Leicester, *et al.* See Devendra P. Varma's Introduction to the Arno Reprint edition of *The Recess, or A Tale of Other Times* (3 vols., New York: Arno Press, 1972).

15. See Ann Henry Ehrenpreis' Introduction to *Emmeline, The Orphan of the Castle* (Oxford English Novels Edition, London, 1971), pp. viii–ix.

16. Ann Radcliffe, *The Castles of Athlin and Dunbayne: A Highland Story* (1821 edition, as reprinted, New York: Arno Press, 1972), p. 7.

17. Reeve, *Old English Baron*, pp. 42–45.

18. Radcliffe, *A Sicilian Romance* (1821 edition, as reprinted in 2 vols., New York: Arno Press, 1971), II, 209–10.

19. Radcliffe, *The Italian, or The Confessional of the Black Penitents* (Oxford English Novels Edition, London, 1968), p. 318.

JONATHAN LAMB

# The Comic Sublime and Sterne's Fiction

The best writers of the early eighteenth century possessed a body of critical theory concerning epic and tragedy which they carefully elaborated, fiercely defended, and hardly ever put into practice. Pope saved bits of his burnt epic *Alcander* to insert as samples of bombast in his *Peri Bathous*, while Johnson was forced to accept the public's judgment against his *Irene*. Historical, political and social developments sapped the confidence and removed the subject matter necessary for the production of epic or tragic works and presented instead scenes of complicated insincerity to which the appropriate literary response was, ironically, the calculated improprieties of mock-epic and burlesque. The deliberate mismatching of style and subject mimicked and mocked the two-facedness of society, and only on these rather self-destructive terms were authors allowed access to the high styles and noble forms they had been reared to admire above all others. It is an extra irony that the age which was proving to itself so decisively the impossibility of ever writing truly great literature should have become fascinated by another contribution to the critical theory of literary grandeur, Longinus' *On the Sublime*. This treatise impelled Pope to write the finest parts of his *Essay on Criticism*; typically, it also provided a format he could travesty in the *Peri Bathous* or *Art of Sinking in Poetry*. Longinus, like the classical critics, seems to have supplied merely the high standards by which low scribbling could be judged, a clue for descending "to the very *bottom* of all the *Sublime*" as Swift called it, and not a model for the true sublime. There is no doubt that the

From *ELH* vol. 48, no. 1 (Spring 1981): 110–43. © 1981 by the Johns Hopkins University Press.

double vision of the satirists, the result of pursuing what was ridiculous in art so as to expose what was vicious in public morality, bred a sort of hopeless idealism, expressed as habitual unions of the highest styles with the lowest subjects, or vice versa, that is detectable in the humblest form of polemic, the threatening letter.[1] But with the possible exception of Horace, Longinus is the critic most congenial to irregular experiments in literature; and certainly as the century advanced he influenced and authorized radical departures in attitudes to epic, as well as to the Bible, metaphor and primitive language, which Northrop Frye has defined as Pre-Romantic "process-writing."[2] In this essay I want to trace a line of development from mock-epic theory and practice to the "process-writing" of Laurence Sterne, not with the intention of contradicting Northrop Frye's conclusions but in an effort to give Sterne's innovations the Augustan context they deserve and a name—the comic sublime.

First of all I want to consider two related aspects of Augustan irregularity—that of forms and that of manners—in order to determine what elements in them were or might be construed as sublime. To begin with manners: by the early eighteenth century the English were strongly aware of peculiarities in their temper which served to distinguish them from the French and which went by the names of singularity and irregularity and later by the more familiar titles of originality and humorism. Nowhere is the expression of this island individuality better known than in the fields of criticism and medicine. Dryden, Pope and Johnson generously season the rules of neo-classical criticism with the exceptions of the wild beauties of English verse by opening appeals, as Johnson puts it, from criticism to nature. Meanwhile an unsteadiness of temperament, induced or aggravated by the weather, exhibits itself as "the English malady," whose "atrocious and frightful Symptoms" are sung in poetry and detailed in medical works. Between the poles of nature and madness, various attempts at eccentric or random writing are made, from the obsessive oddity of John Dunton's semi-autobiographical *Voyage Round the World* to the casual elegance of Shaftesbury's *Miscellaneous Reflections*. Whether the author is a dunce or a man of learning and parts, this irregular method of opening his mind to the world is undertaken as the most honest because the least artificial: he draws his justification from the necessity and the integrity of the national temperament. Even "Mr. Spectator" has the character of "an odd unaccountable Fellow" which is reflected in the loose form of his periodical journalism and which is his warrant for observing society so acutely. It is this sort of unaccountable oddity that eventually characterizes the hero of the comic novel. Adams, Toby and Lismahago have thrived in spite or independent of common forms to become individuals whose minds are open but sometimes unintelligible books; and so they present a double aspect to the social world they have never joined, being both simple and yet honest, eccentric yet virtuous, foolish and yet somehow wise. From the start the odd writer or odd hero represents an equation between social folly and moral worthiness and between irregularity and integrity so tight that to note the one is to note the other. Toby's goodness is inseparable from his being a "confused, pudding-headed, muddle-headed fellow," while Parson Adams' character of perfect simplicity is illustrated by acts of folly and naivety that Fielding concedes from the outset are "glaring."[3]

The *locus classicus* for the discussion of the isolated, non-social and therefore original or humorous nature of moral integrity is Tillotson's sermon "Of Sincerity towards God and Man" and the commentaries offered on it in *The Spectator*. This sermon is a favorite of Addison's and Steele's because it is quoted at length in three *Spectators* (Nos. 103, 352 and 557), and each time it provides a basis for the distinction between the odd value of the private individual and the vicious tendency of public manners. For his part Tillotson mourns the departure of "The old English Plainness and Sincerity, that generous Integrity of Nature and Honesty of Disposition, which always argues true Greatness of Mind, and is usually accompanied with undaunted Courage and Resolution."[4] It has been supplanted by empty terms of art and false offers of service and esteem, the debased currency of "a Trade of Dissimulation." In *Spectator* No. 103 the sermon enforces a compliment just made to the club by its reverend member, namely, "that he had not heard one Compliment made in our Society since its Commencement." Steele takes the opportunity to praise Tillotson for a style free from all "Pomp of Rhetoric" and therefore utterly appropriate to the subject:he discourses as sincerely on sincerity, he declares, as Longinus discourses sublimely on the sublime. In number 352 the sermon offers a text for Will Honeycomb's complaint against the times, far from original, that youth is learning the vices of age and that everything "candid, simple, and worthy of true Esteem" has been sacrificed to fashion and ambition. Addison quotes the sermon in number 557 to make his point that "there is no Conversation so agreeable as that of the Man of Integrity, who hears without any Intention to betray, and speaks without any Intention to deceive"; and he concludes his paper with the fable of the Ambassador of Bantam whose mission to England is an utter failure because he interprets the forms of politesse in their literal meaning, becoming offended in proportion as he becomes offensive. At its simplest, Tillotson's sermon supports the conventional distinction between English bluntness and French ceremony, between the sincerity of natural manners and the hypocrisies of fine breeding. Addison thanks God he was born an Englishman, able to inherit a language "wonderfully adapted to a Man who is sparing of his Words, and an Enemy to Loquacity" (No. 135). The character of Sir Roger de Coverley exhibits the honesty, innocence, oddity and shortness of speech that belongs to an unselfconsciously good man, one who has maintained "an Integrity in his Words and Actions" in spite of all the snares put in the way of simplicity. As we would expect Sir Roger is ignorantly English in the theatre, very good at "Natural Criticism" (No. 335), and his conversation consists of a "blunt way of saying things, as they occur to his Imagination, without regular Introduction, or Care to preserve the Appearance of Chain of Thought" (No. 109). In Addison's scale of singularity Sir Roger's comes somewhere in the middle, for his contradiction of social forms is not complete or systematic, but only "as he thinks the World in the wrong." A combination of country living and a club of thoughtful city friends keeps him well protected from social acerbities like city wits and roving Mohocks, and to this extent he is like Toby, Trunnion, or Bramble whose withdrawals from society are tempered with a limited sociability consisting of family, friends or the traditions of an armed service. At the extremes singularity turns into either madness or heroism, and this is when the contradiction of social forms becomes absolute. At one end is a man like Cato who, refusing to pass his whole life in opposition to his own sentiments, ceases to be sociable: "Singularity in Concerns of this Kind is to be looked upon as heroick Bravery, in which a Man leaves the Species only as he soars above it" (No. 576). At the other end is the unhappy gentleman in the same paper who has a commission of lunacy taken out against him for having followed, in all departments of his life, the dictates of reason at the expense of fashion, form and example. Whether considered heroic or mad, Don Quixote is the literary archetype of this extreme singularity, and his descendents in the eighteenth century novel are those like Parson Adams or Parson Yorick who carry their singular selves into the world's view and risk society's retaliations. But at all points on the scale, singularity argues some sort of opposition to society and an integrity which is irregular in terms of the social forms it ignores but which is consistent and coherent in terms of private values. This "more than ordinary Simplicity" represents for Tillotson "true Greatness of Mind." Tillotson's own sincerity is, for Steele, sublimely self-consistent. For Addison it is potentially heroic.

The confrontation between the singular individual and society at large, whether it is the mild and peaceable pursuit of integrity or the more ostentatious process of self-exemption from social forms, sets up a conflict between a private and the public schemes of value that is echoed in satire as well as in fiction. For the Augustan satirists one of the most vexing problems (and their difficulties with epic are an aspect of it) is that in the very act of defending the common forms and values of their society they see innovative irregularity in such vast array that those forms and values dwindle before their eyes into singularity. Starting from what seem to be the opposite assumptions of the humorist, the satirist ends up in precisely the same confrontation; and it is no wonder that the anecdotes of Swift, Pope and Johnson reveal them in the attitudes of humorists, cherishing modes of eccentric behavior as if to emphasize that their qualities of mind are no longer representative of the society they live in. However, satire offers a major resource to its agents who find themselves in this predicament, and that is its own irregular form. In an Horatian mood Pope confesses,

> I love to pour out all myself, as plain
> As downright *Shippen*, or as old *Montagne*.

As an ingenuous private man, indulging the casual habits of self-revelation, Pope can use the pane in his breast as window and as mirror:

> In this impartial Glass, my Muse intends
> Fair to expose myself, my Foes, my Friends.[5]

Imitating the humorous singularity of the French essayist is, of course, another way of imitating Horace who uses an ambling and indirect method of exhibiting folly, "sometimes an Epicurean, sometimes a Stoic, sometimes an Eclectic."[6] By placing Montaigne, Shippen or Erasmus as middle terms in this sort of Horatian exercise, Pope can claim all the integrity he wants ("My Head and Heart thus flowing thro' my Quill") from the very irregularities which make his satire unobtrusively effective. Simultaneously he defines the characteristics of isolated singularity and he exposes the forces which have driven him to it. And while the "present age" he is publishing mistakes him for verse-man, prose-man, papist, protestant, Whig and Tory, he derives the double benefit of being consistent with himself at the same time as continuing a satirical tradition, quietly reconciling a private and public ideal. Swift makes a similar set of extremes coincide in *A Tale of a Tub* by impersonating the singularity of the very latest writers. His narrator points proudly to the central item in the catalogue of modern irregularities, "the great *Modern* Improvement of *Digressions*," and he compares it with improvements in cookery such as "*Soups* and *Ollio's*, *Fricassées* and *Ragousts.*" He goes on:

> 'Tis true, there is a sort of morose, detracting, ill-bred People, who pretend utterly to disrelish these polite Innovations: And as to the Similitude from Dyet, they allow the Parallel, but are so bold to pronounce the Example it self, a Corruption and Degeneracy of Taste. They tell us, that the Fashion of jumbling fifty Things together in a Dish, was at first introduced in Compliance to a depraved and *debauched Appetite*, as well as to a *crazy Constitution*.[7]

As usual in the *Tale*, the narrator's metaphors have a literal satiric meaning and his literal statements make metaphorical sense as satire. The "Similitude from Dyet" is not a similitude at all but the etymological derivation of the name of satire itself, the *satura lanx* or dish of mixed meats which make up that *"olla*, or hotchpotch, which is properly a satire."[8] Not only does the narrator write satire unconsciously, here he defines it in what he thinks is a novel metaphor. As he pursues the analogy according to the letter, listing all the physical ills that might induce a taste for such food, he loses his grasp on the two senses of *taste*, which in any case suggested merely that bad literature caters for bad sensibilities, and insensibly makes room for the real suggestion, which is that satirical mixtures are produced not to flatter debauched appetites and crazy constitutions but to correct them. By a scheme of subversive, witty necessity observable throughout the *Tale*, what the narrator proposes in the way of idle nonsense resolves itself into specific antagonism to just that sort of nonsense. In this conclusive instance his modern formlessness provides the classically loose form of satire, the illustration of the one being the definition of the other, and Swift's own Horatian integrity finds an inverted image of itself in the glass of modern literary incompetence. To put it another way, the reader experiences simultaneously the cause and effect of satire, the irregularity of dunces and the irregularity of wit which converts the conversions of a crippled imagination back into a consistency that "a great majority among the Men of Taste" (a fairly small club judging by the tone of the "Apology") will enjoy. Like Pope, Swift reconciles his own internal consistency—wit and taste— with the need for public correction by deploying a two way mirror that allows us to glimpse the one while we see the reflection of public folly that calls for the other. It is a combination of "the very *bottom* of all the *Sublime*" with *"the noblest and most useful gift of humane Nature."*[9]

The authorized irregularity of satire means that the satirist is free not only to shadow the follies of the age in the wild dancing light of his own wit, but also to parody other forms of literature. Dryden mentions the *cento* of Ausonius "where the words are Virgil's, but by applying them to another sense, they are made a relation of a wedding-night."[10] Butler's burlesque and Dryden's mock-epic open the road to many experiments in the art of "using a vast force to lift a *feather*,"[11] as Pope calls it, a calculated transgression against the rules of mechanics and proportion. This sort of satire still reflects and even reproduces the ridiculous disparities and inflated assumptions in the behavior of knaves and fools, but its constant use of great literary models puts the possibility of serious imitation of them at a greater remove. It is a two-sided disqualification that the satirists invite: on the one hand they prove that the social values which belong to the production of epic no longer exist, and on the other they develop irregular habits which satire can happily sustain but not the more regulated forms of epic and tragedy. These habits narrow their social circle into the tight circumference of a club, defined by enemies and founded upon literary tastes which can only be satisfied in practice by parody. One of the results, already obvious in Pope, is to establish extra affiliations with literary irregulars like Montaigne. Prior finds much to admire in Montaigne too; while Swift, much to Pope's incomprehension, takes a great delight in Rabelais. Samuel Johnson develops a strong taste for the irregularities of Burton's *Anatomy of Melacholy*, and less notable readers begin to consume macaronic and booby literature. *Don Quixote* exerts a fascination over the minds of satirists and novelists alike. Here we have defined, almost in its full extent, the literary tradition and resources of Laurence Sterne.

Since Cervantes' appeal is so wide, and therefore likely to be representative of irregularities in style and in heroes that the eighteenth century finds so much satisfaction in, it is best to begin with him. "The use of pompous expression for low actions or thoughts is the *true Sublime of Don Quixote*," says Pope.[12] One of Swift's ironic impersonations, according to Pope, is of "Cervantes' serious air." Pope is speaking for many readers who relished the effects Cervantes is able to produce from the distance he sets between himself and the action of the story, those fictional contributors to the narrative whom he makes responsible for its faults, elisions, lies, bombast and parodic historiography. A mock-epic propriety, which matches collisions in style with collisions in dialogue between the knight and the squire and which makes the parodic encounter of high and low styles reflect and mimic the encounters between Quixote's dream and the world, is bound to invite admiration from an age skilled in concocting this sort of heterogeneous mixture. But it isn't simply a compendium of mock-epic devices and a mad hero that *Don Quixote* offers its eighteenth century readership. Stuart Tave puts the date of critical revaluation at about the same time as the performance of Fielding's farce *Don Quixote in England—1738*.[13] After this it is more common to regard Quixote as a humorist, not a madman, and to study the narrative complexity of the story less as a vehicle of satire than as an enquiry into the theory and practice of writing fiction. Even before this, however, the analogy between Quixote's defence of a literary ideal and the efforts of the Tory satirists to preserve something similar must have been evident and have developed the sort of covert sympathy with the knight that exists between him and his chronicler Cid Hamet Benengeli. Swift's outrage at Bentley's attempt to lessen the authenticity of classical texts is not unlike that Quixote feels when Cardenio blackens the name of Queen Madasima; and the way Swift and Pope seem consciously to interpret their lives in terms of Horace's bears comparison with the way Quixote models his career on that of Amadis. *Don Quixote* dramatizes the odd or heroic dependence on books which is to become a major theme of the British comic novel, already apparent in Addison's examples of singularity, one of whom is suspected of madness for reciting Homer out of his window and the other for quoting Milton in his bedroom. Quixote represents that particular sort of integrity which is defined by literary activity, an idealism expressed as a practical demonstration of the neo-classical theory of imitation so that life itself becomes the realization of a literary model. The growing tendency to call attention to the nobility of Quixote's character allows and enshrines this idealism, and when Sterne's Tristram entertains the "highest idea" of the "spiritual and refined sentiments" he finds in *Don Quixote*, or when a critic like Beattie can refer to the "sublimity of Don Quixote's mind," it is clear that the knight's *intentions* can be held to be of a high and even a sublime order, even if his adventures are comic disappointments.[14] This is not to go as far as Romantic critics like Coleridge and Leigh Hunt who abstract the Quixotic humorist from the complex social and literary forces which he reflects and embodies, but it is to acknowledge that "true Greatness of Mind" which Tillotson and *The Spectator* had praised as the accompanying quality of "more than ordinary Simplicity."

As for the Cervantic style and structure, Pope offers some very intriguing comments in his "Postscript." The context is his consideration of Longinus' criticism that by the *Odyssey* Homer's genius had passed its meridian heat and that the sublimity of the *Iliad* had been replaced by narrative and dream. So Pope has in mind the epic, the sublime and Longinus as he pauses in his praise of the beautiful variety of the *Odyssey* to commend *"the true Sublime of Don Quixote."* It is strange that he uses the phrase "the true Sublime" instead of "mock-sublime" or "mock-epic" since the sublime can scarcely be said to exist where there is not some proper and manifest connection between objects, feelings and words. It is possible that Pope was thinking of a part of *Don Quixote* very relevant to his defence of the *Odyssey* as a kind of comic epic. The Canon of Toledo's description of a comic epic in prose is not only applicable to the narrative variety of *Don Quixote* but is also remarkably close to Pope's description of the same thing in the *Odyssey*: the fable may be as various and the hero as diverse as an author chooses to make them, and if the whole is rendered

> in a grateful style, and with ingenious invention, approaching as much as possible to truth, he will doubtless compose so beautiful and various a work, that, when finished, its excellency and perfection must attain the best end of writing, which is at once to delight and instruct, as I have said before: for the loose method practised in those books, gives the author liberty to play the epic, the lyric, and dramatic poet, and to run through all the parts of poetry and rhetoric; for epics may be writ in prose as in verse.[15]

For his part Cervantes, through his Arabian deputy, exploits every opportunity offered by the chivalric epic and this formal interpretation of its real epic potential to invent a mixed fable, mixed hero and mixed narrative style in order to achieve the maximum variety. In the same terms that Cervantes is offering his novel to the public as a comic epic in prose, Pope is defending the variety of the *Odyssey* as belonging to comic epic (the same terms, incidentally, that Fielding will use to found his genre of comic epic poem in prose in *Joseph Andrews*). The phrase "true Sublime" suggests on Pope's part a half-conceived connection between Cervantes' arts of variety and Homer's: "Let it be remember'd, that the same Genius that soar'd the highest, and from whom the greatest models of the *Sublime* are derived, was also he who stoop'd the lowest, and gave to the simple *Narrative* its utmost perfection" ("Postscript," p. 389). He seems to want to say that there is as much sublimity in Homer's stooping as in his rising, but it is to Cervantes he pays the compliment of having discovered a new and yet true sublime. Because Pope is trying to rid the term "sublime" from connotations of action, vigour, fire, and sustained flight he invokes Horace's characteristic preference for the *Odyssey*, and it is likely he is also thinking of other definitions and illustrations of it that Longinus offers. Unfortunately for him and us those portions of sections XXX and XXXI of *On the Sublime* are missing in which Longinus discusses the positive applications of mock-epic, "dressing up a trifling Subject in grand and exalted Expressions."[16] All that remains are two examples from Herodotus to show how vulgar terms can be used in such a way as to have far from vulgar meanings. He returns briefly to the subject in his discussion of hyperboles where he notes their double-edged quality: "they enlarge, and they lessen" (*OS*, p. 91). It is as if Pope, unwilling to start a controversy about a new definition of the sublime, makes Cervantes supply an example of what is missing from Longinus' treatise. What he proposes quite specifically, however, is the question "how far a Poet, in pursuing the description or image of an action, can attach himself to *little circumstances*, without vulgarity or trifling?" Like his *Preface to the Iliad* this "Postscript" exhibits Pope's fascination with circumstantiality and how far it is reconcileable with the faculty of invention and with propriety of expression. Again, Cervantes offers him a fine example of "the *low actions of life...* put into a figurative style"; and again Longinus is being glanced at, who says that an accurate and judicious choice of "adherent Circumstances ... and an ingenious and skilful Connexion of them into one body, must necessarily produce the Sublime" (*OS*. p. 27). Pope is wondering at what point the feather can be cut between the circumstantiality of "stooping" and that of mock-epic, pondering, no doubt, the paradoxical way in which the extremes of burlesque and mock-epic on the one hand and sublimity and propriety on the other seem to meet.

Cervantes offers his English readers a narrative that explores some of the range and effects of comic epic, one which Pope regards in some way as the perfection of mock-epic, its "true sublime"; he also gives them a hero who combines the nobility, or sublimity, of intention with a ridiculous public figure and who therefore represents in its plainest form the mixture of private integrity and public oddity that belongs to the singular or irregular man of sincerity. I want to consider a little more closely the sublime possibilities of this sort of character and to examine how these might be realized when the character becomes an author. Montaigne is the outstanding example of a man whose irregularity of self is expressed in the irregular form of his essays. His rhapsodic style of writing ("without any certain Figure, or any other than accidental Order, Coherence, or Proportion")[17] has the moral value of being utterly devoid of art and, like Sir Roger's irregular conversation, opens a window on to an ingenuous heart. Diderot says of Montaigne that "the licence of his style is practically a guarantee to me of the purity of his habits"[18] and it is that sort of honest casualness that Shaftesbury seeks to represent in his "random essays" or which David Hartley aims for in the introduction to his *Observations on Man* by writing "frequently without any express Design, or even any previous Suspicion of the Consequences that might arise."[19] We have already seen how in the *Spectator* the "true Greatness of Mind" that singularity manifests and protects is given high praise—Steele even compares the natural modesty of "a great Spirit" with the propriety of expression that belongs to the "just and sublime" in literature (No. 350). Addison also considers literary irregularity, and talking of Seneca and Montaigne as originators of loose and immethodical writing he affirms that if it is undertaken by men of learning or genius to read it is like being "in a Wood that abounds with a great many noble Objects, rising among one another in the greatest Confusion and Disorder" (No. 476). In the following paper he realizes the metaphor by describing the irregularity and variety of a humorist's garden where plants "run into as great a Wildness as their Natures will permit." This is called "Gardening ... after the *Pindarick* Manner." These images look forward to those in which Pope will praise Homer ("a wild paradise") and to Johnson's defence of Shakespeare, so that it is no surprise to find Addison using Longinus and Shakespeare in order to praise the exuberant irregularity of genius that cannot be constrained and which bursts its bounds to produce "what we call the Sublime in Writing" (No. 592). By no stretch of the imagination might Addison be suspected of thinking Montaigne's *Essays* sublime. In another paper he laughs at him as "the most eminent Egotist that ever appeared in the World" (No. 562) and considers him diverting in proportion as he is absurd. But Longinus' own standards are more flexible, and he praises warmly those orations of Demosthenes where "Order seems always disordered" and where "he makes Excursions into different Subjects, and intermingles several seemingly unnecessary Incidents" (*OS*, pp. 56, 59). Indeed under the figures of *asyndeton* and *hyperbaton* Longinus includes almost every irregularity, from digression to syntactic breakdown, as aspects of the sublime. As long as they are warranted by pressure of feeling any failure in the order of words, even speechlessness itself, may be powerfully expressive. It is not difficult to see that an author like Sterne, already consciously imitating and incorporating the irregularities of Montaigne's and Burton's prose, is aware of the permission he gets from Longinus to make digressions, apostrophes, starts and gaps. Yorick and Eugenius have both read Longinus, and we are expected to read him too. In a chapter where Tristram irritably dispenses with all rules and the cold conceits they beget, he says, "O! but to understand this, which is a puff at the fire of Diana's temple—you must read Longinus—read away—if you are not a jot the wiser by reading him the first time over—never fear—read him again" (*TS*, pp. 281–2).

It is worth taking Tristram's advice to find out to what degree sublimity can be supported without a splendid or lofty object for the feelings to work on. From Addison to Kames there seems to be an agreement that the sublime belongs to what is eminent, bold, and huge (as well as irregular) so that, in Burke's definition, "the mind is so entirely filled with its object, that it cannot entertain any other."[20] Yet Longinus is not so prescriptive and insists rather on the largeness of soul than the largeness of object, that capacity for "Boldness and Grandeur in the Thoughts" which mean and ungenerous minds can never arrive at. So although the sublime is often the result of considering something immense, like the Creation, it can also be evident in Alexander's quip to Parmenio. What Longinus does expect is a concentration of the faculties which will need no assistance from verbal "Pomp and Garnish" (*OS*, p. 14) and which will convey an apparently unmediated impression of the "Flux and Reflux of Passion." This representation may be so pure and intense that the *cause* of the feelings expressed is reproduced in the audience's imagination. Thus you display "the very Action before the Eyes of your Readers" and mimic the very blows of the assault you are talking about (*OS*, pp. 63, 56). It is a sort of natural propriety that results from and in a naked apprehension of what is experienced, the very opposite of irony. In this sense the mind is indeed filled with its object and the words used to represent this fullness will have an immediacy and propriety because they will be implicated in the very experience they are describing. Montaigne had not heard of Longinus, but with the help of Horace and Plutarch he manages to achieve these sorts of effects (in a domestic way) by associating his mind to his feelings and actions. Free of any allegiance to art Montaigne evolves what he calls "naturalized art" by representing in his irregular essays all the oddities that accident and custom invite him to contemplate. "Grandeur of Soul," he says, "consists not so much in mounting and proceeding forward, as in knowing how to govern and circumscribe itself. It takes every thing for great, that is enough" (III, 456). He limits his faculties to what he is doing and concentrates them on that; so when he dances, he dances; when he sleeps, he sleeps—he even dreams that he dreams—and whatever action or feeling he finds himself experiencing, "I do not suffer it to dally with my Senses only, I associate my Soul to it too" (III, 459). These circumscriptions and associations close the gap between Montaigne's observed and observing self almost to nothing, and they are expressed in words that are entirely fit and apt. In one of his best essays Montaigne discovers, for instance, that the naturalized arts of making love and writing about it are practically the same: "the Action and the Description should relish Theft" ("Upon Some Verses of Virgil," III, 131), hence the sweetest sexual pleasures and the best amorous writing result from obliquity and indirection. The pattern of circumscription is completed with his removal of any difference between what he does and what he writes: "I write of my self and of my Writings, very near as I do of my other Actions; and let my Theme return upon my self" (III, 397). Far from ensnaring himself in baroque tangles of infinite regression, Montaigne's circumscriptions indicate how closely his soul attends to his experience and how faithfully in his "loose and unknit Articles" he represents that attendance. In two ways, then, the *Essays* can be considered as having sublime qualities: Montaigne's capacity for absorption in an experience, no matter how insignificant; and the oblique, digressive and unfinished form in which he renders this absorption. And these qualities both stem from what Montaigne himself chooses to call grandeur of soul.

The mind filled with its object is what Sterne, in his sermon "Search the Scriptures," considers to be the hallmark of the Biblical sublime. Invoking Longinus ("the best critic the eastern world ever produced") he distinguishes between classical poetry which relies for its effects on "the sweetness of the numbers, occasioned by a musical placing of words" and the "beautiful propriety" of the Bible which arises more from "the greatness of the things themselves, than ... the words and expressions."[21] When Yorick derides the French sublime he uses the same standard: "The grandeur is *more* in the *word*; and *less* in the *thing*."[22] It is an important idea that is aired throughout the century and often in a context where the primitive sublime of the Old Testament is being preferred above the classical one. For instance "John Lizard" in *Guardian* No. 86 compares Homer's and Virgil's descriptions of horses with the praise of the war-horse in **Job** 39, and he says, "I cannot but particularly observe, that whereas the classical poets chiefly endeavour to paint the outward figure, lineaments, and motions; the sacred poet makes all the beauties to flow from an inward principle in the creature he describes." He believes this imparts such spirit and vivacity to the images and style "as would have given the great wits of antiquity new laws for the sublime, had they been acquainted with these writings." William Smith, who translated Longinus and who is as partisan as the *Guardian* correspondent in preferring examples of scriptural sublime, praises its "majestic Simplicity and unaffected Grandeur" which consists "not in Ornament and Dress" but in the unmediated confrontation between even "low and common Objects" and what he calls *spirit* (*OS*, pp. 130, 168). This produces a natural propriety in the expression which may seem very close to burlesque but which is in fact the very opposite: "He saith among the trumpets, Ha, ha; and he smelleth the battle afar off." In his *Inquiry* Burke tries to distinguish between refined language, which lacks force in proportion as it is descriptive and exact, and the power of primitive language which gives very imperfect but strong ideas of objects; and he concludes that there are certain natural arrangements of words which are much more apt at conveying the experiences of objects:

> Uncultivated people are but ordinary observers of things, and not critical in distinguishing them; but, for that reason, they admire more, and are more affected with what they see, and therefore express themselves in a warmer manner. If the affection be well conveyed, it will work its effect without any clear idea, often without any idea at all of the thing which has originally given rise to it. (*Inquiry*, p. 180)

It is a short step from this sort of reasoning to Wordsworth's ideas about language in the *Preface to the Lyrical Ballads*. There Wordsworth poses again Pope's question about how far an author may attach himself to little circumstances; and he answers it by saying that as long as there is a natural force linking sensibility to object, language which is necessarily "dignified and variegated" will result. Indeed what occasions the central disagreement between him and Coleridge is his belief in the primitive and constitutive nature of language; for in low and rustic life "men hourly communicate with the best objects from which the best part of language is originally derived ... a more permanent and a far more philosophical language than that which is frequently substituted for it by poets."[23] In his note to *The Thorn* Wordsworth enforces the distinction between the language of conventional signs (including poetic diction) and this much more philosophical language (he uses the term precisely, I think, as a synonym for what was also known as "universal language") by turning, as "John Lizard," Smith, Sterne, and Burke do, to the orientalisms of the Bible for examples of majestic simplicity that might be mistaken by refined critics as embarrassing tautologies and repetitions, as disorder without any braveness. Much more confident than Pope (who feels it necessary to excuse Homer's attachment to low circumstances of cookery and bedmaking in the *Iliad*) these critics identify a kind of sublime which can attach itself very freely to low circumstances and render them in an irregular style, provided the mind is full enough of those objects to guarantee a primitive and natural propriety in the representation of them.

It is ironic that Pope, one of the first to establish Longinian tenets in English criticism, should have received from one of his major critics and apologists, Joseph Warton, so little credit for snatching graces beyond the reach of art. But by looking at the critical debate surrounding Pope and ideas of sublimity we can arrive at some standards for measuring the comic sublime in fiction. It is Warton's view that "Pope's close and constant reasoning had impaired and crushed the faculty of imagination"[24] and out of delicacy he makes his point by quoting Voltaire on Boileau: "Incapable peut-être du sublime qui élève l'âme, et du sentiment qui l'attendrait ... laborieux, sévère, précis, pur, harmonieux, il devint, enfin, le poète de la raison" (*EGWP*, I, xi). Yet those lines of the *Essay on Criticism* which exhibit so well that "liberal and manly censure of bigotry" Warton is supposed to approve of, he selects as an example of a mixed metaphor: "how can a *horse* 'snatch a grace' or 'gain the heart'?" (*EGWP*, I, 136–7). Despite this he goes to some lengths to redeem Pope from Addison's "partial and invidious" comparison between the *Essay* and Horace's *Art of Poetry*, asserting that Pope avoids the irregularity of the Roman by proceeding with "just integrity, and a lucid order" (*EGWP*, I, 101). Just who is being invidious and partial is not quite clear, and Warton manifests most clearly the double vision of the age, able rationally to identify what belongs to the sublime and yet not able to enjoy it: he likes Pope for not being distracted by the warmth and vigour of imagination and yet feels obliged to devalue him precisely because he is bereft of that "acer spiritus ac vis" which mixes metaphors and moves irregularly. Not surprisingly he draws the same distinction between expressive and descriptive poetry that is drawn by Sterne, Burke, and the others when he imagines how Pope's epic might have turned out: "he would have given us many elegant descriptions, and many GENERAL characters, well drawn; but would have failed to set before our eyes the REALITY of these objects, and the ACTIONS of these characters" (*EGWP*, I, 290–1). However, Warton's double vision provides valuable assistance in analysing the qualities of poetry which *he* enjoys while thinking they are unsublime but which Pope and others felt had sublime potential.

Wit, and particularly mock-epic wit, is approached by Warton with the theory of imitation in mind to show that what is admirable in it is also what is unheroic. Like Addison and Pope, Warton reckons that all that is left to a modern poet is novelty of expression, "to shine and surprise" by the manner in which he imitates the just models of classical literature, those changeless repositories of the common sense of mankind. Although Johnson quarrels with Pope's definition of true wit as one which "depresses it below its natural dignity, and reduces it from strength of thought to happiness of language," his own definition of wit as "at once natural and new"[25] merely proposes the problem as a solution since Nature is already the province of Homer and Virgil and, with nothing naturally new under the sun, all that remains is imitation, as Warton points out (*EGWP*, II, 54). One of the advantages Warton sees in modern novelty, however, is its fidelity to real life; and he instances Pope's contribution to the imitation of Horace (Satires, II, vi), Swift's *City Shower*, Gay's *Trivia*, and Hogarth's prints as pieces "describing the objects as they really exist in life ... without heightening or enlarging them, and without adding any imaginary circumstances" (*EGWP*, II, 51–2). His preference for this sort of realism blinds him to the mock-epic and burlesque distortions which allow low and ordinary things to be magnified in this way; and it is such a solid preference that he carries it into a variety of areas, praising Montaigne for giving "so strong a picture of the way of life of a country gentleman in the reign of Henry the Third" and drawing attention to the naturalism of *Don Quixote*: "MADNESS is a common disorder among the Spaniards at the latter part of life, about the age of which the knight is represented" (*EGWP*, II, 152; I, 133). He even goes so far as to adduce the lively, dramatic and interesting parts of the *Iliad* from the "innumerable circumstances" that are included in the narrative. Nevertheless he means to draw a sharp line between the circumstantiality that arises from an heroic inability to generalize and those "DOMESTICA FACTA" which are the proper objects of modern writing and which render the man "skilful in painting modern life ... THEREFORE, disqualified for representing the ages of heroism, and that simple life, which alone epic poetry can gracefully describe" (*EGWP*, I, 291). At one blow Warton demolishes the careful speculations of Pope's "Postscript" aimed at finding the point at which moderns, like ancients, might attach themselves to little circumstances without vulgarity or trifling.

Even if Warton ignores the part played by mock-epic techniques in high-lighting the small circumstances of modern life, when he turns his attention to this kind of wit he defines very neatly the ironic element in it that will always inhibit the unmediated encounter of sensibility and object: "As the poet disappears in this way of writing, and does not deliver the intended censure in his own proper person, the satire becomes more delicate, because more oblique" (*EGWP*, I, 211). Indeed he is right to emphasize the part played by reason in the theory and practice of eighteenth century poetry and wit, because thanks to Locke much of it is directed at the faculty of discrimination. Ideas are united and occult resemblances discovered on the basis of their real incongruity with the purpose of having the rational or moral difference perceived clearly by the reader. Francis Hutcheson points out that it is the *contrast* "between ideas of grandeur, dignity, sanctity, perfection, and ideas of meanness, baseness, profanity, [which] seems to be the very spirit of burlesque, and the greatest part of our raillery and jest is founded upon it."[26] Pope's editor Warburton, glossing the lines on true wit, argues that the image given back to the mind is Fancy's homage to the Judgment and an invitation for the latter's approval of her work.[27] When wit is fully embarked on mock-epic or burlesque associations of ideas, the obliquity and irony of the resemblances is often properly understood insofar as the reader knows the basis upon which they are rationally distinct. To read the fourth book of *Gulliver's Travels*, for example, is to re-master one of the common propositions of logic: that a man is not a horse. The moral function of most mock-epic confusions is to promote the discovery that they ought not to exist in good heads and to prompt the separation of ideas which wit, mimicking the fantasies and misconceptions of fools and dunces, has allied. Burke, who can see the strength of minds "not critical in distinguishing" things, shows that Locke's supposed distinction between wit and judgment which forms the basis of so many theories of wit in this century, is not a distinction at all: "There is no material distinction between the wit and the judgment, as they both seem to result from different operations of the same faculty of comparing" (*Inquiry*, pp. 58–9). Whether wit depends on the resemblance or (as Addison and Hutcheson feel is sometimes the case) the contrast or opposition of ideas, it is the perception of the difference between them, the final and decisive act of the judgment, which determines the ironic value of the union. To the extent that mock-epic and burlesque pursue these judgmental distinctions they have little to do with the sublime possibilities of irregularity.

Yet Warburton picks out an example of what looks like mock-epic contrast in Pope's *Essay on Man* but which behaves in a very different way and to which he gives the name sublime. They are the lines about Newton:

> Superior beings, when of late they saw
> A mortal Man unfold all Nature's law,
> Admir'd such wisdom in an earthly shape,
> And shew'd a NEWTON as we shew an Ape.
>
> (II, ll. 31–4)

To pay a compliment to Newton by comparing him with an ape is to bring it almost within the verge of ridicule, yet a curious encounter between the emotions of pride and humility takes place by means of the comparison. In his note Warburton says:

> And here let me take note of a new species of the Sublime, of which our poet may be justly said to be the maker; so new, that we have yet no name for it, though of a nature distinct from every other poetical excellence. The two great perfections of works of genius are Wit and Sublimity. Many writers have been witty, several have been sublime, and some few have possessed both these qualities separately: but none that I know of, besides our Poet, hath had the art to incorporate them; of which he hath given many examples, both in this Essay and his other poems, one of the noblest being the passage in question. This seems to be the

last effort of the imagination, to poetical perfection: and in this compounded excellence the Wit receives a dignity from the Sublime, and the Sublime a Splendour from the Wit; which, in their state of separate existence, they both wanted.

(III, 50–1 n.)

Warburton's linkage of the terms "wit" and "sublime" recalls Hutcheson's terms "grave wit" and "serious wit," but they stand for opposite ideas; for Hutcheson believes that "In this serious wit, though we are not solicitous about the grandeur of the images, we must still beware of bringing in ideas of baseness or deformity, unless we are studying to represent an object as base and deformed" ("Reflections," p. 109). But there is no doubt that Pope has brought in a base and deformed idea without any intention of demeaning Newton and has succeeded, as Warburton points out, in a "compounded excellence" from which it is impossible to abstract the idea of grandeur from the low circumstances in which it is conceived. In fact Pope seems to have answered the query from the "Postscript" by calculating to a nicety an attachment to little circumstances which is neither vulgar nor trifling and discovering how much real beauty there can be in a low image by uniting it with a sublime but otherwise inexpressible conception. All the negative feeling that might have been aroused by picturing Newton as a showground monkey and the angels as pitchmen and mountebanks is converted into a positive and ascending feeling which is nevertheless contained within the hierarchical limits imposed by the image. The difference between this sublime wit and the mock epic it resembles is that the analogical relation of the lower and higher ideas is not separable into the constituent resembling ideas, partly because one of them is sublimely imprecise and partly because it is only apprehended with the aid of the low image. It is as it were a vertical arrangement from which neither idea can be abstracted or distinguished without entirely losing the effect of their association, and when the reader has climbed by "ape" to "angel" the "ape" can no more be removed than the rung of a ladder one is standing on. Nor would Pope want it to be, since this sort of sublimity is founded quite deliberately on the qualities of the "isthmus of our middle state" from whose limitations not even Newton is exempt.

As a scholar of ancient wisdom and letters Warburton is well placed to discover what Pope is doing. Having understood the necessity of Ovid's delivering on "the most sublime and regular plan, A POPULAR HISTORY OF PROVIDENCE" amidst the superficial irregularities of his *Metamorphoses*, and having grasped the political truths couched by Virgil under Aeneas' descent into the shades,[28] Warburton can discover in Pope's lines a modern version of that sort of necessity where the sublime idea *demands* a primitive vehicle on which to be conveyed. It is as if the wheel has come full circle and out of the ironical contrasts of mock-epic Pope discovers a form responsive to just this kind of necessity, a kind of transcendent burlesque. In a sense all primitive metaphors are a form of burlesque since what is almost beyond conception and expression is fixed in a sensible, material shape that allows it to be thought of and uttered but which is necessarily of a lower order than the mystery it conveys. Thus in Bacon's interpretation of myth, upon which Warburton is modelling his interpretations, the hairy figure of Pan represents the secrets of the universe just as Newton as ape represents the reach of a human mind in establishing the principles of universal motion.

It is significant that two other examples of the sublime selected by Warburton from the *Essay on Man* are chains of imagery that look like arguments but which are designed to embarrass rational inquiry. In lines 35–42 of the first epistle Pope has, says Warburton, "joined the beauty of argumentation to the sublimity of thought" (III, 7 n.), but the argument consists of "the harder reason" which poses a series of unanswerable questions. In the same epistle (ll. 157–160) Pope answers questioning man by referring him to God whom he apostrophizes as the contradictions the questioner wishes to be resolved, making "the very dispensation objected to, the periphrasis of his Title" (III, 23 n.). In both cases Pope is using the rhythms of argument and the strategy of tautology by accommodating himself to Longinus' definition of the apostrophe where the periphrasis turns "what was naturally a Proof into a soaring Strain of the Sublime and the Pathetic" (*OS*, p. 47). In none of these examples does wit assemble ideas on any principle that the judgment can approve. They are overlaid and inseparable and, in the case of Newton, present a mixture of the great and the mean that does not have the effect Hutcheson predicts: "no other effect but to separate what is great from what is not so" (*RL*, p. 114). According to Pope's version of Longinus, he has managed to snatch a grace beyond the reach of argument and reflection "without passing thro' the judgment." It is in celebration of this sublime illogic that Warburton pillories some French critics who had accused the *Essay* of being a rhapsody: "It is enough just to have quoted these wonderful Men of method, and to leave them to the laughter of the public" (*DLMD*, III, 167 n.).

Since I have suggested that in the "Postscript" Pope was considering Cervantes as in some way an exponent of what Warburton calls the witty sublime, I want to take a scene from *Don Quixote* which conforms to its standards, and then compare it with a scene from *Joseph Andrews* and one from *Tristram Shandy*. The first takes place during Quixote's troublesome sojourn at the castle of the Duke and Duchess, just after Sancho's departure for Barataria and immediately before Altisidora begins her practical jokes. The knight is worried by many things: his numberless obligations to his hosts, a feeling that his fidelity to Dulcinea is under threat, an unease about the way adventures are occurring, and most of all the loss of Sancho. In this melancholy state he goes off to bed:

> He therefore shut the door of his chamber after him, and undressed himself by the light of two wax-candles. But oh! the misfortune that befell him, unworthy such a person. As he was straining to pull off his hose, there fell not sighs, or anything that might disgrace his decent cleanliness, but about four and twenty stitches of one of his stockings, which made it look like a lattice-window. The good Knight was extremely afflicted, and would have given then an ounce of silver for a drahm of green silk; green silk, I say, because his stockings were green.
>
> (II, 280–81)

Then Benengeli makes an apostrophe to poverty ("O poverty! poverty! what could induce that great Cordova poet to call thee a Holy Thankless Gift!....") in which he lists all the miserable shifts impoverished honour is driven to in order to disguise its penury. It follows the pattern of many ridiculous incidents in the novel by juxtaposing the two narrative styles Benengeli is so famous for, his careful delivery of "every minute particular distinctly entire" (II, 251) and his talent of "launching into episodes and digressions" (II, 276). It is a perfect example of using pompous expression for a low action and ought to make us laugh at the contradiction between Quixote's chivalric pretensions (mimicked in the high style) and his abject circumstances (minutely chronicled in the low style). Yet the scene does not excite this sort of laughter nor did Benengeli think it would: he predicts that it will not make us laugh outright but that it "may chance to make you draw in your lips and show your teeth like a monkey" (II, 278). One of the reasons for this is that the chapter reminds us of the correspondence that often exists between the narrator and the knight, for it begins with Benengeli's deep regret that he has confined his fancy and parts to the single design of this bare history and it contains an account of why Quixote begins bitterly to regret the constraints his profession is laying him under. In a sense both narrator and knight are lamenting the control now being exercised over the story by the inventions of the Duke and Duchess which keeps them both from a liberty they had previously enjoyed. The laddered stocking and Benengeli's apostrophe are not so remote from each other as might at first appear: the accident represents an aspect of the knight's loss of liberty and the apostrophe represents feelings about that loss which may seem to be in excess of the trivial circumstance but which both the knight and the narrator are experiencing. The connexion between the minor humiliation and Benengeli's commentary on it is made even less burlesque because it is stated that "these melancholy reflections are renewed in Don Quixote's mind, by the rent in his stocking." More than that the green silk gathers other parts of the story together, like the green ribbons Quixote adorned his helmet with, the sneers of the gentry who deride him as one of "your oldfashioned country squires that ... darn their old black stockings themselves with a needleful of green silk" (II, 18), and the nets of green thread that Quixote will get entangled in as soon as he has left this enchanted castle. The colour green, the thread, the stocking all combine to make an image expressive of Quixote's vulnerable idealism, and the little circumstance is given an unobtrusive figurative function which, far from contradicting or being contradicted by the sublime address to poverty, supports, defines and weights it to the point where it conveys a genuine flavor of the pain being felt. Stocking and apostrophe, like "ape" and "angel" in Pope's analogy, offer a new notion of Quixote's heroism; they invite us to consider him as a man whose aspirations are bounded by natural frailties which at once frustrate and ennoble them. In showing our teeth like monkeys at this mixture we respond both to the comedy and the nobility and don't allow one idea (of indignity or nobility) to predominate over the other. The one is crucial to the other.

Parson Adams' entertainment at the joking squire's recalls the indignities Quixote is subjected to at the castle; and when he stands up to vindicate his dignity in front of his tormentors we are presented with a similar case of heroism whose limited range provides a foundation for larger ideas of it:

> "My Appearance might very well persuade you that your Invitation was an Act of Charity, tho' in reality we were well provided; yes, Sir, if we had had an hundred Miles to travel, we had sufficient to bear our Expenses in a noble manner." (At which Words he produced the half Guinea which was found in the Basket.) "I do not shew this out of Ostentation of Riches, but to convince you I speak the Truth."[29]

Although Adams is speaking in his own voice and is therefore free of the burlesque diction that Fielding gives himself permission to use, he provides his own mock-epic inflations by using words like "noble," "riches" and "truth." The coin and the ample gesture with which it is produced do not, as he expects, contradict his appearance as an impoverished naif or warrant the truth of what he says. But they indicate the other values of spontaneity, simplicity and odd integrity which Adams' hosts equally despise and which he is too unselfconscious to estimate. In this respect the production of the half-guinea and words like nobility and truth have, within the limits of the situation, an applicability and a meaning that is not as grand as Adams thinks they have or which they normally possess but which is well above the measurements being made by the squire and his companions. The coin, like

Quixote's stocking, functions both as a little circumstance and as an image upon which thoughts of relative sublimity can be built. Once again, the lower and higher ideas must be taken together, for any attempt to abstract one at the expense of the other would make too little or too much of Adams' qualities.

Sterne refers to his version of the mock-epic as his "Cervantick humour ... of describing silly and trifling Events with the circumstantial Pomp of great Ones,"[30] and probably he conceived of it initially as a means of satire, having enjoyed great success with his imitation of *Le Lutrin, A Political Romance*, and thinking his talents lay that way. The remark is made about the description of Slop's arrival, and it is at that very point in Tristram's narration we see quite clearly how the device has been transformed into a pair of Hogarthian scales on which the *poco più* and the *poco meno*—the insensible more or less—are subtly balanced in order to celebrate the universal "triumph of slight incidents over the mind" (*TS*, pp. 100, 322). Sterne is different from Cervantes and Fielding to the extent that his use of mock-epic and burlesque inflations is never designed to separate ideas by ironic assessments of their comparative value. He has already learned what they discover, and so when uncle Toby gives up the siege of Dendermond to go and help the dying Le Fever, and his nephew avers that it was to his "eternal honour" that he did so and that the "kind BEING, who is a friend to the friendless" (*TS*, pp. 423–24) shall recompense him for his sacrifice, we would be obtuse not to understand the relative but still real value of the sacrifice and the complex significance of Toby's bowling-green campaigns. Since circumstances alone determine the value of things in the Shandean circle, and since every object within its circumference has at least two handles by which it may be grasped, slight incidents and little circumstances very often have large reverberations and little effort is needed on Tristram's part or ours to see constant analogies between the miniature and the grand. Sterne's study of the Bible revealed how "minute circumstances" can be "truly affecting"[31] and what a great pressure they can exert on our feelings and our minds, so he already assumes that little ideas, and even little volumes, can stand for greater ones. But like Cervantes and Fielding, Sterne is careful to control the process so that no falsely sublime ideas supplant those that are anchored in the little circumstances which provide the conditions as well as the images on which the higher ideas can rest. At no point should the comic sublime be mistaken either for sentimentalism or realism because it absolutely depends upon a continuous traffic between high ideas and low circumstances that modifies them both in terms of one another. And always this traffic originates in or is directed towards a peculiar cast of mind which is making no common or logical sense out of the world it perceives.

It is likely that in *Tristram Shandy* the range of devices attributable to the comic sublime will be extensive because the narrative is fully and continuously sensitive to the sorts of character and situation that produce this vertical arrangement of associated or analogous ideas. There is no space to explore all of the range properly, but I want to emphasize those parts which are most prominent and which link Sterne firmly with his Augustan predecessors. First of all it should be plain that his irregular narrative is authorized by Longinus and that all his apparent departures from the rules of formal rhetoric, except for the experiments with typography and idiogram, are classified in *On the Sublime*. Although these irregularities are directed towards comic ends, they are designed to convey the full weight and pressure of Tristram's experience. His ambition to "so manage it, as to convey but the same impressions to every other brain, which the occurrences themselves excite in my own" (*TS*, p. 337) is a plan to generate that corresponding excitement in the reader which Longinus reckons as the acid test of the sublime, that swelling of the mind to the point where it seems "as if what was only heard had been the Product of its own Invention" (*OS*, p. 15). By every means in his power Tristram seeks to banish that impersonality of the narrative voice which Warton says is characteristic of mock-epic, and every invitation extended to the reader to participate in the production of his story is to heighten the sympathy and to dull the judgment. The idea of critical distance is so antipathetic to Tristram (and his author) that the Preface is introduced quite purposely into the body of the text not for any systematic or theoretical statement about the work in hand but simply to "speak for itself." What it speaks is an associationist defence of associationist wit which *illustrates* why there is no need to pass through the judgment to gain its end. It is a contradiction by enactment of Locke's influential counter-definitions of wit and judgment that manages, without any arguments, set dissertations or definitions, to make Burke's point about the judgmental affinities of wit which compares its ideas instead of associating them. It is hard to think of a piece of prose in English which imitates so well Montaigne's skill at thinking in metaphor and analogy, that tautological shifting from illustration to illustration that Tristram calls *dialectick induction* and for which he claims Rabelais' authority too.

I have tried to show in this essay how, with similar social and cultural forces producing the humorist and the mock-epic, ideas of irregularity and sublimity can be attached to both. It is in Sterne's novel that a narrative style which emerges directly from Cervantes' "true Sublime" fits most closely and necessarily round the humorists of the Shandy family so that the hobbyhorse itself, that idol of the cave and image of integrity, becomes the vital tool of narrative representation, better than fame, voice, brush, evacuation or *camera obscura* (*TS*, p. 77). By taking this step Sterne confronts some of the apparently intractable problems which the singular man presents admirers and narrators with. The prime one is that he is likely to be socially invisible or socially unacceptable in proportion to his sincerity; for if irregularity stands in some sort of ratio to integrity then, like Sir Roger de Coverley, he will be hard to understand and yet be insufficiently prepossessing to incline an audience to patience. As a breed he is rare, either because (as Fielding suggests) once discovered the lucky naturalist keeps his habitat a secret or because (the more common explanation) he is especially vulnerable to predators. So the first job is to find the specimen, and the second is to make him speak. Tristram therefore establishes a circle four miles in diameter as his *world* and locates three humorists within its boundaries who can thrive immune from metropolitan knavery. Yet there remains the problem of language and representation. Addison suggests that God alone can understand the language of a thoroughly good and private man:

> There are many Vertues, which in their own Nature are incapable of any outward Representation: Many silent Perfections in the Soul of a good Man, which are great Ornaments to Humane Nature, but not able to discover themselves to the Knowledge of others; they are transacted in private, without Noise or Show, and are only visible to the great Searcher of Hearts. What Actions can express the entire Purity of Thought which refines and sanctifies a virtuous Man? That secret Rest and Contentedness of Mind ... These and the like Vertues are the hidden Beauties of a Soul, the secret Graces which cannot be discovered by a mortal Eye, but make the Soul lovely and precious in his Sight, from whom no Secrets are concealed.
>
> (No. 257)

If Addison says there is no language fit for these perfections, Tillotson in his sermon on sincerity defines the predicament of such a man as linguistic isolation. He will need "a Dictionary to help him to understand his own Language" (I, 7) because current words have turned into the paper money of compliment, "running into a Lie" to participate in conversation which "is little else but driving a Trade of Dissimulation." Expressed in Tillotson's exchange metaphor, the good and sincere man can neither buy or sell, and his perfections are indeed silent ones. It is a theme Sterne returns to frequently in his sermons. His favorite heroes in the Bible are Joseph, who makes himself known to his brothers in an eloquent silence (II, 232), and Job, whose heroic cast is revealed both in his own verbal restraint and in his patience in the face of the mis-constructions his friends place on the few words he utters. Addison's opinion that words and actions, however innocently uttered and performed, are deceitful mediums and "apt to discolour and pervert the Object" (*Spectator*, No. 257) is illustrated in the story of Yorick's life and death. His career is a painful example of how the actions and words of a good man can be either misunderstood or wilfully misinterpreted when they pass through the medium of opinion and prejudice which "so twists and refracts them from their true directions—that, with all the titles to praise which a rectitude of heart can give, the doers of them are nevertheless forced to live and die without it" (*TS*, p. 23). Nevertheless Sterne has devoted his novel to the business of describing the characters of men who have these silent or inaccessible virtues, and he chooses to sensitize us to the language of inarticulateness and dumbness in which this sort of character speaks. It is a double lesson in morality and linguistics.

In *Tristram Shandy* there is an alphabet of hobbyhorsical signs that matches the variety of primitive linguistic devices which Warburton classifies and discusses in *The Divine Legation of Moses*. These are the same devices which critics like Warton, Kames and Burke associate with the sublime, and which Sterne associates with the consistency of hobbyhorsical virtue. First of all there is silence, the primitive muteness of what Longinus calls "a naked Thought without Words" (*OS*, p. 18). It is this sort of silence which in *Tristram Shandy* can be certain proof of pity or can weave dreams of midnight secrecy into the brain. Silence is usually made intelligible by some sort of gesture, what Warburton calls "the voice of the sign," and so the silent disposition of limbs, or the handling of a pipe, or the glance of an eye will often carry the meaning of a hobbyhorsical dialogue. A refinement of the language of gesture is what Warburton calls the speaking hieroglyph, and that takes place when action forms itself into a statement and not just a response. Bridget communicates with Trim by this method. But a subtler form of argument by action is to perform what one is questioned about. Toby proves his hobbyhorse is a hobbyhorse by "getting on his back and riding him about" and Yorick's journeys through his parish are an explanation in the action of why he rides the sort of horse he does. When Toby whistles *Lillabulero* or when Yorick reads the account of Gymnast's fight with Tripet, they are offering examples of this sort of parabolic delivery of a message by gesture. Sometimes these expressive arrangements of the body are accompanied by words, as in Toby's setting the fly free or in Trim's gesture of dropping the hat while reciting a self-evident truth. In the domain of pure language, the primitive belief in the performative function of words is held by Walter Shandy who constantly exhibits his faith in the power of naming and for whom the most expressive sign of the fall of empires is the fact that their *names* "are falling themselves by piece-meals into decay" (*TS*, p. 354). Walter's theory of the auxiliary verbs, which he steals from Obadiah Walker's *Of Education*, is in fact a primitive syntactic basis for a universal language scheme in which, if the word is already known, the thing is known too. In Toby's case we hear another primitive use of the word, which is the extension of its reference by catachresis. For Toby the origin of language is in military science, and that provides him with a fund of literal terms which, when applied to other phenomena such as *trains* of ideas, a *mortar* and pestle, the *bridge* of a nose etc., imitate the process of early language growth by figurative applications of literal words. As for Yorick's puns, they are figurative uses of words that remind us how ideas are formed out of the body's sensations and activities by establishing instant etymologies.

The primitive nature of hobbyhorsical language offers a variety of ways of determining in some detail the characters of the men who use it. Like all primitive language, it both conceals and reveals meaning, and it will offer up its secrets only to those with enough patience and candor to decipher it. Once that effort is made, the hobbyhorse speaks the consistency of its rider and the audience can become as familiar with that consistency as if a Momus glass were placed in the breast. In a comic way certain valuable truths are revealed that were thought to be inexpressible and we learn a tongue that may not be the language of the gods but which God understands. Sterne finds a compendious store of these comic sublimities in Rabelais, and that he regarded them as versions of the sublime is likely from the name he gives to one of his earliest characters. "Longinus Rabelaicus" is the leading figure in Sterne's *Fragment in the Manner of Rabelais* where he is busy producing a *Kerukopaedia*, or institute of sermon-making, that will pay as much attention to the *tune* of the sermon as its content. It will take into account the constitution of the preacher, the disposition of his limbs, the intonation of his voice and all the physical and spiritual accompaniments that belong to saying something with that natural propriety that sincerity demands. Rabelais himself adapts much of his wit from the Bible, and he sees "voices of the sign" and punning as fit vehicles for the carnivalesque union of body and mind which he loves because it is the opposite of hypocrisy and insincerity. Sterne has no tradition of carnival, but he makes moral assumptions about the totality of the human constitution ("the soul and body are joint-sharers in every thing they get"—*TS*, p. 616) of which the hobbyhorse is the odd emblem. Along with the Latitudinarian divines he was so fond of borrowing from, like Tillotson, Clarke, Stillingfleet and Tenison, he sees in Newtonian science a variety of physical proofs of this assumption, and in the work of Cheyne and Hartley he finds physiological accounts of the close relationship between the soul, or mind, and the body. This is the central unifying concept of "sensibility" and the common property of the age, but Sterne typically insists that there is a language appropriate to this union. So the comic sublime is not only the natural language of sincerity, or the constant exchanges between gestural, literal and metaphorical sense that Rabelais passes on; it is also the language of science itself which is supplying the lower, material component of meaning to words like *spirit, inspiration* and *gravity* and unconsciously creating the sort of pun Sterne and Rabelais enjoy so much.[32]

In his narrative Tristram reproduces all the primitivism of his characters' language, even adding primitive cries, parable, metaphor and the literary equivalent of gesture in the form of hieroglyphs. Since I have defined the comic sublime as mounting a higher idea upon a little circumstance or image in order to give a unified expression of a higher truth that has lower relations, I want briefly to strengthen the links between Tristram's narrative and certain effects of Pope and Montaigne by way of insisting on the great difference between Sterne's wordplay and Swift's. If the comic sublime is a response appropriate to the mixed condition of man, where little circumstances provide the impressions that make his elevated ideas, where mind and body are mutually dependent in making sense of things, and where there is a moral as well as physical relation between what is done and what is thought, it follows that it will affirm the inseparability of the ideas it joins, be they in a pun, a gesture, or a metaphor, because they are already linked in the joint activity of the body and mind. It will also follow that in any account of these reciprocal activities, words will tend to reproduce that reciprocity, not merely describe it or, as in mock-epic, establish an ironic distance between the account and the activity, and between the upper and lower elements of the activity itself. Any pun which announces the equilibrium of physical and mental experience *reflects* or *enacts* the very process it is applied to by making the two senses apparent but inextricable:

> In all distresses (except musical) where small cords are wanted,—
> nothing is so apt to enter a man's head, as his hatband:—the
> philosophy of this is so near the surface—I scorn to enter into it.
> (*TS*, p. 165)

The puns on "cord" *quasi* "chord" and on "enter a man's head" (as meaning both the conception of an idea and the pressure of a hatband) are a lowly but thoroughly appropriate illustration of the comic sublime. The one sense is necessary to the other both as explanation and as utterance of Obadiah's "feelings." The causal relation between circumstance and idea is announced by words which proclaim in themselves the inevitable ambiguity of meaning that is made in this way. At first hearing this sort of wordplay sounds frivolous and unnecessary, but it is a testimony to Sterne's solid and coherent faith in sensationism and associationism. And as enactive prose this punning is cousin to some impressive relations. Addison praises Pope and Boileau praises Longinus for having managed to write about the sublime sublimely. Addison has in mind Pope's clever adjustments of the sound to the sense in the *Essay on Criticism*, and Boileau is referring to the famous seventh section of *On the Sublime*. Addison calls it exemplifying "precepts in the very Precepts themselves" (Spectator, No. 253). It is the result of the idea of the object becoming so powerful and exclusive that the quality of the object invades the expression or representation of it. As Demosthenes becomes moved as he talks about an assault, he reproduces the blows in the rhythms of his oration. There is an example of this in the famous attack on Sporus in the *Epistle to Dr. Arbuthnot*. Pope's horror at his enemy's ambiguous qualities mounts with each antithetical example of them until finally he calls Sporus himself "a vile Antithesis," as if the nastiness of Sporus is so perfectly adapted to that rhetorical technique that it becomes infected with his evil and its inoffensive name is converted by association into the most opprobrious epithet Pope can think of.[33] Less impassioned but of the same nature is Montaigne's discovery in "Upon Some Verses of Virgil" that action and description must imitate one another. In constantly elaborating the indissoluble connexions between his mind and his body Montaigne evolves a style that perfectly represents the reciprocity of thought and action, idea and sensation, by slipping with a natural metaphorical ease between them until the book and Montaigne become, as he says, consubstantial, mutually illustrative. The circumscription of Montaigne's experience (dreaming that he dreams, writing that he writes) comes of bending his mind habitually to his body's experience and intensifying the natural relation of the two. Consequently it is pointless in reading his *Essays* to consider his mind as distinct from his body or his style as distinct from the unions it is imitating. In *Tristram Shandy* there are several examples of this sort of circumscription which belong, as the puns do, to the comic sublime. When Tristram plagiarizes an attack on plagiarism, invokes Cid Hamet Benengeli's Invocation, or makes a digression in the very process of writing about digressions, he is comically filling his mind with his object to the degree that description becomes part of the thing described. This tautological reflection in the very prose of the object referred to repeats the effect of puns and literalized metaphors: that of the circumstanced idea, the thing that must always attend the thought it provokes.

Although so much of Swift's wit seems to play up and down the same vertical scale as Sterne's, it always establishes differences, never identities or natural relations. In a discussion of Swift's literalized metaphors, Maurice J. Quinlan points out that it is contrast, and not association, that he is aiming for "in order to reveal an ironic disparity between the two meanings."[34] The apparent resemblance between the two writers (one which Sterne claims along with the common source of Rabelais) is due perhaps to Swift's constant mockery of primitive forms of language, or at least of Baconian approaches to interpreting or imitating those forms. Whatever belongs to type, symbol, analogy, heiroglyph, sign, or mystery is a symptom of dullness and an opportunity for wit to destroy the silly symmetries and literalized notions that foolish minds invent and enjoy. And no matter how cleanly the satirical idea fits over the dunsical one (for example the modern improvement of digressions and the definition of the *satura lanx*), the test presented to the reader is to see and know the difference, and so mount to the disembodied region of the middle air whence wit makes its attacks on the dunces who sprawl in the *matter* of bathos, bombast, and bad magic. Rising properly, in *Tale of a Tub* at any rate, is the condition of having no lead at one's heels and of being free from material considerations. St John of Revelations, Panurge and Jack consume holy texts in order to prophesy, but for sensible folk that sort of bibliophragy is no longer appropriate.

Although this sets Swift at a further remove than the "due distance" Sterne mentions (*Letters*, p. 76), it offers a clearer idea of Sterne's real connections and affiliations. In narrative technique they are with those, like Montaigne, who learn the naturalized art of irregularity, and with Cervantes who both invents a mock-epic narrative and superintends its conversion into the comic sublime. In morality he is close to the genial and masculine sentimentalism of Fielding, who likewise appoints the upper and lower limits in which incorporated minds think and feel. Sterne's interest in the humorist as a figure of real integrity, and in the means by which such a figure expresses himself, is closely involved with his interest in narrative and has much the same line of development, beginning with Cervantes and strengthened by the eighteenth century interest in humorism and irregularity. His physiological interest in the interaction of mind and body places Sterne quite definitely among Newtonians, and quite far from innovators of sublime styles like Chatterton, Smart and Blake whose primitivism has a more mystical basis that is, in Blake's case, profoundly opposed to the mechanist tradition. His interest in language links Sterne with those who were exploring the growth of languages and the structure of ideas, like Warburton, Hartley and Hume; and he owes a good deal less to Locke in this respect than is often supposed. Finally, in his pursuit of the subtler forms of irregularity, a mixture of associationist wit and "sensible" language, Sterne has Longinus to instruct him in how to break rules and find others.

## NOTES

1. See E.P. Thompson, "The Crime of Anonymity," in *Albion's Fatal Tree: Crime and Society in Eighteenth-Century England*, by Douglas Hay. (et. al.) (London: Allen Lane, 1975), pp. 255–344.

2. See Frye's "Towards Defining an Age of Sensibility," in *Eighteenth Century English Literature: Modern Essays in Criticism*, ed. James L. Clifford (New York: O.U.P., 1960), pp. 311–18.

3. See *Tristram Shandy*, ed. James A. Work (New York: Odyssey Press, 1940), p. 85; and *Joseph Andrews*, ed. Douglas Brooks (London: O.U.P., 1971), p. 9. I am indebted to many critics and scholars, chiefly to Stuart M. Tave, *The Amiable Humorist: a Study in the Comic Theory and Criticism of the Eighteenth and Early Nineteenth Centuries* (Chicago: Univ. of Chicago Press, 1960); Ronald Paulson, *The Fictions of Satire* (Baltimore: John Hopkins Press, 1967) and *Satire and the Novel in Eighteenth-Century England* (New Haven: Yale Univ. Press, 1967); and Lionel Trilling, *Sincerity and Authenticity* (Cambridge, Mass.: Harvard Univ. Press, 1967).

4. *The Works of the Most Reverend Dr John Tillotson, Late Lord Archbishop of Canterbury*, 2 Volumes (London: Ralph Barker, 1712), I, 7.

5. Alexander Pope, "The First Satire of the Second Book of Horace," in *Imitations of Horace*, ed. John Butt (London: Methuen and Co. Ltd., 1939), II. 51–52, 57–58.

6. John Dryden, "A Discourse Concerning Satire," *Of Dramatic Poesy and Other Critical Essays*, ed. G. Watson (London: J.M. Dent, 1962), II, 123.

7. Jonathan Swift, *A Tale of a Tub*, ed. A.C. Guthkelch and D. Nichol Smith (Oxford: Clarendon Press, 1958), pp. 143-44.

8. John Dryden, "A Discourse Concerning Satire," II, 146.

9. Jonathan Swift, *A Tale of a Tub*, pp. 18, 44.

10. John Dryden, "A Discourse Concerning Satire," 11, 103.

11. Alexander Pope, "Postscript," *The Odyssey of Homer, Books XIII–XXIV*, ed. Maynard Mack (London: Methuen and Co. Ltd., 1967), X, 387.

12. Ibid, X, 388. Further references to the "Postscript" will be incorporated, in parenthesis, into the text.

13. See Stuart M. Tave, *The Amiable Humorist*, p. 157.

14. See *Tristram Shandy*, p. 22; and James Beattie, "An Essay on Laughter and Ludicrous Composition," *Essays* (Edinburgh: Printed for William Creech, 1776; rpt. New York: Garland Publishing Inc., 1971), p. 603. Further references to *Tristram Shandy* will be incorporated, in parenthesis, into the text under the abbreviation *TS*.

15. Miguel de Cervantes Saavedra, *The Life and Achievements of the Renowned Don Quixote de la Mancha*, trans. Peter le Motteux, ed. J.G. Lockhart (London: J.M. Dent, 1906; rpt. 1970), I, 393–94.

16. Dionysius Longinus, *On the Sublime*, trans. William Smith (1739; rpt. New York: Scholar's Facsimiles and Reprints, 1975), p. 71. Further references to *On the Sublime* will be incorporated, in parenthesis, into the text under the abbreviation *OS*.

17. Montaigne, *Essays of Michael Seigneur de Montaigne*, trans. Charles Cotton (London: 1711), I, 253.

18. Diderot, *Jacques the Fatalist*, trans. Robert J. Loy (New York: Collier Books, 1962), p. 211.

19. David Hartley, *Observations on Man, His Frame, His Duty, and His Expectations* (1749; rpt. Florida: Scholar's Facsimiles and Reprints, 1966), I, vi.

20. Edmund Burke, *A Philosophical Inquiry into the Origin of our Ideas of the Sublime and Beautiful, The Works of Edmund Burke* (London: George Bell & Sons, 1902), I, 88. Further references to *A Philosophical Inquiry* etc. will be incorporated, in parenthesis, into the text under the abbreviation *Inquiry*.

21. Sterne, *The Sermons of Mr Yorick* (Oxford: Basil Blackwell, 1927), II, 230.

22. Sterne, *A Sentimental Journey*, ed. Gardner D. Stout (Berkeley: Univ. of California Press, 1967), p. 159.

23. Wordsworth, "Preface to Lyrical Ballads," *The Prose Works of William Wordsworth*, ed. W.J.B. Owen and Jane Worthington Smyser (Oxford: Clarendon Press, 1967), I, 137.

24. Joseph Warton, *Essay on the Genius and Writings of Pope* (1782; rpt. Farnborough: Gregg International Publishers, 1969), 1, 291. Further references to *Essay on the Genius*, etc. will be incorporated, in parenthesis, into the text under the abbreviation *EGWP*.

25. Samuel Johnson, *Johnson's Lives of the Poets: A Selection*, ed. J.P. Hardy (Oxford: Clarendon Press, 1971), p. 12.

26. Francis Hutcheson, "Reflections upon Laughter," *An Inquiry Concerning Beauty, Order, Harmony, Design*, ed. Peter Kivy (The Hague: Martinus Nijhoff, 1973), p. 109. Further references to "Reflections upon Laughter" will be incorporated, in parenthesis, into the text under the abbreviation "Reflections."

27. See *The Works of Alexander Pope*, ed. William Warburton (London: 1753), I, 104n.

28. William Warburton, *The Divine Legation of Moses Demonstrated* (London: 1837), I, 468; I, 251. Further references to *The Divine Legation* will be incorporated, in parenthesis, into the text under the abbreviation *DLMD*.

29. Fielding, *Joseph Andrews*, p. 220.

30. *Letters of Laurence Sterne*, ed. Lewis Perry Curtis (Oxford: Clarendon Press, 1935; rpt. 1965), p. 77. Further references to *Letters of Laurence Sterne* will be incorporated, in parenthesis, into the text under the abbreviation of *Letters*.

31. See "Self Knowledge," in *The Sermons of Mr Yorick*, I, 41.

32. See Donald Davie, *The Language of Science and the Language of Literature 1700–1740* (London: Sheed and Ward, 1963); and Margaret C. Jacob, *The Newtonians and the English Revolution 1689–1720* (Hassocks: Harvester Press, 1976), who establishes interesting and, in this context, significant links between Newtonian science and Biblical exegesis.

33. See *The Poems of Alexander Pope*, ed. John Butt (London: Methuen and Co. Ltd., 1963), p. 608.

34. Maurice J. Quinlan, "Swift's Use of Literalization as a Rhetorical Device," *PMLA*, 12 (Dec. 1967), 516–21.

SHERIDAN BAKER

# Fielding: The Comic Reality of Fiction

Fielding's achievement in his four novels is immense. *Joseph Andrews* (1742) is not only the first English comic novel but the Declaration of Independence for all fiction. *Jonathan Wild* (1743), though imperfectly, turns Augustan satire into a novel. *Tom Jones (1749)* supersedes and absorbs the drama as the dominant form and, more significantly, culminates the Augustan world of poetry and Pope in the new poetics of prose. *Amelia (1751)* signals the eighteenth century's sombre midday equinox as its undercurrent of sentiment and uncertainty wells up through the cool neoclassic crust. *Amelia* is the first novel of marriage, and it explores a new and modern indeterminacy of character. Notwithstanding Defoe's and Richardson's achievement in fictionalizing the lonely struggle of modernity, Fielding proclaimed the truth of fiction as he gave the novel form. He also gave it mystery with the romantic, and psychic, discovery of identity, acceptance, and success. He gave it its omniscient narrator and comprehensive scope.

Fielding is not of Defoe's and Richardson's rising middle class, where the individual makes himself and the future, where the underdog's struggles are no longer comic. Fielding is a young aristocrat down on his uppers.[1] His is the Augustan perspective, a sophisticated detachment that staves off evils and passionate dogmas through satire and irony, seeking a rational balance between violent extremes. His allegiance is to hierarchy in orderly rank. Like Swift, he prefers Ancients to Moderns. Like Pope, he perceives God's providential creation with calm optimism, and amusement.

From *Tennessee Studies in Literature* Volume 29, published as *The First English Novelists: Essays in Understanding: Honoring the retirement of Percy G. Adams*, edited by J.M. Armistead. © 1985 by The University of Tennessee Press.

He elects himself a Scriblerian. His first major effort, his anonymous *The Masquerade (1728)*, a satire in Swiftian tetrameters, is "By LEMUEL GULLIVER, Poet Laureate to the King of *Lilliput.*" Soon, with his eminent cousin, Lady Mary Wortley Montagu, he is writing a burlesque of Pope's recent *Dunciad (1728)*. His first stage satire and ballad opera, *The Author's Farce (1730)*, is "Written by *Scriblerus Secundus,*" emulating the *Dunciad* in a trip to the underworld of the Goddess of Nonsense. *Tom Thumb* (1730), which imitates Swift's Lilliputian-Brobdingnagian contrasts and, in its final form, Pope's mock-scholarly preface and footnotes, is also by *Scriblerus Secundus*, who becomes *H. Scriblerus Secundus*, with Fielding's initial, in the expanded *Tragedy of Tragedies (1730)*. *The Grub-Street Opera (1731)* is by *Scriblerus Secundus* in all three versions. In short, Fielding set out to emulate the three Augustan masterpieces, all deriving from the brief heyday of the Scriblerus Club (February to June 1714): Swift's *Gulliver's Travels (1726)*, Gay's *Beggar's Opera (1728)*, Pope's *Dunciad* (in three books, 1728). As Sherburn suggests (*"Dunciad"*), Pope confirmed the alliance by borrowing back from Fielding's farces the kaleidoscopic court of Dulness in his fourth book (1742, 1743).

The theater was Fielding's apprenticeship.[2] It gave him stock characters and situations, repeated until they became universal types. It gave him a knack for scene and dialogue, the balanced structural arch of *Tom Jones*, and the long, downward comic slant of fortune that thrusts suddenly upward like a reversed check mark. It gave him social satire and comedy of manners aimed at a serious point.

Fielding's first play, *Love in Several Masques (1728)*, written at twenty-one, forecasts *Tom Jones* in surprising detail. It is intricately plotted. Its hero is Tom Merital, a meritorious rake, a preliminary Tom Jones. Tom's wealthy lady love is an orphan guarded by an aunt and uncle—a stock preliminary Sophia, to be married against her will to save her from the rake. The heroines speak up for the hero, and the aunts respond.

> *Lady Trap:*   I have wondered how a creature of such principles could spring up in a family so noted for the purity of its women. (II.vi)
>
> *Mrs. Western:* You are the first—yes, Miss *Western*, you are the first of your Name who ever entertained so groveling a Thought. A Family so noted for the Prudence of its Women.... (VI.v)

Lady Trap is also an Amorous Matron—the first Lady Booby, Mrs. Slipslop, Mrs. Waters, and especially Lady Bellaston, who, like Lady Trap, has bad breath: "Brandy and Assafoetida, by Jupiter," cries kissing Tom.

Here, at the play's mathematical center, the heroine catches Tom just as Sophia will discover her Tom and Mrs. Waters at central Upton. We also have the stock comic maid, saucy and ingenious, who will become Mrs. Honour. Finally, we have Wisemore, a junior and sourer Allworthy, a virtuous young country squire who introduces Fielding's perpetual contrast with the wicked city and represents the play's moral center, a book-read idealist whom his mistress twice calls Don Quixote. Wisemore will also transform comically into Parson Adams.

In his six rehearsal-farces—no one else wrote more than one—Fielding discovered himself as parodic satirist. In *The Author's Farce (1730)*, he also discovered his autobiographical authorship of comic romances, a comic double self-portraiture in hero and author alike. Harry Luckless, the "author," is young playwright Harry Fielding, luckless with Mr. Colley Cibber of Drury Lane, who appears in no less than two comic versions and two more allusive thrusts. Harry loves Harriot, in the twinnish way of romance, whom his nonentity denies him—courtly love in a London roominghouse. Then Harry stages his show in the Popean realm of Nonsense and becomes Fielding commenting on his work as it goes. In the giddy finale, a pawned jewel proves Luckless a farcical foundling, lost heir of a fabulous kingdom, who may now marry and live happily ever after as Henry I. Fielding's blithe comedy distances his wish for recognition, the universal yearning typical of romance, as we simultaneously fulfill and recognize our fancies in the way of *Joseph Andrews* and *Tom Jones*.

Fielding eventually put nine commenting authors on the stage—seven in the rehearsal-farces (two in *Pasquin*) plus two authorial inductors like Gay's in *The Beggar's Opera*—breaking the bonds of drama to reach for narration. Many of their comments Fielding will repeat less facetiously in his novels. Medly, in *The Historical Register (1737)*, Fielding's last, comes particularly close:

> Why, sir, my design is to ridicule the vicious and foolish customs of the age ... I hope to expose the reigning follies in such a manner, that men shall laugh themselves out of them before they feel that they are touched.

Fielding says of *Tom Jones* (in the Dedication):

> I have employed all the Wit and Humour of which I am Master in the following History; wherein I have endeavoured to laugh Mankind out of their Favourite Follies and Vices.

But *The Historical Register* brought down Sir Robert Walpole's wrath, and the Licensing Act (1737) shut Fielding from the stage. He made himself a lawyer and followed the circuits along the roads of his future novels. He turned to journalism with the *Champion*, the opposition newspaper backed by

Lord Chesterfield and Lord Lyttelton, Fielding's Eton school-friend. He is now "Capt. Hercules Vinegar, of Hockley in the Hole," slaying the Hydras of political corruption like the popular cudgel player and boxing promoter of that name. Like Pope, who had declared himself "TO VIRTUE ONLY AND HER FRIENDS, A FRIEND" in his first *Imitation of Horace* (1733), Fielding is the champion of England against Walpole's government, the future essayist as novelist who will dedicate *Tom Jones* to Lyttelton, believing that it will serve as "a Kind of Picture, in which Virtue becomes as it were an Object of Sight."

Fielding's religious concern deepens in the *Champion*. We can almost see *Shamela* and *Joseph Andrews* accumulating. In the spring of 1740, Fielding pauses in his political championship to write four thoughtful essays about the materialism and vanity of the clergy and the necessity of humble charity. The first (March 29) is untitled. Then in the next issue (April Fool's Day, by luck or design), he satirizes Walpole, along with a new book by "the most inimitable Laureat," none other than *An Apology for the Life of Mr. Colley Cibber, Comedian, Written by Himself*. Cibber had been a standing joke as political sycophant and bad writer ever since Walpole had made him poet laureate in 1730. Moreover, Cibber, from his side of the political fence, had in his *Apology* called Fielding a mudslinger and failed writer. So Fielding interrupts his religious meditation here and returns in several papers to ridicule the vanity and grammar of his old personal and political opponent, whom he will enthrone as an egotistical fraud in *Shamela* and *Joseph Andrews*, as Pope would also in the *Dunciad*. Fielding then continues with his religious essays under the ironic title "THE APOLOGY FOR THE CLERGY,—*continued*."

As Cibber and the clergy mix in Fielding's mind, another new book appears: *A Short Account of God's Dealings with the Reverend Mr. George Whitefield* (1740), written by himself in what would seem Cibberian conceit at God's personal attention. It stirred a controversy between the new Methodist (and old Calvinist) belief that only faith and God's grace warranted Heaven as against the doctrine that "Faith without works is dead" (Battestin, *Moral Basis*, 18), which Fielding had asserted in the *Champion*. Whitefield's *Dealings* would become Shamela's favorite reading, as Fielding mocks Pamela's egotistical piety, and Parson Williams espouses spiritual grace to release the body for pleasure.[3] Fielding turns these negatives positive when he transforms Williams into Adams, who, with Methodist John Wesley, prefers a virtuous Turk to a tepid Christian (Woods, "Fielding," 264). Adams is a lovingly comic portrait of a Whitefieldian enthusiast, who shames the fatness of orthodoxy and nevertheless condemns Whitefield's enthusiastic grace:

> "Sir," answered *Adams*, "if Mr. *Whitfield* had carried his Doctrine no farther ... I should have remained, as I once was, his Well-Wisher. I am myself as great an Enemy to the Luxury and Splendour of the Clergy as he can be." (I.xvii)

But selfless charity was the center of Fielding's religion, and Whitefield stood ready with Cibber to coalesce with pious Pamela, when she arrived in the fall, as symbols of meretricious vanity and hypocrisy.

*Pamela: Or, Virtue Rewarded*, the "real" letters of a serving girl, prefaced by twenty-eight pages of letters praising its moral excellence, is really *An Apology for the Life of Mrs. Shamela Andrews* (1741)—so proclaims Fielding's title page in the typography of Cibber's *Apology*, with "Conny Keyber" as author: *Keyber* being the standard political slur at Cibber's Danish ancestry. Parson Tickletext, who can dream of nothing but Pamela undressed, sends a copy of the new best seller to Parson Oliver so that he too can preach it from the pulpit (as had actually been done in London). Oliver tells Tickletext the book is a sham, doctored by a clergyman who can make black white. The girl is really Shamela, a calculating guttersnippet from London working in a neighboring parish. Richardson's Mr. B. is really Squire Booby; his busybody Parson Williams is really an adulterous poacher of Booby's hares and wife. He sends Tickletext the real letters—Fielding's breezy parodies of Richardson's, which concentrate on his two bedroom scenes, now lifted to peaks of hilarity as Fielding brilliantly condenses two volumes to some fifty pages.

Fielding's title page tells us immediately that something has happened to fiction, now allusively declaring and enjoying in the Augustan way the fictive pretense Defoe and Richardson had pretended real. English fiction has become literate. Here, suddenly, is a book that—like Joyce's *Ulysses*, let us say—generates its being, and its meaning, from other literature as it gets its hold on life. By declaring his letters true to tell us ironically they are not—precisely the comic pose Cervantes shares with his readers—Fielding asserts both the validity and power of fiction, which he will proclaim in *Joseph Andrews*. *Shamela* is probably the best parody anywhere, but it is also a broadly Augustan burlesque of social ills—moral, political, religious, philosophical—in the true Scriblerian mode (Rothstein, 389).

In naming "Conny Keyber" the author, Fielding concentrates his inclusive satire in a bawdy sexual symbol. "Conny" merges Cibber's first name with that of the Rev. Mr. Conyers Middleton, whose dedication to his *Life of Cicero* (February 1741, less than two months before *Shamela*) Fielding closely parodies as a dedication by Conny Keyber to "Miss Fanny, & *c.*" Middleton had dedicated his *Cicero* to John, Lord Hervey, Walpole's propagandist; and Hervey, an effeminate bisexual, had acquired the epithet "Fanny" from Pope's first *Imitation of Horace* (1733), where Pope had saucily Anglicized Horace's Fannius, a bad poet and a homosexual. Now, as Rothstein notes (387), *Conny, coney,* and *cony* (for "rabbit") were all pronounced "cunny"—a version of the still-prevailing obscenity for the female pudendum, and *Fanny* and *et cetera* were both slang terms for the same (382).

In parodying one of Richardson's introductory letters praising Pamela, Fielding writes, "it will do more good than the *C—y* have done harm in the World," wherein one may read both the *clergy* and the *cunny* of Fielding's satirical attack. Later, Shamela reports that her husband gave her a toast so wicked she can't write it and that Mrs. Jewkes then "drank the dear *Monysyllable*; I don't understand that Word, but I believe it is baudy." Williams and Booby likewise drink to and joke about her "*et cetera.*" In short, Cibber, Hervey, Middleton, Richardson, and Pamela, "that young Politician" named on the title page, are all moneysyllabic prostitutes in their various ways. Fielding's slyest touch is in quoting directly another introductory letter telling Richardson he had "stretched out this diminutive mere Grain of Mustard-seed (a poor Girl's little, innocent, Story) into a resemblance of Heaven, which the best of good Books has compared it to." Fielding alters only the parenthesis of this extravagant Biblical allusion (Matt. 13:31): "has stretched out this diminutive mere Grain of Mustard-seed (a poor Girl's little, etc.) into a Resemblance of Heaven."

*Shamela* sharpened Fielding's belief, to be formulated in *Joseph Andrews*, that comedy can be both realistic and morally instructive. No serving maid was ever named Pamela, after the romantic princess in Sidney's recently republished *Arcadia*, nor wrote such letters, if she could write at all. The realistic idiom of Shamela and the housekeepers, and even their calculating morality, amusingly point up the falsity in Richardson's idea of virtue. Tearful Pamela, proud of her dead mistress's clothes, becomes Shamela, wanting to set herself up with Parson Williams, since "I have got a good many fine Cloaths of the Old Put my Mistress's, who died a whil ago." Her language rings colloquially true and yet mimics Richardson at every turn. Shamela actually seems more honest, and Mrs. Jewkes more wholesome, than their prototypes. Nothing seems more typical of Fielding's realistic countryside than Booby riding in his coach with Shamela and catching Williams poaching. Yet as Williams rides off in the coach with Booby's bride, we realize that this is all a mime of an episode in *Pamela* where we find Williams walking, book in hand, at the meadowside; he is met, reconciled, and finally taken into the coach by Mr. B. with his Pamela.

The close parody of Richardson's bedroom scenes taught Fielding the high comedy of sex. The amorous scenes in his plays are heavy. The ladies know what's what. But *Shamela* shimmers with the comic hypocrisies of civilized sex. Pamela wants—not simply for prestige—to submit to her master, but everything she believes in prevents her desire from even breaking surface. Richardson, simply to keep his story going, has her stay when she wants to go, writing into his tale this elemental sexual hypocrisy that gives it the mystic dimension of Beauty and the Beast. In burlesquing it, Fielding learned what it was. His stage ladies wish to appear proper only in the eyes of others; Lady Booby and Mrs. Slipslop of *Joseph Andrews* wish to appear proper in their own eyes as well. A great deal of the comedy in Fielding's novels comes from the universal struggle of hidden passion against propriety or, on the masculine side, of passion against the best of intentions. *Shamela*, more than anything before, brought this to the center of Fielding's comic vision.

Parson Oliver, another step toward Fielding's commenting author, decrying Richardson's lascivious images and meretricious rewards, spells out the moral. He declares the future lesson of *Tom Jones*: Prudence must rule. *Pamela*, he says, encourages young men to impetuous matches that will "sacrifice all the solid Comforts of their Lives, to a very transcient Satisfaction of a Passion." In *Tom Jones*, Fielding will seek "to make good Men wise" by instilling in them "that solid inward Comfort of Mind, which is the sure Companion of Innocence and Virtue." Oliver writes of "the secure Satisfaction of a good Conscience, the Approbation of the Wise and Good ... and the extatick Pleasure of contemplating, that their Ways are acceptable to the Great Creator of the Universe." "But for Worldly Honours," Oliver continues, "they are often the Purchase of Force and Fraud." Tom Jones cries out concerning Blifil, who has defrauded him:

> What is the poor Pride arising from a magnificent House, a numerous Equipage, a splendid Table, and from all the other Advantages or Appearances of Fortune, compared to the warm, solid Content, the swelling Satisfaction, the thrilling Transports, and the exulting Triumphs, which a good Mind enjoys, in the Contemplation of a generous, virtuous, noble, benevolent Action? (XII.x)

*Shamela's* success made Fielding a novelist; he gives *Pamela* another parodic turn in *Joseph Andrews* (1742) and also finally brings Cervantes to English life. At last, Fielding finds his authorial voice in the playful ironies of Cervantes and Scarron:

> Now the Rake *Hesperus* had called for his Breeches.... In vulgar Language, it was Evening when *Joseph* attended his Lady's Orders. (I.viii)

> And now, Reader, taking these Hints along with you, you may, if you please, proceed to the Sequel of this our true History. (III.i)

He now ironically holds up Pamela and Cibber as consummate models for the kind of biography he is writing. He extends the joke of *Shamela* in its next inevitable mutation, transposing the sexes for the more ludicrous effect. Pamela Andrews, who had become Shamela Andrews, will now become

Pamela's equally virtuous, and hence more comically prudish, brother: a footman named Joseph, after the biblical hero who resisted Potiphar's wife. Lady Booby now pursues *her* servant—Squire Booby is her nephew—as Mr. B. pursued his. Richardson's Mrs. Jewkes, "a broad, squat, pursy, *fat thing*" who drinks, becomes Mrs. Slipslop, who also reflects Cervantes's grotesque chambermaid, Maritornes,[4] a libidinous little dwarf with shoulders somewhat humped and a breath with "a stronger *Hogoe* than stale Venison" (I.iii.2). Mrs. Jewkes's salacious lesbianism becomes Slipslop's comic passion for Joseph.[5] Fielding even dares to name his heroine after the obscene "Miss Fanny" of *Shamela*, rinsing the name clean without losing all of its comic pubic potential. In fact, Fielding's Beau Didapper, who attempts to rape the purified Fanny, is none other than Lord Hervey again (Battestin, "Hervey"), the original "Miss Fanny," as if everything of *Shamela* must be converted to new uses. Finally, Mr. B.'s curate Williams becomes, through the wringer of *Shamela*, Lady Booby's curate Adams.

Adams is Fielding's triumph. At twenty-one, as a student at Leyden, Fielding had tried to naturalize Cervantes in his *Don Quixote* in England— eventually a ballad opera (1734). Now, in *Joseph Andrews* ("Written in Imitation of the Manner of Cervantes") he finally creates a thoroughly English Quixote, a country parson drawn from the very life—from Fielding's friend from childhood, the absentminded parson William Young. Like Cervantes, Fielding comically confronts the ideal quest of romance with the satiric picaresque tour of society. Adams is his comic knight, a quixotic Christian benevolist embodying the virtues outlined in the *Champion*. Like Quixote, he is book-blinded, but by the New Testament and classics alike. His tattered cassock replaces Quixote's patchwork armor. His borrowed horse, soon abandoned, a Christian Rosinante, frequently stumbles to its knees. He rescues "Damsels" (Fanny) and stands up for the innocent with his crabstick against the selfish world's wind-mills. Andrews travels the English roads and inns as realistic squire to the daft idealist and, like Sancho Panza, grows in wisdom.

Fielding's parody becomes *paradiorthosis*, as the Greeks would say, an emulative borrowing and bending of a master's words, well loved by Augustans, except that Fielding finds creative joy in allusively reapplying whole characterizations, episodes, and dramatic arrangements. Richardson furnishes his major structure—two wild bedroom episodes at beginning and end, followed by the discovered truth of identity and social elevation of romance, which Pamela had also enacted. It is almost as if Fielding had cut *Shamela* down the middle and pulled the halves apart to accommodate his Cervantic roadway. The first bedroom scenes (I.v-vi), in which first Lady Booby and then Mrs. Slipslop try to possess Joseph—"Madam," says Joseph, "that Boy is the Brother of *Pamela*"—are probably the most hilarious chapters in the English novel. The second and concluding bedroom episode

(IV.xiv) is more broadly comic, a reworking of the old picaresque fabliau about a wrong turn into bed that simultaneously parallels two versions from Cervantes and three from Scarron, as critics from Cross to Goldberg have detected, and primarily into the bed of Mrs. Slipslop, that caricature of Mrs. Jewkes, in whose bed Richardson's second scene of attempted rape is laid, if one may use the term. Even Lady Booby must laugh at the universal selfish scrambling of sex to which intrinsic virtue is impervious (Spilka, 403).

Fielding's central Cervantic journey is linear and episodic, as Joseph becomes both romantic hero and practical companion to idealistic Christianity. When Lady Booby dismisses him, he heads not for home (as Pamela longs to do) or for "his beloved Sister *Pamela*," but to Lady Booby's country parish to see the girl he loves. Fielding's genius is nowhere more blithely evident than in his ability to change his lighting and reveal the young man within the parodic abstraction—this very funny male Pamela—without losing his hero, or his readers. Joseph matures, as Taylor notes, and clearly becomes the romantic hero at an inn, very near the center of the novel (II.xii), which reunites the major characters (except Lady Booby) in much the way the inn at Upton will do at the central climax of *Tom Jones*.

Fielding is reworking an episode from Cervantes he had already used for the whole of *Don Quixote in England*, where the lovers, as Tom and Sophia will be at Upton, are under the same roof unbeknownst to each other. Adams has brought the rescued Fanny, who, like Dorothea in the play and Sophia in *Tom Jones*, has set out across country in search of her lover. Mrs. Slipslop in her coach has picked up Joseph along the road and brought him in "Hopes of something which might have been accomplished at an Ale-house as well as a Palace" (II.xiii). As in Cervantes, our heroine hears a beautiful voice singing. But realism renders romance comic. Joseph's pastoral song ends in sexual climax, with Chloe "expiring." Fanny, only recognizing the voice, cries "O Jesus!" and faints. Adams, to the rescue, throws his beloved Aeschylus into the fire, where it "lay expiring," and enraged Slipslop rides off in disappointment.

Balancing this comic juxtaposition of ideal and sexual love is another structuring episode Fielding will also elaborate in *Tom Jones*. This is Mr. Wilson's story, just on the other side of the central divide between Books II and III, which is, as Paulson ("Models," 1202) and Maresca (199) have noted, Fielding's realistic version of the *descensus Averno* (*Aeneid* VI. 126), the trip to the underworld for truth.[6] Our travelers descend a hill in spooky darkness, cross a river, and find Elysium in the country Eden of Wilson, who tells them the truth about the wicked world of London. Wilson's straightforward account fills out Fielding's social panorama, and Wilson, in the end, neatly fits into Fielding's comic romance as the long-lost father of cradle-switched Joseph, whose white skin (which, as with Tom Jones to come, a lady discovers in succoring the wounded hero) has already disclosed to the reader of romances his unknown nobility.

Fielding comically fulfills the romantic dream of Harry Luckless. He opens his preface by assuming that his readers will have "a different Idea of Romance" from his, never before attempted in English, which will be "a comic Romance." He takes his term from Paul Scarron's *Romant Comique* (1651), the *Comical Romance* in Tom Brown's translation (1700), recently read, which augments Cervantes's authorial facetiousness and claims of "this true History,"[7] and sends its lovers chastely down the picaresque road disguised as brother and sister, in the amusingly incestuous twinship of romance that Fielding will exploit with Joseph and Fanny, the almost identical foundlings of romance from *Daphnis and Chloe* onward. His identical portraits gently parody those typical of Scudéry's romances (Shesgreen, 33–34; Maresca, 200–201), especially in their noses "inclining to the Roman" (I.viii; II.xii). In Joseph's nose and brawny physique, Fielding has again pictured himself both accurately and comically as romantic hero.

"Now a comic Romance," he writes, "is a comic Epic-Poem in Prose." From his bows toward the epic, the twentieth century has largely ignored his, and his readers', context: the vast French romances—which he names, and which had virtually shaped the fancies, manners, and idiom of English elegance—and the new romance of princess Pamela, the serving maid. He is not writing the high life of epic, which can live among modern realities only in mock heroics: "Indeed, no two Species of Writing can differ more widely than the Comic and the Burlesque," touches of which he has indulged here and there to amuse his classical readers. In his conclusion, he insists again on distinguishing his realistic comedy from "the Productions of Romance Writers on the one hand, and Burlesque Writers on the other." His new "Species of writing ... hitherto unattempted in our Language" avoids both the impossibilities of "the grave Romance" and the absurdities of the comic mock-epic. His comic romance will draw from the realities of ordinary life, as his friend Hogarth has done pictorially, to illustrate the vanity and hypocrisy everywhere and eternally evident.[8]

This comic realism he outlines in III.i, which, most likely written before his preface, stands as his Declaration of Independence for fiction. Unlike actual historians, he says, Cervantes has written "the History of the World in general," as have Scarron, Le Sage, Marivaux, and other authors of "true Histories," including the *Arabian Nights*. Fiction is truer than history. It illustrates the typical, the perennially true in human nature in all time and every country: "I describe not Men, but Manners; not an Individual, but a Species." One might add only that typicality is the very stuff of comedy, along with the celebration of life (which Wright and Langer point to)—that central romantic thread on which the comic typicalities are strung, and which *Pamela* seriously exploits: the unknown nobody's becoming somebody in happy marriage. Fielding keeps the wish fulfillment of all us Harry Lucklesses playfully comic, letting us know in his affectionate irony that our deep-seated yearning is real enough, but with no Richardsonian guarantee. Romance encapsulates the central psyche: one's secretly noble self, whom no one appreciates, crying for recognition and riches, especially in the classless world emerging as Fielding wrote, and surely representing his own déclassé impulse. His comic-romantic perspective acknowledges the comic impossibility of the ideal and romantic glories of life, yet affirms their existence and value.

Adams, like Quixote, comically embodies the romantic struggle of the ideal against the cruel realities. As with Quixote, we begin in laughter and end in admiration. For the Duke and Duchess who amuse themselves at Quixote's expense, Fielding gives us an actual practical-joking country squire—son-in-law of the Duchess of Marlborough, indeed (Wesleyan ed., xxiv)—who cruelly abuses Adams for a laugh, and we uncomfortably discover ourselves in company with the laughters at the noble in spirit. In fact, Fielding goes beyond Cervantes, first with Adams and then even with Slipslop, as true nobility rises within the comic bubble without bursting it. When Lady Booby threatens Adams with losing his livelihood if he proceeds to marry Joseph and Fanny, he answers: "I am in the Service of a Master who will never discard me for doing my Duty: And if the Doctor (for indeed I have never been able to pay for a Licence) thinks proper to turn me out of my Cure, G—will provide me, I hope, another." If necessary, he and his numerous family will work with their hands. "Whilst my Conscience is pure, I shall never fear what Man can do unto me" (IV.ii). Adams's comically honest parenthesis deepens the effect as it sustains the amusing characterization, and the scene returns to amusement as Adams awkwardly bows out, mistakenly thinking Lady Booby will understand.

Fielding never again equals this. Neither Quixote, his model, nor Jones to come must stand up for others against tyranny with all they have. And Fielding repeats this feat, in which comedy contains the feeling that would destroy it, when funny old never-to-be-loved Slipslop, the image of the selfish world, turns selfless in Joseph's defense—"I wish I was a great Lady for his sake"—and a chastened Lady Booby mildly bids her goodnight as "a comical Creature" (IV.vi). Evans well illustrates how in *Joseph Andrews* and *Tom Jones* comedy necessarily absorbs the tragic in its broader rendering of the "whole truth" ("World," "Comedy"). *Tom Jones* is the masterwork, of course—bigger, richer, wiser, more Olympian—but because of Adams and his comic depth here achieved, along with the very neatness of the parody, its enduring comic realism, and its joyous energy, *Joseph Andrews* achieves a perfection of its own.

In *Jonathan Wild* (1743), Fielding turns from comic romance for an uneven experiment in sardonic satire. As Digeon suggests, he patched it together for his *Miscellanies* (1743), during a time of sickness and trouble, from previous satirical attempts perhaps beginning as early as 1737, the bitter year when Walpole drove him from the stage. Indeed, a dialogue between Wild and his wife, little suiting them, carries a stage direction: *"These Words to be spoken with a very great Air, and Toss of the Head"* (III.viii).[9] Fielding takes his tone from Lucian, as he had in the dreary *Journey from This World to the Next*, also published in the *Miscellanies*. Although Fielding's Booth calls Lucian "the greatest in the Humorous Way, that ever the World produced" (*Amelia*, VIII,v), and although Fielding claims to have "formed his Stile upon that very Author" (*Covent-Garden Journal*, 52), his Lucianic writings are among his least attractive, uncongenial in a way he could not see.[10]

In *Jonathan Wild*, Fielding tries in a Lucianic-Swiftian way to emulate Gay's *Beggar's Opera* without the Scriblerian verve. Gay had already animated the standing Opposition parallel between Walpole, the "Great Man" of public power, and Wild (executed 24 May 1725), the "Great Man" of London's underworld. As Fielding says in his Preface, "the splendid Palaces of the Great are often no other than *Newgate* with the Mask on."

Defoe's pamphlet on Wild (1725), one of Fielding's sources (Irwin, 19), indicates the difficulty. Defoe "does not indeed make a jest of his story ... which is indeed a tragedy of itself, in a style of mockery and ridicule, but in a method agreeable to fact." Life down here is tragic, not to be viewed from Fielding's comic heights.[11] The vicious life of Newgate is too real for comedy, too dark for Fielding's satire on human foibles. It rises again in *Amelia*, after Fielding's exposure as magistrate, again to cloud his comic optimism.

Nevertheless, *Jonathan Wild* constantly reflects Fielding's characteristic situations, turns of style and thought, as it exposes his uncertainty. His real hero is Wild's victim, Thomas Heartfree, an older merchant-class Thomas Jones, innocently trusting hypocritical avarice; a Booth, married, with children, jailed for debt by the mighty to seduce his wife. Like Adams, Heartfree believes that *"a sincere Turk would be saved"* (IV.i). Like Jones, he extols a good conscience, "a Blessing which he who possesses can never be thoroughly unhappy" (III.v). Not harming others brings him "the Comfort I myself enjoy: For what a ravishing Thought! how replete with Extasy must the Consideration be, that the Goodness of God is engaged to reward me!" (III.x).[12] Fielding has idealized Heartfree from his honest friend, the jeweler and playwright George Lillo (Digeon, 121). But this is the serious middle-class world of Defoe and Richardson, essentially alien to Fielding, in spite of his generous condescension.

Fielding distinguishes "Greatness" from "Goodness" in his preface and opening chapter. The *"true Sublime in Human Nature"* combines greatness with goodness, but the world associates greatness only with the powerful rascal, the "Great Man." Fielding hopes to tell the world that greatness is not goodness (cf. Hatfield, "Puffs," 264–65). But as Dyson remarks (22), no one can believe Wild's great roguery generally typical enough to be of much interest, and Heartfree's goodness is both unconvincing and sentimental.

Of course, Fielding manages some genuine comedy here and there, especially in Mrs. Heartfree's disclaimer of pleasure in repeating compliments to herself (IV.xi). But all in all, *Jonathan Wild* strains at ideas already overworked—Walpole had fallen from power the previous year. Fielding, in ill health and with his wife desperately ill, has tried to clear his desk for his *Miscellanies*, make some badly needed money, and end his career as writer:

> And now, my good-natured Reader, recommending my Works to your Candour, I bid you heartily farewell; and take this with you, that you may never be interrupted in the reading these Miscellanies, with that Degree of Heart-ach which hath often discomposed me in the writing them. (Preface, *Miscellanies*)

A year later, in his preface to his sister's *David Simple* (July 1744), Fielding reiterated his farewell. But before long (Wesleyan ed., xxxviii), Lyttelton prompted *Tom Jones*, with financial support. "It was by your Desire that I first thought of such a Composition," writes Fielding in his Dedication. Lyttelton evidently had proposed something new, a novel recommending "Goodness and Innocence" and the "Beauty of Virtue." Fielding adds its rewards: "that solid inward Comfort of Mind," the loss of which "no Acquisitions of Guilt can compensate." He also adds the lesson most likely to succeed, the one taught Tom Heartfree, "that Virtue and Innocence can scarce ever be injured but by Indiscretion." Prudence is the theme, because "it is much easier to make good Men wise, than to make bad Men good."

Again Fielding's hero, handsome, impetuous, generous, is comically romantic self-portraiture, amusing but now admonitory, played opposite an affectionate version of his dead wife. Again, a Cervantic idealist and realist, now reversed as young Jones and old Partridge, travel English roads in picaresque satire. The story is again the essence of romance: the mysterious unknown foundling, with the qualities and white skin of noble knighthood, discovers identity, paternity, riches, and marriage. Fielding called his new book *The History of a Foundling* as late as six months before publication, and others continued to call it *The Foundling* after it appeared (Wesleyan ed., xliii–xlvi). Indeed his title, usually foreshortened, is actually *The History of Tom Jones, a Foundling*. To keep the comic-romantic expectation before us, across the tops of its pages marches not "The History of Tom Jones," but "The History of a Foundling." But Fielding nevertheless seems to find this generally different from *Joseph Andrews*, with its comically positive Christian championship. *Tom Jones*, though philosophically positive, is morally cautionary. Be wary, or your goodness comes to naught. The old Adam should grow wise before he is old. In this cautionary balance and wiser view, Fielding culminated the Augustan perspective.

Martin Price epitomizes (3) the neoclassic period in the concepts of *balance* and *the detached individual*. Irony and satire stake out for the individual the ground on which he dare not dogmatize. Any stand is extreme, smacking of Commonwealth enthusiasm and bloody fanaticism. With orthodoxy shattered, the emerging individuals of either the middle-class Defoes or the shaken aristocrats must regain their footing, the Defoes in engagement, the aristocrats in detachment. *Tom Jones* embodies the detached Augustan's vision. As Pope in his *Essay on Man* (1733–34) surveyed the cosmic maze in gentlemanly ironic detachment, balancing deism and orthodoxy in a synthesis of divine immanence and contemporary psychology, so Fielding works out the ways of Providence in this conflicting world.

Battestin well makes "The Argument of Design."[13] This evidently unjust and accidental world has really a Providential order. The mighty maze has a plan, comically and affectionately fulfilled. Fielding had declared Pope *"the inimitable Author of the* Essay on Man," who *"taught me a System of Philosophy in* English *Numbers"* (Fielding's preface to *Plutus, the God of Riches*, 1742). Fielding's literary creation reflects the providential order beyond our limited vision:

> All Nature is but Art, unknown to thee;
> All Chance, Direction, which thou canst not see;
> All Discord, Harmony, not understood;
> All partial Evil, universal Good.... (Pope, *Essay*, I:289–92)

Fielding illustrates this *concordia discors*, the Horatian harmony of discords (*Ep.* I.xii.19) that one finds repeatedly echoed in Pope and other Augustans, with a superbly comic "as if," which reflects both the ultimate resolution and its daily dissonance. Chance is really direction: a stupid guide misdirects Jones from the sea toward the army and Upton; Sophia chances upon the same guide to change her direction toward Jones; Blifil's betrayal works out Jones's identity and marriage with Sophia, the name of the "wisdom" he is to obtain (Powers, 667; Battestin, "Wisdom," 204–205; Harrison, 112). Fielding's very sentences reflect the balancing of opposites, the ordered containment of discords, of Pope's couplets as well as of his serenely balancing philosophy (Alter, 61; Battestin, "Design," 297).

All the thorny vines of Nature are really God's Art. And art, in its providential ordering, reflects God's universe. Providence orders the macrocosm; Prudence (semantically linked in Latin) orders the microcosm, man (Battestin, "Design," 191). Fielding the novelist plays God to the world of his creation, illustrating God's ways to man. Fielding sums this in a crucial passage, pausing with ironic detachment in the architectural middle of his comic confusion. He warns the reader not to criticize incidents as "foreign to our main Design" until he or she sees how they fit the whole, for "This Work may, indeed, be considered as a great Creation of our own," of which any fault-finder is a "Reptile" (X.i), a proud and imperceptive Satan in the creator's garden. The analogy, he says in ironic humility, may be too great, "but there is, indeed, no other." The artist brings order out of chaos and reflects God's providential order. Form symbolizes meaning (Battestin, "Design," 301).

Fielding's remarkable ironic balancing of opposites, first comically coupled for him in Cervantes, illustrates both the universal harmonizing of discords and the Augustan sense that opposites mark the norm without defining it: the principle "of Contrast," says Fielding, "runs through all the Works of Creation" (V.i). Everyone notices the contrasting pairing: Tom and Blifil, Allworthy and Western, each with a comically learned spinster sister; Sophia and Mrs. Fitzpatrick, as well as Sophia contrasted successively with her worse and worse opposites, Molly, Mrs. Waters, Lady Bellaston; Thwackum and Square; even the two brothers Blifil and Nightingale. Everything balances as formal artifice ironically orders daily chaos: six books for the country, six for the road, six for the city, as Digeon first noted (175, n.2). Hilles diagrams the remarkable structural balances on the scheme of a Palladian mansion, of which Ralph Allen's at Bath furnished one of the models for Allworthy's—a wing of six rooms angled up to the central six, a wing of six rooms angled down.[14]

For his architectural reflection of providential order, Fielding has heightened the linear episodic structure of *Joseph Andrews* into the arch of formal comedy. The episodic scene from *Don Quixote in England* now becomes the centerpiece. The high hurly-burly of sex and fisticuffs in the inn at Upton spans Books IX and X at the novel's mathematical center. As in the play, our heroine, running off in pursuit of her lover on the eve of forced marriage, arrives at the inn where he is, both lovers unaware of the other's presence. Fielding again comically contrasts sex and love, as Mrs. Slipslop's purpose with Joseph climaxes with Mrs. Waters and Tom, and bedrooms are scrambled as wildly as those concluding *Joseph Andrews*. As in the play, a foxhunting squire with his hounds rides up in pursuit, now converted from the unwanted suitor into Western, the heroine's father. The actual name *Upton* coincides with Fielding's peak of comic complexity (Wright, 89–90). It even seems the top of a geographical arch, as Sophia pursues Tom northward and then Tom pursues Sophia southward.

Fielding combines his favorite dramatic plot of the worthy rake and the heiress with the basic romantic story of the foundling, both in hopeless courtly love. *Love in Several Masques* has proliferated into a novel, complete with the country lover pursuing his mistress into the wicked city, an element repeated in three other plays (*The Temple Beau*, 1730; *The Lottery*, 1732; *The Universal Gallant*, 1735). In fact, four plays from Fielding's burgeoning year of 1730 awaken in *Tom Jones* nineteen years later. Here again is the wicked brother bearing false witness to defraud the hero of his birthright (*The Temple Beau*), the threat of inadvertent incest through unknown identity (*The Coffee-House Politician*, *The Wedding Day*, written c. 1730), and especially the comic pattern of discovered identity already borrowed from romance for *The Author's Farce*.

As readers have frequently noticed, Fielding balances two retrospective stories precisely on either side of his central theatrical peak: a lesson for Tom, a lesson for Sophia. The first is another *descensus Averno*, as if Fielding had lifted Wilson's account of wasted youth from the middle of *Joseph Andrews*, put it before his Cervantic inn, and also put it on Mazard Hill to suggest the greater peak to come. In *Joseph Andrews*, our travelers descend "a very steep Hill"; now Jones and Partridge, their quixotic counterparts, ascend "a very steep Hill" because Jones wants to cultivate his romantic "melancholy Ideas" by the "Solemn Gloom which the Moon casts on all Objects" (VIII.x). Partridge fears ghosts. They see a light and come to a cottage. Jones knocks without initial response, and Partridge cries that "the People must be all dead." Like Wilson, the Man of the Hill has retired from the world of debauchery and betrayal, which he describes for Jones and the reader. But Wilson, with wife and children, lives like people "in the Golden Age," as Adams remarks (III.iv); the Man of the Hill is an embittered recluse. Young Jones rejects his misanthropy and urges Fielding's lesson of prudence—the old man would have continued his faith in humanity had he not been "incautious in the placing your Affection" (VIII.xv). In his *descensus*, Jones has learned the truth. On the other side of Upton, Sophia hears from her cousin Mrs. Fitzpatrick a tale of elopement and amours that illustrates what she should not do with Jones.

Upton emphasizes the balanced theatrical architecture of *Tom Jones*. And many have noticed the theatricality of the city section (Cross, II:202; Haage, 152). Two scenes—with Lady Bellaston behind the bed, then Honour, then both—are pure theater (XIV.ii, XV.vii). Moreover, Lady Bellaston descends directly from Fielding's versions of Congreve's Lady Wishfort, beginning with Lady Trap in his first play. Tom Jones courts her to get at her ward, just as Mrs. Fitzpatrick urges him to court Mrs. Western (XVI.ix), the very ruse of her own ruin (XI.iv), as Fielding thrice deploys Tom Merital's strategem, acquired from Congreve. But Fielding shapes the whole novel in the abstract pattern of five-act comedy: Act I, exposition; Act II, intrigue; Act III, climactic complications; Act IV, unraveling toward disaster; Act V, depression shooting upward into triumph—the playlike ending already traced in Joseph's reprieve from Platonic celibacy and Heartfree's from the gallows.

If we treat the central six books as Act III, dividing the first and the last six books in halves, we find startling references to the theater at each break, except the invocation to Fame that begins the London section, or "Act IV." At "Act V," where the stage expects the final darkness before dawn, Fielding talks, first about the playwright's problem of prologues (XVI.i) and then, in the next Book, most facetiously about the playwright's problem of concluding a comedy or tragedy, and about his own in extricating "this Rogue, whom we have unfortunately made our Heroe," whom he may have to leave to the hangman, though he will do what he can, since "the worst of his Fortune" still lies ahead (XVII.i). "Tragedy is the image of Fate, as comedy is of Fortune," says Susanne Langer (p.333). Indeed, the formal structure of comedy, superimposed on the novel's more realistic vagaries, comments more quizzically on Fortune than a simple affirmation. It sustains with an ironic detachment Fielding's demonstration that the partial evils, the accidents that happen (in his frequent phrase), interweave fortunately in "universal Good." As "we may frequently observe in Life," says Fielding, "the greatest Events are produced by a nice Train of little Circumstances" (XVIII.ii). The author, like the Craftsman of Creation, is shaping our nearsighted joys and blunders, the realities of life.

Life does have odd coincidences. Apparent evils do often prove blessings as life flows on. For Fielding, as Stevick shows, history has meaning, just as his comic "true History" reflects a meaningful actuality. There are people, who, like Jones, have in fact accidentally taken the right road. Possessions, like Sophia's little book with a £100 bill in its leaves, have in fact been lost and luckily recovered—perhaps have even changed a course of life, as when Jones turns from the army to find Sophia. Acquaintances do turn up in restaurants and airports, like Partridge, Mrs. Waters, or Dowling, who seems to dowl his way through apparently random events to conclude the mystery. Accident, bad and good, which Ehrenpreis finds a weakness (22ff.), is actually the very stuff in life from which comedy creates its mimesis.

Fielding's third-person detachment, on which comedy also depends, may seem to deny the inner life that Defoe and Richardson opened for the novel with first-person narration (Watt, *Rise*). But actually, we are perceiving psychic complexities exactly as we do in life—from the outside, from what people do and say. Dowling, apparently only a comically busy lawyer, proves a complex rascal in blackmailing Blifil and keeping Tom from his birthright, yet he is affable and even sympathetic. Bridget, the sour old maid, actually attracts all eligible males. Her secret passions, simmering toward forty, not only beget the illegitimate Tom but thwart her plans for him (Crane, 119) as, again pregnant, she rushes to marry Blifil, whom she has evidently trapped— with his calculated concurrence. She takes a sly pleasure in having Thwackum whip her love-child, when Allworthy is away, for the psychic strain he has caused her, but never her legitimate son, whom she hates, as Fielding tells us directly. She later attracts not only Thwackum but Square, with whom (now that she is past the threat of pregnancy) she has an affair—from which Fielding turns our eyes even as he ironically confirms it, attributing it to malicious gossip with which he will not blot his page (III.vi). Before Tom is eighteen, he has openly replaced Square in her affections, with a hint of the incest that plays comically through Tom's affairs (Hutchens, 40), incurring Square's hatred and his own expulsion from Paradise.[15] Fielding's psychological realism abounds in little self-deceptions: Sophia's about Jones is neatly symbolized in her muff, which appears when love blooms, turns up in Jones's empty bed at Upton, and accompanies him to London, an amusingly impudent visual pun in pubic slang (Johnson, 129–38). Jones has put his hands into it, as Honour reports: "La, says I, Mr. *Jones*, you will stretch my Lady's Muff and spoil it" (IV.xiv).

But Fielding's implied psychology fails with Allworthy. From the first, readers have found him bland if not unreal: the ideal benevolist and ultimate judge, taken in by duplicity, throwing out the good. Fielding seems to have intended a more dignified comic Adams. Allworthy talks "a little whimsically" about his dead wife, for which his neighbors roundly arraign him (I.ii). And we first meet him indeed in a bedroom, absentmindedly in his nightshirt, contemplating "the Beauty of Innocence"—the foundling sleeping in his bed—while Fielding wonderfully suggests that Mrs. Wilkins, "who, tho' in the 52d Year of her Age, vowed she had never beheld a Man without his Coat," believes she was summoned for another purpose (I.iii). Had Fielding sustained this comic view of the imperceptive idealist—he must make him imperceptive at any rate—his book would have fulfilled the perfection it very nearly achieves. But except for some touches about Thwackum's piety and Square's "Philosophical Temper" on his misperceived deathbed (V.viii), Allworthy fades from comic view.

As Hutchens says, Fielding takes an ironic and "lawyer-like delight in making facts add up to something unexpected" (30), and he does the same with the facts that convey personality. Mrs. Western, the comic six-foot chaperone, proud of her little learning and political misinformation, is also the superannuated coquette. Fitzpatrick has fooled her; she treasures in her memory a highwayman who took her money and earrings "at the same Time d—ning her, and saying, 'such handsome B—s as you, don't want Jewels to set them off, and be d—nd to you'" (VII.ix). To avoid forced marriage with Lord Fellamar, Sophia slyly flatters her with the many proposals she claims to have refused. "You are now but a young Woman," Sophia says, one who would surely not yield to the first title offered. Yes, says Mrs. Western, "I was called the cruel *Parthenissa*," and she runs on about "her Conquests and her Cruelty" for "near half an Hour" (XVII.iv). And Western, with his vigor, his Jacobite convictions, his Somerset dialect, his views as narrow as the space between his horse's ears, who has cruelly driven his wife to the grave, yet stirs our compassion as Fielding reveals the feeling that threatens and heightens the comic surface in a Falstaff or Quixote, as he had done with Adams and Slipslop. Western's comic limitations reveal their pathos in London, where— lonely, beaten by Egglane, bewildered—he pleads with Sophia:

> 'Why wout ask, *Sophy?*' cries he, 'when dost know I had rather hear thy Voice, than the Music of the best Pack of Dogs in *England*.—Hear thee, my dear little Girl! I hope I shall hear thee as long as I live; for if I was ever to lose that Pleasure, I would not gee a Brass Varden to live a Moment longer. Indeed, *Sophy*, you do not know how I love you, indeed you don't, or you never could have run away, and left your poor Father, who hath no other Joy, no other Comfort upon Earth but his little *Sophy*.' At these Words the Tears stood in his Eyes; and *Sophia*, (with the Tears streaming from hers) answered, 'Indeed, my dear Papa, I know you have loved me tenderly'.... (XVI.ii)

And the scene soon returns to full comedy as Western leaves in his usual thunder of misunderstanding.

This is the comic irony of character, the comedy of limited view, of the *idée fixe*, which plays against our wider perception and the narrator's omniscience, and in turn makes us part of the human comedy as we think we see all but learn that we do not.[16] Fielding's omniscience guides and misguides us constantly; in his lawyerlike way, he presents the evidence and conceals the mystery, tempting our misunderstandings along with those of his characters, whom we believe less percipient than ourselves, or pretending ironically not to understand motives to guide our understanding: "Whether moved by Compassion, or by Shame, or by whatever other Motive, I cannot tell," he will write of a landlady who has changed her hostile tune when Jones appears like an Adonis and a gentleman (VIII.iv). This is Cervantes's mock-historian elevated to mock-psychological ignorance in the ironic service of psychology. This is Fielding's Cervantic omniscience, which delights us by showing in comic fiction life as it is, comic in selfish imperception, comic in providential blessing.

Fielding's commenting authorship has reached its full ironic power and elegance, and much more pervasively than in *Joseph Andrews*. The earlier twentieth century scorned this kind of "intrusive author." But McKillop (123) and, especially, Booth have well certified the central impact and necessity of Fielding's authorial presence. He has become his own most worthy character, amiable, wise, benevolent, literate, balanced between extremes, engaging us constantly through a long and pleasant journey until "we find, lying beneath our amusement at his playful mode of farewell, something of the same feeling we have when we lose a close friend, a friend who has given us a gift which we can never repay" (Booth, 218). He has shown us the world of Sophias and Toms, Blifils and pettifoggers, but he has also shown us that it contains a wonderfully ironic and compassionate intelligence we have come to know, which is something very like the wisdom of a benevolent God surveying our selfish vices and romantic yearnings.

Booth, of course, insists on the "implied author," a fictive creation clear of biographical irrelevancies. When the author refers to himself as infirm, Booth says that it "matters not in the least" whether Fielding was infirm when he wrote that sentence: "It is not Fielding we care about, but the narrator created to speak in his name" (218). But I dare say readers do care about Fielding as Fielding—Keats as Keats, Whitman as Whitman, Joyce as Joyce—else why our innumerable researches? Booth also oddly implies that Fielding's introductory chapters, which we can read straight through "leaving out the story of Tom," comprise all the narrator's "seemingly gratuitous appearances" (216). But Fielding actually "intrudes" on every page as the authorial voice ironically displaying life's ironies or commenting earnestly, with or without the "I."[17]

Fielding clearly considers that he himself addresses his readers, however much he may pretend, in the Cervantic way, that his history is true, that Allworthy may still live in Somerset for all he knows, or that he has given us "the Fruits of a very painful Enquiry, which for thy Satisfaction we have made into this Matter" (IX.vii). He is playful or straight, facetiously elevated or skeptically glum, exactly as he would be in conversation or anecdote, writing as if he were actually present—as indeed he was when he read his book aloud to Lyttelton and others before publication. He hopes that some girl in ages hence will, "under the fictitious name of *Sophia*," read "the real Worth which once existed in my *Charlotte*," and that he will be read "when the little Parlour in which I sit this Instant, shall be reduced to a worse furnished Box," and all this in a wonderfully mockheroic invocation conveying his actual aims and beliefs as a writer (XIII.i). As Miller says ("Style," 265), "he is Henry Fielding all right." As with Pope—who characteristically begins by addressing a friend, who refers to his garden, his grotto, his ills, his aims, and concludes again in autobiography—the "implied author" seems unnecessary, or irrelevant. Fielding is projecting himself, playing the kind of role we all must play in whatever we do, as teacher, citizen, neighbor, fellow trying to write a scholarly essay, or whatnot. He dramatizes himself, of course, but in a way quite different from those partial versions of himself he comically (or guiltily) dramatized in Harry-Luckless, Andrews, Jones, and Billy Booth.

As Miller well says, Fielding in his comic romance gives us a seamless weave of the real and ideal with life inhering "down to the smallest particle" ("Rhetoric," 235). Many have admired these verbal particles that reflect the universe. Take his "solid comfort." Here is the common reality of life, verbally and emotionally. *Shamela's* Oliver upholds "all the solid Comforts of their Lives." In his preface to the *Miscellanies*, Fielding says that his wife, dangerously ill, gives him "all the solid Comfort of my Life." In *Tom Jones*, he writes to Lyttelton of the "solid inward Comfort of Mind" that will reward benevolence and that Tom will aver as "solid Content" (XII.x). Yet Fielding acknowledges the universal ambiguity even in sincere belief, playing ironically with his favorite term in an extended passage revealing the motives of Bridget and Captain Blifil, who—bearded to the eyes, built like a plowman—bristles virility: Bridget expects a solid phallic comfort; Blifil, the comfort of hard cash.

> She imagined, and perhaps very wisely, that she should enjoy more agreeable Minutes with the Captain, than with a much prettier Fellow; and forewent the Consideration of pleasing her Eyes, in order to procure herself much more solid Satisfaction....
>
> The Captain likewise very wisely preferred the more solid Enjoyments he expected with his Lady, to the fleeting Charms of Person. (I.xi)

That "Minutes" speaks sexual volumes.[18]

With *Amelia* (1751), the realities darken beyond comic affirmation.[19] The Augustan certainties, earned in irony, have faded into the doubts and sentimentalities of the century's second half. Free will now enters the providential scheme (Knight, 389), infinitely more chancey than the happy accidents of comedy. Individual responsibility replaces comic Fortune, now only an "imaginary Being." Each must shape his own luck in an "Art of Life" that resembles the cagey and protective maneuvering of chess. What we blame on Fortune we should blame on "quitting the Directions of Prudence," now active as well as cautionary, for "the blind Guidance of a predominant Passion" (I.i). The world of *Tom Jones*, which had darkened from country to city, reversing the progress of *Joseph Andrews*, now opens in the Newgate of *Jonathan Wild*, with a diseased and vicious Mrs. Slipslop, no longer funny, as Blear-eyed Moll. The subject is the "various Accidents which befel a very worthy Couple," as the husband redeems "foolish Conduct" by "struggling manfully with Distress," which is "one of the noblest Efforts of Wisdom and Virtue"—a struggle and virtue the hero hardly exhibits. In his Dedication, Fielding says that he also wants to expose "the most glaring Evils," public and private, that "infest this Country," and here, at least, he succeeds.

Fielding has attempted another new species of writing. For the first time, he adopts an epic, the *Aeneid*, for his "noble model" as he tells us in the *Covent-Garden Journal* (Jensen, ed., I.186). His serious subject can now sustain the epic parallel his comic romance had prohibited as burlesque mock-heroics. In his Court of Censorial Inquiry, "a grave Man" stands up to defend "poor Amelia" from "the Rancour with which she hath been treated by the Public." He avows "that of all my Offspring she is my favourite Child," on whom he has "bestowed a more than ordinary Pains" (186). Fielding's strange favoritism doubtless owes to his loving fictionalization of his dead wife, complete with scarred nose, whom he elevates to his title and make the virtuous lodestone (Wendt, "Virtue"):

> H. Fielding [writes Lady Mary Wortley Montagu] has given a true picture of himself and his first wife, in the characters of Mr. and Mrs. Booth, some compliments to his own figure excepted; and, I am persuaded, several of the incidents he mentions are real matters of fact. (Cross, II.328)

Fielding is clearly working out some remorse, perhaps for the same infidelities both religious and sexual through which Booth suffers.

Powers demonstrates how closely Fielding parallels the *Aeneid*. Like Virgil, Fielding begins *in medias res* with the long, retrospective first-person accounts of the central action that are typical of epic and new in Fielding.[20] Powers matches characters and actions throughout the book, beginning with Miss Matthews (Dido), who seduces Booth (like Aencas, separated from his wife with a new order to establish), though Powers omits remarking how starkly the chamber in Newgate reflects Virgil's sylvan cave. Fielding's masquerade at Ranelagh matches Aeneas's *descensus*, though moved from *Aeneid* VI to *Amelia* X, where Aeneas meets the resentful shade of Dido and Booth the resentful Miss Matthews. The masquerader's conventional "Do you know me?" in "squeaking Voice" (*Tom Jones*, XIII.vii; *The Masquerade*, 190) now becomes Miss Matthews's caustic "Do'st thou not yet know me?" (X.ii). In the end, Fielding replaces the pious Aeneas's defeat of violent Turnus with Booth's escaping a duel and affirming a new order in his Christian conversion.

As Cross notes, however (II.325), Fielding also characteristically reworks his plot from three of his plays. From *The Temple Beau* (1730), he had already taken the evil brother defrauding the good of his inheritance, with an accomplice, as models for Blifil and Dowling. He feminizes this for *Amelia*. In the play, a father dies and disinherits his heir, abroad in Paris. His brother, through a false witness, had blackened the heir's character "and covered his own notorious vices under the appearance of innocence" (*Works*, VIII.115). Amelia's older sister likewise vilifies her while abroad. She learns in Paris of her mother's death and her disinheritance. But now sister Betty and her accomplices forge a new will reversing the mother's decree to leave her and not Amelia penniless, as Fielding adds a touch from actuality. Four years after the play, Fielding eloped to marry against a mother's wishes, as does Booth. Similarly, his wife's mother died soon after, but nevertheless left her estate to his wife, cutting off her elder sister with a shilling (Cross, II.330).

In *The Coffee-House Politician* (1730), Fielding also foresketches his and Booth's elopement, and introduces the good magistrate who untangles things in *Jonathan Wild* and becomes another self-portrait in *Amelia* (Cross, II.322): the unnamed justice who, about to dine, hears the evidence and resolves, "Tho' it was then very late, and he had been fatigued all the Morning with public Business, to postpone all Refreshment 'till he had discharged his Duty" (XII.vi). Fielding concludes his play with his justice: "Come, gentlemen, I desire you would celebrate this day at my house." Similarly, the justice in *Amelia*:

> Whether *Amelia's* Beauty, or the Reflexion on the remarkable Act of Justice he had performed, or whatever Motive filled the Magistrate with extraordinary good Humour, and opened his Heart and Cellars, I will not determine; but he gave them ... hearty Welcome ... nor did the Company rise from Table till the Clock struck eleven. (XII.vii)

*The Coffee-House Politician* indeed frames *Amelia's* plot, with the instrumental justice at the end, and at the beginning a half-pay army captain, on his way through London streets at night to a rendezvous for elopement who aids a person attacked and is jailed as attacker by a venal judge through false witness—exactly as Booth lands in Newgate at the outset.

*The Modern Husband* (1732) furnishes Fielding's central matter, already worked in *Jonathan Wild*: two influential men, one a lord, ruin and jail a husband in order to seduce his virtuous wife. The husband has an affair and suffers a painful conscience. His extravagance becomes Booth's addictive gambling. His wife's fear of a duel, which keeps the lord's advances secret, becomes the actual challenge Amelia keeps secret. In play and novel, the wife's constancy inspires contrition, confession, and reform. The play's contrasting "modern" couple, who collude in adultery for extortion, become the Trents of *Amelia*.[21]

Except at beginning and end, Fielding's sustained epic parallel has no force, as it would have in the comic contrasts of a mock-epic or a *Ulysses*. It passes unnoticed into Fielding's romance motifs, now similarly forsaken by comedy and indeed more prevalent. Booth has himself smuggled into his lady's hostile household in a basket straight from the flowery thirteenth-century romance of *Floris and Blancheflour*.[22] As Maurice Johnson commented to me in a letter (26 April 1965), this smuggled entry midway in

Book II matches precisely the Grecian warriors' entry into the enemy's citadel inside the Trojan horse, midway in *Aeneid* II. But implausible romance obliterates the epic.

Indeed, in spite of the book's seamy realism (Sherburn, *"Amelia,"* 2; Butt, 27), Fielding's first instance of comic self-portraiture, *The Author's Farce*, now lends surprising and uneasy touches of romance to this more extended autobiographical fiction, no longer comic. Lady Mary, noting the autobiography, complained of *Amelia*, along with *Tom Jones*: "All these sort of books ... place a merit in extravagant passions, and encourage young people to hope for impossible events ... as much out of nature as fairy treasures" (*Letters*, III.93, quoted in Blanchard, 102). The burlesque of wonderful endings, which Fielding initiated in his *Farce* and continued playfully in *Joseph Andrews* and *Tom Jones*, now indeed becomes the fairytale strained by realism. In the play, Harry Luckless has pawned a jewel. His servant's return to the pawnshop enables a bystander to find him and disclose his identity and his kingdom far from London's unjust indifference.

In *Amelia*, this hero's jewel has multiplied. Fielding modifies an episode from Ariosto's *Orlando Furioso*—the story of Giocondo (Canto 28), the same that gives Spenser his Squire of Dames—in which the hero, departing reluctantly from his wife, forgets a little jeweled cross, a farewell gift. Booth, on his departure for war, forgets a little casket, similarly given, which should have contained a jeweled picture of Amelia, lost a month before. Her foster brother and silent courtly adorer—in the submerged incestuous way of romance, which is no longer comic as with Joseph and Fanny—has stolen it. Nothing so clearly illustrates Fielding's fall from comedy as the contrast between this scene and that with Lady Booby in bed and Joseph Andrews beside it. Now, the new noble servant Joseph Atkinson is abed, visited by Mrs. Booth. Fielding's instinctive self-revision—the Josephs, the As, the Bs— here turns romance lugubrious. Atkinson, tears gushing, returns the picture to his lady, who has come to her poor lovesick knight, with words widely adapted—in fiction and actuality both, one suspects—from that famous and monstrous romance so prominent on Fielding's early blacklist, La Calprenède's *Cassandra*: "that Face which, if I had been the Emperor of the World ..." (XI.vi.)[23] Later, Amelia pawns the picture; a second visit to the pawnshop discloses that a bystander has identified her by it, and his information leads to her long-lost inheritance and an estate far from London's unjust indifference.

Harry Luckless's ancient dream of the disinherited and the happy accidents of comedy dissolve into pathos and implausibility in the tragic world of *Amelia*. As Rawson says (70), Amelia's despairs carry the novel's conviction: "There are more bad People in the World, and they will hate you for your Goodness," wails Amelia to her "poor little Infants"; "There is an End of all Goodness in the World"; "We have no Comfort, no Hope, no

Friend left" (IV.iii, VII.x, VIII.ix). This is the modern existential woe of Clarissa:

> What a world is this! What is there in it desirable? The good we hope for, so strangely mix'd, that one knows not what to wish for: And one half of Mankind tormenting the other, and being tormented themselves in Tormenting! (Richardson's *Clarissa* II, Letter vii)

Augustan detachment becomes sentimental involvement. The ironic providential overseer has departed, leaving a less frequent sociologist:

> ... I myself (remember, Critic, it was in my Youth) had a few Mornings before seen that very identical Picture of all those ingaging Qualities in Bed with a Rake at a Bagnio, smoaking Tobacco, drinking Punch, talking Obscenity, and swearing and cursing with all the Impudence and Impiety of the lowest and most abandoned Trull of a Soldier. (I.vi)

The reader, as Coley notes (249–50), has likewise diminished from the "ingenious" to the "good-natured" who enjoys a "tender Sensation." Goodness must demonstrate its sensitivity in faintings and tears (Ribble). Parson Harrison, a realistic Adams, replaces the author as evaluative intelligence, and yet in his uncomic blindness, which drives Amelia to despair, he becomes one of Fielding's most plausible characters in this new indeterminacy of characterization (Coolidge). The quixotic Adams, upholding virtue, now also becomes Colonel Bath, the swordsman upholding only the passé code of honor—pistols were to be the weapons of James's duel.[24] The type no longer represents the comic universals in humanity. The limited view is no longer comically typical but painfully characteristic of human imperfection.

Indeterminacy replaces comic truth in typicality. The psychological complexities authorially implied in a Bridget now become the unreliable testimony of a Mrs. Bennet. Booth agonizes and develops, as against the characteristic comic changelessness of Andrews and Jones (Coley, 251). This is a new age; subjective consciousness breaks through Augustan order and objectivity. Human nature is no longer everywhere the same. Hume's solipsistic feeling has overturned reason, and Hume is clearly Fielding's unmentioned antagonist as he attempts to adjust the new philosophy to the providential Christianity it so profoundly unsettled (Battestin, "Problem").

Booth's Epicurean fatalism wavers toward atheism. Chance is no longer providential direction nor a "blind Impulse or Direction of Fate." Man acts as his uppermost passion dictates and can "do no otherwise" (I.iii; cf.

Thomas). Booth is a prisoner, psychically and physically, throughout the book—limited at best to the Verge of Court (Lepage; Wendt, "Virtue," 146; Battestin, "Problem," 631). In the end, Barrow's sermons free Booth from his passional fatalism, as Harrison frees him from custody for his providential reward. But Fielding's demonstration contradicts his theory that the will can shape the passions and one's fate. Hume's emotive philosophy has persuaded him more than he recognizes. Dr. Harrison bases his strongest argument for religion on Hume's passional doctrine, which Fielding had set out to refute (Battestin, "Problem," 632–33). Harrison asserts that men act from their passions, and that "the strongest of these Passions; Hope and Fear," support the truth of religion (XII.v). Booth converts, and Providence fulfills the dream of escape to Eden with the affluent lady, in the line of Luckless's Harriot, Wilson's Harriet Hearty, Heartfree's Mrs. Heartfree, and Jones's Sophia.

From the first play to last novel, Fielding repeats himself perhaps more than any major writer, working and reworking literary conventions as living paradigms. Even amid the sentimentalities in *Amelia*, his fictive truth persuades us that life is like this: selfish, conceited, agonized, wishful, looking for philosophical certainty. The primordial foundling of romance lives in our dreaming self-pity. The noble Quixote lives in our ideals. When Fielding insulated aspiration in comedy, ironically acknowledging both its truth and probable unfulfillment, he achieved the incomparable *Joseph Andrews* and *Tom Jones*.

## NOTES

1. Genealogists deny his family's connection to the royal Hapsburgs (Cross, 1.2–3), but Fielding and his contemporaries assumed it. "Most members of the family ... have uniformly added the quartering of Hapsburg and displayed their arms upon the double headed eagle of the Holy Roman Empire" (Henley, ed., XVI.xlvi). Fielding used the double eagle as his seal on at least one letter. Oddly, Hogarth's portrait of Fielding shows an unmistakable Hapsburg lower lip. Battestin has recently identified another probable portrait ("Pictures").

2. I borrow extensively throughout from my essays listed in "Works Cited." Historical details and many other points originate in Cross. Texts are Henley for plays; Wesleyan for *Joseph Andrews* and *Tom Jones*; first editions for *Shamela*, *Jonathan Wild*, and *Amelia*.

3. See Evans on the *Whole Duty of Man*, a book central to Fielding's charitable Christianity since childhood. Shamela, like Pamela, approves it but with the major duty of charity missing, and Whitefield condemned it as useless for the Grace of being born again.

4. Paulson, *Satire*, 103–04; Brooks, 161; my "Irony," 142–43; Goldberg, 146–47, 232–33.

5. Golden sees in Fielding's older women assaulting the heroes "the same stuff as the witches of child lore"; the aggressive males are ogres, "grotesques of adults in the child's fantasy" (145). But this wholly ignores the comic, adult perspective.

6. Originating in the *Odyssey* and taken over by Lucian and the romances as well—Ariosto sends Rinaldo to the moon; Cervantes sends Quixote down the cave of Montesinos and both Sancho and his ass down another cavern—the *descensus* became an Augustan favorite: Swift's Glubbdubdrib, Pope's Cave of Spleen (*Rape*) and Elysian shade (*Dunciad*), Fielding's *Author's Farce* and *Journey from This World to the Next*. For the long prevalence of the *descensus*, see Boyce.

7. Lucian also wrote a satiric *Vera historia*, a "true history," and, like Fielding, claimed a new way of writing (Coley, 241). But Fielding's phrase and manner comes directly from Cervantes, underlined by Scarron's more frequent reiteration; see my "Comic Romances."

8. The twentieth century takes "comic epic in prose" as Fielding's generic category, ignoring his defining term, "comic romance," as it also overlooks his romantic plot and Cervantic perspective. Neither he nor his contemporaries thought of his novels as epics, or even as "comic epics" like the *Dunciad*, from which he borrows his remarks on Homer's mock-heroic *Margites*, now "entirely lost." Pope's "Martinus Scriblerus of the Poem" in turn borrows, tongue in cheek, from Aristotle (*Poetics*, IV.12). But Aristotle does not mention loss. Pope says "tho' now unhappily lost." Fielding's similar reference in his preface to *David Simple* has "tho' it be unhappily lost," indicating Pope as his source. As Goldberg (7) and Miller (*Romance*, 8, 16) indicate, *epic* for Fielding means simply "extended narrative." This, for the eighteenth century, was indeed the primary meaning. Johnson's primary definition of *epic* in his *Dictionary* (1755) is: "Narrative; comprising narrations, not acted, but rehearsed." In fact, Fielding has taken "comic epic in prose" from Cervantes's defense of romances (I.iv.20): "Epicks may be well writ in Prose as Verse." Cervantes's discussion clearly indicates that he takes *epic* to mean "any significant narrative," whether history, classical epic, or romance. Fielding also borrows his reference to the *Telemachus* from the Ozell-Motteux translator's footnote to this passage: "The *Adventures of Telemachus* is a Proof of this." J. Paul Hunter errs particularly in a fanciful derivation of *Tom Jones* from the *Télémaque*. See my two articles on this head, esp. "Fielding's Comic."

9. In 1754, Fielding revised this to *"These Words were spoken...,"* along with changing "Prime Minister" (Walpole) to the innocuous "Statesman" (Digeon, 120). Miller sees this passage as imitating Lucian's dialogues (*Essays*, 367n).

10. Saintsbury claims that "Fielding has written no greater book ... compact of almost pure irony" (vii-viii). Digeon finds it "profound and rich in various lessons" (127); Shea, "a highly complex satire" (73). Wendt argues that Fielding deliberately made Heartfree "imperfect" ("Allegory," 317); Hopkins (passim), that the sentimentality is really comic irony; Rawson rightly disagrees with both (234ff., 253–54), and extends his perceptive analysis through the latter half of his book (101–259). Miller observes that Fielding's confident and skeptical perspectives simply reflect different moods, with the usual human inconsistency (*Essays*, 75).

11. Hopkins (225–27) points out that Fielding satirizes Defoe's *The King of Pirates* in Mrs. Heartfree's travels and (less convincingly) Defoe's matrimonial dialogue in his *Family Instructor*.

12. Fielding changed this to read (1754) "that Almighty Goodness is by its own Nature engaged...." Hopkins takes this passage as rendered intentionally ridiculous by *ravishing*, already punned upon sexually in Wild's addresses to Laetitia, and in *ecstasy*. But this is exactly the serious language of Parson Oliver and Tom Jones; see the foregoing discussion of *Shamela*.

13. Battestin, "Design," 290; see also Work and Williams. Preston, Knight, Poovy, Vopat, Braudy, and Guthrie resist the providential reading in various ways. Snow finds

Battestin's providential equation "intriguing but ultimately a misreading of the teasing, obfuscating narrator and his story" (50). But she herself misreads Fielding's reference to secrets that "I will not be guilty of discovering" till the muse of History "shall give me leave" (II.vi). Snow believes that Battestin posits "Fielding's belief in a benevolent deity who, in effect, works like a detective in a murder mystery, perceiving the pattern of cause and effect, discovering the innocent and guilty, and distributing the rewards and punishments" (40). She takes *discover* to mean "find out" (39–40). But this is not Fielding's (or Battestin's) conception of an omniscient deity who eventually *reveals* ("discovers" in the eighteenth-century sense) the benevolent design behind apparently haphazard events.

14. Hilles elaborates Van Ghent's architectural suggestion ("Art," 81). Battestin quotes Palladio himself (pref., bk. IV) on how "these little Temples we raise, ought to bear a resemblance to the immense one of (God's) infinite goodness," in which all "parts ... should have the exactest symmetry and proportion" ("Design," 300).

15. Knight well notices the imperfections in this country Paradise Hall, which Tom's restoration redeems. E. Taiwo Palmer and Combs work out the implication of Fielding's Miltonic expulsion, though this, like Fielding's naming of Allworthy's estate, seems a happy afterthought to authenticate his grand providential design.

16. Stephanson well describes this process in *Joseph Andrews*. See also McKenzie and McNamara.

17. See my "Narration"; Stevick: "Every word is 'told,' nothing is impersonally rendered" ("Talking," 119).

18. Alter also analyzes this passage (42). See also my "Cliché," 358. Hutchens demonstrates the similar ironic shadings in *prudence*, Fielding's central word and concept (101–18). Also see Hatfield (Irony).

19. From the first, readers have found *Amelia* a "failure" (Cross, II:328ff.; Sherburn, *"Amelia,"* 1). See Wolff, Eustace Palmer, Hassall, Osland, Donovan, among others cited passim.

20. Cross, II:326; Digeon, 195–96; Sherburn, *"Amelia,"* 4.

21. Fielding had introduced to the stage a situation aired in two contemporary lawsuits (Cross, I:121; Woods, "Notes," 364).

22. Only this romance, and Boccaccio's version, *Filocopo*, where Fielding probably read it, have the lover carried past hostile guardians in a basket. Dudden calls it a device from the comic stage (811), probably thinking of Falstaff's basket: a means of escape, not of entrance. The chest in *Decameron* II.ix and in *Cymbeline*, and the jars in *Ali Baba*, all serve hostile intentions.

23. Miss Matthews responds to Booth's *"Scene of the tender Kind"* (III.ii), describing his emotional departing from Amelia, with a sigh (nicely leading to his seduction): "There are Moments in Life worth purchasing with Worlds." In *Cassandra*, Statira, widow of Alexander, "emperor of the world," says that she prefers death to "the Empire of the whole World with any other Man" (V.106; also IV.109, IV.204). Lady Orrery classed "the works of the inimitable Fielding" with *"Cassandra, Cleopatra*, Haywood's novels" and "a thousand more romantick books of the same kind" (quoted in Foster, 102). Watt points out that "Amelia" and "Sophia" were the most popular romance names ("Naming," 327).

24. Atkinson's nocturnal "wineskin" battle with his wife, a poor attempt at the bedroom fisticuffs in *Joseph Andrews*, is another remnant from Cervantes, which he had derived from Apuleius (Becker, 146–47; Putnam, I:483n).

## WORKS CITED

Alter, Robert. *Fielding and the Nature of the Novel*. Cambridge, Mass.: Harvard Univ. Press, 1968.

Baker, Sheridan. "Bridget Allworthy: The Creative Pressures of Fielding's Plot." *Papers of the Michigan Academy of Science, Arts, and Letters* 52 (1967), 345–56.

———. "Fielding and the Irony of Form." *Eighteenth-Century Studies* 2 (1968), 138–54.

———. "Fielding's *Amelia* and the Materials of Romance." *PQ* 41 (1962), 437–49.

———. "Fielding's Comic Epic-in-Prose Romances Again." *PQ* 58 (1979), 63–81.

———. "Henry Fielding and the Cliché." *Criticism* 1 (1959), 354–61.

———. "Henry Fielding's Comic Romances." *Papers of the Michigan Academy of Science, Arts, and Letters* 45 (1960), 411–19.

———. "The Idea of Romance in the Eighteenth-Century Novel." *Papers of the Michigan Academy of Science, Arts, and Letters* 49 (1964), 507–22.

———. Introduction to *An Apology for the Life of Mrs. Shamela Andrews*. Berkeley: Univ. of California Press, 1953.

———. Introduction to *Joseph Andrews and Shamela*. New York: Crowell, 1972.

———. "Narration: the Writer's Essential Mimesis." *Journal of Narrative Technique* 11 (1981), 155–65.

Battestin, Martin C. "Fielding's Definition of Wisdom: Some Functions of Ambiguity and Emblem in *Tom Jones*." *ELH* 35 (1968), 188–217.

———. "Lord Hervey's Role in *Joseph Andrews*." *PQ* 42 (1963), 226–41.

———. *The Moral Basis of Fielding's Art: A Study of Joseph Andrews*. Middletown: Wesleyan University Press, 1959.

———. "Pictures of Fielding." *Eighteenth-Century Studies* 17 (1983), 1–13.

———. "The Problem of Amelia: Hume, Barrow, and the Conversion of Captain Booth." *ELH* 41 (1974), 613–48.

———. " 'Tom Jones': The Argument of Design." In Miller, Rothstein, and Rosseau, 289–319. Reprinted as "Fielding: The Argument of Design," ch. 5, in Battestin's *The Providence of Wit: Aspects of Form in Augustan Literature and the Arts*. Oxford: Clarendon Press, 1974.

Becker, Gustav. "Die Aufnahme des Don Quijote in die englische Literatur." *Palaestra* 13 (1906), 122–57.

Blanchard, Frederic T. *Fielding the Novelist: A Study in Historical Criticism*. New Haven, Conn.: Yale Univ. Press, 1927.

Booth, Wayne C. *The Rhetoric of Fiction*. Chicago: Univ. of Chicago Press, 1961.

Boyce, Benjamin. "News from Hell: Satiric Communications with the Nether World in English Writing of the Seventeenth and Eighteenth Centuries" *PMLA* 58 (1943), 402–37.

Braudy, Leo. *Narrative Form in History and Fiction: Hume, Fielding, and Gibbon*. Princeton, N.J.: Princeton Univ. Press, 1970.

Brooks, Douglas. "Richardson's *Pamela* and Fielding's *Joseph Andrews*." *Essays in Criticism* 17 (1967), 158–68.

Butt, John. *Fielding*. Writers and Their Work, no. 57. London: Longmans, Green, 1954.

Coley, William B. "The Background of Fielding's Laughter." *ELH* 26 (1959), 229–52.

Combs, William W. "The Return to Paradise Hall: An Essay on *Tom Jones*." *South Atlantic Quarterly* 67 (1968), 419–36.

Coolidge, John S. "Fielding and 'Conservation of Character.' " *Modern Philology* 57 (1960), 245–59.

Crane, R.S. "The Plot of *Tom Jones.*" *The Journal of General Education* 4 (1950), 112–30.

Cross, Wilbur L. *The History of Henry Fielding.* 3 vols. New Haven: Yale Univ. Press, 1918.

Digeon, Aurélien. *The Novels of Fielding.* London: Routledge, 1925.

Donovan, Robert Alan. *The Shaping Vision: Imagination in the English Novel from Defoe to Dickens.* Ithaca: Cornell Univ. Press, 1966.

Dudden, F. Homes. *Henry Fielding, His Life, Works, and Times.* London: Oxford Univ. Press, 1952.

Dyson, A.E. *The Crazy Fabric: Essays in Irony.* London: Macmillan; New York: St. Martin's Press, 1966.

Ehrenpreis, Irvin. *Fielding: Tom Jones.* London: Arnold, 1964.

Evans, James E. "Comedy and the 'Tragic Complexion' of *Tom Jones.*" *South Atlantic Quarterly* 83 (1984), 384–95.

———. "Fielding, *The Whole Duty of Man, Shamela,* and *Joseph Andrews.*" *PQ* 61 (1982), 212–19.

———. "The World According to Paul: Comedy and Theology in 'Joseph Andrews.' " *Ariel* 15 (1984), 45–56.

Fielding, Henry. *Amelia.* London: A. Millar, 1752.

———. *An Apology for the Life of Mrs. Shamela Andrews.* London: A. Dodd, 1741.

———. *The Complete Works of Henry Fielding, Esq.* Ed. William Ernest Henley. 16 vols. New York: Croscup & Sterling, 1902.

———. *The Covent-Garden Journal.* Ed. Gerard Edward Jensen. 2 vols. New Haven, Conn.: Yale Univ. Press; London: Oxford Univ. Press, 1915.

———. *The History of the Adventures of Joseph Andrews.* Wesleyan ed. Ed. Martin C. Battestin. Oxford: Clarendon Press, 1967.

———. *The History of Tom Jones, a Foundling.* Wesleyan ed. Ed. Martin C. Battestin and Fredson Bowers. [Middletown, Conn.]: Wesleyan Univ. Press, 1975.

———. *The Life of Mr. Jonathan Wild the Great.* In *Miscellanies,* Vol. III.

———. *Miscellanies.* 3 vols. London: A. Millar, 1743.

Foster, James R. *History of the Pre-Romantic Novel in England.* New York: Modern Language Association, 1949.

Goldberg, Homer. *The Art of Joseph Andrews.* Chicago: Univ. of Chicago Press, 1969.

Golden, Morris. *Fielding's Moral Psychology.* Amherst: Univ. of Massachusetts Press, 1966.

Guthrie, William B. "The Comic Celebrant of Life in *Tom Jones.*" *Tennessee Studies in Literature* 19 (1974), 91–106.

Haage, Richard. "Characterzeichnung und Komposition in Fieldings *Tom Jones* in ihrer Beziehung zum Drama." *Britannica* 13 (1936), 119–70.

Harrison, Bernard. *Henry Fielding's* Tom Jones: *The Novelist as Moral Philosopher.* London: Sussex Univ. Press, 1975.

Hassall, Anthony J. "Fielding's *Amelia*: Dramatic and Authorial Narration." *Novel* 5 (1972), 225–33.

Hatfield, Glenn W. *Fielding and the Language of Irony.* Chicago: Univ. of Chicago Press, 1968.

———. "Puffs and Politricks: *Jonathan Wild* and the Political Corruption of Language." *PQ* 46 (1967), 248–67.

Hilles, Frederick W. *The Age of Johnson: Essays Presented to Chauncey Brewster Tinker.* New Haven, Conn.: Yale Univ. Press, 1949.

———. "Art and Artifice in *Tom Jones.*" In Mack and Gregor, 91–110.

Hopkins, Robert H. "Language and Comic Play in *Jonathan Wild.*" *Criticism* 8 (1966), 213–28.

Hunter, J. Paul. *Occasional Form: Henry Fielding and the Chains of Circumstance.* Baltimore: Johns Hopkins Univ. Press, 1975.

Hutchens, Eleanor. *Irony in Tom Jones.* University: Univ. of Alabama Press, 1965.

Irwin, William Robert. *The Making of Jonathan Wild.* New York: Columbia Univ. Press, 1941.

Johnson, Maurice. *Fielding's Art of Fiction.* Philadelphia: Univ. of Pennsylvania Press, 1961.

Knight, Charles A. *"Tom Jones*: The Meaning of the 'Main Design.' " *Genre* 12 (1979), 379–99.

La Calprenède, Gaultier.... *The Famous History of Cassandra*, tr. abridged. London: Cleave et al., 1703.

Langer, Susanne K. *Feeling and Form: A Theory of Art*, New York: Scribner, 1953.

Le Page, Peter V. "The Prison and the Dark Beauty of 'Amelia.' " *Criticism* 9 (1967), 337–54.

Mack, Maynard, and Ian Gregor, eds. *Imagined Worlds: Essays on Some English Novelists in Honour of John Butt.* London: Methuen, 1968.

McKenzie, Alan T. "The Process of Discovery in *Tom Jones.*" *Dalhousie Review* 54 (1974), 720–40.

McKillop, A.D. *Early Masters of English Fiction.* Lawrence: Univ. of Kansas Press, 1956.

McNamara, Susan P. "Mirrors of Fiction within *Tom Jones*: The Paradox of Self-Reliance." *ECS* 12 (1979), 372–90.

Maresca, Thomas. *Epic to Novel.* Columbus: Ohio State Univ. Press, 1974.

Miller, Henry Knight. *Essays on Fielding's Miscellanies: A Commentary on Volume One.* Princeton, N.J.: Princeton Univ. Press, 1961.

———. *Henry Fielding's Tom Jones and the Romance Tradition.* ELS Monograph Series, no. 6. Victoria: *English Literary Studies*, 1976.

———. "Some Functions of Rhetoric in *Tom Jones.*" *PQ* 45 (1966), 209–35.

———. "The Voices of Henry Fielding: Style in *Tom Jones.*" In Miller, Rothstein, and Rousseau, 262–88.

Miller, Henry Knight; Eric Rothstein; and G.S. Rousseau, eds. *The Augustan Milieu: Essays Presented to Louis A. Landa.* Oxford: Clarendon Press, 1970.

Montagu, Lady Mary Wortley. *Letters and Works*, 2d ed., ed. Wharncliffe. London: Tentley, 1837.

Osland, Dianne. "Fielding's *Amelia*: Problem Child or Problem Reader?" *Journal of Narrative Technique* 10 (1980), 56–67.

Palmer, E. Taiwo. "Fielding's Tom Jones Reconsidered." *English* 20 (1972), 45–50.

Palmer, Eustace. "*Amelia*—The Decline of Fielding's Art." *Essays in Criticism* 21 (1971), 135–51.

Paulson, Ronald. "Models and Paradigms: *Joseph Andrews*, Hogarth's *Good Samaritan*, and Fénelon's *Télémaque.*" *Modern Language Notes* 91 (1976), 1186–1207.

———. *Satire and the Novel in Eighteenth-Century England.* New Haven, Conn.: Yale Univ. Press, 1967.

Poovy, Mary. "Journies from This World to the Next: Providential Promise in *Clarissa* and *Tom Jones.*" *ELH* 43 (1976), 300–315.

Powers, Lyall H. "The Influence of the *Aeneid* on Fielding's *Amelia.*" *Modern Language Notes* 71 (1956), 330–36.

Preston, John. *The Created Self: The Reader's Role in Eighteenth-Century Fiction.* London: Heinemann, 1970.

Price, Martin. *The Restoration and the Eighteenth Century*. New York: Oxford Univ. Press, 1973.

Putnam, Samuel. *The Ingenious Gentleman Don Quijote de la Mancha*. New York: Viking, 1949.

Rawson, C.J. *Henry Fielding and the Augustan Ideal Under Stress*. London and Boston: Routledge & Kegan Paul, 1972.

Ribble, Frederick G. "The Constitution of Mind and the Concept of Emotion in Fielding's *Amelia*." *PQ* 56 (1977), 104–22.

Rothstein, Eric. "The Framework of *Shamela*." *ELH* 35 (1968), 381–402.

Saintsbury, George. Introduction to *Jonathan Wild*, Everyman ed. New York: Dutton, 1932.

Shea, Bernard. "Machiavelli and Fielding's *Jonathan Wild*." *PMLA* 72 (1957), 55–73.

Sherburn, George. "The *Dunciad*, Book I." *University of Texas Studies in English* 24 (1944), 174–90.

———. "Fielding's *Amelia*: An Interpretation." *ELH* 3 (1936), 1–14.

Shesgreen, Sean. *Literary Portraits in the Novels of Henry Fielding*. DeKalb: Northern Illinois Univ. Press, 1972.

Snow, Malinda. "The Judgment of Evidence in *Tom Jones*." *South Atlantic Review* 8 (1983), 37–51.

Spilka, Mark. "Comic Resolution in Fielding's *Joseph Andrews*." *College English* 15 (1953), 11–19.

Stephanson, Raymond. "The Education of the Reader in Fielding's *Joseph Andrews*." *PQ* 61 (1982), 243–58.

Stevick, Philip. "Fielding and the Meaning of History." *PMLA* 79 (1964), 561–68.

———. "On Fielding Talking." *College Literature* 1 (1974), 119–33.

Taylor, Dick, Jr. "Joseph as Hero in *Joseph Andrews*." *Tulane Studies in English* 7 (1957), 91–109.

Thomas, D.S. "Fortune and the Passions in Fielding's *Amelia*." *MLR* 60 (1965), 176–87.

Van Ghent, Dorothy. *The English Novel: Form and Function*. New York: Rinehart, 1953.

Vopat, James B. "Narrative Techniques in *Tom Jones*: The Balance of Art and Nature." *Journal of Narrative Technique* 4 (1974), 144–54.

Watt, Ian. "The Naming of Characters in Defoe, Richardson, and Fielding." *RES* 25 (1949), 322–38.

———. *The Rise of the Novel*. Berkeley: Univ. of California Press, 1957.

Wendt, Allan. "The Moral Allegory of *Jonathan Wild*." *ELH* 24 (1957), 306–20.

———. "The Naked Virtue of Amelia." *ELH* 27 (1960), 131–48.

Williams, Aubrey. "Interpositions of Providence and Design in Fielding's Novels." *South Atlantic Quarterly* 70 (1971), 265–86.

Wolff, Cynthia. "Fielding's *Amelia*: Private Virtue and Public Good." *TSLL* 10 (1968), 37–55.

Woods, Charles. "Fielding and the Authorship of *Shamela*." *PQ* 25 (1946), 248–72.

———. "Notes on Three of Fielding's Plays." *PMLA* 52 (1937), 359–73.

Work, James A. "Henry Fielding, Christian Censor." In Hilles, *Age of Johnson*, 137–48.

Wright, Andrew. *Henry Fielding, Mask and Feast*. Berkeley: Univ. of California Press, 1965.

PAULA R. BACKSCHEIDER

# Crime and Adventure

"I SAW," "I SAW," "then I saw." These words occur thousands of times in the prose fiction of Defoe's time. Greedy for knowledge, experience, novelty, and opportunity, early eighteenth-century readers wanted to look through others' eyes at what they could not see and undergo themselves. New World plantations, Caribbean shipping, the Sahara, Siberia's tundra, even elephant herds and Asian idols were exotic and amazing. Freak accidents, gory murders, congenital deformities, and gallows behavior fascinated them. This craving for sensation contributed to a phenomenal rise in the popularity of travel and criminal literature.

The travel and criminal books of the time had much in common and much that appealed strongly to the average eighteenth-century reader. Both forms offered strange tales and vicarious experiences, intriguing personalities, and rambling lives. By Defoe's time, the heroes of these tales were usually restless, often rebellious and uprooted young men hungry for adventure, freedom, and economic gain, and this fact drew the forms closer together. Such men were willing to take risks and even engage in illegal activities from relatively minor, spontaneous theft or smuggling to full-scale, murderous piracy.[1] The narrative patterns of these books were similar, too. They alternated tales of unusual adventures with moral reflections. Moreover, like popular literature of all times, they always concluded by reinforcing the moral values and conventional choices of their readers. These didactic aspects increased their sales by making them acceptable to a larger reading public.

From *Daniel Defoe: Ambition & Innovation*. © 1986 by The University Press of Kentucky.

Daniel Defoe began writing in these forms after they had become popular and even formulaic. He had read them since boyhood, owned large numbers of travel books, and had included "crime reports" in his periodical writings for years. He drew upon his familiarity with them, then added elements from other kinds of writing, and expanded their purposes. More than any other writer, Defoe is responsible for leading other writers to see new potential in these forms and for giving them lasting vitality.

The craze for criminal literature, a craze partly created and certainly fed by Defoe, was at its height in the 1720s.[2] The broadsides ballads, chapbooks, newspapers, pamphlets, "anatomies," and criminal characters of the sixteenth and seventeenth centuries were augmented by the *Old Bailey Sessions Papers, The Ordinary of Newgate, his Account,* and collections such as *A Compleat Collection of Remarkable Tryals* and *The History of the Lives of the Most Noted Highway-men.* From the beginning, pirates were included with domestic housebreakers, infanticides, and frustrated lovers, and travel was often a part of the larger crime stories. Some literature borrowed freely from travel books: *The English Rogue,* for example, drew upon J.H. Linschoten's *Voyage to the East Indies,* and Defoe's *Captain Singleton* from Robert Knox's *An Historical Relation of Ceylon.*

This English crime literature was rigidly formulaic. In almost every case, the reader found a brief statement of the motive for the crime, a detailed account of the crime, and a description of the criminal's death. The Ordinary of Newgate added the facts of the trial (date, composition of the jury, magistrate, proceedings), his sermon, and an additional section that was often an essay on the type of crime committed or a statement allegedly made by the condemned and was similar in many ways to the traveler's "observations."[3] When a pirate was the subject, his life was depicted as miserable and chaotic. Until the middle of the eighteenth century, the motive for an individual crime was easy to overlook because it was assigned, often in single sentences, to a universal sinful tendency in human nature. As the compiler of the first volume of *The Newgate Calendar* said, "The criminal recorder has too often to detail the atrocity of ambition, the malignity of revenge, and the desperation of jealousy...."[4] Furthermore, these crimes and their punishments always took place in a Providential world. Case after case observed that a just God would end the sinner's career sooner or later, and his punishment conformed in degree to that of a condemned *sinner* more than it was appropriate to the specific transgression of a *criminal.*

By 1720 travel literature, too, had become highly formulaic. The traveler was not the Renaissance patriot-dreamer but an opportunistic wanderer. These travelers were usually blown off course, shipwrecked, captured by pirates, or offered unexpected opportunities that put them in strange countries with exotic people, customs, and wildlife. The longer the narrative, the more often such accidents occurred. Factual and pseudofactual travel books described a set list of details about each nation: topography, climate, language, customs, laws, commerce, employments, government, history, religion, and rarities. Because the emphasis was on the place rather than on the protagonist, the narrator was usually unobtrusive for long sections of the book. He gave accurate, detailed descriptions, often including such things as latitude/longitude readings and heights of mountains, arranged information, and relayed curious, novel, or horrible stories with comment or reaction. Until midcentury, fiction duplicated these conventions and adopted their most frequent conclusion: the traveler retired to England grateful to God and usually penitent either for his dissatisfied, restless nature or for specific crimes.

Because historical, psychological, and anthropological as well as fictional accounts of the material in travel and criminal literature are commonplace to us, we must exert our imaginations to comprehend their fascination and power for early modern England. Yet it is a tribute to their writers that we find these subjects so familiar and see the adventure story as ubiquitous. When we consider that their travel and crime literature largely grew from trivial and especially rigid forms, that the heroes and heroines were often criminals, and that writers married the story to an explicitly, blatantly moral commentary called "observations," the enduring popularity of such books is remarkable.

In this chapter, I shall discuss four elements common to travel and crime literature, elements which Defoe recognized as strongly appealing to his age. By exploiting these characteristics and combining the forms and purposes of other literature, Defoe produced four respectably successful novels: *The Farther Adventures of Robinson Crusoe* (1719), *Captain Singleton* (1720), *Moll Flanders* (1722), and *The Four Years Voyages of Captain George Roberts* (1726). Just as he brought his political writing and historical knowledge together in *Memoirs of a Cavalier*, *A Journal of the Plague Year*, and *Colonel Jack*, so he drew upon his knowledge of economic geography, rogue biography, and travel books for the four novels discussed in this chapter.

Defoe understood that a great part of the appeal of criminal and travel stories was the confrontation between ordinary, unheroic individuals and the unknown as these ordinary people struggled to fulfill a rags-to-riches fantasy. Owning less than Crusoe on his island, Defoe's heroes pit themselves against nations and men who apparently have all the advantages on their side. Without much education, "breeding," or money, they live out stories of adventure and economic gain and, in doing so, see almost all of the known world. "Known," however, is far from explored. In fact, the characters face situations, animals, people, and even natural features that are unpredictable and, therefore, horrifying. They cannot tell how much danger they are in. As Sir Walter Scott said, the reader admires "the advantageous light in which it places the human character as capable of ... opposing itself ... to a power of which it cannot estimate the force, of which it hath every reason to doubt the purpose, and at the idea of confronting [that power] our nature recoils."[5]

*Captain Singleton*, Defoe's most complete blending of the criminal and travel forms, came in the wake of the stunning success of *Robinson Crusoe* and while Defoe was one of John Applebee's crime reporters. His narrator, Bob Singleton, offers an entirely different consciousness from Robinson Crusoe. Because of his background, he is a kind of *tabula rasa*, coming to experiences fresh and reacting on the basis of very limited experience. Used by a beggar and then a gypsy to garner greater charity, cast on the parish, and transferred from ship to ship in his youth, Singleton observes all types of petty dishonesty and finally joins an unsuccessful mutiny. Unlike Colonel Jack, Singleton never finds disinterestedly good-hearted people; everyone who gives him food and shelter wants to use him, and most cheat or abuse him. As a marooned mutineer, he is "thoughtless" and "unconcern'd" for he has lost nothing and has no conception of the plight he is in. Never loved, never secure, never even well fed, he cannot imagine himself significantly worse off and lacks the education and experience to fear wild animals, cannibals, or starvation. He is forced to cross an unmapped continent and lacks the education that partially prepares Crusoe for his trip across Asia.

With this kind of character, Defoe gains two advantages: Singleton becomes a clear window to his adventures and to his own nature. Robinson Crusoe is driven to desperation by the memory of his former life and the list of his deprivations; a constant comparison focuses his experience. Singleton is free to share his experiences without the distraction of descriptions of his feelings. Crusoe obsessively searches for his sin; Singleton concentrates on survival. That Defoe and other writers sometimes saw emotion as distraction and directed attention away from it is often explicitly stated through transition phrases such as the one describing the death of Crusoe's wife in *Farther Adventures*: "It is not my Business here to write ..." (2:117).[6] Truthful because he sees no gain for himself and transparent because he has been taught no moral code, Singleton allows the reader to experience and react to his exciting adventures.

Incident after incident challenges the courage and ingenuity of Singleton and the men with him. Many of the episodes are carefully structured for dramatic effect, and the book is rich in strange sights and sounds. Defoe well knows that terror comes from the shock of an unexpected or unfamiliar sight and that sustained, unnatural sounds erode courage and energy. The natives scream, wail, and make strange, eerie sounds, and interpretation is seldom immediate. In a number of places, Singleton and his men watch natives gather, and the white men puzzle over the implications of the sounds they are making. The nights are especially alive: "towards Night we began to hear the Wolves howl, the Lions bellow, and a great many wild

Asses braying, and other ugly Noises which we did not understand" (p. 99). Even the deserts and wildernesses "howl" because of the wind. Huge animals suddenly appear, and the men must learn how to kill, for example, the armored crocodile. Ironically, what experience they have usually misleads them and increases their sense of being in an unpredictable, threatening land. For instance, they mistake the dust from a huge herd of elephants for an army on the march.

For the reader who enjoys exciting confrontations between an ordinary, unheroic person and a variety of adversaries, these books offer more than those by any other contemporary English writer. Defoe pits his protagonists against men, animals, large numbers of men, people who fight in different ways, accidents, the elements, and even natural disasters. The "heroes" scramble, improvise, seem doomed, and yet win. Defoe unified these books by the artistic selection of adventures. For instance, Crusoe's adversaries in *Farther Adventures* are usually men; Singleton struggles with terrain more consistently. Not only does this distinction reflect the state of each continent, but it also contributes to themes in the novels. Crusoe is a supremely social animal, deeply involved in world affairs, and analytical about national character; Singleton has no involvement with any nation and, until he comes to trust Quaker William, hardly distinguishes among men, animals, and weather. He is a lonely speck on the globe, expecting nothing from anything. At one point, he says, "We ... often met with wild and terrible Beasts, which we could not call by their Names, but as they were like us, seeking their Prey, but were themselves good for nothing, so we disturbed them as little as possible" (p. 28). Crusoe shares our prejudices—he expects friendship from those like him and hostility from "heatherns" and Portuguese; Singleton makes no predictions until well into his career as a pirate.

Each of Defoe's adventure stories concludes with a vastly wealthier protagonist, and each contains two of the most popular strains of western rags-to-riches sagas. First, the protagonist is something of a trickster and the book a compendium of tricks. Singleton and Crusoe practice largely on natives in order to survive, but their stories and *The Four Years Voyages of Captain George Roberts* (1726) include significant numbers of descriptions of trading crimes. In order to sell their cargoes, they often must indulge in everything from smuggling to contract swindles. Like the heroes of jestbooks and fabliaux, they rob the anonymous, the selfish, the greedy, and the rich. Need or challenge supplies what motivation is given. Like an intriguing magician, the hero has his audience asking "what will he do next, and how does he do it?"

Sheer cleverness soundly resting upon psychology and ingenuity, even when employed in shameful enterprises, does glorify "the human character." Moll tricking another potential robber at a fire and getting away with her booty; Crusoe's capture of an entire hut of natives whom he forces to watch the destruction of their idol, and Quaker William's seige on the hollow tree full of natives carry the same suspenseful delight. Each has a measure of danger, each is spun out more dramatically than we expect, and each ends with the reader and trickster sharing a triumph that must be kept secret from a more cautious, rigidly moral, and even adult world. Crusoe most explicitly points out this reader/character secret in passages such as that describing the way he and his co-conspirators "appear'd among our Fellow Travellers exceeding busy" the day after they destroyed the idol (3:188-89).

The second element common to western success stories is the idea that hard work is guaranteed to bring material reward. No Defoe adventurer is afraid of hard work. One of the dominating images of *Captain Roberts* is that of him bent over his ship's pump. Often exhausted, ill, alone, and with no reason to believe his effort will do more than determine that he dies from starvation rather than drowning, he pumps on with what Defoe habitually calls "unwearied Industry." Defoe brings alive the position, the rhythm, and the monotony of Roberts's solitary pumping. In the preface of *Moll Flanders*, Defoe tells us that "unwearied Industry ... will in time raise the meanest Creature." Singleton and his men must stop at intervals to build shelters or canoes, and the work is often described as tedious, heavy, and difficult. Often the work is futile, as it is with Crusoe's canoe and twice with Singleton's canoe building, but the faith in the success of work gives the character resilience and enduring interest. In a time when the streets of London could be compared to modern India with maimed and diseased beggars, orphans, scavengers, and pickpockets, Defoe's stories of Singleton and Moll, both "mean Creatures" who rose to appear in a "new Cast" in the world, must have had powerful appeal not only to the laboring poor but to the prosperous who wanted to believe in the work ethic.[7]

Just as the readers of Defoe's *History of the Wars* wanted to know more, to see beyond the bare report, so did those who went from periodical to pamphlet, from a report on a hanging to *The General History of the Pyrates*. The appeals of the periodical survive; modern readers expect to find elaboration of news stories in the paragraphs following the standard who-what-when-where opening, to find editorials, feature stories, and even serialized book chapters and articles on news and newsmakers, to be able to read more in news magazines, and even more in books. Paul Lorrain, one of the Newgate Ordinaries, explained that his *Accounts* brought "Things to Light which were before hidden in Darkness."[8] Even the progression from reports of Jonathan Wild's capture and trial to Defoe's and others' pamphlets to Fielding's *Jonathan Wild the Great* and Gay's *Beggar's Opera* have modern parallels, as anyone who knows the background of John Pielmeier's play *Agnes of God* understands.[9]

The English had always understood *news* to mean reports of the strange, bizarre, and puzzling as well as reports of serious political and economic events. Readers of these papers wanted to *see* more, to know more about aspects and parts of the world beyond their familiar world. Above all, they wanted to know things worth remarking upon. To read the periodicals of the time is to see these novels of Defoe's in miniature:

> We hear from Jamaica, that within these 15 Months past they have hanged upwards of 250 Pirates. [*London Journal*, 10 Nov. 1722]

> We are told, that no less than 16 large Cruisers are preparing to go to the Spanish West-Indies besides those that carry the Imperial Colours....

> Yesterday in the Fore-noon, a Lad about twelve Years of Age, presuming upon the Strength of the Ice, was unfortunately drown'd in *Wood's Close Pond*, a Place remarkable for the Loss of adventurous Youths both in Summer and Winter. He cried out for Help very much, bearing himself up with his Arms, but before the Assistance which was coming could be applied, he sank beneath the Ice, and rose no more. [*Whithall Evening Post*, 23 Dec. 1718]

> Last Tuesday Night a Boy about Eleven Years of Age, and a Girl about Fourteen, were both found dead in a Glass House-Yard in the Minories; and it is supposed they died for Want. [*Universal Spectator*, 6 Feb. 1749]

> [Two hundred eighty Englishmen and women who had been captives] marched in their Moorish habits in good Order through a great Part of this City to the Cathedral of St Paul's to return thanks to Almighty God. [*Whitehall Evening Post*, 9 Dec. 1721]

> ... The Prosecutor deposed, that [Prudence Price] came into the Shop, pretending to buy a Knot, and took her opportunity to take the Goods; and the Prosecutor was positive, that there was no Body else there but the Prisoner when the Goods were gone. Though she denied the Fact, saying, She knew nothing of it; yet was *[sic]* known to be an old Offender. The Jury found her Guilty to the value of 4s. and 6d. [*The Proceedings on the Queen's Commission of the Peace*, 1703][10]

Londoners could turn to the back pages of their papers and read about a man who threw something at a maid but hit and killed his child instead, about a chimney that fell but missed a lady knitting in front of the fire, and about a potential suicide who came to thank his rescuers.

Unlike novel reading, newspaper reading is not almost entirely a solitary activity. Readers look up and remark on various items to companions or refer later to things they've read; they look for paragraphs on people's problems and actions even though they do not expect to see familiar names. Crime and suffering and "human interest" have always sold papers, and some of the best stories have a social nature: the engagement, battle, and outcome in a war; the arrest, trial, and hanging of a criminal; the sighting, arrival, and cargo of a ship. Even grisly notices such as the following appeal to readers' desire for "story": "The Person mention'd in a former Paper to have cut his Throat, and stab'd himself in several Places in the Body, near Kentish Town, proves to be a Mason, and a Person in good Circumstances: He is perfectly recovered ... seem[s] sorry for that rash Action" (*London Journal*, 10 Nov. 1722).

Today's news stories rely on quotations, interviews, columns, and editorials for multiple points of view, while eighteenth-century papers often had a political voice or a "club" of writers. After the popularity of the John Dunton's Athenian Society, Defoe's Scandal Club, and the *Tatler* and *Spectator* clubs, examples are legion. *The Grumbler* (1715) had the Grizzle family, and *The Tea-Table* (1724) included men and women, including the widow of a ship's commander. These periodicals frequently noted the taste for "strange, wild and absurd Notions" and "wandering" among a variety of topics as "Connection, Method, Proportion, Dependency of Parts upon the Whole ... are ... overlook'd by the Generality of Readers...."[11] Gossip and hearsay also appear from the beginning of newspaper history; French *Nouvellistes*, for example, often met travelers on the roads to Paris, interviewed them about things they had seen and done, and then printed their comments about battles, prominent people, or village scandals as authenticated fact.[12] Periodicals had from the beginning included essays and stories with a broad tolerance for speculation, ornament, and even fiction.

As Clara Reeve said in *The Progress of Romance* (1785), "The word Novel in all languages signifies something new"; "The Novel gives a familiar relation of such things as pass every day before our eyes, such as may happen to our friend, or to ourselves."[13] That, of course, is also part of the newspapers' appeal. English journalism from the beginning fed on narrative. The eight to twenty-four page newsbooks, issued whenever enough material warranted publication, continued accounts and included "remarkable" stories often of atrocities or strange accidents. The recognition of the narrative nature of "news" can be seen in satires of typical items such as Addison's "We are informed from Pankridge, that a dozen weddings were lately celebrated ... but are referred to the next letters for the names of the parties concerned" (*Spectator* No. 452). Intensely topical, newsbooks such as *Weekely Newes from Italy, Germanie, Hungaria, Bohemia, the Palatinate, France, and the Low Countries* often included accounts of recent murders and competed directly with pamphlets with titles such as *Three Bloodie Murders* (1613) and *News from Fleetstreet* (1675).[14] An examination of a host of works such as *Sack-Full of Newes* (1557), *Tarleton's Newes Ovt of Pvrgatory* (1589), *Newes from the New Exchange* (1650), and *Strange News from Bartholomew Fair* (1661) indicates that readers associated "news" with the recent, the "remarkable," and the prying. Private family affairs—drownings, suicides, elopements—became public news, and the best journalists spun their material out into fiction or essay, as Ned Ward did in his *London Spy* (1700) or Steele did in *The Tatler*. Just as the early novels promised a variety of "strange and suprizing" adventures, so the early newspapers were expected to produce incidents that would excite amazement in the reader who would respond by remarking, "Just listen to this!"

Like fiction, the papers felt free to report motive. The drowned "lad" had "presumed" upon the strength of the ice, a murderer "could neither bear the thought of forfeiting the esteem of a woman that he courted, nor of marrying her [whom he had seduced]."[15] John Dunton's *Pegasus* (to 1696) included a section called *Observation on Publick Occurrences*, which allowed him space to speculate about motive and moralize. Defoe's books, called the "crude products of the dawn of journalism" by Richard Altick,[16] added the power of a central personality facing unusual obstacles to unify the variety of incidents and the seriality of the journalistic rhythm.

Defoe converted the "characters" of the back pages of periodicals into heroes and heroines. Not one of his protagonists would seem to be worth the notice of more than a single day (usually in a report of the sentence to hanging), yet Defoe makes their lives remarkable. For example, George Roberts is an unprepossessing man sent to Virginia to pick up a sloop and a cargo. Captured by Captain Low, one of the most brutal Caribbean pirates,[17] Roberts is held in a state of constant terror before he is left to die on his stripped ship with two boys. Roberts is a winning combination of wit, courage, and piety. The same dry, religious wit that Bunyan used and that distinguishes Quaker William animates Roberts's character. For instance, Roberts tells us that he answers the swearing, threatening pirates politely on the advice of *Proverbs*: "When your Hand is in the Lion's Mouth, get it out as easie as you can" (p. 30).

Unable to recruit him, the pirates abide by their articles guaranteeing the freedom of married men with children, and they put Roberts on the leaky ship that his implacable enemy, Russell, has stripped of provisions, ammunition, and even sails. Roberts has been firm, sensible, and admirable, but, at this point, he becomes heroic. He and the boys find some food left on board, learn to prepare it and collect fresh water, and even fight and kill a giant shark. The almost constant need to pump out the ship dominates their days and nights. It limits their sleep, saps their strength, and calls for particular endurance and ingenuity from Roberts because his companions are children with limited strength.

Roberts's life becomes a series of frustrations. Because of the children's weakness, he will take so long to lower a boat that darkness comes, and he must pull it up again. He contracts a lingering fever. The younger boy falls asleep on watch, and the older boy and the rowboat are left behind. Now Roberts must pump alone. As he sails from port to port, friendly natives board sometimes to bring food and water but more often to tantalize him with dreams of rescue as they drink his scarce rum or simply swim away. When they spend the night on board but refuse to pump, the tired, debilitated, ill Roberts returns to the hold to pump while three healthy men rest above. Once the natives get him to Salt Point, he can neither climb the peak to get to the fruitful side of the island nor return to the ship. Although he has moments of intense frustration and near-despair, he always rallies and continues to struggle. When trapped on Salt Point, Roberts says, "if I can proceed no farther, and yet at high Water have not here so much Room to stand, or walk upon, as half a Ship's Quarter-Deck[,] I shall be worse than a Person pent up in a solitary close Prison all his Days" (p. 199). *The Four Years Voyages* uses many similar passages to repeat and emphasize Roberts's situation and also to give the reader access to feelings. The metaphor "a solitary close Prison" intensified by the adjectives "solitary" and "close" and the phrase "all his Days" suggest desperation and even horror.

Defoe is a master of these economical summaries. When Singleton and his men are too far from their last supply point to return, Singleton says, "our present Business was, what to do to get out of this dreadful Place we were in; behind us was a Wast[e].... Before us was nothing but Horrour ... so we resolv'd ... to go on as far as we could ... " (p. 138). Beneath the steady words is the vision of suffering and death called up by a statement of the situation and a few adjectives. The spare prose, suggesting rather than milking emotion, is related to journalism; we do not need to be told how a father felt when he accidentally killed his baby nor do we need verbal writhing to imagine Roberts's or Singleton's states of mind. The mastery is in the power to make us see. To allow us to see the water rising toward a barren ledge on Salt Point or to contemplate the vast land Singleton sees before him is a kind of rhetorical discipline that reflects the control, the refusal to despair, that is the character's greatest strength.

Although many modern readers find Defoe's novels episodic, the eighteenth-century reader expected rhythm or narrative intensity and reflective calm. This pattern easily accommodated the taste for collections of the varied and the sensational. Periodicals ended with lists of "Remarkable Providences," "Indifferent Things," and "Remarkable Events," and books of hideous crimes, of lurid love stories, of Oriental tales, of descriptions of exotic animals, of events associated with earthquakes or storms, and of the deaths of virtuous mothers were commercial successes. Writers after Defoe explicitly noted the similarities of the appeal to the taste for the varied and sensational in these collections, precursors of the English novel, and the novel.

Sarah Fielding, for example, wrote in 1757, "From the same Taste of being acquainted with the various surprising Incidents of Mankind, arises our insatiable Curiosity for Novels or Romances; Infatuated with a Sort of Knight errantry, we draw these fictitious Characters into a real Existence; and thus, pleasingly deluded, we find ourselves as warmly interested, and deeply affected by the imaginary Scenes of *Arcadia*, the wonderful Atchievements of *Don Quixote*, the merry Conceits of *Sancho*, rural Innoncence [sic] of a *Joseph Andrews*...."[18] Respectable citizens flocked to Tower Bridge to see two-tailed sheep, hairless dogs, and deformed children exhibited for a few coins, and they gobbled up tales of coney catchers, saints, and kings' mistresses. Prose fiction embraced digressions, interpolated stories, and even other genres to satisfy its readers in the ways that prose fiction since Sidney's *Arcadia* had.

The reader of books such as *The English Rogue*, Chetwood's *Captain Falconer*, or de Serviez's *The Lives and Amours of the Empresses* (tr. 1723) will be immediately struck, however, by the comparative unity of Defoe's narratives and the strength of the personalities of his protagonists. Although *A Journal of the Plague Year* is probably the best example of the use of a collection of anecdotes for thematic and tonal force, in no Defoe novel are the episodes not literary in the strictest sense of the term. That he manages to give his readers the "sights" they wanted even as he subordinates them to his fictional intentions separates his books from those contemporary works most similar to his.

One of the most characteristic marks of eighteenth-century fiction is its use of interpolated, often sensational stories, and Defoe's novels have their share. For example, Crusoe discovers a starving boy gnawing on a half-eaten glove in *Farther Adventures*, and this boy and a servant girl tell their story; the exiled prince tells Crusoe part of his life story; Singleton finds a naked, sun-blotched white man in Africa, and they hear his "history." More often than not, a comparison of these anecdotes with the protagonist's past sets the protagonist in a more favorable light. Sometimes Defoe seems to have his narrators choose among life-histories. Moll, for example, suppresses Jemmy's and Mother Midnight's (noting that they are worth relating) but tells her mother's. This life is the same kind of repetition of Moll's own life and of the themes of the book that the tutor's history is in *Colonel Jack*.

Defoe's interpolated tales and incidents duplicate the plots, rhythm, pace, and types of characters and incidents of formulaic anecdotes, but he invests them with dramatic, even raw emotion. Many of these incidents still manage to carry the kind of moral implications that the anecdotes of the period do; they implicitly (or even explicitly) warn the reader against jealousy, rage, infatuation, or despair. Defoe, however, dramatizes them and draws out their full human vibrations.

Consider the end of Moll Flanders's first love affair. From its beginning, every reader winces at the implications of the class differences, the money given Moll, and the brother's easy "consider yourself married." That he is the *older* brother, that he occasionally is unkind to his family, that Moll is vain, increase the perception that the end is absolutely predictable. The lesson to be learned from the episode is equally unmistakable and utterly familiar. It is a trite story, even in 1722. Yet Defoe can still move us with it. When the lover tells her that his best advice is to marry his brother, Moll "gave him a look full of Horror" and turned "Pale as Death." Although she is sitting down, she nearly falls. Her shock establishes her naiveté and promises deep grief and lengthy suffering. The vivid argument that follows is full of the clichés of betrayed love: "is this your Faith and Honour, your Love," she asks. His answers are the transparent excuses and placating promises of legions of lovers: he tells her "we might love as Friends all our Days, and perhaps with more Satisfaction" than if he married and were disinherited. Moll, of course, has no chance of winning him back. "Can you transfer my Affection?" she asks. And then she raises that question to a higher level of intensity: "Can you bid me cease loving you, and bid me love him?" And yet again the question assumes greater emotional force: "is it in my Power think you to make such a Change at Demand?" The answer, of course, is "no." Moll herself cannot *will* a transfer of affection, and here she apprehends the loneliness and impossibility of what she needs to do. Love is not so simple, temporary, or whimsical. To the end of her marriage to Robin, the older brother's face will appear to her, will haunt her very lovemaking.

Defoe has taken one of the most trite episodes of early English fiction and conduct books and reinvested it with emotional force. Moll's youth, vulnerability, trust, and optimism have been assaulted. The grim life of the working poor that has been her destiny since her infancy is now an emotional reality; she, and we, know this is no Cinderella story and that she will partake fully of the hardships and slurs of her social position. Moll is never again so trusting and vulnerable; only in the grief over separation from Jemmy do we see the same capacity for love. She accepts her lot, but her vulnerability had been established. That she is vulnerable is crucial to the rest of the novel. Without that quality, her actions would be despicable and her regrets hypocritical. It is not incongruous that she thinks of the woman's coming distress when she will discover that items saved from the fire are stolen or that Moll finds the thought of hurting the child she robbed horrifying. The girl who could ask, "is it in my Power ... to make such a Change at Demand?" lives on in the woman. No need to look for psycho-social explanations, although they may be found; the quality of the heart, the genuineness of the human reaction, allows us at our hardest to view Moll with cynicism; we cannot dislike her or wish her hanged.

An equally emotional moment is when Quaker William's widowed sister sends her brother £5 and offers to let him move in with her and her four children. The incident occurs at a time when the narrative, and Singleton's and William's lives, have been arrested for some time. William, who was Singleton's adviser and strategist during their pirate career, has now become the means to his salvation. In addition to *Roxana's* Amy's cleverness and loyalty, William has genuine goodness as well. He has led Singleton to retire with one of his understated, witty observations: "most People leave off Trading when they are satisfied with getting ..." (p. 309). Gradually he brings Singleton to repent, encourages him through a suicidal period, and leads him to new hope. Even as serious, lengthy conversations "continually" give them pleasure and, thereby, signal to the reader that they are sincere converts, they struggle with the questions of converting their wealth into a manageable form and of what use they can most appropriately make of it.

It is after months of discussions that William writes his sister, "a poor relation," whom his money might benefit. At this point, he has given up his own hope to return to England. The irony of the contrast between her meager living from her small shop and the men's vast wealth emphasizes her generosity and moves both men to tears. Their wealth has been troublesome and described as "a Mass," "like Dirt under my Feet," and "no great Concern" when part of it had to be abandoned. For a man who had told William he has no home except where he is and that wherever he has been he has been "cheated and imposed upon, and used so ill" (p. 310), the long-neglected sister's simple, generous gesture seems as wondrous as William's loyalty. Singleton, characteristically extreme in danger or in friendship, first offers his friend's sister £5000 and then urges William to go to England without him. William, however, refuses in the words of the biblical Ruth, "I am resolved I'll never part with thee as long as I live, go where thou wilt, or stay where thou wilt" (p. 331). Over the next two years, William's loyalty and the sister's warm letters work on Singleton until he is willing to go to England disguised, although he still fears that someone will betray him out of avarice. The widow's touching letter, however, serves as the wedge that opens Singleton to an expression of trust and brotherhood and ends the most complete psychological and physical isolation of any eighteenth-century character.

Interested in the classification of experiences and the variations within a category, eighteenth-century readers came to narrative types assured of appropriate anecdotes. The ingenuity and skill of the writer determined how varied, how probable, how exciting, and how integrated these "cases" were. Furthermore, the reader expected certain types of stories with formulaic detail and predictable, exemplary endings. Just as Defoe could give emotional power to, for example, the formula story of the servant girl seduced by her master, he could sift the ingredients of the travel narrative and create a more unified, powerful form.

Readers of travel fiction expected the kind of geographical description found in primarily nonfiction books such as Bartolomé de Las Casas's *An Account of the First Voyages and Discoveries Made by the Spaniards in America* (1699). These passages tended to be specific, detailed, and in the manner of reports to the Royal Society. Las Casas, for example, included letters from other travelers along with his own reports. Representative passages read: "They unshale their Rice from its outward husk by beating it in a Mortar, or on the Ground more often; but some of these sorts of Rice must first be boyled in the husk, otherwise in beating it will break to powder"; or "... Capt. *Avery* ... set all Hands at work in sounding the Bay of the *East* Side of the Island, in 15 Degrees 30 Minutes *South* Latitude, which was large and capacious, unexpos'd to the Fury of the most tempestuous Weather."[19] William Chetwood's *Captain Falconer* is quite typical in the way that he describes fish, insects, birds, and other elements common to nonfiction.[20]

Although Defoe is deeply concerned with geographical accuracy, he subordinates descriptions of the unfamiliar customs and clothing, for example, to the function these places and people serve in motivating adventures and affecting the opinions of his hero. Crusoe, his most self-conscious narrator, contrasts his story specifically to similar contemporary ones: "I shall not pester my Account, or the Reader, with Descriptions of Places, Journals of our Voyages, Variations of Compass, Latitudes, Meridian-Distances, Trade-Winds, Situation of Ports, and the like; such as almost all the Histories of long Navigation are full of, and makes the reading tiresome enough, and are perfectly unprofitable to all that read it, except only to those, who are to go to those Places themselves" (3:83; compare 3:154). Crusoe refers to the "Journals and Travels of *English* Men, of which, many I find are publish'd, and more promis'd every Day ..." and recommends that readers consult those books for locations and details (3: 109). He will give anecdotes and adventures, then data. Crusoe's comments show that Defoe knew these books well enough to have analyzed their contents specifically and to imply that he was aware of the habitual, accepted borrowing of descriptions from one book to another.[21] He has gone beyond the recording of data to a somewhat deeper level of experience.

Defoe finds new fictional usefulness in the natural historians' data. First, he includes descriptions of what the age would call "sublime," then goes on to have his characters make observations that raise the readers' estimation of them. Defoe himself had written an instructive fable about two travel writers for the introduction to the third volume of his *Tour Thro' the Whole Island of Great Britain*. The foolish traveler kept "an exact journal" in which he notes such minutiae as the signs of the inns at which he ate, while the wise traveler takes "minutes ... for his own satisfaction," and these he finds to be "critical" and "significant" and is able to write a "useful account" from them. Rather than a string of trifles, he produces a delightful book with an "abundance of useful observations."

Singleton sees huge waterfalls, deserts, lakes, and rivers, and he comes upon such beautiful sights as the three leopards on the river bank. Crusoe admires the house built of china and the Great Wall and notes the Tonguese who live in underground vaults and cover themselves and their vaults in fur. Descriptions such as these are so brief as to be mere notes; although they give additional credibility and interest to the narrative, they also serve as a vehicle for the characters' perceptive observations, the display of "judgment" so admired in the century. Crusoe finds the Great Wall impractical but he "wonders at it" because it is impressive in size and workmanship and represents monumental human endeavor; in fact, part of its marvelousness comes from its uselessness. Singleton can have the leopard killed and keep its pelt, but he continues to carry the visual image of the tableau of leopards and lush river bank.

These observations were supposed to spring easily from events and sights by the association of ideas and included moral, political, economic, and historical reflections and were sometimes extended into full-scale essays. There are, for example, some similarities between the incident in *Farther Adventures* when Crusoe destroys the idol and Joseph Addison's reflections on the errors of Catholicism after he describes religion in Italy in *Remarks on Several Parts of Italy* (1705). It was not even unusual to separate the recording of facts from the subjective (fictional or personal) commentary, as Defoe does in *Captain Roberts*.[22] Like the contemplation of any sublime object, the reflection upon these descriptions helped the reader understand his world and God's care of his creatures. The alternation of description and "observation" was a rigid convention in travel literature of the seventeenth century and often handled obtrusively, for more value was assigned to the observations than to descriptions. Since one underlying theme in Defoe's works is what should be valued, such "observations" contribute in fictional and artistic ways.

The second use Defoe makes of material common to geographical histories is to motivate adventure. In some ways, the killing of the crocodile in *Captain Singleton* resembles the zoologist's examination of a specimen, and yet it is a good story. The gunner finally runs up to the crocodile, thrusts the barrel of his gun into its mouth, and fires. He is so terrified, however, that he immediately runs away. Before the crocodile dies, it chews the iron barrel until it is marked like a stick worried by a dog. Such experiences try the ingenuity and courage of the travelers and make up the fabric of the plot. Defoe uses his knowledge of African and Asian rivers, of Caribbean sea ports, of climate, and of weather to complicate his plots, as he does when he has Crusoe cross Russia or Roberts lie ill at Salt Point. These episodes build the impression we have that the hero is courageous, persevering, and clever. Because these foes are usually unfamiliar, wild, or unnaturally large, they assume a threat enhanced by near-superstitious awe, the reaction Scott described as "our nature recoils."

By emphasizing characters' perceptions of objects and events or developing their emotional reactions, Defoe made his books unified, coherent linguistic structures. Without losing the appeal of the varied and sensational, he transformed the travel and criminal forms into stories that gave new delight in character and assured their continued vitality.

Finally, Defoe incorporates the satisfaction common to popular fiction, which has always explored fantasies and limits, but concluded by reinforcing the moral order a society believes exists. As press coverage expanded and increasing numbers of authentic and fictional memoirs appeared, readers' fantasies extended to wondering how the choice to join the pirates or to die would be met, what it would be like to be left to starve on a ship or on an island, to be on a ship with a crew of two boys, to be a pirate facing a man-of-war, or to be thrown in Newgate. Defoe knew that fantasies came from the experiences (direct or read) of their readers. From the sight of a boy being pumped comes speculation about his home life. From the shipping news come dreams of shipwrecks, pirates, and cargoes lost. From participation in a rag-tag mob following a constable with a pickpocket comes speculation about the motive for the theft.

Defoe's novels provide situation after situation designed to allow readers to compare their own solutions and fantasies to the action the character finally takes. Fantasies often involve escape from ordinary, social limits, and, more than Defoe's other novels, the four under discussion here free the protagonist from society's bonds. Singleton recognizes no government except the ones he himself designs, Moll insists her situation and her cleverness exempt her from ordinary rules, and Crusoe carries the mentality of the sole ruler of his island through his final trip. Each is a radical individual isolated from the everyday world. No rules exist to help Roberts deal with the pirates, the natives, or his exile on the ship. In fact, most of the dialogue in *The Four Years Voyages of Captain George Roberts* is argument; he reasons, explains, and pleads, and his hearers disagree. Not just cut off from but at odds with majority opinion, these characters are free to behave in ways that we can only imagine. Moll turns thief, Singleton pirate, and Crusoe judge and jury. None finds help from society, and all must make their own ways.

The emphasis in these novels by Defoe is on the adventure, the excitement, the dangers, and the escapes of the hero, and the world in which they operate is removed just enough from the readers' to permit action that would be offensive, improbable, or even impossible in a middle-class English family. For example, once Moll leaves Colchester she is part of a society few know. She is a completely unattached female; she does not even write to anyone in the town that was her home for twenty years. She is in a world in which she can meet and marry highwaymen, prowl the streets, and change her social class. Because Defoe's protagonists' situations are unfamiliar and quite threatening, they can be seen primarily as resourceful characters who exhibit humankind's strengths rather than as dubious examples. Unlike the readers of conduct books and novels such as Defoe's *Roxana* and Penelope Aubin's *Count de Vinevil*, the reader of these novels is encouraged to move from adventure to adventure without pause for moral judgment. The interest is in how Crusoe destroys the idol, not in his motives or in questions of his prudence, inconsistency, or even morality. What serious crimes Singleton commits as a pirate are swallowed up in the sighting and taking of ships; that he may have had to kill men to prevent his capture is acknowledged, but, when the need is debated, another solution occurs; comparable situations that ended, we may suppose, the other way, pass rapidly by the reader.

Injustice, crime, and immorality could appear in these novels and give pleasure to a reading public that demanded morally useful literature because they occur in a Providential world. Just as popular fiction produces popular fantasies so does it embody and support conventional ethical opinion. The reader of such fiction knew that the conclusion would affirm the moral processes and order in the universe. As John Cawelti explains, such novels indulged two human needs—for change and novelty and for order and security.[23] A deeply orthodox writer like Defoe could use this moral world and readers' expectations to increase suspense even as he relied upon it for what Ian Watt has called coherent moral structure.[24] Just as surely as the modern reader wonders if Moll or Singleton will get away with this theft or this piracy, the early eighteenth-century reader would have found reminders of the nature of the world in which these criminals acted.

Defoe establishes the moral framework of these four novels through manifestations of the eternal world that he believes encompasses the temporal one. Perhaps no other aspect of his novels is as foreign and even unattractive to the modern reader. Yet when Defoe depicts his character responding to premonitions, dreams, promptings, and the most conservative religious fundamentalism, he is carrying out one of the enduring imaginative endeavours of the novel. He is, in Richard Gilman's words, bringing us "'news' of the invisible, of what exists beyond the recognitions of the naked eye, as possibility, alternative, redemption through a disbelief in what the world says about itself."[25] No matter how little Singleton knows of religion, he lives in God's world, and the reader (and the retrospective narrator) can locate moments when Providence seems to assert itself. Characters who have some religious education are unable to ignore it; they are never free from feeling the tension between what they do and what they ought to do. Their lives and events in their lives always come to serve as evidence of God's existence.

Lest anyone think religious faith came easily to Defoe's contemporaries, the list of serious, lengthy books proving the existence of

God stands as grim evidence to the contrary. The philosophies of Hobbes, Descartes, Leibnitz, and the steady mathematization of the universe by the new science challenged the pious as never before. In addition, throughout the age, uncomplimentary terms hounded those who took religion too seriously or acknowledged their faith too publicly. Successful businessmen, ambitious politicians, and great literary figures endorsed the Christian rationalism of Addison's *Spectator* no. 465 but went no farther. Defoe's conduct books and his rigid opposition to Occasional Conformity seemed almost as old-fashioned to many of his contemporaries as they do to us. Defoe uses this climate of skepticism to provide themes and psychological tension in *Robinson Crusoe*, *A Journal of the Plague Year*, and *Roxana*. In the four novels discussed in this chapter, Defoe is writing adventure stories, and his emphasis in on the action, the plot, and the setting. One aspect of setting is the eternal world, and Defoe used it for artistic and didactic purposes.

*Captain Singleton* is one of the Defoe novels often criticized for its concluding, unconvincing conversion. In fact, Defoe has constructed the novel so that Singleton lives an amoral life within a highly moral universe. From the beginning of the narrative, the reader finds clues that indicate that God's grace operates in Singleton's life. As retrospective narrator, "Captain Bob" speaks of "a good Providence" that thwarted his numerous plans to murder the Portuguese captains when he was only a youth (pp. 11, 13). At other points, terrifying natural events, such as a violent storm with "Blasts" of lightning, remind him of the "Horrour" of his former life and of his need to repent. Time after time, accident or persuasion prevents Singleton from carrying out cold-blooded murders. Sometimes he and his men are attacked and must defend themselves, sometimes the natives or the ships slip away, sometimes someone suggests a more practical plan. Once Quaker William is taken on board, Singleton has a pragmatic "guardian angel" who stays constantly by him and unfailingly counsels mercy.

In contrast to these weak signs of Providence's plan, as the most devout of Defoe's readers would say, is the powerful tone created by Singleton's life. In brief, dramatic moments and through repetitive incidents, Defoe builds suspense regarding Singleton's ultimate capacity for violence and about his fate. Soon after he and the others are marooned, he suggests they take a boat by force, cruise the coast until they take a larger one, and continue the progression until they have an ocean-going vessel. At this point, he is a teenager, but he has summarized the way most of the pirates built their careers in *The General History of the ... Pyrates* and is cheered by the men.[26] Here Defoe pauses in the narrative to include a striking incident. One of the most sympathetic and intelligent characters, the gunner, stops Singleton, catches his hand, studies his palm, then looks intently into his face and says "very gravely, My Lad, ... thou art born to do a World of Mischief ..." (p. 31). From that point until William Walters persuades Singleton to retire, he lives the most predatory life of any Defoe character. Only a few days after the vote to adopt Singleton's plan, the men's actions give the impression that they are criminals on the prowl. The natives *give* them food and yet they examine the earthenware containers covetously and draw out all the information they can about their neighbors' boats. As the men sail along the coast and cross Africa, they take what they are not given or cannot buy. Animals and men are left unmolested only when they are useless.

As a pirate, Singleton becomes a more ambitious predator. He prowls the seas not for the supplies he needs but for the wealth he wants. The men he captures are as anonymous as the natives and as quickly forgotten. If they are useful, he takes them; if not, his only interest in them is that they not endanger him. Into this world of men constantly on the lookout for an opportunity to rob comes William Walters. He begins to talk of home, retirement, and religion and finally leads Singleton through the process of salvation. He arouses his repentant feelings and then helps him move from suicidal despair to see that "to despair of God's Mercy was no Part of Repentance" (p. 326) and to build a new, reformed life.

Defoe draws upon contemporary opinions about the spiritual to explain Singleton's salvation. Not only is Walters a kind of good angel speaking directly to the pirate, but Singleton's dreams are of calls to repentance, not to evil. For example, he dreams that the devil asks his trade and has come to get him. This dream is no temptation, as those of beautiful, immoral women described in *The Political History of the Devil* are. Walters defines Singleton's suicidal thoughts as "the Devil's Notions" and, in harmony with his consistently wry pragmatism reminds Singleton that "on this side Death [sic] you can't be sure you will be damned at all, yet the Moment you step on the other side of Time, you are sure of it" (pp. 324-25).[27] Walters, his sister, and a dozen or more "accidents" exist as "instruments of God's grace." The fact that they have natural explanations and are treated economically would have seemed appropriate to Defoe's readers, who did not come to adventure fiction for the kind of intense interior drama that spiritual autobiography provided.

The setting of the Providential world is even more crucial in *Moll Flanders*. As I have argued elsewhere, much of the energy of the book comes from the reader's sense that she is being stalked by Newgate Prison, emblem of God's certain justice. Any reader of broadsides, pamphlets, and the Ordinary's *Accounts* would have encountered hundreds of sentences noting the "wonderful" way God "discovers" murderers, thieves, and other criminals and assurances that such actions are always found out. Moll specifically calls Newgate an "emblem" of hell, and Defoe's readers probably would have encountered the metaphor with elaboration before. *The English Rogue*, for example, describes the Compter in the same terms Defoe uses for Newgate: "Hell is a very proper denomination for it, since it is a place to be composed of nothing but disorder and confusion; a land of darkness, inhabited by calamity, horror, misery, and confusion.... A prison is the banishment of courtesy ... the treasure of despair.... Here you may see one weeping, another singing; one sleeping, another swearing ... a living tomb ... a little wood of woe, a map of misery, a place that will learn a young man more villainy ... in six months, than at twenty gaming ordinaries, bowling-alleys, or bawdy-houses...."[28] Prison often acted as symbol of the end of a criminal career, as re-creation of the atmosphere of Hell, and as emblem of the gateway to Hell in the literature of the time, and Moll's constant references to "the Place that had so long expected me" give Newgate more than ordinary meaning.

Having scruples rather than religion, Moll becomes a "creature" of the Devil. Her marriages are the product both of bad luck and the economic realities of her time, but she becomes increasingly predatory with men. She is willing to go beyond exaggerating her means to robbing "tricks." What has been called "hardening" carries the signs of spiritual warfare. A pattern representing the powers of good and evil emerges. Moll commits a crime and then reflects on the sinfulness of the act. At crucial moments, these reflections are intense and extended; for example, she agonizes over marrying Robin and describes "such terrors of mind" after her first robbery. The book becomes the alternation of a predicament quickly solved by an almost incredible opportunity for crime with Moll's guilty reflections on this action. The Devil provides the bait, and her conscience (as good angel) pinches her. The process may be seen in her first robbery. She hears a voice urging, "take the Bundle; be quick; do it this Moment" (2:4). The number of examples of such "promptings" from the Devil that could be drawn from spirit literature is nearly limitless. Richard Baxter, for instance, explains that "The temptations of Satan are sometimes so unnatural, so violent, that the tempted person even feels something besides himself persuading and urging him...."[29] Moll tells us that "'twas like a Voice spoken to me over my Shoulder...." She describes the bundle as the Devil's bait, and, again, this idea was common.[30] Sometimes the temptation was a rehearsal in a dream, sometimes a waking opportunity, but time after time the criminal would cite his need, the irresistible clear stage, and say in all seriousness, "The Devil made me do it."[31]

When Moll is rich, she begins to wonder why she continues to steal. A number of contemporary theologians would have interpreted her behavior as additional evidence for the existence of the Devil. Only Satan's presence, they argued, could explain the number of ways men could sin and the fact that they continued in the face of their friends' warnings and exhortations. Until Moll is thrown in Newgate, she is unreachable, but there she is redeemed by love, as Singleton is. In Newgate, she sees Jemmy and is struck by the belief that she ruined him. He had, after all, spent his entire fortune to trick her into marrying him, and she reasons that his resultant poverty led him to crime. The regret she feels leads her to think of others whom she has led into sin and to pray for mercy. After she is condemned to death, she listens attentively to a minister sent by the Governess and relates a conversion experience.[32] Many elements in the story of Moll and Jemmy suggest Providential action. That their love is so strong that Moll can call him back to her, that they are finally united, and that one sight of him in prison has such a beneficial effect on her distinguish theirs from all of Moll's other marriages. It reinforces her capacity for sympathy for others, for love, and for friendship and reminds us of the girl who would have forgiven and been faithful to the older brother who seduced her had she been able to persuade him to abandon his plan to marry her to Robin. The pause in the narrative of adventure that describes her repentance returns her to society and even to her family. The movement and tone of the novel is broken by the description of Moll's conversations with the minister and, while the pattern of episodic adventures and complicated relationships resumes, the pattern of alternating seized opportunities for sin with reflections on the wrongfulness of the act ceases entirely. For an age that at the very least felt uneasy at rejecting the idea that the world was the field of active battle between the powers of good and evil, Moll's habitual guilty regrets would have seemed the soul's resistance to the Devil's "promptings," "baits," and "hardening."

*Farther Adventures* opens with a re-creation of the beginning of *Robinson Crusoe*. Quite simply, Crusoe is again obsessed with the idea of going to sea. He describes this obsession as "a chronical Distemper" and laments, "I dream'd of it all Night, and my Imagination run upon it all Day.... I talk'd of it in my Sleep, ... it made my Conversation tiresome ..." (2:112). He struggles with this inclination for years, until his wife offers to go with him since she thinks it might be "some secret powerful Impulse of Providence." Her dramatic offer encourages him to conquer his "violent Distemper," and he buys a farm and settles down, only to be cast back into his original state by the death of his wife and his nephew's unexpected offer to take him back to see his island colony. The similarity between the beginnings of the two volumes of *Robinson Crusoe* is deliberate. Many of the same arguments against going to sea are marshalled; Crusoe and his wife are now the aging couple aware of the happiness of the "middle station" of life and the rashness of the proposal, and Crusoe does control his impulse for a number of years. The acceptable reasons for such a trip—poverty and ambition—are not augmented by youth, and none justify Crusoe's journey. At sixty, he "plays the young man" again.[33]

Immediately after the nephew invites Crusoe to join him, Defoe writes, "Nothing can be a greater Demonstration of a future State, and of the Existence of an invisible World, than the Concurrence of second Causes, with the Ideas of Things, which we form in our Minds ..." (2:119). But

Crusoe answers, *"What Devil sent you of this unlucky Errand?"* And so he leaves his children and his comfortable, retired life. A variation of this episode in the book occurs at the end of *Farther Adventures* when the exiled Russian prince refuses to leave Siberia with Crusoe: "How do you know Sir, says he warmly, that instead of a Summons from Heaven, it may not be a Feint of another Instrument? ... let me remain ... banish'd from the Crimes of Life ..." (3:207–8). There is an element of superstition in the opening of *Farther Adventures* that is partially dispelled by the Siberian dialogue. The purpose, the value, of Crusoe's final odyssey is certainly not clear, and he has been involved in "the Crimes of Life" even if he has not committed any of the murders, rapes, and swindlings around him. What good he has done— bringing Christianity to his island and rescuing the prince's son—has been opportunistic rather than planned or even described later as such. He was, as the prince pointed out by implicit comparison, far more likely to find trouble and temptation than goodness.

Furthermore, the philosophical and theological writings of the time overwhelmingly suggest that Defoe's contemporaries would have seen the Devil rather than a good angel prompting the sequence of events that led to Crusoe's final voyage. The progress of Crusoe's decision conforms to Defoe's and dozens of other writers' descriptions of the actions of the Devil in the world. In *The Political History of the Devil*, Defoe tells us that the Devil "is with us, and sometimes in us" but not always suspected. The person who is calm and at peace with himself is "his own man" while the "ruffled," passionate man has the Devil in him.[34] Crusoe's incessant thinking and talking about his desire to travel resembles "possession."

Crusoe obviously regards himself as a Christian in *Farther Adventures*. He reflects on his actions and his duty; he is open to the manifestations of God in the world (3:142, 146–47). Neither a superstitious throwback nor a modern sceptic, Crusoe holds most of the attitudes of men of his time. He listens to the Spanish governor describe the premonitions that prepared him for the invasion of the cannibals: "I am satisfied our Spirits embodied have a Converse with, and receive Intelligence from the Spirits unembodied and inhabiting the invisible World, and this friendly Notice is given for our Advantage ..." (2:166). Crusoe listens to this without comment. The Spaniard is expressing an opinion more common to the Renaissance than the Restoration and, although his anxieties prove to be well-founded, no further mention of the supernatural warning is made. The effect is to introduce the possibility of benign spirits without endorsement.[35] Defoe recounts a similar incident in his *History of Apparitions*. In this book of cases, a ship captain cannot sleep and, in his uneasiness, questions the mate who reassures him; as he leaves, however, he hears a voice say, "Heave the lead!" When he insists the mate do so, they find themselves in dangerously shallow water. Defoe concludes that this warning was not the work of Satan or an angel but "the work of a waking providence, by some invisible agent employed for that occasion...." and uses it to ask, "how will those modern wits ... account for this, who allow no God or Providence, no invisible world, ... kind and waking spirits, who, by a secret correspondence with our embodied spirits, give merciful hints to us of approaching mischiefs ...?"[36] Defoe is expressing a common opinion, one that can be found in books as diverse as Machiavelli's *Discourses on Livy* and Thomas Vaughan's *Magia Adamica*.[37] In *History of Apparitions*, he presents cases in much the way John Aubrey does in one of Defoe's acknowledged sources, *Miscellanies*,[38] and asks if the implications are not clear. In *Farther Adventures*, he uses a similar episode to add drama and to remind the reader that God's care for his creatures may be recognized whether or not man can explain an event rationally. Time after time, in *Farther Adventures* Defoe notes that people cannot always distinguish first or second causes, although second causes almost invariably act.[39]

Even more explicitly, Captain Roberts lives in a Providential world. His dedicatory epistle tells us that his book is a faithful relation of the "Dispensations of Providence." Ready to die in situations in which other Defoe characters compromise, Roberts steadfastly insists that he depends upon "the Blessing of God on my honest Endeavours" (p. 70), and his faith never wavers.[40] Marooned in the leaky ship, he recognizes his nearly hopeless situation but says, "if I was permitted to perish, I ... doubted not but he would ... receive me to his Everlasting Rest; and, what they had intended for my Misfortune, would be the Beginning of my Happiness; and that in the mean Time, I had nothing to do but to resign myself to his blessed Will and Protection, and bear my Lot with Patience" (p. 96). This passage might have been written by a contemporary of Bunyan, but its otherworldliness is undercut by the ingenuity and tenacity of Roberts's efforts to survive. As biblical as Roberts's language is and as many times as he refers to God, his physical survival dominates the narrative.[41] Because Roberts is so religious, he carries the moral world within him; Defoe does not need to supply reminders of it and he lets such incidents as Roberts's delirium on Salt Point pass without extraterrestial nuances.

Far from placing his heroines and heroes in an amoral world, Defoe uses the firmly ordered Christian world as his setting and makes this setting as important to the understanding of his themes as the concrete, historically accurate London Streets and West Indian trade routes. Contemporary readers would have found suspense, delight, and outrage in his books because of it. They would have found affirmation of their hopes and confirmation of their moral choices. Above all, they would have found the mores of their society and their expectations of order and pattern in the narrative and in the world upheld and translated into art. Defoe gave them infinite variety and "surprizing adventures" within a comfortably predictable frame.

## Notes

1. By the 1720s many of these travelers were hard-working, honest merchants. They were, however, often like the men described by Robinson Crusoe's father—the ambitious or the poor. Younger brothers often went to sea.

2. See Peter Linebaugh, "The Ordinary of Newgate and His *Account*," in *Crime in England 1550–1800*, p. 298, and Michael Harris, "Trials and Criminal Biographies: A Case Study in Distribution," in *Sale and Distribution of Books*, pp. 17, 20.

3. John Richetti, *Popular Fiction before Richardson*, p. 29; and Frank W. Chandler, *The Literature of Roguery*, pp. 139–40.

4. Andrew Knapp and William Baldwin, *The Newgate Calendar*, 1:1.

5. Scott, *Essays on Chivalry*, p. 462. Edward Heawood's *A History of Geographical Discovery in the Seventeenth and Eighteenth Centuries* is still the best guide to contemporary geographical knowledge.

6. I do not intend to deny interest in the interior life of characters as treated by such critics as Blewett, Novak, and Zimmerman, but the focus of this chapter is upon action; in chapter 8, I return to the adventure novel and an analysis of character.

7. Some scholars have said that Defoe makes idleness a sin and, therefore, gives this theme a predominantly moral significance (see Ian Watt, *The Rise of the Novel*, pp. 73–74, and Timothy J. Reiss, *The Discourse of Modernism*, pp. 297–327).

8. Quoted in Harris, "Trials and Criminal Biographies," p. 15.

9. Pielmeier's play is loosely based on a murder that took place in Rochester, New York, in April 1975 and came to trial in March 1977. The play was performed in eight cities, including Rochester, before it opened on Broadway in 1982 (see "Newborn a Horricide: Found in Convent," *Rochester Democrat and Chronicle*, 29 April 1975, p. 6B; "Brighton Nun Charged in Death of Infant," *Rochester Democrat and Chronicle*, 30 April 1975, p. 1A; "Lee Remick in Drama," *New York Times*, 12 January 1982, p. C13.

10. J. Paul Hunter discusses the tradition of journalistic treatment of the "unusual, surprizing, and wonderful" and its influence on the novel in a study in progress, tentatively titled "The Contexts of the Early English Novel."

11. [Eliza Haywood], *Tea Table*, no. 22 (4 May 1724).

12. Frantz Funck-Brentano, *Les Nouvellistes*, pp. 23–72.

13. Clara Reeve, *The Progress of Romance*, pp. 110–11; see also Pinkus, *Grub Street Stripped Bare*, pp. 15–17; Davis, *Factual Fictions*, pp. 45–51.

14. On newsbooks, see Davis, *Factual Fictions*, p. 72; G.A. Cranfield, *The Press and Society*, pp. 6, 13, 17; Herd, *The March of Journalism*, p. 13; Sandra Clark, *Elizabethan Pamphleteers*, pp. 23 ff.

15. Knapp and Baldwin, *Newgate Calendar*, 1:18.

16. Richard Altick, *Lives and Letters*, p. 32.

17. Low is the subject of one of Defoe's lives in *The General History of the … Pyrates*. A cruel bully in this collection, Low is eventually marooned by his men and hanged. For a discussion of Defoe's "facts," see Manuel Schonhorn, "*Defoe's Four Years Voyages of Captain Roberts* and *Ashton's Memorial*."

18. Sarah Fielding, Introduction to *The Lives of Cleopatra and Octavia*, p. xlii.

19. Robert Knox, *An Historical Relation of Ceylon*, p. 18, and *The Life and Adventures of Captain John Avery*, p. 9. This life is one that Defoe "answers" in his *King of Pirates* (1719), respectively.

20. William Chetwood, *The Voyages, Dangerous Adventures and imminent Escapes of Captain Richard Falconer*; see, for example, 1: 64–65 and 2: 97–103. Chetwood refers to Royal Society descriptions, 3:86.

21. A number of scholars have documented this practice. See, for example, A.W. Secord, *Studies in the Narrative Method of Defoe*, Percy Adams, *Travelers and Travel Liars*, esp. pp. 142–61, and idem, *Travel Literature and the Evolution of the Novel*, pp. 73, 163–64, 178. *Captain Singleton*, for example, simply copies pp. 188–271 of Knox's *Ceylon*. Boies Penrose dates the practice from Claudius Ptolemaeus's *Geography* (c. 150 A.D.) in *Travel and Discovery in the Renaissance*, p. 5.

22. The practice became standard. See, for example, Arthur Young's *Travels in France*, James Boswell's *Accounts of Corsica*, and Hester Thrale Piozzi's *Observations and Reflections Made in the Course of a Journey through France, Italy, and Germany*. An early example was John Lawson's *New Voyage to Carolina* (1709); even Dionisius Petavius's *The History of the World* is divided into a universal history and "A Geographical Description of the World."

23. John G. Cawelti, *Adventure, Mystery, and Romance*, chapter 1. John Richetti finds similar strains in travel and crime narratives, in chapter 3 of *Popular Fiction*; and see Frederick R. Karl, *The Adversary Literature*, pp. 52–54.

24. Watt, of course, says that *Moll Flanders* lacks such a moral framework (*The Rise of the Novel*, pp. 117ff). Others have found the structure of the spiritual autobiography in the novel; for the fullest argument, see G.A. Starr, *Defoe and Spiritual Autobiography*, chapter 4.

25. Richard Gilman, *The Confusion of Realms*, p. 121. See also Wayne Shumaker, *Literature and the Irrational*: "Aesthetic creativity ... often breaks through the limits of the rationally comprehensible" (p. 147).

26. See the lives of Rackam and White in Defoe, *The General History of the ... Pyrates*.

27. Compare this to Richard Baxter on how despair comes from the idea that "the Day of Grace is past" and leads to suicidal thoughts in *The Certainty of the Worlds of Spirits*. In one anecdote, a man hears a voice saying "Now cut thy Throat.... Do it, do it" (pp. 171–72).

28. *The English Rogue* by Richard Head was published in 1665; Francis Kirkman added a second part in 1668, and Head and Kirkman collaborated on the final two parts, which were published in 1671. The book enjoyed great popularity and saw many editions (see Chandler, *Literature of Roguery*, pp. 211–21). The quotation from *The English Rogue* is from the 1928 edition, pp. 67–68.

29. See Defoe's *System of Magick*, p. 326; Richard Baxter's *Saint's Everlasting Rest* in *The Practical Works of the Rev. Richard Baxter*, 22: 319, and *The Reasons of the Christian Religion*, 21: 87 and 90; Raleigh's *History of the World*, 2:399; and John Aubrey, *Miscellanies* in *Three Prose Works*, pp. 65–66. Aubrey's *Miscellanies* was in a new edition in 1721 and is listed with the books in the Defoe/Farewell library.

30. Baxter, "Witness to the Truth of Christianity," in *The Practical Works*, 2: 339–40; Baxter explains that the devil's "baits" are suited to the age, station, and situation of his victim. Compare this to Defoe, *The Political History of the Devil*, pp. 384–85.

31. The belief in the Devil's promptings was widespread and listed repetitiously in collections of spirit manifestations throughout the period (see, for example, Sir Thomas Browne, *Pseudodoxia Epidemica*, 1: 58). Charles Morton, Defoe's schoolmaster, quoted Browne in his *Compendium Physiace*. Particularly brutal crimes were often ascribed to the devil's inspiration or labeled "devilish ideas" as too wicked for man to have conceived without help.

32. The debate over Moll's sincerity is long-standing. For a recent discussion concluding that Moll is a penitent see Novak, *Realism*, pp. 75–98. Arnold Weinstein finds "Moll's fundamental doubleness" the source of the power of her characterization (*Fictions of the Self, 1550–1800*, pp. 94–95).

33. Compare *Robinson Crusoe*, 1: 3–4 and 2: 111–16.

34. Defoe, *Political History of the Devil*, pp. 241, 423–25.

35. In *The History of Apparitions* Defoe discusses good spirits (see pp. 186, 190, 199). On theologians' unwillingness to deny the reality of spirits and the "threat" of atheism, see Keith Thomas, *Religion and the Decline of Magic*, pp. 591–93. Many pamphlets insisted that disbelief in spirits was a sign of atheism (see, for example, *Satan's Invisible World Discover'd*, p. xviii).

36. On premonitions, see Defoe, *History of Apparitions*, pp. 214–18, 223.

37. Quoted in Aubrey, *Miscellanies*, p. 69; Thomas Vaughan, *Magia Adamica*, p. 132; see also Morton, *Compendium Physicae*, p. 195.

38. Defoe, *History of Apparitions*, p. 192. Among others, Defoe cites Clarendon, Lucian, Tournefort, and Jeremy Taylor as sources. The universal nature of similar reports is always offered as evidence for spirit existence. See, for instance, John Dee, *A True and Faithful Relation*, in which Meric Casaubon argues that he published Dee's account to "promote Religion" and draws examples from Aristotle, Cicero, Remigius, and Bodin. For a modern account, see Aniela Jaffé, *Apparitions and Precognition*, pp. 1, 7–8, 183.

39. Compare, *Farther Adventures*, 3: 62–63: "we do not expect Returns from Heaven, in a miraculous and particular Manner." For a discussion of this central theme in *Robinson Crusoe*, see Backscheider, *A Being More Intense*, pp. 142–44, 168–69.

40. In fact, *Captain Roberts* throws additional doubt on the extent to which Defoe accepted the argument from necessity; in this book only the evil use it, and Roberts rejects it out of hand (see p. 56).

41. On page 84, Roberts remembers, "I humbly besought [God] ... that in all Things I might through the Guidance of the holy Spirit, be directed so as to submit myself entirely to his Will." Roberts's efforts to survive, however, are the subject of his story.

SIMON VAREY

# An Architect's Imagination:
# The Rise of Bath

...it is pointless trying to decide whether Zenobia is to be classified among happy cities or among the unhappy. It makes no sense to divide either into these two species, but rather into another two; those that through the years and the changes continue to give their form to desires, and those in which desires either erase the city or are erased by it.

—Italo Calvino, *Invisible Cities*

...this bathing is profitable for all palsies, apoplexies, caros, epilepsies, stupidity, defluctions, gouts, sciaticaes, contractions, cramps, aches, tumors, itches, scabs, leprosies, cholicks, windyness, whites in women, stopping of their courses, barrenness, abortions, scorbuts, anasarcaes, and generally all cold and phlegmatick diseases, which are needless to reckon up.

—Edward Jorden, *A Discourse of Natural*
*Bathes and Mineral Waters* (1632)

In John Wood's day, visitors to Bath used to be reminded that the city's origins were firmly rooted in British myth. Until about 1700 a grotesque statue of the legendary founder of the city, King Bladud, stood over the north gate, only to be replaced by a new, even worse one, that looked 'more like a dressed Puppet, seated in a Ducking Stool, than the Figure of a famous King', but anyone chancing to miss that could always read, on the south wall of the King's Bath, an inscription that commemorated the fantastic

From *Space and the Eighteenth-Century English Novel.* © 1990 by the Cambridge University Press.

achievements of this curious character.[1] The fanciful inscription 'appearing to some of the last [i.e. seventeenth] Century as a legendary Tale ... was therefore abridged, and, in respect to Time, brought down to the Year 1672', and was then published in Thomas Guidott's *De Thermis Britannicis* in 1691. Particularly well-read visitors might also have known half a dozen different written versions of the Bladud legend.[2]

Geoffrey of Monmouth, the oldest source of the story, explained that at the time of the prophet Elijah, Bladud built Bath, 'and made the hot Baths in it for the Benefit of the Publick, which he dedicated to the Goddess *Minerva*; in whose Temple he kept Fires that never went out nor consumed to Ashes, but as soon as they began to decay were turned into Balls of Stone'.[3] Furthermore, Bladud was so proficient in necromancy that he learned to fly: but not proficient enough, for 'in one of his flying humours',[4] he 'fell down upon the Temple of *Apollo* in the City of *Trinovantum*, where he was dashed to Pieces'.[5] Geoffrey's source on the strange properties of the undying fires was the third-century writer Solinus, who may have been describing Somerset coal when he wrote that this 'perpetual fire never whitens to ash, but as the flame fades, turns into rocky lumps'.[6] As for Bladud, Geoffrey's account, like most of his 'history', was hardly considered reliable: indeed he was often called the inventor rather than 'translator' of the British history.[7] In a more sober commentary than Geoffrey's, William Camden declared: 'I dare not attribute [the baths] original to that art [of magic]'; and in another, John Aubrey's friend Dr Guidott considered nature more likely than any 'Art of Magick' to have 'made the Hot Waters in *Bath*'.[8] Stories of magic and perpetual fires Guidott dismissed as 'feigned matters', and the equally sanguine Dr Edward Jorden thought them 'too simple for any wise man to beleeue, or for me to confute'.[9] Daniel Defoe, never guilty of credulity, acknowledged the 'Antiquity of this Place' but refused to 'come in to the Inscription under the Figure' which claimed that Bladud 'found out the use of these *Baths*, 300 Years before our Saviour's Time ... because even the Discovery is ascribed to the Magick of the Day, not their Judgment in the Physical Virtue of *Minerals*, and *Mineral-Waters*'.[10]

In 1802 a guidebook informed tourists that 'till within these fifty years' the inhabitants of Bath had 'maintained their descent from the necromantic Bladud' with an ardour equal to that 'with which the classical states' adopted their deities.[11] That 1750 or so should mark the *end* of such a belief, rather than its renewal, would have dismayed John Wood, who in 1749 had given the Bladud myth its fullest—and most naively charming—expression. Wood told how Bladud had been expelled from the royal court by his father, Lud Hudibras, because 'by some accident or other', he had contracted leprosy. Incognito, he found a job as a swineherd. The pigs too soon became leprous, but were miraculously cured of their disease when they wallowed in the mud above some hot springs in the west of England. Bladud followed their example, was instantly cured, and when he eventually succeeded to the throne of Britain, he set up his court on the site of the hot springs in 483 BC. The city—Bath, of course—was built three years later.[12] In an earlier version of his story, Wood also had Bladud falling to his death on the steeple of Salisbury Cathedral: he later changed this to Trinovantum, which he triumphantly identified as Bath. (Everyone else identified Trinovantum as London.)[13]

Wood ascribed his story of Bladud and the pigs to oral tradition. Although in 1697 respectable Dr Robert Peirce felt certain that 'there is nothing impossible in it, nor very improbable',[14] by the time Wood was writing, Bathonians had long been something of a laughing stock for perpetuating this ludicrous account of their city's origin, even after 'the famous *John* Earl of *Rochester* coming to *Bath*, the Story of *Bladud* and his Pigs became a Subject for his Wit, and this proved the Cause of striking it out of the Inscription placed against one of the Walls of the King's Bath'.[15] Then in 1711 Martin Powell ran a puppet show of 'The History of King Bladud, Founder of the Bath', so that, to Wood's chagrin, 'the Tradition is now in a Manner lost at *Bath*'.[16] Actually, it was not lost entirely: in 1736 or so 'a tragedy call'd, the TRANSFORMATION: or the *fall of* BLADUD, as he assum'd the seat of *Jupiter*' was advertised as 'ALMOST ready for the Stage', then about 1760 a standard guide book for tourists retailed Wood's account as if it were fact, and in 1775 an anonymous author was still willing to accept Wood's version of the story, and Samuel Foote's allusion to it in a play cannot have been lost on his audience in 1778.[17] Learning of the story on his way through Bath in 1751, Dr Pococke had observed cautiously, 'There may be some foundation for it in tradition'.[18]

One anonymous joker said that 'a belief of Bladud and his swine made one of the necessary qualifications for an introduction into the body corporate', but whether or not anyone, Wood included, seriously believed the Bladud myth, it was a conspicuous means of advertising the efficacy of the naturally hot spring waters, 'Where Pigs were once, and Princes now are boil'd', as another wit put it.[19] Wood knew, of course, that the enduring reason why Bath attracted so many visitors was the fame of the waters' curative power, 'a Fame', he claimed, exaggerating as usual, 'that stirred up the grand Monarch of *France* to compleat the Works of *Bourbon* [in] 1680'.[20] Appealing to primitive hut theory, Guidott thought that in the distant past 'Sick people in all probability ... came hither for relief, first making small Cottages for their Conveniences, which were afterwards improved into fairer Buildings. So that now in this particular, there are few places in *England* that exceed it.'[21] Wood, indeed, placed such high value on the waters that he considered it essential 'to expell all private Property to a proper Distance from the Heads of our Sovereign Fountains, and to enlarge the Bounds of the Baths, to preserve the Springs for the Benefit of Posterity'.[22]

The springs seem to have been in use since the late Mesolithic era (about 5,000 to 4,000 BC), but as Samuel and Nathaniel Buck announced in the caption to their print of Bath, 'not much Credit is given to any Accounts of y^e first discoverers of them, notwithstanding y^e Inscription ... of Bladud ... neither can y^e discovery be attributed to y^e Romans. But there are Proofs that these last contributed to render them commodious and prevent their mixing with other Waters.'[23] Even before the Romans built their baths there, about AD 60–70, sufferers from 'Palsies, Contractions, Rheums, cold Tumors, affects of the skin, aches, &c.' had sought relief by plunging into the steaming waters, rich with 'Bitumen, with Nitre, and some Sulphur'.[24] Visitors in the sixteenth century, overcoming the exhalation of 'an ill favour proceeding from corrupt water mix'd with earth and brimstone' would find 'an effectual remedy to such bodies as by reason of ill humours are dull and heavy' since the heat of the waters would induce sweating, 'and by that means the career of the humour is curb'd'.[25]

The Bladud myth as retailed by Wood epitomized the experience of thousands of ailing visitors, even those who 'look upon the *Baths* as a Pool of *Bethesda*, that cures by Miracle', as some of 'higher quality', and 'ingenious Education' were wont to do.[26] They could bathe in the spring water, too many at a time for Pepys's comfort,[27] or they could drink it. Although Thomas Guidott 'Arrogates to himself the happy discovery that the waters could be drunk,[28] two other seventeenth-century doctors—Edward Jorden and John Radcliffe—are usually credited with the discovery that Bath water was equally effective when drunk, provided it was not contaminated by the water in which infected bodies were immersed, a prospect that made Matt Bramble recoil in perfect disgust.[29] In fact, Ranulf Higden's words suggest that the water had been drunk as early as the fourteenth century: 'the water of this bathe be more troubly and hevyer of savour & of smelle than other hote bathes ben yt I have seen'.[30] Drinking the water, said Jorden, should 'heat, dry, mollifie, discusse, glutinate, dissolve, open obstructions, cleanse the kidneys, and bladder, ease cholicks, comfort the matrix, mitigate fits of the mother, help barrennesse proceeding from cold humors, &c'.[31] Despite a high success rate, such recommendation may seem hard to accept for anyone who has tasted this sulphurous brown liquid,

> that hot, milky, soft, salutiferous Beverage, called *Bath Water*, far beyond any hot mineral Waters for its Delicacy, and supportable, tho' comfortable Heat [120°F], to any other such Water hitherto discovered on the habitable Globe, as it possesses that Milkiness, Detergency, and middling Heat so friendly adapted to weaken'd animal Constitutions, which all other hot Waters want in due Degree ... This Water is admirably grateful to the Stomach, striking the Roof of the Mouth with a fine sulphurous and steely Taste,

or, as Celia Fiennes thought, it 'tastes like the water that boyles eggs, [and] has such a smell'.[32] What is more, it runs straight through anyone brave enough to drink it. Sadly, the *coup de grace* was administered in the winter of 1978–79 when the water had to be declared hazardous to public health after contamination led to a fatal case of amoebic meningitis.[33]

The Bladud legend confirmed the association of Bath with spring waters and hypochondria. In fact, Fiennes noted, 'the town and all its accommodations is adapted to the batheing and drinking of the waters, and to nothing else', for as Defoe wrote, Bath 'would have been a very small City, (if at all a City) were it not for the *Hot Baths* here, which give both Name and Fame to the Place'.[34] An Anglo-Saxon name for the place, Ackmanchester, meaning 'the City of diseased People', is self-explanatory.[35] The Romans seem to have used the place only for bathing: they built no fortifications, and probably established only a small garrison where the Fosse Way crossed the river Avon at Bathwick, and they apparently knew that the water had curative properties, since they separated the water supplies.[36]

The Roman name for the city, Aquae Sulis, draws attention to the waters, of course, but in dedicating their temple the Romans also conflated the names of Celtic and Roman deities, Sul and Minerva, which the Bladud myth also exploits. Yet at least as early as the 1590s the name Aquae Sulis, the waters of Sul Minerva, had become corrupted to Aquae Solis, giving rise to a connotation of Bath with Sol, the sun, thus with Apollo and another set of myths and traditions.[37] No Roman buildings were still visible, but Roman remains were found at Bath during the eighteenth century, some by John Wood's own workmen in 1727: with the meticulous care of an archaeologist, Wood recorded exactly what artefacts had been found, and where, and when (to the hour), before handing over the most interesting specimens to the City Corporation.[38] A gilded bronze head—probably depicting Minerva—was the most exciting discovery until the east end of the Roman baths themselves was excavated in August 1755, alas too late for Wood to cherish: he had died fifteen months earlier, on 23 May 1754.[39] The most important discovery of all was the first-century Temple of Sul Minerva itself, in 1790, which confirmed local tradition and gave genuine substance to myth.

Wood had the sense to see that there was a Bath industry waiting to be exploited. With the leisured classes of British society becoming more mobile all the time, lodging houses could prosper. Bath's natural commodity already meant visitors, who were accommodated in quite expensive lodging houses: ten shillings per week for a suite, and five shillings more for a servant's garret. In the season additional charges were levied on visitors: for subscriptions to balls (twice a week at two guineas each) and concerts, and to the library; for walking in the gardens; for newspapers; and five shillings for pen, ink, and paper at a coffee house.[40] Celia Fiennes considered 'the chargeableness of the Bath' to be 'the lodging and firing, the faggotts being very small', but she conceded that 'they give you very good attendance there'.[41] In his vision of a new city, Wood never contemplated reducing the high cost of anyone's stay, but sought to raise the city's income by providing more, and better lodgings for an increased number of visitors. The poor quality of lodging houses was notorious. Queen Elizabeth had condemned Bath as 'dirty of aspect and nasty of smell' (rather like herself), and although Henrietta Maria diplomatically preferred the English spa to the French, she too had hated the primitive conditions at Bath.[42] Something certainly needed to be done, because in 1727, Wood says, the streets were like 'dung-hills, slaughter houses and pig-styes' and 'the Boards of the Dining Rooms and most other Floors were made of a Brown Colour with Soot and small Beer to hide the Dirt, as well as their own Imperfections'.[43] When the Duke of Chandos visited the city in 1726, he was so appalled by his cramped and unsalubrious lodgings that he resolved to build his own, employing Wood as his architect.

Wood did not initiate the improvement and expansion of Bath as a leisure centre, for that desultory process had already begun before he was born, but he planned the city as we now know it. From its 'very small and mean beginning' Bath expanded so fast that by 1791 it had become almost unrecognizable, as Fanny Burney reported when she returned after eleven years' absence to find a 'City of Palaces—a Town of Hills, & a Hill of Towns'.[44] In 1753 the antiquary William Borlase wrote to Sir Thomas Lyttelton: 'Bath, I find, alters & improves every year, and whatever is new built is spatious, airy, and rich in Pediments, Pillars, Porticoes—Their pavements also make walking in their streets, and even riding too, very secure and easy'.[45] All in all, Mrs Pendarves told Swift in 1736, Bath had become 'a more comfortable place to live in than London', which had 'grown to such an enormous size, that above half the day must be spent in the streets in going from one place to another': she liked London 'every year less and less'.[46] Although large tracts of Bath seemed like an endless, noisy, building site, the city had been transformed in about half a century from a rather squalid, cramped provincial town into an elegant and fashionable resort. Whenever anyone commented on this expansion, the name of John Wood was certain to arise: his 'fame, as an *Architect*, will never be forgotten while the name of *Bath* exists'.[47]

As soon as Wood arrived in Bath in 1727, he gravitated towards Ralph Allen, already something of a local celebrity, whose talent was to make the postal system immensely profitable to the government and to himself.[48] Allen also owned a stone quarry at Widcombe. In addition to several minor projects in the city, North Parade, South Parade, and the Royal Mineral Water Hospital (as it is now known) all owe their existence to the partnership between the architect and the stone merchant, whose combined efforts continued for a quarter-century until Wood's death.

It is customary to attribute the rise of Bath to Ralph Allen, Richard

'Beau' Nash, and John Wood. Because these three were the most conspicuous of Bath's 'developers', they tend to obscure the less spectacular contributions made by the medical men, Tobias Venner, Edward Jorden, Thomas Guidott, George Cheyne, William Oliver, and Robert Peirce, all of whom—whatever their disagreements—industriously advertised and popularized the healthy qualities of the waters, as their predecessors in the profession had done since the mid sixteenth century.[49] Nor should the architects who succeeded John Wood be overshadowed: his eldest son John, who continued his father's work; Thomas Jelly in the middle years of the century; Thomas Atwood and his successor (and ex-assistant) as city architect, Thomas Baldwin, most active during the 1770s; Baldwin's associate John Eveleigh; Robert Adam, who contributed Pulteney Bridge; Jelly's younger partner John Palmer; and John Pinch; the work of these men continued the expansion of the gracious city into the early nineteenth century.

The landowners who initiated the expansion were mostly speculators who rebuilt on their own land, or bought land with a view to speculation, in contempt of local opposition. But some landowners were cautious about building: Wood recorded how Humphrey Thayer hesitated, after buying the old bowling green and Abbey Orchard 'with a View to improve each Piece of Ground by Building, at the Expiration of the under Tenant's Leases': when in 1730 Wood was trying to get his proposed grand circus approved, 'a Person at that Time in London' prevented the scheme from going ahead, and (to Wood's disgust) Thayer, to his dying day—9 December 1737—'would not enter into the Treaty again with the Zeal of one determined to come to the Point'.[50] Whatever pressure was put on Thayer, the case was clearer for Robert Gay, who, as Member of Parliament for the city, declined to pursue one of Wood's building projects, because (Wood said) he was afraid he might lose votes, even though 'it might have been only intended the better to preserve his Interest among the Electors of the City'.[51] Wood permitted himself only the understatement that Gay's decision was 'a Discouragement',[52] but more aggrieved commentators would point out that the overriding consideration for all these men was personal profit. Even Allen, whose 'Charity is seen farther than his House ... and brings him more Honour too', was nevertheless accused in later years of vanity, high-handedness, and an unscrupulous desire for wealth.[53] The city of Bath is a memorial less perhaps to benevolence than to entrepreneurial capitalism.

This expansion of Bath would have been impossible without the Avon Navigation scheme, which finally got under way in the 1720s after fifty years of negotiation, disagreement, and delay. Andrew Yarranton described a proposal which would have connected the Severn and the Thames by way of Bristol and Bath in the 1670s, but 'some foolish Discourse at Coffee-houses laid asleep that design as being a thing impossible and impracticable'.[54] But when the scheme was successfully revived it was Allen who 'did more than anyone else to persuade Henry Duke of Beaufort to pilot through Parliament' the necessary legislation.[55] Wood's part in this project was also considerable: he even refers to digging the canal as something he himself 'had undertaken', and by sending from London 'Labourers, that had been employed on the *Chelsea* Water-Works', he was able to introduce the spade (previously unknown) to Bath workmen, and reduce the cost of earth-removal by one third.[56] Two major advantages of a navigable river between Bath and Bristol were that building materials such as lead could reach Bath more quickly and in larger shipments, and a much greater volume of Bath freestone could be shipped to Bristol, and thence to London, Ireland, and apparently even Lisbon.[57] Wood saw the advantages; it was only when he knew the navigation scheme was certain to go ahead that he began to think seriously of improving Bath.

That Bath freestone was available at all for shipment was due mainly to the entrepreneurial skill of Ralph Allen, whose Widcombe quarry kept the city supplied for over thirty years. Bath is rare among British cities for being almost entirely stone-built, and indeed a significant part of Bath's charm is attributable to the stone's warm golden colour, that 'fine yellow tinct', as Brettingham called it.[58] Bath freestone is soft and prone to crumble before it hardens on contact with air, a fact that even found its way into Richardson's *Clarissa*.[59] These properties make it cheap to quarry, since blasting is unnecessary, but they also make it difficult to work, as London stonemasons found. But those local masons who were accustomed to working with Bath freestone dressed it first, then transported blocks to the building site, where (to Wood's chagrin) rough masons put them directly but carelessly in place.[60] Allen's stone was transported in wooden wagons which ran two miles down the hill from Widcombe along a railway track to his new stone works on the banks of the Avon where the stone was wrought.[61] By reducing the costs of transport, Allen reduced the price of dressed stone, underbidding his rivals for a contract in Bristol in 1740 by 24 per cent.[62] Allen also succeeded in reducing the unit wages of his workmen, but in return he could at least guarantee them employment.

Most of the businessmen responsible for the expansion of Bath had some sense of public duty. Bath, a 'universal Infirmary', as Cheyne called it,[63] became a centre of charity, too, symbolized by the founding of the General Hospital, which opened in 1740 to receive patients from other parts of the country. To enter that institution, it was a requirement to be poor: the costs of maintaining the patients (110 of them by 1755) were borne mostly by the city, by the thirty-two founders of the hospital, and by various private donors. The hospital's 'chief Benefactor' was Allen, who supplied 'all the Wall-Stone, Free-stone ready wrought, Paving-stone, and Lime used in it' at his own expense.[64] Nash donated £1,000 to the building, and Wood charged no fee for his architectural expertise. All three, aided by Dr Oliver, whom God preserve, of biscuit fame, actively canvassed the wealthy to raise funds for the hospital. Oliver was the hospital's physician and Jerry Peirce its surgeon, from its inauguration in May 1740 until May 1761.[65] In 1749 Gwynn thought the vogue for subscribing to hospitals did not spring truly from charity but from 'real *Interest* and *Pleasure*', an attitude that perhaps lay behind the repeated complaints that the insolent townspeople—'a sharking People, scum of all the Nation'—displayed 'a very great Narrowness of Spirit' and fleeced 'Your paralytical people, that come down to be parboil'd and pump'd'.[66] In spite of such criticism Bath became almost as famous for its charity as for its new status as the nation's leading resort.

Bath's rise as a fashionable social resort was due in large part to the efforts of Beau Nash, self-styled 'King of Bath'. This improbable Welsh adventurer instituted rules for proper behaviour to which all visitors—no matter how lofty their status—were obliged to adhere. Richard Graves simply expressed a commonplace when he said that Nash 'had greatly reformed and regulated the manners and behaviour of his subjects in the public room'.[67] But there was a darker side, too. According to Wood, the Gaming Act of 1739 was passed at the request of the Bath corporation, to rid the city of 'fraudulent, and deceitful' gaming and gamesters, and according to the compilers of the 1742 version of Defoe's *Tour*, 'Gaming used to obtain here, as at all publick Places, to a scandalous Degree; but the Act prohibiting that pernicious Practice, has a good deal checked its Progress', but they cannot have known that Nash was, in Goldsmith's words, 'himself concerned in the gaming-tables, of which he only seemed the conductor'.[68] Scandal would follow later.

Long before the arrival of Nash in 1705, Bath had an undesirable reputation for immorality: back in 1572 another Welshman, John Jones, issued a stern warning to male visitors: 'See that altogither whyle ye be there, and lenger, yee auoyde copulation, that is, the vse of women'.[69] The temptations of Bath were evidently undiminished by time. Delicate sensibilities were offended that mixed bathing was permitted: a crusty colonel in one of Thomas D'Urfey's plays finds naked bathing 'very nauseous' and Pander, a character in another light comedy, claims that the 'Class' of demure prudes 'decreases daily' thanks to 'spreading Libertinism'.[70] Dr Jorden (as quoted by Wood) most certainly was not amused: 'The baths are bear-gardens, where both sexes bathe promiscuously', so perhaps he thought they deserved their unpleasant fate: 'passers-by pelt them with dead dogs, cats and pigs': this was considered such a serious problem that a local law was passed, 'That no Person shall presume to cast or throw any Dog, Bitch, or other live Beast, into any of the said Baths', but the law apparently did not prevent anyone from throwing *dead* animals at the bathers. (The fine was 3s 4d.)[71] Although Nash helped to palliate Bath's notoriety, he never entirely suppressed it.[72] Throughout the century, Bath was said to be full of loose women, cheats (as the Bath scenes in Smollett's *Peregrine Pickle* reveal), procurers and profligates: a veritable 'sink of profligacy and extortion', in fact.[73] After his brief account of the antiquity of the city, Defoe admitted:

> There remains little to add, but what relates to the Modern Customs, the Gallantry and Diversions of that Place, in which I shall be very short; the best Part being but a Barren Subject, and the worst Part meriting rather a Satyr, than a Description ... now we may say it is the Resort of the Sound, rather than the Sick; the Bathing is more a Sport and Diversion, than a Physical Prescription for Health; and the Town is taken up in Raffling, Gameing, Visiting, and in a Word, all sorts of Gallantry and Levity. The whole Time indeed is a Round of the utmost Diversion.[74]

Those who continued Defoe's *Tour* added puritanically that Bath 'helps the Indolent and the Gay to commit that worst of Murders, that is to say, to kill Time'.[75]

The story of Nash's reign in Bath is too well known to need repeating, but it is important that despite his own hypocrisy he tried to make Bath a decent, urbane place, to give it a reputation for propriety and so make the ambience of the city attractive to visitors.[76] Nash's personality was inimitable, as his colourless successors soon proved, so that within a few years of his death in February 1761, Bath quickly sank again into unmitigated notoriety. In 1745 Bath was reported to have 'every Thing that can render it delightful & Entertaining, agreable for Persons of that high Rank & Elegancy who resort to It',[77] but such social stratification became gradually less rigid, more democratized. By the early nineteenth century, when sea water was preferred to spa water and Brighton was the rage, Bath's Assembly Rooms were held in general contempt, and the famously decorous social behaviour for which Nash had been largely responsible had become just a fond memory for the nostalgic. Pat Rogers sees Nash as 'the ultimate instigator' of the expansion of Bath, 'not just because he helped to make the town prosperous, or brought the Woods' clientele to Bath, but principally because he created the climate in which architecture of such grandiose ambition could stand without absurdity'.[78] But Nash was only one of the three who made Bath what it was: Allen's commercial enterprise and Wood's imagination built the physical facilities of the city. Together with his son, Wood devised an idiosyncratic Utopia with an astonishingly broad intellectual basis. The Woods were real innovators.

Architectural Utopias had, of course, been in vogue for centuries before Wood turned his attention to Bath, but the distinctive feature of Utopias, by definition, was that they never got built. Among the more recent English attempts, Inigo Jones had 'wanted to transform London into an augustan city in which the architecture would be more than a mere setting for royal policy, but would condition and help its implementation'.[79] Neither Jones's scheme for London's improvement, nor Wren's plans to rebuild the city after the Great Fire, nor even Hawksmoor's bizarre scheme for Cambridge, could be realized. Although Bath turned out not to conform exactly to Wood's systematic proposals, it came closer than practice usually does to theory. The creators of modern Bath built a new, unique city, which enveloped and overshadowed the old. London and, later in the century, Edinburgh, expanded rapidly with additions in a similar architectural idiom, but neither could boast Bath's combination of medicinal virtue, social life, and a concentration of monumental public and private buildings.[80]

By the time Wood the elder had finished with Bath, he had trebled the size of the old city. Even though his most private intentions (discussed in the next chapter) remained in obscurity, Wood gave the city what its visitors wanted: comfortable lodgings, elegant squares, wide streets. He said the older housing within the city walls was neither beautiful nor convenient, 'for there is not a Street, Lane, Alley, or Throng, whose Sides are straight, or whose Surface is upon a true depending Line, to give them the least Beauty: Nor is there any principal Way but what lies in Common to Men and Beasts.'[81] As if these horrors were not enough, the streets also had open sewers, and water dripping down on passers-by from roof spouts. But, Wood prophesied, 'All these Defects, however, seem to be upon the point of decreasing', and with his characteristic note of self-righteousness, 'if the Corporation of the City had come into the Scheme I proposed in the Year 1727, most of them had been removed long before now'.[82] Wood was seeking to accommodate only the well-to-do, since they alone gave the city some substantial return in hard cash, and they alone could afford to squander their money on the other pleasures Bath offered. The scale of the public rooms—particularly Baldwin's Pump Room (1791–92; finished by Palmer, 1793–96) and Wood the Younger's Assembly Rooms (1769–71)—suggests that either the assembly rooms were uncomfortably overcrowded, or relatively few visitors actually attended the public events. Bath may have seemed enormous to Matt Bramble, but the spaces seem very small to me. Although Wood calculated that 12,000 visitors could now be accommodated, his spaces were intended for the use of few people, not for the public at large.

The uniqueness of eighteenth-century Bath consists, in part, in the personal version of Palladianism that John Wood brought to his individual buildings and their disposition. Although he contemplated constructing Assembly Rooms in Bath, 'almost upon the same Footing with the [Earl of Burlington's] Assembly House at *York*', Wood was not quite in the main stream of English Palladianism.[83] Perhaps more than even Burlington's school, Wood realized that the Palladian idiom should be seen to be new and yet remain traditionally British at the same time.[84] The theory behind Wood's architecture is an amalgam of myths and traditions that enabled him to imagine a magnificent city.

Palladio himself recognized one function of architecture as 'ornament' when he praised 'the antients' for building roads 'in such a manner, that also in them might be known the grandeur and magnificence of their minds'.[85] In a much broader conception, Lewis Mumford writes that 'Mind *takes form* in the city; and in turn, urban forms condition mind. For space, no less than time, is artfully reorganized in cities': he adds, 'The city is both a physical utility for collective living and a symbol of those collective purposes and unanimities that arise under such favouring circumstances'.[86] Georgian Bath is a nearly perfect realization of these precepts: the new city was the physical result of the system of financial capitalism that had begun to gather momentum in the last years of the seventeenth century. Bath was built *on* that system's greatest strength, credit; it was built mostly *by* middle-class entrepreneurs and businessmen, who knew how to exploit the network of credit for their own profit.[87] Wood's designs were neither shocking nor controversial, for the spaces of his new city embodied the aesthetic and social ideals of the wealthy and leisured. Although the Palladian revival was not Hanoverian, nor especially Whiggish, Georgian Bath was a good example of Mies vander Rohe's dictum that 'Architecture is the will of an epoch translated into space; living, changing, new.'[88] Yet in an apparent paradox the story of Georgian Bath is the story of John Wood: unlike any other British city, Bath's architecture reveals the hegemony of one mind.[89]

## NOTES

1. John Wood, *An Essay Towards a Description of Bath*, 2nd edn (1749), II, p. 324 and I, p. 8. The crude statue and the solemn inscription (dated 1699) can still be seen, on the south wall of the King's Bath.

2. Guidott printed the inscription in Latin (*De Thermis Britannicis* [London, 1691], p. 16). The sources of the legend include: Wace, *Roman de Brut*, 1667-77 and Layamon, *Brut or Chronicle of Britain*, 2,834–95, both known only in manuscript (e.g. British Library, MS Cotton CAL. A.ix.I). until Sir Frederic Madden edited them for publication in 1847; John Higgins, 'Bladud' (*Parts Added to the Mirror for Magistrates*, ed. Lily B. Campbell [Cambridge: Cambridge University Press, 1946], pp. 132–44); John Leland, *Commentarii de* Scriptoribus Britannicis (Oxford, 1709), pp. 8–11; Spenser, *Faerie Queene*, II. X. 25–26; *Coryat's Crudities* (London, 1611); William Camden, *Britannia*, ed. Edmund Gibson (London, 1695), cols. 69–70. There were other sources still, such as Aylett Sammes, *Britannia Antiqua Illustrata: or, the Antiquities of Ancient Britain* (London, 1676), which simply repeated Camden or Geoffrey.

3. *The British History*, translated by Aaron Thompson (London, 1718), p. 49.

4. William Burton, *A Commentary on Antoninus his Itinerary* (London, 1658), p. 24; cited by Ernest Jones, *Geoffrey of Monmouth*, University of California Publications in

English Vol. 5, No. 3 (Berkeley and Los Angeles: University of California Press, 1944), p. 365.

5. *The British History*, p. 50.

6. Solinus, *Collecteana rerum memorabilium*, quoted by Barry Cunliffe, *Roman Bath Discovered* (London: Routledge & Kegan Paul, 1971, rev. edn 1984), p. 14. See also Samuel Lysons, 'Remains of Two Temples, and other Roman Antiquities discovered at Bath', in *Reliquiae Britannico-Romanae, containing Figures of Roman Antiquities discovered in various parts of England*, I (London: Cadell & Davies, T. Payne, & White, Cochrane, 1813), p. 3. John Jones gave the story currency in his *Bathes of Bathes Ayde* (London, 1572), but Thomas Guidott dismissed it (*A Discourse of Bathe, and the Hot Waters there* [London, 1676], p. 3).

7. E.g. William Lloyd, Bishop of Worcester, declared (around 1703–04) that Geoffrey mingled a few chance truths with his own fictions (see A. Tindal Hart, *William Lloyd 1627–1717: Bishop, Politician, Author and Prophet* [London: SPCK, 1952], p. 229). Cf. Stuart Piggott, 'The Sources of Geoffrey of Monmouth', *Antiquity*, 15 (1941), 269–86, and Ernest Jones, *Geoffrey of Monmouth*, pp. 357–77. For a recent, suprisingly sympathetic view of Geoffrey's history, see Norma Lorre Goodrich, *King Arthur* (New York and Toronto: Franklin Watts, 1986), pp. 41–47.

8. Camden, *Britannia*, col. 70; Guidott, *An Appendix concerning Bathe* (London, 1669), in Edward Jorden, *A Discourse of Natural Bathes, and Mineral Waters*, '4th edn' [actually 5th] (London, 1673), p. 5.

9. *Appendix*, p. 51. Jorden, *Discourse*, 2nd edn (London, 1632), p. 133.

10. *A Tour thro' the whole Island of Great Britain*, ed. G.D.H. Cole (London: Peter Davies, 1927), II, p. 432.

11. *An Historical and Descriptive Account of Bath, and Its Environs* (Bath: R. Cruttwell, 1802), p. 1. Alfred Barbeau, *Life and Letters at Bath in the xviiith Century* (London: Heinemann, and New York: Dodd, Mead, 1904), p. 4, speaks of the Bathonians' pious belief in the legend. The very early commentary by Ranulf Higden accepts that Bladud founded the city, but appeals 'to kendly reason' and a natural cause of the water's heat that 'wassheth of tetres soores and scabbes' (*Policronicon*, 2nd edn [Westminster: Wynkyn de Worde, 1495], fol. xlvi). One hears of Bladud in Bath even today.

12. Wood, *Essay* (1749), I. pp. 71–76.

13. *An Essay towards a Description of Bath* (Bath, 1742), I, p. 8. A contemporary MS annotation in the Henry E Huntington Library's copy exclaims: 'how unguarded Mr. Wood must be to assert this: when there was no Church till 1083 Years after our Saviour.' The Cathedral of Old Sarum was completed in 1258. For Trinovantum as London, see Swift, 'On Poetry. A Rapsody,' 280 (*Poems*, ed. Harold Williams, 2nd edn [Oxford: Clarendon Press, 1958], II, p. 649), and Braun and Hogenberg, *Civitates Orbis Terrarum* (Cologne, 1572–1617; reprinted Cleveland and New York: World Publishing Co., 1966), I, plate 1.

14. Robert Peirce, *Bath Memoirs: or, Observations in three and forty years practice, at the Bath* (Bristol, 1697), p. 175.

15. *Essay* (1749), I, p. 76. I do not know Wood's authority for this anecdote, which, like most Rochester stories, is probably apocryphal but still plausible. Rochester is known to have visited Bath in June 1671 (*The Letters of John Wilmot, Earl of Rochester*, ed. Jeremy Treglown [Oxford: Blackwell, 1980], p. 66).

16. *Ibid.*, Wood refers to *Spectator*, Nos. 14 (16 March 1711), 31 (5 April 1711), and 40 (16 April 1711). See *The Spectator*, ed. Donald F. Bond (Oxford: Clarendon Press, 1965), I, pp. 130, 172.

17. *The Transformation* was apparently never printed. See [Thomas Goulding], *The Fortune-Hunter: or, the Gamester Reclaim'd* [Bath, 1736?], p. [102]. [R. Hippesley?], *Bath and It's Environs* (Bath, 1775), canto III; *The Bath and Bristol Guide: or, the Tradesman's and Traveller's Pocket-Companion*, 4th edn (Bath, 1760?), pp. 1–11; in Foote's *Maid of Bath* (London, 1778), p. 6, Sir Christopher Cripple complains: 'I am shunn'd worse than a leper in the days of King Lud.'

18. Richard Pococke, *Travels through England*, ed. James Joel Cartwright, Camden Society New Series, 42 and 44 (London, 1888–89), I, pp. 4–5.

19. *An Historical and Descriptive Account*, p. 10; [George Ellis?], *Bath: Its Beauties, and Amusements*, 2nd edn (Bath, 1777), p. 3.

20. *Essay* (1749), I, p. 219.

21. Guidott, *Appendix*, p. 12.

22. *Essay* (1749), I, p. 228.

23. Samuel and Nathaniel Buck, *Buck's Perspective Views of Near One Hundred Cities and Chief Towns in England & Wales* (1774). Their view of Bath dates from 1745. See also Barry Cunliffe, 'The Temple of Sulis Minerva at Bath,' *Archaeology*, 36 no. 6 (November-December 1983), 16.

24. Jorden, *Discourse*, pp. 155, 150.

25. Camden, *Britannia*, col. 69.

26. Peirce, *Memoirs*, p. 7.

27. 13 June 1668; *The Diary of Samuel Pepys*, ed. Robert Latham and William Matthews, IX (Berkeley and Los Angeles: University of California Press, 1976), p. 233.

28. Peirce, *Memoirs*, p. 259.

29. Tobias Smollett, *The Expedition of Humphry Clinker*, ed. Lewis M. Knapp, Oxford English Novels (London: Oxford University Press, 1966), p. 45.

30. *Policronicon*, fol. xlvi. Higden died in 1364.

31. Jorden, *Discourse*, p. 151.

32. *The Journeys of Celia Fiennes*, ed. Christopher Morris (London: Cresset Press. 1949), p. 20. Defoe, *A Tour thro' the Whole Island of Great Britain*, 3rd edn (London, 1742), II. pp. 257, 261. This posthumous edition is a revised and expanded version of Defoe. Samuel Richardson apparently supplied some of the additions, and probably edited the whole. George Cheyne wrote the section on Bath water, with the purpose of making it 'a very saleable and entertaining Book to the middling Gentry who want it most and buy most' (to Richardson, 13 December 1740, *Letters of Doctor George Cheyne to Samuel Richardson* [1733–1743], ed. Charles F. Mullett [Columbia: University of Missouri Press, 1943], p. 63). To distinguish this edition of the *Tour* from the one published in Defoe's lifetime. I designate this one 'Richardson, *Tour.*'

33. Cunliffe, *Roman Bath Discovered*, p. 33.

34. Fiennes, *Journeys*, p. 21. Defoe, *Tour*, II, p. 432.

35. Defoe, *Tour*, II, p. 431; James B. Johnston, *The Place-Names of England and Wales* (London: John Murray, 1915), sub; 'Isle of Man'.

36. Cunliffe, 'The Temple of Sulis Minerva', p. 16.

37. See Thomas Gale, *Antonini Iter Britanniarum* (London, 1709), p. 132, who also perpetuates the connection with Minerva. On three maps of Roman Britain and the Roman Empire, Bath was called 'Aque solis' by Abraham Ortelius, *Theatrum Orbis Terrarun* (Antwerp, 1603), the first uniform modern atlas of the world. Lysons thought the corruption of the name was probably a result of a typical error in the Antonine Itinerary ('Remains', p. 9).

38. Essay (1749), I, p. 1.

39. Cf. Benjamin Boyce, *The Benevolent Man: The Life of Ralph Allen of Bath* (Cambridge, Mass.: Harvard University Press, 1967), p. 218. Cunliffe, *Roman Bath Discovered*, p. 12.

40. Wood, *Essay* (1749), II, pp. 417–18.

41. *Journeys*, p. 23.

42. See James Lees-Milne and David Ford, *Images of Bath* (Richmond-upon-Thames: Saint Helena Press, 1982), pp. 23–24, and Cunliffe, *Roman Bath Discovered*, p. 11.

43. *Essay* (1749), I, pp. 170, 216. R.E.M. Peach suggested that only the inferior parts of the city were like this (*Historic Houses in Bath and their Associations* [London: Simpkin, Marshall, 1893–4], I, p. i). Not *everyone* was discontented. Tobias Venner had thought Bath 'beautified with very faire and goodly buildings for receipt of strangers' (*The Bathes of Bathe*, in *Via Recta ad Vitam Longam* [London 1650], p. 345), and in 1687 or earlier, Fiennes was pleased with the lodgings but not with the air (*Journeys*, pp. 17,236).

44. Burney to Mrs Phillips and the Lockes of Norbury Park, August 1791 (*The Journals and Letters of Fanny Burney (Madame d'Arblay)*, ed. Joyce Hemlow, with Curtis D. Cecil and Althea Douglas, I (Oxford: Clarendon Press, 1972), p. 35). See also John Collinson, *The History and Antiquities of the County of Somerset* (Bath, 1791), I, p. 28.

45. British Library, Stowe MS 752, fol. 156, verso.

46. 22 April 1736. *The Correspondence of Jonathan Swift*, ed. Harold Williams, IV (Oxford: Clarendon Press, 1965), p. 475.

47. [R. Hippesley?], *Bath and It's Environs* (Bath, 1775), p. 22.

48. See Boyce, *The Benevolent Man*. Allen said his management of the western postal services had brought the Post Office over £1 1/2 million in forty years (*Ralph Allen's Own Narrative 1720–1761*, ed. Adrian E. Hopkins, n.p.: Postal History Society [1960], appendix 1, pp. 36–38).

49. Cf. Peach, *Historic Houses in Bath*, II, p. 111.

50. *Essay* (1749), I, p. 227, II, p. 245.

51. *Essay* (1749), II, p. 242.

52. *Ibid.*

53. The compliment is from Fielding, *The History of Joseph Andrews*, ed. Martin C. Battestin (Middletown, Conn.: Wesleyan University Press, 1967), p. 235. On Allen's final, troubled years, see Benjamin Boyce, *The Benevolent Man*, pp. 262-98.

54. *England's Improvement by Sea and Land. To out-do the Dutch without Fighting, to Pay Debts without Moneys* (London, 1677–81), I, pp. 64–65, partly quoted by Wood, *Essay* (1749), II, p. 366.

55. Lees-Milne, *Images of Bath*, p. 56.

56. *Essay* (1749), II, p. 241.

57. Richard Graves, *The Triflers* (London: Lackington, Allen, 1806), pp. 63–64.

58. *The Plans, Elevations and Sections, of Holkham in Norfolk*, 2nd edn (London, 1773), p. x.

59. *Clarissa, or the History of a Young Lady*, ed. Angus Ross (Harmondsworth: Penguin, 1985), p. 844.

60. Boyce, *The Benevolent Man*, p. 136.

61. The railway track is pictured in Anthony Walker's well-known engraving of Prior Park (*c.* 1750). The wagons were described by Charles de Labelye, in J.T. Desaguliers, *Course of Experimental Philosophy* (London, 1734), I, pp. 274–79. John Padmore of Bristol devised a simple but ingenious design for brakes that enabled one man to control a stone-laden wagon. See Boyce, *Benevolent Man*, pp. 31–32. The stone works are shown somewhat indistinctly, in Buck's engraving of the city (1745; first published 1774).

62. City of Bristol Record Office, MS 04285, minutes of the Committee of the Exchange and Market, 1739–68. Wood also publicized this reduction in the price of the stone (*A Plan of the City of Bath* [Bath, 1736]).

63. *An Essay of Health and Long Life*, 2nd edn (London, 1725), p. 2. The anonymous author of *Diseases of Bath* reported that Cheyne 'Is said for One he cures a Score to kill' (p. 6).

64. Richardson, *Tour*, II, p. 263.

65. Our anonymous poet considered Peirce 'humane', and, despite his being a surgeon, 'honest' (*Diseases of Bath*, p. 4).

66. Gwynn, *An Essay on Design* (London, 1749), p. 78; *Diseases of Bath* (1737), p. 4; Richardson, *Tour* II, p. 263; Foote, *The Maid of Bath*, p. 2. See also [Goulding], *The Fortune-Hunter*, p. 23; and Richard Graves, *The Spiritual Quixote: or, the Summer's Ramble of Mr. Geoffry Wildgoose* (London, 1773), II, p. 2.

67. Graves, *The Spiritual Quixote*, I, p. 277.

68. Wood, *Essay* (1749), II, p. 388; Richardson, *Tour*, II, pp. 255–56; *Collected Works of Oliver Goldsmith*, ed. Arthur Friedman (Oxford: Clarendon Press, 1966), III, p. 317.

69. *Bathes of Bathes Ayde* (London, 1572), fol. 30, recto.

70. Thomas D'Urfey, *The Bath, or, the Western Lass* (London, 1701), I, i; Gabriel Odingsells, *The Bath Unmask'd* (London, 1725), p. 6.

71. Wood, *Essay* (1749), I, p. 217, II, p. 408. Cf. Humphry Clinker, p. 47.

72. Cf. [Eliza Haywood], *Bath-Intrigues*, with introduction by Simon Varey, Augustan Reprint Society, No. 236 (Los Angeles: Clark Library, 1986); *The Bath, Bristol, Tunbridge and Epsom Miscellany* (London, 1735), especially pp. 11–13; 'Bath Intrigues', an obscene verse, erroneously attributed to Rochester in *The Works of the Earls of Rochester, Roscommon, Dorset, the Duke of Devonshire, &c.* (London, 1732).

73. *Peregrine Pickle*, chs. 68–70; *Humphry Clinker*, p. 57. The spa towns were all notorious (see *Mist's Weekly Journal*, 18 September 1725). Bath society provoked a good deal of satire, of which Christopher Anstey's *New Bath Guide*, first published in 1766 and reprinted continually for four decades, was merely the most famous.

74. Defoe, *Tour*, II, p. 433.

75. Richardson, *Tour*, II, p. 253.

76. A point made by one perfunctory verse, 'Upon Mr N.... s Leaving Bath' (Clark MS P745 M1, a poetical miscellany/commonplace book). The obvious source on Nash is Goldsmith's 'Life of Richard Nash' in *Collected Works*, III, pp. 285–398, some of which is plagiarized from Wood.

77. *Buck's Perspective Views*.

78. Pat Rogers, *The Augustan Vision* (London: Weidenfeld and Nicolson, 1974), p. 56.

79. Joseph Rykwert, *The First Moderns: The Architects of the Eighteenth Century* (Cambridge, Mass.: MIT Press, 1980), p. 139; Rykwert also notes the fashion for Utopias, exemplified in an earlier era by Tomaso Campanella's *Civitas Solis* (Frankfurt, 1623), and Johann Valentin Andreae, who described an imaginary Rosicrucian community in *Christianopolis* (Strasburg, 1619).

80. Lavedan cites Edinburgh's Royal Circus, Ainslie Place, and Morey Place (all early 19th Century), as 'le dernier echo de l'art des deux Wood' (*Histoire de l'urbanisme*, II, p. 467). The standard account of 18th-century Edinburgh is A.J. Youngson, *The Making of Classical Edinburgh 1750–1840* (Edinburgh: Edinburgh University Press, 1966), including very brief remarks on Wood the Elder, p. 74.

81. *Essay* (1749), II, p. 352. On straight lines as the source of beauty, see, for instance, Christopher Wren, *Parentalia* (London, 1750), p. 351.

82. *Essay* (1749), II, p. 352.

83. *Essay* (1749), II, p. 320.

84. Cf. T.P. Connor, 'The Making of *Vitruvius Britannicus'*, *Architectural History*, 20 (1977), 14–30.

85. *The Four Books of Architecture*, translated by Isaac Ware (London, 1738), p. 57.

86. *The Culture of Cities* (New York: Harcourt, Brace, 1938, reprinted 1970), p. 5.

87. For an account of the social and economic development of Bath, see R.S. Neale, *Bath: A Social History, 1680–1850* (London: Routledge & Kegan Paul, 1981).

88. Rykwert, *On Adam's House in Paradise*, p. 18.

89. Wood's dominance in this respect is unusual. Other architects designed buildings in Bath at the same time as Wood, but none rivalled his range or ingenuity. Tradition, at least, ascribed to the Earl of Burlington two houses in Bath: one for himself in the Orange Grove, and one for General Wade in the Abbey Churchyard (see R.E.M. Peach, *The Life and Times of Ralph Allen* [London: D. Nutt, Chas. J. Clark, 1895], p. 66).

JONATHAN LAMB

# The Job Controversy, Sterne, and the Question of Allegory

The fierce debate about the right way to read the book of Job, which was under way fifteen years before Sterne began *Tristram Shandy* and was briskly pursued all the time he was writing and publishing it, is generally acknowledged to have influenced the way he planned and executed his novel. The hints dropped by himself and the literary gossipmongers point to some sort of allegory linking scenes in the Shandy parlour to the disagreements over Job, and the remains of this plan in *Tristram Shandy* indicate that Sterne meant to take sides against his patron William Warburton by dramatising the triumph of the principles of the bishop's leading opponents, Richard Grey, Charles Peters, and Leonard Chappelow.[1] Melvyn New has spelt these hints and fragments into a scenario of literary influence, where Sterne, the ephebe of a repressive yet myriadminded literary father, engages Warburton in a series of sidelong counter-readings aimed at reappropriating the line of Scriblerian wit his patron at once occludes and represents. More recently, Everett Zimmerman has argued the opposite. He suggests that the debate focused Sterne's ideas about fictional and historical narratives, leading him to reject Charles Peters' reading of the book of Job as a genuine relic of pre-Mosaic inspiration in favour of Warburton's view of it as an allegorical treatment of an ancient tale. By setting Sterne this example of how to unite historical and narrative elements into an allegory, Warburton (in Zimmerman's opinion) enfranchises rather than restrains the wit of his protege, ridding him of the superstitions and literalisations that clog the writing of a corroborated documentary history.[2]

From *Eighteenth-Century Studies*, vol. 24, no. 1 (Fall 1990): 1–19. © 1990 by the American Society for Eighteenth-Century Studies.

It is a sign of a good literary quarrel that it will countenance various and contradictory interpretations. In the following account of the Job controversy the emphasis will be laid on the subtlety of the critical questions raised in it, often disguised by the polemical tone of its rival champions (Warburton in particular). This will require a close scrutiny of the main positions occupied by Warburton and his allies on the one hand, and Robert Lowth and his supporters on the other. I will then suggest that there are two indices of the subtlety of the questions debated: First there is a clustering of attitudes so that, for instance, an opinion about history will determine or be determined by an opinion about the sublime, and an opinion about the sublime will be closely linked to an opinion about the value of originality, and so on. Secondly, the writers in this debate often make a shift, sometimes only half-consciously, from discussing the book of Job to imitating it, so that they often reproduce in their literary quarrels the same terms and inflections that are to be found in Job's exchanges with his comforters. This mirror effect, I will finally argue, provides Sterne not with a clear choice between allegory and history, or even one between literary legitimacy or bastardy, but with an intuition about the use to which the rhetorical figure called pleonasm may be put.[3]

In deciding to read Job as an allegory of the plight of the Jews after the Babylonian captivity, Warburton was doing nothing new. Early in the previous century Francis Quarles complains of the "many rash heads" who treat Job as a "feigned thing, or counterfeite Sceane" instead of a "true and faithful record of reall passages."[4] Already the debate between those committed to the historical reality of Job and those preferring a parabolical or allegorical interpretation had been aired on the Continent, with Albert Schultens leading the former and Jean Le Clerc standing up for the latter. What distinguished Warburton's choice of an allegorical reading was the size of his personal investment in it—no less than the whole argument of his life's work, *The Divine Legation of Moses Demonstrated* (1738–41). In this book, constantly under revision and attack and still unfinished when he died in 1779, he undertook to prove by a system of universal illustration that the foundation of the Jewish nation under Moses was unique because it did not depend on the prospect of a future state of rewards and punishments to enforce the people's obedience to the law. What it did depend on was a private assurance from God to Moses that an extraordinary providence would be dispensed to the nascent state, ensuring a strict and invariable correspondence between the degree of obedience to the law and the level of present happiness (that is, the ratio of rewards to punishments). Warburton's positive evidence for this private treaty was nil, so he drew four inferences in support of it. The first was that all pagan social formations (Egyptian, Greek, Roman) did rely on the doctrine of a future state of rewards and punishments. The second was that this doctrine served a purely political purpose and was therefore only believed in by the lower orders, but not by those who promulgated and manipulated it. The third and most ingenious was that Moses' silence on the subject of the future state was itself proof of some hidden contract, otherwise there was no reason for him to forgo such a handy political tool. The fourth was that a common or unequal providence, promiscuously shedding its benefits and penalties on a people unrestrained by the prospect of a future state, would inevitably have provoked lawlessness and the early collapse of the Jewish nation.

The book of Job threatened every one of these inferences. If it could be shown that a set of dialogues explicitly concerned with the question of equal and unequal providence was written before the Mosaic jurisdiction, or even at the same time, then Moses' arrangement with God could no longer be assumed to be secret, since the comforters share it and publish it. The validity of the doctrine is questioned by Job with enough heat ("Wherefore do the wicked live, become old, yea, are mighty in power?" [21:7]) to cast doubt on the extraordinary (that is, equal) providence that is supposed to have preserved the polity in the age of the patriarchs. Furthermore, if the textual crux of the book, verses 19:23–6, is read as Job's prophecy of the coming of Christ and the resurrection of the just, then all secrets are out: the Jews are informed from the very first that a future state of rewards and punishments awaits them. As the prophecy is made at the height of Job's temporal calamities and derives a remedy solely from the quarter of eternity, it puts paid to the idea of an extraordinary providence not simply on the grounds of its manifest failure to work for Job, but more importantly in terms of its irrelevance to all those who believe with him in the superior equity of the hereafter. So Warburton must make "a mere Modern of old Job" if his grand hypothesis is to survive.[5]

His method of modernising Job is closely to inspect the surface of the narrative and dialogues for any anachronism, inconsistency, or omission that might give notice of an ulterior meaning. For example, he turns up references to the law, phylacteries, and the destruction of Pharaoh's host in the Red Sea, indicating a date of authorship some time after the flight out of Egypt.[6] He finds the harsh behaviour of Job's comforters quite inconsistent with common ideas of friendship, and therefore suspects that they are signs of more occult hostility directed not at a historical Job but at the Jewish people as a whole: "Who then will doubt but that ... these *three friends* were the three capital enemies [of the Jews]: SANBALLAT, TOBIAH and GESHEM?" (DLM, 4:270). As for Job himself, a byword in other books of the scriptures both for devoutness (Ezekiel, 14:14) and patience (James, 5:11), he is so prone to blasphemous fits of exasperation that they can only be supposed to represent the sorrows of a nation, not of an individual. Job's speech about his redeemer and the latter day, therefore, is to be taken not as a prophecy of a future state but as a forecast of the end of his afflictions which the outcome of the story will confirm—an alleviation of temporal suffering that is to be applied to the Jews at Jerusalem merely as a promise of better days ahead, not as the day of judgment (DLM, 4:301). Job's sufferings are a fable representing an epoch in Jewish history, carefully constructed by Ezra (the real author) not to depict patience but to counsel it, all by way of consoling the Jews for the loss of the extraordinary providence which, under the rule of Moses, had protected them from unaccountable misery.

Warburton's enterprise is perverse, but at least it is consistent with itself. In choosing to read Job as allegory, he assigns the moral import of the story to what it conceals, omits, or only obliquely represents, and none at all to the events and characters in it (DLM, 4:207 n. i). They are simply the signs of the story's real meaning or (which is pretty much the same thing) the vehicle of the bishop's hermeneutic brilliance. So he doesn't want to talk of impatience as impatience, or heroism as heroism—these are merely the formal devices impelling the fable to its point—and he decidedly does not want to hear of an "original" or "genuine" Job who once existed, since hermeneutically speaking such a Job is an embarrassment, and allegorically speaking an impossibility. According to his hypothesis, Job must be a double character, a sort of involuntary hypocrite constantly representing something other than the sum of his conscious self-manifestations, and therefore incapable of ever saying anything that coincides with the real drift and meaning of his story. Although Warburton joins his opponents in praising the sublimity of Job, he is not convincing. His deliberate neglect of the pathos of Job's complaints is accompanied by a very perfunctory salute to the ornaments, figures, and luxuriant descriptions with which Ezra's rewritten tale is replete. Everything he calls sublime is a copy or supplement of an inconsiderable original, for "The truth is, the language of the times of Job had its grandeur, its purity, and sublimities; but they were of that kind which the learned missionaries have observed in the languages of certain warrior-tribes in North America" (DLM, 4:231).

Richard Grey, Charles Peters, Thomas Sherlock and others in the numerous band of Warburton's opponents are no less consistent on the other side. They lay their emphasis squarely on the authenticity and the great age of the text, arguing that the story is not merely probable, but strictly and historically true: The story of Job is "the most antient extant ... neither Allegorical, nor properly Dramatic,"[7] "a plain and orderly relation of facts."[8] "This Narrative is Matter of Fact."[9] "The history of Job and his sufferings, is not a studied parable, or an artfully contrived drama; but a matter of real fact and truth."[10] "The question is a question of fact."[11] In some cases the stress is naively laid, as when Leonard Chappelow takes the dialogues between Job and his comforters to be originally transcribed in Arabic from the spoken word; or when William Hawkins and Charles Peters argue that Job is the author of his own story.[12] In some of the paraphrases it can lead to an absurd particularisation. Sir Richard Blackmore, an anti-Warburtonian *avant la lettre*, furnished Pope with some of his best specimens of the art of sinking in poetry because the paraphrast was so keen to furnish the facts of the matter:

> The Putrefaction from my running Boils,
> In loathsome manner all my Vest defiles:
> Close to my Sores it sticks, as to my Throat,
> The narrow Collar of my seamless Coat.[13]

No less ridiculous is Edward Young's careful weighing of the reasons that led him to call Leviathan not a whale but a crocodile: "Moses being (as we may well suppose) under an immediate Terror of [them] from their daily Mischiefs and Ravages around him [in the Nile]."[14]

In their efforts to specify the incidents and localise the narrative of Job, many of the anti-Warburtonians respond to inconsistencies and irregularities as authentic symptoms of passion, not as signatures of a coded message. The pathos of the hero's confrontation with his three friends, the terror he suffers as he tries to account for what has happened to him, and the urgency of his declared faith in the ultimate justice of the divine scheme, all strike them as undisguised ebullitions of the heart, rendered in just the language that a nomadic chieftain, of large soul but small vocabulary, would be expected to use. Peters instructs Warburton, "Human nature in those days was human nature ... what the heart felt, the tongue uttered" (p. 41). Job's message is as plain as can be—"I know that my redeemer liveth"—and the sublimity of his language is not owing to verbal ornaments added by a civilised translator at a later date but to "the passionate Rhapsodies and Exclamations of Man conscious of the Truth and Goodness of his Cause" (Worthington, p. 511). Knowing that Hebrew was not Warburton's strong suit, his opponents turn to the original to analyse the language, to study the sources of its sublime figures and inflections. They show how these arise with "the force and spirit of original genius," from a definite historical situation (Lowth, *A Letter*, p. 80), bearing all the marks of "a real genuine thing" and a "real original conversation" (Peters, pp. 97, 99).

Thomas Sherlock, the most eminent of Warburton's opponents until Robert Lowth took over the leadership of the quarrel, lays it down for a maxim that "metaphors do not arise out of nothing."[15] Lowth's far-reaching contribution to biblical scholarship and literary criticism in the later eighteenth century depends on his dedication to the same principle: "It is the first duty of a critic to remark the situation and habits of the author, the natural history of his country, and the scene of the poem."[16] His decisive *Letter to the Author of the Divine Legation of Moses* (Oxford, 1765) put an end to the debate because his authoritative dating and placing of the poem, together with a magisterial taste for the sublime of Hebrew poetry, were both founded on close attention to the little circumstance ("low and trivial as it may appear to some" [*Lectures*, p. 81]) that can distinguish a fine original from an ornamented copy. His analysis of the metaphors in Job showed no trace of the geography found in those of the Psalms, indicating instead an Arabian setting and an earlier date of composition; but not so early as to be bereft of the benefits of Egyptian civilisation—Lowth is icily contemptuous of Warburton's assertion that the language of an original Job would be on a par with that of the warrior tribes of North America (see *A Letter*, pp. 75, 79). His attention to details of Hebrew customs and prosody also reveals a repetitive parallelised verse structure which is not, as Warburton suggests, owing to poverty of language, but the fruit of choices made among a considerable variety of synonyms and figures, perfectly adapted to represent those perturbations in which "all the affections and emotions of the soul, its sudden impulses, its hasty sallies and irregularities, are conspicuously displayed" (*A Letter*, p. 86; *Lectures*, p. 157).

The plan of getting back to the site of Job by studying the original language yields fascinating results. Having established a link between the Hebrew for weary *(naketah)* and the Arabic verb to unhinge or dismember *(nakadah)*, Leonard Chappelow runs some astonishing parallels between the figurative structure of Job's complaint and various etymologies of ruin (pp. 142, 244–6). And George Costard, officially a Warburtonian but by bent a Lowthian, traces the etymology of the word *hermeneut* itself back, via the Hebrew verb *aram* (to heap up), to the cairns of stones which first marked the borders of property and which were eventually improved into those columnar effigies known as *herms*. He hints at a connexion between these teasing resemblances and the subject of his prior pamphlet, the stone in which Job wants to carve the state of his case.[17] The two most powerful verses of Job—"Oh, that my words were now written! oh, that they were printed in a book! That they were graven with an iron pen and lead in the rock for ever!"—exercise the minds of all those who want to follow the Hebrew original to its source in actual facts. Sherlock takes it to be some sort of literal monument (p. 172); and Grey agrees that it is a "standing Monument of his Appeal to God," an engraved epitaph (p. 88). Peters seems to beckon to Costard when he compares these verses (19:23–4) with 21:29, "Have ye not asked them that go by the way? and do ye not know their tokens?" observing, "It was the custom of the ancients to bury near the high roads, and in the most public and conspicuous places; and to erect a pillar or monument over the dead, to preserve his memory" (p. 240).[18]

As well as providing this sort of situational detail, the original language shows Job to be no hypocrite, but a man who has taken all guards from his tongue and who is, as he says, speaking in the bitterness of his soul and the anguish of his spirit (10:1; 7:11). Peters and Grey understand the subject of the story to be the question of the hero's integrity, impeached by his friends and turbulently defended by Job who deeply resents this last provocation. "I have all along shewn," cries Grey in rejoinder to Warburton's polemic, "that Job and his Friends are not arguing a speculative Question ... but maintaining and denying a personal Accusation" (Grey, p. 87). "The question debated," echoes Peters, defending his hero against the imputation of playing a "double part," "was not whether God's providence was equal or unequal, but whether Job was wicked" (Peters, p. 67). It is not hard to see how they lump Warburton with the comforters as someone equally interested in finding a hidden motive in what the patriarch says. "Poor Job!" Grey exclaims, "what will these allegorical Reformers make of thee at last?" (p. 63 n. w).

The parallel is never lost sight of. Warburton damages Job's character by searching for the inconsistencies that will disclose the *moral* of the fable, forcing him and his story to the point of exegetical unmasking the learned commentator calls "exposing the true face of the Subject" (DLM, 4:277). This "true face" is the same lesson about providence chanted so pitilessly at Job by the comforters ("Yea, the light of the wicked shall be put out, and the spark of his fire shall not shine" [18:51]), who are incredulous at his refusal to acknowledge how well he exemplifies it. So the hostility of the anti-Warburtonians to allegorical reading and to the injustice of the comforters includes a contempt for the sententious, proverbial language that Job is tormented by and sacrificed to. According to Chappelow, Job specifically rejects as trite the sententious wisdom of his friends while being impelled himself into an antithetical mode of speech, based on the two prime figures of excess, the tautology and the pleonasm (pp. 190, 236–46). Peters believes that all the comforters' artful maxims serve the master-maxim that the wretched must be guilty. He argues that their remorseless imputation-by-proverb is quite at odds with the grandeur and daring irregularities of Job's complaint, which is misnamed *parable* in the translation since the Hebrew *mashal* means strong language, not an apologue or moral fable (pp. 49, 67, 138, 36). The difference detected between the arranged speeches of the comforters and Job's disorderly spontaneities helps further to define his sublimity as passionate energy exceeding all bounds of received wisdom, and to counterdefine these bounds as suspect piety, whether they masquerade as friendly advice or as a talent for ingenious exegesis.

The convenient linkage of destructive sententiousness in the story to the allegorising and moralising habits of some of its readers has some unfortunate results for the anti-Warburtonians, dramatically and esthetically. If Job's decisive retort to the comforters' mockery is made in the nineteenth chapter, what of the remaining twenty-three, including Elihu's important speech of moderation, and God's mighty blast from the whirlwind? Even if these contained some allusion to the mercy apparently vouchsafed to suffering humanity in Job's prophecy of the resurrection, they come too late dramatically to improve on it—and in fact they seem flatly to contradict it. One reason that the anti-Warburtonians are so happy to assimilate Job to an historical model rather than a dramatic or allegorical one, is that it leaves these troublesome questions of artistic symmetry and authorial intention to one side.

For the same reason they prefer to talk of sublimity as a profoundly irregular phenomenon, blossoming in the interstices between the cruel interpretations of the comforters and the rhetoric of divine omnicompetence. But here they have to attempt a risky distinction between the sublime of Job's preceptless and terror-stricken excesses and God's prodigious exercise in ostensive sublimity. They must remain unimpressed as inexorably God matches the manifestations of nature to the plenitude of his creative intention, reappropriating them piece by piece until the whole (to coin one of Warburton's own phrases) is transformed into the periphrasis of his power and his title.[19] This is difficult on two accounts. The first is the weight of Longinus' authority. His preference for language with performative virtues leads him to single out the Mosaic creation, alone of all the poetry of the septuagint, as sublime, specifically the verse where God creates light in talking of it. Although the God of Job doesn't actually create the war-horse and leviathan, his discourse about them has the same flavour. The second difficulty is that Job seems clearly to recognise the difference between his own refrain and God's voice, and to deprecate the emptiness of the sounds he makes. Even before its spectacular irruption into his debate, Job has characterised the continuity of the divine tongue with what it mentions: "If I speak of strength, Lo, He is strong" (9:19) Being no more than sign of this strength, Job's voice is continuous with nothing that is entire or proper to himself, only with what is absent, divided, and strange. Excess is therefore not an option or a respite for him, it is the necessary consequence of being unable any longer to act like himself. When Peters says, "a person under an excessive load of grief [may be supposed] to forget himself a little, and to talk inconsistently" (p. 45), he tries to blunt Warburton's argument with an appeal to probability. But Job himself quite clearly announces the correlation between the abjection of self-division and his role as an incarnate proverb: "He hath broken me asunder ... and set me up for his mark ... He hath made me also a byword to the people.... Now I am their song, yea I am their byword" (16:12; 17:6; 30:9).

Here Job enters the debate on the side of William Warburton, admitting that his story has a moral, even if he can't fathom it, and that it depends on his not being like himself, not in the way of a probable manifestation of grief but in the way of allegory. The anti-Warburtonians provide no consistent response to this paradox. Peters, Grey, and Sterne stick to the primitivist position, arguing that the repetitions of a straightforward and innocent man in distress are bound to strike the uncorrupted ear as sublime. Job's example, says Sterne, speaks "truer to the heart" because both historically (as the first extant book) and dramatically (as the first words the patriarch speaks after a week of mute misery) his speech bears the true stamp of "the words of that being, who first opened the lips of the dumb, and made the tongue of the infant eloquent."[20] Even Warburton's slighting reference to the American Indians is a gesture in this direction, subsequently defended in a careful commentary on the beauties of primitive language by his lieutenant, Richard Hurd.[21]

Lowth is much more careful. While defending the purity of the Jobian sublime (by which he means Job's speeches, not God's), he never concedes that it is a spontaneous overflow of powerful feeling or one determined solely by the surrounding circumstances. He always supposes that there is someone selecting words and figures, both in the spirit of the feelings represented and of the ordonnance of Hebrew verse.[22]

As for Job, sunk in text and denied God's creative liberty of voice, he longs to become a reader of himself. He wishes his enemy had written a book, for then he would know what he, as sign, was supposed to mean. His desiderated epitaph is an elaboration of this wish. In the absence of an enemy's pen, he will have someone write on his behalf of the pain of being God's writing. He is aware of the parallels between the rock and his own flesh, since both will be inscribed with an identical message, one that cuts and defaces its medium. It is quite specifically a matter of writing and a question of being the writer or the written upon. "Thou settest a print upon the heels of my feet," Job tells God, "thou writest bitter things against me" (13:26–27). It is also a matter of literal disfigurement: "My flesh is clothed with worms and clods of dust; my skin is broken and become loathsome. ... My face is foul with weeping" (7:5; 16:16). The further Job is from the goal of a sympathetic reading and writing his story, and consequently the more tattered and punctured his integument, the more he sees himself as a figure in an allegory, communing with other sententious incarnations: "I have said to corruption thou art my father: to the worm, thou art my mother, and my sister" (17:14). In the parable of his imbecility, he hopelessly asks Destruction and Death if they know the whereabouts of Wisdom (28:22). Although Warburton has followed God and the comforters in trying to keep Job in this allegorical enclosure, the fact that he has written a book makes him something like the redeemer Job expects. He is not backward in claiming a nearer relation to Job than that assigned him by his opponents. What he comes up with is a mixture of Job and God adjusted to the fact and figure of writing:

> Job's *life*, by means of the devil and false friends, was an exercise of his patience; and his *history*, by means of criticism and his commentators, has since been an exercise of ours. I am far from

> thinking myself unconcerned in this mischief; for by a foolish
> attempt to support his name and character, I have been the
> occasion of bringing down whole bands of hostile critics upon
> him.... Most of their [books] were professedly written against me,
> but all, in reality, bear hardest on the good old patriarch....
> Though I am reckoned ... amongst Job's persecutors; yet I have
> this to say for myself, that the vexation I gave him was soon over.
> If I scribbled ten pages on his back, my adversaries and his have
> *made long furrows* and scribbled ten thousand.
>
> (*Appendix*, p. 559, n. B)

Like God, Warburton provokes Job's tragedy with an unsolicited testimonial, "a foolish attempt to support his name and character." This in turn requires a little vexatious writing upon the person of the esteemed old man; but in the sequel, the writer's modest and candid inscription is multiplied by mockers into such voluminous scribblings that he and Job are almost equally overwhelmed with mimic penmanship. The more closely Warburton reads in Job's predicament a reflection of his own, the less allegorical it might seem. Furthermore, his "redemption" of the patriarch by writing, keeping him in countenance by multiplying the significant marks on his skin, seems to intersect with Costard's etymology of *herm*, where the heaping up of words culminates in a sort of face. But the "true face" of the subject of Warburton's hermeneutics is not Job's, it is the argument of his brainchild, *The Divine Legation*.

The scribblers themselves are not behindhand in grasping the parallel Warburton is attempting to draw, so they perversely elaborate it. Warburton's "ten pages"—otherwise *The Divine Legation*—is his epitaph, a message inscribed not on the rock but on Job's back, where it will be attentively read by posterity: "A work which he intends (no doubt) shall live as long as time itself shall last," jeers Peters. Grey laments the unlucky transformation Job's allegorisers force him to endure (p. 63 n. w); and Tillard sighs in mock relief at his lucky escape from the furrows of the bishop's plough: "Had Mr. Warburton honour'd my Name with his own in his immortal Works, what a pitiful Figure should I have made 50000 Years from hence."[23] The only "face" they can perceive in Warburton's labours is the unconquerable brazenness of his own—"the most impudent man living," as Bolingbroke called him.

Notwithstanding his immodesty, Warburton is closer to Lowth's primary insight than critics like Sterne (of the *Sermons*) and Peters, who simply equate the struggle for utterance with the sublime in what amounts to an affective symptomatics. In supposing that original simplicity and primitive integrity cannot be represented without the double vision and calculated effects of art, he anticipates, albeit very clumsily, the grounds of Lowth's claims for the complexity of Hebrew prosody. Indeed, if Warburton had been able to defend the name and character of Job by locating the point where the techniques of allegory conspire to expose the double character of writing itself, he would have satisfied Grey's most serious criticisms, all of which turn on the sacrifice made by the interpreters of Job's character to the point of the moral. Although Warburton allows that there is a kind of allegory where such a dual emphasis may be placed, he specifically excludes Job from this category: "In that sort of allegory, which is of the nature of the book of Job, or the APOLOGUE, the cover has *no moral import;* but in that sort which is of the nature of a NARRATIVE WITH A DOUBLE SENSE, the *cover has a moral import*" (*Appendix*, p. 561 n. E). The furrows ploughed into Job's already furrowed back, then, disperse the figurative power Lowth identifies in Job's complaints, at the same time as they compound the wounding effects of the comforters pseudo-consolations. Warburton's marking of Job's already marked skin, so far from being the writing upon writing Job calls for in his epitaph, is merely the fifth attempt to read Job's disfigurement as the exemplary "true face" of this unequivocal narrative.

For all its concern with the questions of allegory and figurative language, the Job controversy is always in danger of running aground on literalisms. The arguments in favour of an unequal providence, raised on assumptions about Job's authenticity as an historical individual, are in the end as reductive as the Warburtonian defence of an equal providence on the basis of an allegory held exactly to represent a period in the Jewish Dispensation. Both depend on an historicising move which transforms rhetorical effects into signs of the times, evidence of real events that is equivocal only to the extent that it is imperfect. What saves the debate, and keeps it a place in Sterne's fiction, is the effort made by some of the leading anti-Warburtonians to use their knowledge of the original circumstances and language of Job not just to run a metaphor or figure down to its source, but rather, as Lowth says, "to discover the connexion between the literal and the figurative meaning" (*Lectures*, p. 84).

In the exchange between Warburton and Lowth about the difference between primitive iteration and Hebraic parallelism, the figure they choose to talk about is the pleonasm. Warburton says, "The *Pleonasm* evidently arose from the narrowness of a simple language: the hebrew, in which this figure abounds, is the scantiest of all the learned languages of the east.... When the speaker's phrase comes not up to his ideas (as in a scanty language it often will not) he endeavours of course to explain himself by a repetition of the thought in other words" (DLM, 3:156). Spotting the contradiction between scantiness and "other words," Lowth points out that Hebrew poetry relies not on copiousness of thought coupled with privation of words, but the very reverse: "If you reduce the Psalmist to a single term or two, you strike him dumb, be he never so fond of Pleonasm." And he concludes, "the Pleonastic

Character must arise from the Abundance of parallel terms and phrases in the language" (*A Letter*, p. 86). The distinction is important, since it takes repetition and parallelism out of the sphere of symptomatics and assigns them a place among the figures of iteration, of which the pleonasm is the chief. In this group of figures the slight degree of difference between the same words or phrases invites the reader to a double sense of their literal meaning and their figurative expansion.

Despite his naive claims for the historical authenticity of the Job dialogues, Chappelow analyses the pleonasms in them very skillfully. As an anti-Warburtonian, he wants to identify in Job a species of sublimity outside the sheer grandeurs of God's rehearsal of his creation, but he finds little of it in the usual place—the inspired verses of the nineteenth chapter. He is attracted instead to examples of repetition that accompany Job's allusions to the lamentable condition of his body, "a miserable object of broken bones and disjoynted members," "every part in a state of separation" (*A Commentary*, 2:125–26). Although these are translatable (such as, "He breaketh me with breach upon breach"), the full effect is only appreciated in the original, where the multiplication of syllables produce words that sound alike in their stuttering compound forms, but which are not identical:

> *He hath broken me asunder: jeparpereni:—Shaken me to pieces:* jepatzpetzeni: The words which Job uses are no doubt particularly chosen ... you see in what manner the letters are doubled and increased from their simple radixes *pur* and *putz*: How exactly they agree in form, in sound and cadence.... That observation which is frequently made concerning the beauties of Poetry, may properly be applied here; viz. that Job's words are an *"echo to the sense"* (1:244).

Chappelow also discovers that when these minute discriminations get lost in translation, as in "a land of darkness, as darkness itself" (10:22), they result in "a plain and manifest tautology" (1:153) because it is impossible to reproduce in English the differences between similar words (here the differences between the synonyms for darkness being used by the Hebrew poet).[24] In effect Chappelow is confirming in advance Lowth's objections to Warburton's definition of the Hebrew pleonasm as tautology by default.

In his search for a sublime appropriate to Job, then, Chappelow (clearly thinking of the strong who talk of strength [1:70]) locates a version where the weak talk of weakness, and the shattered of breaking. It is not so much that this sublime language is an echo to the sense, as that it turns repetitive language of excess into a vertical figure in which two not quite identical terms are mounted one on top of the other: *jeparpereni* upon *jepatzpetzeni*, darkness upon "darkness," breach upon "breach." These pleonasms are fundamentally different from the tautologies of perfection where talk of strength is continuous with strength itself; nor do they have anything in common with the self-evidence of God's instances of his power in the whirlwind speech. There words are understood to share the virtue they mention, to mark and exercise it at the same time. But in the representation of privation and loss, the necessary failure of language perfectly to deliver what is imperfect keeps words from ever coinciding with themselves or with things. That difference, whether it is heard in the variation between *naketah* and *nakadah*, or revealed in the inverted commas that distinguish "breach" from breach, opens up a space for the substitutions and deferments that Job associates with writing. Job acknowledges that his alienation from himself is equal to his inability to decipher the meaning he represents in God's allegory, and that his only comfort is to hope for a further alienation that will fix him forever in script. He waits for the *goel*[25]—the substitute, the standin or, as the Authorised Version has it, the redeemer—who will read the writing in the rock: the writing on writing which Job also wishes might stand in for him and speak on his behalf. In this arch-pleonastic form the pain of being legible by virtue of one's disfigurements is eased by its very excess. The overdoing of the undone leaves a message for the future whose interpretation, if we accept Costard's etymology, will preserve word upon word as a figure in stone with a face.

There are a number of ways of charting Sterne's transition from the simple anti-Warburtonian stance of his sermons, where he declares his belief in the primitive integrity, noble simplicity, historical authenticity, and sublime originality of Job, to the ambidexterity of his fiction, where he enjoys putting each of these pristine notions in company with its opposite. The quickest one is to see how well he exploits the resources of the pleonasm. The thirtieth chapter of the seventh volume of *Tristram Shandy* follows the hero's discovery that many a disaster carries its consolation with it, and that losses may under certain circumstances be construed as gains. No sooner has he announced this paradox than he seems to contradict it with the case of a double inconvenience, which he sets out carefully in the form of a pleonasm that recalls the vexations furrows upon furrows that Warburton complained of:

VEXATION

upon

VEXATION.

The lower vexation as it were is to be in Lyons and unable to see its sights; the upper, the vexation that detains him, is an ass which has torn a hole in Tristram's breeches with its pannier. The modulation of vexation upon vexation into breach of breeches is insisted on with another pleonastic arrangement: a reference to the

REVIEWERS
of
MY BREECHES

who are charged with assessing their degree of equivocality.

This is not the first time Tristram has used typography to emphasise the vertical relation of the two terms of a pleonasm. The epitaph lying draped under the dark veil of Tristram's black page is arranged as one, with apparently identical words placed on top of one another, except that the upper phrase is inflected as the epitaph proper ("Alas, poor YORICK!"), and the lower as an elegiac echo ("Alas, poor YORICK!"). Like the breach of breeches, this pleonasm recalls one of Job's. The inscription on Yorick's plain marble slab is the Shandean version of Job's rock, inscribed with a history of the written. Writing on writing is achieved in Yorick's case by cutting into the stone words that have already been printed in a text. The *goel* is the reader of this writing, who, like the reviewer of the breeches, is expected to appreciate the difference between the apparently identical words.

The margin for failure in the *goel*'s task is explored in the chapter of *A Sentimental Journey* where Yorick identifies himself to the Count de B**** by pointing to the graveyard scene in *Hamlet*. The challenge to the Count complements the test set to the reader of Yorick's epitaph: just as there are two ways of intoning "Alas, poor YORICK!" so "there are two Yoricks." But the difference is obliterated because the Frenchman is unable to tell an English clergyman and a Danish jester apart: "'Twas all one, he replied." As Yorick ruefully contemplates his disfigurement, which leaves his own countenance as bare as "the idea of poor Yorick's skull," he is reminded of a colleague whose commitment to univocal readings kept him from looking "into sermons wrote by the king of Denmark's jester." Gardner D. Stout takes this to be an allusion to William Warburton.[26] The parallels between the bishop and the count are certainly close. Because their talent for conceiving ideas is not matched by a facility for combining them, they ignore the differences that transform words on words into figures, and read unredemptively in pursuit of single meanings that not only reduce pleonasms to empty tautologies (Yorick is Yorick) and stale literalisms (Job is the Jews), but also leave the "true face" of the subject little better than a deathshead.

NOTES

This essay was completed at UCLA, with the help of an ASECS short-term fellowship. I would like to record my gratitude both to the staff of the Williams Andrews Clark Memorial Library and to the American Society for Eighteenth-Century Studies for their generosity and encouragement.

1. "An allegory has been run upon the writers on the Book of Job. The Doctor [Warburton] is the Devil who smote him from head to foot, and G[re]y, P[ete]rs and Ch[appel]ow his miserable comforters. A group of mighty champions in literature is convened at Shandy-hall. Uncle Toby and the Corporal are thorns in the private tutor's side, and operate upon him as they did on Dr Slop at reading the sermon; all this for poor Job's sake." Letter published in the *St James Chronicle* (April, 1788) and reprinted in Alan D. Howes, *Sterne The Critical Heritage* (London: Routledge and Kegan Paul, 1974), pp. 57–60. Howes incorrectly identifies Grey as Zachary Grey, the editor of *Hudibras*. The correspondent refers to Richard Grey, editor of a Hebrew text of Job, who had a running battle with Warburton about the dating and interpretation of the book and who is praised by Lowth as a worthy ally in the dispute. Zachary Grey fights on another of Warburton's many fronts—his edition of Shakespeare—publishing *An Answer to Certain Passages in Mr Warburton's Preface* (1748). A brief but authoritative survey of the Job controversy is to be found in Martin C. Battestin, *The Providence of Wit* (Oxford: Clarendon Press, 1974), pp. 197–200.

2. See Melvyn New, "Sterne, Warburton, and the Burden of Exuberant Wit," *ECS* 15:3 (1982), 245–74; and Everett Zimmerman, "*Tristram Shandy* and Narrative Representation," *The Eighteenth Century: Theory and Interpretation* 28:2 (1987), 127–47.

3. I have discussed Sterne's fondness for this figure from the inside out, as it were, in *Sterne's Fiction and the Double Principle* (Cambridge: Cambridge Univ. Press, 1989), especially pp. 105–57.

4. *Job Militant* (London, 1624), p. [i]

5. J. Tillard, *A Reply to Mr. Warburton's Appendix* (London, 1742), p. 141.

6. *The Divine Legation of Moses Demonstrated*, 9 vols. (London, 1758), 4:223 [Book VI, Section ii].

7. Robert Lowth, Letter to Warburton, September 6, 1756, printed in the Appendix to *A Letter to the Author of The Divine Legation* (Oxford, 1765), p. 106.

8. Charles Peters, *A Critical Dissertation on the Book of Job* (London, 1757), p. 94.

9. Daniel Bellamy, *A Paraphrase on the Book of Job* (London, 1748), p. 11.

10. Leonard Chappelow, *A Commentary on the Book of Job with a Paraphrase*, 2 vols. (London, 1752), p. xiv.

11. Richard Parry, *A Defense of the Bishop of London's Interpretation of Job* (Northampton, 1760), p. 43.

12. *Tracts in Divinity*, 3 vols. (Oxford, 1758), 1: 340; Peters, p. 93.

13. Sir Richard Blackmore, *A Paraphrase on the Book of Job* (London, 1700), p. 129.

14. *A Paraphrase on Part of the Book of Job* (London, 1719), n. 24.

15. *Four Dissertations* in *The Works of Bishop Sherlock*, 4 vols. (London, 1830), 4:163.

16. *Lectures on the Sacred Poetry of the Hebrews*, trans. G. Gregory (London: S. Chadwick & Co., 1847), p. 77.

17. George Costard, *Two Dissertations* (Oxford, 1750), pp. 38–41; and *Some Observations on the Book of Job* (Oxford, 1747), pp. 21–24.

18. It is only to be expected that Warburton would resist the equation of rock with grave-stone: "Their Rock is not as our Rock," he says, meaning that his rock stands for God, in whose extraordinary providence Job is beginning to have faith. See DLM, 4:301 n. x.

19. "He makes the very dispensation objected to the periphrasis of his title," is how Warburton glosses the lines of the *Essay on Man*: "Who knows but he, whose hand the

lightning forms,/ Who heaves old Ocean, and who wings the storms." *The Works of Alexander Pope*, 10 vols. (London, 1753), 1:104 n. His taste for the splendour of God's illocutionary tour of nature is reinforced by his belief that only a civilised poet could possess sufficient information about astronomy and natural history to be able to compose it.

20. See "Job's Expostulation with his Wife" and "Job's Account of Life," *The Sermons of Mr. Yorick*, 2 vols. (Basil Blackwell: Oxford, 1927), 1:175, 112.

21. [Richard Hurd], *A Letter to Thomas Leland* (London, 1764), reprinted in *Two Tracts of a Warburtonian* (London, 1789), pp. 238–59.

22. See Robert Lowth, *A Letter to the Author of the Divine Legation of Moses* (Oxford, 1765), pp. 71–78. Although this was followed by John Towne's vicious *Remarks on Dr Lowth's Letter* (1766), it marked the end of the dispute and, as far as Warburton was capable of one, a capitulation.

23. Charles Peters, *An Appendix to the Critical Dissertation* (London, 1760), p. 36; J. Tillard, *A Reply to Mr. Warburton's Appendix*, p. 141. Warburton's image of ploughing is taken from Psalm 129:3 where the psalmist complains of despiteful usage, "The plowers plowed upon my back: they made their long furrows." It seems to have been a byword for destructive commentary on monuments of patience. Richard Preston accuses the critics of Boetius of being "like Plowers plowing upon his Back, and making their Furrows long": *Of the Consolation of Philosophy*, 2 edn. (London, 1712), p. ix.

24. Hugh Broughton, one of the translators of the King James version, tried hard to give the effect of the original pleonasm in English, rendering Job 16:14 as, "He hath breached in me breach overagainst breach": *Job, to the King* (London, 1610), p. 35.

25. Costard discusses the various meanings and translations of this important word in *Some Observations on the Book of Job*, p. 37 n. 1.

26. *A Sentimental Journey through France and Italy*, ed. Gardner D. Stout (Berkeley: Univ. of California Press, 1967), p. 222 n.

PATRICK REILLY

# Fighting the Pharisees

Toward the close of the novel the newly enlightened Allworthy, swinging between self-reproach for having been so long blind to Tom's goodness, and censure of Tom for the sustained imprudence that mitigates his myopia, breaks off to pay his auditor the supreme Fielding compliment: "hypocrisy (good Heaven how have I been imposed on by it in others!) was never among your faults" (853). For this much else can be forgiven. It is better to be a sinner than a hypocrite. There is always hope where there is no hypocrisy; only the hypocrite, the Pharisee, stands obdurately outside the pull of salvation. Hypocrisy, says Hazlitt, is the only vice that cannot be forgiven, because even the repentance of a hypocrite is hypocritical.[1] Fielding, indeed, provides a perfect exemplum in his final depiction of the groveling Blifil, despicable and degraded, sorry not for his sins but for their detection. Be what you will, a thief like Black George, a coward like Partridge, a highwayman like Anderson, a kept man like Jones, and you still have a chance of rescue; but the Pharisee is damned.

Yet scholars tell us that the historical Pharisees may have been maligned and misreported.[2] They were, after all, the one element of traditional Judaism to survive the destruction of Jerusalem and the dispersal of its people. As such they inevitably attracted the hostility of the early Christians, who rightly identified them as their most dangerous religious competitors. St. Paul told King Agrippa that he had been brought up as a Pharisee, within the strictest sect in Israel (Acts 26:5). Perhaps, paradoxically,

From *Tom Jones: Adventure and Providence.* Boston: Twayne Publishers (1991): tv727–61. © 1991 by G.K. Hall & Co.

it was their very virtues that provoked their enemies to a defamation so successful that the name itself has become a synonym for corruption. It is highly possible that Pharisaism has been made out to be worse than it really was.

The truth of this must be left to the scholars to determine; for the purpose of the argument here, Pharisaism will be understood in the traditional, possibly slanderous, sense of the word. Yet even here, on the evidence of the Gospels themselves, it soon becomes clear that Pharisaism sustains two very different, perhaps even contradictory, interpretations, initially distinguishable as deception and self-deception. The first, most obvious definition of Pharisee is hypocrite, fraud, pious dissembler, someone whose virtue is a pose, an act, a performance; who deceives others, but knows himself. Tartuffe at once comes to mind, or Square, posing as the Stoic wise man who has overcome the body, chastising Tom for his shameful surrender to sexual passion, before being himself found crouched humiliatingly with the *other* female utensils beside Molly's bed. Both John the Baptist and Jesus denounce the Pharisees along these lines. The Baptist calls them "snakes" and warns them to prove by their actions (the only acceptable proof) that they have turned from sin: "every tree that does not bear good fruit will be cut down and thrown into the fire." Words alone, faith without works, are futile; the test is action: "He will reward each one according to his deeds" (Matt. 3:7–10). The branch that does not bear fruit is simply firewood. Fielding, as we shall see, is a fervent advocate of the Baptist's ethos; in *Joseph Andrews* he specifically invites the reader to join him in condemning the pernicious doctrine of faith without works as the bane of true Christianity.[3]

Jesus, if anything, surpasses the Baptist in virulence. The Pharisees are blind guides, rapacious engrossers of widows' houses, serpents, broods of vipers, persecutors of the prophets, and enemies of the just; above all, they are barren ritualists, sterile legalists, obsessively preoccupied with appearances and forms while flouting in their hearts the basic religious and moral decencies: "Woe to you, Scribes and Pharisees! because you are like whited sepulchres, which outwardly appear to men beautiful, but within you are full of dead men's bones and of all uncleanness. So you also outwardly appear just to men, but within you are full of hypocrisy and iniquity" (Matt. 23:27–28). Against no other sin does Jesus fulminate so fiercely; the invective is pitiless, the rage almost ungovernable, as he strips bare the impudicity of this bogus virtue.

Yet there is another and different type of Pharisee, neither hypocritical rogue nor fraudulent trickster. The Pharisee presented by Jesus in his parable is not some Palestinian precursor of Tartuffe, but a good man, sincere and devout, speaking the simple truth. He *had* done all he said—prayed, fasted, paid tithes, given alms; he was *not* lying when he thanked God that he was not greedy, dishonest, adulterous, like other men. True, he despised the publican at the back of the temple, but what good man would not? Publican, tax collector—such words were mere synonyms for rogue and swindler, people with whom it was morally impossible to share the same table. To associate with such was in itself a contamination, about as sensible as becoming the crony of lepers or sharing a needle with heroin addicts. For Jesus even to suggest that the tax swindler found more favor with God than the devout Pharisee was outrageous—but, then, so too was his parable of the prodigal son. In having the abandoned, disreputable wretch come off better with his father than the upright son who stayed at home, Jesus must have seemed to many of the righteous in Israel to be undermining the very foundations of morality and justice.

If Jesus lashed the first kind of Pharisee for deceit, this second kind was equally scandalized by what they could only interpret as his own disgraceful laxity. The Pharisee believes above all in the law as a system of ritualized external performances; believes that he has been elected by God to be the vigilant custodian and scrupulous servant of the law; and believes that everyone who deviates from the law, however minutely, should be punished in accordance with God's command. Simon the Pharisee was genuinely shocked when Jesus allowed the prostitute to anoint his feet with the precious ointment; surely a true prophet would have recognized the identity of the ministrant, and surely a good man would have driven her away in loathing? Simon, a good man himself, would certainly have done so. This second kind of Pharisee was distinguished by true zeal for the law, for cultic purity and ritual exactitude, for ostentatious devotion, and for works of supererogation as evoking, almost compelling, God's favor.

Jesus, by contrast, displays an astonishing freedom toward the law, which the Pharisee could only regard as criminal negligence. Not for him the pious legalism, the stern Sabbatarianism, of the strict moralist. However much he revered the law, he never hesitated to act against it when he thought fit, whether it meant healing on the Sabbath or preventing the stoning of the adulteress. Although not abolishing the law, he did not shrink from placing himself (and mankind) above it. No wonder the Pharisees were outraged by his friendship with gluttons, drinkers, loose livers, law breakers; this, reinforced by such parables as the prodigal son and the Pharisee and the publican, must have seemed morally subversive, destructive and offensive, to many decent, godfearing Israelites. Jesus as moral teacher is altogether too slack, too lackadaisical, for the hard-line Pharisee mentality.

Yet, paradoxically, Jesus, the forgiver of sinners, the bender of rules, coming between the hard-liners and their righteous prey, the adulteress, is also, in another sense, much harsher, more condemnatory, than his adversaries. Legalism is, after all, intended as a friendly, a consoling, service to humanity, relieving man's conscience, providing security. If you avoid certain actions, if you scrupulously perform others, then you can rest easy in the assurance of God's favor; so taught the Pharisees (so they teach still), freeing man from the anguish of his dubious salvation. Jesus, making light of the purity regulations, of the need for clean hands, insisted instead that only purity of heart counted with God. The consequence is that he is at once more demanding and more lenient than his opponents. The Pharisees condemned violence against others as sinful; Jesus points to the anger that fuels violence as the root offense. The Pharisees warned men against the act of adultery; Jesus tells us to avoid the very thought, since he who dreams of adultery has already committed it. Sin is not, as the Pharisees taught, an act, something done, external; it is a wish, something desired, internal. Hence Jesus' rage against the self-righteous sinner, hence the striking metaphor of the beautifully whitened tombs that house dead men's bones. Such "piety" simply masks a craving for public acclaim; it ministers to vanity, to a theatricality that has already had its reward.

Salvation is, accordingly, a much more problematic and nerveracking matter than that computed by the Pharisees, those actuaries of virtue. Even the "good" Pharisee, visiting God to discuss his spiritual balance sheet much as he might visit the bank manager about his financial one, has got things hopelessly confused. Against the Pharisees, fixated on moral accountancy, forever balancing merit against sin, Jesus insisted that there was no question of merit at all. Salvation is not the reward of merit but the largesse of grace; it has nothing to do with man's deserving, but is simply God's gift, free, unconditional, like the good heart that Tom Jones was born with. It defies and affronts human calculation, as the parable of the laborers in the vineyard, with its scandal of equal pay for all, so disconcertingly displays. We are not to compute what God owes us, a vulgar error to which, as Jesus points out, good people are especially prone. The sinner is too busy asking for mercy to demand his deserts. It's the person conscious of his own worth, in particular of his superiority to the scapegrace at the rear of the temple, who reminds God of the fine fellow he is; it's the man who has toiled all day in the vineyard who is indignant when he learns that some Johnny-come-lately is to receive the same wages as himself.

However humanly understandable such resentment may be, it is, Jesus insists, totally inappropriate when applied to the relationship between God and man. Yet it seems rooted in human nature—how difficult it is not to be continually comparing ourselves with others. Nevertheless, Christ is remorseless to those who do compare themselves with others, invariably to their own advantage. For it is not the tax collectors who find it hard to repent; it is the devout, convinced as they already are of their own justification. Anyoone without selfcriticism takes himself too seriously, while simultaneously taking God and his fellowmen too lightly. It was, after all, the good people who engineered the Crucifixion, and who thought they were thereby serving God by punishing the blasphemer. If the good people renege on their duty of punishing sinners, the consequences for the public good will be disastrous: so ran, so still runs, the argument.

Every other consideration aside, this last point should alert us to the significance of all this for an understanding of *Tom Jones*. Almost from the opening page the novel becomes the forum for a debate as to how we should deal with sinners and try to reform sin. Allworthy is continually reprehended for what Thwackum, as leading Pharisee, regards as his criminal lenity in handling sin; Thwackum, by contrast, trusts to the whip as the infallible recipe for promoting virtue. But the most cursory reader of Fielding's novel soon discovers that it goes much deeper than a seminar on effective penology, on rehabilitation and retribution; in *Tom Jones* Fielding set out to scrutinize, to appraise and evaluate, the various forms and manifestations of Pharisaism, to provide a complete taxonomy of the malady, from the most impudent hypocrisy to the most deep-seated self-righteousness. Unless we remind ourselves that Fielding is to the Pharisees what Samson was to the Philistines—their fated foe and destined destroyer—we shall inevitably go astray, baffled by the apparent contradictions in the man and his work. The next chapter will examine how the struggle against Pharisaism conditioned the very style and form of the novel, how the need to expose the Pharisee— not merely the Pharisee as character *within* the text, but the Pharisee as potential reader *of* the text—shaped the kind of fiction that the pioneering author chose to create. For the moment it will suffice to point to the magisterial element in Fielding's art. *Tom Jones* has been described as an exercise in the pursuit of true judgment;[4] it seeks to educate, to train its reader to be a good judge—which, by definition, means to avoid being a Pharisee. The Pharisee is the worst of judges, at once too severe and too indulgent, too possessed by arrogance in his dealings with others, too lacking in spiritual modesty, in moral imagination, when interrogating himself.

To be a good judge of the text, one must see from the outset how provocatively and aggressively it challenges Pharisaism. Those who miss this are at risk of falling into various errors concerning Fielding and his book. The less harmful blunder is the myth of the genial Fielding, a jolly fellow, always ready, like his hero Tom, for another glass and another woman, reckless and unrefined, but full of a vulgar vitality, so that his book, though not really important, is a jolly good read and a triumph of the Augustan picaresque. Far more damaging than this good-natured, if trivializing, estimate is the more hostile view of Fielding as a bad man, corrupt and corrupting, a cynical debunker of any real goodness, whose vicious book— Dr. Johnson knew no more corrupt work (Rawson, 181)—is the appropriate poisonous fruit of his own contaminated self. To recognize Fielding as the foe of the Pharisees is to avoid each of these critical pitfalls.

Fielding enters the arena as a comedian, but I shall postpone until the final chapter a consideration of his comedy, aside from pointing out that he is a comedian not because he is careless but because he is Christian—his comedy stems from faith much more than from experience: *credo quia impossibile est*. He enters the fray as adversary of the Pharisees on two main counts: he proposes, not, as Dr. Johnson would have it, a cancellation of morality, but a revaluation of values, a new league table, as it were, of sins, in direct subversion of the priorities of Pharisaism; and he recommends a "new" way (really as old as the Gospels, but continually ignored) of dealing with transgressors—namely, recourse to punishment only as a last, desperate, unavoidable resort, rather than as the panacea preached so avidly by the Pharisees. Denouncing those who instinctively reach for the whip, who love to lash, he links together the most disparate types—self-righteous moralists, hidebound Calvinists, snarling, malicious critics—but all united as condemners of men (302, 468, 509). Fielding follows Jesus in condemning the condemners. Conversely, he brings pardon to sinners, leaning over backwards to palliate any fault, to excuse any offender, thief, highwayman, fornicator, just as long as he is not also a hypocrite.

This antipathy to the hypocrite is not simply the thoughtless, instinctively defensive reaction of the jolly dog, *l'homme moyen sensuel*, toward the censorious sneak who would spoil his fun. It is a pondered condemnation, grounded in the most strenuous moral objections to hypocrisy as the sin against the Holy Spirit, the unforgivable sin that bars the route to heaven, the defect that drew from Jesus his fiercest invective. Ideally, a man should exhibit his true self to the world, not only *being* but *acting* himself, matching word to deed, motive to action, performance to promise, existence to essence, in perfect concordance. Outside and inside should mesh in exact congruence. Such perfect symmetry will, admittedly, be achieved only at the Last Judgment, when reputation and reality finally meet in permanent, indissoluble unity; on earth there will always be a discrepancy, an unavoidable disproportion, between truth and seeming. The choice is between presenting to the world the false face of the Pharisee, or, as Fielding recommends, wearing a face that is not more but less comely than the real one. What good is it, morally speaking, to have the face of an archbishop and the heart of a miller? Better, declares Fielding, to seem worse than to seem better than you are, better—the question of worldly success apart—for a man to misrepresent himself downwards, to be his own traducer, the concealer of his true worth, than to pose as a better man than he truly is or to claim virtues not his own. Better for Tom Jones to seem a drunken and libidinous wastrel than for Blifil to seem the impassioned liberator of caged birds.

When we press Fielding to justify this preference, we touch the core of his Christian comedy. In his optimistic secularization of Christian eschatology, his earthly rendition of the Last Judgment, the *parousia*, all things will be revealed in time, with an inevitable reappraisal and revision of reputations. In that there must be such a revision, let it be upwards. When the day of disclosure comes, woe to the man who has been valued above his deserts, whose reward has exceeded his merit; such a man, like a moral bankrupt, has been living beyond his means; when, at Judgment Day, the checks inevitably bounce, he will be the more discomfited. Conversely, the man who has been devalued or misprized will be justified and raised to his proper level.

Fielding could have cited the highest scriptural authority for his preference in Christ's advice to those about to attend a feast. Those who presumptuously claim the first place at table run the risk of humiliation when the lord of the feast decides his own seating arrangements. The wise guest will guard against the shame of being publicly ordered to a lower place; only the spiritually modest will hear the gratifyingly welcome words: "Friend, go up higher! Then thou wilt be honored in the presence of all who are at table with thee. For everyone who exalts himself shall be humbled, and he who humbles himself shall be exalted" (Luke 14:7). No Pharisee will ever be the recipient of these words; having already arrogated to himself the place of honor at the Lord's table, he will suffer either dismissal to a lower station or banishment from the feast altogether.

It is in this sense that Fielding's otherwise misleading opening metaphor of the novel as feast and the novelist as restaurateur is so strikingly pertinent. Fielding's novel is not an inn where we can sit where we choose and eat what we will; if we do behave in this unmannerly fashion, we will, as we shall see, be quickly ordered to take our unwelcome custom elsewhere (51). I shall be considering later the series of metaphors by which Fielding attempts to define his relationship to the reader. For the present it is enough to say that if the novel is a feast, it is so in the sense of the passage just quoted from the Gospel of St. Luke—a feast in which the guests, characters and readers alike, will be judged and allocated. Blifil, the chief Pharisee, lacking the proper garment, will be bound hand and foot and cast into exterior darkness (scarcely the kind of treatment to be encountered in the average hotel), while Tom, unjustly banished from Paradise Hall, at least partly as a consequence of his own self-depreciation, will be restored to his true position as Allworthy's heir.

Fielding's fondness for parable has often been remarked, usually in terms of a predilection for the illuminating cameo, the striking vignette, the revealing incident, within the text, that provides the clue to the essential moral meaning. What has not been adequately recognized is that *Tom Jones*, considered as a total structure, is a complex and elaborate extension of one of the simplest yet most profound of the parables, that of the two sons. Beneath the ample flesh of the panoramic display of eighteenth-century English society is the bare skeleton of the parable, providing the armature of the work. When the father ordered his first son to go and work in the vineyard, the boy refused; but, afterwards, countermanding his own words, he obeyed the command and performed the work. By contrast, the second son instantly promised to obey, but did nothing. For each, word and deed clash, and appearances are misleading: the good son seems disobedient and ungrateful, the bad son a model of filial rectitude. No one can miss the parable's meaning. Certainly, the Pharisees, who had been harrying Jesus and to whom the parable was addressed, did not. When Jesus asked them which of the two sons had done his father's will, they, giving the only possible answer, walked straight into the trap set for them: "Amen I say to you, the publicans and harlots are entering the kingdom of God before you" (Matt. 21:28–32).

Just as unmistakable as the parable's meaning is its pertinence to the central concern of Fielding's novel. Once again we have the two sons (technically Bridget's, but, in terms of the legacy of golden girl and golden mountain, the possession of Sophia and Paradise Hall, they are Allworthy's boys, only one of whom can be finally fortunate); the novel's resolution shows the long-deluded Allworthy that the apparent rapscallion is the true son who has really done the father's will, while the dutiful yes-man, so punctiliously pious, is really a rogue and a hypocrite. The reader, if not Allworthy, should have no difficulty in making these identifications from the start. When we hear that young Master Blifil possessed "a zeal surprising in one so young," alarm bells should start to ring; is not this, above all else, the spoor of the Pharisee, made all the more unmistakable by the youth of the offender? (135). When, much earlier, his uncle, the doctor, is described as having "a great appearance of religion," we intuit instantly that this is bogus, a front for a very different reality (75). Distrust appearances: things are not what they seem; God's judgment is not man's; the best of men are blunderers (Allworthy is not all-seeing), while the worst are cheats. Fielding is doing little more than give body to the moral teachings of Jesus, applying the Gospel's ethical insights in his new fiction. Gide accused Fielding of being unable to conceive a saint, which is simply a pejorative way of saying that he distrusted a too visibly strenuous striving after virtue—as did Jesus when he warned those doing good not to let the hand know what the right was up to.

Tom, in contrast to his mealymouthed rival, is thoughtless, giddy, with little sobriety of manner, wild and impulsive—which is promising, because it means he is his natural self rather than an unnatural impostor, a tearaway but not a prig. How can we fail to see in this description of the two boys—the elder born to be hanged, the other a model youth—a replication of the parable's antithesis: the first defying the father, the other all sweet obedience? But, lest we do, Fielding supplies throughout the text a succession of incidents and situations that drive home the Gospel provenance of his fiction. Tom's friendship with Black George exposes him to the same charge brought by the Pharisees against Jesus for his unsavory associations with the dregs of Jerusalem: would a good man consort with publicans and harlots?

Thwackum and Square likewise attempt to blacken the boy in Allworthy's estimate by pointing to the company he keeps. Tom is by no means a messiah (though by the later stages of the novel this identification will cease to be so farfetched or outrageous), but we do find him suffering for the sins of others and taking all the blame for sin upon himself. The parallel with Jesus extends to his enemies' slander. The Pharisees accused Jesus of casting out demons with the help of demons; thus his seeming good was really evil. Square follows suit when he persuades Allworthy that the apparent goodness of Tom is really corruption, that he relieved the Seagrim family as a path to Molly's bed, helping the parents in order to debauch the daughter. Of course, Tom is *not* Jesus—but just as surely his enemies *are* the Pharisees, the enemies of Jesus.

The clinching proof of this is supplied when that even more utterly improbable *alter Christus*, Squire Western, uses the very words of Jesus to the Pharisees in condemnation of Tom's detractors. It occurs as the culmination of a series of visits by the foremost Pharisees to the bedside of Tom, who lies recuperating from the broken arm he suffered when rescuing Sophia (203–204). Thwackum, Square, Blifil, each arrives in turn, ostensibly to comfort the sufferer, but really to tell him what a bad lot he is and how deserved or, in Square's case, how trivially insignificant is his anguish. Thwackum assures Tom that the broken arm is a sign from heaven, a judgment upon the sinner—not, of course, to encourage Tom to repent, since that is impossible, but to give him a foretaste of the pangs of hell, his inevitable destination. An angry God, alert to the affair with Molly, has broken Tom's arm, in much the same way, if we are to accept certain contemporary views, that he has sent AIDS today as a visitation on sinful man. Square, for his part, tells the sufferer that pain is contemptible, a trifle that the Stoic wise man easily ignores, before accidentally biting his own tongue and giving way to an outburst of grief and anger. Blifil visits seldom and never alone, because isolated proximity to a sinner (the AIDS analogy again) can be a risky business.

Western is the last of the visitors—rowdy, drunken, trying to force beer down the patient's throat, riotously disturbing his much-needed rest, but, redeeming all else, good-natured and meaning well (204–205). The point is vital to an understanding of Fielding's ethic. The road to *heaven* is paved with good intentions. An ostensibly virtuous act (the freeing of a bird, telling the truth) when motivated by malice is an abomination; conversely, a reckless or even technically sinful act (Tom's lie to save Black George from punishment) may be forgiven or even commended, provided the motive is good. Fielding anticipates the insight of T. S. Eliot's saintly martyr: the greatest treason is to do the right deed for the wrong reason.[5] Just as clearly he also anticipates Graham Greene's insight concerning his saintly sinners: that to damn oneself for the good of others, like Scobie or the whiskey priest, may be the highest virtue of all. The smug hypocrites who tiptoe demurely and maliciously toward Tom's sickbed are in far worse moral case than the rowdy, well-meaning drunkard.

Admittedly, Western's defense of Tom against the hypocrites has its selfish side; Tom broke his arm protecting Western's daughter, so the squire is most unlikely to take the same churlishly uncharitable view of the injury as Thwackum. Nevertheless, his stinging rebuke to Tom's vilifier is astonishing as we hear the violent, uncontrollable drunkard unwittingly echoing the words of Christ to the Pharisees: "I have had a battle for thee below stairs with thick parson Thwackum.—He hath been a telling Allworthy, before my face, that the broken bone was a judgement upon thee. D—n it, says I, how can that be? Did not he come by it in defence of a young woman? A judgement indeed! Pox, if he never doth anything worse, he will go to heaven sooner than all the parsons in the country" (205–206). Expletives and imprecations apart, we are listening to the judgment of Jesus: "the publicans and harlots are entering the kingdom of God before you." Not those who talk, serving God with their tongues only, however mellifluous, but those who do their father's will, however low their social reputation: these are the true heirs of the kingdom. But Thwackum was doubtless as affronted to hear Tom preferred above him as were the righteous in Israel to hear of the new, shockingly subversive order of entry into the kingdom.

The sickbed visits reveal, in addition, the classic Pharisee explanation of human suffering. Thwackum's only surprise is that it has taken God so long to vent his righteous anger on the sinner; still, he takes comfort in the deliciously incontrovertible fact that "Divine punishments, though slow, are always sure" (203). George Santayana said of the Puritan mentality that it thought it was beautiful that sin should exist so that it might be beautifully, inexorably punished. Thwackum's nose twitches eagerly at the hint of sin; he hunts sinners as Western hunts hares, with meditations full of birch, and his spiritual inheritor is Kafka's Whipper with his chilling claim: "I am here to whip."[6] At the novel's close he is as unteachable as ever, still preaching his infallible remedy for sin—scourging, still condemning Allworthy for the reprehensible lenity which allows vice to flourish. It is appropriate that, unlike Square, he does not repent. Square is, like Tartuffe, an impudent imposter, but Thwackum is the full-fledged Pharisee, the genuine article, who really does see himself as God's hit man—he is Alceste, a *self*-deceiver, a good man. What has a good man to repent who has done nothing wrong? Conversion in *Tom Jones* is apparently easier for the brazen atheist than for the convinced Christian—but, then, the devout were the most implacable foes of Jesus.

Thwackum as Pharisee knows the reason for Tom's broken arm: not a horse's hoof, but the hand of God. There is, for such a mentality, no mystery in suffering, no tragic, inexplicable incommensurability between the victim and his torment. On the contrary, all is as smoothly rational as a mathematical proof, as openly verifiable as a scientific experiment. Nothing is hidden, all is visibly ascertainable. Sinners suffer. If a man sins, expect the suffering; if a man suffers, seek the sin. That not only Pharisees are afflicted by this mania to turn pain into a science, to become actuaries of anguish by identifying the infallible, comforting system of cause and effect here as in the rest of the physical world, is shown by the question put to Jesus by his own disciples when they encountered the man blind from birth (John 9:1–5). Who, they demanded to know, was the sinner, the man or his parents, that he should be born blind? The sightless eyes prove guilt; all that remains is to identify the culprit.

In denying that anyone was guilty, man or parents, in rejecting altogether the relevance of guilt to the question, Jesus simultaneously attacked the assumption, axiomatic to Pharisee thought, that anguish belongs to the intelligible scientific world of cause and effect and that there is a logical explanation for pain; suffering is, rather, a mystery, not to be contained within the syllogisms and sorites of any rational system. The sufferer may be innocent, or, still more inexplicable, virtuous. When the healthy Thwackum tells the ailing Tom that sickness is the badge of sin, he is arrogantly proclaiming his own right to heaven while consigning Tom to hell. He is also advancing the basic arguments of Pharisaism: that the world is divided into saints and sinners, elect and reprobate, sheep and goats; that this division is visibly identifiable; and that the manifestly good have been commissioned by God to chastise the manifestly wicked. The moral mission of Jesus was to persuade us to abandon such pernicious beliefs. In *Tom Jones* we see Fielding waging the same campaign against the same enemies.

In this campaign Fielding's chief philosophical weapon is his insistence on a distinction between existence and essence, which thereby undermines the simplistic Pharisee reliance on external signs and appearances as the infallible index of God's favor or disapproval. The true judgment toward which Fielding summons us is a perilous activity, because in judging others we inevitably judge ourselves, a risk so complacently overlooked by arrogant Pharisaism. Fielding knows, no one better, how seduced our assessments can be by external appearances, how easily bribable our verdicts are by considerations of status and wealth (184). It is surprising, in view of his own essentially conservative temperament, that Fielding should so forcibly remind us how sin, or, more precisely, punishment for sin, is socially determined, dictated by class considerations. The candor of the Duchess of Buckingham's stinging rebuke to John Wesley makes this class animus splendidly clear: "It is monstrous to be told that you have a heart as sinful as the common wretches that crawl on the earth."[7] There speaks the voice of unabashed class Pharisaism. The Duchess is very willing to judge, but not to be judged. Sin is the prerogative of the lower orders, and the cultivated no more admitted its presence in their hearts than they did the canaille in their drawing rooms.

Fielding, from the privileged position as insider, scion of the aristocracy, warns us against such partisan bias. He knows how severe we are disposed to be on "whores in rags," how much more accommodating when the whores are wearing the latest Dior creations; and he challenges us to say what really offends us—the whores or the rags (445). Incarceration in Bridewell and being whipped at the cart's tail are for poor sinners like Molly; a rich sinner like Lady Bellaston will never suffer such a fate. Ironically, Fielding tells us that the otherwise ineffectual, indeed counterproductive, Bridewell inculcates at least one good lesson in those who suffer there: it teaches the poor to respect anew the gulf between the classes, because faults in them are punished there that are overlooked in their superiors (184). In another type of man such an insight might have instigated a demand for revolution, for the overthrow of an unjust society and the foundation of a new polity in which all were equal before the law, but Fielding is no revolutionary—it is a moral, individual reformation that he proposes, not a political and collective restructuring.

In any case, it goes much deeper than allowing our judgments to be swayed by the prestige of rank or wealth. The appearances that pervert true judgment may be more than the insignia of social status. Deeds themselves may be a deception, totally misleading the onlooker as to the true inner worth of the actor. To be a good judge it is not enough to be good-natured or well-meaning; indispensable though these attributes be, they are necessary but not sufficient conditions of true judgment. One must be able to see through acts, to recognize that a chicken thief may be the Good Samaritan or that setting a bird at liberty may, in certain circumstances, be irrefutable proof of perfidy (*JA*, 70; *TJ*, 158). The good judge must be judicious, able to emancipate inner truth from surface appearance.

Central to this quality of judiciousness for Fielding is the need to be able to separate act and motive, deed and doer, and here the contrast with Swift is instructive. Swift, following the Baptist, insists on deeds as the sole reliable indicator of moral worth. A man is what he does—there is no spurious essence to defend us against an inculpating existence, no laudable inner self to which a man can legitimately appeal against the incriminating evidence of his actual behavior. A man is the sum of his actions and nothing else. Swift supplies a catalog of sordid, vicious habits as a description of how Yahoos behave; if, under oath, you are forced to confess these habits as your own, then you, too, are a Yahoo and there is no more to be said: *causa finita*. Fielding, far less rigorous, exhibits the generosity of a benevolent judge rather than the relentless pursuit of a Swiftian prosecutor. Not what a man *does* but what, at heart, he *is* is what counts. This consoling distinction between existence and essence is, as Coleridge notes, the defining characteristic of Fielding as moralist.[8]

The distinction has its Gospel source in Jesus' dismissal of the key Pharisee argument that decorum is the test of virtue, external observance the infallible proof of inner purity. The Pharisee declared that the godly man is he who follows certain rules and performs certain acts, while the reprobate is marked by his failure to do either: virtue is performance. Jesus countered by suggesting that performance is simply that, that a man who acts may be no more than an actor, a player—and Fielding reminds us that player and hypocrite are the same word in Greek (300). It follows that acts in themselves are not reliable indicators of vice or virtue: the ostensibly good man may be a sham, the apparent scoundrel a hero.

Fielding insists against Swift that a man may fail himself in his actions, may libel his true essence, commit treason against his real self—a man, in short, may be better than his deeds. Deeds deceive. Tom Jones gets drunk and this is wrong, but a wise and compassionate judge (he cannot be one without the other) will consider the mitigating circumstances, the commendably ungovernable joy at Allworth's miraculous recovery from seemingly imminent death. Blifil frees a bird from a cage not because he loves birds or freedom but because he hates Tom. Even had the bird escaped, Blifil would get no credit; that the poor creature is instantly devoured by a predator simply helps to illuminate the malice that freed it in the first place. For Swift and John the Baptist doing is the mirror of being; the filthy deeds of men reveal their rotten hearts, and they must repent, that is, act differently, or perish. Fielding and Jesus, less confident of the unerring testimony of acts, doubtful of Burke's assurance that conduct is the only language that never lies,[9] call for a profounder, more sympathetically intuitive assessment: a man may look guilty, like Tom or the publican, and be justified, while another, applauded for his goodness, may, like Blifil and the Pharisee, be in moral peril. Conduct can be as mendacious a language as any other. The distinction between existence and essence, deeds and nature, may be a consolation for the publican in the parable, Tom in the novel, and the accused sinner in general, but it has a contrary, an accusing and threatening import for Blifil and the tribe of Pharisees he represents.

Despite Coleridge's telling insight, it would, nevertheless, be a blunder to attribute to Fielding, of all men, an antinomian contempt for conduct. Far from upholding faith against works or slighting the importance of deeds, Fielding repeatedly stresses the indispensability of action, agreeing with Tillotson that "that man believes the gospel best who lives most according to it" (Rawson, 397); good living is for Fielding the soul of religion, with doctrinal purity trailing a long way behind. What might seem like an irresolvable contradiction in Fielding, a confusion as to the value, efficacy, or testimony of actions—on the one hand dismissing them as indicators of inner worth, on the other insisting that without them faith is empty—is once again unriddled with the help of the Gospels.

The contradiction between Jesus and the Baptist is more apparent than real. Superficially, it may seem that the Baptist upholds, while Jesus decries, the value of works; in truth, both regard action as crucial: we are *not* saved by faith alone, if by this is implied a disregard for deeds. Fielding's practical Christianity accords perfectly with Christ's warning that not the mouthers of the Father's name but the doers of the Father's will shall inherit the kingdom; in Fielding's secularized reprise the kingdom belongs to those who have good hearts, benevolent impulses, and actions to match. That the issue mattered greatly to Fielding is plain from its recurrence throughout his work. In *Joseph Andrews* he invites us to join him in condemning "the detestable doctrine of faith against good works"; in *Jonathan Wild* it is dragged in when Heartfree outrages the Newgate ordinary by arguing that a good pagan is more pleasing to God than a Christian rogue (*JA*, 70; *JW*, 165). Apart from rounding off the set of Heartfree's virtues, this has little to do with the plot, but that further serves to emphasize how large the theme bulked in Fielding's thought. It is not enough to *say* you believe; belief must be translated into action; otherwise you are the Baptist's dead branch, fit only for the fire.

Still, it would be hard to deny that, for Fielding, essence finally determines existence. Blifil, bad from birth, twisted in mind and nature, is incapable of a good action; what seems like one in such a man is pure illusion—it *must* be perverted at its root. What Calvin alleged against all men—that their seeming virtue is a mere skin over pollution, their good deeds simply a screen for corruption—is taken up and employed by Fielding against a certain type of man, of whom Blifil is his representative figure. Hence the paradox in Fielding: actions are *not* all-important when sundered from the hearts in which they are conceived and nurtured. Whatever he *does*, Blifil is rotten to the core. When Fielding ostentatiously refuses to make windows into Blifil, to journey into that heart of darkness—"it would be an ill office in us to pay a visit to the inmost recesses of his mind"—has not the visit, for all practical purposes, in the very moment of its renunciation, been devastatingly paid? (157). Do you need a tour of the whited sepulchre before you recognize how loathsome it is? (We shall see later how decisive this reticence is in determining Fielding's narrative mode, so antithetical to the prying intrusiveness favored by Richardson).

All of this, unarguably, is fully compatible with Christ's insistence that it is the heart, the motive, the desire, that finally determines the nature and quality of the deed. If the heart is Pharisaic, the deed, regardless of appearances, cannot be good. If Blifil frees a bird, seek the corruption; if he insists on telling the truth about Bridget's death to her dying brother, unearth the malice behind such murderous probity; if he pursues Sophia, not with fornication but with a respectable Christian marriage in mind, expose the sadistic perversion of his intent. What a man *is* must color what he does; the wicked soul can perform only wicked acts. How can a bad tree bear good fruit? All these acts—freeing a bird, telling the truth, courting a woman—may be good in themselves; but so, too, is going to the synagogue to pray. Everything depends upon the how and the why of its doing. So it seems obtuse to complain, as some readers do, that Blifil gets a raw deal simply because he lacks a good heart, or to advance as the chief argument on his behalf what is, in fact, the chief accusation against him. His heart *is* corrupt, his nature vicious. How did they become so? No more than Jesus does Fielding tell us how the pharisee became a Pharisee; but, just as devastatingly as Jesus, he reveals the heap of bones strewn behind the gleaming facade.

Lest we risk missing this, Fielding, at the moment of Allworthy's final enlightenment, his insight into Blifil's perfidy, has him utter the explicit word of condemnation, the word chosen by Christ himself to denounce the Pharisees: "that wicked viper which I have so long nourished in my bosom" (845). Who can doubt that Blifil is here assuming his true place in a tradition of biblical obloquy that begins with the serpent of Eden and culminates in the vipers of Jesus? The source becomes completely unmistakable as Mrs. Miller, on her knees, prays the Christian prayer for the forgiveness of the adulterous woman, Mrs. Waters: "may Heaven shower down its choicest blessings upon her head, and for this one good action, forgive her all her sins be they never so many" (845). The very words of the Gospel are repeated in an eighteenth-century London drawing room; we might call it plagiarism but for the inescapable fact that Fielding so deliberately emblazons his "theft"; he wants us to detect it, to recognize in him the heir of Jesus, the foe of the Pharisees.

The novel exhibits the whole panoply of Pharisaism, with its parade of hypocrites representing every conceivable type, every possible subset: the immitigable villain posing as good man (Blifil), the sanctimonious frauds denouncing the sins they commit (Square, Bridget, Mrs. Wilkins), the sadist who really believes that his bloodlust is sanctioned by heaven (Thwackum). All, the villainous Blifil included, are comic, for reasons that will be examined in the final chapter, but the nature of the comedy, the categories of laughter, vary from one type to another.

In his onslaught on hypocrisy Fielding pioneers the mimetic style that Joyce was to bring to perfection in *Dubliners*. What at first glance seems like straight authorial reportage becomes, on inspection, an ironic dissection of the hypocrite trained in the narrator's sights. Bridget, we are told, cared so little for beauty (which she lacks) that she never mentioned it (54). Suspicions are aroused; the very proof offered of her contempt turns into its opposite—the suggestion that she indeed cared deeply about it and that the lack rankled badly. The case is clinched when we detect her obvious relish of the fact that so many beautiful women end up ruined, a speculation rounded off with a pharisaical acknowledgment to God for having so graciously exempted her from the odious gift: I thank thee, God, that I am not like other women—

the prayer of the female Pharisee. The narrator pretends to find it strange that the ugliest women are the most circumspect, though the reader who knows his La Rochefoucauld will find no mystery there. Just as the trained bands eagerly present themselves for duty when there is no danger, so ugly women are punctiliously chaste because no man is interested—the women so keen on prudence do not need it.

The insight has an importance transcending the case in question. For example, it is contemptibly easy for men who have no way with women to attack Tom Jones for succumbing to temptation, yet only a charmer like Tom, overcoming the temptations so plentifully and readily offered, has a right to condemn Tom's indiscretions. Milton makes a similar point in the key argument of *Areopagitica:* only those who have been exposed to and solicited by temptation have ceased, morally speaking, to be children and may now be treated as moral beings;[10] conversely, there is something shamefully facile in pillorying the sins we are never likely to have a chance of committing. "By God, Mr. Chairman, at this moment I stand astonished at my own moderation."[11] Lord Clive, brought back from India to face charges of peculation in Parliament, implicitly challenges his accusers; those who have not been in his position are incapable of appreciating the modesty of his conduct, for the truly surprising thing is not his extortions but his abstentions. Similarly situated, what would his accusers have done?

Tom, had he been so minded, might have advanced a similar selfexculpation. Despite his reputation among critics as a squire of dames, Tom is really a naif where women are concerned, comically deluding himself that he is pursuer and seducer when he is really the prey. In any case, balancing his three lapses (with Molly, Mrs. Waters, and Lady Bellaston) are the three victories he wins in the final section of the novel: the rebuff of the sexual advances of Mrs. Fitzpatrick; the refusal of Mrs. Waters's sexual gambits on her prison visit; and, most heroic of all, considering his penniless condition consequent on abandoning Lady Bellaston, added to the apparently irrecoverable loss of Sophia, his rejection of the young, rich, and pretty widow Mrs. Hunt in her offer of honorable, profitable marriage (773, 811, 735). If only those capable of Tom's abstentions were to attack him, the number of his condemners would be much reduced.

Fielding's earlier ironic exposure of Bridget's hypocrisy warns those who condemn Tom, whether character or reader, to be scrupulously honest in scrutinizing their motives; envy of the successful philandereer, chagrin at one's own sexual incompetence, may so easily be alchemized into a spurious moral indignation. It is Christ's recurring charge against the Pharisees: their seeming virtue, forever expressing itself in the indictment of others, masks an inner corruption. Fielding similarly insists that the condemnation of sinners is not necessarily a proof of virtue. Who is more likely to chastise Tom's monetary recklessness than the avaricious Blifil, who more zealous to expose his drunkenness than his strategically abstemious adversary, who more eager to pillory his imprudent though healthy sexuality than the pervert who dreams not of love, nor even of sex, but only of violation? The accuser is not necessarily holy: it is Fielding's key ethical insight, as it is also Christ's. "That higher order of women," so avid to condemn their frailer sisters, may well be impelled by envy and chagrin. By the time the narrator tells us that these touchy women are severely left alone by men—"from despair, I suppose, of success"—his cheek is fairly bulging with his tongue, and the cause of their touchiness not hard to infer (54). How easy it is to parade necessity as a virtue, to alchemize incapacity into merit, or to elevate spite into principle! On this topic Fielding has nothing to learn from Nietzsche. With Fielding in the vicinity there is no chance of perpetrating such a fraud; like a moral weights-and-measures man, he may at any moment arrive with his true scales to verify the standards we habitually employ. It is the hypocrite-trader who has most to fear.

Allworthy's housekeeper, among the first of the frauds to be exposed, is clearly a cheat of this kind. Finding the child in his bed, Allworthy rings for the elderly Mrs. Wilkins, but is so engaged with the infant, so oblivious of self, that he forgets he is undressed. But Mrs. Wilkins is not forgetful of self. Here, Fielding insinuates, is the crude reality behind the tense Richardsonian myth of imperiled female servants and lustful masters, the truth underlying the fantasy of procrastinated rape on which Fielding's great rival had based his work and built his reputation. The contrast is between the abstracted man, so absorbed with the discovery of the foundling child that he forgets he is in his shirt (the eighteenth-century euphemism for naked), and the shrewd, calculating woman, her mind concentrated on how she can turn a nocturnal summons to her master's bedroom to her own material advantage. Paradoxically, the scandalously naked man is a paragon of virtue, while the respectably clothed matron is a sexual schemer, who, summoned in the night, first visits her mirror, not to make herself decent but seductive, not to conceal but to advertise her charms. That Mrs. Wilkins is not a nubile young charmer like Pamela simply makes her vamping ambitions more risible, but not less reprehensible. Her failure is not to her credit; she is still a scheming female, though laughably without a hope of success, a joke who tried to be a threat. She finds her master as she hopes—naked—and her strategic swoon, in the best Pamela tradition, could only have facilitated the sexual onslaught she anticipates, had her innocent employer ever entertained any such desires (56).

Overcoming the disappointment of her master's sexual indifference, she immediately exhibits that salient trait of Pharisaism, the lust to punish. Not the child's welfare but the mother's chastisement is her first thought. Transplant her to New England and she will easily take her place among those demanding harsher penalties for Hester Prynne; transplant her to the

Palestine of Christ and she will be strong for the stoning of the adulteress. Her mind hankers after punishment—Bridewell and the cart's tail—no whipping being too severe for such sluts, especially one who has so patently tried to incriminate Allworthy. Allworthy is astonished at the onservation. For a magistrate he seems curiously naive, quaintly assuming, in advance of Kafka's Joseph K., that only guilty men are accused. The more knowing Mrs. Wilkins reminds him that "the world is censorious," but it is a world projected from her own suspicious mentality and made in her own image; she is the scandalmonger (57). Fortunately for Tom, Allworthy rejects the role of Laius that Mrs. Wilkins would have him play—the "father" threatened by an infant son who deals with the threat through infanticide. Here, as at the climax of the novel, Tom is, at worst, a comic Oedipus, which is to say a false Oedipus, a *not*-Oedipus, entirely appropriate in a work that is a Christian comedy rather than a pagan tragedy.

The housekeeper's attitude toward the child is reminiscent of Gulliver's toward the Yahoo infant: "it goes against me to touch these misbegotten wretches, whom I don't look upon as my fellow creatures. Faugh, how it stinks! It doth not smell like a Christian" (57). The absurdity of the complaint (do Christian babies come toilet-trained?) should not mask the malice or the consciousness of difference, of superiority, which is the Pharisee's hallmark; this same sense of election inspires her brutal solution of the problem. She is for wrapping the child in a basket and leaving it on the highway; the odds are about two to one in favor of survival till morning, but, even should it die, it will be for the best, since, in the idiom of the *Modest Proposal*, what future happiness can there be for such a misbegotten wretch? This is funny, but in the way that Swift or Joe Orton is funny: there is savagery in the humor.

In the parade of the Pharisees, Mrs. Wilkins, in addition to being the first of the punishers, hence the first contributor to a key debate in the novel that will continue almost to the last page, is also the first of those who prophesy a disastrous finale for Tom. But for the moment his is not to be the fate of Oedipus; when the unheeding Allworthy commands that, rather than be exposed to the elements, the child is to be cared for, the timeserver at once switches and plays the third of a series of rapidly assumed roles, that of the motherly woman following on outraged moralist and shocked maiden. Forgetting her recent abhorrence, she takes the child, the "sweet little infant" (somehow miraculously freshened), into her arms—a testimony less to her capacity for conversion than to a shrewd awareness of the dangers of defying an employer (58). Mrs. Wilkins lacks the courage of her odious convictions; she can pretend love for a Yahoo child provided it pays to do so. Like the lawyer in *Joseph Andrews* who insists, for purely selfish reasons, on caring for the injured man (JA, 69), Mrs. Wilkins is still wrong even when she does right, supplying yet another instance of Eliot's greatest treason.

Once again Fielding exhorts us to search behind the deed for the all-decisive motive. Tom will turn out to be the opposite of the timeserving housekeeper, because he does the wrong deed for the right reason: telling a lie to save Black George, getting drunk to celebrate his benefactor's recovery, while Blifil, his uncle's would-be killer, sits discreet and sober, harvesting all the false credit of an outward decorum. Throughout the entire scene between Allworthy and Mrs. Wilkins we have an exposure of the doublethink that Fielding tended to associate with the basic Richardsonian situation of beleaguered maiden and rampant rapist; the man is naked not because he is lascivious but because he is virtuous; the woman, epitome of outward respectability, is obsessed by thoughts of self.

These same thoughts of self are clearly visible in Fielding's reprise of the parable of the laborers in the vineyard, the deathbed declaration of Allworthy's will. The metaphor of the indignant laborers who feel they have been bilked by the boss coalesces with the repulsive image in St. Matthew of the vultures gathering round the corpse (Matt. 20:1–16; 24:28) to shape Fielding's description of the bogus deathbed scene in which the household assembles to hear Allworthy's bequests. However dissimilar laborers and vultures are, they are linked by a rapacious resolve to grab as much as they can get. When the vulture has been schooled by Pharisees, it is also convinced that its deserts are greater than its share.

Only by recognizing its parable origin will we be prevented from misconstruing this episode. After Allworthy's recovery, the narrator informs us that the illness had never been so serious as what the doctor diagnosed (233, 225). But we would be wrong to conclude that we are dealing with a hypochondriac and an inept doctor, because the latter decides and the former believes that death is imminent; far from being a hypochondriac, Allworthy tends to neglect himself, while the fact that the doctor confuses a bad cold with incipient rigor mortis is not, in this context, necessarily a proof of folly. Quite apart from the fact that the plot requires Allworthy to be unavailable when the lawyer Dowling calls, Fielding needs a deathbed to develop another aspect of his theme, the debunking of Pharisaism. We are at this point reading a parable, not a psychologically realistic fiction. Parable will not tolerate too strict a psychological scrutiny, is discomfited when we ask it too many specific and particularized questions. Where did the woman get the precious jar of ointment? No matter, it is what she did with it that counts. Why was the man who sowed tares in the corn the farmer's enemy? Could it be that he had cause, or was at least mitigated, in seeking revenge? These are misguided speculations, as totally out of place here as they would be appropriate to realistic fiction. In this parable of the field we simply have the datum, not the explanation, of enimity; all else is irrelevant to the story's understanding. Christ's only interest is in the practical problem: Now that the field *is* in such a condition, what are we to do with it? The parameters of parable are strict, and this holds equally for Fielding's bogus deathbed scene. We are not meant to speculate about hypochondria or the medical incompetence that mistakes a snuffle for the death rattle. Fielding needs a deathbed (better in a comedy that it should be bogus) so that he can display certain attributes of human nature: cupidity, resentment, envy, sense of injured merit, and so on. His only aim is to lay bare the rancor and disgruntlement of the beneficiaries, the laborers in Allworthy's vineyard.

Allworthy does not fear death. If a pagan like Cato could despise it, how much more easily can a Christian fortified by the infinitely superior promises of his religion do so. He likens his approaching death to that of a faithful laborer at harvest end, summoned to receive his reward from a bountiful master—a splendidly appropriate prelude to the modern rendition of the parable that follows (225–26). Allworthy, too, is a bountiful master and has gathered his friends for the final comfort of witnessing their satisfaction at the legacies provided. He is, of course, yet again woefully mistaken. Only Tom and Blifil are unresentful. Tom, grief-stricken at the approaching death, is heedless of legacies. Blifil *is* satisfied with the fortune left him, so satisfied, indeed, that he tries to hasten the benefactor's demise by communicating, against the doctor's advice, the sad news of Bridget's passing, using his own mother's death as a means of killing off his uncle.

Everyone else—Mrs. Wilkins, Thwackum, Square—is angry and discontented, each resenting the other's share, each convinced that he or she has been cheated. All shed, of course, the tears obligatory on such occasions (229)—when was a Pharisee ever found wanting in ritual exactitude? But this is rote mourning, mere eye-service. That Fielding is not the naive Polyanna, the Shaftesburian simpleton, invented by some critics, optimistically viewing human nature through the rosiest-tinted glasses, is shown in the chapter heading: "Containing matter rather natural than pleasing"(229). The resentment of the rancorous Pharisees is, regrettably, a natural reaction, not some monstrous aberration of ingratitude imported from another species on another planet. Mrs. Wilkins fumes privately against her employer's failure to reward her own superior merit: "now we are all put in a lump together"(230)—precisely the complaint of the disgruntled laborers, made all the more outrageously comic in the light of her self-confessed peculations, the fact that, like the unjust steward, she has been robbing her master for years.

Both she and the similarly disappointed Thwackum comfort themselves in the standard way of envious Pharisaism: their enemy, who is ipso facto God's enemy too, is headed for hell—"he is now going where he must pay for all" (230). The narcissism of the Pharisee is comically yet arrestingly manifested, not merely in the relish of another's everlasting torment, but also in the notion that God will send Allworthy to hell for not giving Thwackum more money. It is not so much having God in your corner as having him in your pocket. Small wonder that they concur so readily with Blifil's resolve to tell the "dying" man the sad news of his sister's death; those who condemn you to hell will scarcely shrink from condemning you to death. That Blifil can hypocritically cite obedience and truth as justifying his disclosure merely highlights the Pharisaism, because here obedience is the sin and truth a means of murder (232). Even without knowing Blifil's malicious motive—and quite apart from the stunning dishonesty of pleading truth while withholding from his uncle the greatest truth of all, that of Tom's parentage (withheld on a first reading, be it noted, not only from Allworthy but also from the reader)—the sensible argument against such formulaic rigidity is that circumstances later cases, that one must always take the context into account. Should a man in danger of dying be told bad news? Is truth and idol to which everything else must be sacrificed? Accused of desecrating the Sabbath, Jesus retorted that the Son of Man is lord of the Sabbath, thereby upholding human love and need against an inflexible, inhuman code. Even were his reverence for truth genuine, Blifil would still stand convicted; it is merely a mask for murder exposes him as a monster.

It is one of the triumphs of Fielding's art that even a monster like Blifil should finally be seen as comic, or, at least, should easily and without any sense of strain take his position within the total comic structure of the work. A character like Square provides a very different kind of comedy and provokes a very different brand of laughter. Why do we laugh at Square? The preface to *Joseph Andrews* will tell us: "To discover any one to be the exact reverse of what he affects" is, says Fielding, the essence of the ridiculous (JA, 29), and Square is the foremost example of the ridiculous in *Tom Jones*. When the Pharisee is caught with his trousers down, he is comic, especially when the debagging reveals a man who is just the same as other men. We laugh because Fielding contrives through his art that we must. Note the obvious relish of the narrator in the "wicked" rug that fell and left the shivering philosopher exposed (215). The normal, straightforward, moral explication of the transferred epithet would be that the rug is wicked because it *hid* the wrongdoer, but here the narrator ironically condemns it for *ceasing* to hide him. The narrator may say "unhappily," but he is clearly overjoyed that the rug fell—all the more so if Molly, in her simulated rage as she plays the role of betrayed maiden, really did unintentionally displace it; God's ways are wonderful indeed—would it not be deliciously apt if she *acted* herself into her predicament?

"With shame I write it, and with sorrow will it be read" (215); but we know there is nothing of the kind, on both counts. For shame substitute elation, for sorrow, delight. As the rug falls the narrator describes how the "philosopher" Square (just in case the reader has forgotten his vocation) is crouched, in the position of a soldier punished by being tied neck to heel, or of a miscreant disgustingly excreting in the public street, "among *other* female utensils" (215). It is the linking of "philosopher" and "other" that does all the comic damage; the pretentious self-elevated man is revealed with as much dignity as a dildo or a jordan. The spectacle of his large, staring eyes gazing from beneath Molly's nightcap would be risible enough in any man; in the philosopher it is sidesplitting. In *The Mechanical Operation of the Spirit* Swift ridicules the philosophic claim to have raised the soul above matter, and nominates the unfortunate Thales as the archetype of those philosophic blunderers. Walking along, his eyes fixed dreamily on the stars, he falls into a ditch, a slimy hole in the earth, the appropriate nemesis of such abstracted visionaries.[12] Square, unlike Thales, is simply a fraud, and the manner of his exposure makes it impossible, as the narrator says, for any spectator to refrain from "immoderate laughter" (215).

Such laughter is the revenge of reality on phony aspiration, of life on pretension. The wise and grave man, normally preening himself on his pedestal, is found skulking shamefaced in Molly's bedroom, and the hoot of comic incongruity that erupts from the perception that the wise and grave man is no different from you and me. Square is not being ridiculed for being a sexual creature, but for pretending *not* to be a sexual creature, for posing as superior to other men. Not the fornicator but the Pharisee is targeted; his present behavior is natural enough, it is his previous rhetoric that is intolerable. "Philosophers are composed of flesh and blood as well as other people" (216): only let *them* remember this and there will be no need for *us* to remind them. If they are superior at all, it is in theory, not practice; their speculations may be more refined than ours, but their conduct is no different.

The inescapable question presents itself: why does Fielding find it funny? Why is he not more incensed against the hypocrite? Is this yet further evidence of what some critics regard as a laxity or compliance, a too ready indulgence toward sin, in Fielding himself? Fielding might well have posed a counterquestion: what is there to get angry about? Why rage against nature? Had Square been honest with us from the start about his natural impulses, the case against him would scarcely be worth pursuing. We are all in the same fallible boat, all sons of Adam; even the gravest of men may sometimes stoop to reading certain books and looking at certain pictures. This genial forbearance in Fielding is, after all, an essential element in all comedy; it is the arrogant, the rigorous, the overstrict who are the targets of leveling comedy, which seeks to bring them down to their proper place alongside ordinary mortals. Comic nemesis invariably attends comic hubris. The Duke in *Measure for Measure* may talk contemptuously of love, but he will end up a married man for all that. Not what Square does but rather the secrecy with which he does it—this is Fielding's target and he merrily takes aim.

Where Jesus gets angry at the hypocrite, Fielding is amused; Jesus finds no mirth in sin, Fielding forever unearths comedy. What Square says to Tom—"I see you enjoy this mighty discovery and—taste great delight in the thoughts of exposing me" (218)—might be even more appropriately directed at Fielding himself. Far from shaking his head over Square's deplorable behavior, Fielding enjoys it immensely: "I was never better pleased with thee in my life"; the reader senses a second, authorial voice here reinforcing and echoing Tom's words (219). Tom has, of course, a personal stake in Square's humiliating exposure—it gets him off a very difficult moral hook with Molly; but even allowing for this selfish interest, there is a patently uncensorious note in this, a live-and-let-live attitude. Tom *is* pleased at the discovery for selfish reasons, but he is also pleased to find Square for once behaving like a man instead of a philosophic calculating machine. It is, admittedly, splendidly convenient; nevertheless, Fielding does not cheat—there is no manipulation of puppets to provide Tom with an easy escape. Square *is* a fraud, Molly a trollop; they act according to their natures, predictably, consistently, as we can see in retrospect, and the scene ends not just with Tom happy but with everybody happy: a genial conclusion from a genial narrator.

It is this genial temperament that makes Fielding unsympathetic to any form of Pharisaism, including that curious type that assumes its superiority, not to others, but to itself, claiming an immunity from nature, a status out of this world. Fielding has been faulted for his tolerance of sinners; he is, we are told, too good-humored for indignation, too pleased with life to demand reform.[13] "Ye must be perfect even as your Father in heaven is perfect": the exhortation is inconceivable in Fielding's mouth. Indeed, he cautions us against the itch for perfection as ruinous to social intercourse and self-repose: "Men of true wisdom and goodness are contented to take persons and things as they are, without complaining of their imperfections, or attempting to amend them" (112). Let ill alone, advises Fielding, rest easy in reality instead of hankering after some impossible utopia. It is good advice, even for villains; if Blifil had not schemed to ruin Tom, he would have ended up as Allworthy's heir.

The personal note is unmistakable as the narrator tells us that he requires the kind of friend who both sees and overlooks faults, and assures us of his own readiness to reciprocate: "Forgiveness ... we give and demand in turn" (112). Echoes of the Lord's Prayer are easily audible in Fielding's definition of a friend: someone who forgives. Will the God who made us be any less generous, less friendly? Fielding comes close to anticipating Heine: *"Dieu me pardonnera—c'est son métier."* Conversely, "there is, perhaps, no surer mark of folly, than an attempt to correct the natural infirmities of those we love" (113), as the perfectionist zealot of Hawthorne's *The Birthmark* so tragically learns. As with the finest china, so with the best of men: in each may be an incurable flaw; but what witlessness to discard either for the sake of one defect. And how can what would be folly in man become wisdom in God? He, too, loves us as we are and is not so unreasonable as to demand an unprocurable faultlessness. Fielding's God predictably resembles Fielding.

The rigorous moralist may command us to sin no more; Fielding is content if our failings should be no worse than flesh is heir to. Pascal, pondering with bemused indignation the human penchant for diversion,[14] would have identified Western's sudden forgetting of his beloved runaway daughter to go chasing after a fox as another instance of this reprehensible distraction in man, this zany inability to concentrate upon what really matters; Fielding relishes the eccentricity too much to censure his madcap squire; the author-God loves Western too much to wish him changed (555). The humorist evicts the moralist.

Man is what he is, whatever fools and fanatics say. Even grief must eat at last; Fielding offers this as a fact, not as a stricture (748). What for Orwell in *Nineteen Eighty-four* is a source of anguish—the fact that the aspiring spirit is demeaningly shackled to a subversively feeble body—is accepted by Fielding with cheerful good humor. Contemplating Tom at Upton, Fielding lightheartedly tells us that heroes, self-esteem and the world's adulation notwithstanding, are finally mere flesh and blood: "However elevated their minds may be, their bodies at least (which is much the major part of most) are liable to the worst infirmities, and subject to the vilest offices of human nature" (453). There is no hint here of Paul's anguished prayer to be delivered from the body of this death. Heroes and philosophers have bellies and genitals like other men, and these organs require a like satisfaction as in lesser mortals: "To say the truth, as no known inhabitant of this globe is really more than man, so none need be ashamed of submitting to what the necessities of man demand"(453). No one is excluded from this general amnesty. Fielding adumbrates Brecht's *erst essen*, though in a very different sense; only after he has satisfied his hunger does Tom think of sex. The lady is no more to blame than the hero. Tom is an irresistible combination of Hercules and Adonis, and has, if more were needed, just saved her life. Only a prude will blame her for falling for so attractive a champion.

Fielding's indulgence toward his erring characters reaches its Everest point in an especially audacious piece of special pleading, when, employing the metaphor of love as feast, he tells us that Mrs. Waters is not too "nice," that is, squeamish or scrupulous, to dine where she knows that someone else has a prior claim, or has, indeed, dined previously—her suspicion that Tom loves someone else does not prevent her present enjoyment. This, the narrator concedes, may not be as refined as we might wish, but it is at least more wholesome and less spiteful than the niggardly attitude of those ascetic females who will happily forego enjoying their lovers provided no one else does. We are, presumably, to prefer Mrs. Waters's sexual largesse, her openhearted spirit, to the spiteful hoarding of a puritanism that denies the self and everyone else (461). It would, of course, be completely unreasonable to blame Fielding for not anticipating AIDS and the possibly catastrophic consequences of Mrs. Waters's generosity today; but neither, from our ambiguously privileged position, can we regard such promiscuity with the same casual indulgence as Fielding. Morally, we may still agree with him; medically, we cannot.

In fairness to Fielding, it should be said that he is *not* the irresponsible advocate of a sexual free-for-all. Tom, admittedly, seems to open the door to this in his perhaps too ready palliation of Square: "what can be more innocent than the indulgence of a natural appetite?" (218). Still, he takes a very different line in his stern rebuke to Nightingale over his treatment of Nancy (668), and Allworthy, surely not here Fielding's butt, has at the start of the novel denounced "the vice of incontinence" (186). Yet most readers will surely rise from *Tom Jones* feeling that we are too obsessed with sexual weaknesses, exag-gerating their importance in the graph of human imperfection, often condemning as wicked or sinful what is simply a datum of life, an inescapable fact of experience—or, at least, that this is what the author *wants* us to feel. It has to do with the revaluation of values, the restructuring of the league-table of sins, that we shall examine in the next chapter. Consider the narrator's comment on Tom's inability to resist the temptation to snatch a glance at Mrs. Waters's splendid breasts—what reader, whatever his own views on the matter, believes that Fielding condemns this as sinful rather than accepting it as natural? (444).

So the general point about Fielding's tolerance is valid. Swift's truth about man is intended to shame us, Fielding's to deliver us from shame. We must not scourge ourselves for what is trivial or unavoidable; we must live at peace within the limitations of the body, refusing to allow the aberrations of an extravagant Platonism to impose upon us, always remembering our first fealty to flesh and blood. Blood is thicker than Platonism. Depressed at Sophia's resolve never to marry against her father's will, Tom is, nevertheless, conforted to read in the same letter that she will just as surely not be coerced into an unappealing marriage. No man is so incredibly exalted, so much an enthusiast of love, as to wish his mistress married to another, even if this marriage were to make her completely happy. Such selfless devotion, if it exists at all, must be "a gift confined to the female part of the creation"; certainly, the narrator has heard only women claiming to possess it, "though I cannot pretend to say, I have ever seen an instance of it" (756). Do women exceed men in love—or is it simply that men exceed women in honesty? To tell such a truth shames only the devil, not the self. It is this calm, unextravagant fidelity to fact that identifies Fielding as the ancestor of Jane Austen, as witness Emma's sensible refusal to allow any "flight of generosity run mad" to enter her brain.[15]

Fielding no more approves of self-deceivers than he does of outright cheats: each is the foe of truth. Take Tom's thicket adventure with Molly: "With sorrow we relate, and with sorrow, doubtless, will it be read" (238)—but the historian must tell truth, however distressing or unpleasant. So

Fielding begins the chapter in which the drunken Tom, dreaming of Sophia and swearing eternal constancy to her, ends up copulating in the bushes with Molly. It echoes an earlier irony as Fielding zestfully prepares to pull the rug away from Square: "with shame I write it, and with sorrow will it be read"— but there are crucial differences. Square plots like a boudoir Napoleon the seduction of Molly; all goes according to plan until Tom's unexpected visit and the accident of the rug. Moreover, Square has not only posed as the Stoic wise man, apathetically superior to appetite, but has implacably condemned Tom for his shameful surrender to passion. Hence the reader, far from repining, is delighted to discover the sham behind the rug—Square, too good to be true, gets his thoroughly deserved comeuppance. Far from shame and sorrow, the reader shares the narrator's joy in the unmasking.

Tom's self-deception is of a less flagrant kind. Love, says Woody Allen, is the answer, but while we are waiting for the answer, sex can raise some pretty interesting questions. Such opportunism does not really fit the case of the drunken, surprised Tom, taken almost unawares amid his ecstatic protestations. Tom, drunk and vulnerable, has not reckoned on meeting an avid Molly. The target is not so much his conduct after Molly's arrival as his rhetoric before it. Should any man, never mind one as drunk and unguarded as Tom, so recklessly give such verbal hostages to fortune? As always in Fielding, comic nemesis waits in the wings. As background, Fielding supplies all the stock software of conventional pastoral romance—grove, stream, nightingale, smitten lover. Tom is exalted—and also inebriated and irresponsible. In the earlier exposure scene, the consciously hypocritical Molly, her new lover still hidden behind the rug, declaims like a tragic heroine: "I can never love any other man as long as I live" (215). Tom, less consciously culpable, is a self-deceiver: "But why do I mention another woman?" (239). To which the short, ironic answer is: because Molly is just around the corner. As Tom, in the throes of an absurdly hyperbolic devotion, vows to tear out his eyes rather than look at another woman, there are echoes not only of a comic Oedipus but of an inappropriate Gospel: if thine eye offends thee, pluck it out. But in comedy men are no better than men and self-mutilation is out of place; all Tom's high-flown protestations end laughably with the hero leading Molly into the thicket. Know thyself: the treasure of pagan wisdom is not to be despised by the Christian hero.

To know oneself: is there a more exacting moral and intellectual discipline? Of all writers Fielding is most acutely aware of how deep-seated, perhaps ineradicable, is the human talent for self-deception. A hypocrite is someone who.... But who isn't? So pervasive is the malady that even the good characters seem occasionally at risk of lapsing into pharisaical self-esteem. Does not our first view of the good Mr. Allworthy provoke a certain unease, however slight or qualified? "A human being replete with benevolence, meditating in what manner he might render himself most acceptable to his

Creator, by doing most good to his creatures" (59). Is it not just a trifle lush, excessive, a shade too programmatic and self-conscious? Tom, in the first flush of his heroic resolve to sacrifice himself rather than pursue Sophia to her ruin, is temporarily suffused with a glow of self-congratulation and pride in his own achievement, though the reality of loss quickly reasserts itself and conceit withers (289). Sophia herself is not above the insidious seductions of self-flattery. She is tempted to obey her father's command to marry Blifil from motives of duty and religion, but also from the "agreeable tickling in a certain little passion," neither religious nor virtuous in itself, but often acting as the auxiliary of both (329). Had not Mandeville scandalously and subversively proposed that virtue is mere vanity?[16] Hypocrisy is, it seems, a pit into which anyone can fall.

It is therefore, deliciously surprising and artistically superb that Fielding should end his onslaught on hypocrisy (for, morally, that is what *Tom Jones* is) with an instance at once innocent and delightful, as Sophia, in docile submission to her father's will, meekly agrees to marry the man for whom she yearns. Thy will be done, says the obedient handmaid of the Lord. What splendid consummation when duty and desire are one, and obedience is self-gratification. *E'n la sua volontade è nostra pace.*[17] To love the Lord's commands: it is, with the Virgin as archetype and model, the highest aspiration of the Christian soul.

## NOTES

1. William Hazlitt, "Characteristics," in *The Collected Works of William Hazlitt*, vol. 2, ed. A. R. Waller and Arnold Glover (London: J.M. Dent and Co., 1902), 392.

2. For instance, Hans Küng, in *On Being a Christian*, trans. Edward Quinn (Glasgow: Collins, Fount Paperbacks, 1978), 202–11.

3. *Joseph Andrews*, ed. R. F. Brissenden (Harmondsworth, Middlesex: Penguin, 1977), 93; hereafter cited in the text as *JA*.

4. By John Preston, *The Created Self: The Reader's Role in Eighteenth-Century Fiction* (London: Heinemann, 1970), 114–32.

5. *The Complete Poems and Plays of T.S. Eliot* (London and Boston: Faber and Faber, 1969), 258.

6. Franz Kafka, *The Trial*, trans. Willa and Edwin Muir (Harmondsworth, Middlesex: Penguin, 1953), 97.

7. Quoted in Roland Stromberg, *Religious Liberalism in Eighteenth-Century England* (Oxford: Oxford University Press, 1954), 144 (note).

8. In Compton, 34–35.

9. Edmund Burke, *Reflections on the Revolution in France*, ed. Conor Cruise O'Brien (Harmondsworth, Middlesex: Penguin, 1969), 200.

10. John Milton, "Areopagitica," in *Selected Prose*, ed. C.A. Patrides (Harmondsworth, Middlesex: Penguin, 1974), 212–13.

11. Lord Clive quoted by Thomas Babington Macaulay, in *Lord Clive*, with introduction and notes by K. Deighton (London: Macmillan; New York: St. Martin's Press, 1960), 84.

12. *The Prose Works of Jonathan Swift*, vol. 1, ed. Herbert Davis (Oxford: Basil Blackwell, 1939), 190.

13. A. E. Dyson, *The Crazy Fabric: Essays in Irony* (London: Macmillan; New York: St. Martin's Press, 1965), 14–32.

14. Blaise Pascal, *Pensées*, trans. A.J. Krailsheimer (Harmondsworth, Middlesex: Penguin, 1966), 70–71.

15. Jane Austen, *Emma*, ed. Ronald Blythe (Harmondsworth, Middlesex: Penguin, 1966), 418.

16. Bernard Mandeville, *The Fable of the Bees*, ed. Philip Harth (Harmondsworth, Middlesex: Penguin, 1989), 88–91.

17. Dante Alighieri, *Divine Comedy*, "Paradise," 3, line 85.

JOHN M. WARNER

# Mythic and Historic Language in Smollett

In *The Dialogic Imagination*, M. M. Bakhtin describes how the novel incorporates various genres both artistic and extra-artistic which, "as they enter the novel, bring into it their own languages, and therefore stratify the linguistic unity of the novel and further intensify its speech diversity in fresh ways" (321). He concludes that the consequent "novelistic hybrid is an *artistically organized system for bringing different languages in contact with one another*, a system having as its goal the illumination of one language by means of another, the carving-out of a living image of another language" (361). In this chapter I will explore some of the different languages we can find in Smollett's work; in this way I shall follow Bakhtin's injunction that the real task of stylistic analysis lies in "uncovering all the available orchestrating languages in the composition of the novel, grasping the precise degree of distancing that separates each language from its most immediate semantic instantiation in the work as a whole" (416).

Since Bakhtin theorizes this condition of multiple languages for *all* novels, readers may believe that undercuts my hypothesis of a special kinship between the novels I am studying. Bakhtin, however, recognizes within the broader genre different kinds of development where we can differentiate uses of language. For example, he argues that although "we find the same parodic stylization of various levels and genres of literary language" in Fielding, Smollett, and Sterne, the "distance between these levels and genres is greater than it is in Dickens and the exaggeration is stronger" (308). Although Bakhtin recognizes that a "sharp opposition between two stylistic lines of the

From *Joyce's Grandfathers: Myth and History in Defoe, Smollett, Stern and Joyce*. © 1993 by The University of Georgia Press.

novel comes to an end" toward the beginning of the nineteenth century, he does allow for their continued development "off to the side of the mainstream of the modern novel" (414). In this way, he corroborates my idea that we can find a line of descent from Defoe, Smollett, and Sterne to Joyce's *Ulysses* "off to the side" from the realist tradition.

The tensions within Smollett's work, and particularly in his use of language,[1] are tensions between what Bakhtin calls "unitary" language and heteroglossia (by which he does not mean polysemousness, as many modern critics seem to believe). For Bakhtin, unitary language "constitutes the theoretical expression of the historical processes of linguistic unification and centralization." Always posited rather than something given, it makes its "real presence felt as a force for overcoming this heteroglossia, imposing specific limits to it, guaranteeing a certain maximum of mutual understanding and crystallizing it into a real, although still relative, unity— the unity of the reigning conversational (everyday) and literary language, 'correct language'" (270). One way of describing the parameters of Smollett's career would be to say that he moves from being a writer who overvalues unitary language to become a novelist who "welcomes the heteroglossia and language diversity of the literary and extraliterary language into his own work not only not weakening them but even intensifying them" (Bakhtin 298).

Unlike Joyce, whose pre-*Ulysses* experiments with the diachronic and synchronic tensions in narration are all intrinsically valuable, Smollett did not achieve a finished fiction in any of his earlier writings. Nevertheless, several of these novels interestingly reflect the struggles with language and voice he was finally able to resolve in *Humphry Clinker*. There, he achieved a sophisticated sense of the value of illuminating the language of history by juxtaposing it against a mythic voice. While Smollett only sporadically attempts in his first novel the mythic language he uses so effectively later, he does use a historical mode as a means to stabilize both the rather frenetic voices of the satirist and of the narrator Roderick. Roderick Random is involved in a world dense with historical references.[2] Beyond this background of historical detail, we find extended sequences which Smollett takes both from his own personal experiences and from the history of his time. These lengthy episodes find Roderick playing different roles; sometimes he is merely their reporter, and other times he participates as a fictional character within episodes which are based more or less directly on history.

For example, in the episodes dealing with the expedition to Carthagena, Smollett draws upon his own experience and his interpretation of historical event. This heading for chapter 33 will suggest economically how Smollett chose to incorporate these materials into his novel.

A breach being made in the walls, our soldiers give the assault, take the place without opposition—our sailors at the same time become masters of all the other strengths near Bocca Chica, and take possession of the harbour—the good consequence of this success—we move nearer the town—find two forts deserted, and the channel blocked up with sunk vessels; which however, we find means to clear—land our soldiers at La Quinta—repulse a body of militia—attack the castle of St. Lazar, and are forced to retreat with great loss—the remains of our army are re-imbarked—an effort of the admiral to take the Town—the oeconomy of our expedition described. (184)

In this particular chapter Roderick figures less as a character within a fiction than as a spokesman for Smollett's interest in writing history.

But in other instances in the series of chapters dealing with the Carthagena campaign (31–34), Roderick plays much more the role of a fictive character participating in a fiction loosely based on historical reality. For example, he describes how his ship is assigned to batter the port of Bocca Chica. During this encounter Dr. Macshane, the surgeon who has been Roderick's enemy throughout his sea career, prostrates himself on the deck in terror while Roderick is scarcely able to refrain from doing so. Roderick then remarks:

And that the reader may know, it was not a common occasion that alarmed us thus, I must inform him of the particulars of this dreadful din that astonished us. The fire of the Spaniards proceeded from Bocca Chica mounting eighty-four great guns, besides a mortar and small arms; from fort St. Joseph, mounting thirty-six; from two faschine batteries, mounting twenty; and from four men of war, mounting sixty-four guns each.—This was answered by us, from our land battery, mounting twenty-one cannon; our bomb battery, mounting two mortars, and twenty-four cohorns, and five men of war, two of eighty, and three of seventy guns, which fired without intermission. (181)

Whether this is actual history or not, it certainly introduces the language of historical realism into a fictional scene. After this brief synopsis, we are switched back directly to a fictional episode as Roderick amputates the wounded hand of his friend Jack Rattlin.[3]

Smollett frequently uses this historical voice to stabilize a more frantic narrative voice. For example, the following brief paragraph covers six months of Roderick's life in only six lines, but it does so in a way that seems historically real to the reader: "In less than a fortnight after, we made the land of Guinea, near the mouth of the river Gambia, and trading along the coast as far to the southward of the Line as Angola and Bengula, in less than six months disposed of the greatest part of our cargo, and purchased four hundred negroes, my adventure having been laid out chiefly in gold dust" (409–10). In contrast with those passages describing Roderick's "adventures" which cram as much action into every moment as they can, this passage suggests a more historical sense of the way time actually seems to unfold. Smollett thus at times introduces the manner of history into his novel proper.

As analysis of "The *History* of Miss Williams" (my emphasis) will show, Smollett uses what Bakhtin calls "unitary" language—a "correct literary language attuned to the speech of everyday"—to present not just his historical material but also that fictional material that aims at being taken as history. Miss Williams is a woman Roderick becomes engaged to in his fortune-hunting days, only to discard when he finds her in bed with another man. Later he finds Miss Williams, destitute and pox-ridden, deathly ill; then he saves her by feeding her and curing her pox. He also listens to her story. This "history," as Smollett labels it, is spread out over two chapters, interrupted in the second by a "scene" in which Miss Williams is falsely arrested and collects a guinea in damages which enables her and Roderick to move to more comfortable quarters before she finishes her story. This story itself has a number of narrative features which set it apart from the main narrative. For one thing, the story is linear, not cyclical. Miss Williams, proud of her intellectual powers, nevertheless foolishly allows herself to be seduced, becomes pregnant, and leaves home. Her path afterward is the downward one from courtesan to street-walker until Roderick saves her from dying of starvation. Thereafter, she will become a maid (Narcissa's in the main story), permanently losing her social class and making no return to her place of origin. There is, for her, no mythic return. Related to this is her "growth" or change as a character. Intellectually proud, vain of her beauty, she learns from experience and accepts the humble role of lady's maid as the most she can hope for. While myth frequently involves its characters in marriage and the family romance, more historic narrative emphasizes the unique story of the individual. Within her own history Miss Williams does not marry; it is only when she is absorbed into the main narrative that she does (and even then only to Strap, who is much beneath her previous social level).

Linguistically, the most interesting thing in this history is its univocal quality, the monotone of its narrative. Whereas the main narrative has linguistic variety acquired from the use of anecdote, caricature of characters, romantic interchanges, and satiric interludes, Miss Williams's story is all told in one color; it aims for what Ian Watt would call a "realism of presentation." Moreover, while the novel as a whole is written in the past tense, an interplay of time sequences is achieved between the past-tense of the story and the present-tense of the chapter headings (e.g., chapter 50 heading: "I long to be revenged on Melinda, apply to Banter ... He contrives ... I make ... grow melancholy" etc.). The heading of chapter 22 is simply "The History of Miss Williams"; there is no juxtapositioning to an ongoing present. Finally, the language itself is invariably abstract: "After this mutual declaration, we contrived to meet more frequently in private interviews, where we enjoy'd the conversation of one another, in all the elevation of fancy and impatience of hope, that reciprocal adoration can inspire" (120). Although all parts of the novel are touched by this stiffly correct style, it is only in Miss Williams's story that it is so consistently maintained. (The one linguistic concession to mythic usage is the name of her first seducer, "Lothario.")

Perhaps the most significant feature of her history is its total lack of humor. Deeply attracted to the writing of history,[4] Smollett must have understood that the reality of events of his time left little room for comedy. John H. Burke, Jr., has argued that Fielding refused to yield to "historical pessimism" and abandon the comic mode. Rather, he "filtered history out of his prose fictions" (60–63). By deemphasizing historic reality, Fielding kept open for himself the possibility of comedy. Unlike Fielding, or at least the Fielding of *Joseph Andrews* and *Tom Jones*, Smollett was not willing to abandon diachronic history. Nor was he willing, in the novel proper, to abandon comedy. But, in the section of the novel that comes closest to history in its narrative method and language, he eschews comedy; Miss Williams's story is baldly serious. (The introduction of the comic scene of Miss Williams's being falsely accused and taken to jail occurs within Roderick's narrative and not in her "story." It suggests that Smollett felt the need for some comic relief even within this relatively short history.)

Were I concerned with the intrinsic merits of *Roderick Random* rather than its foreshadowings of later, more successful accomplishment in *Humphry Clinker*, I would want to demonstrate its language of satire and also the dynamic voice of the irascible, rather than romantic, side of its narrator. Along with the historic voice, these languages work in more fruitful conjunction than in any other of Smollett's early fictions. For my purposes, however, it is more important to concentrate on peripheral and even implicit language patterns than on these more central ones. And, after all, these other voices have been carefully explored before: see particularly the work of Ronald Paulson and Damion Grant. My own essay on Smollett's development as a novelist also considers these language patterns. If G. S. Rousseau's notion that there is a "dearth of incisive critical writing about Smollett's works" (68) remains true, perhaps an approach that emphasizes seemingly tangential aspects of *Roderick Random* rather than reworking often discussed material can be justified as an effort to articulate a coherent overview of Smollett's career that can explain how he came in *Humphry Clinker* to achieve a worthy predecessor to Joyce's *Ulysses*.

In the preface to *Roderick Random*, Smollett writes that romance "owes its origin to ignorance, vanity, and superstition" (xxxiii). The twenty-six-year-old Smollett's early position on myth is euhemeristic, not Vichian. The "heathen mythology ... is no other than a collection of extravagant Romances" (xxxiii) by means of which the family and adherents of famous men magnified their virtues and, imposing on the gullibility of the vulgar, deified them. With the advancement of learning and taste in the classical period, tragedy and epic replaced mythology and romance. Reborn in the dark ages of religious superstition, romances "filled their performances with the most monstrous hyperboles" (xxxiv) until Cervantes "reformed the taste of mankind, ... converting romance to purposes far more useful and entertaining, by making it assume the sock, and point out the follies of ordinary life" (xxxiv).

The word "converting" is ambiguous; does he mean altering the purpose but maintaining the form of romance, or does he mean eliminating it altogether? The militant rationalism both toward the "superstition" of the ancient myths and the "imposition of priest-craft" (xxxiv) in medieval times would suggest that Smollett meant to eliminate romance (and myth) altogether. Yet, since his novels follow the pattern of romance,[5] it seems more likely that he wants to maintain the form of romance but within a more rationalistic frame. What I shall be arguing is that Smollett wants to keep the form of romance as a way of giving minimal shape to what would otherwise be formless satiric panoramas. What he discovers, however, is that romance demands its own language. As long as he adheres to the euhemerist view of myth, he is unable to find that language. Only as he, perhaps as the result of exposure to "Vichian" ideas of myth, widens his concept of mythic language does he finally resolve this problem in his last novel. A certain susceptibility to the ideas I have been exploring is hinted even in this rather cockily rationalist preface when Smollett gives as one reason for making his hero a Scotsman the idea that he "could represent simplicity of manners in a remote part of the kingdom, with more propriety, than in any place near the capital" (xxxv). Alongside the neoclassic concern for propriety, we discover the nostalgia for the primitive—a kind of capsulization of the tensions I see in Smollett.

Narcissa's romance, which is the antithesis of Miss Williams's history, can serve as a model of Smollett's early interest in, if not myth as I have been defining it, romance archetypes that operate in a way different from his historical voice. Disguised as a footman, Roderick introduces her by remarking that he saw her aunt approach, "accompanied with the young lady, whose name for the present shall be Narcissa" (219). Since the name is never changed, this remark seems rather peculiar. Perhaps Smollett meant to give her a more fully rounded characterization and consequently to alter her name to something less archetypal—like Melinda, the name of the woman Roderick courts for her fortune and who later marries Narcissa's brother.

Instead, as the story proceeds, he actually emphasizes more fully her archetypal nature. Narcissa might seem an unfortunate archetype to evoke for a heroine—and very inappropriate to the bland, unself-centered woman Smollett portrays; but I think Smollett really intends us to see her as a kind of anima-figure of Roderick himself. *He* is the Narcissus, and through identification with her he enters her mythic world. Miss Williams similarly tries to draw Roderick into her historic world by making him a "double" of her seducer, Lothario: "He was the exact resemblance of you, and, if I had not been well acquainted with his family and pedigree, I should have made no scruple of concluding him your brother" (119).

The main feature of Narcissa's world is that it is cyclic, not linear. Although at the end of the novel she lives in Scotland rather than in England, nothing has changed in her life; she is in the same social class, economic bracket, and emotional state. She has achieved no insight to mark her experience as linear; even her passion is marked by stasis rather than growth and condemns her, as Robert Caserio says such passion must (236), to perpetual childhood rather than the life of an adult. Her pregnancy, which might mark entry into mature life, is treated in a mythic way to emphasize the synchronicity of family romance rather than the individual development on which historical narration is based: "My dear angel has been qualmish of late, and begins to grow remarkably round in the waist; so that I cannot leave her in such an interesting situation, which I hope will produce something to crown my felicity" (435). Miss Williams's pregnancy and miscarriage marked clear stages in her development as an individual; pregnancy simply marks the mythic "return" Narcissa and Roderick have made at the end of the novel.

Narcissa remains, then, not a character but simply a type of the romantic heroine, featureless throughout. What interests one is why she, and the romance pattern she signifies, figure as largely as they do in the book, and why Smollett was so unsuccessful at energizing them. The answer to the first question is that the "romance" she embodies offered Smollett a means by which to achieve a pattern for his fiction. Much as Defoe used providential time, Smollett relies on archetypal patterns of return to structure what could otherwise become miscellaneous satiric gatherings. The answer to the second question is made clear to us by Roderick himself; he has no language to signify his meaning: "But, alas! expression wrongs my love! I am inspired with conceptions that no language can convey!" (351). He remarks, in describing his secret garden meeting with Narcissa before beginning his last sea journey to the new world, "Because my words are incapable of doing justice to this affecting circumstance, I am obliged to draw a veil over it" (406). And when he returns from that voyage and remeets Narcissa, he exclaims: "Heavens! what was my situation! I am tempted to commit my paper to the flames and to renounce my pen for ever, because its most ardent and lucky expression so poorly describes the emotions of my soul" (425).

Since this is the first time that the narrator has made the reader conscious of him as someone actually using a pen and paper, we can only wonder whether Smollett articulates his own frustration here.

Certainly, the language Smollett uses when forced to describe Roderick's passion rings very hollow: "Good heaven! what were the thrillings of my soul at that instant! my reflection was overwhelmed with a torrent of agitation! my heart throbbed with surprizing violence! a sudden mist overspread my eyes! my ears were invaded with a dreadful sound! I panted for want of breath, and in short, was for some moments intranced!" (337). Although there is some suggestion of mythic response here as Roderick's feelings become translated into actual physical responses, there is none of the linguistic skill used to make Win Jenkins's prose credible. In contrast, Roderick's language in responding to Miss Williams (now Narcissa's maid) may not convey any more realistic sense of character, but at least it is not so silly as his romantic speeches. "The sentiments of this sensible young woman on this, as well as on almost every other subject, perfectly agreed with mine; I thanked her for the care she took of my interests, and promising to behave myself according to her direction, we parted" (342). The slight note of the Machiavel in this speech suits, in fact, our sense of Roderick as a dynamo—as "random" as his culture is, according to James H. Bunn (469). Unfortunately, Smollett is unable to achieve any language to catch Roderick in his static role as lover. Awakening from their first night of connubial bliss, Roderick writes: "I was distracted with joy! I could not believe the evidence of my senses, and looked upon all that had happened as the fictions of a dream!" (430). *We* cannot believe his language.

While Smollett is far from mastering a synchronic language, there are clear indications, even in this first novel, that he is searching for one. Roderick's early master, Mr. Lavement, has a French accent that challenges the correctness of unitary language: "Ah! mon pauvre Roderique! you ave more of de veracité dan of de prudence—bot mine vife and dater be diablement sage, and Mons. le Capitaine un fanfaron, pardieu!" (111). Compare the credibility of this voice with Roderick's own more correct one a page later: "Sir, appearances, I own, condemn me, but you are imposed upon as much as I am abused—I have fallen a sacrifice to the rancour of that scoundrel ... who has found means to convey your goods hither, that the detection of them might blast my reputation, and accomplish my destruction" (113). In his speech to Roderick's dying grandfather, Captain Bowling (Roderick's uncle) also shows Smollett's experiments with accent and dialect to attain greater credibility: "What! he's not a weigh? How fare ye—how fare ye, old gentleman?—Lord have mercy upon your poor sinful soul.... Here's poor Rory come to see you before you die and receive your blessing.—What, man! don't despair—you have been a great sinner, 'tis true,—what then? There's a righteous judge above, isn't there?—He minds me no more than a porpuss.—Yes, yes, he's a going—the land crabs will have him, I see that;—his anchor's a peak, i'faith!" (12). The speech clearly points to Trunnion's great death scene in *Peregrine Pickle*, where an effect of mythic language is achieved.

In conception Smollett's most coherent novel,[6] *Peregrine Pickle* is in fact almost unreadable for the modern taste. Very damaging is the inclusion of so much adventitious satire in Peregrine's own story. The stale pranks of the foreign tour and the absurd machinations with Cadwallader Crabtree at Bath and in London create an unbridgeable gap between Perry as satirist and as character in a romantic story. Moreover, the long interpolated histories of Lady Vane and MacKercher's relation to the Annesley claimant work against the unity of the story. It is not just that they are interpolated stories—one could skip them—but that the language they introduce into the novel works against the idea of peripety and moral growth that is voiced in the more central plot.

There has been much speculation about Smollett's relationship with Lady Vane, about why he included her memoirs in *Peregrine Pickle*, and about whether he had a hand in their writing. Most critics agree that Smollett probably smoothed out the memoir if did not actually write it—perhaps at Lady Vane's dictation.[7] I would argue that Smollett, possibly unconsciously, uses Lady Vane's story to qualify Peregrine's fictive one. Smollett "creates" the story of Peregrine's pride and its consequences. He develops it quite carefully, in much fuller detail than anything else in his fiction, to show that his hero must learn to curb his false pride and develop a true one if he is to achieve full maturity. As a consequence for doing so, he is rewarded with a restored fortune and Emilia. But Smollett then includes the "history" of Lady Vane to give a diachronic version of the same theme. Married first for love, the lady is soon widowed. At the advice of her friends, she then marries Lord Vane, who can fill neither her emotional nor her sexual needs. Thus begin her "adventures" (real rather than imagined, however) as she moves from one lover to another, trying both to escape the persecutions of her husband and to find the romantic attachment her heart desires. Her search for this ideal love offers a parallel to Peregrine's passion for Emilia. Like Perry, she makes the point of not being bound by historical necessity; but, of course, her memoirs show that she must continually submit to her sicknesses, her lack of money, her loss of lovers, her family, and her husband's demands. At the end of her story, she has not integrated her mythic world and the world of reality. Instead, she has returned to her mad husband and is trying to make the best of her situation. Her story historicizes the idea Smollett wants to develop. If Lady Vane has "learned" anything from her experiences, it is not a character-reversing revelation—perhaps more appropriate to fiction than to real life—but rather the need to accommodate her wishes to reality as best she can. In that way, her "history" offers a corrective mirror to Peregrine's adventures, much as Miss Williams's history does to Roderick's earlier adventures. Linguistically, Lady Vane's story works in the same monochromatic way as that of Miss Williams, offering a further undercutting to the tonal variety of Peregrine's fable of moral development.

Another illustration of the historicist impulse in *Peregrine Pickle* is the inclusion of the long story of MacKercher and the Annesley case. Lewis M. Knapp and Lillian de la Torre have shown that Smollett closely modeled this material on a manuscript copy of the Annesley *Case* and that he probably got from MacKercher himself the details of his life (30–32). In other words, he directly imported historical materials into his novels. Why? Since the Annesley material describes a famous historical instance where a son has been unjustly debarred from his rightful inheritance by a cruel parental figure, its relation to Peregrine's case seems obvious. In the beginning of the novel, Peregrine's mother takes an unnatural dislike to her son and forces her henpecked husband to disown him. But Peregrine's father has neglected to make a will, and at his death Peregrine inherits the family estate, which seems a just reward for the moral growth he has achieved.

The Annesley claimant does not fare so well. The alienation between his mother (and her family) and his father makes the young boy totally dependent on his dissolute father. Upon his death, the boy's uncle, playing Peregrine's mother's role, plots to have his nephew killed, gives out the story that he has died, and takes over the estate. Spared death, the boy is sent as an indentured slave to America. After years of struggling to become a free man, he turns up as a sailor in the Carthagenean campaign, where the rumors of his claim begin to surface. (Undoubtedly Smollett heard them at that time.) Befriended by MacKercher—who plays a role parallel to Trunnion's in Peregrine's story, he returns to England and enters a suit against his uncle. Though he wins a judgment against the uncle, the latter is able to use the law to delay the carrying out of the court decision. In Smollett's version, MacKercher and his protégé are jailed after the former's fortune has been expended trying to achieve justice for the claimant. In life, the latter died before any final decision that would have reinvested him in his rightful position was reached.

The differences between Smollett's historical and his fictional treatment of this theme of the wrongfully disinherited son are instructive. There is no happy ending in the Annesley case; the villains of the piece (apparently one of the few additions Smollett made to the *Case* was to underline the blackness of one of these [Knapp and de la Torre 31]) are not defeated; the hero does not win out. A generally pessimistic tone prevails as history seems to reveal little other truth than that entrenched might will prevail. Peregrine's story, however credibly, incorporates a mythic pattern. Having largely squandered one fortune and having behaved unpleasantly throughout, he, in fact, seems undeserving of a happy ending. Yet Smollett's "myth" demands that the cyclic pattern be completed, and he restores the same fortune to Perry that he had given Roderick. The one concession to historic reality seems to be that Peregrine has achieved more genuine self-insight and knowledge of his flaws than Roderick ever attained. One wonders whether Smollett has not included the story of the Annesley case to placate his sense of historical reality. This kind of narration, he tells the reader, can be trusted, for it tells things as they really are. Again, the language of the Annesley case is a rigorously "correct" one which eschews the tonal variety of Peregrine's fictive story. Language is also made to mirror things as they are.

The MacKercher-Annesley material is interesting on another level, too. Knapp and de la Torre have shown that MacKercher was a close friend of Smollett, and the inclusion of the material clearly was meant to puff MacKercher's generous behavior as well as to publicize the claimant's case. But, at least unconsciously, Smollett is involved in the projection of certain anxieties of authorship. As author, he guides Peregrine through certain experiences, uses him to express satiric views of many different sorts, creates many humorous, even farcical scenes around him, involves him in romantic and sexual scenes, and crowns it all by having his hero undergo a growth experience that justifies his being rewarded with a beautiful wife and large fortune. As an eighteenth-century intellectual aware of the process of historicization in his century, Smollett could not have been very comfortable with this fictional representation of experience; and he projects that discomfort in the figure of MacKercher. A self-made man like Smollett himself, a figure of force and power as Smollett undoubtedly thought himself after the success of *Roderick Random*, MacKercher is, nevertheless, totally impotent before historical necessity. All his efforts to guide his protégé are foiled. He expends all his powers—money, influence, social stature—in vain. The life that he is trying to make for the claimant cannot be made; the entrenched powers of reality are simply too strong to be overcome. A tribute to his friend, Smollett's picture of MacKercher also projects a recognition of the impotence of the imagination before historical forces.

One way out of this impasse for the creative writer would be to revive archaic forms of knowing which had been subsumed by historical modes. These could give larger play to imaginative truth. Smollett does, in fact, give voice to a nostalgia for the mythic in *Peregrine Pickle's* extended emphasis on family romance. Although his earlier criticism stressed Smollett's satire, Ronald Paulson has recently, quite brilliantly, commented on this mythic aspect of *Peregrine Pickle*. Studying the way the earlier chapters of *Peregrine* and *Tom Jones* give an extensive prehistory of their heroes, he concludes that they generate a "myth" in which they describe their heroes' withdrawal (or expulsion) from Eden. In Defoe the son as rebel had defied the father and left, but in this version of the mythos, the parents are seen as the original fallen Adam and Eve figures who visit their sins upon their son, who, "having inherited his original sin (unlike Crusoe, who created it himself), reenacts the parents' fall" (Paulson 72). While archetypal patterns operate in the background of all Smollett's fiction, Paulson seems right to find the first part of *Peregrine Pickle* to be structured more explicitly around a version of the family romance. This concentration on the family leads, Paulson feels, to better writing on Smollett's part. "Though his reputation is first and foremost as a writer of the episodic picaresque narration, Smollett always becomes a tighter, more intense, and more interesting writer when he gets to a small hierarchical group" (65).

The use of myth does, then, intensify the synchronic effect of the tighter plot. Why does Smollett abandon it less than a quarter of the way through the novel? We have to recognize that this sort of synchronic vision was not Smollett's congenial material. Smollett does achieve in the family scenes at the opening of this novel a Richardsonian blending of historicism and myth, a muting of the extreme needs of both that permits the emergence of the realist school. Unlike Richardson, Smollett could not work continuously within the framework of a small family group which gave him the opportunity to explore the mythic dimensions of character. He needed myth; but he also needed history. His effort to write a coherent novel of the realist sort in *Peregrine Pickle* did not suit his talents. Even within the earlier, more tightly knit part, other kinds of narrative impulses intrude on the story. Perry's pranks as a child are meant to illustrate the growth of his pride; nevertheless, they are excessive in number and often more indicative of Smollett's propensity to satire than to characterization. And, as I have illustrated, within the larger framework of the novel, we find Smollett more attuned to historicity than to myth.

The basic problem again is that of language. Smollett clearly has an interest in myth and synchronic vision, but he has not yet found a way to express it. As in *Roderick Random*, there are a few hints of what will come in Win and Tabby's letters. Deborah Hornbeck's letter to invite Perry to an assignation foreshadows Win Jenkins's later efforts: "Heaving the playsure of meating with you at the ofspital of anvil-heads, I take this lubbertea of latin you know, that I lotch at the *hottail de May cong dangle rouy Doghouseten*" (219). Smollett's second attempt at comic polysemy, this letter is a great improvement over the one "Clay-render" wrote Roderick. There the whore's literary pretensions, seen in her classical allusions, were undercut by her comic misspellings; here, Deborah has no pretensions. Her language simply shows an inevitable interweaving of the physical with the abstract.

As many critics have pointed out, the single most effective passage in the novel is the great scene of Trunnion's death, and its power derives largely from Smollett's language:

> Swab the spray from your bowsprit, my good lad, and coil up your spirits. You must not let the top-lifts of your heart give way, because you see me ready to go down at these years; many a better man has foundered before he has made half my way; thof I trust, by the mercy of God, I shall be sure in port in a very few glasses, and fast moored in a most blessed riding: for my good friend Jolter hath overhauled the journal of my sins; and by the observation he hath taken of the state of my soul, I hope I shall happily conclude my voyage, and be brought up in the lattitude of heaven. (392)

The first thing we note about this passage is the near absence of any abstracting or generalizing language. Except for "the mercy of God" and "the state of my soul," all of Trunnion's speech is cast in concrete naval terms. Yet it is a concreteness that accommodates a dimension of feeling as well. The phrase to keep your heart up had become an empty cliché. Trunnion's revivification of the metaphor in his injunction to Perry not to "let the top-lifts of your heart give way" not only renews the metaphor but also makes the emotion credible. The rich specificity of his language opens up the spiritual dimension of his death as well. We see this effect in the wonderful phrase "fast moored in a most blessed riding," as well as in "lattitude of heaven," where what might be empty clichés are wonderfully revivified by Trunnion's language. That language is concretely specific, yet brilliantly inclusive, enabling the reader to respond to his death on a number of levels. We see, first, the death of the man who has been so deeply fixated on his professional life; yet Trunnion convincingly enacts the death of Everyman, as well as that of the Christian. Smollett achieves this effect by stressing the synchronic aspect of language, its ability to hold many dimensions in suspension at the same time.[8] The hostess's speech describing Falstaff's death does the same thing; critics have frequently noted the similar effect of the two death scenes. Since Smollett's larger purposes in *Peregrine Pickle* are more realistic and historicist, he puts much less emphasis on verbal ingenuity in Trunnion's speech than in the Hornbeck letter; thus he keeps Trunnion within the framework of his action yet also stresses his archetypal significance.

Richardson, of course, achieves the ultimate accommodation of myth and realism in Clarissa's death scene. His task was easier than Smollett's since he did not have to deal with the stylizations of comedy as well as those of myth. The synchronic emphases in Smollett's scene press beyond the limits of realistic fiction. Trunnion is simply too much larger than life to fit into the tradition of comic realism established later by Austen and Trollope. Dickens creates similar figures; but he uses sentiment to integrate their archetypal reverberations into his realistic frame. One remarkable feature of Smollett's scene is how free it is of any overtone of sentimentality.

In one sense, we could simply say that Smollett's use of language in this death scene is "poetic" in contrast to the historic language we have largely been tracing in his earlier fiction. Vico, of course, found the distinguishing feature of early societies to be their innately poetic quality. We cannot conclude that Smollett had renounced his early euhemeristic view of myth for something like a Vichian one on the solitary example offered by Trunnion's death scene. Nevertheless, *Peregrine Pickle* illustrates Smollett's problems in trying to create a language suitable to the romance forms he uses to structure his fiction.

This difficulty continues in *Ferdinand, Count Fathom* and *Sir Launcelot Greaves*. In both these later novels, Smollett can effectively add a historic voice to the perpetual voice of satire; but whether he follows the Gothic or the Cervantic pattern, he cannot discover a consistently adequate language for elements which demand an extra-rational, intuitive understanding. Since I in no way challenge the general critical view that these are Smollett's weaker achievements, one example will be enough to illustrate my point. Following an unknown woman in order to return her lost purse, the love-maddened Sir Launcelot is surprised to find that she is his beloved Aurelia. During the course of an interview, he learns that she did not intentionally send him a letter of rejection and that she still loves him. The scene reaches an incredible climax:

> So saying, he approached this amiable mourner, this fragrant flower of beauty, glittering with the dew-drops of the morning; this sweetest, and gentlest, loveliest ornament of human nature. He gazed upon her with looks of love ineffable; he sat down by her; he pressed her soft hand in his; he began to fear that all he saw was the flattering vision of a distempered brain; he looked and sighed, and, turning up his eyes to heaven, breathed, in broken murmurs, the chaste raptures of his soul. (168)

The language here is not ironic, just turgid; and Smollett's novel suffers from his inability to give his hero a credible romantic voice.

An affinity between *Ulysses* and *The Expedition of Humphry Clinker*, besides their interest in the mythic dimension of language, is their use of their authors' lives. Smollett appropriates his own historical experiences, his autobiography, for the basis of his fiction as freely as Joyce does. The novel is not a simple rewrite of Smollett's historical journey to Scotland from May to August 1766. It is a novel, fiction, but fiction that has a basis in the reality of place and person. Although Jery's story of Tim Cropdale's tricking Birkin out of a new pair of riding boots may be a fabrication, the garden and house where the joke occurred were as real as 7 Eccles Street is in Joyce's Dublin.

Jery's letter of June 10 is, in fact, Smollett's sly joke as his fictional character describes a visit to the home of his creator, the historical Smollett. The actual antics of the hack writers who sponge off S—t (as he is referred to in the novel) and then abuse him behind his back may be "fictional," but undoubtedly the scene reflects Smollett's historical attitude toward his peers. In a similar way, the Mr. Smollett whom the characters in the novel visit during their tour of Scotland is James Smollett, the novelist's cousin, who had inherited the family estate at Bonhill. The Bramble party actually stays at Cameron House rather than the older family home, just as Smollett and his wife did in 1766. While Bramble calls James Smollett's home a "Scottish paradise" (244), he does not return to a mythic center as Roderick and Perry do, but he visits a concrete, historical spot—a diachronic rather than a synchronic place.

Perhaps Smollett's most interesting use of himself in the novel occurs during Bramble's meeting with Mr. Serle. The fictional story of Serle's aid to Paunceford and the latter's ungenerous treatment of his benefactor after he acquires great wealth had its origin, as Lewis M. Knapp has shown (290–92), in a real incident in which Smollett experienced the ingratitude of one Alexander Campbell. Here we have the very Joycean situation where real characters serve as the basis for a fictional episode. Interestingly, the story is followed just a few pages later by Jery's story of Tom Eastgate and George Prankley. Eastgate, wishing a living in Prankley's power to give, has long suffered the latter's rudeness till he is informed that the position will be given to someone else. Although a cleric, he challenges Prankley to a duel and frightens him into giving him the living. The story, entirely fictional as far as one can tell, offers a rich counterpoint to the fiction based on historical truth. An act of ingratitude is not suffered mildly but gets its comeuppance; justice wins out. We note how this episode reverses the effect of Miss Williams's story in *Roderick Random:* her "history" qualified the romance of fiction; Eastgate's fiction alleviates the grimness of history.

Like Joyce, Smollett uses other historical figures besides himself in his fiction. Sometimes he does so in a much more flatly historicist way than Joyce ever does. In Matt Bramble's letter of May 19 from Bath, he speaks of the landscape painting of Mr. T—(John Taylor), which he admires greatly. In a slightly more novelistic way, he recounts in his July 4 letter from Scarborough the story of his old acquaintance H—t (William Hewett) and his eccentric voyages. At points like this, the fiction is very close to historical anecdote. More Joycean is Smollett's treatment of the actor James Quin. Satirized in both *Roderick Random* and *Peregrine Pickle,* Quin is treated more evenhandedly here. Jery's letter from Bath of April 30 begins with a realistic description of Quin's personality and habits, but then quickly transforms the historical figure into an actor within the drama of the book. He first draws Quin into an opinion about one of the novel's central themes, the effects of democracy on society; involves him in an anecdote about watching women competing for favors at a tea party; and creates a humorous interchange between Quin and Tabitha over whether he is a descendant of Nell Gwynn. Progressively, Quin moves from being a real person into being a real person observing a fiction, and finally into a real person involved as a character in a fiction.[9]

The larger affinity between *The Expedition of Humphry Clinker* and *Ulysses* is, of course, their use of language. Recognizing Smollett as Joyce's linguistic grandparent will help to establish a context for his experiments; but perhaps more importantly, looking at Smollett through Joyce's eyes can make us aware how Vichian his interests had become in his last novel. Smollett here addresses his language theme both abstractly and dramatically. The abstract articulation of the theme summarizes the idea of language as a mode of historical recording which we have been addressing in Smollett's earlier novels. The dramatic projection embodies an idea of language as myth which has been a slowly gathering ground swell throughout his fiction. The spokesman for the historical attitude toward language within the novel is Lismahago, whose perspective is even more conservative than that of Samuel Johnson. In arguing with Jery whether English is spoken with more propriety at Edinburgh or London, Lismahago asserts that "the Scottish dialect was, in fact, true, genuine old English, with a mixture of some French terms and idioms, adopted in a long intercourse betwixt the French and Scotch nations; that the modern English, from affectation and false refinement, had weakened, and even corrupted their language, by throwing out the guttural sounds, altering the pronunciation and the quantity, and disusing many words and terms of great significance" (194). Johnson regretfully accepted the inevitability of change in language; Lismahago apparently believes the Scots have resisted and can resist the "affectations and false refinement" which corrupt language. As he demonstrates, an ambiguity has grown up in England about the word *gentle*. Does it mean mild and meek or noble and high-minded? The Scots, however, do not have trouble with the word because they have retained its original, true meaning (194).

Inevitably, such discursive passages reveal a good deal about Smollett's own sense of language.[10] And we recognize throughout much of the novel that one of the pressures on the letter writers is to use language in a way consistent with this essentially conservative position. That is, they are to use a "correct" language which permits them to represent, as unequivocally as possible, a historical reality. In doing so, they often turn language into a very abstract, emotionless instrument. Even Lydia, whom Smollett tries without much success to characterize as a sentimental girl, expresses herself in emptily abstract terms: "Unexperienced as I am in the commerce of life, I have seen enough to give me a disgust to the generality of those who carry it on—There is such malice, treachery, and dissimulation, even among professed friends and intimate companions, as cannot fail to strike a virtuous mind with horror; and when Vice quits the stage for a moment, her place is immediately occupied by Folly, which is often too serious to excite anything but compassion" (296). Although such language is colorless in emotional terms, it does have the advantage of being clear and unambiguous. Liddy expresses herself with a great deal of confidence that she can say exactly what she means. It is in response to such linguistic usage that generations of critics have built up "historicist" readings of *Humphry Clinker*. Language in the novel often reflects reality in such a way as to suggest to us that a true "history" is being given.

This conception, of course, reflects the high value that Smollett's age placed on the post-mythic, logical world of diachronic history. History, says an essay which has been attributed (probably wrongly) to Smollett, "is the inexhaustible source from which [the poet] will derive his most useful knowledge respecting the progress of the human mind, the constitution of government, the rise and decline of empires, the revolution of arts, the variety of character, and the vicissitudes of fortune" (Cunningham III 299).[11] Much of Smollett's work does reflect an effort to record the processes of actual life in what Bakhtin calls unitary language. Still, as the writer of this essay concluded, it is "not that the poet or painter ought to be restrained to the letter of historical truth" (Cunningham III 299). And another aspect of Smollett's fiction is his exploration of a mythic mode of expression. A historicist, Smollett nevertheless felt a "revolutionary nostalgia" for the intuitive language of myth.

This theme is dramatized, not developed discursively, in the letters of Win Jenkins and Tabitha Bramble.[12] As we see when we look closely at Win's and Tabby's letters, their language is not abstract but intensely concrete. It evokes not the age of consciousness with its emphasis on logic and rationality but an earlier stage which, as Barfield says, did not postulate but simply assumed a reality in which there was no differentiation between spirit and body. Smollett's "nostalgia" for myth parallels Barfield's idea of poetic diction; it is an effort to *re*use language in such a way as to recapture its lost emotional overtones and meanings. A letter of Win's dated April 26 begins: "Heaving got a frank, I now return your fever" (41). Both misspellings suggest the inevitable attachment of mind to body. The abstract "favor" becomes a physical "fever"; and an indefinite "having" becomes a concrete "heaving." The misspellings undoubtedly show Win's sexual nature; but it would be reductive, I think, to suggest that was their only purpose. And her reference to "handsome Christians, without a hair upon their sin," shows that her mind also works the other way, elevating the physical "chin" to the spiritual idea of sin.

While we regard the idea that Smollett is trying to create an ideolect for Win as naive, we would be more likely to accept the notion that he is trying to mirror in written form the sound of her Welsh dialect. Actually, Smollett's purposes are more complex because they depend as much on how we *see* the words as how we *hear* them. The effect of inscription is synchronic; writing is a configuration in space that allows us to perceive multiple meanings. We visually perceive "sin" and think of what that spelling means in our own pronunciation; then we have to figure out by context what Win means. Were we to hear the passage read to us, there would not be the ambiguity. Speech, in fact, is more diachronic than writing. Pronunciation and intonation, for example, limit ambiguity. In speech, meaning is sequentially determined, for each new word affects and limits the possibilities of meaning in the following words. Smollett is not just trying to make us *hear* the passage the way Win would speak it in her dialect; rather, his primary emphasis is on the *visual* aspect of the words which awakens the reader to their multiple overtones. The Welsh might pronounce *favor* as *fever;* but Smollett clearly wants us to think first of the meaning of *fever* and then understand how, for Win, the abstract *favor* still echoes with the physical implications language had in earlier, mythic times. Consistently, by making us both *see* and hear Win and Tabby's language, Smollett evokes in their letters the lost unity between matter and spirit.

A longer passage from this letter reveals the brilliance of Smollett's imagining:

> Dear girl, I have seen all the fine shews of Bath; the Prades, the Squires, and the Circlis, the Crashit, the Hottogon, and Bloody Buildings, and Harry King's row; and I have been twice in the Bath with mistress, and na'r a smoak upon our backs, hussy—The first time I was mortally afraid, and flustered all day; and afterwards made believe that I had got the heddick; but mistress said, if I didn't go, I should take a dose of bum-taffy; and so remembring how it worked Mrs. Gwyllim a pennorth, I chose rather to go again with her into the Bath, and then I met with an axident. I dropt my petticoat, and could not get it up from the bottom—But what did that signify? they mought laff, but they could see nothing; for I was up to the sin in water. To be sure, it threw me into such a gumbustion, that I know not what I said, nor what I did, nor how they got me out, and rapt me in a blanket—Mrs. Tabitha scoulded a little when we got home; but she knows as I know what's what—Ah Laud help you!—There is Sir Yury Micligut, of Balnaclinch, in the cunty of Kalloway—I took down the name from his gentleman, Mr. O Frizzle, and he has got an estate of fifteen hundred a year—I am sure he is both rich and generous—But you nose, Molly, I was always famous for

keeping secrets; and so he was very safe in trusting me with his flegm for mistress; which, to be sure, is very honourable; for Mr. O Frizzle assures me, he values not her portion a brass varthing—And, indeed, what's poor ten thousand pounds to a Baron Knight of his fortune? and, truly, I told Mr. O Frizzle, that was all she had to trust to—As for John Thomas, he's a morass fellor—I vow, I thought he would a fit with Mr. O Frizzle, because he axed me to dance with him at Spring garden—But God he knows I have no thought eyther of wan or t'other. (42)

In the diachronic world of the travel book, we would have the Circus, the Crescent, the Octogon, the Bladud Buildings, and Harlequin's Row of eighteenth-century Bath. But Win's language probes beneath the historic scene to a more synchronic reality where flesh and spirit intertwine in a more universal way. This is, perhaps, most obvious in "Crashit" for "Crescent." Once a living symbol both for virginity (Diana) and religion, the word *crescent* had become what Barfield calls a "dead metaphor." The deliberate emphasis on the excremental in Win's naming is a poetic evocation of a former mythic unity—perhaps the only way centuries of abstraction can be purged from the word.[13] Similarly, "Bloody Buildings" suggests a more archetypal physical presence than does Bladud, as well as evoking a vaguely sexual tone. "Circlis" also has sexual overtones, suggesting "clitoris." In naming Harlequin's Row "Harry King's row," Win shows the tendency of myth toward the particular and concrete rather than the abstract; and calling squares "Squires" demonstrates the tendency of myth to anthropomorphize.

This tendency toward mythopoeia is persistent throughout the passage. Win has spelled the word *know* correctly three times in her letter; nevertheless, she says, "But you nose, Molly ..." In mythic time one does "know" with other organs than the intellect; knowing is a matter of the senses rather than an abstraction, not unrelated to the way dogs "nose" one another and, perhaps for that reason, used only in relation to her fellow servant and not her social superiors. "Sin" for chin is repeated; Win thinks she describes only her physical state when she says, "I was up to the sin in water," but of course she evokes her spiritual condition as well. She transforms the Divinity in "Ah Laud help you!" The abstract "Lord" becomes the concrete lauds of the prayers, suggesting the physical direction Win's spiritual yearnings will take later in the book.

John Thomas is a "morass fellor" rather than a morose fellow, reflecting Win's inarticulate sexual impulse. That impulse also motivates her transformation of Sir Ulic Mackilligut into "Sir Yury Micligut, of Balnaclinch, in the cunty of Kalloway." This mythic vision of the knight evokes venality on both the sensual ("Bal," "cunt") and economic ("gut," "clinch") levels as does Win's later description of his "flegm" for her mistress.

The synchronic vision can sometimes yield, Smollett suggests, a truer sense of things than the historical perspective.

We could examine the mythic implications of many other words (for example, "smoak," "heddick," "bum-taffy," "gumbustion") in this passage; but it will be more productive to pass on to another letter written as Win is about to set off in a "cox and four for Yorkshire." The coach appears prominently in the diachronic travel narrative: it breaks down and needs to be repaired by Humphry Clinker; it overturns in midstream and nearly kills Matt Bramble, etc. Win's journey, as the pun on *cock* reveals, concerns itself with the more synchronic reality of sex and family romance. (Smollett gives her four "stud" too: Humphry, Dutton, John Thomas, and Archy M'Alpin—called Machappy by Win.) Win goes on to describe how Humphry has been wrongly imprisoned: "The 'squire did all in his power, but could not prevent his being put in chains, and confined among common manufactors, where he stud like an innocent sheep in the midst of wolves and tygers.—Lord knows, what mought have happened to this pyehouse young man, if master had not applied to Apias Korkus, who lives with the ould baliff, and is, they say, five hundred years ould, (God bless us!) and a congeror" (152). In her synchronic way, Win concretizes the writ of habeas corpus into a mythological figure of a five-hundred-year-old conjurer. The biblical expression "sheep among wolves" had become a cliché by this time; but we note how Win renews its mythic potentiality by using the word "stud" (to say nothing of "common manufactors"!), thereby re-introducing the physical and sexual into what had become a spiritual banality.

The letter concludes with a wonderful conflation of religious and sexual meanings:

> Mr. Clinker ... is, indeed, a very powerfull labourer in the Lord's vineyard. I do no more than yuse the words of my good lady, who has got the infectual calling; and, I trust, that even myself, though unworthy, shall find grease to be excepted.—Miss Liddy has been touch'd to the quick, but is a little timorsome: howsomever, I make no doubt, but she, and all of us, will be brought, by the endeavours of Mr. Clinker, to produce blessed fruit of generation and repentance.—As for master and the young 'squire, they have as yet had narro glimpse of the new light.—I doubt as how their harts are hardened by worldly wisdom, which, as the pyebill saith, is foolishness in the sight of God.
>
> O Mary Jones, pray without seizing for grease to prepare you for the operations of this wonderful instrument, which, I hope, will be exorcised this winter upon you and others at Brambleton-hall. (152)

From a strictly historicist position, I suppose we could say that Win's malapropisms satirically "express the reality behind the spiritual concerns of Methodism" (Rothstein *Systems* 127). Certainly, Tabby's "infectual" calling suggests Methodism as a kind of fever while Win's expectation of "grease" from Humphry's "instrument" suggests that it is merely a sublimation of sexual drives. But Smollett's purposes are more inclusive. "Quick," as in "the quick and the dead," has been reduced to its abstract meaning of "life," but clearly the quick to which Liddy has been touched is much more concrete. And it will, at the end of the novel, "produce blessed fruit of generation." Smollett here revivifies the mythic meaning of the word, and does not, I think, so much satirize the spiritual as ask us to recognize its foundation in the concrete. The spiritual reality of the Bible can withstand being called the "pyebill"; in fact, like the metaphor quick, it is revivified by being brought back into contact with its mythic origin. Jery and Matt's insistent rationalism, on the other hand, is undercut by the word "hart," which demonstrates that it, too, has a basis in the animal.

My argument is not to deny particular satire, but to suggest that Smollett's ultimate purposes are more inclusively to place historical reality in relation to myth, to juxtapose the diachronic and synchronic realities of words. In a marvelous phrase, Win tells Mary Jones to "pray without seizing for grease." Clearly, Win wants no one else touching Humphry's wonderful instrument, however much she wants them to be spiritually moved by it. Here the historical thrust, so to speak, perfectly balances the mythic one. "As for me," Win remarks in a later letter, "I put my trust in the Lord; and I have got a slice of witch elm sowed in the gathers of my under petticoat" (295). Christian revelation *and* pagan superstition: both together allow Win to "deify the devil and all his works" in "the new light of grease" (295).

Often skewing toward the scatological as Win's have toward the sexual, Tabitha's letters also demonstrate a rich use of language. She writes to Mrs. Gwyllim, housekeeper of Brambleton-hall: "I hope you keep accunt of Roger's purseeding in reverence to the butter-milk. I expect my dew when I come huom, without baiting an ass, I'll assure you.—As you must have layed a great many more eggs than would be eaten, I do suppose there is a power of turks, chickings, and guzzling about the house; and a brave kergo of cheese ready for market; and that the owl has been sent to Crickhowel, saving what the maids spun in the family" (264). "Accunt" is one of Tabby's favorite words, conflating as it does her interests in economy and sexuality. "Purseeding" is more subtle since "purse" underlines her meanness in money matters while "seeding" shows her interest in matrimony ("mattermoney," as Win calls it [337]) and procreation. Tabby's gross materialism is revealed in her "reverence to" (reference to) the buttermilk as a source of income; but the word "dew" for due has some of the same effect as seeding. It evokes an innocence and a timeless cyclicity that work against Tabby's mean-spirited commitment to the present. Similarly, "baiting an ass" for bating an ace suggests a concrete sexual impulse beneath Tabitha's principles of accounting. That alliance with the synchronicity of myth comes out in her pursuit of a husband, which despite Matt's and Jery's sneers, reflects strongly her sexual rather than her economic appetite.

Tabby's economic drives, aligned with diachronic historical impulses, may seem to have mastery over her; but her language always knows better. In her first letter to Mrs. Gwyllim, she writes: "The gardnir and the hind may lie below in the landry, to partake the house, with the blunderbuss and the great dog" (8). And, of course, "partake" is what they do, as on her instinctive level she too feels is her "dew." In the passage we have been analyzing, she consciously speaks about her poultry when she says, "I do suppose there is a power of turks, chickings, and guzzling about the house." Her language evokes, however, an image of Falstaffian excess, one that accords not incongruously with Tabby's own libidinal drives.

As Lismahago becomes the overt spokesman for the conservative view of language within the novel, Win dramatizes the counter view of mythic language in some of her letters. Unlike Liddy, who tries to say what she means, Win says more than she means because her language regains some of the vibrancy of myth:

> I pray of all love, you will mind your vriting and your spilling; for, craving your pardon, Molly, it made me suet to disseyffer your last scrabble, which was delivered by the hind at Bath—O, voman! voman! if thou had'st but the least consumption of what pleasure we scullers have, when we can cunster the crabbidst buck off hand, and spell the ethnitch vords without lucking at the primmer. As for Mr. Klinker, he is qualified to be clerk to a parish—But I'll say no more—Remember me to Saul—poor sole! it goes to my hart to think she don't yet know her letters—But all in God's good time—It shall go hard, but I will bring her the A B C in ginger-bread; and that, you nose, will be learning to her taste. (106)

Win thinks Humphry's command of language qualifies him to be clerk of the parish; we may think hers entitles her to be the clerk's wife. Her first sentence seems entirely carnal as she cautions Mary to be careful of her "spilling," with obvious sexual overtones. But this phrase, "I pray of all love," sets up a nice tension between body and spirit that climaxes with the sentence, "Remember me to Saul—poor sole!" Sal, the fellow servant girl, is, of course, a poor soul, a spiritual abstraction. But through the power of Win's language, she is "Matthew-murpheyed" into Saul, the New Testament saint, who has become, paradoxically, a physical body—a sole. And when we remember that the fish was a symbol for Christ who incarnated the spirit in the flesh, our admiration for the unifying aspect of Win's—and Smollett's—language increases.

Deconstructive critics, who seem to exult in the condition of the fall, can certainly point to the slipperiness of a language where "consumption" contends with conception and "sculler" spars with scholar. Win, however, knows in her "hart" that "all in God's good time" Sal/Saul, the poor soul/sole, will know her letters: "It shall go hard, but I will bring her the A B C in ginger-bread; and that, you nose, will be learning to her taste." Mythic language, the A B C in gingerbread, allows for the recovery of lost unities; it also, Smollett discovered, allows for the creation of credible voices for his characters. Win's and Tabby's language, to speak only of that one aspect of characterization, is the most convincing that Smollett gave to any of his characters.

While a deconstructive reading of the comic play on words in these letters can be made,[14] it seems more reasonable to conclude that Smollett had come to share Vico's and Boulanger's feeling that "words bore with them a set of emotive tones which were clues to the true temper of antiquity" (Manuel 218). A passage from Tabby's first letter speaks to this idea: "let none of the men have excess to the strong bear" (8). Pointing to the confusion between "excess" and "access," we could argue that language is unstable, a purely arbitrary and undependable system of signifiers. But we could also argue that the play on "excess"/"access" is a perfect illustration of the power of mythic language to reflect deeper unity rather than perpetual disunity. What Tabby's language really shows is her desire not for deprivation but for fulfillment (and particularly on an animal level, as in "bear" for beer).

As we saw, the archetypal "return" of Roderick Random was quite unconvincing because of Smollett's failure to find an adequate language. Only in *Humphry Clinker* does Smollett achieve a fruitful orchestration of different languages that leads to a convincing closure where myth is integrated with history.[15] Closure is focused in this last novel more around the achievement of an ideal mode of life than around the weddings which resolve its ostensible marriage plot. Always present in Matt's testy sense of the inadequacies of modern society, the idea of an ideal state gets its first extensive development as the characters travel in Scotland. In his letter marked Cameron, Sept. 6, Matt Bramble speaks of a "Scottish paradise" (244). He describes the marvelous foods they eat, the scenery they can view, the company with whom they visit, and he gives a brief history of the clan system. His is the point of view of the historian as he describes enthusiastically the world around him. Indeed, the idea that the Scottish material strays too far from novelistic convention has become a commonplace in Smollett criticism, where it is assumed that his enthusiasm for his native country caused him to lose sight of his novel as a novel (letters from Tabby and Win are nearly submerged in Matt and Jery's more reportorial letters).

As Smollett prepares to modulate from his satiric attack on the ills of society to his picture of its ideal realization, this emphasis on historical language is, however, necessary. By establishing the credibility of a good society on this realistic level, he readies his readers to accept a larger vision which includes a mythic dimension. Two letters by Matt and Jery as they cross back from Scotland to England further this process of modulation. Jery's letter marked Carlisle, Sept. 12, describes, first of all, the episode of the return of one Brown, a captain in the East Indies, who returns home to discover his ancient father at work paving a street. Having been security for his landlord and lost the money Brown had sent him, the old man is reduced to penury, another son having gone to jail for his debts. While Brown, unrecognized, talks to his father, the other son calls out from the prison window that his brother William has returned. His mother, hearing the cry, calls out, "Where is my bairn? where is my dear Willy?" (255). As if the scene were not sufficiently melodramatic and incredible already, Jery remarks that Bramble "was as much moved as any one of the parties concerned in this pathetic recognition.—He sobbed, and wept, and clapped his hands, and hollowed, and finally ran down into the street" (255). What is interesting to us is that this seemingly incredible story had a basis in historical fact. According to Robert Anderson, Smollett changed only the name of the real hero, which was White, into Brown (XI, 415, quoted in Parreaux, xxi). Clearly, Smollett here takes the material of history and turns it not into factual story but into a myth of return and reconciliation.

The second event Jery deals with is the "death" and "rebirth" of Lismahago. Traveling along the dangerous Solway sands, the group perceives Lismahago's dead horse and presumes he has been drowned. He is discovered alive at Carlisle, however; and it is at this point that Jery and Matt decide to encourage him to wed Tabby. Having seen the failure of his ideal vision of his native Scotland, Lismahago will have to embrace history in the vinegary arms of Tabitha. His story is the reverse of Brown's mythicization of history.

Matt's letter on crossing into England describes two "supernatural" events. In one, a story is recounted about how a man has received visionary foreshadowings of a visit from a group of friends (260–61); the other describes how a pragmatic Scotsman has been severely whipped by the ghost of his long dead grandfather (261–63). We soon discover that the latter "ghost" was Lismahago, who was mistaken for his dead father as he beat his nephew for desecrating the family home to commercial ends. A "historical" explanation for this supposed visionary scene is given; yet the other episode is left unexplained. Smollett here interweaves the mysterious and the rational as a part of the general orchestration of event and language that marks the end of the novel.

In the closing pages of the novel, the search for an ideal mode of life is explored in visits to four different country houses. The visit to Lord Oxmington's, which culminates in near strife as Bramble takes umbrage at the lord's condescension, symbolizes all that is wrong in a historical England which has perverted tradition and class standards. We are given a view of how the aristocracy has betrayed its historic social role, as well as of Bramble's quixotic defiance of that betrayal. The visit with Baynard and his wife describes how the lower gentry have also betrayed the ideal of the good life by aping the manners of those above them. Only the timely death of the wife saves Baynard from the bad end her extravagance has made otherwise certain. Under Bramble's guidance, Baynard is able to save himself from the spiritual and monetary bankruptcy Smollett sees as endemic in certain strata of contemporary English society.

The episode at Sir Thomas Bullford's offers a comic interlude which modulates history into myth. "Sir Tummas Ballfart," as Win calls him (295), is a Falstaffian lord of misrule who leads us from the everyday world of historical contingency into the holiday of comic release. The episode in which he figures properly comes, then, just before the climactic recognition scene. His main joke is on Lismahago, who is forced, through Sir Thomas's trickery, to expose himself in a scanty nightshirt at the top of a ladder. In parting, he tells Tabby that she should "remember him in the distribution of the brides's favours, as he had taken so much pains to put the captain's parts and mettle to the proof" (294). The pun on metal/mettle/and sexual organ is evidence that we are entering a freer linguistic world; and Win's reentry into the novel after a long absence confirms that the ideal state offered at the end of the novel will be presented in a wider spectrum of voices and language than that used to describe the "Scottish paradise."

The overturning of the coach in a river between the Bullford and the Dennison scenes plays an obvious archetypal role. During this symbolic death/rebirth sequence, not only is Humphry Clinker revealed as the natural son of Matt; but Bramble's own regeneration as a freer, more flexible person is confirmed. Metamorphosis, as applied to change in places and customs as well as in character, is as persistent a theme in *Humphry Clinker* as the idea of metempsychosis is in Joyce's *Ulysses*. Humphry first "metamorphosed" (81) his bare posteriors with a suit of clothes, making him acceptable to Tabby's virgin eyes. He is "metamorphosed into Matthew Lloyd" (306) when it is discovered he is Bramble's natural son. Lydia describes how her lover Wilson has been "metamorphosed into George Dennison" (321); and Win also comments on how Wilson has been "matthewmurphy'd" (323) into a fine young gentleman. Concerned as they were with change, both Smollett and Joyce were fascinated with the possibility of transforming history into myth—and also with the possibility that such transformations might be "murphy" tricks, as in Joyce's use of the seaman W.B. Murphy in the Eumaeus chapter of *Ulysses*.

The Dennison estate reflects Smollett's image of the ideal society. Dennison has achieved, Bramble says, "that pitch of rural felicity, at which I have been aspiring these twenty years in vain" (307). Byron Gassman points out that "the disappearance of precise geographical notation here helps remove the novel's final vision of England from historical and geographical particularity. The effect is as if the travellers were still in England, but not the England bound by the historical latitude and longitude of George III's precarious kingdom" (*Criticism* 107). The estate and what it represents thus take on mythic proportions. Much of the description is in Dennison's own voice; the language is more concrete and specific than Bramble's ordinarily more abstract and analytical style. The effect of distancing—Dennison being quoted by Bramble who in turn is separated from Smollett—lends an authority and resonance to this voice not always found in Smollett's fictions.

While Smollett thus introduces some of the synchronic effect of Win's and Tabby's letters into his picture of the Dennison estate, his purpose is not to substitute mythic understanding for rational knowledge. His "revolutionary" nostalgia is not for a simple return to intuitive modes of being. In fact, in Jery's letter that narrates Tabby's response to discovering the truth about Humphry, her myth is turned to history. Here, instead of *seeing* Tabby's own inscribed language with its synchronic effect, we *hear* her through Jery's ears: "'Brother, you have been very wicked: but I hope you'll live to see the folly of your ways—I am very sorry to say the young man whom you have this day acknowledged, has more grace and religion, by the gift of God, than you with all your profane learning, and repeated opportunity—I do think he has got the trick of the eye, and the tip of the nose of my uncle Loyd of Flluydwellyn; and as for the long chin, it is the very moral of the governor's—Brother, as you have changed his name pray change his dress also; that livery doth not become any person that hath got our blood in his veins'" (306). The effect here is to historicize Tabby, to make her a much more conventional character than her own letters do. Since we inevitably bring echoes of the synchronic energies of those letters to our reading of Jery's transcription of her voice, Tabby retains much of her buoyancy as a character; yet her language has been remarkably flattened.

Thus, while Smollett maintains a variety of languages at the end of the novel, we do notice how each has taken on some of the color of the others. This idea is most triumphantly illustrated in Win's last words, the last of the book itself: "Present my compliments to Mrs. Gwyllim, and I hope she and I will live upon dissent terms of civility.—Being, by God's blessing, removed to a higher spear, you'll excuse my being familiar with the lower sarvents of the family; but, as I trust you'll behave respectful, and keep a proper distance, you may always depend upon the good will and purtection of Yours, W. Loyd" (337). We hear Win assuming the voice of the establishment in this passage, removing herself from the free play of democracy to the privilege of class (the reverse of Matt's own journey). Yet we also note how brilliantly Smollett reveals in the phrase "higher spear" all the emotion and sexuality that counters pure economic abstraction. Win's sexual energies will always be warring on her abstract sense of place, humanizing her. This idea is brought out most tellingly in the phrase "dissent terms of civility," which not only summarizes the dichotomy between the changing (history) and the unchanging (the mythic) which we have been tracing but also suggests how they must ultimately coexist.

*Humphry Clinker* is not "torn between" its mythic and historic visions, but rather exploits them in individual and effective manipulations of form, structure, and especially language. Understanding what Joyce has done in a nonrealistic form helps us to look back and better understand Smollett's similar achievement. Joyce took his own chance encounter with a Mr. Alfred Hunter and transformed it into the adventures of a modern Ulysses occurring within a single archetypal day. Smollett took his own trip to his native Scotland from May till August 1766 and fashioned it into a symbolic journey from spring to the rebirth of the Christmas dinner promised in Matt Bramble's last letter. Joyce's novel demonstrates both the historical world of Dublin 1904—drawing upon actual events, places, persons, and things—and the mythic world of Bloom's family romance. Smollett's five letter writers undertake a trip through a historical England and Scotland filled with real persons (including the author himself!) and events; but they also enact their family romance, moving from an initial estrangement to an ultimate harmony with one another.

The central point of comparison between the two novels lies in their use of language; but we find similarities also in the reconciliation of sons and fathers, the growth of the hero into a wiser perception of his relation to life, the emphasis both novels place on human excretions and the scatological, etc. What seems to lie behind all of these is their authors' persistent interest in the relation between what is ever renewed and what is perpetually changing. When Joyce violates the standards of realism to exploit the incompatibilities as well as the harmonies of synchronic and diachronic vision, we consider that he has written a masterpiece. Perhaps we owe *Humphry Clinker* a similar consideration. One modern critic has said that *Humphry Clinker* "is too much a 'gossiping novel,' too much of a pleasant potpourri of events, persons, data, observations, criticism, and moralizing ever to submit to the kind of analysis that discovers a single underlying principle dictating form and content to a work of fiction" (Gassman *Bicentennial Essays* 168). Not a novel in the realist tradition, neither is it a mere potpourri. It is a deeply original exploration of the relation between myth and history.

## Notes

1. Although a few of Smollett's critics have declared him a univocal writer (Copeland, Rosenblum, and especially Sekora), most have seen his work expressing deep tensions. These have been interpreted variously as those between the country and the city (Evans), sensibility and violence (Daiches), Augustan values and the expressive and affective theories of the later eighteenth century (Grant), Christian and secular world views (New), and, most interestingly for my study, between realism and mythopoeia in Byron Gassman's reading of *Humphry Clinker.*

2. As innumerable scholars have demonstrated, the texture of the world Smollett has created for Roderick can be traced directly to sources in eighteenth-century politics, law, medicine, etc. To indicate just one example, John F. Sena has shown that Smollett's picture of Narcissa's strange aunt is "derived almost entirely from contemporary medical theories of hysteria" (270).

3. The introduction of Melopoyn's story differs somewhat from Smollett's use of the Carthagenean material. While in prison, Roderick listens to the difficulties the poet has had in trying to get his tragedy on the stage. The two chapters Smollett devotes to this story are based on his own experiences with his play *The Regecide.* Much like Joyce, then, Smollett is using biographical reality as the basis for fiction. "Earl Sheerwit" is a thinly veiled picture of Lord Chesterfield, and "Marmozet" clearly reflects a satiric image of David Garrick himself. Thus we know that the story *is* history; yet the way the story is colored and told keeps us from believing its historical reality. What does emerge as "true" is the indignation in the language of the "I" who responds to the story. We sense that it is Smollett rather than the fictional character Roderick whose anger we hear.

4. David Green maintains that Smollett's *History* is a "greatly underestimated work" which emphasizes not the grand movements of history as did his contemporary historians but rather the psychology and motivation of individuals (301).

5. See, for example: Rosenblum, "Smollett and the Old Conventions," 389–401; New, "'The Grease of God': The Form of Eighteenth-Century Fiction," 240–43; Treadwell, "The Two Worlds of *Ferdinand Count Fathom,*" 144–49; and Copeland, "*Humphry Clinker:* A Comic Pastoral Poem in Prose?," 493–501.

6. *Peregrine Pickle* is Smollett's closest approach to the traditional novel as Watt defines it. As Rufus Putney demonstrated more than forty years ago, there is a "plan" to the novel that involves Peregrine's overcoming a false pride (1051–65). One of the central features of plot, as we have seen, is the idea of peripety, upon which the moral development of the main character depends. In this novel, Smollett tries to demonstrate such growth in Peregrine. Confined to jail, Peregrine, as Boucé suggests, confronts both the reality of the social world whose false values have misled him and his own flaws which are ultimately responsible for his downfall. Although Peregrine is rescued by the deus ex machina of his father's death intestate, Smollett clearly tries to show his hero's moral growth under the face of circumstances. This tighter plot leads to a more intense emphasis upon a small group of characters who figure consistently in Peregrine's growth rather than the more miscellaneous relationships Roderick has. These characters are also more fully individualized than those in Smollett's first novel.

7. Although rumors circulated from the first that Smollett was well paid for publicizing Lady Vane's story, James L. Clifford doubts this was so. Instead, he suggests that for Smollett Lady Vane "may have symbolized the rebel condemned by society. Her very frankness in admitting her many affairs, and her insistence that it was love which had been her undoing, evidently made an immediate appeal" (xxvi).

8. Damian Grant says that "Smollett has succeeded in colouring Trunnion's whole expression with a dense network of images, until it seems almost another created language" (139).

9. In an extended discussion of Smollett's blending of historical detail and fiction, Thomas R. Preston points to this scene to demonstrate that it is "not the individual items, factual or fictional, but the new mixture, the comic fusion of historical, factual, and fictional elements that constitutes the reality" ("Introduction" xlv). Preston's discussion helps one to see how Joyce could have found in Smollett a model in incorporating historical personages into his fiction.

10. In his study of Smollett's work in the *Critical Review*, James Basker points out a critique of Warton's language, whose "insistence on purity and correctness links Smollett to a century-long tradition of linguistic conservatism" (94). Lismahago's view of language is clearly the one held by Smollett himself in 1756. The novels themselves, however, demonstrate the breaking away from a unitary language toward heteroglossia.

11. Cunningham himself did not believe these six essays from *The British Magazine* were Goldsmith's, although he included them in his edition. Caroline Tupper, on the basis of both internal and external evidence, attributed them to Smollett (325–42). While accepting that the essays are not Goldsmith's, Ronald S. Crane feels that Tupper's "suggestion that the real author was Smollett is hardly more than a plausible guess" (xix).

12. The history of the response to these letters reads like a microcosm of Smollett scholarship, moving as it does from more literal, historical responses to freer considerations of Smollett's artistic purposes. W. Arthur Boggs first approached these letters from a linguistic angle, attempting to describe the realism of their idiolect. He concluded that unlike Scott, Mrs. Gaskell, and Thackeray, who "have recorded actual dialects with remarkable fidelity," Smollett has created "a rich and persuasive speech which turns out to be no speech at all" (337). When V.S. Pritchett suggested in *The Living Novel* (1946) that Joyce and Smollett might "have had not dissimilar obsessions" in their chamber pot humor and that there was "some hint of Anna Livia in the Welsh maid's letters in *Humphry Clinker*" (22), ground was broken, if only superficially, for a less literal, more "poetic" reading of the letters. Damian Grant's reading shows affinities with modern deconstructionist theory. For him, Win and Tabby's letters are "a significant testimony to the willfulness of words, and a spirited exposure of the simple model of language proposed by the empirical tradition." Smollett's distortion of language has been "pushed beyond the point where it has any significant moral implications, into the sphere of pure linguistic virtuosity" (94–95). Eric Rothstein returns to a historical view, suggesting that Smollett has been using these women's speech to overcome an English prejudice against the "outlandish jargon" of the Scots (70). Perhaps rounding out a cycle in Smollett scholarship, Thomas R. Preston extends Bogg's analysis of dialectical usage in the letters ("Introduction" xxxv-xxxvii), though he draws our attention to Sherbo's critique of such efforts (li).

13. Owen Barfield points out that in the twentieth century "the expression 'I have no stomach to the business' is still by no means purely psychic in its content. It describes a very real sensation, or rather one which cannot be classified as either physical or psychic." He continues by suggesting that, on the general model of language development this meaning of this word will also split into two, and "the physico-psychic experience in question will have become as incomprehensible to our posterity, as it is incomprehensible to most of us today that anyone should literally feel his 'bowels moved' by compassion" (80n). Robert Adams Day ("Sex, Scatology, Smollett") and William Park ("Fathers and Sons—*Humphry Clinker*") have pointed out an excremental motif in Smollett's work.

Rather than following their psychological explanations, I would suggest that some of the same physico-psychic feeling we have for the metaphor "stomach to the business" persisted in Smollett's response to "bowels moved by compassion." The persistent emphasis on excrement in Smollett's fiction functions as part of an effort to recall an earlier unity of body and spirit.

14. Grant, in fact, argues that Smollett demonstrates the "wilfulness" of words, that his "imagination has gone to work, picking at the seams of language, revealing the abyss that opens (or is temporarily concealed) under our everyday handling of words" (96).

15. From one perspective or another, a wide variety of critical studies have stressed the archetypal, mythic aspect of *Humphry Clinker*. Many have called attention to its circular movement (one of the earliest of these was B.L. Reid's "Smollett's Healing Journey"). Paul-Gabriel Boucé also notes this pattern (202), while Byron Gassman argues that a "mythic kingdom" materializes in the last pages of the novel (*Criticism* 107). Accepting that romance archetypes lie behind Smollett's fiction, Michael Rosenblum suggests, however, that in his last novel Smollett parodies these conventions (393). And Melvyn New finds Smollett "most solidly within the romance tradition, except for his final work ... which thrusts the romance further from the center of consideration than any previous fiction" (240).

LOIS E. BUELER

# The Tested Woman Plot

The very notion of a moral test points to a fundamental feature of our Western ethical system. To say that one of the most elemental story types of Judeo-Christian culture describes the testing of a person's obedience to moral law is to say, first of all, that we construe morality legalistically. Not all cultures do so. Nor is a legalistic ethics the only ethics in the Western tradition, a fact we shall explore later. But it is unquestionably the dominant one, in which Hebraic and classical influences reinforce each other to conflate religious with civil morality and make law, whether sacred or secular, the controlling structure. When the legalistic tradition assumes narrative form in the story of moral demonstration, it focuses on obedience to the law. This legalistic bias imposes in turn upon the story's structure, and what it imposes is key structural features of the law itself.

To begin with, in our familiar Western story of the moral test, moral law is couched as prohibition. Theoretically, the Judeo-Christian ethical ideal can be summed up in positive terms: doing justice, loving mercy, and walking humbly with God represent the Jewish epitome, to which the Christian injunction to love God and one's neighbor constitutes a gloss rather than an extension. But in practice, in this legalistic tradition behavior tends to be scrutinized negatively, in terms of shalt-nots. The story of moral demonstration, then, has as its central issue the violation of a prohibition. Furthermore, the test tends to center on a single discrete action rather than on the sum of a character's intentions or behavior. It becomes a test of

---

whether a character has violated a specific requirement rather than how well he or she has behaved in general. A third feature is that, since obedience to law means obedience to authority, the story of the moral test explores and sometimes questions the hierarchical relationships through which authority is expressed. Because in our tradition moral law is divine in its ultimate origins, even when expressed through human institutions, either overtly or by implication the story of the moral test provides a mechanism for bringing into question the authority not just of man, but of God.

We can see these features starkly at work in the story of Adam and Eve. The Genesis story involves not the weighing of entire lives, but a single test of obedience. The issue is stated in the form of a prohibition which derives its force from the authority of its divine promulgator. Lest we have any doubt, Genesis validates this authority by framing the Garden narrative in the narrative of the Creation. In the story of the Edenic test, the Creator commands His creatures. There can be no stronger moral imperative.

But in the Edenic narrative we also see a seemingly unnecessary dramatic complication. The test requires only two participants, God and his creature, but we find a cast of four. The test might just as well have been directed by God, but instead it is directed by the serpent. It might just as well have targeted Adam, but instead it targets Eve. This multiplication of characters is motivated by the fact that moral tests occur only when moral authority is in disagreement or disarray—or at least appears to be so. The story of the Garden is constructed to demonstrate competing claims and allegiances. By putting the test on Eve, by placing her at the bottom of a hierarchy in which not just God but Adam and the serpent exercise authority, the Genesis story allows the playing off of one claim against another and opens the way to a questioning of the very concept of authority.

The multiplication of characters we see in the story of the Garden tells us something absolutely central about the tested woman: in plot terms she is a structural convenience, a device that makes possible the exploration of hierarchical relationships among authority figures. Like Adam, Eve is God's creature. But she is also Adam's wife and subject to Adam's marital authority. The serpent's approach, therefore, is made in part as though for Adam's benefit and Eve must weigh her obligation to Adam as well as to God. The approach is also made in terms which insinuate that the serpent himself is a superior being, superior in knowledge and by implication in authority and therefore worthy to be obeyed. Not Good against Evil, but one Good against another seeming Good—that is the stuff of the moral test, and that is what Eve is subjected to. Making Eve rather than Adam the object of the test is a simple way to introduce the competing claims which make a moral test possible. It gives dramatic form to the real issue: to what degree man, having been created in the image of God, has the right to share in His authority.

For exactly this dramatic reason, women are favorite objects of moral tests throughout Western literature. All manner of authority—civil and religious, parental and marital—can be exercised upon women by a variety of male figures, whether human or divine, for the ultimate purpose of establishing to whom that authority rightly belongs and how it is to be shared. Always these tests involve obedience. Usually they are focused on sexual behavior because in a patriarchal world it is a woman's sex that not only determines her hierarchical status but constitutes the very purpose for her existence. Sexual obedience or chastity, the appropriate reservation of her sexual and thus her reproductive services, is therefore her primary moral obligation because it is her primary social obligation: it is where her honor chiefly lies.

In the account I am giving, we see a telling conflation at work. The legalistic tradition out of which the story of the test arises, a tradition in which obedience to a prohibition is the moral key, comes to focus on a figure whose social identity is primarily defined in terms of her obedience to a prohibition. Unlike a man, a woman occupies her appropriate place in such a patriarchal society by means of, and only by means of, the fact that her sexual services are appropriately reserved or restricted in obedience to patriarchal prerogative. Her virtue—all her virtue—lies in what she does not do, what she refuses to do. In effect she becomes emblematic of an entire moral system based on prohibition. (Following the reductive logic of that system, we can see why it is no accident that modernly the word "virtue" refers primarily to women's chastity.) But when morality is based on prohibition and on prohibition alone, when the only virtue lies in refusal, then virtue can be demonstrated only under pressure. Without the occasion which allows its violation it is mere potential. Thus the prelapsarian Adam and Eve have no moral character; they just are. We have no basis for a moral estimate because there has been no opportunity for disobedience and therefore no moral choice. The same effect holds for the woman whose moral character is exclusively defined in terms of the passive virtue of chastity. Until she either violates or refuses to violate the prohibition which defines her, she has no moral character. Only a test which forces a choice can make her morality actual.[1]

Thus moral innocence really means moral ignorance, lack of knowledge of the test. Yet we must allow that in this moral system no woman after Eve totally lacks moral character. The moral genealogy is too potent, cultural expectations are too strong. For in the tradition with which we are dealing, a woman's sex also determines her psychological makeup, which is more passionate, more changeable, and more subject to temptation and vice than that of more rational males. Given the opportunity, women can be expected to err, as did Eve. "She is chaste whom no man hath solicited," sneers the bawd Dipsas in Ovid's *Amores* (I, 8). Only the extraordinary woman, supported by an unusual measure of divine grace, will be capable of virtuous behavior.

Interestingly, however, the great majority of stories about the testing of a woman work against the cultural expectation of female moral collapse. Though the fallen woman is a stock figure in Western literature, there is little to be said about her per se. It is the woman virtuous in the face of opportunity who is at the heart of the stock story. Perhaps this should not surprise us. The tale of the exercise of extraordinary virtue calls forth the dramatic power created by moral heroics and the reversal of audience expectations. Nevertheless, the testing plot has the same essential structure whether the woman stands or falls. The reason, which we shall explore shortly, is that its real dramatic and moral point lies not with the choice itself, but with the way authority interprets and responds to that choice. Further, occasions for choice may be repeated. And since once obedient does not mean always obedient, with each occasion the tested woman may fall, or the fallen woman may encounter new tests which allow her redemption. Thus the sequence may be played over and over, since the plot of the test, like the plot that is Christian life, ends definitively only with death.

The Tested Woman Plot is the literary formalization of the moral patterns and assumptions evident in the story of Adam and Eve. This formalization is always dramatic in the broad sense—that is, it consists of a narrative of human actions, employing human characters. And it is always centered on the test of a woman's obedience—usually her sexual obedience—to patriarchal authority. This brief survey of the plot's ethical background has alluded as a matter of course to archetypal features of Western patriarchy with which feminist cultural and literary criticism has made us thoroughly familiar. Among Richardson critics, both Carol Houlihan Flynn and Margaret Ann Doody give accounts of some of the ways this archetype found form in eighteenth-century literary convention and permeated Richardson's work.[2] Within this background, whose general familiarity I am assuming, my focus is the architectonics of the plot.

The two-stage event sequence typical of the Tested Woman Plot grows directly and naturally from the nature of the concept of obedience itself. The action of obedience requires at least two participants, the one who commands and the one who obeys. As a moral virtue, then, obedience has two components, fact and reputation. That is, it examines not just what the subordinate does, but what the superior thinks of it. This means that the plot which tests obedience contains a structural peculiarity: when exhibited in full it has two stages, a *fact* stage and a *reputation* stage. The first stage involves the occasion for disobedience itself, the point at which the woman takes or refuses an action of clear moral significance. To put the matter in terms both crude and familiar, it is the "will she or won't she?" point, the point at which her potential nature becomes actual. Schematically, the *moral issue* of this stage is *virtue* and its *essential dramatic action* is *choice*. To keep the terminology clear, I call this stage the *Test*. Although the Test may be spoken of as a temptation, it is significant that the woman faced with an occasion for sin may actually feel no desire to be unchaste or disobedient. The occasion for error does not necessarily induce the desire to err; the woman does not necessarily feel "tempted" in the ordinary sense of the word. On the other hand, she may experience a psychological struggle—a weighing of the appeals of competing claims or a desire to capitulate to worldly pressures.[3] In either case, the Test is the point at which she must choose to obey or disobey.

The second plot stage involves reputation—the opinion of others about the tested woman's action. It takes the form of an inquiry into the choice that occurred in the previous stage. In this second stage, the *moral issue* is *truth* and the *essential dramatic action* is *judgment*. I call this inquiry or demonstration the *Trial*, understanding that the trial is only sometimes formal or forensic. Once the woman's choice has been made, the Trial is a demonstration conducted by the authority figures to whom she owes obedience. If she has been disobedient, the Trial stage establishes that fact and metes out punishment. Even if she has been obedient, the Trial stage of the plot nevertheless goes on; in fact, most tested woman stories involve virtue upheld, if not always rewarded. During this Trial, the woman may simply be declared virtuous. Or she may face an honestly mistaken accusation based on genuinely misleading evidence against which she must be defended. Or she may be slandered by someone who wishes her downfall.[4] That the Trial goes on no matter what the woman's behavior underlines its fundamental purpose: it is conducted for the benefit, not of the woman, but of the men who command and judge her. The Genesis story is not for the edification of Eve. It is played out to educate the patriarchs Adam and Abraham and their seed forever, as *Paradise Lost* exhaustively establishes.

This two-stage event sequence invites richly productive literary variations without losing its essential shape. It may be entered at a number of different points, so that some of the required episodes occur before the story begins. Always, however, the antecedent portion of the plot is understood to have happened. Thus when *Othello* opens, the Test is already over. Desdemona has already made her choice—she has already left her father without his permission—and the entire first act is devoted to replaying that choice from a variety of perspectives. In the first act of *The Winter's Tale*, Hermione neither has been nor is being wooed illicitly, and thus has no sense of making a choice, so from one perspective the Test never occurs. But because Leontes in his madness thinks it has, the Tested Woman Plot is precipitated.

There is even greater variation in the way the Tested Woman Plot ends. The story cannot end until the truth has been demonstrated, it is true, but the Trial stage may be carried on largely or wholly without the woman's presence, even after her death.[5] Since the Trial concerns the woman's reputation rather than her ongoing actions, the record of her life is required for its conduct, but her physical presence is not. Some portion of the Trial typically is worked out without the woman present, whether her absence is caused by incarceration, casting away, sickness, madness, or actual death. A Tested Woman story is therefore open to striking variations of tone and mood depending on structural choices related to the timing of the Trial. The key manipulations involve how the truth about the woman emerges, when the male authority figures who surround her are able to come to a reconciliation among themselves, and whether she survives to see her vindication.

Many of these variations are exhibited by Shakespeare's four calumniated woman plays. The slandering of an innocent woman's chastity is the best-known variation on the Tested Woman Plot,[6] and Shakespeare uses it in *Much Ado About Nothing*, a comedy; *The Winter's Tale* and *Cymbeline*, both tragicomedies; and *Othello*, a tragedy. Thinking about these plays as a group clarifies the degree to which genre is a function of plot manipulation. In fact, seeing the variations at work in this one version of the Tested Woman Plot brings home a wider literary truth, the degree to which the manipulation of plot timing defines genre. The comic conclusions of reconciliation and joy are made possible because the plots buy time for the accused woman. The collapse of Hero and Hermione in the face of sudden, brutal, and seemingly unmotivated slander allows them to be hidden away as dead. Imogen's disguise and flight, along with the bloody sign which gives her out for dead, accomplishes the same thing. "Truth," says the Chorus of *The Winter's Tale*, "is the daughter of Time," and in the time bought by the women's absence change can be effected. *Othello*, on the other hand, allows no time. The claustrophobic physical and temporal concentration of its central three acts gives Desdemona no protection, Othello no possibility for reflection, and Desdemona's would-be defenders no working space to understand or to act. Iago uses this concentration as his chief tool, twisting and conflating dilatory time to his purposes. These variations suggest that if the woman can buy time for a fair trial—as the Duchess of Malfi tries to do, as Clarissa tries to do—she can hope that truth will out.

What time works toward is the face-to-face encounter among the men who surround the tested woman and whose competing claims have created the conflict to begin with. The Trial stage of the plot is constructed to seek the point at which the men will meet, examine the evidence about the woman, and know the truth. Iago's task is to prevent such an encounter, killing whoever might give evidence, sealing Othello off. Part of the tension of act 4, scene 1 arises because Cassio and Othello are together on stage yet inaccessible to each other: Cassio appears precisely when the swooning Othello is incapable of hearing him; Othello "oversees" Cassio's conversation with first Bianca and then Iago precisely without being able to hear them. In the comedies, the male encounters are timed beneficently. In the wonderful last scene of *Cymbeline*, father and husband and slanderer and faithful servant all meet, tell their fragments of the truth, and reach understanding and reconciliation before Imogen is reintroduced to them. In *The Winter's Tale* and *Much Ado*, the men meet and learn the truth, lay blame and take blame, perform acts of explanation and expiation, before Hermione and Hero can be reborn to them.

The genre variations in these versions of the Tested Woman Plot are owing, however, to something more than the timing within the separate plot lines that leads to the meeting and reconciliation of the competing men. They are also caused by the sequence in which the information reaches us. This feature is particularly clear in *Much Ado*, which is a romp because of the precise rhythm by which the Dogberry discovery action is interspersed with the Don John slander action. We first meet Dogberry within stage seconds after Don John has made his accusation against Hero. At the very moment that Conrade and Borachio boast about their part in the phony window scenario, we are hearing Dogberry and company overhearing. The arrival of Dogberry and crew to give evidence to the magistrate Leonato delays Leonato's departure for his daughter's wedding, where we know he will hear her slandered. Because we see these scenes in the order we do, we detect and rejoice in the providential workings of the plot. The mood established by the plot is a feature not just of the timing of the events in relation to each other, but the order and manner in which they are revealed to us. The powerful final scenes of *The Winter's Tale* and *Cymbeline* have very different flavors, although in terms of plot events they are rather similar. In one, the joyful surprise of the recovery of Hermione surprises us as well, while in the other our pleasure in the reconciliation of the men stems in part from our pleasure at sharing the event with Imogen herself. These variations remind us of what no merely formalist description of plot can convey: the power inherent in the manner and order of the telling.

In addition to its two-stage event sequence, the Tested Woman Plot is structured by a fixed set of characters or, more accurately, character functions. The woman herself is routinely categorized primarily by her familial position of Maid, Wife or Widow, more or less enriched by conventional expectations regarding female moral psychology. She is surrounded by a cluster of competing men, often far more vividly characterized,[7] who attempt to exercise authority over her. This exercise of authority is divided into four stereotyped functions—temptation, accusation, defense, and judgment—which to be dramatic must be carried out by characters who act as tempter, accuser, defender, or judge. Although for convenience I will refer to the tempter *figure*, it is crucial to recognize that function and character are not the same thing. In some stories the four authority functions are allotted to four characters, but in others they are combined so that a single man exercises more than one, or even all.

The *tempter* offers the woman the occasion for disobedience, thus serving as antagonist of the Test stage. His motives are various and may be mixed. As importunate lover or would-be rapist he may desire sexual or psychological possession of the woman. Or, since a test is the only way a woman can make her chastity active, he may offer the opportunity for disobedience in the hope that she will reject it. His motives may be confused or hidden, even from himself, so that he is genuinely uncertain which response he desires. Occasionally the opportunity for disobedience is offered by a male or female bawd, but the approach is always on behalf of a man who seeks illicit possession of the woman.[8] And usually the tempter knows whose patriarchal rights he seeks to violate. His real target, it is fair to say, is the man already in possession.

The *accuser* acts as antagonist of the Trial stage, bringing the woman's actual or supposed disobedience to public attention. He may be the injured party, the person in whom patriarchal ownership resides. He may be the tempter under a different guise who, having succeeded in his seduction, flaunts his possession or, having been rebuffed, revenges himself by a false accusation. Or the accuser may be a third party who brings a charge against the woman from a desire to protect or injure the possessor.[9]

In the Test stage, the *defender* may appear to strengthen the will of the woman against the blandishments of the tempter, though his presence is not required because it is she, finally, who must do the choosing. But because of its judicial or even forensic nature, the Trial stage does require a defender. He may be a new character. He may be the tempter or accuser who has repented his attempt or withdrawn his accusation. In frankly allegorical versions, the defender may even be God Himself who, in addition to strengthening the tested woman's will, converts tempter, accuser, or judge to a recognition of her virtue, appoints a human champion, or performs a retributive or revelatory miracle.[10]

The *judge* renders the decision in the Trial stage. Because he is the final arbiter, he is typically the highest-ranking character in the story, frequently an actual magistrate. Sometimes he is a neutral figure who reaches a frankly judicial decision. At least as often, he is not a disinterested party at all but the man in legal possession to whom the woman directly owes obedience. In this case he may have served as accuser, as defender, or even as tempter.[11] No matter who acts as judge, however, the crucial point of the Tested Woman Plot, the resolution toward which it moves, is the acceptance of that judgment by the man in duly constituted possession of the woman. It is this man—the husband, the father, or their surrogate—who must understand the truth about the woman. Judgment is rendered on his behalf, not hers.

Thus the plot's ultimate moral and social resolution is not primarily between the woman and the men to whom she owes obedience, though that is usually either cause or side effect. What is ultimately important is reconciliation among the male functions which have laid claim to her allegiance. Even when an abused woman is triumphantly vindicated, the real point is the reintegration of male authority. It is the comprehension of the misled men, the expiation of their guilt, the reconciliation with their friends, or the unified front against their common enemies that is the victory. The abused woman may be welcomed back from grave or exile, received back into a marriage, or made the rallying point of a political or military campaign,[12] but the health that is celebrated is that of the patriarchal establishment which has regained a hold upon itself. The plot uses the exemplary figure of the tested woman to educate and correct, not just its audience or the woman, but the male figures who comprise its own hierarchy.

The foregoing description of the character functions and event sequence of the Tested Woman Plot begins to help us account for the "tensions of myth" that Angus Ross finds at the heart of *Clarissa*. It establishes that some of the tensions are created by the interplay between the underlying structure and the form of the literary representation. In literature based on myth, for instance, we feel a conflict between our response to the characters as "people," folks like us, and our implicit understanding that they are in some sense the creatures of the mythic structure. We expect the characters, especially those in literal narrative, to be motivated by recognizably personal concerns, but we also detect and take comfort in the cosmic design of the plot, a design that seems to lie very deep in our collective expectations. Some light is thrown on this vexing and fruitful tension between what the character "is" and what the character "has to do in the story" by Vladimir Propp's study of the morphology of the folktale. Roughly speaking, the folktale is an intermediary form between the patterns of myth and the realizations of literal narrative. In his formalist analysis of this intermediary form, Propp demonstrates the extent to which the shape of the plot of a folktale, its morphology, is effectively the same thing as the stereotyped interactions of its character functions. The characters in a folktale do the things the tale type does; the folktale is the things they do.

Of course the relationship between events and characters in plays and novels is by no means so rigid. But the "rules" generated by Propp's analysis, because broadly applicable to the Tested Woman Plot, provide a possible explanation of its structural features. Propp maintains that in a given folktale the functions of characters serve as stable elements (as in the Tested Woman Plot there are always the functions of temptation, accusation, defense, and judgment). The number of character functions is limited (the Tested Woman Plot has four in addition to the testee), and their sequence is uniform (first temptation, then accusation and defense, and finally judgment). But functions are independent of the characters who fulfill them and may therefore be distributed among the characters in a variety of ways. (In the Tested Woman Plot a single character may take on a variety of functions;

furthermore, a given social role like the family friend may be the tempter in one version, the accuser or defender in another.) This is why motivations "are the most inconstant and unstable elements of the tale." The overall morphology of a folktale hooks the functions together by means of one or more "moves," each proceeding from a choice among a stereotyped set of openings, through a series of intermediary functions, to one of several possible terminal functions.[13] Even this extremely brief description of Propp's work suggests its affinities with the above analysis of the Tested Woman Plot. Propp helps most by giving us tools for working against our modern expectations of psychologically realistic literary motivation, showing the degree to which the proto-literary structures of the folktale are motivated by impersonal forces. Instead of the language of human psychology—desire, fear, despair, hope—that of the motivations of Propp's tales is physical— balance, disruption, unity, stasis, the language of the cosmic dance of myth.

Yet the Tested Woman Plot is a potent literary artifact precisely because it carries moral significance, which means that human motivation— some version of human psychology—does matter crucially after all. There must be some connection between the character's social role, life purpose, even "personality," and the function she or he performs. The Test/Trial sequence of the Tested Woman Plot unquestionably has affinities with the simpler moves of Propp's folktale morphology. But this sequence also exhibits causal relationship, a teleological drive, the purpose of which is first to force and then to judge the characters' moral choices. Plot structure is inextricably bound to moral demonstration, constituting the most important difference between the Tested Woman Plot, a tightly constrained literary artifact, and the folktale types from which it sprang.

This brings us to the heart of the tension. To the degree that a literary plot displays moral dilemmas and drives toward a morally based conclusion, it must be centrally concerned with the deliberate acts of individual characters. Functions and motivations cannot be too arbitrary or unstable. They must be rationalized sufficiently so that behavior can be understood in terms of the currently available moral psychology; it is that rationalization which allows for conflict within the individual psyche. Given the architecture of this plot, we expect psychological complications distinctive to the two stages. In the Test or Fact stage, whose moral issue is virtue and whose dramatic action is choice, the psychological complication involves *intention*. In the Trial or Reputation stage, where the moral issue is truth and the dramatic action is judgment, the psychological complication involves *interpretation*.

Introducing *intention* and *interpretation* into the architectonic scheme introduces moral ambiguity or, more accurately, draws our attention to the ambiguity already present. Take the tempter and his intention. Like Angelo, the tempter may not be certain what he wants, whether he would have

Isabella chaste or have her body his, whether it is not her very chastity that tempts him. So he can find himself faced with a psychological dilemma of his own making, in which desire struggles with duty. The tested woman, by contrast, may face a dilemma not of her own making that pits one obligation against another. Such a dilemma is most cruel, most unresolvable, when the two moral demands emanate from the same source of authority. Suppose that a woman is confronted with the moral requirement to maintain her chastity, which is her honor, in the patriarchal interests of her family. Suppose that the life of the head of that family can only be saved by the loss of that honor. Then we have Isabella's dilemma, which becomes Claudio's as well. What has this to do with intention? Angelo knows, and it is how he tempts. If this act is done to save your brother's life, are you not honoring your deepest obligations? Does not the virtue of your intention make the act possible? In fact, does not your very powerlessness excuse you? If your intention is vacated by my force, have I not eliminated your morality, and thus your dilemma, altogether? So argues Tarquin with his dagger at Lucretia's breast.

Even subtler forms of ambiguity are associated with the problem of intention. Because its authority is ultimately divinely based, the Judeo-Christian tradition internalizes authority as virtue and, particularly in the Protestant tradition, insists upon the primary moral authority of the individual conscience. One may imagine a Tested Woman story in which the woman's sense of her personal integrity is pitted against all sources of worldly authority. Then the problem of intentionality becomes stark: is the widowed Duchess who enters into a clandestine liaison unsanctioned by family, church, or social custom finally only a headstrong, self-indulgent, albeit charming, whore? How about the equally charming and headstrong young woman who has fled her father's house to secretly marry a foreigner unacceptable to her family by age, race, and social background? In these situations the Tested Woman Plot is raising the issue behind Mr. Harlowe's curse. Is the decision of the Duchess or Desdemona to place her confidence against the wishes of those in authority over her a sign of her wickedness? Or is it heroic virtue? Or is it something very much more psychologically ambiguous and morally strenuous than either? With these questions, the most interesting version of the Tested Woman Plot is afoot.

Whence come some of the more ambitious moral ambiguities possible to the Trial stage. In theory, the Tested Woman Plot operates to bring Reputation into harmony with Fact. The act of interpretation is supposed to be an act of truth-seeking. But what patriarchal authority finds convenient to recognize as truth is not necessarily consonant with what a given version of the plot has actually demonstrated or suggested. Authority figures may have to be painfully educated into the capacity to see and interpret accurately. The Tested Woman Plot, moreover, contains another hermeneutical layer involving the way readers or audience join in. All readers actively construct

literary texts, but the readers or viewers of stories based on the Tested
Woman Plot, do more. They come to perform the actual plot functions. For
instance, readers or viewers cannot regard the Duchess of Malfi as simply a
headstrong, self-indulgent whore, though that is what her brothers call her.
Her view of herself must count for something, and so must our view of her
accusers. Thus we carry out the act of moral interpretation while it is going
forward among the authority figures in the plot, as a reading of the criticism
of Webster's play will demonstrate.[14] Although we were mere observers of
the Test stage, by the very fact of that observation we become participants in
the Trial. We too know a version of the facts; we too accuse, defend, and
judge. This fact provides a literary explanation for why the plot has two
stages and why the authority functions are distinguished and allotted as they
are. In the Test stage, the Tempter operates without our participation,
though not without our connivance. But Defender, Accuser, and Judge, the
authority functions of the Trial stage, are our functions as well.

It is the Trial that implicates us most deeply in the Tested Woman Plot
because it forces us to take parts. As my final chapter suggests, this parttaking
is one reason for the nature of the critical debate about *Clarissa*. Yet I have
implied that we connive at the Test as well. For one thing, the Test carries
out the simple but titillating dramatic function of getting things underway,
unbalancing and complicating so that in due time balance and clarity may be
restored. In addition, the Test makes us voyeurs of a rich and disturbing
phenomenon, the provocation of virtue. The provocation of virtue is what
usually sets the Tested Woman Plot going, and to understand how it works,
we turn to the plot's most seminal rendition, the story of Job.

The greatest test case in the Judeo-Christian tradition, the Book of Job
schematically displays the two-stage structure and competing character
functions of the Tested Woman Plot. In the brief opening, Yahweh provokes
the test by praising the most virtuous of his creatures. Satan the Adversary, the
functionary of the heavenly court who acts as Tempter, returns the challenge
by arguing that untried virtue is no virtue at all: "Doth Job fear God for
nought? /... But put forth thine hand now, and touch all that he hath, and he
will curse thee to thy face" (1:8,10). Job's Test proceeds in the interest of
forcing him to a choice, first by severing him from all external sources of
happiness, then by tormenting his body. Having provoked and permitted the
Test, God absents himself while Satan puts Job to the question. Will Job retain
his faith in God or, given the overwhelming evidence of his rejection by the
Creator, will he separate himself, curse God as his wife advises, and thereby
find the only possible relief in death?[15] At the end of chapter 2, the conclusion
of the Test stage, Job has made his choice. Though confusion and grief silence
him temporarily, he does not curse God. What follows is the Trial, the
examination of Job's case. Satan the Tempter disappears from the story, his
function concluded. The friends step forward to act as Accuser and Defender,

arguing on the one hand that Job must have brought this misery upon himself, on the other that however undeserved his lot he is obliged to accept the inscrutability of his suffering. In agony of spirit Job refuses both positions. He examines and confirms his sense of his own integrity, presents his own case, and while not questioning God's right to act as He wills, insists that only the Creator can weigh his life. Eventually ceasing to act the Tempter, God takes up His more appropriate functions of first Defender and then Judge, accepting Job's account and handing down an award of multiple damages.

The Book of Job, however, tests a man, not a woman. How can we call it a version of the Tested Woman Plot? Because it reminds us yet again that for this plot the woman is only a paradigmatic convenience in literal stories in which the authority figures are male human beings. Secular literature has an enormous problem in trying to render the story of Job or, for that matter, the story of Adam and Eve. The problem is God. A literature in the Judeo-Christian tradition which wishes to raise and examine the issue of authority without being frankly a theodicy must sublimate downward, substituting human power for divine. But in a literary form in which God may be brought on stage—epic poems, miracle plays—the books of Genesis and Job make prime plot material. The story of Job is one of the central models of the Tested Woman Plot for the very reason that it demonstrates what the plot is really about: the relationship between ultimate superior and inferior. When God the ultimate authority can enter the story as a dramatic character, a woman is not necessary. A man may be tested directly because he can confront that authority directly.

The Book of Job does more than display the architecture of the plot, however. It is also centrally informing about the origin of the Test, that most difficult moment of all the plot to understand or rationalize. The story has as its starting point Job's virtue: "There was a man in the land of Uz, whose name was Job: and that man was perfect and upright, and one that feared God and eschewed evil" (1:1). The fact of Job's virtue and his prosperity once established, the tale is framed with an account of the heavenly court or debate, in which God makes a boast and Satan issues a challenge:

Now there came a day when the sons of God came to present themselves before the Lord, and Satan came also among them.

And the Lord said unto Satan, Hast thou considered my servant Job, that there is none like him in the earth, a perfect and an upright man, one that feareth God, and escheweth evil?

Then Satan answered the Lord, and said, Doth Job fear God for nought?

Hast not thou made an hedge about him, and about his house, and about all that he hath on every side? Thou hast blessed the work of his hands, and his substance is increased in the land.

But put forth thine hand now, and touch all that he hath, and he will curse thee to thy face.

And the Lord said unto Satan, Behold, all that he hath is in thy power; only upon himself put not forth thine hand. So Satan went forth from the presence of the Lord.

(1:6–12)

So the test begins.

In this exchange God does exactly what Posthumus does in *Cymbeline*. God deliberately holds up for admiration the perfection of His servant Job, the human partner who analogically stands to Him as the wife to her husband. Like Iachimo, Satan immediately challenges the boast, and he and God together set the terms of the test. The boast/challenge pattern is so bold and its significance so central to the Tested Woman Plot as to demand examination. What provokes Satan to attempt to violate Job's perfection? What provokes God to test his servant? The interpretive clues are found in the terms of the wager and in traditional views of the nature of the participants. Satan's response is the easier to understand, for it is caused by envy. God's description —"there is none like him in the earth"—establishes Job as first among men. Although in the universal hierarchy he is God's inferior, within his own rank he is preeminent, responsible for the physical and spiritual well-being of a great clan (1: 2–5). Sketchily characterized in this story, Satan lacks such preeminence. One of the heavenly courtiers, he is distinguishable primarily for his busyness in going to and fro on the earth and in challenging God's estimate of His creature. Satan's power to harm Job is a power delegated and circumscribed by God. He is portrayed, in short, as the quintessential lieutenant.

In the face of this sketchiness, we are justified in appealing to the traditional elaboration of Satan's character which infuses Christian readings of the Book of Job. The envy implied in Satan's challenge is traditionally ascribed to his nature as a fallen angel, the once brightest son of God now reduced to a perpetually discontented instrument of temptation and chastisement. So strong is this tradition that when Milton's Satan makes his first testing approach to Christ in *Paradise Regained*, by denying envy as his motive he confirms the tradition:

Envy they say excites me, thus to gain
Companions of my misery and woe.

(I, 397–98)

Christ, giving him the lie, naturally cites the experience of Job:

> What but thy malice mov'd thee to misdeem
> Of righteous Job, then cruelly to afflict him
> With all inflictions.
>
> (I, 424–26)

Since the terms in which God holds Job up for inspection imply a comparison of Job's righteousness with the blemishes of the tarnished Lucifer, Satan's response is first to deny that Job is as perfect as he appears to be and then to seek to fulfill his own prophecy.

By raising the issue of Job's essence and his relationship with God, the boast has activated the issue of Satan's essence and his relationship with God. By rebellion Satan lost his position as God's most favored partner; with the creation of man he lost his position as heir. But he has lost none of his desire and only part of his capacity: that is the frustration. Coupled with his limitless aspiration to be powerful and perfect is a limited power to act. Having his attention called to God's servant Job is thus a triple affront: Job's relative perfection reminds Satan of his own imperfection, God's total power over his servant reminds Satan of his own limited power, and Job's most favored status with God reminds Satan of his own alienation from God. Satan's response is to attempt both to exercise power over Job and to reduce Job's status. Satan does not seek Job's death; he is indifferent to Job's existence as such. It is Job's virtue that he wishes both to own and to eliminate, for he wishes to make Job like himself. Here is the lure and the paradox of violation, which by transforming its victim at once possesses and destroys. Satan's power must operate on Job's will, though the means may be his goods, his family, or his flesh. In order for violation to occur, Job must be brought to curse God of his own free will. Job must destroy himself by taking evil into himself, thereby providing Satan with the ultimate thrill.

If Satan seeks to violate, God seeks to prove. God's situation is the opposite of Satan's because by definition He is the One in possession. He describes Job in the same words by which the narrative frame opens its account, and the implication is clear: God knows What Is; He knows that Job is a perfect and an upright man, one that fears Him, and eschews evil. Why then should God seek to establish what He already knows? Why should He seek to have what He already possesses? The wager gives us a partial clue. Satan's challenge provokes God's pride of possession; what He knows He must demonstrate to those who doubt. The creature Job reaches the height of his perfection and value only if acknowledged. The acknowledgment of the power and perfection of God's creation is the compulsion of the entire tale: that Satan acknowledge the perfection of God's servant Job, that Job acknowledge the mystery of God's creative power, that Job's friends acknowledge both Job's righteousness and the power and justice of God's dealings with him, that all God's creatures say of Him the thing that is right (42:7, 8). Proving, then, means demonstrating.

But proving also means testing, for God is stung by Satan's challenge into admitting a degree of uncertainty. In this ethical frame, virtue untried is no virtue at all, since true virtue lies in the refusal to do evil. Satan's prediction is that Job, if sufficiently tormented, will cut himself off from God as God has seemed to cut himself off from Job. Job's response to increasingly severe tests reinforces that uncertainty. Truly he has not feared God for nought, for he is first among his people in possessions, power and prestige. The initial test completed and Job's family and possessions stripped from him, it is also true that he finds consolation in his physical and spiritual integrity, his very reduction to his essential form: "Naked came I out of my mother's womb, and naked shall I return thither: the Lord gave, and the Lord hath taken away; blessed be the name of the Lord" (1:21). When the original wager is repeated and its boundaries extended to Job's body, he still insists upon his own integrity and justifies his own righteousness. Job does not curse God, as God would have known had He, in Jung's evocative phrase, consulted His own omniscience.[16] But Job does maintain his own case, he does stand on his own separateness, he does insist upon a response.

For God, then, the provocation of Job's virtue is that it is both His and not His, as Job is both His and not His. God may dictate the situations under which that virtue will be tested, but its essence is up to Job to create, its limits up to Job to define. To possess Job's virtue fully, God must find a way to ask for it. And Job must willingly give it. Thus, when the crisis comes, when Job ends his words at the end of chapter 31, stopping what has been a fruitless plea for dialogue, the test suddenly falls on Yahweh. It is He who must make it possible for Job to express the bond between creature and Creator.

This God does by an appeal to the ineffable majesty of His creation. But it is as much how He appeals as what He appeals to that matters. After all, Elihu has spent six chapters taking the same position, that God's power is beyond man to fathom and His ways beyond man to comprehend. But Elihu has *told* Job. God, when He responds to Job out of the whirlwind, *asks*. He takes the initiative for commencing what is to be a dialogue: "Gird up now thy loins like a man; for I will demand of thee, and answer thou me" (38:3). When Job in his humility refuses to answer (40:4–5), God repeats His proposition: "Gird up thy loins now like a man: I will demand of thee, and declare thou unto me" (40:7). The extraordinary sequence of statements and questions by means of which He describes His creation is not simply rhetorical. They demand interpretation. They demand that Job become aware by their means of the full import of the nature and power of the Godhead, an awareness out of which he may formulate the relationship between Creator and creature. This is what Job performs in his response. He humbles himself before God; he acknowledges God's omniscience and omnipotence as it is appropriate that he should. But the definition of God's power comes from Job. The servant defines the master.

The Book of Job gives us help with the commencement of the Test because it gives us a paradigm for the relationships and motives of the testers. Satan the dispossessed seeks by attacking the property and the body of Job to violate Job's spirit, transforming it by taking possession of it. God the possessor seeks by stimulating demonstration of Job's obedience to reassure Himself of His possession. In both cases the object of desire is the will of the virtuous man, for both parties desire the gift of virtue willingly bestowed. Satan clearly plays the Tempter. But equally clearly his behavior is sanctioned—even, by means of the boast, activated—by God. Though by right of pride, possession, and omniscience God should play Job's Defender, for the duration of the test He is symbiotically linked with the Tempter. In literary versions of the Tested Woman Plot not every man who feels the lure of violation is overtly sanctioned by the man in possession. But many are. For many more, as in *Clarissa*, the sanction is covert; the possessor and the man who longs for possession cooperate, through the force of their assumptions about authority, hierarchy, and the nature of women, to carry out the Test.

## NOTES

1. This tradition of obedience to a prohibition, developing as it does into an ethics of refusal, certainly results in the "complicity" William Warner finds at the heart of the "Lady and the Serpent" construct with which he ends his reading of the novel. "Thus the virgin purity of the Lady makes the Serpent's role as violator plausible; the Serpent's attack makes the Lady seem chaste" (*Reading Clarissa*, 261). Unlike Warner, I do not view this "complicity" accusatorily; moreover, by "seem" I would seek to emphasize the idea of demonstration, where Warner insinuates a falsified appearance.

2. Chapters 2 and 3 of Flynn's *Samuel Richardson: A Man of Letters* usefully survey eighteenth-century convention and opinion about the nature and position of women. In *A Natural Passion: A Study of the Novels of Samuel Richardson*, the rich, judicious scholarship of Doody's chapters on pre-Richardsonian novels of love and seduction, on the heroic drama, and on the Virgin Martyr theme provide a helpful background for my thesis in this book.

3. In the terms of the distinction made here, Imogen in Shakespeare's *Cymbeline* is a prime example of a tested woman who feels no desire to be unchaste. By contrast, Bianca in Middleton's *Women Beware Women* is conscious of, and stirred by, the Duke's seductive appeal.

4. Beatrice-Joanna of Middleton's *Changeling* is disobedient and punished; in the anonymous *Edward III* the Countess is simply declared virtuous; Dame Christian Custance of Udall's *Ralph Roister Doister* faces an honest but inaccurate accusation; Shakespeare's Desdemona is the victim of deliberate slander.

5. Webster's Duchess of Malfi is the most powerful example of a tested woman whose trial occurs after her death; *Othello* displays a very swift version of the same plot move.

6. In *The Slandered Woman in Shakespeare*, Joyce Sexton rightly groups these plays as variations of a single type-story, "four tracings of one basic pattern" (11). I of course am situating them within the larger pattern of the Tested Woman Plot.

7. In *Endeavors of Art* (especially chapter 9, "Character," 216–58), Madeleine Doran surveys Renaissance attitudes towards dramatic decorum, attitudes which help account for treatments of class, gender, and motivation. One can summarize Renaissance dramatic practice as being based on a doctrine of types which stemmed from Aristotle's discussion of appropriateness in the depiction of character and was formalized by classical rhetorical advice such as Cicero's list of arguments from the person in *De inventione*.

8. As examples we have, for the tempter seeking possession, Tarquin in *The Rape of Lucrece* (Shakespeare's poem; Heywood's play); for the tempter hoping for a virtuous repulse, Vindice to his sister Castiza in *The Revenger's Tragedy*, probably by Middleton; for the tempter confused about his motives, Angelo in Shakespeare's *Measure for Measure*; for the use of a female bawd, Marina's test in Shakespeare's *Pericles*; for the use of a male bawd, Vindice.

9. An example of the successful seducer who flaunts his possession is Brachiano in Webster's *White Devil*; of the rebuffed tempter turned accuser, Iachimo in *Cymbeline*; of the possessor as accuser, Leontes; of the accuser who attempts to protect the possessor, Aurelio in Ford's *Lady's Trial*; of the accuser who attempts to injure the possessor (by turning him into chief accuser), Iago.

10. An example of the tempter become defender is Adurni in *The Lady's Trial*; of the accuser turned defender, Caraffa in Ford's *Love's Sacrifice*. God does not quite appear as a character in the literal drama, though a divinely inspired accident strikes dead the incestuous tempter of Tourneur's *Atheist's Tragedy* and a dream visitation from Jupiter confirms Imogen's purity and shakes the accusing Posthumus out of his lethargy. In the biblical and saints' tales from which so much of the literal drama takes its impetus, God takes a more active role. Thus He features as chief persuader in various versions of the Constance story, as for instance Chaucer's Man of Law's Tale; in the Susanna story He performs the miracle of opening Daniel's eyes and loosening his tongue in Susanna's defense.

11. We find an at least putatively neutral judge in the Duke of Shakespeare's *Measure for Measure*; the accuser as judge in Leontes of *The Winter's Tale* and Monticelso of *The White Devil*; the defender turned judge in the husband Frankford of Heywood's *Woman Killed with Kindness*; the tempter turned judge in the King of the anonymous *Edward III*.

12. We find male comprehension in *Othello*, expiation in *The Duchess of Malfi*, reconciliation in *Much Ado About Nothing*, a politically united front in Webster's *Appius and Virginia*. We see the wife received back into a marriage in *Cymbeline*, featured as the figurehead of a political campaign in *The Rape of Lucrece*, and, in the form of a calumniated wife/daughter duo, returned from both grave and exile in *The Winter's Tale*. In his monograph entitled *The Rapes of Lucretia*, Ian Donaldson sees this prototypal version of the story as divided between a Lucretia-focused action and a Brutus-focused action and helpfully discusses the range of political and psychological emphases to be found in its various literary treatments.

13. In *The Morphology of the Folktale*, Propp analyzes a large group of (primarily Central European) folktales from which he formulates a set of folktale "rules" or operating procedures. The rules that seem to me most generally significant as well as most salient to the Tested Woman Plot are the following:

A—The morphology of a tale is based on the functions of its characters (19–20).

B—Functions of characters serve as stable, constant elements in a tale, independent of how and by whom they are fulfilled, and the number of these functions is limited (21).

C—The sequence of functions is uniform (22).

D—Functions are defined independently of the characters who fulfill them (66) and may be distributed among characters in a variety of ways (79–83).

E—Motivations ("both the reasons and the aims of personages which cause them to commit various acts"), which are largely responsible for giving individual versions their distinctive coloring, are "the most inconstant and unstable elements of the tale" (75).

F—The overall morphology of a tale consists of one or more "moves," each proceeding from a choice among a stereotyped set of openings through a series of intermediary functions to one of several possible terminal functions (92–96).

14. Changing patterns of accusation, defense, and judgment of the Duchess are part of the history of Webster's sources; see Gunnar Boklund, *The Duchess of Malfi: Sources, Themes, Characters* (1962). Matteo Bandello's *Novelle* (1554), which provides the first account of this real-life horror story, frames the tale with a critique of revenge murders, though it makes no explicit moral commentary on the Duchess herself. But subsequent Renaissance versions, including Webster's main source William Painter (*Second Tome of the Palace of Pleasure*, 1567), increasingly inveigh against the Duchess's actions and character. Webster, of course, both redresses and complicates the balance. Twentieth-century criticism, from as early as E.E. Stoll's case (*John Webster* [1905], 118) that the play is a permutation of Kydian revenge tragedy in which the victim has become hero and her torturers the villains, has to a great extent focused upon the moral, political, sociological, and sexual ramifications of the Duchess's behavior. The most famous disagreement, perhaps, is William Empson's scathing review, "'Mine Eyes Dazzle'" (*Essays in Criticism*, 1964), of Clifford Leech's position in *Webster: "The Duchess of Malfi"* (1963) that Elizabethan audiences would have regarded the Duchess as wanton. Joyce E. Peterson's monograph, *Curs'd Example: The Duchess of Malfi and Commonweal Tragedy* (1978), passes particularly "hard and grievous" judgment on the Duchess. By contrast, D.C. Gunby ("*The Duchess of Malfi*: A Theological Approach," 1970) announces that "to find the positive values which the play offers, we must first consider the character of the Duchess and then her relationship with Bosola. I do not intend to discuss the already exhaustively treated— and it seems to me, peripheral—questions of the Duchess's guilt, or the propriety of the remarriage of widows. It is obvious, after all, where our sympathies are meant to lie: the moral issues are never in doubt" (189).

15. That "blasphemy [will] bring its certain and immediate consequence" of death, a consummation surely to be wished under the circumstances, is the interpretation preferred by Samuel Terrien in his exegesis in *The Interpreter's Bible*, 921.

16. "It is amazing to see how easily Yahweh, quite without reason, had let himself be influenced by one of his sons, by a *doubting thought*, and made unsure of Job's faithfulness. With his touchiness and suspiciousness the mere possibility of doubt was enough to infuriate him and induce that peculiar double-faced behaviour of which he had already given proof in the Garden of Eden, when he pointed out the tree to the First Parents and at the same time forbade them to eat of it. In this way he precipitated the Fall, which he apparently never intended. Similarly, his faithful servant Job is now to be exposed to a rigorous moral test, quite gratuitously and to no purpose, although Yahweh is convinced of Job's faithfulness and constancy, and could moreover have assured himself beyond all doubt on this point had he taken counsel with his own omniscience" (C.G. Jung, *Answer to Job*, 375).

LOIS E. BUELER

# The Don Juan Plot

In *Clarissa*, Richardson's conscious adherence to the Tested Woman Plot is unmistakable. But while this plot accounts for much that is both distinctive and unexpected in the novel, it cannot adequately account for Lovelace. It does not explain his relationship with Morden or the manner of his death. Nor does it explain why, when his plot purpose is lost, he can neither change his function nor quit the story. The problem is not merely that in Lovelace Richardson has conceived a most compelling Tempter. It is that the plot in which Clarissa finds herself seems not to be precisely the plot of which Lovelace believes himself a part.

I think that in a sense this explanation is accurate. In addition to the Tested Woman Plot, Clarissa exhibits the pull of another entire structure, the Don Juan Plot. The Don Juan Plot is no mere rake's progress, any more than the Tested Woman Plot is simply the story of a woman abused. As a genuine plot, it exhibits a strong coherence of both events and character types. And the feature that most accounts for Lovelace's treatment is that its Tempter protagonist maintains his singularity to the point of, even in despite of, death. But Richardson seems to handle the Don Juan Plot less masterfully than the older structure, perhaps because it is comparatively simplistic and lacks the rich variety of the testing plot, perhaps because it is innately less well suited to his positive didactic purposes. Some of the difficulties of *Clarissa* stem from the cross-purposes set up by his attempt to graft the Tested Woman Plot with a plot which is its structural antitype.

Unlike the truly venerable Tested Woman Plot, the Don Juan Plot is

From *Clarissa's* Plots. © 1994 by Associated University Presses, Inc.

essentially an Enlightenment artifact. The first literary version, Tirso de Molina's play *El Burlador de Sevilla*, was published in 1630. The story was immediately popular, especially among dramatists, and renditions, the more hackneyed the more typical, were legion. According to Leo Weinstein's study *The Metamorphoses of Don Juan*, in the slightly more than 100 years before *Clarissa* there were thirty-one literary treatments, virtually all of them continental. To modern readers the best known of the pre-Richardson versions is surely Molière's *Dom Juan, ou Le Festin de pierre* (1665). The greatest rendering of the Don Juan Plot, however, is unquestionably the Mozart/Da Ponte *Don Giovanni*. Written and performed in 1787, the opera naturally had no influence on Richardson. But partly because of the structural starkness of opera, partly because it was the last great version uncontaminated by the Romantic glorification of self-aggrandizement, *Don Giovanni* tells us much about the plot's essential structure and, as we will see later, is therefore helpful to our understanding of *Clarissa*.

The one significant English version of the Don Juan Plot before Richardson is Thomas Shadwell's *Libertine*, published in 1676. Its chief virtues are energy and a strict adherence to the already stereotyped plot. Shadwell, who took positive pride in being a hack, vaunts himself in the play's preface on having spent no more than five days writing any of the acts, and from the reading I do not doubt him. *The Libertine* remained part of the standard London stage repertory for decades, enjoyed the additional fame of incidental music written by Henry Purcell for a revival in 1692, and was performed at Drury Lane until as late as 1740. It probably even served as the source for the Don Juan pantomime produced by David Garrick some time before his death in 1779.[1] Richardson is unlikely to have read Tirso, Molière, or other continental Don Juan plays, though he could have heard of them. But he probably read or attended Shadwell's play: Jocelyn Harris ("Richardson," 198–200) catalogues not just the similarities of character and event which we would expect whatever Richardson's source, but verbal echoes of Shadwell which in a few instances go beyond the stageravisher commonplaces. By the time of *Clarissa*'s composition, at any rate, the Don Juan Plot was part of English theatrical lore.

One of the striking features of the Don Juan story, at least in its seventeenth-and eighteenth-century renditions, is its schematic rigidity—hence Shadwell's quickie. The plot always contains three agonistic groups of characters. *Don Juan himself*, the constant focus of the plot, is often abetted by a cluster of fellow rakes and usually accompanied by a servant whom he bullies and patronizes. He preys upon *a succession of woman victims*, both high-born and low-born, against one or two of whom he has especially offended either by promising marriage or by killing the father, the husband, or the betrothed. At the end he faces *the figure of Death*, usually a stone statue representing the slain relative.

These characters are involved in a characteristic, virtually an inevitable, event sequence. Early in the play Juan or his cronies engage in *a defense of libertinage*, which is associated with *a cataloguing of Juan's female victims*. Throughout the first part of the plot, we are entertained with *the alternating seductions of highborn and lowborn women*, and, at some point, *Juan's killing of the male relative of one of the women*. Midway through the story Juan issues *an impious invitation to the statue of the slain man* and the statue comes to life to issue *a counter-invitation*. Juan arrives *at the tomb or crypt* to which he has been invited, where the statue welcomes him in funereal surroundings, often to a stone feast. There, in a swift winding down of the plot, Juan *refuses the statue's demand that he repent*, boldly accepts the *statue's handshake of Death*, and *descends into Hell*.[2]

Because this plot, unlike the Tested Woman Plot, is singlemindedly focused on the protagonist, it is not surprising to find in him the same kind of stereotypicality we find in the plot structure. Two psychological traits are consistently associated with the Don Juan character. One is that Juan is less the lover than the trickster, the "burlador" of Tirso's title. He is conspicuous for his strongly histrionic flair, frequently involving role-playing and costume changes, and for his delight in improvisation. He is typically far more interested in the pleasurable challenges of his devious and often cruelly exploitive pursuits than he is in the sexual pleasure that is his putative goal. Even more famously, Don Juan is marked by his impiety or disregard for Providence, his "libertinage." This trait may take the form, as it does in Tirso's play, of his bold refusal to fear the Divine power in which he professes belief. Or it may appear as the frank unbelief of late Renaissance and Enlightenment freethinking or "atheism": the "Nature, thou art my God" strain of Shadwell's John. In either case, Juan's impiety is related to his abuse of promises, especially the promise of marriage, as a means to seduce. And it accounts for his provocation of Death, for the invitation to the statue, always an impious invitation, comes first from him.

Such in fact is what "libertine" means, to Juan, to Shadwell, and to the Enlightenment. Though in the letters of a real-life Rochester or the dialogue of a stage Horner the sensational (and, I might add, the politically safe) emphasis is on *sexual* libertinism, which is characterized by James Grantham Turner as a *"mélange* of Ovidian seduction-theory and Epicurean philosophy" ("Lovelace," 71), *libertine* is by no means a restrictedly sexual description. More broadly, it names Juan's refusal to be bound by Christian doctrine and moral causality. This trait is reflected at the end of the story in his unflinching willingness to accept the Statue's handshake despite the threat of hellfire. In terms of the event sequence as a whole, his libertinage is reflected in the importance of the issue of promises. Don Juan seduces by promising fidelity, usually marriage. But he never returns. The heart of the matter, one of the features that makes the Don Juan Plot the antitype of the

Tested Woman Plot, is thus the attitude of its protagonist toward contract. The Tested Woman Plot contains a team of male characters who, in a highly synchronized though vigorously agonistic dance, cooperatively act out the common contractual assumptions of a patriarchal society. The Don Juan Plot, by contrast, focuses on a single individual who violates those assumptions. But he violates them by negation, by not holding them. It is not that Don Juan breaks real contracts, it is that he makes specious or phony ones, casually, nonchalantly, as the nonbeliever can blaspheme with nonchalance, there being for him no such thing as blasphemy. It is in this regard especially that Don Juan is the trickster. He is a confidence man, a speculator in phony promises and phony contracts, a professional hypocrite.[3] To the patriarchalist by right of nature (the father) and the patriarchalist by right of contract (the husband) has been added their antitype, the patriarchalist by right of fraud. Thus Juan the libertine is the antitype of Lothario the seducer, who never promised more than pleasure, and who longs to pay what he promised.

Don Juan's attitude toward contract may be understood as an expression of his attitude toward time. Jean Rousset, to whose tight and suggestive structural analysis of the Don Juan myth I am much indebted, calls Don Juan a "paladin of the present moment" (*Le Mythe de Don Juan*, 101) and links his inability to maintain contract with his lack of a sense of continuity:

> A man living only in the present cannot know either past or future, so how can he deliver on what he has promised? At the moment he commits himself, he simply cannot conceive that later he might be called to account. He cannot conjugate the future, it escapes him, because it lies outside the framework of his desire.... And when the future does intrude upon the present, the moment of contract has already been swallowed up in a forgotten past. For Don Juan lacks memory as well as foresight. (100; my translation)[4]

Don Juan's failure to acknowledge the past and future in the present is most marked in his relations with women. But it is manifested everywhere in his human relations. Such at least is the implication of the blackly comic ending of Molière's *Dom Juan*, in which the servant Sganarelle howls his anguish as his master descends into hell: "Mes gages! mes gages!" My wages, my wages: the play ends on the theme of the broken contract. For Don Juan, only the promise to Death is unimpeachable.

Readers have always seen that *Clarissa* shares themes and motifs with the Don Juan story. The most striking involve the characterization of Lovelace himself, some of whose Juanesque features are even exaggerated by the novel's extension. Lovelace's histrionic flair is pronounced: he adopts roles, dons disguises, delights in the improvisation of seductive ploys. Bullying and exploiting his gap-toothed manservant Will, surrounded by his admiring, imitative gang of fellow rakes with whom he exchanges paeons to the life of libertinage, he catalogues and takes a craftsman's credit for the dizzying succession of gentlewomen, shop girls, and innkeepers' daughters who have challenged his attention and his skill. When they are not at hand, he fantasizes: Imagine the triumphant serial seductions of Anna Howe (interfering creature) *and* her mother *and* the maid![5] Or he literally dreams, as when in the Mother H. sequence his concubine Clarissa continues on the warmest of terms with his concubine Anna, and his children by the two women marry "(for neither have dreams regard to *consanguinity*)" in order "to consolidate their mamas' friendships" (L271, [20 June], 922). Such self-congratulatory *sprezzatura* is pure Don Juan, and it is one of the triumphs of Richardson's art. He is not finally writing a Don Juan novel, but in this regard he has created the most typical and unquestionably the most attractive Juan in literature.

One thing Lovelace is not, however, is an atheist, an unbeliever. As Leo Weinstein reminds us (*The Metamorphoses of Don Juan*, 18–19), Tirso's type specimen is no atheist either; believing in the risk, nay the certainty, of eternal damnation, he runs it with bold aplomb. But by the mid-eighteenth century the issue of religious libertinage was so closely associated with the Don Juan figure that Richardson went out of his way to protect himself from its charges and to deny Lovelace its taint. Richardson protests as much in the postscript to the third edition: "But the reader must have observed that, great, and, it is hoped, good use, has been made throughout the work, by drawing Lovelace an infidel, only in practice, ... " And Richardson goes on to remind the reader of Clarissa's consolation to herself that "'he is not an infidel, an unbeliever,'" which means that she can continue to remain hopeful on his behalf. Richardson knows, as does Clarissa, that if Lovelace were a religious libertine he could not keep it to himself: "It must be observed that scoffers are too witty in their own opinion (in other words, value themselves too much upon their profligacy), to aim at concealing it."[6]

Nevertheless Richardson protests too much, is obliged to do so because the theme of the abuse of contract figures so strongly in his portrayal. The Lovelace Richardson has created is a man who does not comprehend moral causality. He can abuse the promise of marriage by the subtleties of pretense, implication, and plausible denial because like Don Juan he is incapable of genuine contract with a woman. He acknowledges as much to Belford: "It would be strange if I kept my word—In love-cases, I mean; for as to the rest, I am an honest moral man, as all who know me can testify" (L 439, 26 Aug., 1270). We are entitled to our doubts about Lovelace's honesty with regard to "the rest." Concerning "love-cases" we can have no doubts; we know that the succession of seductions which preeminently characterizes the Don Juan

stalls with Clarissa only because she is unattainable on the only terms
Lovelace knows with women. No matter what he had promised, were she
snivelingly acquiescent or even adoringly compliant she would be a mere
number in the ledger; he would instantly move on. This is one of the
underlying psychological reasons why *Clarissa* is not a courtship story. To the
degree that he partakes of the Don Juan type, Lovelace does not hold the
same psychological ground toward contract as those around him. Lovelace
does not truly court Clarissa, unlike Solmes, who truly does court her (that
is the horror), or Hickman, who truly courts Miss Howe. Lovelace perverts
the gestures and language of courtship with their implications of contract,
and he perverts even formal contract itself. When after the rape Clarissa
holds up the marriage license to him (L 260, RL to JB, [15 June], 887), she
is not attempting to hold him to a promise. She is not begging for marriage,
as she makes unequivocally plain the moment her wits are hers to command
(L 263, RL to JB, 18 June], 901): *"The man who has been the villain to me you
have been, shall never make me his wife."* Instead she is signaling her belated
understanding of the total fraudulence of his language of commitment.

Actually Richardson wants to have it both ways. By maintaining that
Lovelace is a practicing rather than a professing atheist, Richardson is
arguing that his unbelief is psychological rather than theological. This is
precisely Richardson's point about him throughout—and Clarissa's and
eventually Belford's point. Lovelace has no emotional, no psychological,
teleology, no sense that a person's mental and emotional habits build upon
themselves to construct the creature he becomes. Especially is this true
regarding death, whether his own or that of others. Because people prepare
their ends by the way they have lived, worthy preparation requires
consciousness of an ending. Belford contrasts the deathbed terrors of Belton
and Mother Sinclair with his own moral reformation and Clarissa's beatific
passing in order to lift his friend beyond the solipsistically compelling
moment and educate him into a sense of spiritual causality. It is not a point
that takes with Lovelace. Commenting on Belton's guilt over causing the
death of the brother of a woman he seduced, Lovelace excoriates the
messenger: "Why didst thou not comfort the poor man about the rencounter
between him and that poltroon Metcalfe? He acted in that affair like a man
of true honour, and as I should have acted in the same circumstances. Tell
him I say so, and what happened he could neither help nor foresee" (L 422,
23 Aug.). As for foreseeing his own responsibility, though he accepts first
grudgingly, then hysterically, that Clarissa's death is somehow his doing, he
hopes that his own unlooked-for death will balance and thereby expiate it.
That hope reads very much like the last of his improvisational quickchange
schemes.

The portrayal of Lovelace's moral psychology represents Richardson at
work upon some of the most promising material of the Don Juan character.

Every Richardsonian innovation deepens and complicates Juan's nature. For instance, Lovelace differs conspicuously from the type specimen in the staying power he brings to his intrigue with Clarissa. The typical Don Juan seduction—the sighting, the subterfuges, the pitch, the conquest—is over in a mere moment; from night to night, we are to believe, Juan moves from woman to woman, not merely because his inevitable success allows him to do so, but because he is too impatient, too mercurial, to do otherwise. As Lovelace says it, "Variety has irresistible charms. I cannot live without variety" (L 261,16 June, 897).[7] This character trait is influenced in part by genre. It is all very well for critics to speak Juan's philosophical entrapment in the present, but such an emphasis on the momentary and the instantaneous is also an economical literary means for making the dramatic point about his prowess. The two-hour play, especially if contaminated by the specious demands of the dramatic unities, will often attempt to get its drive from frenetic repetition of the act itself. It is a quick and dirty way to write the commercial dramatic property, and we see Shadwell embracing it with gusto. Richardson, however, reveling in the leisure and extension of his enormous novel, brings us a Juan uncharacteristically patient in design, with uncharacteristic wind and bottom for the chase, a Juan who seems to enjoy delaying as much as pressing his suit. Telling Belford how much he craves variety, Lovelace can go on to assuage that craving by reveling in a new scheme to redeploy the Widow Bevis and the rest of the Hampstead crew. If we are examining the capacity to understand and control human behavior, Lovelace is a character for whom the causality of intrigue and enforcement has the most constant fascination.

Which is why his moral emptiness is so strange, and for Clarissa so deceiving. For months and months, she simply cannot comprehend that a man of such wit, such imaginative élan, such an ability to imitate the various passions and behaviors of others, such control and patience and staying power, can remain so unchanged by what he does. It is as though he has no life other than the life of his various roles and intrigues and seduction ploys. And there we have an explanation of Richardson's technique. Within Lovelace's theatrical life, so to speak—within his life in the Don Juan role— there is past and future aplenty. But there is nothing beyond that role, with the result that nothing he performs really matters to him morally or spiritually. Lovelace is an infidel only in practice because the practice, the stage role, is all there is. Richardson has gained his literary effect by lifting the most histrionic of characters from drama into the novel, elaborating him in all the ways novelistic extension allows, yet never releasing him from his theatrical bondage to the eternal present. It is this bondage that is finally the source of his existential despair.[8]

James Grantham Turner makes clear that Lovelace's bondage is typical of the double bind of the Enlightenment libertine in general. The libertine sexual code was a double program of indulgence in the life of the senses and of tactically intricate and method-driven mastery of women. Supposedly spontaneous behavior was coupled with set procedures designed to prove fixed maxims: that women like "an uncontrollable passion," that they want to be seduced and even raped by men of "violent spirit," that the greatest prudes are the greatest lechers, that "every woman is at heart a rake." The paradox, says Turner, is that this "experimental and tendentious approach to seduction ... undermines the libertine's claim to originality. The intense assertion of individual rebellion and individual libido turns out to be quite conformist, since it aims to prove an existing theory, an established (if scandalous) ideology of female submission and female arousal. It confirms a script already written" ("Lovelace," 72). The libertine's entrapment in the already written script extends far beyond his sexual behavior. Turner cites Claude Reichler's suggestion that "the central problem of libertinism, once it had rejected traditional religious beliefs, was to maintain an authentic self in a world increasingly constituted by 'representations'. Reichler traces the oscillation of the libertine character between two extreme positions—a fierce individualism that underestimated the power of social forces, and a compliance to social conventions which, though intended to be ironic and self-liberating, eventually traps the self within the mask."[9] In Lovelace Richardson has vividly dramatized this self-defeating libertine code.

In this discussion of Richardson's use of the Don Juan Plot, I have thus far commented on striking aspects of theme and characterization. A plot structure is more than a collection of themes and character traits, however, or even of discrete events. A plot has an inevitable direction. With the same compulsion by which the Tested Woman Plot seeks judgment of the woman, the Don Juan Plot seeks not just the challenge of women but the challenge to Death. The type story—and the plot logic—drives toward a confrontation with the supernatural that annihilates the protagonist. This plot feature seems strongly linked with the phenomenon of Juan's histrionic entrapment. H.G. Tan (*La Matière de Don Juan*, 113–17) points out that the essence of the Don Juan story is the act itself—even the act repeated—rather than language about or contemplation of the act. This is why the Don Juan story is uniquely at home in drama rather than fiction, in fact at home in drama of a very particular style and pacing. The act in question is the act of seduction, during which for the fleetest of moments Juan escapes from himself by his participation in the desire of another. But since her seduction transforms the woman into his mere adjunct, his creature, it is an act that can only be repeated with someone new. Hence the typical sequentially introduced cast of female characters in the typical Don Juan play. The typical way to put an end to this progression is by means of death, for the exquisitely simple reason that there is no other way off the existential treadmill. In fact Juan typically goes to his death by literally falling off the stage through the trap door.

Another way to stop the treadmill would be to have Don Juan fall genuinely in love. But although such a plot move is the frequent recourse of the nineteenth century, it bears no relation to what the original Don Juan story is about. If Juan were able to repose his confidence in an other, if he could have faith in her otherness instead of seeking to possess and destroy it, he would not be the mechanical man he is. In his momentary accesses of conscience, Lovelace knows this: "To be *excelled by a WIFE.... To take lessons, to take instructions*, from a WIFE!—.... I am so goaded on—Yet 'tis poor too, to think myself a machine—I am *no* machine—Lovelace, thou art base to thyself, but to *suppose* thyself a machine" (L 202, 23 May, 658). But Juan the libertine, the infidel, the everlastingly self-creating man of the original plot, cannot have faith. "So now, Belford, as thou hast said, I am a machine at last, and no free agent" (L 246, 10 June, 848). He challenges Death because it is the only way to bring about his own release.

Now Jean Rousset denies that Lovelace is a Don Juan figure because he has not fought with Death—"il [se] manque d'avoir combattu contre le Mort" (*Le Mythe de Don Juan*, 17). Rousset is correct to see the challenge to Death as the signature event of the Don Juan Plot. He is wrong, however, to deny its presence in *Clarissa*. Richardson has a realistic novel to conduct, one that hardly lends itself to talking statues or stage traps opening over Hell Mouth. But the key elements of the Don Juan Plot's conclusion do appear, some of them intriguingly displaced for the sake of realistic psychological demonstration.

In the Don Juan Plot, with its economy of male roles and plot moves, the lethal fight with the protecting male relative directly sets up the encounter with Death because it makes possible the dead man's metamorphosis into the stone statue. In *Clarissa*, the fight with the relative actually precedes the novel's opening, since Lovelace has had his duel with Brother James before Miss Howe's first letter. Only James's self-esteem is slain in the encounter, though that death is enough to ruin the peace of the Harlowe family forever. James is too contemptible to stand as the figure of Death, however, and besides, the Tested Woman Plot has used him up elsewhere. This then is where the seemingly incompletely used Morden comes in. His name, like those of Lovelace and Clarissa, announces his symbolic meaning. He is the representation of Death, the character whom Lovelace will be compelled by his despair to encounter. Lovelace's psyche knows this with a certainty terrible in its prescience. The dream he recounts to Belford in his letter of 22 August (L417, 1218–9) plays out the funereal final sequence of the Don Juan Plot. In the dream we have the assembled family members dressed in mourning, the supernatural appearance of Morden, his demand for Lovelace's repentance, Lovelace's refusal, the opening of the floor and Lovelace's descent into Eldon. As in the Don Juan story, so in the dream Morden does not kill, for the fight that Lovelace attempts as one man with another is prevented. Morden is catalyst only, the sign of the presence of Death which is the occasion by which Lovelace passes to judgment.

In the novel's realistic denouement, however, Morden does kill. It is a puzzling ending to the Tested Woman Plot, since it is an ending specifically forbidden by Clarissa herself, the terms of whose death and will have become a sacred trust to Morden as well as Belford. The Tested Woman Plot, after all, seeks judgment of the woman and reconciliation among the family; nothing done to Lovelace will aid in either. But grafting Don Juanesque elements onto the story has given Lovelace a plot of his own to which he may respond beyond or even despite the exigencies of Clarissa's story. So it is with his death. Not that Morden pursues him. Morden simply makes himself available, on the Continent where a duel may be more easily arranged than in England and where national borders offer escape, and Lovelace finally cannot but seek him out. The initial approach comes from Lovelace, as it must: "I have heard, with a great deal of surprise, that you have thought fit to throw out some menacing expressions against me" (L. 534.1, 10–21 Nov., 1479). The subsequent exchanges lead with stately scrupulosity to the dueling ground. As in Don Juan's encounter with the Statue, impetuous improvisation has no place here; no pickup match just because the principals happen to find themselves surveying the field. And no broken faith either. The challenge to Death has for Lovelace, as for Don Juan, an unimpeachable seriousness unavailable to him in his relations with women. Not that Lovelace expected to die, the French valet assures Belford. We however know differently, we and Lovelace's psyche. We know that the Tested Woman Plot has no more use for him, and the Don Juan Plot only this one end.

The Don Juan Plot focuses almost claustrophobically on its protagonist, which means that it teaches us most about Lovelace. But it also teaches us about Clarissa because it corroborates our understanding of the way the Tested Woman Plot responds to his plot. Which means, of course, how he chooses to seduce and she to refuse. To examine the relationship of seduction and refusal in the light of the Don Juan Plot, I wish to invoke the evidence of Mozart's opera. The fact that opera as a genre has little space for anything but music means that plot and characters are trimmed to their essentials. What the Da Ponte libretto chooses to regard as essential especially illuminates the plot's female characters, and thus the plot possibilities open to a Clarissa. Don Juan is the seducer of hundreds of women. Most versions of the plot, as for instance Molière's, characterize at least four, giving thereby the illusion of infinite numbers. *Don Giovanni*, however, has only three characterized women, giving thereby the impression of the closed set. Operatically, the reason has to do with manipulating the limited number of naturally available vocal slots and creating optimal musical configurations and partnerships. But a deeper dramatic economy seems to be operating. The three women of *Don Giovanni* embody three forms of female obsession, counterparts to the three styles wherewith Don Juan brings women to the point of submission. Clarissa is pressed by Lovelace to succumb to the temptations of all three of these forms. It is these women's obsessions—the "idols of the Don Juan Plot"—that she comes specifically to understand and to refuse.

The first is the temptation of the flattery of power. This is Don Giovanni's way with the peasant Zerlina—the generic lower-class woman. It is Don Juan's only way with lower-class women; hence the psychological redundancy of Molière's second peasant. Flattery is always a power move, which is why it rarely occurs between equals. Flattery practiced by a superior on an inferior, further, always combines a promise and a threat: that such a man as Il Cavaliere desires such a woman as Zerlina promises to enhance her, does enhance her, but the power to enhance carries with it a reminder of the power to ruin. Such flattery is one of Lovelace's styles as well. The possibility of marriage need not be part of the enhancing and threatening attention he bestows—no one pretends in the Rosebud episode that it is—but with Clarissa the prospect of marriage is part of the campaign. Clarissa is expected to be flattered by Lovelace's attention. Arabella and the rest of the Harlowes are. They are also fearful of Lovelace's social power, since his capacity to flatter reflects hierarchical position: it arises from perceived inequality. The fact that marriage is socially acceptable between the socially unequal Clarissa and Lovelace represents one of the most brilliant moves on Richardson's part, for that possibility makes the seeming obligation of Clarissa to marry her violator all the stronger—as Lovelace knows. The world would regard marriage as a social as well as moral victory for Clarissa. How could anyone lose—so long as the will to marriage proceeds from the one in power?

The second temptation for the women in Mozart's opera is the temptation of passion, Don Giovanni's way with Donna Elvira. Elvira's bitterness is palpable—she cannot reconcile herself to having been wooed, won, and abandoned—but her consuming passion is not the desire for vengeance but a cruelly masochistic love. When she experiences renewed hope that Giovanni loves her, it is because Leporello, in the costume of his master, has been assigned to court her as a diversionary measure. She pours out her soul to a servant and a mask, and is again both caught and cheated. But Don Giovanni does not want Elvira; he has had her. For him, the awakening of her capacity for passion is merely one style of seduction. This style is part of Lovelace's enterprise as well. Though he commences his courtship of Clarissa intent primarily upon flattery and compulsively attentive to the slights her family has visited upon him, as he begins to understand her complexity and self-containment he turns to the awakening of passion as his putative central goal. That she is cold and he will thaw her, that she is reluctant and he will make her willing and then eager and finally utterly dependent, becomes increasingly his fantasy. The rape belongs in part to this second style of seduction and obsession because Lovelace designs it as a form of sexual tutelage and when it does not take even proposes to perform it again on a fully conscious victim.

The third temptation of the opera, represented by Donna Ana, is the temptation of vengeance for the rape attempt and her father's death. We know next to nothing about the rape attempt except what we learn subsequently about Ana's family and situation: she had a father; she has a fiancé who loved and honored her father; she did not know Don Giovanni; she was broken in upon by him; she fought off his attack and her screams sent him running; her father met him, and death, in the courtyard; she and Ottavio vow vengeance. Ana is the woman indifferent alike to the temptations of position and passion. The rape was designed to break through her indifference, but it failed. Yet Giovanni takes her too—in fact, her bondage is more long-lived than that of either of the other women, for as the opera ends she requires of Ottavio a year of wan abstinence while she completes her psychological recuperation. How has Don Giovanni managed her seduction? He killed her father as recompense for the failure of the rape, it is true, but that death gave Giovanni himself no satisfaction. And while it punishes Ana, it does not control her—unless she allows it to. But allows it she does. Vengeance becomes her fixation. Lovelace's motive for rape is likewise in part the motive of Clarissa's perceived indifference: this she cannot ignore! Though from his viewpoint rape has its uses in furthering the style of flattery (now she must admit my generous offer of marriage) and in furthering the style of the awakening of passion (now she knows what sex is and will want more), Clarissa herself comes during the last few weeks of her life to perceive the danger of the rape primarily in terms of this third category of obsession. If she allows herself to become obsessed by the desire for vengeance, the rape will be a recurrent event and Lovelace will possess her indeed.

Again and again we have seen how Lovelace's real agenda, to force Clarissa's hand, her body, her will, underlies his pretense to persuasion. "What does it mean to persuade?" asks Paul Ricoeur. "What distinguishes persuasion from flattery, from seduction, from threat—that is to say, from the subtlest forms of violence?" (*The Rule of Metaphor*, 11). That distinction is what Clarissa must learn to make. Those "subtlest forms of violence" are exactly what Don Juan practices, which is why understanding his plot helps us understand hers.

At the beginning of this chapter I described the Don Juan Plot as the structural antitype of the Tested Woman Plot. We are now in a position to see how this antithesis works psychologically, and how Richardson attempts to take advantage of it. In the bald plot terms of character function and event sequence, the Tested Woman Plot is antithetical first because of its focus on one woman. Thus *Clarissa* lacks the unending sequentiality of Don Juan's women. These women people Lovelace's past, to be sure, but his present becomes compulsively focused on Clarissa. Here we have Richardson's technical method for crossing the two plots, a method which ends the unending sequentiality of female characters while continuing the endless attempts at seduction. For, says Richardson's novel, suppose Don Juan were to meet an unattainable woman? The result would not be love, exactly; it would be a frustrating of the capacity to move on. By definition Don Juan the seducer never loses and never gives up. But suppose that, without losing, he could nevertheless not win? Suppose he were forced, not to move on to the next woman, but to move always back to the same woman, so that the infinite variety of technique—which he and we enjoy the most but cannot see to its full effect because the shift in prey obscures it—were to become the heart of the presentation of his character? Were this to occur, we would have a perfect meeting of plots, for just as Don Juan returns again and again to the attempt, the Tested Woman is again and again attemptable. The most mesmerizing feature of *Clarissa* lies here, in the variety with which Lovelace acts out his single compulsion.

But no dramatic action can remain so poised forever and Richardson unbalances it by showing us the terror of psychic entropy. Even success, Lovelace intuits, would turn pale: "The worst respecting myself in the case before me, is that my triumph, when completed, will be so glorious a one, that I shall never be able to keep up to it. All my future attempts must be poor to this" (L 171, [3 May], 559). But the actual worst turns out to be the absence of that completed triumph. Suppose that Don Juan began to lose his capacity to recreate himself because he began to sense that while he cannot win at what is his game, he cannot stand to move on without winning? And cannot change the game, because to do so would be to change his nature? "If I give up my contrivances, my joy in stratagem, and plot, and invention, I shall be but a common man" (L 264, 19 June, 907). Yet suppose he cannot tolerate any longer the situation he is in, because it has come to resemble stasis, and stasis is against his nature? For the actor must act, or he ceases to exist. What then?

Then he can rape. To Don Juan, rape is intended as a form of seduction. It is seduction by means of the language of the body and it is predicated on the assumption of his irresistibility. He does not see, or he pretends not to see, that it is violation. He believes, or pretends to believe, that it is merely the most forceful and passionate expression of the source of his essential attraction, his desire. If he can only bring that essence home to the woman, she will despite her misery consider herself blessed—for to be the object of desire is to be blessed. Then he can at last move on, unless stopped by that force external to the woman which is death. In play after play, this is the way the Don Juan Plot goes. But that plot shape is possible only if a certain notion of integrity, from which stems the notion of violation, has lost its centrality.

Imagine however that at a certain moment in the eighteenth century this new plot finds itself coupled to the Tested Woman Plot, in which the ideas of integrity and violation remain central, so that the woman whom Juan attempts is precisely the prototypal tested woman. And imagine that when Juan employs his ultimate tool of seduction—rape—he discovers that although stasis has been broken, it has not been in the direction of seduction at all, which would make him all-important to the woman, but in the direction of its opposite, the removal of the woman from his sphere of influence. We know that though the Tested Woman Plot requires the figure of the Tempter, for the woman cannot be tested unless he is present and active, it requires him only during the testing action itself. The Test completed, he loses his function. Once her plot moves into the Trial action, the Tempter has only historic interest. The rape, in short, signals "end of Test" but it also signals "end of Tempter." It is not that the Tempter has lost the woman, for he may never have had her. It is that he has lost the action to another action that has no room for him. The Tested Woman Plot has moved into its second phase, which Don Juan never recognized as the purpose of the first action, and he made it happen. The drama will continue but it will not be his drama; he can get back into it only by changing his function.

To the typical Renaissance Tempter of the Tested Woman Plot, the function change we are describing is not felt as existential trauma because the "character" and the "function" are different matters. Sometimes, the play needing a certain function, it creates for the purpose a character who is dropped when the function is dropped. At other times, in the interests of dramatic economy, one of the characters already in the plot gets to perform a certain function. Such a character does not define himself by his function, he takes on that function. It is not that he is Tempter, but that he plays the Tempter and so long as he does so behaves in certain ways. But in the Don Juan Plot the protagonist *is* the Tempter. His plot is supposed to honor his centrality and to remain his until his death. It is a plot both about how he does not change because he cannot change, and about how he does not have to change because his essential nature is what controls his plot and carries it to its necessary conclusion.

Take Don Juan's plot away from him and what happens? He can do what Lovelace does: flail about in an attempt to find a place for himself. Lovelace tries out a dizzying variety of plot continuations, none of which really carries conviction. Intermittently and halfheartedly he proposes to resume his Juanesque game by pretending that because he has raped Clarissa he has seduced her and is now free to go on to other women. But this move is stymied by her refusal to be seduced, even seduced by the compulsion to seek revenge.[10] More determinedly, Lovelace tries to pretend that Clarissa is still psychologically susceptible to him so that he can plan concubinage or marriage as the next state to which she is to be reduced. But this does not work because she is no longer psychologically available. Or he can attempt to take on one of the functions available in the Trial action of the Tested Woman Plot, acting as Defender against those who would maintain her fault or make her miserable because of it. Lovelace repeatedly attempts a specious version of this move, ranging from the mad demand for Clarissa's heart and bowels to charges against her family, recriminations against Belford, and protestations of the power of his remorse. But because the Defender must seek and speak truth, whereas Lovelace cannot see the truth either about himself or about Clarissa, this move does not work either. His remaining option is to carry out the conclusion of the Don Juan Plot, the point of which is existential annihilation. This is what Lovelace does, inviting the encounter with Morden who leads him to Death.

In so describing Lovelace we are describing failure. This failure is surprising, almost tantalizing, because it seems not just a moral failure but a failure of the artistic imagination in a character who seems in some ways the consummately imaginative artist. Despite his increasing at-least-purported willingness to encounter Clarissa on her own terms, Lovelace cannot bring her or his relationship to her into any kind of accurate focus. He never manages to see and describe, for more than a few sentences at a time, what is actually there. Iris Murdoch might be thinking of him when she sees the moral problem and the imaginative problem as essentially the same: "The chief enemy of excellence in morality (and also in art) is personal fantasy: the tissue of self-aggrandizing and consoling wishes and dreams which prevents one from seeing what is there outside one" ("On 'God' and 'Good'," 78). Such is the case with Lovelace, whose personal fantasy cripples and finally destroys not just his morals but his art.

## NOTES

1. See Montague Summers's introduction to *The Libertine* in *The Complete Works of Thomas Shadwell*, 3, 11–14.

2. In *Le Mythe de Don Juan*, Jean Rousset provides the most interesting and thorough analysis of the structural elements of the Don Juan Plot; my description is based largely on his distinctions and terminology. Leo Weinstein's *The Metamorphoses of Don Juan* summarizes and analyzes the major versions of the story and provides a catalogue of works based on the Don Juan plot. I am indebted, here and throughout this chapter, to them both.

3. H.G. Tan, *La Matière de Don Juan et les genres littéraires*, 52–53, points out the importance of the theme of "la dénonciation de l'hypocrisie" in Molière's version of the Don Juan story.

4. Rousset *(Le Mythe de Don Juan*, 101): "un paladin de l'instantané";(100): 'L'homme livré au seul présent ne se connaît ni passé ni avenir, comment tiendrait-il ce qu'il a promis? Il ne conçoit pas, au moment où il s'engage, qu'on puisse lui en demander compte plus tard; le futur est un temps qu'il ne sait pas conjuguer, qui échappe à sa compétence, parce qu'il renvoie au-delà de son désir actual; ... Et quand ce futur se réalise inopinément dans le présent, l'engagement remonte à un passé déjà tombé dans l'oubli. Don Juan n'a pas plus de mémoire que de prévision" (100).

5. [Thursday, 25 May], Lovelace to Belford—This letter appeared first in the third edition of 1751, though it was summarized by Richardson in editions one and two. Ross, who does not print the letter but does give it a number, argues (16–17) that it was actually written for, but omitted from, the first edition. It appears in the AMS edition as Letter 42, vol. 4 (252–61), and in the Everyman edition as Letter 109, vol. 2 (418–25).

6. *Postscript*, AMS ed., vol. 8 (291–92); Everyman ed., vol. 4 (559–60).

7. Jean Rousset, arguing that the essential Don Juan, the Don Juan of drama, can be characterized as "l'improvisateur contre la permanence" *(Le Mythe de Don Juan*, 95–103), emphasizes his trait of working to the moment rather than to plan, of seizing the target of opportunity: "Don Juan ... brûle d'impatience, il conquiert à la hâte, il court d'une proie à l'autre; pressé de prendre et de passer, il ne se donne ni le temps ni la peine de projeter à froid, de méditer ses rapts; peu doué pour la prévision et les longues trames, il attaque parce que l'occasion l'entraîne. C'est la rencontre imprévue, c'est la chance de l'instant qui décident pour lui" (96). ("Don Juan ... burns with impatience, he conquers in haste, he rushes from one prey to another; compelled to hit and run, he devotes neither time nor energy to thinking ahead or deliberating his assaults. Lacking foresight, unequipped by nature for the long haul, he attacks because an opportunity presents itself. The unexpected encounter, the luck of the moment, decides it all"—my translation.)

8. Though beginning from a rather different perspective, Cynthia Griffin Wolff arrives at a similar description of the incoherence of Lovelace's character: "At first the reader may be deluded—believing, with Clarissa, that the disguises merely serve to hide the real Lovelace from our view. As the novel progresses, however, we gradually come to realize that there is no real Lovelace behind the mask, that the mask itself is Lovelace, and that the formlessness of his nature, the very absence of a coherent identity, makes it impossible for him to limit himself by engaging in any social role" *(Samuel Richardson and the Eighteenth-Century Puritan Character*, 105).

9. J.G. Turner, "Lovelace and the Paradoxes of Libertinism," 73–74. Claude Reichler's work is *L'Age libertin* (Paris: Minuit, 1987).

10. Terry Eagleton remarks that Clarissa's most demoralizing double bind is "the truth that it is not so easy to distinguish resistance to power from collusion with it," and he goes on, "Few people are likely to bulk larger in a woman's life than the man who has raped her...." This is why, as I have argued, Clarissa's refusal of the seduction of revenge is so important: "What will finally strike Lovelace impotent ... is the fact that he cannot secure Clarissa's collusion" *(The Rape of Clarissa*, 82–83).

DAVID E. HOEGBERG

# Caesar's Toils:
# Allusion and Rebellion
# in *Oroonoko*

But those who came prepared for the business enclosed him on every
side, with their naked daggers in their hands. Which way soever he
turned he met with blows, and saw their swords levelled at his face and
eyes, and was encompassed, like a wild beast in the toils, on every side.[1]

Plutarch's "Life of Caesar"

Included in the new sixth edition of the *Norton Anthology of English Literature*,
Aphra Behn's *Oroonoko* has passed a literary milestone, raising anew the
question of how it fits into and plays against the literary "canon" it is more
and more coming to inhabit. While *Oroonoko*'s literary indebtedness has often
been noticed, critics have seldom examined how specific literary allusions
contribute to the novel's structure and meaning.[2] Citing English heroic drama
and French romance as immediate precursors of Behn's work, they view her
either as slavishly derivative or as holding a politically conservative ideology.[3]
One view produces a picture of Behn as a marginally competent artist
following older models, while the other ignores the possibility that Behn's use
of convention might be in part subversive. Its subversion does not lie,
however, in portraying successful rebellions against those in power—
Oroonoko and Imoinda are defeated both at home and abroad—but in
revealing the mechanisms by which power operates, including both physical
force and subtle forms of mental or psychological control.[4]

Robert Chibka has already done extensive work on the role of deceit by
whites in manipulating Oroonoko,[5] but consciously crafted deceit is only one

From *Eighteenth-Century Fiction*, vol. 7, no. 3 (April 1995). © 1995 by McMaster University.

form of mental control. I would like to extend Chibka's work to consider the role of plot in the novel's structures of domination, not only the plot of *Oroonoko* itself, but the way it alludes to and incorporates pre-existing classical narrative models, especially those of Achilles and Julius Caesar. At every stage of his life, Oroonoko is dominated by texts that shape his career in ways he cannot control.[6] While his authority to act as an independent being is wrested from him, the authorship of his life story is complicated by literary allusions so that questions of constraint and freedom become wrapped up with questions of literary indebtedness and originality. In *Oroonoko*, the allusions form a supplement to Behn's text that deepens the analysis of power and its problems. If the main plot tells the story of Oroonoko's struggles against the old king, the English captain, and Byam, the allusions—and the processes of mental control they suggest—tell a story of Oroonoko's struggle against less tangible forces of ideology and belief.

To read Behn's allusions as more than literary homage or political nostalgia we must look beyond the standard heroic qualities associated with each character. When considered in a static or synchronic mode, warrior heroes such as Achilles and Caesar, by virtue of their fighting skill and devotion to honour, often become symbols of aristocratic male virtue. The synchronic view, however, may ignore the narratives or plots that place the hero in relation to other characters and in cultural, geographical, and historical contexts that add complexity to the messages or implied ideologies of the story. (In the *Iliad*, for example, Achilles comes to question some aspects of the aristocratic system he represents. Should he not, therefore, be seen as a symbol of radicalism as well as a warrior hero?) The diachronic view acknowledges contextual elements—webs of relations and changes over time—that make characters more than "stock" figures. The potential for complexity is compounded when heroic narratives become the models or scripts for another character's behaviour, since the weaving of one narrative into another increases the number of contextual variables affecting the "meaning" of the allusion.[7] The allusions can thus be seen as sites of ideological struggle and not only as examples of the dominant ideology against which struggle is mounted.[8]

Before I discuss the first heroic allusion in *Oroonoko*, let me illustrate the more general process of mental control that forms one of the novel's central concerns. Oroonoko's native culture in Coramantien instils in him several important values that function like scripts to limit and shape his actions. We learn that Oroonoko and Imoinda are required by custom to inform the king of their intent to marry: "There is a certain Ceremony in these cases to be observ'd ... 'twas concluded on both sides, that in obedience to him, the Grandfather was to be first made acquainted with the Design: For they pay a most absolute Resignation to the Monarch, especially when he is a Parent also."[9] The respect they are obliged to pay is accompanied by, or encoded in, a "Ceremony" or model for action, while the king's power arises in part from his ability to manipulate such scripts for his own ends. Influenced by his "Court-Flatterers," he decides he wants Imoinda for himself and turns to another cultural custom, the "Royal Veil" or "Ceremony of Invitation," by which any woman he chooses is "secur'd for the King's Use; and 'tis Death to disobey; besides, held a most impious Disobedience" (p. 140).

In these scenes Behn describes the actions of both parties as tied to ritualized narrative or diachronic patterns known within the culture. Furthermore, these patterns have a certain power over the participants that can override their resistance to specific rulers and events.[10] Oroonoko and Imoinda fall automatically into the "ceremony" of obedience to the king, with no thought that this may be against their interests ultimately. The king takes a more consciously manipulative approach, assessing his interests first and then choosing an appropriate "ceremony." A combination of custom and the king's desire—internal belief and external political power—forms the text that ensures Oroonoko's romantic misery. The intangible bonds hold him more securely than physical bonds, as he recognizes when he cries:

> were she in wall'd Cities, or confin'd from me in Fortifications of
> the greatest Strength; did Inchantments or Monsters detain her
> from me; I would venture thro' any Hazard to free her; But here,
> in the Arms of a feeble old Man, my Youth, my violent Love, my
> Trade in Arms, and all my vast Desire of Glory, avail me nothing.
> (p. 142)

The old man's strength lies in his political power, which is linked to his symbolic place within the cultural belief system, and against this Oroonoko is restrained by his own virtuous will, which shuns "impious Disobedience." Even the king's death would not free him from the bonds of custom:

> If I would wait tedious Years; till Fate should bow the old King to
> his Grave, even that would not leave me *Imoinda* free; but still
> that Custom that makes it so vile a Crime for a Son to marry his
> Father's Wives or Mistresses, would hinder my Happiness; unless
> I would either ignobly set an ill Precedent to my Successors, or
> abandon my Country, and fly with her to some unknown World
> who never heard our Story. (pp. 142–43)

Oroonoko sees that he can gain Imoinda only by escaping custom through criminal acts, thus becoming a social outsider, or by fleeing to another "World," something he will do, though not by choice.

Despite his inclination towards obedience, Oroonoko rebels against the king by planning to see Imoinda in secret, but his arrangements are neither well designed nor effective. He is caught making love to Imoinda when he might have been wiser to use the time to escape and, although he has the opportunity to bring her away with him when the king's guards retreat, he leaves her to be punished for his crime.

Oroonoko's motives are hard to fathom here. Even when he chooses rebellion, there is something that steers him towards acquiescence to the king's power, and when he breaks laws, he does not go far enough to secure Imoinda for himself. The outcome of his ill-planned rebellion, therefore, is that Imoinda is more than ever lost to him. Could he not have anticipated this result? Why did he not mount a military coup or escape with her when he had the chance? Such questions can be answered by arguing that it is Behn not Oroonoko who is inept: Oroonoko's reasoning is inscrutable because the narrative here is poorly constructed, and it is poorly constructed because the author cares more about setting up the reunion in Surinam than she does about psychological realism.

I prefer to assume that Behn used the long African section of her novel to make some serious points about the nature of political power. Oroonoko's actions become more plausible if we see here the work of a kind of hegemony that keeps his beliefs and choices within the prevailing discourse of power. According to Antonio Gramsci, hegemony is "the 'spontaneous' consent given by the great masses of the population to the general direction imposed on social life by the dominant fundamental group."[11] The word "spontaneous" is in quotation marks because the consent of the masses is not without cause: it is caused by the prestige of the dominant group, that is, by a pervasive belief in the dominant group's superiority and in the superiority of the laws that protect it. Throughout this section of the novel, custom and law work to fulfil the king's desires and to frustrate Oroonoko's, yet Oroonoko acts like one who believes he can achieve no more than an inconsequential and symbolic resistance. Although he may question specific acts of the king, he neither questions nor flees from the system that gives rise to the king's prestige (and his own).

Behn places her allusion to Achilles in the context of Oroonoko's repeated attempts to circumvent the king's authority without assaulting the underlying belief system. The king sells Imoinda into slavery but tells Oroonoko that he has killed her. Oroonoko's response to the news of Imoinda's "death" is to withdraw from warfare and refuse to fight the king's enemies. This departure from the king's script follows a script of its own drawn not from African culture but from European tradition. In a virtual summary of the *Iliad*, the narrator describes how Oroonoko withdraws from battle after his favourite woman is taken by the king. The chiefs of the army beg him to return to the battlefield, "But he made no other Reply to all their Supplications than this, That he had now no more Business for Glory; and for the World, it was a Trifle not worth his Care" (p. 157). Without him, Oroonoko's troops are routed by the enemy, "who pursued 'em to the very tents" (p. 158). At last Oroonoko enters the battle and turns defeat into victory by fighting, like Achilles, "as if he came on Purpose to die" (p. 159).

Oroonoko cannot escape from one script without entering another. Following Achilles' script, he returns to battle, is reconciled with the king, makes a triumphant return from the wars, and is "belov'd like a Deity" (p. 160), but he has lost the person dearest to him. The allusion to Achilles functions on several levels at once. By further defining Oroonoko's character it both ennobles and confines him. Behn increases our appreciation of Oroonoko's military prowess, and at the same time condemns him to live Achilles' painful life. Did she intend to compliment Oroonoko without understanding the full implications of her allusion? Does her use of a tragic pattern indicate a form of racism that will not allow a black hero to succeed? The context of the allusion I have described suggests that Behn, while she may be racist in other ways, is here concerned to show the difficulties inherent in *any* attempt to resist state power. Harming one's enemies may harm one's friends as well, so that both action and inaction are loaded choices. Achilles and Oroonoko, although from different eras, places, and racial backgrounds, face similar obstacles.

They also share a rather ambiguous political position. Achilles is dissatisfied with his treatment by Agamemnon but has the power to question and retaliate only because he is a strong and respected leader who has benefited in the past from the established system of conquests and rewards. Similarly, Oroonoko's ability to court and claim Imoinda arises from his status as prince, general, and member of the courtly inner circle. Both Oroonoko and Achilles, as men, have privileges that effectively limit the scope of any rebellion they might mount. Disputing over women, they are unlikely to challenge the custom that gives them the right to engage in such disputes in the first place, that is, the commodification of women. While part of the heroism of these figures *is* their questioning of authority, neither story allows for full-scale revolution or social reorganization. One effect of Behn's allusion, therefore, is to deepen rather than simplify our sense of the complexities involved in political struggle, for rebellions take place *in* cultural contexts.

There is also the level of Oroonoko's consciousness to be considered. He has been educated in European ways, can converse in French, English, and Spanish, and "knew almost as much as if he had read much" (p. 135). Imitating Achilles may, therefore, be a conscious choice. If so, it is interesting that he chooses a European hero to imitate, as if, having exhausted the options offered by his own culture, he were searching for a new, more effective script. Achilles' script brings him glory. Immersing himself in the male world of camps and battles, he begins to overcome his grief, but he does not gain political or romantic power. Although he tries to act independently, Oroonoko is not in control of his own destiny, but is subjugated by alien texts.

Oroonoko's return and reconciliation with the king coincide with the arrival of the English ship and the beginning of a new phase in his career. Now a colonial power replaces the domestic state power in Oroonoko's life, functioning in a similar way but with more horrifying results. Like the king, the captain uses deceit to maintain power over Oroonoko, and Behn shows that colonial power also has a subtle literary or narrative dimension. At the moment of Oroonoko's capture by the captain, the narrator adds another text to the list of those confining Oroonoko. She writes: "It may be easily guess'd, in what Manner the Prince resented this Indignity, who may be best resembled to a Lion taken in a Toil; so he raged, so he struggled for Liberty, but all in vain" (p. 162). The figure of a lion in toils has a complex literary history that must have been familiar to Behn. It is an allusion to Plutarch's "Life of Julius Caesar," which appeared in a new translation between 1683 and 1686. Describing Caesar's assassination by the senators, Plutarch says that Caesar "was encompassed, like a wild beast in the toils, on every side" (p. 892). Although Oroonoko will not be dubbed "Caesar" by his white owner until he arrives in Surinam, Behn suggests that, from the moment of his capture, he is already caught up in Caesar's script. Plutarch's image of a beast in toils occurs at Caesar's death, but Behn uses the allusion early in her story, thereby suggesting that Oroonoko's end is already written at the time of his capture. For Oroonoko, to be renamed "Caesar" is to have his life symbolically rewritten. Thereafter, try as he might to rebel, he plays the part in a white colonial drama of one who is too strong and dangerous a leader to be trusted, whose popularity with the masses threatens those in power. Like Julius Caesar, Oroonoko will be undone, not only by enemies, but also by those who appear to be his friends and, like Caesar, he will be remembered as a martyr defeated not by honourable battle but by treachery.

This allusion has another source, which provides a colonial parallel to Oroonoko's predicament. In act one, scene two of Dryden's *The Indian Emperour*, Montezuma, King of the Aztecs, observes that he is surrounded by romantic enemies, the result of involvements that he, his two sons, and his daughter have with relatives of his old antagonists in *The Indian Queen*, Zempoalla and Traxalla: "My Lyon-heart is with Loves toyls beset, / Strugling I fall still deeper in the net."[12] No sooner has he spoken than he learns that he is surrounded by military enemies as well. A guard enters and announces that the Spaniards, led by Cortez, have surrounded them. Montezuma and his group are "compast round" (line 196) and "inclos'd" (line 204) by "swarming bands / Of ambush'd men" (lines 193–94). Although Montezuma had used the "toyl" metaphor in the context of love, events on stage show that it is also an accurate description of colonialism, as he is caught simultaneously in the net of love and in the net of Cortez's conquest.

Although Dryden may have had Plutarch in mind when he used this image,[13] there is no other evidence in the play suggesting a parallel between Montezuma and Caesar. It fell to Behn to link these two heroes to Oroonoko by means of an image that could be traced back to both texts. Her explicit use of the name "Caesar" suggests that Plutarch is the more important of the two predecessors, yet Dryden's play may have given Behn ideas about depicting a colonial struggle in literature. Like Oroonoko, Montezuma is a strong leader who resists enslavement and, although he scoffs at the Spaniards' religious rhetoric, always acts honourably towards his enemies. Dryden interweaves gender and colonial conflicts in his play in a way Behn might also have found useful. Finally, Dryden contrives to have the lion-in-toils simile enacted onstage when Montezuma is tied up and tortured by the priest; as we shall see, Behn uses a similar technique at the end of her work.

As if this were not enough, Behn herself had used a similar image in 1677 in a play entitled *Abdelazer; or, The Moor's Revenge*. Its titular hero is prince of the north African kingdom of Fez, which has been conquered by Spain, its king having been killed and Abdelazer taken captive to Spain. Although he is treated well by the Spanish king and becomes a general, he nevertheless refers to his captivity as "Slavery"[14] and tries to avenge himself by claiming not only the throne of Fez but also that of Spain. Through a combination of martial prowess and court intrigue he almost succeeds but is captured by the Spaniards and executed. Just before he is stabbed to death, Abdelazer says:

> As humble Huntsmen do the generous Lion;
> Now thou darst see me lash my Sides, and roar,
> And bite my Snare in vain; ...
> And like that noble Beast, though thus betray'd,
> I've yet an awful Fierceness in my Looks,
> Which makes thee fear t'approach; and 'tis at distance
> That thou dar'st kill me; for come but in my reach,
> And with one Grasp I wou'd confound thy Hopes. (p. 96)

The similarity to the threats Oroonoko hurls at his hunters before being taken in the woods and to the stabbing of Caesar is obvious.

To say that Behn associates this image with the exercise of colonial power is not to say that she always sympathizes with the colonized: Abdelazer is guilty of several moral outrages that mitigate his claim to justice, and the narrator's ambivalence towards Oroonoko has been well documented.[15] Yet in both these images, and especially in *Oroonoko*, Behn is searching for a way to express not only the rage of the colonial victim but also the pervasive nature of the encompassing power, which is represented by the snare or net.

By moving the image to the beginning of Oroonoko's captivity, as in Dryden, rather than placing it at the end, as in Plutarch and *Abdelazer*, she emphasizes the scripted nature of Oroonoko's slavery, its tendency to follow an existing pattern to a preordained conclusion.

Instead of the word "snare," she employs the less common "toil," used also by Plutarch and Dryden. A look at the etymology of this word may help to explain her choice. The English word "toil" for a hunter's net comes from the Old French *toile* and the Latin *tela*, both meaning a web or net. Other words that come from the same Indo-European root-syllable are "text," from the Latin *texere*, to weave, and "technology," from the Greek *tekhne*, art, craft, or skill.[16] Etymology shows the conceptual links between linguistic or narrative skill (textuality), physical skill (technology), and military aggression (hunting), thereby deepening Behn's allusion. When used as a hunter's tool, the toil ensnares the unsuspecting victim, symbolizing the hunter's power over his prey and his disguise, since toils are always hidden. By analogy, the toil suggests the colonialists' ability to hide their selfish and acquisitive motives behind language that appears benign and selfless, as seen in the captain's actions. It represents also the power of texts or narratives to shape proceedings in a colonial situation—the web of words used to ensnare Oroonoko includes not just the deceit practised by the captain and Byam but also the name "Caesar" and the biography that goes with it. All three aspects of the word may be seen in the captain's capture of Oroonoko.

Caesar's political position, like that of Achilles, is complex. His ambition to become dictator rested upon successful foreign conquests, which gave him the wealth necessary to buy influence and popular support and to make his army intensely loyal. Similarly, Oroonoko's threat to colonial power in Surinam is possible because he has won the loyalty and admiration of the other slaves, who constitute a majority of the population.[17] His symbolic status stems from the power he used to conquer and sell them into slavery in the first place. The ideological contradictions that critics have noticed in the text appear in the allusions as well.[18] That Behn complains about the unjust power used against Oroonoko and Caesar without questioning the colonial power that they also used illustrates a limitation of her critique, but does not entirely undermine it. Her allusions to Achilles and Caesar glorify a certain kind of resistance to unjust rule staged from positions within the aristocracy. At the same time, Oronooko's ultimate failure—and that of his literary models—indicates Behn's pessimism about the very resistance she praises.

The script of Julius Caesar's life does not account for every detail of Oroonoko's captivity, but it does provide a trajectory for it. He is kept on the trajectory by his enemies and ostensible friends, who do not intend to deceive him, but who are also subject to the hegemony of colonial ideology. Trefry names Oroonoko "Caesar" in homage to Oroonoko's nobility of birth and demeanour and later professes his "Abhorrence" (p. 168) at Oroonoko's capture and promises to free him, but good intentions cannot prevent Caesar's fate from overcoming Oroonoko. Since, as we have seen from the position of the lion-in-toils image, Oroonoko is *already* living Caesar's life, Trefry's homage implies his unwitting consent to the direction imposed by the colonial powers.

The narrator plays a similar role in colonial events, declaring herself Oroonoko's ally yet participating in his subjection. She says she "entertained" Oroonoko and Imoinda "with the Lives of the *Romans*, and great Men, which charmed him to my Company; and her, with teaching her all the pretty Works that I was Mistress of, and telling her Stories of Nuns, and endeavoring to bring her to the Knowledge of the true God" (p. 175). While Oroonoko does not like the narrator's proselytizing, the other entertainments seem pleasant enough to him, yet the word "charmed" here suggests that there is a mechanism at work which he does not see, a kind of narrative magic charm that casts its spell on him. By telling stories about the "Lives of the *Romans*,"[19] the narrator teaches Oroonoko the significance of his new name and of his lines in the white script that will end with his death. Whether the narrator intends it or not, the effect is the same. Although she claims to be on their side, her "entertainment" of Oroonoko and Imoinda gives them clearly circumscribed places in the colonial system. In this respect she is similar to the "Cast-Mistresses" of Coramantien, who assist the king in the education and control of his sexual servants.

A similar point can be made about the narrator's activities as a writer. She excuses the practice of renaming slaves on the grounds that their native names are "likely very barbarous, and hard to pronounce" (p. 169). Trefry's choice of "Caesar" she finds especially appropriate because it

> will live in that Country as long as that (scarce more) glorious one of the great *Roman*: for 'tis most evident he wanted no Part of the personal Courage of that *Caesar*, and acted Things as memorable, had they been done in some Part of the World replenished with People and Historians, that might have given him his Due. (p. 169)

Here the narrator begins to lament that Oroonoko's story will not be as well known as Caesar's. His due, she feels, is to become famous for the martyrdom he has suffered. Unable to save Oroonoko, the narrator wants at least to make his sufferings and accomplishments known. "But his Misfortune was, to fall in an obscure World, that afforded only a Female Pen to celebrate his Fame" (p. 169). The use of a modesty trope indicates that Oroonoko is confined by the text of the novel itself.[20] The narrator hopes to establish Oroonoko as Caesar's equal by writing his "Life," thus liberating him from Plutarch's text and giving him one inscribed with his own name.

But she fears that her biography, written by a "mere" female, is doomed to obscurity, censure, or both. There is an uneasy relationship here between racial and gender prejudices: through literary skill the narrator may be able to overcome her readers' prejudice against black protagonists, but her skill cannot change the fact of her own femaleness. Oroonoko, in his literary reincarnation, will thus continue to suffer the neglect and confinement that characterized his life, not because of racism, but because the narrator is confined in a sexist literary power structure.

The narrator's next sentence confirms her declaration of textual impotence. "For the future therefore I must call *Oroonoko Caesar*; since by that Name only he was known in our Western World" (p. 169). She "must" call Oroonoko by the name that entangles him in the white drama, the word "therefore" connecting this necessity causally to the foregoing discussion of female inferiority, as if she, too, were caught in the colonial script and contributed to his sufferings because powerless to do otherwise. Thereafter, Oroonoko's original name does not appear in the text except when he uses it. The narrator's subjection to the narrative convention of naming mirrors her subjection to the political system in Surinam, and henceforth she plays a dual role in the text, as advocate for the down-trodden prince and as participant in the prejudice and distrust that ensure his final defeat. Like Brutus in Plutarch's narrative, she has Oroonoko's "intire Confidence" (p. 177), but she turns out to be part of the conspiracy against him.

The narrator is a key figure in the "Actions and Sports" (p. 176) that the whites use as "Diversions" to turn Oroonoko's mind and energies away from rebellion. These activities serve white colonial interests by making the land safer for colonization. Oroonoko kills a tiger that had stolen a cow and another that had "long infested that Part, and borne away abundance of Sheep and Oxen, and other Things, that were for the Support of those to whom they belong'd" (p. 181). He also catches one of the dreaded "Numb-Eels," which were supposed to render someone unconscious merely by a touch of the bait on his fishing line (pp. 182–83). The shift here from human interaction to combat against monsters suggests the use of another narrative model, Hercules' twelve labours, often taken as civilizing actions to subdue the savage and monstrous elements of the Mediterranean world. The script of Hercules, like that of Achilles, ennobles Oroonoko by endowing him with superhuman strength. It also helps to disarm his otherness by giving it a familiar literary form and by directing his violence away from the monstrosity of slavery itself. Hercules, however, performed his most famous exploits at the command and in the interests of another and, like Oroonoko, he was caught in debasing servitude to an unworthy master.[21] The allusion to Hercules is thus not merely conservative in its ideological thrust; it highlights the exploitation by whites of Oroonoko's labour. The ideological conflict in this allusion centres on Hercules' dual role in relation to acts of exploitation. Each successful labour proves the injustice of his enslavement, but each act also kills or subordinates another being whose right to autonomy is never entertained. Similarly, Oroonoko's Herculean adventures separate him from savage native elements which he tames (including the disgruntled Amerindian villagers) and from other African slaves left behind on plantations, thus proving his right to freedom by showing his "legitimate" superiority over those who will remain enslaved.

The colonial diversion, with its Herculean overtones, is presented as a narrative "Digression" (p. 189), showing once again that Oroonoko cannot leave one script without entering another. The last part of the novel recounts Oroonoko's attempted rebellion against the scripts in which he has become entangled. As in Coramantien, the rebellion has two phases, an overt "criminal" act of defiance that fails, followed by his sullen withdrawal from society. Oroonoko rouses his fellow slaves to mutiny, but, as in Coramantien, there are problems with his plan. Although his rhetoric is high-flown, he does not appreciate the practical obstacles to a successful escape. A slave named Tuscan warns him that the women and children are "unfit for Travel in those unpassable Woods, Mountains and Bogs" that surround them (p. 191). Oroonoko's response is theoretical; he tells them "That Honour [is] the first Principle in Nature" (p. 191) and that "the more Danger the more Glory" (p. 192). Attempting to encourage the slaves, he cites the example of Hannibal, "a great Captain, [who] had cut his Way through Mountains of solid Rocks" (p. 192). Oroonoko has learned well the "Lives of the *Romans*, and great Men" (p. 175) taught him by the narrator, but Hannibal is an inauspicious choice since his efforts, too, were doomed: he crossed the Alps but failed to achieve his goal of conquering Rome.[22] In mentioning Hannibal Oroonoko invokes another script for heroic failure.

The pitiful white militia defeats the slaves not by superior force but by "perplexing" them. Their whips inflict pain but are not deadly. Whips also have a symbolic value, however, which the English augment by crying out *"Yield and Live! Yield, and be Pardon'd!"* as they fight (p. 194). As in Herodotus, where the Scythians resort to whips to put down a slave revolt, the use of whips forces the Africans to "remember they are slaves" and causes them to lose courage.[23] The whites also attack their eyes and faces to demoralize them further (p. 194), a tactic Julius Caesar himself is said to have used successfully against Pompey's cavalry.[24]

In this victory, hegemony is again a factor. Language and symbols are the primary colonial weapons: victory by the whites is complete when Byam makes "use of all his Art of Talking and Dissembling" to obtain Oroonoko's surrender (p. 195). Oroonoko is not at first convinced by Byam's professed deference, but Trefry, himself deceived into "believing the Governor to mean what he said" (p. 196), makes the decisive plea, again becoming an unwitting instrument of the colonialist cause. The narrator's failure to prevent the treacherous whipping of Oroonoko follows a similar pattern. She fears, with other whites, that Oroonoko will come and "cut all our Throats," even though he has specifically promised that he "would act nothing upon the *White* People" (p. 176). She distrusts that promise, she says earlier, because of his "rough and fierce" spirit, a view that now helps to cause her absence at a crucial moment.

Equally prejudicial is the immediate division of the white camp along gender lines: the "Females," accepting their role as weaker beings, "fly down the River, to be secured." While the narrator says that she has "Authority" to preserve Oroonoko, her actions place her firmly within the female stereotype. Her betrayal comes from those deep-seated aspects of culture that are hardest to shed. Oroonoko's suffering may thus be said in a broad way to be caused by the prejudice of European culture against blacks and women. The narrator's "spontaneous" consent to the male-dominated system helps to perpetuate Oroonoko's subjection in the colonial system. The subtle, unconscious workings of hegemony explain why she believes she has "Authority" when, in fact, she does not.

With the failure of his first plan, Oroonoko begins to plot a more radical escape through death. He also plans to "take a dire Revenge" on Byam for subjecting him to the *"contemptible Whip"* instead of merely killing him, proof that the whip's symbolic value is not lost upon Oroonoko: "No, I would not kill myself, even after a Whipping, but will be content to live with that Infamy, and be pointed at by every grinning Slave, till I have completed my Revenge; and then you shall see, that *Oroonoko* scorns to live with the Indignity that was put on *Caesar*" (p. 199). This is the first time Oroonoko's original name has appeared in the text for some thirty pages and it comes as a bolt of lightning. It shows for the first time that he distinguishes between his two identities of prince and slave. One is a maker of dramas, the other a character in someone else's drama. As Oroonoko begins to compose a script to compete with the powerful white script, he reclaims his former name in a symbolic attempt to summon his princely power. "The Indignity that was put on *Caesar*" is not only the indignity of whipping, it is also the indignity of treacherous assassination. Oroonoko's new script will be a script of suicide to pre-empt the script of assassination already composed for him by the colonists. His ultimate failure to escape Caesar's toils indicates how deeply he is bound in the colonial net.

After Oroonoko reclaims his former name, he begins to re-enact sections of his African life. In addition to imitating other literature, Behn's novel now begins to imitate itself, as if Oroonoko's earlier life as a prince, which has already become the stuff of legends enjoyed by the narrator, Trefry, and others in Surinam, has become a script to be reused. As we might expect, Oroonoko is no more successful now than he was then. After he has killed Imoinda, he wastes himself in grief and remorse:

> He remained in this deplorable Condition for two Days, and never rose from the Ground where he had made her sad Sacrifice. ... but offering to rise, he found his Strength so decay'd, that he reeled to and fro, like Boughs assailed by contrary Winds; so that he was forced to lie down again, and try to summon all his Courage to his Aid. He found his Brains turned round, and his Eyes were dizzy, and Objects appear'd not the same to him they were wont to do. (pp. 203–4)

His condition here parallels directly the Iliadic episode, mentioned above, in which Oroonoko, believing Imoinda to be dead, languishes "for two Days, without permitting any Sustenance to approach him" (p. 158), yet when he rises to do battle he is able to do "such Things as will not be believed that human Strength could perform" (p. 159). In both cases, Oroonoko is certain his beloved is dead and starves himself, but in the second instance his original strength and determination have been eroded by the ordeal of slavery. Both his body and his "Brains" fail him this time, suggesting that the colonists' linguistic weapons, deceptions, and whipping have affected his mind. In spite of himself, he has internalized the colonists' view of himself as their inferior.[25]

Whereas Oroonoko's Achillean script was partially successful in Coramantien, here it is disastrous. Achilles himself had the favour of gods who could "distil nectar inside his chest, and delicate / ambrosia, so the weakness of hunger [would] not come upon him," but Oroonoko has no such protecting deities. Thetis promises to preserve Patroklos's dead body from decay while Achilles takes his revenge upon Hektor,[26] but Oroonoko's enemies discover him by the "Stink" of Imoinda's decaying body (p. 204).

As the search party surrounds him, he grasps wildly for narrative models, finding three different ones from different parts of his past. The image of a dizzy and weak Oroonoko warning his pursuers to "approach no nearer, if they would be safe" (p. 204) and that *"Fatal will be the Attempt of the first Adventurer"* (p. 205) is a pathetic re-enactment of the scene in which Oroonoko leaps naked from Imoinda's bed, grabs a nearby battleaxe, and promises "the certain Death of him that first enters" (p. 153). This time his attackers are not scared off but merely delayed. Once again the whites rely on language more than on action, entreating Oroonoko to give himself up while they keep a safe distance (p. 205). As he holds off the whites, who approach him like hunters surrounding a lion, he "cut a Piece of Flesh from his own Throat, and threw it at 'em" (p. 205), in imitation of yet another heroic script, this time taken from the culture he observed on his visit to the Indian village.[27] Finally, he imitates the tiger he himself had killed during his "Herculean" adventures, who "feebly wounded him" in the thigh with her claws as she died (p. 180); Oroonoko can only wound Tuscan feebly in the arm before falling completely into the hunters' power (p. 206). His capture in this manner provides a graphic staging of the lion-in-toils simile, itself an echo of Plutarch's description of the death of Caesar, thus re-enacting and completing his subjection to the role of Caesar written for him by his masters.

By killing Oroonoko, the whites ironically give him exactly what he wants. The "Barbaric" Bannister does what all Oroonoko's well-meaning friends are unable to do: he liberates the slave from his hated captivity. Behn suggests that the actions of the whites backfire another way: the "rude and wild ... Rabble" and the "inhuman ... Justices" who presided at Oroonoko's execution, she says, "after paid dear enough for their Insolence" (p. 208), implying that some power, perhaps the Lord Governour when he finally arrived, made them atone for their crimes. The passage corresponds to one in Plutarch's "Life of Caesar":

> But the great genius which attended [Caesar] throughout his lifetime even after his death remained as the avenger of his murder, pursuing through every sea and land all those who were concerned in it, and suffering none to escape, but reaching all who in any sort or kind were either actually engaged in the fact, or by their counsels any way promoted it.[28]

By condemning Oroonoko to the fate of Caesar, the whites also condemn themselves to the fate of Caesar's enemies, unconsciously admitting their guilt. While "Caesar" may be subject to their power, they are themselves subject to a divine principle of justice that pursues and finally punishes them. Behn suggests that Caesar's toils return to ensnare the hunters, subjecting them to a part of the text they perhaps did not read carefully enough.

There remain several different levels on which we can read Behn's literary allusions. The allusions are the most striking examples of a process of "scripting" that goes on throughout the novel, in which those in power shape the lives of those they dominate by means other than what Gramsci would call "direct control." Whether the narrative model is a famous story, a ritualized "ceremony," or a new pattern composed by the powerful for a specific situation, some degree of hegemony or "spontaneous" consent appears to be involved on the part of Oroonoko and his friends. In Oroonoko's case this can be seen in those actions he consciously controls: his plan of seeing Imoinda in private, his withdrawal from the battle, and his impractical plan for the slave mutiny are actions where he displays an internal lack of will, judgment, or foresight. In situations beyond Oroonoko's control, such as the whipping, execution, and imposition of Caesar's name and biography upon him, hegemony can be seen most clearly in his allies.

When the narrator and Trefry help to keep Oroonoko subdued, they are involved unknowingly in colonial machinery. The failure of acts of resistance is due as much to internal factors as to external force or control. The allusions suggest that it is difficult for people to think and act independently of the cultural biases and patterns that surround them, whether they are natives of the culture in question or displaced aliens. Allusions are a particularly appropriate means of making this point, since they force readers to rely on prior knowledge that is usually acquired from the same education and cultural indoctrination that gave rise to the hegemony.

If hegemony is effective, it may be argued, then Behn's message is essentially conservative. Behn's Toryism and her refusal to criticize slavery have been widely acknowledged, and the evidence discussed here could be used to bolster that view of her. She may evoke our sympathies for Oroonoko, but the failure of his attempted rebellions establishes a pattern that begins to carry the weight of destiny. The pattern of failure could reassure a white, aristocratic audience that such uprisings are always doomed and that, while subjects and slaves may have legitimate complaints, they can never really change the status quo.

To portray the mechanics of power, however, is in some sense to criticize them, even when no solution is offered. The detail with which Behn depicts the multiple and subtle means of control used on Oroonoko and his friends works against the continuing effectiveness of such control, for if hegemony depends upon belief, then it can be upset by changes in belief fostered by literature. The subversive potential in the novel is emphasized if we interpret it not as a modified romance to entertain aristocratic readers but as an extended disquisition on the nature of power both domestic and colonial. I have called for a consideration of Oroonoko's predecessors not as figures but as narratives. All the men are great aristocratic warriors, but all are also caught in complex webs of power and engaged in political struggle. Their stories can therefore be said to have power and rebellion as their main subject. Behn uncovers a tradition of resistance in the midst of the literary tradition, although, as I have suggested, it does not extend to those on the lowest rungs of society.

Furthermore, although none of the heroes can usurp authority for himself, each is the beneficiary of an apotheosis of sorts after death. According to legend, after his death at the hands of Deianira, Hercules was made a god by Zeus. By an act of senate after his death, Julius Caesar was worshipped as a god in Rome. Achilles, though not deified, enjoys a reputation for greater virtue, cunning, and strength than Agamemnon, as a result of Homer's contrasting characterization of the two.[29] Thus in some sense all three heroes triumph over their oppressors. Each story contains a coda in which previously inescapable powers, including death itself, are re-evaluated and shown to be malleable.

As we have seen, Oroonoko's story has a similar coda hinting at the later downfall of his oppressors. In the final paragraph the narrator hopes that Oroonoko's "glorious Name" will, along with Imoinda's, "survive to all Ages" (p. 208). In light of the other narrative models, this plea for lasting fame may be read as a call for a re-evaluation of the power structures that doomed Oroonoko to failure.

## NOTES

1. Plutarch, *Lives of the Noble Grecians and Romans* trans. John Dryden, revised by Arthur Hugh Clough (New York: Modern Library, 1932), p. 892.

2. Exceptions include Adelaide P. Amore on the parallels between Oroonoko and Christ in her introduction to Aphra Behn, *Oroonoko, or, The Royal Slave: A Critical Edition*, ed. Adelaide P. Amore (Lanham, New York, and London: University Press of America, 1987), pp. xxxii–xxxiii; Laura Brown on the links to literature memorializing Charles I in "The Romance of Empire: *Oroonoko* and the Trade in Slaves," *The New Eighteenth Century*, ed. Felicity Nussbaum and Laura Brown (New York and London: Methuen, 1987), pp. 57–59; and Margaret Ferguson on the parallels with Shakespeare's *Othello* in "Juggling the Categories of Race, Class and Gender: Aphra Behn's *Oroonoko*," *Women's Studies* 19 (1991), 169–73.

3. See Martine Watson Brownley, "The Narrator in *Oroonoko*," *Essays in Literature: Western Illinois University* 4 (1977), 174–81; Katherine M. Rogers, "Fact and Fiction in Aphra Behn's *Oroonoko*," *Studies in the Novel* 20 (Spring 1988), 1–15; William C. Spengemann, "The Earliest American Novel: Aphra Behn's *Oroonoko*," *Nineteenth-Century Fiction* 38 (1984), 384–414; Rose A. Zimbardo, "Aphra Behn in Search of the Novel," *Studies in Eighteenth-Century Culture* 19 (1989), 277–87.

4. My distinction here is similar to one between "direct control" and "hegemony" made by Antonio Gramsci, "The Intellectuals," *Selections from the Prison Notebooks*, ed. and trans. Quintin Hoare and Geoffrey Nowell Smith (New York: International Publishers, 1971), p. 12.

5. Robert L. Chibka, " 'Oh! Do Not Fear a Woman's Invention': Truth, Falsehood, and Fiction in Aphra Behn's *Oroonoko*," *Texas Studies in Literature and Language* 30 (Winter 1988), 510–37.

6. Sandra M. Gilbert and Susan Gubar discuss the idea that authors are owners and masters of the characters in their texts in *The Madwoman in the Attic: The Woman Writer and the Nineteenth-Century Literary Imagination* (New Haven and London: Yale University Press, 1979), p. 7.

7. My use of the terms "synchronic" and "diachronic" as well as the idea of well-known myths as "scripts" that can shape social interaction is influenced by the work of Victor Turner, *Dramas, Fields, and Metaphors: Symbolic Action in Human Society* (Ithaca and London: Cornell University Press, 1974), especially pp. 35–36 and p. 123.

8. I am here taking issue with Laura Brown where she argues that "In Behn's text 'reductive normalizing' is carried out through literary convention, and specifically through that very convention most effectively able to fix and codify the experience of radical alterity, the arbitrary love and honor codes of heroic romance" (p. 49). Mary Louise Pratt's essay, from which the phrase "reductive normalizing" is taken, makes a distinction between "informational" and "experiential" discourses that is similar to the synchronic/diachronic distinction I employ. The typical way of normalizing the colonial native is to reduce

him/her to a static list of "manners and customs." Experiential narratives may be equally reductive, Pratt argues, but have a greater potential for parody, dialogism, and critique because they portray "situated human subjects" (p. 150). See Pratt, "Scratches on the Face of the Country; or, What Mr. Barrow Saw in the Land of the Bushmen," in *"Race," Writing, and Difference*, ed. Henry Louis Gates, Jr. (Chicago: University of Chicago Press, 1986), pp. 138–62.

9. Aphra Behn, *Oroonoko, The Works of Aphra Behn*, vol. 5, ed. Montague Summers (New York: Benjamin Blom, 1915), p. 139. References are to this edition.

10. See Turner: "Religious myths—and their episodic components—[can] constitute dramatic or narrative process models which so influence social behavior that it acquires a strange processual inevitability overriding questions of interest, expediency, or even morality" (p. 122).

11. Gramsci, p. 12

12. *The Works of John Dryden*, ed. Edward Niles Hooker and H.T. Swedenberg, Jr. (Berkeley: University of California Press, 1956–), vol. 9 (1966), I.ii.182–83. Further references in the text are to line numbers of this scene.

13. See James Winn, *John Dryden and His World* (New Haven and London: Yale University Press, 1987), p. 388, for Dryden's contribution to the translation of Plutarch's *Lives*.

14. Aphra Behn, *Abdelazer; or, The Moor's Revenge*, vol. 2 of *Works*, p. 14. As lines are not numbered in this edition, references are to page numbers. Cf. Margaret Ferguson's article above, which first directed me to this play (p. 179n31).

15. In addition to Brown, Chibka, and Margaret Ferguson, see for example Moira Ferguson, *Subject to Others: British Women Writers and Colonial Slavery, 1670-1834* (New York: Routledge, 1992), chap. 2; Wylie Sypher, *Guinea's Captive Kings: British Anti-Slavery Literature of the XVIIIth Century* (Chapel Hill: University of North Carolina Press, 1942), pp. 110–13; Michael Echeruo, *The Conditioned Imagination from Shakespeare to Conrad* (New York: Holmes and Meier, 1978), p. 80.

16. See the *OED*, s.v. "toil" and *The American Heritage Dictionary*, Appendix of Indo-European Roots, s.v. "teks-."

17. The concern of white colonists over the power of a multitude parallels that of Caesar's adversaries in Plutarch's narrative. At one point, Caesar is elected high priest over Catulus and Isauricus: "When the votes were taken, [Caesar] carried it, and excited among the senate and nobility great alarm lest he might now urge on the people to every kind of insolence" (Plutarch, p. 858).

18. Margaret Ferguson finds that Oroonoko and the narrator are "both victims and beneficiaries of the international system of the slave trade" (pp. 168–69); Moira Ferguson notes the irony of Oroonoko's "temporary identification with slaves whom he may have originally sold into slavery" (p. 31) and discusses other ways in which the novel is complicated by class distinctions. The point is also discussed in Stephanie Athey and Daniel Cooper Alarcon, "*Oroonoko's* Gendered Economies of Honor/Horror: Reframing Colonial Discourse Studies in the Americas," *American Literature* 65 (Sept. 1993), 437.

19. Some editions of *Oroonoko* print "Loves of the *Romans*." See for example *Oroonoko*, ed. Lore Metzger (London and New York: Norton, 1973), p. 46. Mary Vermillion notes that only "Lives" is consistent with the first edition of *Oroonoko* published in 1688; see "Buried Heroism: Critiques of Female Authorship in Southerne's Adaptation of Behn's *Oroonoko*," *Restoration: Studies in English Literary Culture, 1660-1700* 16 (1992), 37n13. Although "Loves" indicates a more specific type of story, it does not alter my point.

20. Behn used this kind of deference ironically, both here and in other works, to assert

her superiority; see Larry Carver "Aphra Behn: The Poet's Heart in a Woman's Body," *Papers on Language and Literature* 14 (1978), 414–24; Judith Kegan Gardiner, "Aphra Behn: Sexuality and Self-Respect," *Women's Studies* 7:1/2 (1980), 67–78. Gilbert and Gubar discuss the "bitter irony" of such poses when used by female writers (p. 62).

21. For an outline of Hercules' story, see Apollodorus, *The Library*, trans. James George Frazer (Cambridge: Harvard University Press, 1921), II.iv–II.vii. Hercules' comment to Odysseus in *Odyssey* 11 is also relevant here: "For I was son of Kronian Zeus, but I had an endless spell of misery. I was made bondman to one who was far worse than I, and he loaded my difficult labors on me"; see *The Odyssey of Homer*, trans. Richmond Lattimore (New York: Harper and Row, 1965), p. 184. For a translation that predates Behn, see that of George Chapman in *Chapman's Homer: The Iliad, the Odyssey, and the Lesser Homerica*, ed. Allardyce Nicoll (New York: Pantheon, 1956). For further discussion of transformations of the Hercules model in the sixteenth and seventeenth centuries, see Eugene M. Waith, *The Herculean Hero in Marlowe, Chapman, Shakespeare, and Dryden* (New York: Columbia University Press, 1962).

22. On Hannibal see Plutarch, pp. 213–32, 372–88.

23. Herodotus, *The Histories*, trans. Aubrey de Selincourt (New York: Penguin Books, 1954), book 4, p. 272.

24. Plutarch, p. 881.

25. Athey and Alarcon also discuss the parallels between these two scenes, but they focus on the acts of violation that precede the arrival of Oroonoko's pursuers (p. 436).

26. Homer, *Iliad*, trans. Richmond Lattimore (Chicago: University of Chicago Press, 1951), book 19, pp. 401, 392–93.

27. Soldiers competing for the "Generalship" in war cut off their own noses, lips, and eyes, says the narrator, "so they slash on 'till one gives out, and many have dy'd in this Debate. And it's by a passive Valour they shew and prove their Activity" (p. 188).

28. Plutarch, p. 894.

29. See Apollodorus, II.vii.7; Plutarch, p. 893; and Homer, *Odyssey*, book 24. In book 24 of the *Odyssey* Achilles has a chance to gloat a bit when he says to the soul of Agamemnon that his political status as "lord over numerous people" did not prevent him from suffering an early and inglorious death. Agamemnon then goes on to describe the grand funeral of Achilles, at which both gods and mortals mourned and brought gifts even greater than those normally reserved for a king's funeral (Lattimore translation, pp. 346–47).

MICHAEL SEIDEL

# *Gulliver's Travels* and the contracts of fiction

## I FICTIONAL BONA FIDES

Mariners lie like old sea dogs. In James Joyce's *Ulysses* (1922), the adventuring hero, Leopold Bloom, never leaves the confines of his native city, but he does run into an old sailor named Murphy who boasts of his travels to several remote regions of the world. Bloom has his doubts about Murphy, "assuming he was the person he represented himself and not sailing under false colours after having boxed the compass on the q.t. somewhere."[1] Listening to the yarns and finding something out of joint about them makes Bloom "nourish some suspicions of our friend's bona fides" (512).

What does it mean to nourish suspicions about a narrator's bona fides? This is the very question that haunts Jonathan Swift's *Gulliver's Travels* (1726), and for good reason. *Gulliver's Travels* has been a notable gathering place, almost a convocation, for the severer sort of Western Critic who sees its satiric action as a vicious attack on the political and cultural institutions of eighteenth-century British civilization in the guise of a satiric send-up of travel literature.[2]

But what if Swift's satiric travel narrative is directed not simply at the experience of modern political, social, and intellectual life in England and Europe, but at the narrative bona fides of those middling fictional subjects who emerged during the early decades of the eighteenth century in England precisely to endorse the modern, progressivist, commercial vision of the

From *The Cambridge Companion to the Eighteenth-Century Novel*. © 1996 by Cambridge University Press.

world that Swift's satire bemoans? The novel is the literary form positing the fitness of a low-life, pseudoprofessional, or merchant-class narrator—Moll Flanders, Robinson Crusoe, Colonel Jack, Captain Singleton—to record the contingencies and changing valences of modern life. As such, it was a likely and predictable Swiftian target.[3]

In most of his work, Swift is a master at what might be called satiric deauthentication. His satire cuts to the core of self-representation in the literature of his age, and offers complex challenges to the supposed bona fides of a host of figures whom he sets up as representatives of modern consciousness. No satirist has ever been craftier at allowing his satiric subjects free voice in their own annihilation. His career is based on a kind of satiric ventriloquism where egophiliac narrators talk themselves into states of exhaustion or lunacy. In *A Tale of A Tub* (1704), Swift worms into the voice and rots out the discursive ramblings of a hack for hire; in the *Bickerstaff Papers* (1708–9), he finishes off a scandal-mongering, lying astrologer; in *Argument Against the Abolishment of Christianity* (1708), he turns inside out the equivocations of a trimming, secular, free-thinking religious apologist; in *A Modest Proposal*, he reveals the motives of an ambition-driven, calculating political economist; in *Gulliver's Travels*, he ruins the life of a one-time ship's surgeon turned professional merchant adventurer. Swift's best satire always recreates the manner in which the modern mind conceives, writes up, and enervates its own condition.

For Swift, the early novelistic experiments of the 1720s in England provided a tantalizing space for his satiric powers to run loose over new terrain. He distrusted virtually everything represented in the early novel: its individualistic psychology; its brief for class mobility; its delight in a burgeoning of the British economy; its adjustable ethics and morality; its increasing tolerance of opinion; its role in the proliferation of knowledge; its success as a product of the increasingly commercial literary industry. From Swift's satiric viewpoint, the novel was exactly the narrative form his age deserved, one that removed the time-tested values of cultural inheritance and substituted the subjective experience of a serviceably dim and limited commercial intelligence.

Though first-time readers are more likely to set the satiric perimeters of *Gulliver's Travels* around all of European civilization, there is a way of reading the narrative and drawing the loop around Gulliver as parody of the middling fictional subject as well. In this sense—one perfectly confirmed by other works of Swift—it is less Gulliver's rendition of his civilization that exists at the narrative center of the *Travels* than what the *Travels* tell us about Gulliver as representative of his civilization. Gulliver may be the primary critic of civilization by the end of his account, but he is also, and this is crucial to any productive reading of the work, the primary product on display of that civilization from the beginning of his account. The first items the

Lilliputians discover in Gulliver's pockets are a watch and some loose silver coin and gold: time and money, the modern Englishman's credo.

Gulliver is a blustering modern figure at the beginning of his voyages: his middle-class cocksureness, his professional acumen, his receptive linguistic ear, his interests in politics, social values, civic engineering, and military strategy are all inestimable resources for the contemporary subject negotiating the early eighteenth-century world. Gulliver in Lilliput is an outsized version of the new man of his age. By the time we begin to understand the satiric focus of the narrative, we also begin to understand the satiric implication of what Swift has done to and with Gulliver in the first adventure. Gulliver's physical size is partly a satiric image of the inflated status of the subject in modern fiction. In Swift's writing, to blow something up is to set it up for satiric action, as deflation necessarily follows inflation. The more complex pattern (exercised on Gulliver's mind) is, of course, previewed in the second book of the adventures in the land of giants. Gulliver the maximalist becomes, for purposes of the satiric narrative, Gulliver the minimalist. This has a structural role in the plot of the fantasy, and also a subtle role in the more ranging satire on the fictional bona fides of the narrator in the early eighteenth-century novel. Where the novel generally works to render its authenticating subject secure, Swift's satire destabilizes the body and then the mind of its central character. By the end of the *Travels*, Gulliver is not even certain what it is to be human, and his behavior suggests as much.

Gulliver is the expert whose knowledge is limited, the sailor who knows little about the sea, the modern jingoist patriot who is also the national turncoat, the world traveler who speaks only to the horses in his barn, the surgeon who cannot operate, the translator who cannot locate idioms or contexts. What are we supposed to make of Gulliver, the linguistic expert, who derives the place-name of his third voyage, "*Lapute* was *quasi Lap outed; Lap* signifying properly the dancing of the Sun Beams in the Sea and *outed* a Wing, which however I shall not obtrude, but submit to the judicious Reader?"[4] Just *how* would the judicious reader know? More likely, the injudicious reader hears the Spanish *la puta*, or whore, which gets closer to Swift's satiric point about Gulliver inside his narration: it's all something like prostitution, a selling of one's narrative produce to all comers.

As narrator, Gulliver loses credit as his adventures develop. It is not that Gulliver exhibits the same greed, corruption, hypocrisy that constitute the satiric matter of his harangues against British life to his Houyhnhnm Master in the fourth voyage, but that he is self-infatuated, self-obsessed, and deranged. He begins by thinking moderately well of himself and ends by thinking himself a superior member of an inferior species. Swift constructs a narrative subject who ironically does all he can to invalidate the literary form that conveys him. Snickering readers have long joked about the satiric significance of Gulliver's medical mentor, a Master Bates, in this respect. It is fairly well established by now that the pun was at least possible in 1726, and if so, it means Gulliver was trained not only in surgery but in a sort of narrative onanism, the same impulse that marked the self-projecting capacity of the unstable narrator in Swift's *A Tale of A Tub*.

Gulliver has, in a modern idiom, an image problem. The narrative sets out to present him with one. He doesn't know whether he looks good small or big; he doesn't know whether the features of his face look better symmetrically disposed or awry; he doesn't know whether his pathetic body would serve him better shaped like a horse's; he doesn't know whether his sounds and smells are as offensive to everyone else as they are to him. In short, he is uncertain about the material reality around him. Even at the beginning of his voyages he is all too ready to adopt an unsettling perspective in relaying information. When he urinates in Lilliput he refers to the "Torrent which fell with such Noise and Violence from me" (9). Why does *he* choose such words? The Lilliputians have reason to record the noise and violence, but not Gulliver. Similarly, in Brobdingnag Gulliver describes the way whales from his world swim into Brobdingnaggian waters: "These Whales I have known so large that Man could hardly carry one upon his Shoulders" (89). What does Gulliver think when he makes such an observation? Swift's deadpan narrative ventriloquism encourages the question.

When Gulliver returns home after his voyages he assumes the most absurd things. Looking at his wife after his visit to the land of giants he concludes "she had been too thrifty, for I found she had starved herself and her Daughter to nothing" (124). It is one thing to think them small; it is another to misconstrue completely why they would look so. Gulliver gets worse and worse. At the finale of his narrative he is a bundle of nervous tics; he has difficulty filtering out human things; he thinks that horses speak to him (has anyone ever asked how English horses come to speak Houyhnhnmese, a language derived from an unknown place 10,000 miles away?). *Gulliver's Travels* is so thoroughly satiric that its resolution is its worst narrative crisis, and the hero's homecoming the most foreign and alienating experience of all. Gulliver returns home in exile, as detached from his land and time as the infamous Struldbruggs or immortals of voyage three of the *Travels*. Indeed, the pattern for the Struldbrugg episode is not unlike the mental pattern for the *Travels* at large. Gulliver is set up to represent the best hopes of progressive modern life and is brought through to the alien side where he can comprehend neither the values nor, in some cases, the language of his native land. The course of the Struldbruggs, though long in *their* lives and adventures, is shortened for Gulliver. At their end, the Struldbruggs live at home the way Gulliver will in his—"like Foreigners in their own Country" (183), despised and hated by one and all.

Gulliver is an Odysseus gone sour; a homecomer who, in a satiric version of narrative rest, is depressed and drained by his very resources as a human being. His last observation on his human life is a deeply contradictory remark about not wishing any yahoo with a tincture of pride—though all yahoos, including himself, possess it—to appear in his sight. This is also the last reference to the fictional subject in the *Travels* and the last reference to the form that inscribes the self, the novel. Gulliver wants nothing human to appear before him. The modern subject faces only the raw dilemma of being alive.

Swift's attack on modern consciousness was not new in *Gulliver's Travels*. For years he was associated with the famous Scriblerus Club (whose very name identifies and mocks modern writing). The primary task of the Scriblerians was to collect and satirize all forms of contemporary literary expression represented by absurdly imagined figures of eighteenth-century political and cultural life. Out of the club came John Arbuthnot's British proto-imperialist, John Bull, John Gay's highwayman spoiler, MacHeath, and Alexander Pope's (under Arbuthnot's direction) expert-in-everything, Martin Scriblerus. *Gulliver's Travels* was originally supposed to have been an early part of the Scriblerian enterprise in 1713. Pope proposed that Swift get busy on a chapter for the *Memoirs of Martinus Scriblerus* in which Martin would visit the land of pygmies, giants, and mathematicians before voyaging to a land where he discovers a "vein of Melancholy proceeding almost to a disgust of his Species."[5]

Swift dawdled with the assignment at the time it was given, but never abandoned it. He waited until 1726, changed characters, expanded the satire, but to a certain extent kept wearing his Scriblerian hat. At the Academy at Lagado during Gulliver's third voyage, we hear of a giant word machine (actually diagrammed in the text) by which "Contrivance, the most ignorant Person at a reasonable Charge, and with a little bodily Labour, may write Books in Philosophy, Poetry, Politicks, Law, Mathematicks and Theology, without the least Assistance from Genius or Study" (156). It is difficult to read such a passage, let alone imagine the random, whirling words tossed out by the machine, and not think Swift had a typical Scriblerian target like Daniel Defoe in mind.[6] Defoe represented the voice of modernity—the prolific journalism, the conduct books, histories, gazeteers, mock biographies, the novel. It was almost as if Swift needed to have the century produce the literary symptom of Daniel Defoe full-blown before he could scourge the malady in *Gulliver's Travels*. In this sense, Defoe's impulsive traveler, the narrating merchant-adventurer Robinson Crusoe, provided Swift with a better satiric model for Gulliver than Martin Scriblerus.[7]

It is no accident that so many of the specifics of Swift's narrative ingest and redispose the Crusoe story in a form more suitable to satire. A pointed example occurs late in the adventures when Gulliver considers for the space of a few paragraphs what for Crusoe had been a life's adventure.

> My Design was, if possible, to discover some small Island
> uninhabited, yet sufficient by my Labour to furnish me with
> Necessaries of Life, which I would have thought a greater
> Happiness than to be first Minister in the politest Court of
> *Europe;* so horrible was the Idea I conceived of returning to live
> in the Society and under the Government of *Yahoos.* For in such
> a Solitude as I desired, I could at least enjoy my own Thoughts,
> and reflect with Delight on the Virtues of those inimitable
> *Houyhnhnms,* without any Opportunity of degenerating into the
> Vices and Corruptions of my own Species. (248)

For Crusoe, this is a fictional opportunity that generates an entire narrative.
For Gulliver, a native islander shoots him in the knee with an arrow, and he
swims off the island in despair. So much for Swift's commentary on the value
of the Crusoe saga. Would that the novel form itself, as a literary
phenomenon, had enjoyed such a quick demise. That it did not do so was yet
another symptom for Swift of the corruption of values and literary tastes in
his age.

Crusoe is an image of the reconstituted self that Swift so distrusted, the
Iland whose fictional experience reinforces the idea of enterprise, liberty, and
self-sovereignty in the modern world.[8] The novel—whether called the
personal memoir, the true history, the life and adventure, the confession—
generally builds character; it devises strategies to make character paramount
and also to build confidence in character. Characters in the early novel work
by repeating key impulses, and succeed by integrating those impulses with
possibilities offered to them in the worlds in which they circulate. The
desires, wants, compulsions of the ordinary man or woman become the stuff
of fiction. Life is a series of calibrations and negotiations, compromises and
accommodations. The relatively inconsequential self becomes the filter for
human experience where, as Defoe puts it in his own musings on *Robinson
Crusoe,* "all reflection is carried home, and our dear self is, in one respect, the
end of living."[9]

Defoe lets us know that Crusoe's subjective "Story is told with
Modesty, with Seriousness, and with a religious Application of Events to the
Uses to which wise Men always apply them (viz.) to the Instruction of others
by this Example, and to justify and honour the Wisdom of Providence in all
the Variety of our Circumstances, let them happen how they will."[10] In his
parody of the Crusoe-like subject, Swift makes a mockery of this egocentric
contract for fiction, and any moral justification that would tag along with it.
He parodies the language of modern fiction while debasing the enterprise:

> I hope the gentle Reader will excuse me for dwelling on these and
> the like Particulars, which however insignificant they may appear

to grovelling vulgar Minds, yet will certainly help a Philosopher to enlarge his Thoughts and Imagination, and apply them to the Benefit of public as well as private Life, which was my sole design in presenting this and other Accounts of my Travels to the World. (73)

Of course all these particulars—the circumstantial voicings of the modern narrative self—are about Gulliver's disposing of his excremental waste in Lilliput, perhaps one of the many images for Swift that serve satirically for the new forms of eighteenth-century fiction.

Swift's satire tends to suck the lifeblood right out of the novel, to ignore the nuances of character, to present human response as reflexive, to doubt the unique and individual workings of the human mind. It is almost axiomatic in satiric representation that the subjects under scrutiny participate in a kind of thoughtless, soulless arena where individuals do not really count. Swift's characters act as if no one in his or her right mind would judge and scrutinize human actions on the basis of particular contingencies or necessities. Satire is essentially about the ways in which individuals reveal their selfish and egotistical desires; character for the satirist is always comically distilled as nothing but self-seeking. In Swiftian satire, the subject is an embarrassing monster who is meant to provoke in us an almost visceral disgust with the ways in which individuals misrepresent their real motives. Characters are always invalidated by their actions, and satire means stripping them of their narrative bona fides that the emerging novel grants them so fully and readily.

## II  NARDACS AND LIARS

Gulliver is a Nardac. There can be no dispute about that. After his waylaying of the Blefuscan fleet in the service of the Lilliputians, Gulliver is made a Nardac "upon the Spot, which is the highest Title of Honour among them" (34). So what, then, is a Nardac? Nardac seems an arbitrary name until other anagrammatic matters provide a retrospective license of sorts to rearrange the order of its letters. In Laputa, during a discussion about anagrams and excrement, Gulliver claims special knowledge because of his unnarrated travels in a place, "Tribnia (by the natives called Langden)" (163). "Langden" and "Tribnia" are, by the simple disposition of the anagrammatic draw, "England" and "Britain." Few readers have, or ought to have, trouble rearranging these geographically disposed letters. After all, the Laputa episode itself, whatever implications can be drawn from *its* letters, invites readers to scramble letters by diagramming a machine that does just that.

As is often the case in narrative, incidents that occur later in a sequence have a kind of throw-back potential in focusing questions that may not have even occurred at first. We can ask with good cause whether the order of the

Nardac is anything more than a scrambled Canard?[11] A *canard* is a hoax or joke. It is a concoction, as Sterne might put it, full of cock and bull; or, as the Marx Brothers might swim in, duck soup.

The Order of Canard brings Swift's readers close, perhaps perilously close, to a series of tricky fictional questions in *Gulliver's Travels*. What honor ought the reader best bestow upon Gulliver's story? To what extent does that story look like a hoax consisting of jumbled territorial letters inside the head of a traveler who may now be a lunatic, sojourning in Tribnia, by the natives called Langden? Are all of the *Travels* a canard, part of whose fictional content is the notion that the traveler never leaves the mental spaces that literally project his ground? Is the possessive in *Gulliver's Travels* not only a function of grammatical belonging but of subjective parody? Do the travels belong to Gulliver in the sense that the distraction of his ego-driven mind is the only thing that could have really produced them? Is the actual fiction a much more complicated narrative satiric investigation about the kind of mind that would imagine fantastical places from the mixed up, local, and nonsensical jumble of experiences that constitute a version of modern or *nouveau* British madness? Though Gulliver seems hardly touched by the modern world—exactly the King of Brobdingnag's point when, in a backhanded compliment, he exempts Gulliver as a traveler from the corruptions of the odious little race of vermin to which he belongs—perhaps he is really driven mad by it *before* he ever voyages anywhere?

To put these questions differently, what happens to the standard reading contract of fiction—the naive one that asks us to give the narrator his or her due and believe what is told us—if we assume Gulliver never left England? If we dismiss the naive reading contract that allows the voyages their fictional credibility, what is the point of reading on in the narrative? But what if another contract offers a different way of reading the *Travels?* What if the attitudes Gulliver strikes—especially his behavior at the end—become symptomatic of the delusionary madness of a depressed and self-persecuted modern? Swift and his age knew madness under several names, one of them melancholy—maybe that is why Gulliver marries a woman named Mary Burton, who sports the surname of the greatest expert on madness in the seventeenth century, Richard Burton.[12] Swift named as melancholy what we would name depression in its less manifest state and paranoia in its raving state. Essentially paranoia is a form of overactive imagination, as Swift explained the malady (even if he did not identify it) earlier in *A Tale of A Tub*. The delusion of special grandeur brings all paranoid experience into its own special compass, and imposes its vision upon the world as a form of power, the power of self-projection.

Why would Swift want to include the possibility that the *Travels* are Gulliver's stay-at-home invention, the fancy of homebound lunacy? One argument, perfectly consistent with everything Swift ever wrote (and, more important, perfectly consistent with the manner or mode of Swift's approach to the satiric nature of narrative voice), is that madness approached the very condition assumed as necessary for the modern form of the prose memoir or novel: the obsessive self-centeredness of the narrator. The narrator in the early *Tale of A Tub* is an abstraction of the later Gulliver in this sense. We learn to read the whole of the *Tale* as a projection of the reality of a lunatic whose several returns to Bedlam are all homecomings. The result looks like a tale told by a crazed teller. Swift's earlier modern writer in the *Tale* was supposed to be at work on two treatises, one called "A Description of the Kingdom of *Absurdities*," and another, "A Voyage into *England*, by a Person of Quality in *Terra Australis*, translated from the Original." Perhaps Swift produced both years later in *Gulliver's Travels*, an account more like a voyage into England or, at least, into the subjective *terra incognita* of Gulliver's disturbed brain than it is the comic record of travels to which we extend fictional credit only because we are told they occur. The presumed person of quality voyaging into England is the satiric travesty of Gulliver as novelistic canard, a person returned from somewhere near the Australia of his mind bereft not only of quality at the end of his travels, but of his senses.

To pose the possibility that Gulliver never leaves England is to raise notions about points of access into any fiction. Readers generally proceed by following the terms of a fictional contract until it is violated or altered. The center of the new narrative tradition building around the time of Swift's *Travels* and continuing after it, was the contract of good faith established between writers and readers of novels based on a key premise: relatively unexceptional characters could produce a relatively engaging narrative if enough circumstantially probable things happened to them. Only under the narrative contract of veracity do these narratives gain credit. That is, if we believed them to be improbable, they would lose the credit they sustain by masquerading as true stories.

Defoe begins his narrative of Robinson Crusoe by insisting that he "believes the thing to be a just History of Fact; neither is there any Appearance of fiction in it" (3). By this he means that within its fictional contract, the events laid out are strictly probable. Even if the novel takes place within an imaginary topography—say, Crusoe's island—that topography bears a resemblance to a place that might well exist. Those reading the narrative can, by a none-too-wrenching leap of the imagination, credit the possibility of the story actually taking place somewhere and to someone. Swift has Gulliver's cousin Sympson make the same assessment in the *Travels*: "There is an Air of Truth apparent through the whole; and indeed the Author was so distinguished for his Veracity, that it became a Sort of Proverb among his Neighbors at *Redriff*, when any one affirmed a Thing, to say, it was as true as if Mr. Gulliver had spoke it" (viii). But the choices Swift makes in constructing Gulliver's narrative, the contradictions and inconsistencies he allows Gulliver, contribute to the reader's suspicion that the contractual truth of this fiction is really the delusionary nature of Gulliver's adventures.

Gulliver's diction is tangled throughout when the subject is truth-telling, even if by the time he writes the *Travels* he is liege to Houyhnhnm ideology where there is no word for "lie" in the language. How convenient! Nonetheless, Gulliver keeps bringing up the possibility of lying. Does anyone imagine him "so far degenerated as to defend my Veracity?" (vii). How far degenerated does one have to be not to defend one's veracity? Gulliver's repeated defense of his veracity is one of those clues that all may not be as it seems. That he protests his abiding veracity is evidence of the extent to which Gulliver believes the claim, however much the untruth may have entered his consciousness as vision. The lengths to which a narrative subject will go to convince himself that his beliefs are definitive is one of Swift's major satiric strategies in representing the modern object of fiction. When Gulliver fronts the issue of his veracity again, late in the adventure, he selects for support the words of that infamous snake-in-the-grass Sinon, the Greek deserter during the Trojan War. Sinon is in the midst of telling the grandest lie in literary history to the Trojans concerning a gift horse that bears some looking in the mouth. Of course Sinon is only lying about a horse whereas Gulliver thinks he is telling the truth about a Houyhnhnm. When the Trojans express doubts about his story Sinon protests, "Though Fortune may have made me wretched, she has not made me a liar," and Gulliver finds the sentiment apt just after his own ringing claim that in all things he "would *strictly adhere to Truth*": "—*Nec si miserum Fortuna Sinonem / Finxit, vanum etiam, mendacemque improba finget* [Though Fortune has made Sinon wretched, she has not also made him a liar] *Aeneid*, II, 79–80" (256). Actually, at the very instance that Sinon protests his veracity he may well believe, like Gulliver, that his wretchedness supersedes his lie, a belief based primarily on its articulation.

It is because Gulliver cannot and could not recognize the implications of the Sinon allusion for his own account of horse culture in Houyhnhnmland that is so very powerful. The strength of Gulliver's belief in his veracity is precisely what clues the reader to disbelieve it. Gulliver's is not the imposter's lie but rather the lunatic's lie. He remains convinced that what is in his head is true, and he is willing to cite any scrap of material that has also lodged itself in his memory to support it, even if that scrap of material is profound countertestimony for his readers. Gulliver is so deluded that Sinon serves him as a character reference, which is, in a way, what Sinon is.

Some would insist that the fiction of the *Travels* resists a reading that would posit Gulliver as having made up all his voyages because there are still unaccountable bits of fictional information left over from the naive reading contract that the reader must dispose. For example, the *Travels* had to have taken place because we are told how Gulliver digs into his pocket on the way home from Lilliput and Brobdingnag and actually produces live artifacts of those tiny and gigantic civilizations. But this is simply to give the prior contract—the naive one—too much credit. Paranoids are perfectly capable— within the reading contract that assumes madness—of imagining actions that seem perfectly real to them, and then imagining a cast of characters who, unlike the rest of world, partake of the very fantasies created for and by the lunatic. There is the famous joke of the paranoid who complains to his shrink that he is covered with butterflies. "Good god," the shrink shouts, "don't brush them off on me." This joke is based on a double fictional contract: the naive one that the butterflies exist and the revised one that the patient and the shrink *think* they exist. Such is the kind of double contract that gets written for *Gulliver's Travels* as part of its satiric agenda.

## III SCURRY POINTS

When anything occurs in fictional narrative that challenges, threatens, or alters the terms of an original or naive reading contract, readers are well advised to seek counsel. Doubting Gulliver's veracity or unscrambling the letters of Nardac and, later, Tribnia and Langden, compel just such radical alterations of the reading contract. A word like canard, all jumbled up as a special honor bestowed upon the narrator, forces a readerly double take. Exactly who is swimming in the duck soup? Maybe Gulliver and maybe all travelers who have been adhering to the wrong clauses of the wrong reader's contract and who continue to do so as they read on.

The *Travels* are filled with hundreds of narrative words, phrases, and incidents that force the savvy reader to pay most attention at the very moment the reading contract appears in doubt or in jeopardy.[13] These are what can be called scurry points, where readers are sometimes explicitly asked and sometimes implicitly required to reconstrue the contracts under which they are proceeding. In its 1726 version, *Gulliver's Travels* begins narrative life as a voyage memoir. Whether actual or counterfeit, it is fair enough to say that the fiction seems to proceed as a faithful record of Gulliver's experience abroad until we encounter a race of people roughly six inches tall in a place named Lilliput. Gulliver, no more than his readers, is ready for the Lilliputians. He senses their abnormality, their deep strangeness. Even as a character inside a fiction he does not assume the suspension of the laws of probability; rather, he asks for the suspension on the basis of a new reader's contract that *has* to be rewritten because of things that have occurred to him. After all, he simply came upon the Lilliputians. Readers tentatively grant him fictional license to proceed with his record. This seems an acceptable addendum to the naive fictional contract, understood by readers as part of a general theory of literature.[14]

The amended contract does not demand that we should expect such a race as the Lilliputians (neither does Gulliver before he encounters them), only that we should credit Gulliver's surprise discovery. Nonetheless, there is another option based on a more radical scurrying of the reading contract at the beginning of *Gulliver's Travels*. We have to recall something about the method and sequence of the work's publication history here. In 1735, nine years after the original publication of the *Travels*, Swift added prefatory material—a letter from Gulliver to his cousin Sympson, and a letter from Sympson to the reader. When he did so, he was obviously concerned enough about readers missing the course of Gulliver's mental history that he reimagined it.

Presumably compiled from notebooks and journals written close to the time of the voyages, even the 1726 *Travels* are recollected after Gulliver is represented to have gone crazy or at least to prance and whinny like a horse in his stable. But we have to reach the end of the *Travels* before we can entertain any notion of the already disturbed Gulliver establishing the sequence of his own distraction. This is a nifty trick. The new prefatory material simply emphasizes the process Gulliver has already undergone and places it at the beginning of the narrative. Swift might have wished the reader to infer in 1726 the proposition he reinforces in 1735: Gulliver was entirely mad when he turned over his manuscript to his cousin Sympson. At the very least, the letter opens the prospect that Gulliver suffers from a sort of delusion whose major symptom is the travels themselves.

We now begin with a potentially different contract. Gulliver represents in writing the state of mind that, first and foremost, produces the *record* of the adventures, not the adventuring. The private vocabulary of the prefatory Sympson material scurries the narrative in stranger ways than Gulliver's own bewildering encounter with a race of little people. As readers we hear words in the first paragraph of the narrative that are completely alien: first *Houyhnhnm*, and, a few lines later, *Yahoo*. No first-time readers could incorporate these into the clauses of any naive fictional contract without worrying over them. The difficulty resides not simply in the strangeness of the words, but in the way they are presented by the text as if readers *should* know what they mean. Gulliver speaks a kind of foreign language as if it is a lingua franca, circling around from the ending of the 1726 version to the beginning of the 1735 version. The *Travels* become satirically supplemented. By the narrative device of adding what can be seen as a coda to the preface, Swift begins with a paranoid hero rather than building to one. The implication is that we missed something the first time around. Indeed, we did.

Of course, Gulliver's letter is for his cousin, who, presumably, does know what the words mean. But even if Sympson knows full well to what Gulliver refers, there is still something in the tone and insistence of the references that renders Gulliver fictionally suspect. *Something* has made

Gulliver insane or unsettled at home, and the travels are the fable we get from him as an explanation. If the Sympson letter scurries the narration long before the first odd marvel, the Lilliputians, pop into the text, just what sort of a person conceived and wrote these things in the first place? Who, after all, uses a private vocabulary with such urgency? Depending upon where readers pick up the narrative thread Gulliver is literally a different narrator within two reading contracts. Readers have the option of beginning where they once might have arrived. Gulliver is a traveler in one contract; a madman in another.

With this in mind it is possible to return to the anagrammatic aside in Laputa about "Tribnia by the natives called Langden." The letters of the anagram collapse the naive and the novelistic spaces of the narrative: the external territory to which Gulliver may travel, and the locally mapped place from which only his mind may wander. Two reading contracts become one. We begin to substitute the contract of insanity for the naive indulgence of the adventures. In the most subtle of satiric strategies, Swift takes the novelistic reading of the *Travels* a step further than it might wish to go. That is, he returns the plot to probable grounds. He takes away the fantastic and the marvelous by assuming that his main character has imagined all that he experiences, with the exception of the madness that has made him imagine it. This is a perfectly naturalistic reading with enough clues strewn about the narrative that it is both a likely and a contractual reading. But what does it do to the new subject of fiction? Exactly what Swift wished to do. It unsettles him; it loosens the mental screws that make such a subject reliable; it depicts instability where that other innovator of novelistic form, Daniel Defoe, depicts substantiation.

Defoe suggested in defending his Crusoe fable that an island scene "placed so far off, had its original so near home."[15] By this he means that the story novelists have to tell is always in some sense a version of the mental experience of the author. The topography of the plot is a plausible extension of the narrating or authoring self. As satirist, Swift goes Defoe one better—he not only writes a narrative in which faraway places reflect local experiences, but he writes a narrative about a man so mad that his projected adventures *become* the equivalent of the jumbled letters of his home. Gulliver himself points readers to those who think he made these journeys up as "a meer Fiction out of mine own Brain" (vi); and he imagines his countrymen will "believe that I *said the Thing which was not*: that I invented the Story out of my own Head" (206). He even admits that his flirtation with lunacy occurred to him during his voyages: "I feared my Brain was disturbed by my Sufferings and Misfortunes" (198). Moreover, some "will not allow me to be Author of Mine Own Travels" (vi). That is, he not only didn't write them but he didn't actually make them. He has no authority to foist them off, and he has authored them only insofar as he made them up.

Oddly enough, he says he was "very little Sunburnt in all my Travels" (71), without exactly explaining why. Later, when he speaks to horses in his stable, his readers may stumble upon the quixotic truth. All the languages that come back from his voyages are in a way local. He is the only translator. And at the end is he transcribing nothing more than horse sounds? *Yahoo* sounds like a horse, a sort of wheeze and sneeze. And *houyhnhnm* is obvious— it doesn't even need translation. Gulliver ends up talking to horses in his stable because he probably began that way. We do not hear much about Gulliver's life in England, but he says things in Lilliput that make us think of him as hopelessly paranoid, presumably as the result of experiences at home rather than abroad. There are hints early on that Gulliver has a reputation in England that is not easily explained. For instance, what does he mean when he seeks to justify his cleanliness to satisfy "some of my Maligners" (13). These maligners have no history other than as readers of the book—they are in England, not in Lilliput. But the English at this point are supposedly all yahoos with an inherent disposition to nastiness and dirt. What goes here? Is Gulliver making up the maligners? Or is he persecuted at home for being crazy rather than for being dirty?

Lilliput is his first delusionary place, a fantasy of power, a combination of niceness and prissiness and barely suppressed violence: eating, bashing, squashing. Gulliver's first projection miniaturizes the world for purposes of overpowering it. It is not for nothing that the first voyage of the narrative makes Gulliver into so dominating a figure. But he is even persecuted by the little people. To do so much and still to be blamed is the paranoid's greatest fear and, in a complex neurotic way, his greatest delight. Gulliver is both perpetrator and victim. His locutions are revealing. Of a leading Lilliputian minister he says, "Skyresh Bolgolam, who was pleased, without any Provocation, to be my mortal Enemy" (25). It sounds as if Gulliver has practiced this phrase often; it falls easily off his tongue. His sense of persecution folds neatly into his proclamation as a truth-teller. Of his Lilliput adventures he says that "Posterity shall hardly believe them, although attested by Millions" (66). Who are these millions? If millions attest, why wouldn't posterity believe? Posterity has believed much more from far fewer.

By the last voyage to Houyhnhnmland, the paranoid feast is expanded. Gulliver speaks as if England had been a nightmare of persecution for him in contrast to Houyhnhnmland: "here I did not feel the Treachery or Inconstancy of a Friend, nor the Injuries of a secret or open Enemy" (p. 241). There "was neither Physician to destroy my Body, nor Lawyer to ruin my Fortune; nor Informer to watch my Words and Actions, or forage Accusation against me for Hire" (242). All of modern civilization seems out to get Gulliver; more so at home than out of the country. But when did these things happen? Gulliver's travels seem to allegorize experiences in England for which we have no narrative record.

It is in the most strikingly modern land of the entire adventures, Laputa, the land of projectors, that Gulliver is most explicit about his circumstances. He, too, claims (like Defoe) to have "been a Sort of Projector in my younger Days" (152), and he unabashedly makes further proposals throughout this book, venturing his "poor opinion" on such paranoid matters as the possibility of swallowing information wafers or analyzing excrement for political plots. His treatment could be the most revealing clue about his state of mind in England that led him to make Laputa and the other places up: "I thought my self too much neglected, not without some Degree of Contempt" (147). This is a key to Gulliver's psyche. Gulliver has nothing—no dignity, no centrality, no stature—and his experience in the most modern place of his travels is, as he describes it, the most melancholy of all. The modern inhabitants of Laputa are, for good satiric measure, the closest to mad, suffering from a sense of exaggerated doom, moving too fast toward their own conclusion. That is, they are unsettled in ways similar to Gulliver, displaying "continual Disquietudes, never enjoying a minute's Peace of Mind" (137). They "neither sleep quietly in their Beds, nor have any Relish for the common Pleasures or Amusements of Life" (138).

What Gulliver says of Laputa can be extended metaphorically to the condition that inspires the projected travels of a madman: "I was weary of being confined to an Island where I received so little Countenance, and resolved to leave it with the first Opportunity" (147). This is a parable of Gulliver's life. He leaves his own native England by making up his travels, which then provide an imagined antidote for his insignificance as modern man within his own culture. The fervor with which he ends up attacking European civilization makes less sense had he actually traveled for so many years than if he never left—precisely the point made to Gulliver by the King of Brobdingnag. The extraordinary harangue Gulliver later produces about life in his own country for his Master Houyhnhnm, with barely the vocabulary to do it in his host's language, reveals the image of England he carries around in his head. Gulliver is so steeped in satiric details that articulating them makes them real. Metaphorically, cataloguing abuses is equivalent to an obsession with them. His *Travels* are, as is so often the case in Swiftian satire, the articulated version of his madness. The Master Houyhnhnm senses as much when he points out that the information provided by Gulliver is enough to turn even a sane horse mad: Gulliver's "Discource had increased his Abhorrence of the whole Species, so he found it gave him a Disturbance in his Mind, to which he was wholly a Stranger before" (215). The process, though not the timing, is something that Gulliver well knows. Of course he may have made up the Master Houyhnhnm to image himself as narrator. The greatest truth about Gulliver is his fullest lie, the abiding satiric contract of the *Travels*.

## NOTES

1. James Joyce, *Ulysses* (New York: Random House, 1984), 52. Subsequent references are to this edition. To box the compass is to go virtually nowhere. Ships set their compasses before voyages by sailing back and forth between light beacons on coastal points.

2. In the anonymous *Gulliver Decypher'd: or Remarks on a late Book, intitled, Travels into Several Remote Nations of the World. By Capt. Lemuel Gulliver* (London, 1727), the *Travels* are said to be "design'd only for a Satyr upon those Writers that affect the marvelous and improbable, and upon the wild and monstrous relations of Travellers" (43). Of course, within such a frame, the *Travels* are demonstrably a reflection of the wider social, political, and ethical orders of England: the corrupt practices of Lilliputian court life begin the attack; the King of Brobdingnag widens it; the shades summoned from the republics of the ancient world in Glubbdubdrib reiterate it; and the Master Houyhnhnm rearticulates and sustains it.

3. J. Paul Hunter makes a cogent case for just such a notion in "*Gulliver's Travels* and the Novel," in Fredrick N. Smith, ed., *The Genre of Gulliver's Travels* (Newark, Del.: University of Delaware Press, 1990). Hunter writes, "the *Travels* work as a kind of parodic answer to the early novel and as a satire of novelistic consciousness" (56).

4. *Gulliver's Travels*, Norton Critical Edition, ed. Robert A. Greenberg (New York: Norton, 1970), 135. All subsequent citations are to this readily available edition.

5. Alexander Pope, *The Memoirs of the Extraordinary Life, Works, and Discoveries of Martinus Scriblerus*, ed. Charles Kerby-Miller (London and New York: Oxford University Press, 1966), 165.

6. At the time Swift was given the Scriblerian assignment, he thought of Defoe as the archetypal downclass modern writer, his "mock authoritative Manner" being "of a Level with great Numbers among the lowest Part of Mankind" (*Examiner*, 15 [16 November 1710], reprinted in Herbert Davis, ed., *Prose Works of Jonathan Swift* [Oxford: Blackwell, 1966], III: 14).

7. Early on, Jonathan Smedley, in *Gulliveriana: or, a Fourth Volume of Miscellanies. Being a sequel of the Three Volumes, published by Pope and Swift* (London, 1728), recognized the connection: "This pious Author seems to have taken his Hint, if not from the celebrated History of *Tom Thumb*, from the Author who a few Years ago obliged the World with the Travels of *Robinson Crusoe [sic]*." Cited in Kathleen Williams, ed., *Swift: the Critical Heritage* (London: Barnes and Noble, 1970), 91.

8. Richard Braverman's "Crusoe's Legacy," in *Studies in the Novel*, 18 (1986): 1–26, has a great deal to say about the *I* in island.

9. *Serious Reflections during the Life and Surprizing Adventurers of Robinson Crusoe*, reprinted in G. H. Maynadier, ed., *The Works of Daniel Defoe* (New York: G. D. Sproul, 16 vols., 1903), III: 4.

10. *Robinson Crusoe*, Norton Critical Edition, ed. Michael Shinagel (New York: Norton, 1975), 3.

11. The question was posed to me exactly this way by a student in the mid-1970s, whose name has long since passed the territorial borders of my memory. I gladly credit that student with the question and its implications.

12. Richard Burton's great *Anatomy of Melancholy* is a book so diverse and grand that the critic Northrop Frye considered it a Menippean satire and names his own *Anatomy of Criticism* after it.

13. For example, consider the name of the Lilliputian capital, Mildendo. It sounds like mid-London, or, fitting for Lilliput, Demilond. Better yet, it suggests the inhabitants,

Dildo men, which, when we ponder what later happens to Gulliver among the young maids of honor in Brobdingnag when he is of Lilliputian size, makes the fiction not only satirically prescient but prurient. Gulliver becomes a kind of dildo for one of the queen's young female attendants ("wherein the Reader will excuse me for not being over particular" [96]). Even though he refuses to dwell on the details, the earlier training Gulliver received from Master Bates enjoys a curious supplement. Gulliver becomes the instrument of his own earlier training.

14. The first translator of *Gulliver's Travels* into French, the Abbé Desfontaines, wrote in his 1727 preface to the volume of the fictional contract implicit in giving the improbable its space: "That is the poetic system. If we condemn it, we must now reduce all fictions to the boring intrigues of romances; we must look with utmost scorn at Ovid's *Metamorphoses*, and those which are scattered through the poems of Homer and Virgil, since all this is based solely on inventions which are wholly lacking in verisimilitude" (excerpted from Williams, ed., *Swift: the Critical Heritage*, 80–81). The theory is validated by Aristotle (*Poetics* 1460a): "Homer has taught other poets to tell an untrue story as it should be told, by taking advantage of a logical fallacy. When one event is followed by a second as a consequence or concomitant, men are apt to infer, when the second event happens, that the first must have happened or be happening, though the inference is false" (*On Poetry and Style*, trans. G. M. A. Grube [New York: Bobbs-Merrill, 1958], 53). Augustine makes the equally pertinent distinction between fable and deception: "What I call the fabulous kind of falsehood (*mendax*), the kind which is committed by those who tell fables. The difference between deceivers and fabulists is this, that every deceiver wants to deceive but not every one who tells a fable has the desire to deceive" (*The Soliloquies of Saint Augustine*, trans. Thomas F. Gilligan [New York: Cosmopolitan Science and Art Service, 1943], 105). (2.9.16)

15. *Serious Reflections*, III: xiii.

THOMAS KEYMER

# Serializing a Self

## THE USES OF DEFERRAL, SCHEHEREZADE TO SMOLLETT

In Addison's inaugural number of the *Spectator*, the presiding persona of the new journal efficiently describes his life, starting three months after conception and ending at the present day. He then outlines an ambitious scheme for conveying his opinions (to which will be added 'other Particulars in my Life and Adventures ... as I shall see occasion'). The wording of his proposal is arresting: wishing 'to communicate the Fulness of my Heart', he intends using the serial 'to Print my self out, if possible, before I die'. In the incremental form of diurnal instalments, his language seems to promise, the private will become public, the impalpable will be made material, the fugitive will be fixed. Accumulating in regular bulletins ('I shall publish a Sheet-full of Thoughts every Morning'), the taciturn self of Mr Spectator will be transformed into an eloquent text—or will be so transformed 'if possible'.[1] The confidence of Addison's persona is only fleetingly disrupted by this qualification, however, and whatever factors might jeopardize his chances of printing out the self before death are left unmentioned. He does not speculate about any possible mismatch between the fluidity of subjectivity and the linearity of prose, or between the endlessness of opinions and the finiteness (even when repeated daily) of a single folio half-sheet. He does not even worry about the possible effect on his project of sudden death (a prospect that leaves him 'not at all sollicitous'[2]); and though other casualties

From *Sterne, the Moderns, and the Novel.* © 2002 by Thomas Keymer.

arise during the *Spectator's* run (Sir Roger de Coverley is the notable case),
Mr Spectator himself is immune. Ongoing reports of his ongoing opinions
and life accumulate serenely for a further twenty-one months, and little sense
of incompleteness or failure on his part colours the journal's close. It was left
to imitators like Edward Moore's weekly *World* (1753–6) or the fortnightly
*Ladies Magazine, or the Universal Entertainer* (1749–53) to contrive, when
winding up their journals, a more playful effect of business left undone. The
first ends abruptly, and in an imported persona, when its fictional manager,
Adam Fitz-Adam, fatally crashes his chaise; the second breaks off in midflow
when its ailing editor, 'Jasper Goodwill', dies of that most Shandean disorder,
consumption.[3]

None of these periodicals, of course, makes any serious move towards
fictional autobiography. At most they gesture in that direction by using
sketchy fictional situations and progressions to frame their miscellaneous
matter—a characteristic perhaps exaggerated by Michael G. Ketcham, who
finds in the *Spectator* 'a proto-Shandeanism where ... a faintly comic narrator
moves through a series of associations, shifting between incidents and
reflections'.[4] Yet in articulating the ambition of turning the self into a text
while also intimating the possibility of failure, Addison momentarily
pinpoints the fundamental problem for all autobiographical writing, which is
that completeness, one way or another, must always elude it. The difficulty
is directly encountered in more genuine serial autobiographies of the period,
which in their very mode of production conveyed a sense that to represent
identity in all its shifting complexities—to print the self out in full—required
a form of writing more flexible and extensive than conventionally seamless
memoirs could provide, and a form of writing, too, that would never end.
Underpinned by a sense of flux that was commonplace at the time (Sterne is
not unusual in his observation that 'in the same day, sometimes in the very
same action, [men] are utterly inconsistent and irreconcileable with
themselves' (*Sermons*, 11.104)), these serials were able to register identity
with new alertness to its ongoing twists and turns. Inherently, the subjects
and meanings they sought to define were never closed or resolved. In
avoiding false closure of their own, however, works of this kind inevitably
courted arbitrary closure from without—the kind of closure Sterne describes
in a more famous sermon, 'Job's Account of the Shortness and Troubles of
Life', preoccupied as it is by the unpredictability with which 'cruel distemper
or unthought of accident' arrives to cut off life (*Sermons*, 10.98). As several of
these works were to demonstrate, to document one's life in serial form was
to cultivate a mode more responsive than others to the instability of identity
over time, but one also more vulnerable to the very contingencies it sought
to catch.

In the extracts from his *Journal* that John Wesley issued in twenty-one
instalments between 1739 and 1791 (the year of his death), the patterned

certainties of spiritual autobiography are discarded for a more provisional and discontinuous mode of writing, in which a spiritual life of unceasing struggle is monitored and held up for inspection in ongoing interim reports. As Isabel Rivers writes, 'serialization effectively emphasized that Wesley's quest was never complete': he had engineered a form in which the experience described could never be final, stability and conclusiveness were never on offer, and spiritual recognitions could never accumulate fully enough to complete the work of self-examination.[5] Serial autobiography could also lend itself to less high-minded purposes, as in the case of *An Apology for the Conduct of Mrs. Teresia Constantia Phillips* the notorious (and probably ghostwritten) serial memoir that Phillips published and sold from her own address in seventeen shilling numbers in 1748–9. Although Philips complained in successive instalments about the ruses practised by her enemies to curtail or delay publication (she also feared piracy, and anticipated Sterne's unusual precautions against forgery by announcing that 'to prevent Imposition, each Book will be signed with her own Hand'), the work proved successful enough in broadcasting Phillips's intended message about herself while also spinning out a lucrative scandal.[6] A more troubled case exists in the contemporaneous *Memoirs of Laetitia Pilkington*, even though Pilkington shared much of Phillips's exuberant ingenuity in exploiting the plasticity of the mode (notably when threatening, in her opening instalment, that 'if every married Man, who has ever attack'd me, does not subscribe to my *Memoirs*', these men would be named and shamed in later instalments[7]). Published in three volume-length parts of 1748, 1749, and 1754, Pilkington's autobiography is discontinuous in chronology and digressive in style, its fractured structure and inclusive instincts posing a conspicuous ongoing threat to any prospect of reaching adequate closure. 'In the narrative, written a decade before Sterne's *Tristram Shandy*, the trivial is always disrupting the linear description of the past,' as Felicity Nussbaum puts it.[8] Description of the past was then more conclusively disrupted by Pilkington's death in 1750, which left her third volume unpublished, and perhaps unwritten. 'The Author intended another Volume of these Memoirs, but died before she had compleated it; and ... no such Third Volume will ever be published,' reads a note in the 1751 reissue of volumes 1 and 2. The posthumous volume of 1754, which brings Pilkington's interrupted narrative to an off-the-peg providentialist conclusion, was at least augmented, and perhaps substantially forged, by her son.[9]

But what of *Tristram Shandy*, that work so finely attuned to all that is most hostile to first-person writing: the impenetrability of identity ('Don't puzzle me' (7.33.633)); the insufficiency of language ('Well might *Locke* write a chapter upon the imperfections of words' (5.7.429)); the unavailability of permanence ('Time wastes too fast' (9.8.754))? Serialization gave Sterne the ideal medium in which to work out such concerns, specifically by dramatizing the way Tristram's struggle to control his writing coexists, with ever more desperate imbrication, with the struggle to prolong his life. That Tristram is progressively ailing as he writes, losing his life even as he endeavours to write it, gives urgency to what might otherwise seem a merely playful meditation on the impossibility of fixing the self (or the memories and opinions that constitute a self) in serial print. In contriving this unfolding tale, Sterne had a wealth of serial precedents to play on.

The boom in eighteenth-century serialization can be pinpointed with reference to the original and revised versions of Fielding's book-trade satire, *The Author's Farce*. The original play of 1730 makes no allusion to the trend; the 1734 revision, however, adds a new trick to the cynical repertoire of Mr Bookweight, a Curll-like dealer in false imprints, cribbed translations, and bogus pamphlet-wars. 'Write me out proposals for delivering five sheets of Mr. Bailey's English Dictionary every week, till the whole be finished,' he orders Mr Quibble, who should use as his model 'the proposals for printing Bayle's Dictionary in the same manner'.[10] His finger on the pulse as ever, Fielding was adjusting his satire to register an innovation that (in the words of its historian, R. M. Wiles) 'accelerated the book trade more than any other single force affecting the reading habits of our ancestors between 1700 and 1750'.[11] By making prestigious books available in cheap instalments ('in Scraps', sneered one contemporary, 'that the Purchaser may not feel the Price'[12]), serial publication not only expanded the book-buying market but also made its exploitation newly efficient. Costs could be spread and returns speeded and recycled; purchasers could be locked in by systems of subscription, with demand accurately predicted; slender packets of sheets could be distributed to provincial areas that had once seemed commercially inaccessible (this being the decade when an expanding post-road network was first used for monthly magazine distribution on a national scale).[13]

The trend towards piecemeal issue of large multi-volume works peaked in the early 1730s (Wiles identifies 1732 as the crucial year) with several immensely successful publications that Sterne would later use. The five-volume second edition of Bayle's *Dictionary Historical and Critical* (1733–8), which Sterne borrowed from York Minster Library and used in 'Slawkenbergius's Tale', had originally been published in 148 fortnightly parts. In the sale catalogue of his library (lot 2) is the ten-volume rival version in monthly parts, *A General Dictionary, Historical and Critical* (1733–41), which took even longer to appear.[14] As this protracted project reached its close, the fifth edition of Chambers's *Cyclopaedia* (1741–3) came out in weekly sixpenny numbers of three sheets each, as opposed to the lump-sum price of four guineas for the simultaneously available fourth edition of 1741; and this pattern was repeated when the sixth edition of 1750 was accompanied by a serialized seventh in 1751–2.[15] Although it is the second edition (1738) that Sterne may have owned (lot 236), the Florida editors use the serialized text of 1741–3 in annotating *Tristram Shandy*, and Judith Hawley has shown that he used this edition specifically (s.v. 'Circumcision') in a mock-learned passage in volume 5.[16] Chambers as much as Bayle must have been in Sterne's mind as he contrived, in 'the slow progress my father made in his *Tristra-pædia*' (5.16.448), his domestic analogue for the situation in which the hapless compilers of these serial encyclopaedias were caught, their openings becoming obsolete before their endings could appear.

Probably the most spectacular success of all was Sterne's principal source for the campaigns of Uncle Toby, Nicholas Tindal's long-running translation and continuation of Rapin de Thoyras's *History of England*. Although the relevance of this work for *Tristram Shandy* was not documented until 1936, the popularizing effect of serialization had made it one of the best-known histories of the century (and netted its publishers, even before the continuation began, as much as £10,000): 'no Book in our Language had ever more Buyers or Readers,' as the *Daily Gazetteer* averred.[17] When Tristram thinks better of his plan to transcribe a lengthy passage from Rapin, there are complex resonances to his joke that this would be to charge the reader 'for fifty pages which I have no right to sell thee' (7.6.584). Here was a work notorious for the quarrels about copyright that had surrounded its lucrative run; a work that had already been extensively plagiarized elsewhere;[18] and a work that many of Sterne's readers would already have owned. First launched in monthly octavo numbers that sold at a rate of thousands weekly, and grew into a fifteen-volume first edition of 1725–31, Rapin's *History* was so successful that by the end of its run rival publishers were cashing in with a serial translation of their own. Tindal's publishers responded with a second edition in weekly folio numbers (1732–5), and his continuation began in 1736. Two combined editions of the history and continuation are listed in the sale catalogue of Sterne's library, the second weighing in at twenty-eight octavo volumes.[19]

The handsome editions that resulted from these processes could never wholly erase their serial origins, and occasionally Tindal makes explicit the relentless pressures of the mode. Like many similar publications, his work got off to a shaky start (one witness reports that he 'was for some Time not a little dubious, as to its success; and strongly inclin'd to drop his Design; and yet it is well known to what a vast Account it turn'd at last'), and he used a sequence of dated volume dedications to document his progress.[20] The impression left is of a frantic ongoing juggling act between his various duties as translator-historian, parish priest, and naval chaplain. In July 1726 he is in the Baltic, dedicating to his admiral a volume on the Norman conquest; September 1728 sees him back in his Essex parish, dedicating to the British merchants of Lisbon the volume of medieval history he wrote while ministering there; in March 1747 he is in another parish, dedicating to the Duke of Cumberland a volume on the 1720s.[21] Altogether this herculean task occupied Tindal for several decades, not least because, once the commitment to continuation had been made, it became, more accurately, sisyphean (and tantalizing with it). He began with intentions of abridging his massive source, but 'soon dropt his Design, and resolv'd not only to give the Publick a full and fair Translation, but also to add some *Notes* and *Observations* relating to *Antiquities, Curiosities, remarkable Occurrences, Characters* ... and several other Particulars and Circumstances'. Even when he had finished translating and begun his own continuation, Tindal was still doggedly adding opinion to transaction, so that 'nothing is omitted to render the Work as comprehensive and useful as possible'.[22] The result was predictable. In 1736–7 his first effort at continuation promised on its title page to fill the gap *'from the Revolution to the Accession of King George I'*, yet by the time this update drew to a close, in 1747, he had spent ten years describing no more than thirteen, and was only just at the point getting George II crowned. The more he wrote, the more he had to write; and the manufacturers of paper were profiting indeed. In the 1750s two further editions of the continuation advertised coverage *'from the Revolution to the Accession of King George II'*, but as *Tristram Shandy* entered gestation the title of a newly extended fourth edition (1758–60) was revised to read *'A Continuation of Mr. Rapin de Thoyras's History of England, from the Revolution to the Present Times'*. For the first time, Tindal had explicitly embraced the Shandean project of describing a subject that would accumulate without limit, dooming his work to a rolling state of incompleteness no matter how fast he produced it. Volume 21 of this continuation appeared in September 1760, to be sneered at by Smollett (who was now doing well himself as a writer of serial history) in the *Critical Review*.[23] Undeterred, Tindal's publishers (who now included the printer of *Tristram Shandy's* later instalments, William Strahan) launched a further update almost as soon as its predecessor was complete. By the time this fifth edition drew to a close in 1763, Tindal's work had been kept a-going for almost forty years—its only serious rival in bulk and longevity being a publishers' venture partly owned and printed by Richardson, the twenty-volume *Universal History from the Earliest Account of Time to the Present* (1736–50), several volumes of which Sterne borrowed from York Minster Library in 1754. At the same crucial stage for *Tristram Shandy*, this massive serial was revived in the form of a forty-four-volume *Modern Part of an Universal History* (1759–66), about a third of it compiled by Smollett, who at one stage wrote in desperation to Richardson of having to fill sheets with material 'which all the art of man cannot spin out to half the number'.[24]

The phenomenal success of serial publications like Tindal's Rapin attracted much conservative hostility, partly because it was attributed to marketing more than merit, and partly because it gave a dangerous currency to knowledge. Complaining that 'you have Bayle's *Dictionary* and Rapin's

*History* from two Places, with the daily Squabbles of Book sellers and Translators about them', the *Grub-Street Journal* worried about the democratization of reading entailed by serial form. Poor men now 'spend Six-pence upon a Number of Rapin' while their families starve, the journal protested, adding that to extend this sort of material to men 'designed by Nature for Trade and Manufactures ... was the Way to do them Harm, and to make them, not wiser or better, but impertinent, troublesome, and factious'.[25] Fielding (whose various comments on the Whig-Republican extremism of Tindal's Rapin partly explain the strength of this anxiety) was more amusingly scathing about serials, but his hostility was no less real. *Tom Jones* sarcastically admires the miracle of literary commodification through which 'the heavy, unread, Folio Lump, which long had dozed on the dusty Shelf, piece-mealed into Numbers, runs nimbly through the Nation'. *Joseph Andrews* fakes up a classical provenance for the practice, reporting that Homer not only divided his work into books 'but, according to the Opinion of some very sagacious Critics, hawked them all separately, delivering only one Book at a Time, (probably by Subscription)'. He thereby pioneered the art 'of publishing by Numbers, an Art now brought to such Perfection, that even Dictionaries are divided and exhibited piecemeal to the Public; nay, one Bookseller hath ... contrived to give them a Dictionary in this divided Manner for only fifteen Shillings more than it would have cost entire'.[26]

Serial works like this were an easy target. Although the contemporaneous example of Chambers's *Cyclopaedia* (which cost much the same whether bought outright or in parts) suggests fairer dealing than Fielding alleges, there were obvious disadvantages to users. The publishers of one medical dictionary in weekly numbers, 'alphabetically digested', pulled the plug midway through the letter 'B', presumably without compensating buyers, and such abrupt curtailments were not uncommon. Even a multivolume work by the indefatigable Tindal fell behind schedule after one number and collapsed after two.[27] Moreover, as Fielding well knew, text in this early phase of serial publication would be divided to suit the needs of production, not reception, so that a subscriber's weekly or monthly purchase would be simply a fascicule of so many sheets, utterly lacking the integrity of a Homeric book, and often beginning or ending in mid-sentence. Distinct in kind from the serialization in volumes that Sterne would later practise, this primitive mode of serialization never lost its dual reputation for cozenage and dumbing down: in the 1760s Hume preferred 'publishing in Volumes than in Numbers' because the latter method 'has somewhat of a quackish Air', while Samuel Bishop wrote scathingly that '*Scribblers*, from hand to mouth, who write and live, | In weekly *Numbers*, mental *Spoon-meat* give'.[28] Even so, it remains surprising that Fielding—a prolific writer of periodical journalism, and a novelist adroit in his games with fictional time—could see no redeeming potential in the serialization of books.[29] By the simple expedient of harmonizing printers' units with authorial divisions, thereby giving each number of a part-issued work an integrity of its own, serialization had more than commercial opportunities to offer, not least in the medium it established for manipulating through time the experience of reading. Here was an opportunity that novelists in particular could exploit.

Far more of the period's fiction than we commonly suppose reached its full extent through part publication, sometimes a volume or two at a time, sometimes in units that anticipate the more slimline Victorian norm. As J. Paul Hunter has argued, this tendency implies a grounding assumption in eighteenth-century fiction 'that stories are interwoven, seamless, continuous, and relatively endless', and encouraged readers to look for continuation more than resolution in the novels they consumed.[30] Well-known works like *Robinson Crusoe* and *Pamela* generated sequels, and Defoe was especially assiduous in scattering continuation nodules along his path as he wrote, most of which (like the volumes on Moll's 'governess' and highwayman husband tentatively projected in the preface to *Moll Flanders*) he never returned to exploit.[31] Other works inhabit a grey area between serial fiction and *roman fleuve*. Trilogy may be the best term for Sarah Fielding's linked publications of 1744–53, *The Adventures of David Simple, Familiar Letters between the Principal Characters in David Simple, and Volume the Last*, but there are closer connections between the three parts of Aphra Behn's *Love-Letters between a Nobleman and His Sister* (1684–7) or Eliza Haywood's *Love in Excess* (1719–20), which William Beatty Warner has described as using serialization to open the amatory novel 'to a potentially endless repetition on the market'.[32] Decades later, Henry Brooke's *The Fool of Quality* (1766–70) is a genuine serial novel in five more or less annual volumes. Several translated works are relevant, most obviously Marivaux's *La Vie de Marianne*. Written and published in eleven parts between 1731 and 1742, and serially translated in a three-stage English edition of 1736–42, the text plays explicitly on the dilatoriness of its own production, provoking complaints at the time (as W. H. McBurney and M. F. Shugrue report) 'that if a month of Marianne's life occupied six parts of the novel, the reader would need more than a lifetime to finish the work'. Eventually, Marivaux abandoned the novel without a conclusion, prompting a second English translator, Mary Collyer, to round off her version in fortnightly numbers, *The Virtuous Orphan* (1742), with a twelfth and final part of her own devising.[33]

More journalistic in character, though moving towards serial fiction in their limited continuities of focalization and setting, were open-ended satirical sequences like John Dunton's six-part ramble *The Night Walker* (1696–7) and Ned Ward's fictionalized journal *The London Spy* (1698–1700). Published in sixpenny numbers of four sheets each, *The London Spy* was designed to go on 'Monthly, as long as we shall find Encouragement', and ran eventually to eighteen numbers and two volumes. (The continuing vigour of its mode in Sterne's day is shown by Goldsmith's satirical essay series *Chinese Letters*, which began almost simultaneously with *Tristram Shandy*, attacked Sterne's first instalment in June 1760, and was fleetingly mocked in return in Sterne's third instalment of December 1761.)[34] Preceding *The Night Walker* was another Dunton periodical, *A Ramble round the World* (1689), which collapsed very soon, but was later revived (as *A Voyage round the World*, 1691) into an experimental fusion of autobiographical and fictional material that Dunton 'had been sweating at the best part of this seven Years', as his prologue declares. In a passage that looks forward to Tristram's glee at galloping amongst the critics and splashing a bishop (*TS* 4.20.306–7), Dunton adds: 'I first send out this *First Volume* by way of *Postilion*, to slapdash, and spatter all about him, (if the Criticks come in his way) in order to make Elbow-room for all the rest of his *little Brethren* that are to come after.' Twenty-four of these little brethren are envisaged altogether, but the project then peters out after three, closing with the narrator's lament that because of his digressiveness—'How many Miles (*alias* Pages) *am I again out of my way?*'—he must now suspend his present thread and 'reserve it for the next Volume'.[35]

The same period also saw begin to develop the tradition of magazine fiction described by Robert D. Mayo, who traces its inauspicious origins back to the failure, after six chapters in three instalments, of a projected twenty-four-part Cervantic imitation of 1681 entitled 'Don Rugero'. In the early eighteenth century, periodicals often ran intermittent background fictions, spun out over time and dropped when convenient. The inaugural *Tatler*, for example, promises 'from time to time ... to be very exact in the progress' of the lovelorn Cynthio, who is eventually killed off six months and eighty-four numbers later. Mayo establishes the 1740s as the decade in which more sustained kinds of fiction written expressly for magazine publication (and sometimes making serious efforts to exploit the advantages of periodicity) become significant. The richest period comes in the early 1760s, but a noteworthy prior example exists in 'A Story Strange as True': this skilfully managed serial tale ran intermittently through seven numbers of the *Gentleman's Magazine* in 1737–8, terminating (though with unfulfilled hints about future resumption) in the same number as a contribution that has been attributed to Sterne.[36]

Sometimes there could be a compelling logic to serialization. It was perfectly appropriate for publication of Antoine Galland's *Arabian Nights' Entertainments* to be an extended event, both in the Grub Street translation that closely followed the first French edition (1704–17) and in unauthorized newspaper serializations of the 1720s.[37] The work's framing situation (in which a narrator staves off execution by repeatedly deferring narrative closure) catches to perfection the characteristic elasticity of serial writing, as well as the hovering threat of sudden curtailment.[38] Scheherezade's dilemma is not exactly Tristram Shandy's—where he lives 364 times faster than he writes, she has only a day to live, and narrates 1,001 times more slowly—but in each case the proliferation of gratuitous narrative that typifies the work could not have been better enacted. By the same token, the halting publishing process that so infuriated Marivaux's early readers could intensify a series of games with narrative time that anticipates *Tristram Shandy*. By recurrently promising, from part 3 onwards, an interpolated tale that fails to materialize until part 8 ('I am not in a condition to undertake it present'; 'I find I must defer it'), *La Vie de Marianne* looks forward to Tristram's seven-year procrastination of his 'choicest morsel' (*TS* 4.32.401). Serialization could also enrich a fictional exploration of subjective duration and objective time that is incipiently Shandean. 'These various sensations and reflections, though so long in relating, passed through my mind almost in an instant':[39] when Marianne makes this remark in Marivaux's second instalment, for which readers had already waited thirty months, her words set up an intricate three-way discrepancy between relative rates of thinking, writing and reading. Sterne plays similarly with anisochrony in *Tristram Shandy*'s famous chapter on consciousness and time, which begins when 'two hours, and ten minutes ... since Dr. *Slop* and *Obadiah* arrived' seem 'almost an age' to Walter (3.18.222)—the difference being that here Sterne brings Walter's imagination into jokey harmony with the real-time experience of his readers, for whom Slop's arrival in the previous instalment had happened a year ago.

At this earlier point, Tristram talks of synchronizing the rates of action and reading, thus preserving 'the unity, or rather probability, of time'. Because it is 'about an hour and a half's tolerable good reading' since Obadiah was sent for Slop, Obadiah has now had 'time enough, poetically speaking ... both to go and come', and his return can be described (2.8.119). Here Sterne makes Tristram as absurdly fussy as ever. Yet in aspiring to equivalence of duration between narrated time and reading, he seeks only to replicate an effect that serialization had already made commonplace. Again, the *Arabian Nights* provides an arresting example, its three-year serialization from 1723 in 445 thrice-weekly numbers of *Parker's London News* tracking rather closely the 1,001 nights in which Scheherezade's narrative prolongs its flight from death. No doubt as much by chance as design, a similar effect was often achieved by newspaper piracies of diary or epistolary fiction. When *Robinson Crusoe* was serialized thrice weekly in the *Original London Post* (1719–20), the duration of reading did not exactly match an isolation that lasted decades, but the sense given of Crusoe's steady notching of days must still have been enhanced by the reader's slow-paced access to the text. Similarly, when Behn's *Love-Letters between a Nobleman and His Sister* was run over four months in the *Oxford Journal* (1736), or when Richardson's *Pamela* was serialized in *Robinson Crusoe's London Daily Evening Post* (1741–2), the diurnal rhythms of each narrator's life and writing could be replicated in the reading.[40] Just as these epistolary narrators write 'to the moment', so their readers were required to read to the moment. It is worth noting that the *Pamela* controversy generated a spate of serials in various media, as though anything connected with the novel was recognized in the trade as best delivered and accessed in serial form. When Sterne's sometime bookseller Caesar Ward and his London partner published their opportunistic *Pamela's Conduct in High Life* in volume-length instalments of May and September 1741, they appropriated the novel, in effect, as an open-ended serial, thus anticipating not only the plan of *Tristram Shandy*—Richardson described their intention 'to try the Success of one first (and still more and more Volumes ... so long as the Town would receive them)'—but also the difficulties later presented to Sterne by spurious continuations.[41] Other serializations include a second unauthorized continuation, *Pamela in High Life* (published in three parts of autumn 1741 to match a three-part piracy of the original); *Pamela Versified* (a fifteen-part serial dropped after two instalments); and unlicensed serializations of *Anti-Pamela* and *Joseph Andrews* in a farthing newspaper, *All-Alive and Merry* (1741–3).[42]

Perhaps it was because of this capacity to simulate in the reading the undifferentiated continuum of time in *Pamela* that Fielding refused to see any potential in part-published narrative. In *Tom Jones* he distinguishes himself from 'the painful and voluminous Historian' who narrates the past at a constant rate whatever its eventfulness, and likens such histories to 'a News-Paper, which consists of just the same Number of Words, whether there be any News in it or not'. With this talk of a drudging seriality analogous to newspaper journalism, Fielding may have been pointing at Tindal. Yet in his use of the term 'Historian' to include a novelist like himself, as opposed to that lesser historian who 'seems to think himself obliged to keep even Pace with Time', it is hard not to detect a sideswipe against Richardson (as well as a hint that Sterne would develop in Tristram's own painful accretions). He, by contrast, would follow a strategy that Richardson had ignored (and that Tristram, later, would fail to get near) by mixing 'some Chapters ... that contain only the Time of a single Day, and others that comprise Years' (*TJ* 2.1.75–7).

In using serialization to enhance and dramatize the distinctive effects of 'writing to the moment', Richardson may even have taken his cue from serial appropriations of *Pamela*. In *Clarissa*, too, narrators progressively disclose themselves in the increments of epistolary exchange, and Richardson now chose to reinforce this gradualist effect by spreading publication over a period corresponding to the action. *Clarissa* came out in three instalments (two volumes in December 1747, two in April 1748, three the following December), and this schedule tracked the pace of a fiction covering a calendar year. Richardson thereby enhanced the potential of non-retrospective epistolary narration to stage intimate periodic reports of what he called 'the unfoldings of the Story, as well as of the heart', prolonging an effect so addictive that one reader thought *Clarissa* had 'no other Fault but its not continuing as long as the Faculty is left for Reading'.[43] By timing instalment breaks to coincide with moments of unresolved crisis, moreover, Richardson showed as keen a sense of the cliffhanging pause as any Victorian serialist, so replicating the more local effects created when narrators tease their addressees by breaking off (as Lovelace puts it to Belford) 'without giving thee the least hint of the issue of my further proceedings'. Awaiting the second instalment, one provincial reader lamented that 'we are left wholly in the dark as to the catastrophe. Miss Clarissa is a most amiable character, but we leave her in so perplexing circumstances that I think long for the other volumes.'[44]

Behind all this lay a dramatization of decline and death that, though wholly unlike *Tristram Shandy* in tone, pioneered its effects of prolongation. By involving readers so intimately with his heroine, and then leaving them an interval of several months to imagine her flourishing future, Richardson used serialization to render her untimely death with dramatic force. At the same time, he involved his narrators in an incipiently Shandean struggle to compensate for Clarissa's death by first enshrining her life in narrative, slowing the final volumes with exhaustive accounts by Belford and others, even as Clarissa herself despairs of the capacity of language to organize and render meaning.[45] Richardson cannot have foreseen the doggedness with which readers would exploit the apparent openness of the novel (which, unusually for serial fiction, had been fully drafted years beforehand) by besieging him with requests for a happy ending, and was soon complaining of the trouble arising 'from publishing a work in Parts which left everyone at liberty to form a catastrophe of their own'.[46] But he was able, in response, to turn to advantage the capacity of serial writing to pursue a conversation with readers. By hearing in the gap between instalments the case for a happy ending, he was able to revise the third instalment, and append an answering postscript, in light of their responses and desires: with this move, like *Tristram Shandy*, *Clarissa* inscribes within itself the history of its own reception.

Different anticipations of Sterne's project arise from the serialization in 1753–4 of *Sir Charles Grandison*, which Richardson was forced by copyright infringements to compress into four months.[47] Even so, the time-lapse method enabled him to restage several of *Clarissa's* main effects, such as his incremental drawing out, in the reading, of Clementina's emotional and mental breakdown. Yet there was also an interesting departure from *Clarissa's* method. Where the relentless logic of the earlier novel could lead to only one outcome (albeit one that readers tried to avert by besieging Richardson between instalments with requests for a happy ending), in *Sir Charles Grandison* he sought to experiment with a soapopera-like continuity of action that frustrated the desire for closure of any kind. The final volume tails quietly off with several plotlines unresolved, prompting readers to plead for further volumes and Richardson himself to propose a participatory scheme in which members of his circle would continue writing the novel by assuming a narrator apiece.[48] Privately anxious that 'some other officious Pen (as in Pamela in High Life, as it was called) will prosecute the Story', he sometimes suggested that the open-endedness of *Grandison* made formal resumption an option: eighteen months later he was still asking a correspondent to 'give me your Opinion, should the Humor return, as to proceeding, or closing, as at present'.[49] But publicly he insisted that the work, though strictly speaking unconcluded, could not be taken further. In a open letter to a reader *'who was solicitous for an additional volume to ... Sir* CHARLES GRANDISON; *supposing it ended abruptly'*, he observed 'that in scenes of life carried down nearly to the present time ... all events cannot be decided, unless, as in the History of *Tom Thumb the Great*, all the actors are killed in the last scene; since persons presumed to be still living, must be supposed liable to the various turns of human affairs'. From these assumptions, *Sir Charles Grandison* became literally interminable, but would have to continue in the imagination of readers rather than on the page. It would be up to them to marry Clementina to Jeronymo or not, as the fancy might take them. Halving matters amicably, he asks his addressee: 'Do you think, Madam, I have not been very complaisant to my Readers to leave to them the decision of this important article?' (*SCG* 3:467; 3:470; 3:468).

Commenting on the relative absence of major novelists from the sale catalogue of Sterne's library, Nicolas Barker notes the presence of the volume of *Grandison* in which Richardson reprinted this teasing document (lot 2486).[50] But he misses the significance of lot 1481, 'British Magazine, or Monthly Repository for Gentlemen and Ladies, 2 vols ... 1760', a fiction-bearing periodical that (like Lennox's *Lady's Museum* in the same year) may have been launched by its founder-editor, Smollett, as a way round the adverse market conditions affecting novels at the time. Its leading item, *Sir Launcelot Greaves*, marks the culmination of all the traditions and processes described above, and remains the leading product of a minor boom in magazine fiction in the *Tristram Shandy* years that, though it proved a false start, significantly anticipates the Victorian serial mode. These years saw the first appearance as magazine or newspaper serials of works by leading writers like Goldsmith and Lennox, as well as anonymous Shandean imitations like *The Disasters of Tantarabobus* (1762) or, a few years later, *A Sentimental Journey, by a Lady* (1770–7).[51] The vogue began with Smollett's novel, which started its run through the first two volumes of the *British Magazine* in January 1760, a few weeks after volumes 1 and 2 of *Tristram Shandy* appeared. Coexisting in the magazine's pages with other serial items like 'The History of Omrah' (an oriental tale by Goldsmith) and a lengthy history of Canada (which was probably also by Smollett),[52] it closed after twenty-five parts in December 1761, the month which also saw published volumes 5 and 6 *Tristram Shandy*.

Each successive part was termed a chapter, but Smollett was doing more here than string out something otherwise indistinguishable from non-serial fiction in the Fielding mould. On the contrary, he saw (as Fielding had missed, and as modern theorists of narrative time repeatedly miss) that serialization, by subjecting the temporal experience of the reader to limited but definable regulation, could further complicate the kind of interplay between *Erzählzeit* (the time of narrating) and *erzählte Zeit* (the narrated time) for which *Tom Jones* is often praised.[53] The duration and interruptions of reading are always on Smollett's mind as he writes, as is the elasticity of his publishing mode. His novel never commits itself to a specified length until its final month, and, although it does reach conventional closure at this point (unlike 'The History of Canada', which peters out unfinished after more than three years), Smollett begins joking about premature curtailment as early as Chapter 3, which (placed pointedly below the conclusion of Goldsmith's short-lived 'Omrah' tale) is headed 'Which the reader, on perusal, may wish were chapter the last'.[54] In a sense, the whole work unfolds as an ingenious set of variations, practically enacted, on the seminal chapter from *Joseph Andrews* in which Fielding mocks the practice of serialization while defining the strictly spatial divisions between his own chapters as places for readerly repose. Now, in Smollett's hands, chapters become units of time as well as space, and opportunities for the manipulating novelist to procrastinate, withhold, and frustrate. His first instalment breaks mischievously off at its critical point, asking the reader to 'wait with Patience' for the 'comfort and edification' provided in the following number. Another picks up the mock solicitude with which *Joseph Andrews* acknowledges that a chapterless volume 'fatigues the Spirit', concluding that, 'as the ensuing scene requires fresh attention in the reader, we shall defer it till another opportunity, when his spirits shall be recruited from the fatigue of this chapter'.[55] The underlying joke is always the same: that Smollett's reader cannot simply, like Fielding's, resume reading at will the next day, but instead has been stranded for a month.

There are other ways in which *Sir Launcelot Greaves* wears its serial origins on its sleeve. There is no authority for Sir Walter Scott's account of Smollett despatching scribbled instalments from Berwickshire to London ('when post-time drew near, he used to retire for half an hour, to prepare the necessary quantity of copy ... which he never gave himself the trouble to correct, or even to read over'[56]), but the novel was clearly written *pari passu* with publication, and its instalments play not only on their own discontinuous mode of production but also on intervening texts and events. That Smollett was monitoring Sterne and his imitators as he wrote is clear not only from his annotated listings of new publications in the *British Magazine* but also from the novel's madhouse scene, written at a time when volumes 1 to 4 of *Tristram Shandy* had already established Toby's hobby horse and its effect on communication as central themes. When one inmate rants about sieges ('why don't you finish your second parallel?—send hither the engineer Schittenbach—I'll lay all the shoes in my shop, the breach will be practicable in four and twenty hours—don't tell me of your works—you and your works may be damn'd'), another starts off about doctrine: 'Assuredly, (cried another voice ...) he that thinks to be saved by works is in a state of utter reprobation.'[57] The whole exchange—not only the shoemaker's besieging obsession but also the methodist's hobby-horsical misprision—flows straight from Uncle Toby. Evidently, Smollett grasped very well Sterne's Lockean intimation that the association of ideas 'is really Madness', and that anyone giving in to its motions will 'be thought fitter for *Bedlam*, than Civil Conversation'.[58]

It may also be that the relationship of influence or borrowing between these overlapping texts could work in both directions, with serialization establishing an ongoing dynamic of mutual exchange. Sterne's teasing suspension of Toby's amours at the end of the 1765 volumes ('but the account of this is worth more, than to be wove into the fag end of the eighth volume of such a work as this' (8.35.729)) had obvious precedents in *Sir Launcelot Greaves*, which, though starting later, was now completed: 'But the scene that followed is too important to be huddled in at the end of a chapter, and therefore we shall reserve it for a more conspicuous place in these memoirs.' Perhaps an even more intricate dynamic was at work, given the launch and development during the first year of both *Sir Launcelot Greaves* and *Tristram Shandy* of Lennox's *Harriot and Sophia*, which pioneered the style of sentimental instalment break that is now a standard convention in television soaps. Typically, Lennox uses the break to freeze her action at suspenseful moments, leaving a character 'motionless with astonishment' at the end of one month's instalment, or 'reliev[ing] her labouring heart with a shower of tears' at the end of another.[59] The technique irritated as many readers as it pleased, or so it would seem from the announcement of a rival magazine when launching a six-part imitation of its own in July 1760: this novel, *The Fortune-Hunter*, would be 'divided in such a manner that the portion, in each number, shall make a complete story, in itself, without torturing curiosity, by abruptly breaking off, in the most affecting parts, (the design of which conduct is too plain)'.[60] Smollett's flippant obstructions of reading playfully court this same objection, and Sterne's habit of freezing characters in awkward postures while Tristram breaks off—the conspicuous instance is the end of volume 8, which leaves Mrs Shandy bending at a keyhole for two years—renders parodically literal Lennox's device.

DYING BY NUMBERS

The directness with which *Tristram Shandy* plays on individual serial works, as opposed to the generic conditions they all expose, will always be debatable. But in many cases the points of contact are close and suggestive. It would be possible, for example, to read *Tristram Shandy* as an elaborate comic subversion of the Spectatorial project, in which the lucubrations that Addison's urbane persona offers for 'the Diversion or Improvement' of his readers give way to the crack-brained efforts of a provincial buffoon 'to write my life for the amusement of the world, and my opinions for its instruction' (*TS* 3.28.253). Certainly, Tristram's decision to mingle life with opinions as he writes —'expecting that your knowledge of my character, and of what kind of a mortal I am, by the one, would give you a better relish for the other' (*TS* 1.6.9)—calls to mind the famous premiss from which the *Spectator* begins, which is 'that a Reader seldom peruses a Book with Pleasure 'till he knows whether the Writer of it be ... of a mild or cholerick Disposition, Married or a Batchelor, with other Particulars of a like nature, than conduce very much to the right Understanding of an Author'.[61] Tristram's more teasing strategy is to keep his readers guessing, and after twelve further chapters he is still warning them 'not to take it absolutely for granted ... "That I am a married man"' (*TS* 1.18.56). Later Sterne brings to the surface the absurdity of Tristram's pretensions to a Spectatorial lineage by having him compare a banal observation 'struck out by me this very rainy day, *March* 26, 1759' with a point more fully explained by 'the great *Addison* ... in one or two of his Spectators' (*TS* 1.21.71), and he jokes elsewhere about the inauspiciousness of the Shandean environment for a project of Spectatorial ambitions. There is a fragile defiance in Tristram's eschewal of Addison's fashionable urban milieu in favour of his own circumscribed world 'of four *English* miles diameter' (*TS* 1.7.10), and even in Languedoc he is 'confident we could have passed through Pall-Mall or St. James's-Street for a month together ... and seen less of human nature' (*TS* 7.43.648). None of these connections (or comic distortions) is in itself of particular significance, but cumulatively they keep in play a jocoserious sense of Tristram writing under an anxiety of Spectatorial influence, vainly pursuing the same goal of printing himself out before death.

It has been argued before that *Tristram Shandy* is not only derivative but also parodic of dictionaries of knowledge like the *Cyclopaedia*, the original version of which Chambers was labouring to compile in the very decade (according to the implied chronology of *Tristram Shandy*) that sees Walter struggle with his *Tristapœdia*.[62] Chambers had worried in his preface about the 'little measure of Time allow'd for a Performance to which a man's whole Life scarce seems equal', going on to note that even 'the bare Vocabulary of the Academy *della Crusca* was above forty Years in compiling'. Ten years later he was still lamenting the 'infinite Labour' demanded of the writer of encyclopaedic works, and complaining that 'the very evil they were intended to remove has seized them; I mean, Multitude and Voluminousness'.[63] The absurdity of his dilemma (brought to an end by his death after the third edition, which left further updates, as well as a two-volume *Supplement* of 1753, to be compiled by other hands) may well have been among Sterne's inspirations. Tristram's own work is at one point proclaimed 'this cyclopædia of arts and sciences' (*TS* 2.17.141), and in the *Tristapædia* passage Sterne reinforces the point with a complex set of connections and synchronizations between slow-moving encyclopaedic fiction and slow-moving fictive encyclopaedia. Three years and five volumes into *Tristram Shandy* we learn that 'in about three years ... my father had got advanced almost into the middle of his work'. The glacial pace of this project puts Tristram in mind of della Casa's *Galateo*, a romance on which its author 'spent near forty years of his life' (*TS* 5.16.445–6); this in turn suggests the run he projects for his own sprawling text. With this inter-locking set of *mises en abyme*, *Tristram Shandy* deftly implies the vanity of systematizing Enlightenment desires, as the vast and shifting bodies of knowledge to be digested and codified in projects like the *Cyclopaedia* endlessly outrun their vehicle.

This preoccupation with textual interminability should also prevent us dismissing Tindal's translation and continuation of Rapin as nothing more significant for Sterne than a repository of military-historical information. In the increasingly outlandish prolixity of Tindal's work (which was in its fourth decade of intermittent production as *Tristram Shandy* began), and in the relentless chase to keep up with passing time in which it embroiled its compiler, Sterne had before his eyes another extreme case of the dilemma he gives his narrator. At one point he makes the analogy plain. An earlier chapter to leave Mrs Shandy frozen in eaves-dropping posture overtly relates Tristram's organizational problems to those of Tindal's volumes (each of which would end with a badly integrated update of ecclesiastical history): 'In this attitude I am determined to let her stand for five minutes: till I bring up the affairs of the kitchen (as *Rapin* does those of the church) to the same period' (*TS* 5.5.427). Nor were such disruptions of historiographical continuity exclusive to Tindal. Even Hume is included in Smollett's strictures against digressions by historians in which 'the chain of events is broken',[64] and this complaint makes clear the extent to which serial history falls within Sterne's parodic reach. By identifying *Tristram Shandy* as a work 'the great humour of which consists in the whole narration always going backwards', Horace Walpole nicely catches its wry relationship to projects like Hume's, in which volumes on the Tudors (1759) followed earlier volumes (1754, 1756) on the Stuarts—a 'piece of irregularity' in Hume that made Smollett wonder sarcastically why he should have chosen 'to reverse the order of history'.[65]

As all these sources combine to make clear, there stood behind Sterne a diverse and vigorous tradition of serial writing, encompassing a variety of genres from essay periodical and encyclopaedia to historiography and fiction, and a variety of publishing modes from diurnal broadsheets and weekly fascicules to monthly magazines and annual volumes. Sterne knew this tradition well, having used (and probably owned) some of its best-known products, before starting to write and publish *Tristram Shandy*, and it continued to impinge on him as he continued to publish and write. The resulting text bears its trace in many ways and at many points. It is now clear, indeed, that *Tristram Shandy's* parodic anticipation of Victorian serial fiction is directly rooted in Sterne's responsiveness to comparable forms of paradox and impasse in earlier serial writing. Again and again, eighteenth-century serialization had posed a central question for *Tristram Shandy*: how, if at all, can adequate closure ever be reached by a text that forgoes once-and-for-all publication in favour of indefinite ongoing production, typically in the attempt to encompass a large subject of indefinite or ongoing extent? How, if at all, can such a work ever complete its task and decisively *conclude*, as opposed to being arbitrarily terminated by force of circumstance or admission of defeat? Here were special exemplifications of the larger anxiety about the human capacity to comprehend and signify, to make one's mark before death in an unstable world, that is the central joke (and the central lament) of *Tristram Shandy*. Nowhere could this anxiety be more persistently explored than in serial form, which spreads and develops Tristram's seven-year-long story of frustration and failure over the seven years in which its presentation to the public remained an ongoing event.

It is often observed that *Tristram Shandy* becomes more straightforwardly novelistic as its volumes progress, and that a coherent story about the past gets more accessible: '*Tristram Shandy* moves away ... from mock-learning and Scriblerian satire towards a mock-sentimental comic narrative,' as Judith Hawley puts it.[66] No less important than the past-tense story Tristram tells about Toby's amours, however, is the quiet but insistent present-tense story of his own acts of telling, jeopardized as these increasingly are by chronic authorial sickness. Now the strictly literary or technical threats to completeness that dominate the playful opening of *Tristram Shandy* become, as the narrator's life-expectancy plummets, urgently corporeal. Here, in Tristram's struggle to complete his tale before interrupted by death, we find a brilliant concentration of all the questions about the capacity of writing to contain experience that serial writing inherently raises. Using the serialist's special predicament to literalize the sense of ineffability widely held in the period to vex all human art (Reynolds writes memorably of an ideal 'residing in the breast of the artist, which he is always labouring to impart, and which he dies at last without imparting'[67]), Sterne contrives a dramatization that draws for its full impact on its publishing mode—its status not as a static work but as an inexorable performance over time, the various stages and implied ending of which are quietly marked in each successive instalment. While contriving this story of parallel literary and physical defeat in ways informed by many prior serializations, moreover, he may have found precedents of particular relevance in recent serial fiction: in *Clarissa*'s incremental disclosure of decline and death, the interminability of subject matter in *Grandison*, or Smollett's gradualism in unfolding the stages of madness in *Sir Launcelot Greaves*.

Initially, the unavailability of closure, and the resulting proliferation of text, are an exuberant joke for Tristram. Even before his fantasy of an eighty-volume serial autobiography gives way to panic, however, an inauspicious context is established for this ambition. *Tristram Shandy* is a work famously preoccupied by time, by its flight, and by the pressures it exerts in a culture newly enabled to calibrate its passing in ever finer units. 'I wish there was not a clock in the kingdom,' Walter exclaims (3.18.224): quite apart from Tristram's increasingly anxious measurements of narrated time, narrating time, reading time and their various relations, the work contrives several brilliantly comic exemplifications of the passage of time and its capacity to thwart achievement. Paradoxically, it is the winding of a house clock that jeopardizes Tristram's inheritance of 'memory, fancy, and quick parts' (4.19.354), the very qualities he needs to thrive in a time-bound world. A newer and more stressful chronometry is in play when he rails against the 'hypercritick' who measures a narrative gap 'to be no more than two minutes, thirteen seconds, and three fifths' (2.8.119) or a soliloquy of Garrick's to have paused in mid-sentence 'three seconds and three fifths by a stop-watch' (3.12.213). Here Sterne is quick to detect the changes wrought to consciousness by a technology that was already making the minute discrimination of passing time a portable and permanent accompaniment of daily life.[68] The onward march of time is relentlessly active for Tristram, rendering ever more futile his hope of making his represented past catch up with the fugitive present. By the sixth year and fourth instalment of *Tristram Shandy*, there is something painful in his quiet joke about the two great tourist attractions (Lippius's clock and a thirty-volume history of China) that he hopes to visit in Lyon. If time would only stand still, Tristram might finish the book: 'Lippius's great clock ... had not gone for some years—It will give me the more time, thought I, to peruse the Chinese history' (7.39.642). The joke becomes more pointed still if Sterne was remembering (along with the Peking-printed volumes that really were in Lyon) another serialized *folie de grandeur* that echoes his own: a fifty-two-part translation of Du Halde's *Description ... de la Chine*, which, projected in 1735 and published head to head with a rival serialization from 1737, had almost ruined its publisher, Edward Cave, by the end of its halting run in 1742.[69]

The passage of time matters, of course, because it brings ageing and death to the individual, and to civilization as a whole (as Walter laments) 'decay, and ... a perpetual night' (5.3.422). On this score, too, *Tristram Shandy* gets off to an unpromising start. On its title page an epigraph from Epictetus hints in context at the terrors of the notion of death,[70] while the preliminary dedication to Pitt locates its comic impulse alongside 'the infirmities of ill health, and other evils of life'. (Here life itself is 'this Fragment', as though doomed to be broken off, denied wholeness or completion.) Clearly there is no need to go to the *Sermons*, nor even to the desperate final stages of *Tristram Shandy*, to find in Sterne a preoccupation, however variable tonally, with what Tristram calls 'the chances of a transitory life' (7.9.589). Yorick's consumptive death displaces Tristram's birth in the first volume, and as the work proceeds Sterne shows none of the scruples that made Richardson refuse to continue *Grandison* for fear of seeming to wield 'a murdering Pen'.[71] Among his more lingering victims are Yorick (1.12.35), Le Fever (6.10.513), Trim (6.24.544), and Uncle Toby (6.24.545); among the more premature and tragicomic are Bobby ('got from under the hands of his barber before he was bald' (5.3.424)) and Le Fever's wife (6.7.507), who is killed in mid-embrace by a stray shot. '*Nothing in this world, Trim, is made to last for ever*' (8.19.684): the same could not be truer of *Tristram Shandy*.

All these problems—the proliferation of text; the passage of time; the fact of mortality—meet in the question of Tristram's own health. Struck by the limitless proliferation of matter implied by the inclusiveness of his literary ambitions, he soon devises his famous solution: 'not to be in a hurry;—but to go on leisurely, writing and publishing two volumes of my life every year;—which, if I am suffered to go on quietly, and can make a tolerable bargain with my bookseller, I shall continue to do as long as I live' (1.14.42). Here he seems in little doubt of his ability to achieve his goals, and he remains so even as he comes to see that his work will need to be 'kept a-going these forty years, if it pleases the fountain of health to bless me so long with life' (1.22.82). There seems no question at the end of this first instalment about his ability to produce the next. Yet in the context of his fleeting admission earlier of consumptive illness ('I can now scarce draw [breath] at all, for an asthma I got in scating against the wind in *Flanders*' (1.5.8)), qualifications like 'as long as I live' or 'if it pleases the fountain of health' look more significant and pressing than Tristram himself seems to see. Already, ominous notes are sounded by the implication that the text has no natural conclusion of its own, will be coterminous with Tristram's life, and will always depend for its prolongation on his prospects of health.

The ominous notes grow louder as the work proceeds. A year later the second instalment, by setting a marbled page in place of Yorick's black one (3.36.268), and by talking of the work as designed to secure Tristram's own immortality (4.7.333), plays insistently on the traditional ambition of finding in art a permanence unavailable in life. Yet at the same time the marmoreal product that Tristram seeks to leave behind him looks increasingly vulnerable. Again he talks in terms that imply the inevitable fragmentariness of his project, 'being determined as long as I live or write (which in my case means the same thing)' (3.4.191). A brave face is put on the problem by the famous passage in which he finds himself 'one whole year older' than when he began the text, 'and no farther than to my first day's life'; but while celebrating the limitless publishing opportunity thus provided, Tristram also foresees its sudden curtailment. He would lead a fine life out of writing his life, he says, 'was it not that my OPINIONS'—the digressive impulse that forever disrupts his narrative line—'will be the death of me'. Now it is as though a vicious circle is at work, in which the demanding task of immortalizing oneself in writing threatens first the life to be immortalized, and thus in turn the immortalizing text. Moreover, Tristram knows as well as Defoe in *Moll Flanders* that 'no Body can write their own Life to the full End of it, unless they can write it after they are dead'.[72] As he whimsically acknowledges, at least two volumes of his work will always be lacking—or maybe more: 'write as I will, and rush as I may into the middle of things ... I shall never overtake myself—whipp'd and driven to the last pinch, at the worst I shall have one day the start of my pen—and one day is enough for two volumes—and two volumes will be enough for one year' (4.13.342). Now he starts to prioritize more urgently, and even as he suspends the text for a year he itches to get its key sections written. The closing paragraphs of volume 4 make clear his pressing reason for this new sense of purpose. His head 'akes dismally', and he ends by mentioning the more ominous ailment that threatens the capacity of 'true *Shandeism*' to open his own 'heart and lungs': another pair of volumes will come in another year's time, he promises, 'unless this vile cough kills me in the mean time' (4.32.401–2).

Dying in mid-text, of course, has always been an occupational hazard for the narrative writer. In the seventeenth century Dorothy Osborne was disappointed when the long romance *La Prazimène* cut out *in medias res* ('I never saw but 4 Tomes of her and was told the Gentleman that writt her Storry dyed when those were finnish'd'), and the abrupt curtailment of John Chalkhill's *Thealma and Clearchus* halfway through line 3170 elicited a wry marginal note in the first edition: 'And here the Author dy'd, and I hope the Reader will be sorry.' A few years before *Tristram Shandy*, Fielding registers the same hazard in his valedictory *Journal of a Voyage to Lisbon*, where the question of whether he will live to complete the work becomes 'a matter of no great certainty, if indeed of any great hope to me'.[73] *Tristram Shandy* is unusual, however, in making the threat of its own untimely curtailment a prominent and recurrent concern, and in using serial production to render the uncertainty active. Where Fielding's reader can immediately turn to the volume's end to see that, though posthumously published, the *Journal* has indeed concluded, *Tristram Shandy's* original reader is always kept guessing. A winter later, the appearance as promised of volumes 5 and 6 makes clear that Tristram is hanging on; but little headway is made with his promised matter, and the instalment is haunted by untimely death in the twin examples of Bobby and Le Fever. Unlike previous instalments, moreover, this one breaks off without commitment to a specific date of resumption. Then follows an unusually lengthy pause of three years, during which it may well have seemed that Tristram's projected eighty volumes had already met their inevitable end: by mid-1763, at any rate, one reader had playfully drawn from the non-appearance of volumes 7 and 8 the conclusion that Tristram had now succumbed to disease, and contributed to Robert Lloyd's *St James's Magazine* an 'Elegy on the Decease of Tristram Shandy' (*CH*153). When the silence was at last broken in January 1765, volumes 7 and 8 make clear how close a call it has been. 'Now there is nothing in this world I abominate worse, than to be interrupted in a story' (7.1.576); yet it is not only the anecdote that Tristram is telling Eugenius, but also his *Life and Opinions* as a whole, that are almost cut off in the visit from Death that grimly kicks off this instalment.

Clark Lawlor has shown how one of the running jokes of *Tristram Shandy* lies in its subversion of the standard contemporary assumption that, by leaving the mind clear in its slow advance, consumption encouraged its victims to prepare for death in a serene and orderly manner. 'Indeed a certain messenger of death; but know that of all the Bayliffs, sent to arrest us for the debt of nature, none useth his prisoners with more civility and courtesie then the Consumption,' writes Thomas Fuller—though he also warns that 'too often an ill-use is made thereof, for the prisoners to flatter themselves into a possibility of an escape'.[74] Clearly Tristram has long been failing to settle his accounts with the control of the ideal consumptive, and now, when death civilly calls and courteously leaves, he flatters himself into the least appropriate of escapes. 'I will gallop,' he says (7.1.577), his verb laden with ominous irony (and the submerged pun here on 'galloping consumption'—a term in use by 1674—returns three chapters later). There is new desperation in Tristram's voice, moreover, as he now recalls his earlier proposals to write two volumes a year for forty years, 'provided the vile cough which then tormented me, and which to this hour I dread worse than the devil, would but give me leave' (7.1.575). Here again what is jeopardized, quite explicitly, is Tristram's ongoing text (now scaled down in panic by half its length) as well as his ongoing life: 'for I have forty volumes to write, and forty thousand things to say and do, which no body in the world will say and do for me, except thyself; and as thou seest he has got me by the throat (for Eugenius could scarce hear me speak across the table) ... had I not better, Eugenius, fly for my life?' (7.1.576–7). Now a series of punning links between Tristram's flight through France and the simultaneous progress of his writing hints that little more of either life or text can be left to come. When in the following chapter he imagines himself being 'overtaken by *Death* in this passage' (7.2.578), 'passage' suggests not only the crossing to Calais but also the words he writes while crossing. When he hopes to keep 'a stage, or two' ahead of Death in his journey (7.7.585), moreover, there is yet another glance at the volume-stage analogy from *Joseph Andrews*, implying that very few further volumes can now be in prospect. As he proceeds, Tristram recognizes that Death 'might be much nearer me than I imagined' (7.10.590), envisages his own deathbed (7.12.591–2), and shifts to a scriptural register to present himself as one 'who must be cut short in the midst of my days' (7.14.595).[75]

At the end of this volume, renewed urgency marks Tristram's resumption of his story with a resolution 'that I might go on straight forwards, without digression or parenthesis' (7.43.651). When he begins volume 8 with 'a thing upon my mind to be imparted to the reader, which if not imparted now, can never be imparted to him as long as I live' (8.2.656), his confidence of beginning further volumes seems to have gone, and his anxious repetition of the phrase 'as long as I live' a few pages later (8.5.661) reinforces the threat. From that point on, the work is studded with reports of Tristram's now critical health, and with anticipations of sudden death. A 'vile asthma' torments him in the following chapter, and a broken pulmonary vessel has cost him two quarts of blood (8.6.663). A fever attacks him as he writes a chapter of volume 9, and costs another 'fourscore' ounces of blood— a measurement that ominously parallels the forty-year, eighty-volume project now struggling to survive. The crisis prompts Tristram, keenly aware of his own impending death, to issue a Grandisonian invitation to his readers: 'any one is welcome to take my pen, and go on with the story for me that will' (9.24.779).

It is in this final volume of 1767, beginning with the sentiment that 'time and chance ... severally check us in our careers in this world' (9.1.735), that Sterne most clearly indicates that Tristram's life and text are now approaching their end. At one point, for example, Tristram imagines his work swimming 'down the gutter of Time' with Warburton's *Divine Legation of Moses Demostrated* and Swift's *Tale of a Tub* (9.8.754). The contribution of this passage to Sterne's serial campaign of Warburton-baiting has been finely documented;[76] but there is larger significance in Tristram's readiness to bracket his own work here with this odd couple, which have almost nothing in common except a conspicuous appearance of incompleteness. The promised third part of Warburton's five-volume *Divine Legation* (1738–41) had still not materialized a quarter of a century later (though a fragment did posthumously appear in 1788). No doubt *A Tale of a Tub* was finished as far as Swift was concerned, but not for the hack persona of the work, who merely pauses 'till I find, by feeling the World's Pulse, and my own, that it will be of absolute Necessity ... to resume my Pen'.[77] It looks likely here that Sterne had Swift's teasing ending in mind even before his opening volumes had appeared: Dodsley may not have picked up the hint when Sterne first proposed to him 'two small volumes, of the size of Rasselas ... to feel the pulse of the world' (*Letters*, 80), but with hindsight the echo of Swift's phrase (amplified by the reference to Johnson's work, with its famous 'conclusion, in which nothing is concluded')[78] carries a clear implication. Like *A Tale of a Tub*, this work too will end with its narrator's (as distinct from its author's) task unfinished.

More explicit is Tristram's mournful continuation of the 'gutters of Time' passage. As he apostrophizes to Jenny (whose precise identity, promised six years earlier, he has still not got round to disclosing):

> Time wastes too fast: every letter I trace tells me with what rapidity Life follows my pen; the days and hours of it ... are flying over our heads like light clouds of a windy day, never to return more—every thing presses on—whilst thou art twisting that lock,—see! it grows grey; and every time I kiss thy hand to bid adieu, and every absence which follows it, are preludes to that eternal separation which we are shortly to make.—(9.8.754)

Time merely 'presses upon' Tristram earlier in his narrative (5.35.474), and the change of verb at this point is laden with grim implication. Time wastes too fast, while Tristram has been wasting time, and wasting from a consumptive disease that also attenuates his text. The parallel acts of living and writing, linked throughout the work in an increasingly urgent mutual chase, are now approaching their joint extinction—and 'shortly'. At the height of the Ossianic vogue described in a later chapter of this study, the tropes of mutability and mortality used here are commonplace enough. What is not commonplace is the seven-year publishing process through which Sterne dramatizes the relentlessly declining health that first jeopardizes and now, it seems, is about to defeat Tristram's efforts to fix in print his life and opinions.

## EPITASIS, CATASTASIS, CATASTROPHE

In his classic account of the ending of *Tristram Shandy*, Wayne Booth bases his argument that in volume 9 Sterne 'completed the book as he had originally conceived it' on several internal factors: the absence of the usual forward-looking serial break at the volume's end; the *a priori/ a posteriori* joke that links the dedications to volumes 1 and 9; above all, the culmination of volume 9 with Toby's amours, which are trailed from the second instalment (and implicitly, Booth would have it, from the first) as the 'choicest morsel' of the work. *The Life and Opinions of Tristram Shandy* becomes 'an elaborate and prolonged contradiction of [its] title-page', its real focus being instead 'the amours and campaigns of Uncle Toby', which now—albeit limply—reach their climax.[79]

Booth's argument for closure has since been reinforced on other grounds,[80] and it might be added that his case about the long-awaited delivery of Tristram's 'choicest morsel' gains weight by analogy with the structuring principles of Slawkenbergius, who retains his own best story 'for the concluding tale of my whole work; knowing ... that when I shall have told it, and my reader shall have read it thro'—'twould be even high time for both of us to shut up the book' (4.1.325). Other, more pervasive evidence for finding closure in volume 9 has been obscured by Booth's conflation of Sterne's design and project with Tristram's own, and by his focus on the narrated time of the volume (the years 1713–14, in which Toby conducts his amours) as opposed to its time of narration (1766–7, in which Tristram is dying of consumption). Whereas *Tristram Shandy* does indeed appear to have run its course as a novel of Sterne's, it has barely got itself started as an autobiography by Tristram, and in this sense the *Life and Opinions* title page is contradicted, and its subject displaced, not only by Booth's past-tense plot about Uncle Toby's amours and campaigns, but by a present-tense plot about Tristram's decline and death. Intermittent but pervasive, this present-tense plot—an unfolding performance of terminal disease, from Tristram's troubled breathing in the first instalment to his full-blown consumption in the last—is quite as important as the plot about Toby, and even more conclusive. Booth would have seen as much had he lingered on the passage in which Toby's campaigns are trailed as 'no uninteresting under-plot in the epitasis and working up of this drama' (2.6.114). The terminology here—which returns when Slawkenbergius discusses the '*Epitasis, Catastasis...Catastrophe*' sequence in neoclassical aesthetics (4.317)—begs the question of what the *over*-plot will be, and what the *catastrophe* will be;[81] yet elsewhere the answer is made clear. The key passage comes when, foreseeing his own death in volume 7, Tristram pointedly resumes this language: 'I never seriously think upon the mode and manner of this great catastrophe, which ... torments my thoughts as much as the catastrophe itself, but I constantly draw the curtain across it' (7.12.591). The catastrophe of Tristram's life, and thus of his otherwise interminable *Life and Opinions*, will be his death. This, as we know from the opening of volume 7, will be sudden and peremptory; and now we seem to be being told that it will happen when the curtain is down. With its newly urgent sense of time wasting and death advancing, the brisk and slender fifth instalment—almost an emblem, in its physical attenuation and galloping pace, of Tristram's condition—brings us right to this juncture.

The over-plot of Tristram's consumptive decline, then, confirms the inference Booth draws from the under-plot of Toby's amours, which is that Sterne is tacitly winding his serial up. The medical history that moves to the surface of volumes 7 and 8 precludes the possibility of many more volumes to come, and specific telltale passages in volume 9—the 'tragicomical completion' of Walter's prediction (9.2.737); the imminence of Tristram's 'eternal separation' from Jenny (9.8.754); the desperate, massive phlebotomy of chapter 24—suggest that this is the last. The subsequent non-appearance of further instalments confirms the point, and lends the blank page at the end of volume 9 a meaning quite as emphatic, in retrospect, as the black page of volume 1 (which also marks a consumptive death, as though in another version of the *a priori/a posteriori* symmetry between these volumes). Here is an ending that practises on a grand scale Sterne's favourite rhetorical figure of the aposiopesis, in which a speaker halts in mid-flow, as though unable to proceed, but usually in such a way as to imply the unspoken conclusion.[82] Now the entire serial halts in mid-flow, and the unspoken conclusion is clear: Tristram's race to prolong his life and complete its transcription has now been lost, the absence of continuation implying his sudden death—'gone! in a moment!' as Trim would put it (5.7.431)—and the terminal interruption of his text. Without any further volumes, the 'forty thousand things' he wants to say in volume 7 go with him to his grave; for it is not the explicit fact of Toby being caught by Widow Wadman but the implicit fact of Tristram being caught by death that is the catastrophe of *Tristram Shandy*, a structural aposiopesis in which Sterne deftly rounds off his serial while highlighting Tristram's failure to complete his own. As noted above (p.140), an adroit member of the Lloyd—Churchill circle of wits had already made this inference in print in July 1763, some months after volumes 7 and 8 had failed to appear on schedule; but now Sterne's implication looks much stronger. Here indeed is a conclusion in which nothing is concluded, or one in which (to borrow another Johnsonian distinction) Tristram's life and ongoing efforts to transcribe it are 'ended, though not completed'.[83]

Volume 9, then, evidently marks the culmination of *Tristram Shandy* as a seven-year dramatization of terminal disease, in which the frustration of human ambitions to control and fix inherently fugitive things—experience, memory, identity—is encapsulated by a story of consumptive decline, premature death, and the leaving of unfinished business. While this picture fits in with other arguments for closure that have previously been made, however, it is important to make two qualifications to Booth's influential account, driven as it is by a formalist agenda that makes him overstate the definitiveness and premeditation of the ending. The first is that, while bringing *Tristram Shandy* to implied closure, Sterne cannily stops short of making the closure explicit and binding, so tempering whatever drive towards coherence he may have had with the characteristic pragmatism of the serialist. Here Booth neglects the tendencies shared between volume 9 of

*Tristram Shandy* and the endings of other serial works of the period, from Tindal's *Continuation* to *Sir Charles Grandison*, which were typically arbitrary, provisional, or accompanied by a get-out clause. Simply in generic terms, an unequivocal, irreversible conclusion of the kind Booth wants to find would be alien to Sterne's project, anticipating as it does the postmodern quality that Umberto Eco calls 'variability to infinity' or 'the infinity of the text'— that quality in which 'the text takes on the rhythms of that same dailiness in which it is produced and which it mirrors'.[84] More specifically, we cannot rule out the possibility of Sterne returning to reopen *Tristram Shandy*, not only because of the inexplicit nature of his aposiopetic conclusion, but also because of the many undeveloped nodules for continuation scattered earlier in his path. Seventy-one volumes remain to be written, after all, before Tristram's ambition will be fulfilled, their contents including (among much else) a map 'which, with many other pieces and developments to this work, will be added to the end of the twentieth volume' (1.13.40); a section 'where the instrumental parts of the eloquence of the senate, the pulpit, the bar, the coffeehouse, the bed-chamber, and fire-side, fall under consideration' (2.17.141); 'the catastrophe of my great uncle Mr. *Hammond Shandy*, [who] rushed into the duke of *Monmouth's* affair' (3.10.198); the 'rich bale', to be unloaded 'hereafter', of Tristram's tour through Europe with his father and uncle (7.27.618; 7.28.621); the collection of 'PLAIN STORIES' he intends to deliver once Toby's amours are written (7.43.648). Evidently enough, Sterne was treading a careful line, in ways reminiscent of the kind of 'opportunistic seriality' that William Beatty Warner has found in formula fiction by Haywood and others in the 1720s.[85] By confining to implication his indications that the text is complete (and complete only from his own standpoint, not from Tristram's), he leaves the door to resumption ajar in case of any future need. A moribund hero, in fiction at least, could always be revived.

The likelihood of any such need was now very remote, however, and not only because the sensibility vogue had now made *A Sentimental Journey* a more promising vehicle for Sterne's writing than *Tristram Shandy*. Sterne was dying himself, and must have known it by mid-1762, when he suffered the traumatic pulmonary haemorrhage—'I was likely to bleed to death' (*Letters*, 180)—that finds its echo in volume 8. Throughout the novel, indeed, the terminal decline of Tristram's health shadows Sterne's condition, and both follow, as Lawlor has shown, the classic course of consumption as then understood.[86] Here it is easy enough to detect implied closure in volume 9, but much harder to agree with Booth that this closure marks completion of the book as 'originally conceived'. Sterne had suffered a similarly dangerous medical episode as early as the 1730s (*EMY* 61), and it is always possible that he was executing a long-held plan to use serialization as a way of rending active and dramatic a narrative in which literary ambition is choked by progressive disease. But the closeness with which Tristram's condition tracks Sterne's over the years of serialization more plausibly suggests that the relationship was causal, with the phasing and trajectory of *Tristram Shandy* developing in improvised response to the ungovernable rhythms and crises of its author's own health. In this light, *Tristram Shandy* looks very much more unstable than Booth would have it, its shape emerging not so much from elaborate forward planning as from adroit extemporization over the years, with Sterne using the contingencies of his own condition to direct the work as he wrote, published, and sickened. It would not be entirely frivolous to imagine a counterfactual scenario in which, instead of declining, Sterne grows stronger during the period of serialization, and writes not the *Tristram Shandy* we have but the alternative *Tristram Shandy* we glimpse in John Croft's 'Anecdotes of Sterne': 'Sterne said that his first Plan, was to travell his Hero Tristram Shandy all over Europe, and ... finish the work with an eulogium on the superior constitution of England and at length to return Tristram well informed and a compleat English Gentleman.'[87]

Indeed, there is a sense in which Booth's clinching indicator of prestructuring and closure—the transition from Toby's campaigns to Toby's amours—is also governed by contingency. These amours can begin in earnest only once Toby has been released from his war-gaming obsession by the end of Marlborough's wars at the Peace of Utrecht, an event apparently triggered in the novel by the protracted run-up to the real-time Peace of Paris (which was widely anticipated after the second instalment of *Tristram Shandy*, negotiated and signed after the third, and obliquely registered—'AND SO THE PEACE WAS MADE' (7.35.638)—in the fourth). Only then can the 'choicest morsel' be introduced in the volumes of 1765–7, its emergence depending as much on the course of international diplomacy as Tristram's convulsions depend on the state of Sterne's lungs. At the very least, these two large contingencies, public and private, regulate *Tristram Shandy's* pace, and it may be right to see Sterne as activating his implied conclusion when he did only because one circumstance—the ending of the Seven Years War—now allowed it, while the other—his rapidly declining health—now required it as an urgent matter.

Where all this leaves us with Sterne's last work, *A Sentimental Journey through France and Italy*, is an even more puzzling question. Its second and last volume stops with Yorick no further forward in his tour than the south of France, though Sterne had earlier envisaged a work 'of four volumes' (*Letters*, 284). In a notice tipped in to several copies of the first edition of February 1768, Sterne acknowledges that subscribers 'have a further claim upon him for Two Volumes more than these delivered to them now', and promises the remainder 'early the next Winter'. A month later, however, he was dead. The result is that we can only guess whether the mismatch between title and text in *A Sentimental Journey* is just another

Shandean joke about the impossibility of fulfilment, complicated further by a playful advertisement, or whether this notice is sincere evidence that a longer project was cut off. Perhaps there is a middle option, which is that Sterne, knowing the imminence of his own death and anxious not only to provide for his daughter but also to join (as he says in a letter) 'ces Heros, qui sont Morts en plaisantant' (*Letters*, 416), was perpetrating the kind of fraud that Charles Churchill wittily alleges against Johnson in his Shandean poem *The Ghost*: 'He for *Subscribers* baits his hook, I And takes their cash—but where's the Book?'[88]

One sure conclusion may be drawn, however, from the modulation out of *Tristram Shandy* of *A Sentimental Journey*, and from the door to resumption that Sterne left ajar in both these works. His ongoing strategy for success in the faddish, unstable literary culture of the 1760s was to defer closure, generate continuations and spin-off projects, and so cultivate a mode of writing able to absorb and respond to new texts, trends, and tastes as they emerged, holding its position at this culture's cutting edge with a kind of self-renewing fashionability. The ambiguously sentimental turn in later volumes of *Tristram Shandy*, and the sideways propagation of *A Sentimental Journey* from the Maria episode in volume 9, mark the best-known case of this responsiveness to shifts in marketplace demand. Alert not only to the cultural force of sensibility in general, but also to the growing popularity of the new sentimental fiction (Sarah Scott's *Millenium Hall* (1762), Frances Brooke's *Lady Julia Mandeville* (1763), and Goldsmith's *Vicar of Wakefield* (1766) were among the conspicuous successes), Sterne reacted with a vein of writing delicately poised, in its handling of sentimental themes and tropes, between participation and parody. However, the provenance of much of the stock in trade of 1760s sentimental novels in earlier examples (the massively influential *Grandison*, with Sarah Fielding's *David Simple* and forgotten works like Guthrie's *The Friends: A Sentimental History*) makes it difficult to identify specific sentimental elements in Sterne's later volumes as simple or certain cases of improvisatory engagement with newly emerging texts. One must look in less predictable directions, and to other genres. In the remaining chapters of this book, I turn in detail to two poetic examples of contemporaneous literary projects—one public and intensely voguish, the other as yet confined to a coterie in which Sterne moved—that more plainly highlight *Tristram Shandy's* distinctive capacity to shift, or even mutate, in mid-publication.

## NOTES

1. *Spectator*, ed. Donald F. Bond, 5 vols. (Oxford: Clarendon Press, 1965), 1:5 (no. 1, 1 Mar. 1711); see also Stuart Sherman's chapter on Addison in *Telling Time: Clocks, Diaries, and English Diurnal Form, 1660–1785* (Chicago: University of Chicago Press, 1997), 109–58.

2. *Spectator*, 1:34 (no. 7,8 Mar. 1711).

3. Morris Golden, 'Periodical Context in the Imagined World of *Tristram Shandy*', *The Age of Johnson*, 1 (1987), 237–60 (at 248); Robert D. Mayo, *The English Novel in the Magazines 1740–1815* (Evanston, Ill.: Northwestern University Press, 1962), 212.

4. Michael G. Ketcham, *Transparent Designs: Reading, Performance, and Form in the Spectator Papers* (Athens, Ga.: University of Georgia Press, 1985), 98.

5. Isabel Rivers, '"Strangers and Pilgrims": Sources and Patterns of Methodist Narrative', in J. C. Hilson et al. (eds.), *Augustan Worlds* (Leicester: Leicester University Press, 1978), p. 194; see also Isabel Rivers, *Reason, Grace, and Sentiment: The Language of Religion and Ethics in England, 1660–1780* (Cambridge: Cambridge University Press, 1991), ch. 5. The term 'serial autobiography' is Felicity Nussbaum's: see *The Autobiographical Subject: Gender and Ideology in Eighteenth-Century England* (Baltimore: Johns Hopkins University Press, 1989), 1–29 and (on Wesley) 80–102.

6. R. M. Wiles, *Serial Publication in England before 1750* (Cambridge: Cambridge University Press, 1957), 143–6, 355; for Paul Whitehead's likely authorship of Phillips's *Apology*, see Virginia Blain, Patricia Clements, and Isobel Grundy (eds.), *The Feminist Companion to Literature in English* (London: Batsford, 1990), 852. Sterne's signature in every copy of volume 5 (see *LY* 113) prompted the *Critical Review* to note that he was following 'a precaution first used' by Philips (*CH* 138–9).

7. *Memoirs of Laetitia Pilkington*, ed. A.C. Elias, Jr., 2 vols. (Athens, Ga.: University of Georgia Press, 1997), 1:93.

8. Nussbaum, *Autobiographical Subject*, 193.

9. 3rd edn., 2 vols. (1751), 2:364; for Jack Pilkington's role, see introduction to the Elias edn., 1: xxvii. The posthumous volume of 1754 appears as lot 2492 in the sale catalogue of Sterne's library (on the status of which, see above, p. 60).

10. Henry Fielding, *Dramatic Works*, 3 vols. (London: Smith, Elder & Co., 1882), 1:215 (II.iv). Samuel Foote picks the same target in *The Author* (1757) with passing reference to a sozzled hack named 'Master *Clench*, in *Little Britain*', who 'has a Folio coming out in Numbers' (I.i).

11. Wiles, *Serial Publication*, 2; see also John Feather, *A History of British Publishing* (London: Croom Helm, 1988), 114–15.

12. *Comedian*, 6 (Sept. 1732), referring to John Kelly's translation (in rivalry to Nicholas Tindal's) of Rapin's *History of England*; cited in Wiles, *Serial Publication*, 108.

13. See Thomas Keymer, introduction to *The Gentleman's Magazine*, 16 vols. (London: Pickering & Chatto, 1998), 1:vii-xl (at pp. xvi-xx).

14. C.B.L. Barr and W. G. Day, 'Sterne and York Minster Library', *Shandean*, 2 (1990), 18–19; Wiles, *Serial Publication*, 287, 175; see also, on the serialization of Bayle and other biographical dictionaries on the Baylean model, Isabel Rivers, 'Biographical Dictionaries and their Uses from Bayle to Chalmers', in Isabel Rivers (ed.), *Books and their Readers in Eighteenth-Century England: New Essays* (Leicester: Leicester University Press, 2001), 137–69 (at 149–52).

15. On the complex bibliography of the *Cyclopaedia*, see L.E. Bradshaw, 'Ephraim Chambers's *Cyclopaedia*', in Frank Kafker (ed.), *Notable Encyclopaedias of the Seventeenth and Eighteenth Centuries* (Oxford: Voltaire Foundation, 1981), 123–40; also Wiles, *Serial Publication*, 8, 327.

16. Judith Hawley, 'Laurence Sterne and the Circle of Sciences: *Tristram Shandy* and its Relation to Encyclopaedias' (diss., University of Oxford, 1990), 188, referring to *TS* 5.27.459–5.28.463.

17. Theodore Baird, 'The Time-Scheme of *Tristram Shandy* and a Source', *PMLA* 51 (1936), 803–20; Wiles, *Serial Publication*, 237. A total print run of 18,000 copies in the

thirty years after 1725 is estimated by Philip Hicks, who calls the work 'England's most successful book serialization, the groundbreaking one for the entire industry' (*Neoclassical History and English Culture: From Clarendon to Hume* (London: Macmillan, 1996), 147; see also p. 148, citing the *Gazetteer* of 12 Mar. 1736). For the complex bibliography of the various Rapin editions before 1750, see app. B of Wiles's study.

18. See e.g. Fielding's *Journey from This World to the Next*, in *Miscellanies, Volume Two*, ed. Bertrand A. Goldgar and Hugh Amory (Oxford: Clarendon Press, 1993), 86–97: chs. 20–1 are closely based on Tindal's Rapin, which Fielding owned in the folio edition of 1732–3.

19. Lot 7, in five folio volumes, probably combines the second edition of 1732–5 with the first edition of the continuation (1735–6); lot 1019, in twenty-eight octavo volumes, probably combines the first edition of 1725–31 with the uniform octavo continuation in thirteen volumes of 1744–7. Also in the catalogue is Thomas Lediard's rival continuation in weekly folio numbers of 1735–6 (lot 278).

20. *A Letter to the Society of Booksellers* (1738), cited in Wiles, *Serial Publication*, 136.

21. *The History of England*, 15 vols. (1725–31), 2: A2; 6: A2; *The History of England... Continued from the Revolution to the Accession of King George II*, 13 vols. (1744–7), 13 [28]: A4$^V$.

22. *The History of England*, 1: A3; *The History of England ... Continued*, 1 [16]:A2$^V$.

23. James G. Basker, *Tobias Smollett: Critic and Journalist* (Newark, Del.: University of Delaware Press, 1988), 260; see also, on the serialization and profitability of Smollett's historical works, pp. 104–9.

24. Barr and Day, 'Sterne and York Minster Library', 10,16; *The Letters of Tobias Smollett*, ed. Lewis M. Knapp (Oxford: Clarendon Press, 1970), 78 (4 Apr. 1759).

25. *Grub-Street Journal* (19 Sept. 1734), cited in Wiles, *Serial Publication*, 236–7.

26. *TJ*, 13.1.684; *JA*, 2.1.77. On the politics of Tindal's Rapin, see *JA*, 3.1.162; *TJ*, 6.2.273.

27. See Wiles, *Serial Publication*, 8 (Chambers); 121–2 (*Dr. Colbatch's Legacy, or, The Family Physician*, 1732); 119–20 (Tindal's *History of Essex*, 1732).

28. Hume to Andrew Millar, 17 May 1762, cited by Basker, *Tobias Smollett*, 109; Bishop, 'The Book', ll. 51–2, in Samuel Bishop, *Poetical Works*, 2 vols. (1796), 1: 229.

29. Mayo illustrates 'the reluctance of the journals to emulate the novel' with reference to Fielding's *Champion*. Here connected narrative never develops: even 'the "Voyages of Mr. Job Vinegar", which appeared in thirteen instalments between March and October, 1740, studiously seems to avoid a narrative structure' (*English Novel in the Magazines*, 76).

30. J. Paul Hunter, 'Serious Reflections on Farther Adventures: Resistances to Closure in Eighteenth-Century English Novels', in Albert J. Rivero (ed.), *Augustan Subjects: Essays in Honor of Martin C. Battestin* (Newark, Del.: University of Delaware Press, 1997), 276–94 (at 282).

31. Defoe's groundwork was not wasted, and shortly before *Tristram Shandy* an enterprising writer picked up the loose threads in a thee-part work, *Fortune's Fickle Distribution ... Containing First, The Life and Death of Moll Flanders. Part II The Life of Jane Hackaway Her Governess. Part III The Life of James McFaul, Moll Flanders' Lancashire Husband* (1759).

32. William Beatty Warner, *Licensing Entertainment: The Elevation of Novel Reading in Britain* 1684–1750 (Berkeley and Los Angeles: University of California Press, 1998), 116.

33. Marivaux, trans. Mary Collyer, *The Virtuous Orphan*, ed. W. H. McBurney and M. F. Shugrue (Carbondale, Ill.: Southern Illinois University Press, 1965), p. xxxvii.

34. Wiles, *Serial Publication*, 77, 80–1; *TS Notes*, 146, 371. For further interaction

between Sterne and Goldsmith's vehicle, the *Public Ledger*, see Anne Bandry, '*Tristram Shandy*, the *Public Ledger*, and William Dodd', *Eighteenth-Century Fiction*, 14 (2002), 309–22.

35. John Dunton, *A Voyage round the World*, 3 vols. (1691), 1: 26; 3: 416; see also J. Paul Hunter, *Before Novels: The Cultural Contexts of Eighteenth-Century English Fiction* (New York: Norton, 1990), 336.

36. Mayo, *English Novel in the Magazines*, 24–6, 34–5, 6, 273–98, 165–6; Kenneth Monkman, 'Did Sterne Contrive to Publish a "Sermon" in 1738?', *Shandean*, 4 (1992), 111–33.

37. Antoine Galland, *Arabian Nights' Entertainments*, ed. Robert L. Mack (Oxford: Oxford University Press, 1995), p. xxv; Wiles, *Serial Publication*, 35, 38; Mayo, *English Novel in the Magazines*, 59. An eight-volume *Arabian Nights* in French (The Hague, 1714) is in the sale catalogue of Sterne's library (lot 2262).

38. The point is nicely caught in Hilary M. Schor's study of Gaskell's serial fiction, *Scheherezade in the Marketplace: Elizabeth Gaskell and the Victorian Novel* (Oxford: Oxford University Press, 1992).

39. Marivaux, trans. Collyer, *The Virtuous Orphan*, 163, 201, 57; see also the comments by McBurney and Shugrue on this second resemblance (introduction, p. xxxvii), and by Wayne Booth on the first ('The Self-Conscious Narrator in Comic Fiction before *Tristram Shandy*', *PMLA* 67 (1952), 163–85 (at 174)).

40. Wiles, *Serial Publication*, 27, 69, 51–2. It was probably this *Pamela* serialization that first generated the famous story about villagers ringing the church bells on hearing of Pamela's marriage: see Thomas Keymer, 'Reading Time in Serial Fiction before Dickens', *Yearbook of English Studies*, 30 (2000), 34–45 (at 38–9).

41. *Selected Letters of Samuel Richardson*, ed. John Caroll (Oxford: Clarendon Press, 1964), 44 (Aug. 1741); on the spurious *Tristram Shandy* volumes, see *LY* 87–8, 264; also Anne Bandry, 'The Publication of the Spurious Volumes of *Tristram Shandy*', *Shandean*, 3 (1991), 126–37.

42. See the chronology of publications in *The Pamela Controversy: Criticisms and Adaptations of Richardson's Pamela 1740–1750*, ed. Thomas Keymer and Peter Sabor, 6 vols. (London: Pickering & Chatto, 2001), 1: xxi–xxix.

43. *Selected Letters of Richardson*, 289 (14 Feb. 1754); Forster MSS, xv, 2, fo. 34 (commentary by Jane Collier).

44. *Clarissa*, 6: 280; '*Your Affectionate and Loving Sister*': The Correspondence of Barbara Kerrich and Elizabeth Postlethwaite, 1733–1751, ed. Nigel Surry (Dereham: Larks Press, 2000), 83 (2 Mar. 1748).

45. On this Shandean dimension, see Thomas Keymer, *Richardson's Clarissa and the Eighteenth-Century Reader* (Cambridge: Cambridge University Press, 1992), 222–9.

46. *Selected Letters of Richardson*, 117 (17 Dec. 1748).

47. See T.C.D. Eaves and B. D. Kimpel, *Samuel Richardson: A Biography* (Oxford: Clarendon Press, 1971), 375–86.

48. Ibid. 384–6, 403–13.

49. *Selected Letters of Richardson*, 296 (25 Feb. 1754); Liverpool Public Library MSS, cited by Eaves and Kimpel, *Samuel Richardson*, 412 (letter of 12 Sept. 1755).

50. Nicolas Barker, 'The Library Catalogue of Laurence Sterne', *Shandean*, 1 (1989), 9–24 (at 17).

51. Charlotte Lennox's *Harriot and Sophia*, originally serialized in Lennox's *Lady's Museum* (Mar. 1760–Jan. 1761), was separately published as *Sophia* (1762); Oliver Goldsmith's *Chinese Letters* was serialized in the *Public Ledger* (Jan. 1760-Aug. 1761) and

separately published as *The Citizen of the World* (1762). *The Disasters of Tantarabobus* was in the *Universal Museum* (Jan.-Aug. 1762), and *A Sentimental Journey, by a Lady* (1770–7) was in the *Lady's Magazine* (which after eighty parts and 270,000 words abandoned the work uncompleted 'on account of the desire of *many* Correspondents'): see Mayo, *English Novel in the Magazines*, 341–4.

52. Louis L. Martz, *The Later Career of Tobias Smollett* (New Haven: Yale University Press, 1942), 180. For Goldsmith's authorship of 'Omrah', see Basker, *Tobias Smollett*, 195.

53. See Keymer, 'Reading Time', 34–5.

54. *British Magazine*, 1 (Mar. 1760), 124.

55. *JA*, 2.1.76; *Sir Launcelot Greaves*, ed. David Evans (Oxford: Oxford University Press, 1973), 7 (ch. 1, Jan. 1760), 119 (ch. 14, Jan. 1761).

56. Lionel Kelly (ed.), *Tobias Smollett: The Critical Heritage* (London: Routledge, 1987), 354.

57. *Sir Launcelot Greaves*, 185–6 (ch. 23, Oct. 1761). See also Basker's demonstration that, having reviewed a Shandean imitation (*Yorick's Meditations*) in the *Critical Review* for July 1760, Smollett plagiarized it in chapter 10 (Sept. 1760) of *Sir Launcelot Greaves* (*Tobias Smollett*, 259).

58. John Locke, *An Essay Concerning Human Understanding*, ed. Peter H. Nidditch (Oxford: Clarendon Press, 1975), 395.

59. *Lady's Museum*, 1 (Mar. 1760), 44; 1 (Nov. 1760), 666.

60. *Royal Female Magazine*, 2 (July 1760), p. ii, cited by Mayo, *English Novel in the Magazines*, 286.

61. *Spectator*, 1: 4; 1: 1 (no. 1, 1 Mar. 1711).

62. See Hawley, 'Sterne and the Circle of Sciences'.

63. Chambers, *Cyclopaedia* (1728), 1: 1; 'Some Considerations Offered to the Public, Preparatory to a Second Edition of Cyclopaedia' (*c.*1738), in Robert DeMaria, Jr. (ed.), *British Literature, 1640–1789: An Anthology* (Oxford: Blackwell, 1996), 699, 698.

64. *Critical Review*, 2 (Dec. 1756), 386; see Basker, *Tobias Smollett*, 108.

65. *CH* 55 (Walpole to Sir David Dalrymple, 4 Apr. 1760); *Critical Review*, 7 (Apr. 1759), 289.

66. Judith Hawley, '"Hints and Documents" (2): A Bibliography for Tristram Shandy', *Shandean*, 4 (1992), 49–65 (at 55).

67. Robert R. Wark (ed.), *Discourses on Art* (New Haven: Yale University Press, 1975), 171.

68. As John Sutherland notes, state-of-the-art dials were just beginning to be marked in units of a fifth of a second, and second hands had been fitted since the 1740s with stop levers to enable users to freeze a result ('Slop Slip', in *Can Jane Eyre Be Happy?* (Oxford: Oxford University Press, 1997), 25–30 and 225–6n.).

69. See *TS Notes*, 481–2; Wiles, *Serial Publication*, 307.

70. Elizabeth Carter's 1758 translation is cited in *TS Notes*, 37: 'MEN are disturbed, not by Things, but by the Principles and Notions, which they form concerning Things. Death, for Instance, is not terrible ... But the Terror consists in our Notion of Death.'

71. *Selected Letters of Richardson*, 296 (25 Feb. 1754).

72. Daniel Defoe, *Moll Flanders*, ed. G. A. Starr (Oxford: Oxford University Press, 1981), 5. Sterne may also have known the solution offered in a minor memoir novel from the sale catalogue, *Memoirs of the Life and Adventures of Signor Rozelli* (lot 1680). In the final sentence, with wonderful bathos, the hero receives extreme unction and 'prepared for Death, which however did not come, since I lived after that to compose these *Memoirs*'; a brisk editorial postscript then notes his death after two further months (4th edn., 2 vols. (1740), 2:231).

73. *Letters to Sir William Temple*, ed. Kenneth Parker (London: Penguin, 1987), 131 (24–5 Sept. 1653); *Thealma and Clearchus* (1683), 168; *The Journal of a Voyage to Lisbon*, ed. Thomas Keymer (London: Penguin, 1996), 82.

74. *The Collected Sermons of Thomas Fuller, D.D.*, 1631–1659, ed. J. E. Bailey and W.E.A. Axon, 2 vols. (London: Gresham, 1891), 2:386 ('Life out of Death', 1655); partly quoted in Clark Lawlor, 'Consuming Time: Narrative and Disease in *Tristram Shandy*', *Yearbook of English Studies*, 30 (2000), 46–59 (at 56).

75. The Florida editors note parallels here in Psalms and Jeremiah; see also Sterne's lengthy gloss on Job 14:2, in which he plays relentlessly on Job's term 'cut down' (*Sermons*, 10.91–102).

76. Melvyn New, 'Sterne, Warburton, and the Burden of Exuberant Wit', *Eighteenth-Century Studies*, 15 (1982), 245–74 (at 273–4).

77. Jonathan Swift, *A Tale of a Tub*, ed. A.C. Guthkelch and D. Nichol Smith, 2nd edn. (Oxford: Clarendon Press, 1958), 210.

78. Samuel Johnson, *Rasselas*, ed. J. P. Hardy (Oxford: Oxford University Press, 1988), 122.

79. Wayne Booth, 'Did Sterne Complete *Tristram Shandy?*', *Modern Philology*, 48 (1951), 173, 180.

80. Objections to Booth's case are made in Arthur H. Cash and John M. Stedmond (eds.), *The Winged Skull: Papers from the Laurence Sterne Bicentenary Conference* (London: Methuen, 1971): see Marcia Allentuck, 'In Defense of an Unfinished *Tristram Shandy*. Laurence Sterne and the *Non Finito*', 145–55; R. F. Brissenden, '"Trusting to Almighty God": Another Look at the Composition of *Tristram Shandy*', 258–69. More recently, Booth has been supported by Mark Loveridge, who argues for 'poetic closure' in volume 9 ('Stories of COCKS and BULLS: The Ending of *Tristram Shandy*', *Eighteenth-Century Fiction*, 5 (1992), 35–54), and by Samuel L. Macey, who finds in it the fulfilment of Sterne's intricate time-scheme ('The Linear and Circular Time Schemes in Sterne's Tristram Shandy', *Notes and Queries*, 36 (1989), 477–9). The case for an unrealized twelve-volume plan is made by Peter de Voogd, 'The Design of *Tristram Shandy*', *British Journal for Eighteenth-Century Studies*, 6 (1983), 159–62. Closest to my own position is Melvyn New, who finds Booth's question 'answerable in the affirmative only if we understand that while Volume IX is indeed the concluding volume, the work could have admitted of additional materials before it' (*Laurence Sterne as Satirist: A Reading of Tristram Shandy* (Gainesville, Fla.: University of Florida Press, 1969), 189; see also Melvyn New, *Tristram Shandy: A Book for Free Spirits* (New York: Twayne, 1994), 104).

81. For these terms, see *TS Notes*, 145,316–17.

82. A mock example from *Peri Bathous* seems relevant here: '"I can no more", when one really can no more' (*The Prose Works of Alexander Pope, vol.2.1725–1744*, ed. Rosemary Cowler (Oxford: Blackwell, 1986), 207).

83. Preface to the *Dictionary*, in Samuel Johnson, *Poetry and Prose*, ed. Mona Wilson (London: Hart-Davis, 1968), 317.

84. Umberto Eco, 'Interpreting Serials', in *The Limits of Interpretation* (Bloomington, Ind.: Indiana University Press, 1990), 83–100 (at 96).

85. Warner, *Licensing Entertainment*, p. 116.

86. 'The Asthma usually ends in a Consumption in lean Bodies' (John Floyer, *A Treatise of the Asthma*, 3rd edn. (1726), 175, cited by Lawlor, 'Consuming Time', 50).

87. *Whitefoord Papers*, ed. W.A.S. Hewins (Oxford: Oxford University Press, 1898), 228.

88. *The Poetical Works of Charles Churchill*, ed. Douglas Grant (Oxford: Clarendon Press, 1956), 126 (*The Ghost*, bk. 3 (1762), ll. 801–2).

# Chronology

| | |
|---|---|
| 1660 | Daniel Defoe is born in London; Restoration of the Stuart monarchy and the accession of Charles II. |
| 1662 | The Royal Society is chartered. |
| 1665–6 | The Great Plague and Great Fire of London occur. |
| 1677 | Milton's *Paradise Lost* is published. |
| 1677 | Mary, daughter of James II, marries William of Orange. |
| 1678 | Bunyan's *Pilgrim's Progress* is published. |
| 1685 | Death of Charles II; is succeeded by his brother, James II; Monmouth's rebellion takes place; Louis XIV revokes the Edict of Nantes; end of religious toleration in France. |
| 1687 | Isaac Newton's *Principia Mathematica* is published. |
| 1688 | William of Orange lands in England and James II is forced to abdicate. |
| 1689 | Samuel Richardson is born in Derby; accession of William III and Mary to the throne. |
| 1690 | Publication of Locke's *An Essay Concerning Human Understanding*; William defeats James II's forces at Battle of the Boyne in Ireland. |
| 1694 | Founding of the Bank of England. |
| 1695 | Licensing of the Press Act expires and is not renewed. |
| 1697 | William Hogarth is born in London. |
| 1700 | Deaths of John Dryden and of the Duke of Gloucester, only |

son of Princess Anne; the protestant succession of the English throne passes to the House of Hanover.

1701    Act of Succession secures the continuation of the protestant line through the House of Hanover; the Society for the Propagation of the Gospel is founded in London.

1702    Death of William III and accession of Queen Anne; England declares war against France and Spain, beginning the War of Spanish Succession; the Asiento Guinea Company is founded in order to exploit the slave trade between West Africa and the Americas; publication of the *Daily Courant*, London's first daily newspaper.

1703    While imprisoned, Daniel Defoe begins publication of the weekly paper, *The Review*; birth of John Wesley, founder of Methodism.

1704    English capture Gibraltar; Duke of Marlborough defeats the French at Blenheim; death of John Locke.

1705    Edmund Halley correctly predicts the return, in 1758, of a comet last seen in 1682; His Majesty's Theatre opens in London.

1707    Henry Fielding is born in Sharpham Park, Somerset; England and Scotland are united as Great Britain under the Act of Union.

1708    The University of Oxford founds its first Professorship of Poetry.

1709    The British Parliament passes a Bill for the naturalization of foreign-born Protestants; the first Copyright Act is passed in Great Britain; Steele and Addison publish the first issue of *The Tatler*, the first major British periodical; Samuel Johnson is born.

1711    Addison and Steele's *Spectator* begins publication; the South Sea Company is founded; David Hume is born.

1712    The Newspaper Stamp Act exploits the popularity of new publications as a means of raising tax revenue; Jean-Jacques Rousseau is born.

1713    Treaty of Utrecht is signed with France, ending the War of Spanish Succession; Laurence Sterne is born in Clonmel, Ireland.

1714    Death of Queen Anne and accession of George I.

1715    Jacobite rebellion; death of Louis XIV of France; a Riot Act is passed for the suppression of rebellions and civil disturbances; Thomas Fairchild first successfully produces an artificial hybrid plant; Gabriel Daniel Fahrenheit develops the temperature scale that bears his name.

1716    James Stuart, the "Old Pretender," leaves Britain to return to exile in France; birth of Thomas Gray.

1719    Daniel Defoe's *Robinson Crusoe* is published.

1720    War with Spain declared, a conflict which lasts through 1729; the South Sea Company fails, causing thousands of British investors to lose their savings in the "South Sea Bubble," a stock-market crash on Exchange Alley; first year for serial publication of novels in newspapers.

1721    Tobias Smollett is born in Dumbarton, Scotland; Robert Walpole is appointed First Lord of the Treasury and Chancellor of the Exchequer.

1722    Defoe publishes *Moll Flanders* and *Journal of the Plague Year*.

1723    In England, The Workhouse Act or Test forces the poor to enter a workhouse; Richard Price and Adam Smith are born.

1724    Defoe publishes *Tour around the Whole Island of Great Britain*; birth of Immanuel Kant.

1725    Defoe publishes *A New Voyage Round the World*, *The Complete English Tradesman* (through 1727) and *Jonathan Wild*; Francis Hutcheson publishes *The Original of Our Ideas of Beauty and Virtue*.

1726    Swift's *Gulliver's Travels* is published; death of George I and accession of George II;  faced by continued Jacobite opposition in Scotland, the British government builds military roads throughout the Highlands.

1728    Oliver Goldsmith is born.

1729    Edmund Burke is born.

1730    James Thomson publishes *The Seasons*; John and Charles Wesley found the Methodist sect at Oxford.

1731    Births of William Cowper and Erasmus Darwin; Daniel Defoe dies.

1733    Latin is abolished as the language of the English courts.

1737    Theatrical Licensing Act is passed in Britain, limiting the number of playhouses and establishing government censorship of performances; birth of Edward Gibbon.

1738    Birth of the future King George III.

1739    "War of Jenkin's Ear"—a trade war between Great Britain and Spain develops due to British attempts to circumvent the Peace of Utrecht; Britain declares war on Spain; David Hume's *A Treatise of Human Nature* is published.

1740    Samuel Richardson publishes the first part of *Pamela*; birth of James Boswell.

1741    Britain is involved in the War of the Austrian Succession with Empress Maria Theresa of Austria against France, Spain, Bavaria, Prussia and Saxony; David Hume publishes *Essays, Moral and Political*.

1742    Henry Fielding publishes *Joseph Andrews*; England enters the Austrian Wars under the ministry of Carteret; William Pitt the Elder criticizes the use of English resources in a Hanoverian conflict.

1743    George II defeats the French at the Battle of Dettingen in the War of the Austrian Succession; Britain is at war with France in America and in India; birth of Anna Laetitia Barbauld.

1744    Alexander Pope and Giovanni Battista Vico die; "King George's War" breaks out in North America, as the continental conflict expands to the French and English colonial possessions; Britain begins to expand into the Ohio Valley.

1745    Charles Edward Stuart ("Bonnie Prince Charlie"), "the Young Pretender," lands in Scotland and leads the Jacobite uprising; Jonathan Swift and Robert Walpole die.

1746    Battle of the Culloden and defeat of the "Pretender" ("Bonnie Prince Charlie") and his allies; Benjamin Franklin performs his experiments confirming that lightning is a form of electricity.

1747    Thomas Gray publishes "Ode on a Distant Prospect of Eton College"; Samuel Richardson publishes the first volumes of *Clarissa*; Thomas Warton publishes *Pleasures of Melancholy*; Anna Seward is born.

1748    Smollett's *Roderick Random* is published; the Treaty of Aix-la-Chapelle ends the War of the Austrian Succession; Adam Weishaupt, founder of the Order of the Illuminati is born; John Cleland's *Memoirs of a Woman of Pleasure* (*Fanny Hill*) is published.

1749    Henry Fielding's *Tom Jones* is published; Britain expands its colonial territories in North America—George II grants lands to the Ohio Company, Georgia becomes a Crown Colony, and Halifax, Nova Scotia, is founded; David

Hartley publishes *Observations on Man*; Charlotte Turner, later Smith, and Johann Wolfgang von Goethe are born.

1750    London is struck by two small earthquakes; Samuel Johnson begins publishing *The Rambler* (until 1752).

1751    Britain passes a Gin Act for the prevention of public alcoholism; William Hogarth engraves the drawings *Gin Lane* and *Beer Street*; the British calendar is altered to make January 1 the first day of a new year; death of Frederick Lewis, Prince of Wales.

1752    Frances Burney and Thomas Chatterton are born; Charlotte Lennox publishes *The Female Quixote*; Benjamin Franklin invents the lightning conductor.

1753    French troops from Canada march south, seizing and fortifing the Ohio Valley; Britain protests the invasion and claims Ohio for itself; British parliament institutes a land tax of two shillings on the pound and passes a Marriage Act regulating the holding of weddings; the Act of Parliament in England allows the naturalization of Jews, which is subsequently repealed after anti-Semitic protests; British Museum receives a royal charter; births of Elizabeth Inchbald, William Nicolson and Sir Timothy Shelley, father of Percy Bysshe Shelley.

1754    Fielding dies in Lisbon; the Anglo-French War begins in North America with France taking Fort Duquense.

1755    French defeat British forces under General Braddock in North America; Smollett publishes his translation of Cervantes' *Don* Quixote; Samuel Johnson publishes his *Dictionary of the English Language*; Rousseau publishes *Discourse on the Origin of Inequality*.

1756    Seven Year's War with France begins; Lord Clive campaigns against the French and the Nawab of Bengal in India; one hundred and twenty British prisoners die in an infamous prison soon known as the "Black Hole of Calcutta"; Tobias Smollett begins *The Critical Review*; William Godwin is born in March; Wolfgang Amadeus Mozart is born.

1757    Publication of Burke's *Philosophical Inquiry into the Origin of Our Ideas of the Sublime and Beautiful*; Horace Walpole publishes Thomas Gray's *Odes*, including "The Progress of Poesy" and "The Bard"; William Blake is born; David Hartley dies.

| 1758 | Britain begins its political administration of India; Lord Clive becomes Governor of Bengal; Britain takes the French fort of Louisburg in Canada; the French abandon Fort Duquesne and Britain begins the construction of Fort Pitt (modern Pittsburgh) on the site; Samuel Johnson begins publishing *The Idler* (through 1760); return of Halley's Comet; Mary Darby, later Robinson, born. |
|---|---|
| 1759 | First two volumes of Sterne's *Tristram Shandy* are published; Wolfe defeats the French under Montcalm at Quebec; the British Museum opens; Samuel Johnson publishes *Rasselas*; Robert Burns and Mary Wollstonecraft are born. |
| 1760 | Death of George II and accession of George III; Montreal surrenders to the British, ending French military power in Canada; Josiah Wedgewood opens pottery works in Staffordshire; Laurence Sterne publishes *Sermons of Yorick*; William Beckford is born. |
| 1761 | Tobias Smolett begins publishing his edition of a new translation of Voltaire's *Works*; Jean-Jacques Rousseau publishes *Julie, ou la nouvelle Héloise*; Adam Smith publishes *Considerations Concerning the First Formations of Languages, and the Different Genius of Original and Compounded Languages*; death of Samuel Richardson. |
| 1762 | Rousseau publishes *Émile* and *The Social Contract*; Horace Walpole begins publication of *Anecdotes of Painting in England* (through 1771); births of Joanna Baillie and Helen Maria Williams. |
| 1763 | Peace of Paris ends the Seven Years' War with France; Britain proclaims its government of Quebec, Florida and Grenada; James Boswell meets Samuel Johnson; Boswell leaves for his tour of the Continent and meets Voltaire and Rousseau. |
| 1764 | Horace Walpole's *The Castle of Otranto* is published; The British Sugar Act is amended to tax the American colonies; James Hargreaves invents the spinning jenny; James Watt invents the condenser—the first step towards a steam engine; the London Literary Club is founded by Johnson, Burke, Walpole, Goldsmith and others; Edward Gibbon first conceives his *Decline and Fall of the Roman Empire*; Anne Radcliffe is born. |
| 1765 | The Stamp Act for taxing the American colonies is passed in the British parliament; the Virginia Assembly challenges the Crown's right to the tax; at the Stamp Act Congress in |

New York, a declaration of rights and liberties is drawn up by colonial delegates; Samuel Johnson publishes *The Works of William Shakespeare* and Thomas Percy publishes *Reliques of Ancient English Poetry*; Richard Young dies.

1767      Britain taxes imports of tea, glass, paper and dye to America; A non-importation agreement is made at a Boston meeting; the New York assembly is suspended for refusing to quarter troops; Rousseau publishes *Dictionnaire de Musique*; he settles in England and receives a pension from George III; August Wilhelm von Schlegel is born.

1768      The Massachusetts Assembly is dissolved for refusing to collect taxes; a Colonial Secretary is appointed to the British government; Thomas Gray is appointed professor of modern history at Cambridge; publishes *Poems*; Captain Cook's first voyage to Australia and New Zealand; Royal Academy of Art is founded; Laurence Sterne publishes *A Sentimental Journey through France and Italy*; Joseph Wright paints *Experiment with the Air Pump*; Maria Edgeworth is born; birth of Napoleon Bonaparte; Laurence Sterne dies.

1770      The writers and publishers of the "Junius" letters, attacking corruption in public life, are tried for seditious libel; James Cook discovers Botany Bay, Australia; Goethe completes the first part of *Faust* and Goldsmith publishes *The Deserted Village*; Ludwig van Beethoven is born; Thomas Chatterton dies; G.W. Hegel, James Hogg and William Wordsworth are born.

1771      Births of Charles Brockden Brown, Walter Scott and Dorothy Wordsworth; Thomas Gray dies; Smollett's *Humphry Clinker* is published; Mackenzie's *The Man of Feeling* is published; Tobias Smollett dies.

1772      Samuel Taylor Coleridge is born; the Boston Assembly demands the right of secession from Britain.

1773      The Boston Tea Party, a protest against colonial tea duties, takes place in December; a Correspondence Committee is set up in Virginia; Samuel Johnson and James Boswell tour the Hebrides islands of Scotland; Goldsmith's *She Stoops to Conquer* is performed in London.

1774      The British Parliament refuses a petition to remove Massachusetts Governor Hutchinson; Britain closes the port of Boston in retaliation for the protests; the first Constitutional Congress meets in Philadelphia, where a non-importation protest is decided upon; Goethe publishes *The Sorrows of Young Werther*; Oliver Goldsmith dies. Robert Southey is born.

1775    The American Revolution begins with the battles of Lexington, Concord and Bunker Hill; the second Continental Congress is called in Philadelphia, appointing George Washington commander-in-chief of American forces; Jane Austen is born, Charles Lamb, Matthew Gregory (Monk) Lewis, William Savage Landor and Charles Lloyd are born.

1776    American Declaration of Independence is signed; Adam Smith's *Wealth of Nations* is published; first volume of Edward Gibbon's *Decline and Fall of the Roman Empire* is published; Thomas Paine begins publishing *The Crisis*, which runs through 1783; Richard Price publishes *Observations on Civil Liberty and the War with America*; David Hume dies.

1777    Britain is defeated by American forces in battles at Princeton and Bennington, but is victorious at Brandywine and Germantown, Pennsylvania; French volunteers under Lafayette arrive in support of the Americans; the British General Burgoyne loses two battles in New York; James Cook publishes *Voyage towards the South Pole in 1772-5*. Samuel Johnson begins writing *The Lives of the Poets*; Richard Brinsley Sheridan produces *The School for Scandal*.

1778    The American colonies reject a British peace offer and sign treaties with France and Holland; Washington is victorious at Monmouth, New Jersey; the British capture Savannah, Georgia; the British Parliament passes the Catholic Relief Act, freeing Catholics from restrictions on land ownership and inheritance; James Cook discovers Hawaii; Frances Burney's *Evelina* is published; deaths of Rousseau and Voltaire.

1779    British forces surrender to the Americans at Vincennes; French forces take Grenada and St. Vincent from the British; the U.S. Congress sends an army into the Wyoming Valley in order to attack Native American warriors; Spain declares war on Britain and lays siege to Gibraltar; Warren Hastings fights the first of the Mahratta conflicts in India.

1781    General Lord Cornwallis surrenders to Washington at Yorktown, Virginia to close the American Revolution.

| 1782 | Thomas Grenville and Benjamin Franklin meet in Paris to negotiate an end to the American Revolutionary War; Frances Burney publishes *Cecilia*; William Cowper publishes his *Poems*. |
| 1783 | Treaties of Paris and Versailles end the American War of Independence; George Crabbe publishes *The Village* and Hannah Cowley publishes *A Bold Stroke for a Husband*; William Blake's *Poetical Sketches* is published; births of Marie Henri Beyle (Stendhal) and Washington Irving. |
| 1784 | Charlotte Smith publishes *Elegiac Sonnets, and Other Essays*; Denis Diderot and Samuel Johnson die; Leigh Hunt is born. |
| 1785 | Edmund Cartwright patents his power loom; Thomas Love Peacock and Thomas De Quincey are born; William Cowper publishes *The Task*. |
| 1786 | Robert Burns publishes *Poems, Chiefly in the Scottish Dialect*; William Beckford publishes *Vathek* and Helen Maria Williams publishes *Poems, in Two Volumes*. |
| 1787 | U.S. Constitution is signed in Philadelphia. |
| 1788 | King George III of England experiences the first of his bouts of insanity; Lord Byron is born; Thomas Gainsborough dies. |
| 1789 | French Revolution begins; the Bastille in Paris falls in July; first United States Congress is held in New York, with Washington elected President; America ratifies the Bill or Rights; William Blake publishes *Songs of Innocence* and *The Book of Thel*. |
| 1790 | Edmund Burke's *Reflections on the Revolution in France* is published; Ann Radcliffe publishes *A Sicilian Romance*; Mary Wollstonecraft publishes *A Vindication of the Rights of Man*; Benjamin Franklin dies. |
| 1791 | Thomas Paine's *The Rights of Man* is published; Elizabeth Inchbald publishes *A Simple Story*; Ann Radcliffe publishes *The Romance of the Forest* and Charlotte Smith publishes *Celestina*; death of Wolfgang Amadeus Mozart. |
| 1792 | Mary Wollstonecraft publishes *A Vindication of the Rights of Woman*; Charlotte Smith publishes *Desmond*; and Coleridge composes a Greek Sapphic Ode, "Ode on the Slave Trade," written during freshman year at Cambridge; Susanna Rowson publishes *Rebecca*. |

1793          Execution of Louis XVI of France; France declares war
              against England.

1794          Ann Radcliffe publishes *The Mysteries of Udolpho*; Thomas
              Paine publishes *The Age of Reason*.

1795          Goethe publishes *Wilhelm Meisters Lehrjahre*; John Keats is
              born.

1797          Death of Mary Wollstonecraft; Mary Shelley is born.

1798          Wordsworth and Coleridge publish the first edition of
              *Lyrical Ballads*.

1799          House of Commons rejects abolition.

# Contributors

HAROLD BLOOM is Sterling Professor of the Humanities at Yale University. He is the author of over 20 books, including *Shelley's Mythmaking* (1959), *The Visionary Company* (1961), *Blake's Apocalypse* (1963), *Yeats* (1970), *A Map of Misreading* (1975), *Kabbalah and Criticism* (1975), *Agon: Toward a Theory of Revisionism* (1982), *The American Religion* (1992), *The Western Canon* (1994), and *Omens of Millennium: The Gnosis of Angels, Dreams, and Resurrection* (1996). *The Anxiety of Influence* (1973) sets forth Professor Bloom's provocative theory of the literary relationships between the great writers and their predecessors. His most recent books include *Shakespeare: The Invention of the Human* (1998), a 1998 National Book Award finalist, *How to Read and Why* (2000), *Genius: A Mosaic of One Hundred Exemplary Creative Minds* (2002), and *Hamlet: Poem Unlimited* (2003). In 1999, Professor Bloom received the prestigious American Academy of Arts and Letters Gold Medal for Criticism, and in 2002 he received the Catalonia International Prize.

JAMES R. FOSTER (1890– ) is the author of "Peregrine Pickle and the Memoirs of Count Grammont" and co-author of the *Concise Dictionary of American Grammar and Usage*.

MARGARET ANNE DOODY is Andrew W. Mellon Professor of Humanities and Professor of English at Vanderbilt University, Nashville Tennessee, where she also directs the Comparative Literature Program. She is the author of numerous books and articles, including *The Daring Muse: Augustan Poetry Reconsidered*, *Frances Burney: The Life in the Works*, and *The True Story of the Novel*.

JONATHAN LAMB is Professor of English at Princeton University. He is the author of Sterne's *Fiction and the Double Principle*, and *The Rhetoric of Suffering: Reading the Book of Job in the Eighteenth Century*.

SHERIDAN BAKER has been Professor of English at the University of Michigan and former editor of *Papers of the Michigan Academy of Sciences, Arts, and Letters* and of the *Michigan Quarterly Review*. His poems have been published in the New Yorker and other magazines. He is the author of *Ernest Hemingway: An Introduction and Interpretation*, 1967 and *The Harper Handbook to Literature* (with Northrop Frye and George Perkins).

PAULA R. BACKSCHEIDER has been Associate Professor of English at the University of Rochester. She is the author of numerous articles and books, including *Daniel Defoe: His Life*, *Moll Flanders: The Making of a Criminal Mind*, and editor of *Revising Women: Eighteenth-century "Women's Fiction" and Social Engagement*.

SIMON VAREY is the author of *Henry Fielding, 'Joseph Andrews': A Satire of Modern Times*, and *Henry St. John, Viscount Bolingbroke*.

PATRICK REILLY has been a Reader in the English Department at the University of Glasgow. He is the author of *The Literature of Guilt: From 'Gulliver' to Golding*, and *Jonathan Swift: The Brave Desponder*.

JOHN M. WARNER is the author of "Renunciation as Enunciation in James's The Portrait of a Lady,'" and "Symbolic Patterns of Retreat and Reconciliation in 'To the Lighthouse.'"

LOIS E. BUELER is Professor of English at California State University. She is the author of *The Tested Woman Plot: Women's Choices, Men's Judgments, and the Shaping of Stories* and "The Failure of Sophistry in Donne's Elegy VII."

DAVID E. HOEGBERG has been Assistant Professor of English at Indiana University, Indianapolis. He is the author of "The Anarchist's Mirror: Walcott's Omeros and the Epic Tradition" and "'Master Harold' and the Bard: Education and Succession in Fugard and Shakespeare."

MICHAEL SEIDEL is Professor of English and Chairman of the Department at Columbia University. He is the author of numerous books, including: *Satiric Inheritance: Rabelais to Sterne*, *Robinson Crusoe: Island Myths and the Novel*, *Exile and the Narrative Imagination*, and *James Joyce: A Short Introduction*.

THOMAS KEYMER is Elmore Fellow and Tutor in English at St Anne's College, Oxford and Lecturer in English Language and Literature, University of Oxford. He is the author of *Richardson's 'Clarissa' and the Eighteenth-Century Reader*, "Dying by Numbers: 'Tristram Shandy' and Serial Fiction II."

# Bibliography

Adams, Percy G. *Travel Literature and the Evolution of the Novel*. Lexington: University Press of Kentucky, 1983.

Adamson, William Robert. *Cadences of Unreason: A Study of Pride and Madness in the Novels of Tobias Smollett*. New York: Peter Lang Publishing, 1990.

Allen, Walter Ernest. *The English Novel: A Short Critical History*. London: Phoenix House, 1954.

Alter, Robert. *Fielding and the Nature of the Novel*. Cambridge: Harvard University Press, 1968.

Armistead, J.M. *The First English Novelists: Essays in Understanding*. Knoxville: University of Tennessee Press, 1985.

Backscheider, Paula R. and John J. Richetti, eds. *Popular Fiction by Women: 1660–1730*. Oxford: Clarendon Press, 1996.

———. *Daniel Defoe: His Life*. Baltimore: Johns Hopkins University Press, 1989.

Barker, Gerard. *Grandison's Heirs: The Paragon's Progress in the Late Eighteenth-century English Novel*. Newark, DE: University of Delaware Press, 1985.

Basker, James G. *Tobias Smollett: Critic and Journalist* Newark: University of Delaware Press, 1988.

Battestin, Martin C. and Ruthe R. Battestin. *Henry Fielding: A Life*. London and New York: Routledge, 1989.

———. *A Henry Fielding Companion*. Westport, Conn.: Greenwood Press, 2000.

Beasley, Jerry C. *Tobias Smollett, Novelist*. Athens, Ga.: University of Georgia Press, 1998.

Bell, Ian A. *Henry Fielding: Authorship and Authority*. London and New York: Longman, 1994.

Blewett, David. *Defoe's Art of Fiction*. Toronto: University of Toronto Press, 1979.

Boege, Fred W. *Smollett's Reputation as a Novelist*. Princeton: Princeton University Press, 1947.

Brown, Murray L. "Learning to Read Richardson: *Pamela* 'speaking pictures,' and the Visual Hermeneutic." *Studies in the Novel* 25 (1993): 129–51.

———. "*Emblematica Rhetorica*: Glossing Emblematic Discourse in Richardson's *Clarissa*." *Studies in the Novel* 27 (1991): 455–76.

Castle, Terry. *Masquerade and Civilization: The Carnivalesque in Eighteenth-century Culture and Fiction*. Stanford, CA: Stanford University Press, 1986.

Clifford, James L., ed. *Eighteenth Century English Literature: Modern Essays in Criticism*. New York: Oxford University Press, 1960.

Cohan, Steven. *Violation and Repair in the English Novel: The Paradigm of Experience from Richardson to Woolf*. Detroit, Mich.: Wayne State University Press, 1986.

Davis, Lennard. *Factual Fictions: The Origins of the English Novel*. New York: Columbia University Press, 1983.

DePorte, Michael V. *Nightmares and Hobbyhorses: Swift, Sterne, and Augustan Ideas of Madness*. San Marino: The Huntington Library, 1974.

Doody, Margaret Anne. *A Natural Passion: A Study of the Novels of Samuel Richardson*. Oxford: Clarendon Press, 1974.

———. *Frances Burney: The Life in the Works*. New Brunswick, NJ: Rutgers University Press, 1988.

———. *The True Story of the Novel*. New Brunswick, NJ: Rutgers University Press, 1996.

——— and Peter Sabor, eds. *Samuel Richardson: Tercentenary Essays*. Cambridge, UK and New York: Cambridge University Press, 1989.

Douglas, Aileen. *Uneasy Sensations: Smollett and the Body*. Chicago: University of Chicago Press, 1995.

Dussinger, John A. *The Discourse of the Mind in Eighteenth-Century Fiction*. The Hauge: Mouton, 1974.

Earle, Peter. *The World of Defoe*. London: Weidenfeld and Nicolson, 1976.

Epstein, Julia. *The Iron Pen: Frances Burney and the Politics of Women's Writing*. Madison: University of Wisconsin Press, 1989.

Flynn, Carol Houlihan. *Samuel Richardson, A Man of Letters*. Princeton, N.J.: Princeton University Press, 1982.

Furbank, P.N. and W.R. Owen, eds. *The Canonisation of Daniel Defoe*. New Haven and London: Yale University Press, 1988.

Grant, Damian. *Tobias Smollett: A Study in Style*. Manchester: Manchester University Press; Totowa, N.J.: Rowman and Littlefield, 1977.

Gwilliam, Tassie. *Samuel Richardson's Fictions of Gender*. Stanford, Calif.: Stanford University Press, 1993.

Hunter, J. Paul. *The Reluctant Pilgrim: Defoe's Emblematic Method and Quest for Form in "Robinson Crusoe."* Baltimore: Johns Hopkins University Press, 1966.

———. *Occasional Form: Henry Field and the Chains of Circumstances*. Baltimore and London: Johns Hopkins University Press, 1975.

James, Eustace Anthony. *Daniel Defoe's Many Voices. A Rhetorical Study of Prose Style and Literary Method*. Amsterdam: Rodopi, 1972.

Kahrl, George M. *Tobias Smollett: Traveler-Novelist*. Chicago: University of Chicago Press, 1947.

Kelly, Lionel. *Tobias Smollett: The Critical Heritage*. London: Routledge & Kegan Paul, 1987.

Keymer, Thomas. *Richardson's "Clarissa" and the Eighteenth-century Reader*. Cambridge: Cambridge University Press, 1992.

———. *Sterne, the Moderns, and the Novel*. Oxford and New York: Oxford University Press, 2002.

Kinkead-Weekes, Mark. *Samuel Richardson, Dramatic Novelist*. Ithaca: Cornell University Press, 1973

Konigsberg, Ira. *Narrative Technique in the English Novel: Defoe to Austen*. Hamden, Conn.: Archon Books, 1985.

———. *Samuel Richardson and the Dramatic Novel*. Lexington: University of Kentucky Press, 1968.

Kreissman, Bernard. *Pamela-Shamela: A Study of the Critiques, Parodies and Adaptation of Richardson's Pamela*. Lincoln, NE: University of Nebraska Studies, 1960.

Lamb, Jonathan. *Sterne's Fiction and the Double Principle*. Cambridge and New York: Cambridge University Press, 1989.

———. *The Rhetoric of Suffering: Reading the Book of Job in the Eighteenth Century*. New York: Oxford University Press, 1995.

Lynch, James J. *Henry Fielding and the Heliodoran Novel: Romance, Epic, and Fielding's New Province of Writing*. Rutherford: Fairleigh Dickinson University Press, 1986.

Mace, Nancy A. *Henry Fielding's Novels and the Classical Tradition*. Newark, Delaware: University of Delaware Press, 1996.

Martz, Louis L. *The Later Career of Tobias Smollett*. New Haven: Yale University Press, 1942.

McAllister, John. "Smollett's Semiology of Emotions: The Symptomatology of the Passions and Affections in *Roderick Random* and *Peregrine Pickle*. *English Studies in Canada* 14 (1988): 286–95

———. "Smollett's Use of Medical Theory: *Roderick Random* and *Peregrine Pickle*." *Mosaic* 22 (1989): 121–30.

McKeon, Michael. *The Origins of the English Novel: 1600–1740*. Baltimore: Johns Hopkins University Press, 1987.

McKillop, Alan Dugald. *The Early Masters of English Fiction*. Lawrence: University of Kansas Press, 1956.

Mullan, John. *Sentiment and Sociability: The Language of Feeling in the Eighteenth Century*. Oxford: Clarendon Press, 1988.

Novak, Maximillian. *Realism, Myth, and History in Defoe's Fiction*. Lincoln, NE: University of Nebraska Press, 1983.

———. *Daniel Defoe, Master of Fictions: His Life and Ideas*. Oxford and New York: Oxford University Press, 2001.

Pagliaro, Harold E. *Henry Fielding: A Literary Life*. New York: St. Martin's Press, 1998.

Paulson, Ronald. "Satire in the early novels of Smollett." *Journal of English and Germanic Philology*, vol. 59 (1960): 381–402.

———. *Satire and the Novel in Eighteenth-century Fiction*. New Haven and London: Yale University Press, 1967.

———. *The Fictions of Satire*. Baltimore: Johns Hopkins University Press, 1967.

Rawson, Claude. *Henry Fielding and the Augustan Ideal Under Stress*. London: Routledge and Kegan Paul, 1972.

———, ed. *The Character of Swift's Satire: A Revised Focus*. Newark: University of Delaware Press; London: Associated University Presses, 1983.

Rivero, Albert J., ed. *Augustan Subjects: Essays in Honor of Martin C. Battestin*. Newark: University of Delaware Press, 1997.

Richetti, John. *Defoe's Narratives: Situations and Structures*. Oxford: Clarendon Press, 1975.

————. *Popular Fiction Before Richardson: Narrative Patterns 1700–1739.* Oxford: Clarendon Press, 1969.

————. *The English Novel in History, 1700–1780.* London: New York: Routledge, 1999.

Robbins, Bruce. *The Servant's Hand: English Fiction from Below.* New York: Columbia University Press, 1986.

Rosengarten, Richard A. *Henry Fielding and the Narration of Providence: Divine Design and the Incursions of Evil.* New York: Palgrave, 2000.

Scheuermann, Mona. *Social Protest in the Eighteenth-Century English Novel.* Columbus: Ohio State University Press, 1985.

Skinner, John. *Constructions of Smollett: A Study of Genre and Gender.* Newark: University of Delaware Press; London: Associated University Press, 1996.

Spector, Robert D. *Smollett's Women: A Study in an Eighteenth-Century Masculine Sensibility.* Westport, CT: Greenwood Press, 1994.

Spencer, Jane. *The Rise of the Woman Novelist: From Aphra Behn to Jane Austen.* Oxford: Basil Blackwell, 1986.

Starr, George A. *Defoe and Spiritual Autobiography.* Princeton: Princeton University Press, 1965.

Tadié, Alexis. *Sterne's Whimsical Theatres of Language: Orality, Gesture, Literacy.* Aldershot, England and Burlington, Vermont: Ashgate, 2003.

Todd, Jane. *The Sign of Angellica: Women, Writing and Fiction, 1660–1800.* New York: Columbia University Press, 1989.

Trilling, Lionel. *Sincerity and Authenticity.* Cambridge, Mass.: Harvard University Press, 1967.

Turner, Cheryl. *Living by the Pen: Women Writers in the Eighteenth Century.* London and New York: Routledge, 1992.

Uphaus, Robert W. *The Idea of the Novel in the Eighteenth Century.* East Lansing, MI: Colleagues Press, 1988.

Van Ghent, Dorothy Bendon. *The English Novel, Form and Function.* New York: Rinehart, 1953.

Van Sant, Ann Jessie. *Eighteenth-century Sensibility and the Novel.* Cambridge: Cambridge University Press, 1993.

Varey, Simon. *Henry Fielding.* Cambridge and New York: Cambridge University Press, 1986.

————. *Joseph Andrews: A Satire of Modern Times.* Boston: Twayne Publishers, 1990.

Warner, John M. *Joyce's Grandfathers: Myth and History in Defoe, Smollett, Sterne, and Joyce*. Athens: University of Georgia Press, 1993.

Watt, Ian. *The Rise of the Novel: Studies in Defoe, Richardson and Fielding*. Cambridge: Cambridge University Press, 1957.

# Acknowledgments

"Sentiment from Afra Behn to Marivaux" by James R. Foster. From *History of the Pre-Romantic Novel in England*. New York: The Modern Language Association of America (1966): 19–44. © 1949 by The Modern Language Association of America. Reprinted by permission.

"Deserts, Ruins and Troubled Waters: Female Dreams in Fiction and the Development of the Gothic Novel" by Margaret Anne Doody. From *Genre*, vol. X, no. 4 (Winter 1977): 529–72. © 1977 by The University of Oklahoma. Reprinted by permission.

"The Comic Sublime and Sterne's Fiction" by Jonathan Lamb. From *ELH* vol. 48, no. 1 (Spring 1981): 110–43. © 1981 by the Johns Hopkins University Press. Reprinted with permission of the Johns Hopkins University Press.

"Fielding: The Comic Reality of Fiction" by Sheridan Baker. From *Tennessee Studies in Literature Volume* 29, published as *The First English Novelists: Essays in Understanding: honoring the retirement of Percy G. Adams*, edited by J.M. Armistead. Knoxville: The University of Tennessee Press (1985): 109–42. © 1985 by The University of Tennessee Press. Reprinted by permission.

"Crime and Adventure" by Paula R. Backscheider. From *Daniel Defoe: Ambition & Innovation*. Lexington: The University Press of Kentucky (1986): 152–81. © 1986 by The University Press of Kentucky. Reprinted by permission.

"The Rise of Bath" by Simon Varey. From *Space and the Eighteenth-Century English Novel*. Cambridge and New York: Cambridge University Press (1990): 65–80. © 1990 by the Cambridge University Press. Reprinted with permission of Cambridge University Press.

"The Job Controversy, Sterne, and the Question of Allegory" by Jonathan Lamb. From *Eighteenth Century Studies*, vol. 24, no. 1 (Fall 1990): 1–19. © 1990 by the American Society for Eighteenth Century Studies. Reprinted by permission.

"Fighting the Pharisees" by Patrick Reilly. From *Tom Jones: Adventure and Providence*: 27–61 © 1991 by G.K. Hall & Co. Reprinted by permission of the Gale Group.

"Mythic and Historic Language in Smollett" by John M. Warner. From *Joyce's Grandfathers: Myth and History in Defoe, Smollett, Stern and Joyce*. Athens and London: The University of Georgia Press (1993): 57–88. © 1993 by The University of Georgia Press. Reprinted by permission.

"The Tested Woman Plot" by Lois E. Bueler. From *Clarissa's* Plots. Cranbury, N.J. and London: Associated University Presses (1994): 22–40. © 1994 by Associated University Presses, Inc. Reprinted by permission.

"The Don Juan Plot" by Lois E. Bueler. From *Clarissa's* Plots. Cranbury, N.J. and London: Associated University Presses (1994): 100–116. © 1994 by Associated University Presses, Inc. Reprinted by permission.

"Caesar's Toils: Allusion and Rebellion in *Oroonoko*" by David E. Hoegberg. From *Eighteenth Century Fiction*, vol. 7, no. 3 (April 1995): 239–58. © 1995 by McMaster University. Reprinted by permission.

"*Gulliver's Travels* and the contracts of fiction" by Michael Seidel. From *The Cambridge Companion to the Eighteenth Century Novel*, ed. John Richetti. Cambridge, UK and New York: Press Syndicate of the University of Cambridge (1996): 72–89. © 1996 by Cambridge University Press. Reprinted by permission.

"Serializing a Self" by Thomas Keymer. From *Sterne, the Moderns, and the Novel*. Oxford and New York: Oxford University Press (2002): 113–49. © 2002 by Thomas Keymer. Reprinted by permission.

# Index

Characters from novels are listed by first name, last name *(title of book)*.